Handbook of Career Counseling for Women

Second Edition

WITHDRAWN

Edited by

W. Bruce Walsh
Ohio State University

Mary J. Heppner
University of Missouri

 LAWRENCE ERLBAUM ASSOCIATES, PUBLISHERS
2006   Mahwah, New Jersey   London

Lawrence Erlbaum Associates, Inc., Publishers
10 Industrial Avenue
Mahwah, New Jersey 07430
www.erlbaum.com

Cover design by Tomai Maridou

Library of Congress Cataloging-in-Publication Data

Handbook of career counseling for women / edited by W. Bruce Walsh, Mary Heppner.—
2nd ed.
p.   cm. — (Contemporary topics in vocational psychology)
Includes bibliographical references and index.
ISBN 0-8058-4888-6 (c. : alk. paper)
ISBN 0-8058-4889-4 (pbk. : alk. paper)
1. Vocational guidance for women.   I. Walsh, W. Bruce, 1936–   II. Heppner, Mary J.
III. Series.

HF5382.6.H36   2005
331.702′082—dc22   2005040062
                                                                          CIP

Books published by Lawrence Erlbaum Associates are printed on acid-free paper,
and their bindings are chosen for strength and durability.

Printed in the United States of America
10 9 8 7 6 5 4 3 2 1

Contents

Preface

Tell me, what is it you plan to do
With your one wild and precious life?

—Mary Oliver

The last refrain of Mary Oliver's poem *The Summer's Day* encourages us to think about our lives as wild and precious, and subsequently dares us to look at them critically and think about the choices we are making. In many respects, the authors of the chapters in this book are in quest of a similar goal: to give career counselors the knowledge, awareness, and skills to work with diverse girls and women to make their lives as authentic, meaningful, and rewarding (in whatever ways they define that) as they possibly can be.

This new edition builds on the 1994 text entitled *Career Counseling for Women* which was edited by W. Bruce Walsh and Samuel H. Osipow. Like that edition, we have solicited the help of some of the finest scholars in the field to develop 14 chapters that are designed to help career counselors work with diverse girls and women as they pursue the ever widening choices in their lives. As editors, we feel enormously grateful to the authors as they worked to develop chapters that examine the intersections of various social identities such as race, class, and sexual orientation within their specific content focus. As we read each chapter, we were very excited about the creativity of their thinking and the many ideas provided to help counselors expand and affirm women's life choices.

This edition unfolds with a chapter written by one of the true pioneers of career counseling for women, Helen Farmer. Her chapter focuses on the history of this field and provides the social–historical context for its development. The chapter is a brilliant example of how social forces (women's and civil rights movements), professional organizations, and dedicated individuals came together to develop the focus for career counseling of women.

Next, a scholar who has had enormous influence on the field of career counseling, Nancy Betz, discusses basic issues and concepts in the career development and counseling of women. This chapter communicates the critically important role that career has in a woman's life and explores the barriers and facilitators that continue to affect women's development. Dr. Betz wrote this chapter as an overview of the issues that are explored in more depth in the ensuing chapters.

The needs of women living at or below the poverty level is the topic of a chapter written by Mary J. Heppner and Karen O'Brien. These authors challenge us to critically analyze the classism and middle class assumptions that much of the research and practice in career counseling exemplifies. The authors present factual information about women and poverty, as well as offer ideas for ways career counselors can effectively advocate for poor women.

Assessment is often a major part of career counseling and the chapter by Susan Lonborg and Gail Hackett reviews critical gender issues in many forms of qualitative and quantitative assessment. Although the field has come a long way from the "pink" and "blue" versions of the Strong Vocational Interest Blank, there are still a host of subtle and complex ways that gender can influence the career assessment process. The likelihood of girls and women to underrate their abilities compared to men with the same actual ability, or the gendered lens that men and women use when thinking about different occupational settings, are part of the more nuanced way that gender bias can occur. The chapter provides a wealth of information about assessment and the competencies career counselors need when working with girls and women.

The role of critical feminist theory in career counseling with women is presented by Krista Chronister, Ellen Hawley McWhirter, and Linda Forrest. In their chapter, they describe the use of a critical feminist approach that "helps clients make decisions that are congruent with their multiple identities (e.g., ethnicity, gender, class, sexual orientation) and advance their empowerment, as they define it." The chapter provides powerful case examples of applying this approach to the lives of diverse women and is a highly affirming framework with which to counsel girls and women.

Lucia Gilbert's work on dual-career and dual-earner families spans decades. She has clearly contributed definitive work on this critically important topic. Now she and Lisa Kearney discuss critical issues for career counselors to understand as they work with diverse dual-earner couples. Since less than

5% of American families with children living in the home have a full-time employed father and full-time homemaker mother, issues of dual-earners are crucial for career counselors to understand. The chapter provides very helpful data to indicate what factors are critical for having successful dual-earner relationships.

The next four chapters examine the unique career development needs of women in the four major racial and ethnic groups in the United States. First, Rosie Bingham, Connie Ward, and Melissa McGhee Butler provide a framework and technique for working with African American women. They introduce a "think aloud" technique for delineating the metacognitive process that occurs in counseling and helps the counselor formulate hypotheses to guide the counseling process. Saba Rasheed, Samuel Lewis, and Riddi Sandil provide a very engaging sociohistorical and demographic perspective on Asian women in the United States, their differences as well as similarities and what unique career development needs they may have. They also apply models of counseling and assessment techniques that have been developed to be sensitive to working with diverse individuals. Their rich case examples bring to life the importance of sociocultural context in working with these girls and women. Then Lisa Flores, Rachel Navarro, and Lizette Ojeda discuss the career development of Latinas. After highlighting the importance of understanding between-group differences, the authors describe central Latina values such as familismo, allocentrism, personalismo, simpatia, and respeto, and discuss how these core values may influence the career planning and counseling process for Latinas. Perhaps no other racial/ethnic group within the United States has received less attention in psychology in general and career development in particular as Native Americans. Through their chapter, Charlotte McCloskey and Laurie Mintz provide a critically important historical context for the modern issues faced by Native women. The chapter describes the obstacles and barriers faced by Native women and also their strengths and incredible resiliency as well as offering suggestions to career counselors for intervening with Native women.

Kathleen Bieschke and Elizabeth Toepfer-Hendey provide a chapter examining the unique career counseling needs of lesbian girls and women. Specifically, they use an ecological model of career development to help contextualize and understand the career behavior of lesbian women including vocational choice, role management, and identity management issues.

Although the numbers of legal immigrants coming into the United States is large and growing, this population has been largely invisible in the psychology literature broadly and in the career development literature more specifically. Oksana Yakushko reviews the existing literature and starts to develop a framework for understanding and working with the career needs of immigrant women including examining the key influences that shape the career experiences of immigrant women.

With the rapid growth in science, technology, engineering, and mathematical (STEM) occupational fields, it is critical for career counselors to have knowledge of these fields and the lives of women who enter them. Ruth Fassinger and Penelope Asay begin their chapter with rich case examples and proceed to examine these cases from the perspective of challenges faced by women in these traditionally male STEM fields. Interventions that may be helpful to women considering these fields are explored as well as recommendations for changes needed in STEM workplaces to make them more conducive to women.

Joyce Russell examines the career counseling needs of women in management positions and the fact that even though management is now seen as a sex neutral field, there remains a large gap between men and women who rise to higher levels of management within organizations. The chapter reviews the major issues confronting women in management today and discusses counseling approaches that may offer assistance to these women.

We hope that you find this book as rich with ideas and suggestions as we did reading these chapters. We also hope they offer you help in understanding your own career development and those of your clients, students, daughters, and other important girls and women in your lives.

W. Bruce Walsh and Mary J. Heppner

Chapter 1

History of Career Counseling for Women

Helen S. Farmer
University of Illinois at Urbana-Champaign

The theory and practice related to career counseling for women have gone through major changes in the past 50 years. During the 1950s and 1960s little attention in the literature was given to career counseling for women. However, with the advent of the amendments to civil rights and higher education legislation in 1972, including Title VII and Title IX related to sex equity in education and the workplace, there was a flowering of interest in career counseling for women and the literature exploded with theory, research, and practice applications.

Each decade from the 1980s to the present brought forward new priorities within the American Psychological Association (APA), Division 17 (Counseling Psychology), some of which were either directly or tangentially related to women's career counseling. In the 1980s new priorities directly affecting a woman's career development included a growing awareness of the effects of sexual orientation for lesbian and bisexual women on discrimination in the workplace as well as in school, especially high school. Other career-related issues that came to the fore in the 1980s included the need to help women with multiple role planning, and with wanting both a happy, healthy family and a challenging, satisfying career. The AIDS crisis, child sexual abuse, and violence against women were also critical issues for counselors in the 1980s that, although only indirectly related to women's career counseling, had debilitating effects on victims, who often neglected their career development.

In the 1990s professionals concerned with career counseling for women began to focus more on how career issues differed for different subgroups

1

of women. Diversity issues such as poverty, aging, sexual orientation, and multiculturalism were and continue to be dominant themes for theory, research, and practice in counseling. These issues have a direct impact on career counseling for both women and men, and have thus brought women's and men's issues closer together.

WITHIN THE APA: RELEVANT GOALS, GUIDELINES, STANDARDS, AND PRINCIPLES

The recent plethora of APA-approved guidelines and principles in the 1990s and in the 21st century on ethnically, linguistically, and culturally diverse populations, lesbian and gay parenting, lesbian, gay, and bisexual clients, ethical principles, and multicultural education, training, research, practice, and organizational change for psychologists (APA, 1993, 1995, 2000, 2002, 2003a) has given direction to efforts to increase equity for multicultural persons, and lesbian, gay, and bisexual persons. The APA Council is currently reviewing *Guidelines for Psychological Practice With Girls and Women* (Hansen, 2005).

Measurement guidelines also provide important information related to gender-fair assessment practices in career counseling: The American Educational Research Association, APA, and the National Council on Measurement in Education's (1999) *Standards for Educational and Psychological Testing* as well as earlier versions of these standards, such as the National Institute of Education's *Guidelines for Assessment of Sex Bias and Sex Fairness in Career Interest Inventories* (Diamond, 1975), and Gump and Rivers' (1975) guidelines for the use of interest tests with Black women and minorities.

Although these guidelines, standards, and principles have little to say directly to the practice of career counseling with women, they do indicate ways for career counselors to provide equitable services to women, persons of color, the poor, lesbian, gay, and bisexual persons, and the disabled. Guidelines for career counseling for women, if and when they are developed, could build on existing guidelines and standards, incorporating features found in the relevant literature of the past 50 years.

A crucial goal of career counseling for women is to improve the quality of life for women as individuals, and for groups of women such as women of color, lesbian and bisexual women, disabled women, poor women, and aging women. Another goal is to improve the quality of our society by increasing the opportunities for all women to contribute to pressing societal needs. Each new emphasis within the field of career counseling for women as it emerges seizes our attention because of the urgent need to change attitudes, behaviors, and social policies among individuals and institutions in our society. This book addresses many serious concerns related to career counseling for women that still remain. The Appendix provides a chronological list of events that contributed directly and indirectly to the evolution of career counseling for women.

SOCIAL EVENTS IMPACTING WOMEN'S CAREERS

Some of the positive events in America affecting the career development of women during the past century include: (a) developments in technology that simplified homemaking chores, (b) the contraceptive pill and related prochoice advances, (c) the civil rights movement and related legislation, (d) the War on Poverty, (e) the Cold War stimulating a race to beat the Russians in space and increase our scientific competence, (f) the women's rights movement, and (g) the gay rights movement. In combination with these changes, legalization of contraceptives, growth of labor unions, and civil rights legislation increased the opportunities for women in poverty and women of color to choose employment that paid better and to be less burdened by heavy family responsibilities. The 1950s were a time when technological advances were easing the workload of running a home. Dishwashers, duomatic laundry machines that combined washing and drying in one machine, disposable diapers, and frozen foods—all reduced the time and energy required for homemaking tasks, leaving time for at least part-time employment.

The Right to Choose: Contraception, Abortion, and the Pill

The right of women to choose whether or when to have babies evolved slowly during the 20th century. The use of contraception was still controversial in the 1950s and in some states, such as Connecticut, it was illegal. Margaret Sanger was jailed in the 1930s for her support of women's reproductive rights. Sanger worked in the slums of New York City and found many destitute women who lacked the resources to care for their large families. During that same period, women of affluence were able to obtain both contraceptives and abortions. Lack of access to birth control procedures prevented many women from working and pursuing professional-level careers. The establishment of the Planned Parenthood Federation in the 1930s and the repeal of anticontraception laws in many states by the end of the 1950s were positive steps for women who wished to have both a career and a family. With the development of the contraceptive pill in the 1960s, the foundation was laid for women to more easily plan the timing of conception, and limit the number of children they had.

Prochoice initiatives supporting abortion rights received a boost in the 1970s when the Supreme Court voted in favor of *Roe v. Wade* (1973). This choice is, however, still controversial, and forbidden by many religious institutions except when there is a clear health threat to either the mother or the fetus, or conception is the result of rape.

The Women's Movement: Impact on Career Counseling

Several important events related to the women's movement early in the 20th century impacted women's career development opportunities. In the 1920s following World War I, there was the passage of legislation giving women the vote in federal and state elections. As early as the 1920s, within the field of psychoanalysis, Karen Horney (1926) took a stand critical of Freud's theories of women's sexuality (Quinn, 1987). Hall and Lindzey (1978) classified Horney's theory along with those of Adler, Fromm, and Sullivan, as a social-psychological theory. Horney's theories predate the feminist emphases on the effect of context and of sex-role socialization on personality. Her theory contrasted with Freud's biological determinism and the idea that for women biology is destiny. Horney's theories were popular in academic psychology departments in the 1950s, but later came under criticism from feminists during the sexual revolution of the 1960s and 1970s, which was strongly critical of psychoanalytic concepts (Unger & Crawford, 1992). However, Hall and Lindzey's classification of Horney within the social-psychological theoretical school cast a more positive light on Horney's contributions. Horney also emphasized the importance of empowering women and encouraging them to be self-reliant, and less dependent on men and mothering for their economic and emotional needs. Horney (1945) described her goals for counseling women as follows:

> The woman must acquire the capacity to assume responsibility for herself, in the sense of feeling herself the active responsible force in her life, capable of making decisions and of taking the consequences. With this goes an acceptance of responsibility toward others, a readiness to recognize obligations in whose value she believes, whether they relate to her children, parents, friends, employees, colleagues, community, or country. (p. 241)

In the 1950s and early 1960s, two other writers stimulated the women's movement that erupted in the latter half of the 1960s. Simone de Beauvoir, a French economist and longtime companion of the French writer Jean-Paul Sartre, wrote a book which appeared in English translation in 1953 entitled *The Second Sex* (1949/1953). In this book she made a compelling argument for women to achieve economic independence from men. Betty Friedan wrote *The Feminine Mystique* (1963), urging middle-class housewives to return to work in order to give meaning to their lives. The 1960s was the decade during which the women's movement reached its apex, with many civil rights marches for the Equal Rights Amendment (ERA), bra burnings, and the establishment of both the National Organization for Women (NOW) and the Women's Bureau within the U.S. Department of Labor.

Within the APA, the Committee on Women in Psychology (CWP) and the Women's Program Office were formed in 1972. APA, Division 17 established an ad hoc committee on women in 1970, formalized as the Committee on Women in 1982 and as the present Section for the Advancement of Women (SAW) in 1996. The history of the accomplishments and challenges faced by SAW and its parent committees were described in Farmer (2002) and are not repeated here. However, it is important to note some contributions of the ad hoc committee during the 1970s. This committee sponsored the publication of three special issues of *The Counseling Psychologist*: Fitzgerald and Harmon (1973), Birk and Tanney (1976), and Hill et al. (1979). The Fitzgerald and Harmon issue contained an article focused on women's career counseling (Vetter, 1973). The Hill et al. issue contained the principles concerning the counseling and therapy of women. These principles were later approved by several APA divisions, including Division 17, and in 1986 Fitzgerald and Nutt published a rationale and implementation statement related to these principles. In 1984 the Committee on Women, Division 17 sponsored a special edition of *The Counseling Psychologist* on the career development of women (Whiteley, 1984). The major contribution in this issue was by Helen Astin (1984). Other landmark articles by psychologists during this period include Broverman, Vogel, Broverman, Carlson, and Rosenkranz' (1972) article on sex-role stereotypes and Gilligan's (1977) article on women's moral development.

Brooks and Forrest (1994) provided a helpful description of the impact of feminism on counseling in general, and suggested that career counseling for women would do well to adopt many of the feminist emphases in both research and clinical practice. Brooks and Forrest noted that the feminist emphasis on social action has been adopted by many career counselors for women and that it would be desirable for more career counselors to adopt the feminist concept of a nonhierarchical client–therapist relationship. These authors lamented the lack of attention to feminist recommendations for conducting research, such as those that encourage input from participants.

The guidelines for psychological practice with girls and women mentioned earlier and currently under review by the APA Council, if and when adopted officially, should provide further guidance for provision of feminist career-counseling practice. These guidelines are commendable on several counts. First, the application of these guidelines to adolescent as well as adult women recognizes that socializing experiences that occur early in a woman's life contribute significantly to career problems or lack thereof

later on. Second, the inclusion in these guidelines of multicultural and lesbian and bisexual women's concerns and how to address them is consistent
with the current efforts to integrate these women's needs into the theory
and practice of career counseling for women. Other career-counseling
practices that owe a debt to the feminist movement are described later in
this chapter in the section on practices.

Sex Equity for Women: Participation in the Labor Market

Ferment in American society during the 1960s raised women's career aspirations and determination to reduce gender bias in education, employment, and society in general. By 1970 the groundwork had been laid for the
1972 amendments to both the 1964 Civil Rights Act and the Higher Education Act (Association of American Colleges, 1972) that addressed equity in
education and employment for girls and women. In addition, affirmative
action legislation was amended to include women and government sanctions for ensuring enforcement of this legislation. This sex equity legislation required test publishers to follow federal guidelines to reduce sex bias.
Measures used frequently by career counselors, such as career interest inventories, were subject to these federal guidelines (Diamond, 1975). This
legislation also led to federal funding for retraining teachers and counselors in gender-fair practices (Farmer & Backer, 1977).

The Cold War with Russia led indirectly to an increase in women pursuing science careers. After the Russian launching of the spacecraft Sputnik
in the late 1950s the American government responded by making funds
available to improve science education in schools, and to increase the number of highly trained scientists in American space programs. Following the
passage of amendments to the Civil Rights Act and the Higher Education
Act (Association of American Colleges, 1972), funding was made available
to schools and universities to increase girls' and women's participation in
science education and careers. In the 1980s during Ronald Reagan's presidency, federal funding for sex-equity initiatives was sharply reduced (Klein,
1985). However, when the administration changed, later in the 1980s the
National Science Foundation established special funds to support women's
research and to initiate programs in education aimed at increasing the participation of women in science and technology education and careers.
These initiatives resulted in positive gains for women in these fields, but
women still lag behind men, especially in the hard sciences, as we enter the
21st century (National Science Foundation, 2000).

Census figures for 1940 show that 4% of women with children under the
age of 18 were working. During World War II many women were employed,

filling positions left vacant by men in the armed services. Women were particularly needed in factories producing materials needed for the war effort. However, in the years following World War II many women dropped out of the workforce to raise families, and to make their employment positions available to men.

During the 1950s there were an increasing number of labor unions supporting both skilled and unskilled laborers. This movement was of critical importance to both men and women in these sectors of our economy and contributed to women's ability to support themselves economically. In the 1950s women were beginning to break with the interrupted career pattern described by Super (1957) and to continue to work while raising their preschool children. In 1956, 40% of women with children ages 6 to 17 were employed, and an additional 18% of women with children under age 6 were employed (U.S. Department of Labor, Women's Bureau, 1969). During the 1960s, women 25 or younger increased their labor force participation even more during their childbearing years (U.S. Department of Labor, Women's Bureau).

Rapoport and Rapoport (1969), in a study conducted in England, identified the increasing prevalence of married couples in which both spouses were employed. Rapoport and Rapoport's work motivated research in America on the dual-career couple (Gilbert, 1987, 1994). By the mid-1980s the dual-career couple had become the norm in America (Farmer, 1985). Gilbert (1994) reported that only 10% of American families fit the traditional model of a two-parent family with children, a wage-earning husband, and a homemaker wife. By 1994 56% of women with children under the age of 6 were employed and, of these, 69% were employed full time. Researchers involved in career counseling for women have developed several procedures and assessment devices to help dual-career couples with planning and stress reduction (Farmer, 1984; Nevill & Super, 1986a, 1986b; Weitzman, 1994), some of which are described later in this chapter.

The lack of role sharing by men in the home (Gilbert, 1987, 1994) combined with the continuing wage gap between working women and working men (still approximately 75%, U.S. Bureau of the Census, 2001) attests to a continuing lack of sex equity in the workplace in the United States. For most women, shifting between career and family roles has not been easy, especially when women are required to engage in parenting, homemaking, and employed work. Stresses develop from the division of labor at home, finding adequate child care, the distribution of power and responsibility within the marriage, and the various pulls of employment demands. Sekaran (1986) noted that many women and men experience interrole conflict and that satisfaction in a career and in life depends on the resolution of these conflicts.

Sexual Harassment in the Workplace
and in Higher Education

Sexual harassment in the workplace and in higher education, although long-standing, has become more and more visible since the early 1980s when the federal government issued guidelines on this behavior (Fitzgerald, 1993, 2003; U.S. Equal Employment Opportunity Commission, 1980). These federal guidelines make it clear that sexual harassment is any behavior, verbal or physical, that interferes with a woman's work performance or that creates an intimidating, hostile, or offensive work environment. Since these guidelines were disseminated many university and college administrators have developed guidelines for sexual harassment that apply not only to relationships among employees, but also to relationships between faculty and students.

In the late 1980s media attention to the accusations leveled at Supreme Court justice nominee Clarence Thomas by Anita Hill during his confirmation hearings raised the level of public awareness and made it clear that sexual harassment in higher education and the workplace is not well understood by the average student or worker. Government enforcement and campus guidelines on sexual harassment to date have been unsatisfactory for many reasons, including the difficulty in obtaining evidence that will stand up in a court proceeding, and the continuing attitudes in society suggesting that women ought to be "good sports" and take men's sexually explicit jokes as harmless social repartee. The rare instance in which the perpetrator is fired or punished in some way continues to make headline news.

Riger (1991) contended that the low rate of reporting harassment is a result of gender bias in the harassment grievance policies rather than an absence of harassment or lack of assertiveness by victims. For example, courts have ruled that behaviors classified as creating an intimidating, hostile, or offensive work environment must be repeated in order to constitute evidence of harassment. Some have held that these incidents must be shown to affect the victim's mental health. Furthermore, the "reasonable person rule" has been invoked to establish whether a reasonable person would be offended by the behavior. The problem is that the definition of a reasonable person is different for men and women.

Louise Fitzgerald (cited in Dittman, 2003) questioned whether there is adequate protection for women who come forward with a complaint. Fitzgerald said that "these cases cost plaintiffs more in anguish and humiliation than the monetary awards they receive for damages. This is because victims must endure a discovery process in which intimate details of their personal lives are often publicized in open court and their characters are questioned" (Dittman, p. 24).

In 1993 the *Journal of Vocational Behavior* editors published a special issue on sexual harassment in the workplace (Tinsley & Stockdale, 1993). This special issue provided ample evidence of the harmful effects of sexual harassment on women's career development and employment. This special issue also reported some gains in reducing sexual harassment since 1980 including: (a) Behaviors formerly viewed as a woman's problem are now increasingly viewed as a societal problem and (b) victims are increasingly turning to grievance staff in employment or campus settings where they find some validation and acknowledgment of the seriousness of the sexual harassment behaviors they are experiencing.

Civil Rights: Related Legislation and Federal Programs

The civil rights movement involving minority groups in America can be traced back at least to the 19th century, even before the Civil War. However, the second half of the 20th century saw the most important gains for the civil rights of minorities in America, many of which (e.g., affirmative action) also resulted in backlashes by majority White Americans (Smith, 1983).

During Eisenhower's presidency, in *Brown v. Board of Education* (1954) the Supreme Court supported desegregating public schools. This decision set in motion efforts by local school boards to integrate their schools through busing and other means.

During the 1950s there was increasing agitation to support labor unions and increase the economic security and lifestyle of working men and women at the unskilled and skilled labor levels. Also, there were marches on state legislatures to increase protection for the poor by enforcing rent-control policies and housing standards related to heating and plumbing. Some have described the 1950s as the do-nothing decade. However, there were strong leaders engaging in social action in the 1950s who laid the foundation for the Civil Rights Act (1964) and the War on Poverty in the 1960s.

Martin Luther King, Jr. appeared on the national scene in the 1950s and, among other initiatives, he led nonviolent marches in the South aimed at integrating all-White restaurants and removing discrimination in seating on public buses. Martin Luther King, Jr.'s "I Have a Dream" speech in 1963 at the march on Washington for jobs and freedom paved the way during the Johnson administration for the Civil Rights Act passed in 1964. It was followed by Executive Orders No. 11,246 (1965) and No. 11,375 (1968) that established rules governing the affirmative action required of federal educational and employing institutions (Farmer & Backer, 1977).

During his administration (1963–1968) President Johnson also established a War on Poverty that included programs such as Head Start for preschoolers, the Office of Economic Opportunity (OEO), and the Job Corps (Smith, 1983). The purpose of OEO was to retrain the unemployed, improve access to employment opportunities through affirmative action, and provide training to upgrade the skills of racial and ethnic minorities. The Vietnam War (1965–1972) led to a reaction against the work ethic of success by the younger generation, who were disillusioned by the government's handling of the war and by the loss of lives in a conflict that to many seemed unjustified. Many who rebelled against the war also rebelled against the established norms for success in America, replacing these with a desire for a simpler life, and the need to treat all persons with respect and to provide equal opportunities for all in education and employment.

Civil Rights Gains and Continuing Needs

By the 1970s the number of Americans living in poverty had declined from approximately 38 million in the early 1960s to approximately 24 million in 1969 (Smith, 1983). In 2001 34.6 million Americans still lived in poverty, although that represented a smaller percentage, because the overall population in the U.S. had grown (U.S. Bureau of the Census, 2001). Unrest in the inner cities of the nation (e.g., the Watts riots in southeast Los Angeles) in the late 1960s contributed to a backlash against the perceived privileges being given to minorities and the poor. In the 1980s much of the federal funding for poor and minorities was redistributed to the states to manage and benefits varied depending on the state.

The Civil Rights Act has been amended several times since 1964, most notably in 1972 when several categories in addition to minorities were identified to benefit from greater equity in education and employment, including women and older adults (Association of American Colleges, 1972). The Disabilities Amendment to the Civil Rights Act in 1990 marked another legislative triumph for civil rights in America. Some civil rights were granted to lesbian, gay, and bisexual (LGB) persons in the 1990 amendment, but LGB persons are still ineligible for the full complement of civil rights legislated for married couples, minorities, the poor, and women.

The civil rights situation for minorities in America in the 21st century is still lacking in many respects and the playing field is still uneven. California restricts immigrant rights that affect mainly Chicano (i.e., Mexican American) illegal immigrants. The U.S. Bureau of the Census (2001) reported that the poverty rate for African Americans remains three times higher than for White Americans and the unemployment rate is twice as high; and that 20% of African Americans have no health insurance. The high school dropout rate for African Americans has declined from a high in 1970 of 11% to 5% in 1994. This contrasts sharply with the dropout rate for Hispanics of 33% in 1994 (Sue & Sue, 2003). In a challenge to affirmative action legislation in higher education the Supreme Court in 2003 ruled against undergraduate admissions policies at the University of Michigan in *Gratz v.*

Bollinger. However, at the same time, the Supreme Court did not reject the use of racial preferences to encourage diversity in higher education. Their rationale was their recognition of the continuing reliance of admissions officers on standardized test results, which discriminate unfairly against minorities. Discrimination complaints to the Equal Employment Opportunity Commission have increased in the past 10 years and the amount awarded to plaintiffs has nearly tripled to a high of $141.7 million in 2002, suggesting that there is still much to do to eradicate discrimination in the workplace.

Following the 1954 Supreme Court decision supporting desegregation of the schools and the subsequent Civil Rights Act (1964) and related revisions (Association of American Colleges, 1972), implementation of civil rights laws have been far from smooth and many areas of controversy remain, especially concerning affirmative action legislation, sexual harassment in education and the workplace (Fitzgerald, 1993, 2003), and gay rights (Fassinger, 1996). Neville, Lilly, Duran, Lee, and Browne (2000) found that a tendency toward colorblindness in the racial attitudes of some White persons is a continuing cause for concern. For example, some believe that "everyone who works hard, no matter what race they are, has an equal chance to become rich" (p. 62). The negative effects of ethnic minority discrimination on women's career development have been described by Ward and Bingham (1993) and Bingham and Ward (1994).

Over the past 50 years the number of Americans with a minority ethnic or cultural background (Black, Hispanic, Asian, Native American) has grown; in 1980 they represented 18% of the population and by 2000 they were over 30%. Population projections during the 1980s alerted educators and employers to the changing ethnographic mix in America and they were urged to prepare to better serve this multicultural population.

Smith (1983) noted that in order for American society to continue to progress toward racial justice, the unemployment of racial minorities had to improve significantly. Smith pointed to skill training programs, training adults in the skilled trades and in technology, as potentially benefiting minorities and the poor. If such programs are to succeed, however, Smith noted, the government needs to target some of the barriers to success such as lack of adequate child care for trainees, transportation needs, and work adjustment needs. These issues remain and their resolution continues to dominate domestic politics in the 21st century.

Multiculturalism and the APA

The Office of Minority Affairs was established within the APA in the 1980s. Concern for the provision of better services for multicultural groups is also evidenced in the APA's *Ethical Principles and Standards* (APA, 2002), *Guidelines for Providers of Psychological Services to Ethnic, Linguistic, and Culturally Di-*

verse Populations (APA, 1993), and *Guidelines on Multicultural Education, Training, Research, Practice, and Organizational Change for Psychologists* (APA, 2003a). Division 45 (Ethnic and Minority Issues) was formed within the APA in 1986 and acquired its own journal, *Cultural Diversity and Ethnic Minority Psychology*, in 1998.

There have also been an increasing number of journal articles and books devoted to the psychological needs and related services for our multicultural population. Within the APA, Division 17's journal *The Counseling Psychologist* has published several special issues on this topic since 1994 during the editorial tenures of Gerald L. Stone, P. Paul Heppner, and Robert Carter (April 1994; July 1994; January 1998; July 1998; November 1998; March 1999; January 2001; July 2001; May 2002; May 2003). Other journals related to counseling and career development such as the *Journal of Counseling Psychology*, the *Journal of Vocational Behavior*, and the *Journal of Career Assessment* have also given extensive space to multicultural issues during this period.

Numerous books on multicultural counseling have been published in the last decade. Sue's (1981) book, *Counseling the Culturally Different*, was an early entrant, and is now in its fourth edition under a slightly different title (Sue & Sue, 2003). The *Handbook of Multicultural Counseling* (Ponterotto, Casas, Suzuki, & Alexander, 2001) is in its second edition, *Counseling Across Cultures* (Pedersen, Draguns, Lonner, & Trimble, 2002) is in its fifth edition, and *A Handbook for Developing Multicultural Awareness* (Pedersen, 2000) is also in its fifth edition. Sue's earlier publication (1975) focused on Asian American counseling needs. Arredondo (2002) and Vasquez (1998), among others, addressed Hispanic women's career-counseling needs; Gump and Rivers (1975), Helms (1984, 1990), Smith (1983), Bingham and Ward (1994), and Bowman and Tinsley (1991), among others, outlined the counseling needs of African American women; and La Fromboise and Jackson (1996) and La Fromboise and Howard-Pitney (1995), among others, addressed the counseling needs of Native American women. Cook, Heppner, and O'Brien (2002) provided a model comparing the career development of women of color with White women. In 1994 Walsh and Osipow published *Career Counseling for Women*, which included a chapter on ethnic minority women by Rosie Bingham and Connie Ward (1994).

Tinsley (1994) edited a special issue of the *Journal of Vocational Behavior* on racial identity and vocational behavior. Bingham and Ward (1994) described several ways in which the racial identity status of the client affects career counseling. Fassinger (2000) cautioned that focus on racial identity status should be balanced with a recognition of the effect of discrimination and the behavior of majority persons on minority clients.

In summary, the APA broadened its focus in the 1980s to include an Office of Minority Affairs, and Division 45, Ethnic and Minority Issues. A burgeoning number of books and journals focusing on multicultural issues has emerged in the past 20 years. However, the literature specifically addressing minority women's career-counseling needs, theory, research, and practice is still relatively sparse.

Lesbian and Bisexual Women

Prior to 1970 the psychological research literature on homosexuality focused on its presumed pathology (Croteau & Bieschke, 1996a). The Kinsey reports on the sexual behavior of Americans reported that lesbian and gay sexual orientations were more common than previously thought (Kinsey, Pomeroy, & Martin, 1948; Kinsey, Pomeroy, Martin, & Gebhard, 1953), a finding indicating that same-gender sexual orientation is neither unusual nor unnatural (Morin & Rothblum, 1991). There was also some research evidence in these early years indicating that homosexuals were, on average, as mentally healthy as heterosexuals (Hooker, 1957; Sue & Sue, 2003). Hooker, for example, found evidence that clinicians could not differentiate between projective test data from gay and heterosexual men.

In the 1950s LGB persons' situation in society was limited both with respect to employment, and by exclusion from various legal rights enjoyed by "straight" citizens. Coming out as a homosexual was much more hazardous than it is today (Fassinger, 1996). During the 1960s social movements related to women's liberation, the sexual revolution, and the gay rights movement all contributed positively to a change in the way the mental health profession viewed LGB persons. Many graduate training programs in counseling psychology in the 1960s taught that homosexuality was deviant behavior and that therapists should try to change it in their homosexual patients and clients. However, prior to 1970, psychiatrists and psychologists had experienced little success, if any, in trying to change the sexual orientation of their homosexual patients and clients using behavioral therapy techniques (Morin & Rothblum, 1991). Meanwhile, Thompson, McCandless, and Strickland (1971) reported research findings supporting Hooker's (1957) study indicating that lesbians and gay men were similar to heterosexual women and men on measures of psychological adjustment and self-esteem.

The APA and LGB Concerns

Following the 1973 lead of the American Psychiatric Association, the APA Council in 1974 approved a statement declaring that homosexuality was not a mental illness. In 1975 the APA Council passed the following resolution: "Homosexuality, per se, implies no impairment in judgment, stability, reliability, or general social or vocational capabilities: Further the APA urges all mental health professionals to take the lead in removing the stigma of mental illness that has long been associated with homosexual orientation" (Garnetts, Hancock, Cochran, Goodchilds, & Peplau, 1991, p. 971). Also in 1975 the APA adopted the following resolution concerning the civil and legal rights of LGB persons (Conger, 1975):

> The APA deplores all public and private discrimination in such areas as employment, housing, public accommodation, and licensing against those who engage in or who have engaged in homosexual activities and declares that no burden of such judgment, capacity, or reliability shall be placed upon these individuals greater than that imposed on any other persons. Further, the APA supports and urges the enactment of civil rights legislation at the local, state, and Federal level that would offer citizens who engage in acts of homosexuality the same protections now guaranteed to others on the basis of race, creed, color, etc. Further the APA supports and urges the repeal of all discriminatory legislation singling out homosexual acts by consenting adults in private. (cited in Garnetts et al., 1991, p. 971)

Such resolutions contribute to social attitude change but related state and federal laws have changed slowly. In 2003 the Supreme Court ruled that state laws against sodomy violated the due process clause of the 14th Amendment. As recently as 1986 the Supreme Court had upheld such laws (see *Bowers v. Hardwick*, cited in Hertzberg, 2003). This 2003 action by the Supreme Court was long overdue and has led to renewed support for legalizing LGB marriage in the states where it is illegal (Hertzberg, 2003).

The APA Council appointed a task force on the status of gay and lesbian psychologists to monitor APA involvement in and support for LGB civil rights. This task force became the standing Committee on Lesbian and Gay Concerns in 1980. At about the same time, the *Journal of Homosexuality* was launched. APA, Division 17 took notice of these changes within the APA and *The Counseling Psychologist*, in a special issue in 1979 on counseling women, included a short article by Kingdon (1979) on counseling lesbian women. Kingdon concluded her article with eight helpful recommendations.

In the 1981 APA revision of their ethical principles a statement was included about sexual orientation: "As employees or employers, psychologists do not engage in or condone practices that are inhumane or that result in illegal or unjustifiable actions. Such practices include, but are not limited to, those based on considerations of . . . sexual preference" (Keith-Spiegel & Koocher, 1985, p. 456). The establishment of Division 44 within the APA in the 1980s, now the Society for the Psychological Study of Lesbian, Gay, and Bisexual Issues, was an important step in the process of improving psychological services for LGB clients.

By 1992 the APA ethics revision contained several references to sexual orientation. The 1992 revisions relating to LGB persons were in Ethical Principle D (respect for people's rights and dignity), and in standards on human differences, other harassment, and use of assessment in general and with special populations. A committee organized by Division 44 developed the *Guidelines for Psychotherapy with Lesbian, Gay, and Bisexual Clients* which were approved by the APA Council in 2000 (APA, 2000). In the most recent APA (2002) ethics revision, Principle E, Standard 2.01, and Standard 3.03 addressed practices with LGB clients. Note that principles and standards are enforceable by the APA, whereas guidelines are aspirational statements.

During the years since 1974, the APA has written more than 11 amicus curiae addressing lesbian and gay civil rights. Garnetts et al. (1991) surveyed 2,544 psychotherapists and obtained data on their attitudes and practices with LGB clients. They concluded that "to bring individual practice into accord with APA policy will require continued and expanded efforts to educate practitioners about sexual orientation" (p. 964).

Research journals devoted to LGB issues have appeared and cooperation on projects between Division 44 and other APA divisions has evolved (i.e., Divisions 12, 17, and 35). However, discrimination against LGB persons has continued in our society, as they are excluded from employment areas, the armed services, and housing. Discrimination against LGB couples prevents them from receiving government benefits available to married persons. In 1998 the APA Council adopted the following policy statement (APA, 2003b):

> Whereas providing the legal benefits that the license of marriage offers to same-sex households (including, but not limited to, property rights, health care decision-making, estate planning, tax consequences, spousal privileges in medical emergency situations and co-parental adoption of children) is justified as fair and equal treatment. . . . Therefore, be it resolved, that APA supports the provision to same-sex couples of the legal benefits that typically accrue as a result of marriage to same-sex couples who desire and seek the legal benefits. (pp. 1–2)

A central career development issue faced by lesbian and bisexual women as well as gay men is related to their sexual identity development, which occurs later than for most heterosexuals (Fassinger, 1996; Morgan & Brown, 1991). Many LGB persons do not become aware of their sexual identity until adolescence or adulthood. The timing of coming out to self and others "confounds the vocational development of lesbians in several critical ways" (Fassinger, p. 162). A study by Driscoll, Kelley, and Fassinger (1996) focused on lesbian identity and disclosure issues in the workplace is a good example of needed research on career barriers for adult lesbian and bisexual women. Fassinger noted that there is a need to rethink some of the common assumptions related to the career development of women in order to comprehensively integrate lesbian and bisexual women's experience into theory and practice.

In 1996 a special issue of the *Journal of Vocational Behavior* (Croteau & Bieschke, 1996b) was devoted to the vocational issues of lesbian women and gay men. Fassinger (1996) commented on some of these articles, proposing a way to integrate their suggestions. Using the same theoretical framework adapted by Betz and Fitzgerald (1987) for career counseling with women in general, Fassinger outlined a list of unique barriers and facilitative factors related to lesbian and bisexual women's career development. She said that lesbian and bisexual women are confronted with major barriers to accessing certain occupations, such as teacher of small children and residence hall director. Lesbian and bisexual women also often lack support from family and friends and occupational role models of LGB persons who are satisfied and successful. Occupational stereotypes limit choices considered by lesbian and gay persons.

As Fassinger (1996) noted:

> Discrimination problems documented in the literature include disclosure issues in hiring, wage inequalities, legal prohibitions, retention and promotion problems, harrassment and abuse, surveillance, poor work evaluations, under-utilization of abilities and job tracking, hate crimes and violence, social and collegial ostracism, hostile work climate, limitations of future options, and dual public-private identities. (p. 166)

Fassinger indicated that a central problem confronted by lesbian and bisexual women is sexual identity management in the workplace: "Although existing legal protections for lesbians and gay men are more extensive in the pubic than private sector, no Federal or national standards exist for addressing employment discrimination based on sexual orientation" (p. 166).

The AIDS crisis came to the fore in the 1980s and at first it was considered by some to be an LGB disease. This view has since been changed but at the time it added to the burden that LGB persons carried. Crawford (2003) reported that women in the United States now constitute 25% of persons with AIDS and 75% of these are women of color. We now know that AIDS is transmitted through the exchange of blood, contaminated needles shared by illegal drug users, and unsafe sexual practices. For lesbian and bisexual women who want to be checked for HIV or AIDS the issue of their sexual identity comes to the fore in spite of various laws to protect AIDS patients. Fear of reprisal at work because of this disease is a serious issue for lesbian and bisexual women.

The AIDS crisis did have some positive effects. Research to identify ways to maintain the health of AIDS and HIV-positive patients has been funded to some degree. Also, federal funding was made available to provide clean needles to illegal drug users, and to provide safe-sex educational programs. By the 1990s it was clear that the AIDS crisis had become an international health crisis and its cure continues to elude researchers. By 1995 medical science had found a combination of prescription drugs capable of transforming HIV from a death sentence to a chronic illness. The focus of the health community is now on helping HIV patients to both obtain and take these medications.

THEORETICAL DEVELOPMENTS RELATED TO WOMEN'S CAREER DEVELOPMENT

Theory related to women's career development evolved slowly during the 1950s and 1960s, then accelerated rapidly during the 1970s, and has continued to evolve during the past 30 years. Several excellent reviews of theory development related to women's careers and career counseling have been written in the past 20 years (Betz & Fitzgerald, 1987; Brown, Brooks, Borow, Brown, Collin, Dawis, et al., 1996; Fitzgerald, Fassinger, & Betz, 1995; Osipow, 1983). Theories specifically designed to address the career development of women emerged in the 1970s and 1980s (Astin, 1984; Betz & Fitzgerald; Farmer, 1976, 1985; Gottfredson, 1981, 1996; Hackett & Betz, 1981). Some common themes may be found in these relatively new theories. They do not discard the older career development theories of Ginsberg, Ginsberg, Axelrod, and Herma (1951) and of Super (1957) or the trait-and-factor personality theory of Holland (1959). These older theories of career development and choice provide important foundational concepts that apply to both men and women. However, most of these older theories were viewed as giving less consideration to the effects of socialization and of the current context on women's career development (Farmer, Altman, Carter, Cohn, Conrad, Giurleo, et al., 1997; Fassinger, 1996; Fitzgerald et al.). Theories are currently emerging that are more relevant for various subgroups of women who experience discrimination of various kinds and who have career development needs similar to the men in their subgroup but different from those of middle-class heterosexual White women (Bingham & Ward, 1994; Fassinger; Helms, 1984, 1990).

Theory Related to Women's Career Development Before 1970

Super (1957) described seven career patterns: stable homemaking, conventional, stable working, double track, interrupted, unstable, and multiple trial. Among these were three unique to women: stable homemaking, double track (combining homemaking and career), and interrupted (to have children). The basis for these unique career patterns was Super's belief that homemaking and childrearing were focal organizing elements in women's career choices and paths, a view echoed in Ginsberg, Ginsberg, Axelrod, and Herma (1951) and Ginsberg, Berg, Brown, Herma, Yohalem, and

Gorelick (1966). Although these patterns did describe what women were doing at this time, these authors did not address ways to use this information to increase women's self-actualization through their careers. Ginsberg et al. (1951) and Ginsberg et al. (1966) noted that women have a more difficult time figuring out what career to choose because they also have to consider whether to marry and, if so, whether to have children. Ginsberg et al. (1966) stated further that many girls cannot realistically plan on a career until they know what kind of man they will marry, because a woman's financial status and potential freedom to continue her education or career are partly dependent on the attitudes of her husband toward educated working women. Zytowski (1969) also described a series of career patterns unique to women. Psathas (1968), a sociologist, noted that culture and current context play an important role in women's participation in the workforce. He pointed to the important effects of social class and social mobility on the career choices of women, similar to Ginsberg et al. (1951) and Super. Psathas also noted the important role played by marriage and family in the career choices of women.

One may deduce from Ginsberg et al. (1951), Psathas (1968), Super (1957), and Zytowski (1969) that there was a growing consensus toward the end of the 1960s on at least one aspect of theory related to women's career choice, a consensus that recognized the central role of marriage and family in women's career choices, and agreement that women's career choices were more complex than those confronted by men and involved more variables (Harmon, 1970). There was at that time also a beginning awareness of the greater importance of context and environmental factors in women's career choice compared to men's (Psathas).

Career Development Theory: Relevance for Heterosexual Women

Many theorists now agree that a major deterrent to women's optimum career development is rooted in the roles of most heterosexual women not only as childbearers, but also as childrearers and homemakers (Farmer et al., 1997; Fitzgerald et al., 1995; Gilbert, Hallett, & Eldridge, 1994; Harmon & Meara, 1994; National Science Foundation, 1997). These role expectations make women's career development and choice process more complex than that of men's because most women have to consider how marriage and family will fit with their career role (Farmer, 1971; Fitzgerald & Crites, 1980; Ginsberg et al., 1966; Harmon, 1970; Hackett & Lonborg, 1994).

Some theorists have contended that for desirable changes to occur, changes that would facilitate career equity for women compared to men, men's attitudes and behaviors related to work and homemaking need to change (Farmer, 1971; Gilbert, 1987, 1994; Hansen & Rapoza, 1978; Harmon & Meara, 1994; Harmon, 1997). This view is critical of theories of women's career development that focus on changing the work environment and changing women's socialization experiences but neglect to address the interdependence of women's and men's roles in society, especially their homemaking roles, but also their career roles. The literature related to home–career conflict (Farmer, 1971, 1984, 1997), role stress (Hall, 1972; Sekaran, 1986), multiple role planning (Nevill & Super, 1986a; Weitzman, 1994; Weitzman & Fitzgerald, 1996), and dual-career couples (Gilbert, 1987, 1994) has developed largely in response to this issue. Career practice in relation to this issue is discussed later in this chapter.

The dual-earner couple had emerged in America by the 1980s as the modal pattern. Gilbert (1987, 1994) has been conducting research on dual-career couples for nearly two decades and has provided useful theory and research evidence for career counseling with women and men. Gilbert (1987) identified three relationship patterns among dual-career couples: conventional, participant, and role sharing. She reported that about one third of the dual-career couples she studied fit into each of the three categories. The one third in the role-sharing category may provide role models for young women and men who are planning ahead for their careers. Recently Barnett and Hyde (2001) suggested that the dramatic increase in women's participation in the workforce and the related increase in dual-career couples have actually decreased stress in the family. That is, multiple roles in role-sharing families contribute to their mental, physical, and relationship health. In the past three decades since sex equity legislation was passed, men's and women's homemaking and parenting roles have changed. Men are now more interested and involved in parenting (Gilbert, 1994) and most are willing to help their partners with homemaking chores. However, few men view parenting and homemaking as their responsibility, but rather feel they are available primarily to help out. Equitable sharing of homemaking and parenting is still very rare in the U.S. population as a whole.

The response of working women to their multiple roles was at first an attempt to do it all, as shown in the literature of the 1970s and early 1980s. Women tried to be super moms and executive managers at the same time. More recently women have backed off from wanting it all to compromising some roles in order to benefit others. Most women take primary responsibility for raising their children (Gilbert, 1987, 1994). With a newborn, finding quality day care is a major task confronting parents who both work. The United States lags behind most European countries in terms of the amount of available quality child-care facilities. Tipping (1997) reported that many of the employed women she interviewed rejected the use of day care, preferring to make arrangements with family members or friends to care for their babies. They did this because available, affordable day care did not meet their quality standards.

There are some positive signs, however. There are some large business institutions that now provide on-site child care for their employees. Also, many higher education institutions now permit tenure rollbacks for faculty who need to take time out to raise small children (Hyde, 1995).

Career Development Theory: Relevance for Minorities

Women of color experience combining home and career roles somewhat differently from White women (Bingham & Ward, 1994). Black women are more likely to have had mothers who worked, and who expected them to have a career (Bingham & Ward). Also, single women who are heads of households and living in poverty work to survive and put bread on the table, making combining home and career roles a necessity, not a choice.

Smith (1983) provided some useful comments on the relevance of current career theories for minority women and noted two basic viewpoints in the literature criticizing career development theories and their relevance for minorities. Some positions emphasize severe limitations in the application of these theories to racial minorities. Others recognize the overall value of the current theories while pointing out their shortcomings. Super's (1957) and Ginsberg et al.'s (1951) life-stage development theories are thought to have limited application to racial minorities because of their experiences of discrimination and their lack of economic resources (Cohn, 1997; Smith). Successful navigation through the career development stages posited by Ginsberg et al. and Super implies a life relatively free from stress related to poverty and discrimination, a life that permits progress through each stage and mastery of associated tasks. Smith noted that such progress and mastery simply does not occur for many minorities growing up in America.

Smith (1983) challenged the assumption of many career development theories that "dignity exists in all work" and that work is satisfying and fulfilling. According to Smith, this assumption "neither reflects the reality of many individuals' work lives nor the career literature that shows there is in American society a clear hierarchy by which jobs are ranked from very high to very low in desirability" (p. 187). For many workers in America work may simply mark the passage of time or represent a means of survival, and at the same time lack desirability. Also, for many Americans, especially racial and ethnic minorities, there is no "free and open labor market" and their freedom to choose an occupation is severely limited. The reason for many minorities' unemployment is the prevailing economic and social conditions in America. An emerging minority group in America, the 6 million Muslims living here, many of whom are regarded by employers and their neighbors as potential terrorists, and who have difficulty in finding meaningful work should be added to our list. Harmon and Meara (1994) also noted the lack of relevance of many of our career development and choice theories for the poor Black or White.

Career choice theories such as Holland's (1997), which are based on matching a person's career interests to a compatible occupation, also rely on the assumption of an open labor market, one that allows individuals to freely choose a career based on their interests. Such theories are unrealistic about minority persons' freedom to choose, and fail to consider the minorities' lack of experiences that would develop a broad range of career interests, and their alienation growing up in the public school system (Cohn, 1997; Smith, 1983).

Career Development Theory: Relevance
for Lesbian and Bisexual Women

A special issue of the *Journal of Vocational Behavior* edited by Croteau and Bieschke (1996b) was devoted to the vocational issues of lesbian women and gay men. Three articles analyzed the relevance of vocational theories such as Holland's (1997), Super's (1990), and Lent, Brown, and Hackett's (1994) for LGB persons. Fassinger (1996) commented on these articles by proposing a way to integrate their suggestions. Mobley and Slaney (1996) noted that Holland's congruence theory needed to be supplemented with consideration of employment setting attitudes toward LGB individuals, and the likelihood of harassment and discrimination. Morrow, Gore, and Campbell (1996) reviewed the relevance of the Lent et al. sociocognitive framework for explaining the career development of lesbian women and noted that issues unique to lesbian career self-efficacy would need to be considered. Dunkle (1996) noted that Super's life stages were more difficult for lesbian women to work through because of sexual identity issues and societal bias and discrimination. Fassinger noted also that pervasive discrimination, harassment, and hostility in the workplace make disclosure of sexual orientation a critical decision for lesbian and bisexual women. She also noted some facilitating factors in lesbian and bisexual women's career development. For example, they tend to be more androgynous in their sex-role concepts and more open to occupations nontraditional for their sex. Also, they do not anticipate depending on men for their future financial security and therefore are likely to take their career planning seriously. Lesbian and bisexual women are less likely to be affected in their career development and choice process by home–career conflict (Fassinger) because they typically have egalitarian relationships. If and when they choose to adopt or bear children, and to share childrearing in some fashion, they are likely to adopt a role-sharing pattern. Fassinger's suggestions related to career development theory for LGB persons, similar to the approach used by

Betz and Fitzgerald (1987) for women in general, seems promising, especially in light of the need for research in this area.

Social Learning Theory and Women's Career Development

Several career development theorists have agreed that there are unique barriers to women's career development and that these barriers are found primarily in their environment, more specifically in their socialization leading to role expectations, and in the current gender biases in their family of origin, school, and workplace. Bandura's (1969, 1977, 1989, 1997) social learning theory and related research was adapted by several researchers (Betz & Fitzgerald, 1987; Farmer, 1976, 1985, 1997; Hackett & Betz, 1981; Lent, Brown, & Hackett, 1994) to help explain women's career development and choice processes. Also, in the 1970s, Krumboltz, Mitchell, and Jones (1976) and Mitchell and Krumboltz (1996) adapted Bandura's theory in their formulations related to career development. The emphasis in these theories is to identify both barriers and facilitating factors related to women's career development.

Some of the identified barriers to women's career development include: fear of success (Horner, 1969); the societal expectation that homemaking is the primary role for women, leading to a restricted range of career options (Farmer & Bohn, 1970; Harmon, 1970); mathematics identified as a critical filter in the job market (Sells, 1975); the null environment in the classroom for girls and women related to their academic achievements (Betz, 2002; Freeman, 1979); lack of career self-efficacy, that is, confidence in their ability to negotiate the various career development tasks (Hackett & Betz, 1981); widespread bias against employment of women of color except in the most menial positions (Smith, 1983); the continuing salary gap between employed men and women (National Science Foundation, 2000); sexual harassment in the workplace (Fitzgerald, 1993); and bias against lesbian and bisexual women in the workplace, especially if they are "out" (Fassinger, 1996).

A potential facilitator that has received a lot of attention since Hackett and Betz (1981) introduced it is occupational self-efficacy and the broader career self-efficacy noted earlier. Studies have shown that self-efficacy is related to persistence at a task until mastered, and engaging in a task, that is, choosing to try it (Bandura, 1989). The importance of performance self-efficacy for women was demonstrated by Hackett, Esposito, and O'Halloran (1989), who found that self-efficacy beliefs (i.e., "I can do it") were more determining of career choices than actual abilities. That is, they found that even when a woman had the necessary grades for entry into a particular college major, she was unlikely to choose that major unless she believed she could perform well in it. In this study performance self-efficacy was found to predict career commitment, educational aspiration, and nontraditionality of career choice (Betz & Hackett, 1997; Hackett & Betz, 1992).

Two other theories that complement the social-learning-based theories of women's career development are those of Gottfredson (1981, 1996) and Astin (1984). These theories fall outside the social learning framework, although they both incorporate some social learning principles.

Gottfredson's and Astin's Theories

Gottfredson's theory highlights the importance of sex-role socialization, social class, and ability on women's career choices. It should be noted that her theory is intended to apply to both women and men. Unlike social learning theory, she draws on sociological theory (Holland, 1959; Hotchkiss & Borow, 1996; Sewell & Shaw, 1968), self-concept theory (Super, Starishevsky, Matlin, & Jordaan, 1963; Tiedeman & O'Hara, 1963), and cognitive development theory (Kohlberg, 1966) in deriving her theory of the compromise and circumscription processes related to career choice.

Early reactions to Gottfredson's theory were mixed: Some praised it as one that offered an explanation for women's constricted occupational choices (Farmer & Seliger, 1985), others criticized it for its suggestion of the "serious restrictive effects of societal sex role norms on women's aspirations" (Betz & Fitzgerald, 1987, p. 26). Gottfredson's subsequent writing (1996) suggests that she is a realistic but not a deterministic theorist. She would prefer to see preventive interventions in the elementary and middle schools, interventions that are shown to be effective in reducing the typical circumscription and compromises made by women in their occupational choices. However, she does not preclude the notion that adult women can benefit from career-counseling interventions and from new career opportunities in the workplace. Empirical evidence supporting Gottfredson's theory is summarized in Gottfredson.

Astin's (1984) theory of women's career development is grounded in motivation and personality theory. Commentators on Astin's theory have frequently identified her description of the potential effect of the current "opportunity structure" as a timely reminder that change is possible in the present when new opportunities open up (Osipow & Fitzgerald, 1996). Harmon (1984) noted that "[Astin's] description of how the socialization process and the opportunity structure interact to produce social change . . . is a major contribution" (p. 127). Although there has been little research to validate Astin's theory there are studies that demonstrate the powerful effect of context on career aspirations, for example, Farmer and Bohn (1970) and Lockheed (1975).

Summary: Career-Counseling Theories for Women

The newer social learning theories (Hackett & Betz, 1981; Lent et al., 1994; Mitchell & Krumboltz, 1996), Gottfredson's (1981, 1996) theory of circumscription and compromise, and Astin's (1984) theory of the opportunity structure all address the limitations on many Americans' career choices, and their lack of exposure to experiences that would allow for progress through the career development stages. Theories of the career development of women have brought to the fore the importance of context and socialization experiences in shaping women's career choices. Subsequently, multicultural theorists and theorists concerned with the career development issues of LGB persons have found this emphasis compatible with the career development needs of these groups. Research has yet to demonstrate which interventions might reduce the effects of early socialization experiences on minority and LGB persons. Gottfredson's and Astin's theories complement the theories based on social learning and are applicable to both women and men.

ASSESSMENT AND CAREER COUNSELING FOR WOMEN

Published measures developed for career counseling, especially measures assessing abilities, interests, values, career beliefs, and role salience, are frequently used in career counseling for women. Following sex equity legislation in 1972, publishers of these measures instituted procedures to ensure that they were not biased in favor of either sex. In fact, federal guidelines (Diamond, 1975) laid out the criteria for publishers to meet that would result in sex-fair measures. In addition to these published measures, some assessment measures have been developed by researchers in the past 30 years that are relevant to the career development of women and are potentially useful to career counselors for women.

It is important to note that, historically, counselors and therapists have had mixed feelings about the value of assessment in counseling (Patterson, 1966). Counselors with a Rogerian theoretical orientation and those with an existentialist orientation have had little confidence in the usefulness of assessment in counseling. Some multicultural counselors have criticized the use of tests in counseling multicultural women because of their bias in favor of White middle-class individuals (Flores, Spanierman, & Obasi, 2003; Ward & Bingham, 1993). Career counselors have also been advised to be cautious in the use of some career-assessment measures with LGB clients (Chung, 2003). These differences among counselors in their use of career assessment in counseling have changed little in the past 50 years (Hackett & Lonborg, 1994). In this section of the chapter I focus on what has changed to benefit women in career-counseling assessment, rather than detail the controversies over the usefulness of assessment or the fine points of how best to reduce bias in measurement.

As noted earlier in this chapter, the *Standards for Educational and Psychological Testing* jointly developed by the APA and other organizations (American Educational Research Association et al., 1999) and the APA's (2002) *Ethical Principles of Psychologists and Code of Conduct* provide guidance for the use of tests in counseling, including career counseling for women. Relevant from this broader context also are guidelines developed for counseling women in general, such as those found in Brown (1990) and Hackett and Lonborg (1994), which address the importance of gender-role analysis in counseling women and the importance of the interview procedures within which assessment occurs. Although assessment of career interests, values, and abilities provides results that may well reflect a woman's socialization, they can also be useful shortcuts to provide information to the client that can lead to discussion. A special issue of the *Journal of Career Assessment* was devoted to career assessment for women (Walsh, 1997). Also, the first edition of *Career Counseling for Women* (Walsh & Osipow, 1994) contained a chapter on career assessment for women (Hackett & Lonborg). Both publications provide useful information on this topic. Changes made in published measures used in career counseling that are responsive to sex equity guidelines and civil rights requirements provide potential benefits for men, women, minorities, and the poor in our society.

Goals for career assessment for women evolved early in the 1970s, following sex equity legislation, and dominant among them was the desire to expand the career options considered by a woman client (Hackett & Lonborg, 1994; Walsh & Betz, 2001). This goal was based on data indicating that women typically constrict their career choices to those they think are compatible with their sex (Gottfredson, 1981, 1996). A second goal was to encourage women clients to think about how their early experiences in the family and at school had influenced their thinking about work and careers, and about the suitability of particular careers for them. A third goal was to help women clients plan realistically for their future multiple roles, especially those related to career and family.

In the following section the history of career interest measurement and the ways in which it has changed in the past 30 years are briefly reviewed. Next, the assessment of career-related values is discussed. Third, role-salience measures are described. Then some of the newer measures developed for multiple-role planning are discussed.

Interest Measurement and Career Assessment for Women

There were few references to gender differences within the field of career assessment up to and during the 1950s. An exception was the work of E. K. Strong, who developed the Strong Vocational Interest Blank (SVIB; Strong, 1927) to assess a person's interests and relate these to occupations in which satisfied employees had similar interest patterns. The SVIB was intended for use with high school seniors, college populations, and adults. Strong found significant sex differences in responses to SVIB items and as a result he developed a second form of the SVIB (Strong, 1933) that had occupational norms and scales for what Strong termed "women's occupations" (i.e., teacher, nurse, librarian). In practice, however, counselors tended to use the male form with female clients, because the men's form gave women scores on occupations not included in the women's form, and potentially enlarged the occupations that women might consider. The problem with this approach, of course, was that these occupations were normed primarily on men, and mean scores were not representative of employed women's interests in that occupation. Several research studies during the 1950s and 1960s used data from the SVIB to identify women with homemaking versus career interests (Gyspers, Johnston, & Gust, 1968; Hoyt & Kennedy, 1958) and proceeded to develop SVIB interest profiles for these two categories. Harmon and Campbell (1968) provided a further distinction by developing norms for the SVIB interest profiles of nonprofessional women.

With the passage of the Title IX Amendment to the Higher Education Act (Association of American Colleges, 1972) the focus shifted from the homemaking versus career distinctions in interest patterns to removing gender bias from interest measures consistent with the legislation (Diamond, 1975). Interest measures were criticized in the 1970s because they typically used sexist occupational titles and test items that were biased toward experiences more familiar to men than to women, and yielded scores that rarely encouraged girls to explore occupations nontraditional for their gender (Diamond). At the same time that sex equity in interest measurement was being addressed, more equitable career interest measures for minority women became an issue (Gump & Rivers, 1975).

The National Institute of Education (NIE) issued guidelines for reducing sex bias in interest measurement consistent with civil rights amendments requiring sex equity in education and employment (Diamond, 1975). Sex bias was defined in the NIE guidelines as "any factor that might influence a person to limit—or might cause others to limit—his or her consideration of a career solely on the basis of gender" (Farmer & Backer, 1977, p. 125). The guidelines further suggested that administration of interest inventories be:

preceded by an orientation dealing with possible influences from the environment, culture, early socialization, traditional sex role expectations of society, home-versus-career conflict, and the experiences typical of women and men as members of various ethnic and social class groups on men's and women's scores. Such orientation should encourage those taking the measure to examine any stereotypic sets they might have toward activities and occupations and should help them to see that there is virtually no activity or occupation that is exclusively male or female. (Diamond, pp. xxvi–xxvii)

Interest inventories that increase exploration of occupations beyond those clients have already considered, especially those occupational fields not typical for their gender, are responsive to the NIE guidelines.

The NIE guidelines (Diamond, 1975) stimulated publishers of the most frequently used career interest measures to revise these measures. Other contributors to the literature on gender bias in interest measures include Cole (1973), Raymond (1974), and Tittle and Zytowski (1978). From the mid-1970s to the mid-1980s interest measure publishers attempted to eliminate sexist language in occupational titles, to use the same form of the test for both sexes, to provide norms on all occupational scales for both sexes with an explanation of which norms were used to develop the scale, and to use items equally reflective of experiences familiar to both sexes (see, e.g., the current version of the Strong Interest Inventory [SII; Harmon, Hansen, Borgen, & Hammer, 1994], the Kuder Career Search [Zytowski, 1999], the Self-Directed Search [SDS; Holland, Fritzsche, & Powell, 1994], and the ACT-IV UNIACT [Prediger & Swaney, 1995]).

Because women consistently obtain higher scores on Holland's (1997) Social career interests (teaching, nursing), and men obtain higher scores on Holland's Realistic career interests (technical, engineering), interest measurement often reflects the status quo, that is, what is rather than what could be. Preventive interventions are needed to change the limiting effects of girls' socialization experiences on their occupational choices. Walsh and Betz (2001), Hackett and Lonborg (1994), and Gottfredson (1996) remind us that the best way to increase the likelihood that women will consider occupations nontraditional for their gender is to provide experiences early in childhood that would stimulate interest in and competence for those occupations.

Assessing Career Self-Efficacy and Agentic Self-Concepts

A recent addition to the SII is the Skills Confidence Inventory (SCI; Betz, Borgen, & Harmon, 1996), which provides information for women on their confidence in their ability to perform tasks related to particular occupations and to the six Holland Interest Scales (Holland, 1997). The addition of the SCI to the SII allows the counselor to identify a match or mismatch between a woman's interests and skill confidence levels. When a mismatch is found for a woman client, especially when interest is high and confidence is low, the counselor can work to help the client obtain experiences that might lead to an increase in her confidence to perform well in that occupation. Betz and Hackett (1997) noted that there are several other career-assessment measures that combine assessing interests and skills. Examples are Holland's Self-Directed Search, the Campbell Career Interest and Skill Inventory (Campbell, Hyne, & Nilsen, 1992), and the ACT Career Planning Program, which includes UNIACT (Prediger & Swaney, 1995).

An agentic self-concept has been found related to both self-efficacy and to nontraditional career choices for women (Betz & Fitzgerald, 1987; Farmer, Waldrop, Anderson, & Risinger, 1995). The Bem Sex Role Inventory (BSRI; Bem, 1981) may be useful in assessing a woman's self-concept with respect to expressive and agentic characteristics. High scores on agentic characteristics were found earlier to be related to nontraditional career choices by women (Farmer, 1985). Spence and Helmreich (1978) provided another example of a measure of agentic characteristics in their Personal Attributes Questionnaire.

Work-Related Values and Career Assessment for Women

Although assessment of values has received less attention in career counseling than assessment of interests and abilities, consideration of work values is critical to making a satisfying career choice (Brown, 1996; Dawis, 1991; Katz, 1975; Nevill & Super, 1986b; Super, 1990). In fact, work values according to Super, Starishevsky, Matlin, and Jordaan (1963) emerge into consciousness during late adolescence and then remain relatively stable throughout life. Women may need help both in clarifying their work values and in identifying careers that allow them to satisfy these values. For example, research has shown that women who choose a science career may do so primarily because they value contributing to societal problems through science (Farmer et al., 1995), whereas men may do so because of the prestige a science occupation offers or the potential for earning a high salary (Farmer, Rotella, Anderson, & Wardrop, 1998).

A measure developed by Nevill and Super (1986b) assesses 21 work values and has been used with high school, college, and adult clients. The results of this assessment provide a useful description of a person's work-related values (Super, 1990). Katz (1973) developed a computer-assisted career-planning program called SIGI (System of Interactive Guidance and Information), renamed SIGI-PLUS (Educational Testing Service, 1985), that incorporates assessment of values as well as interests, and self-estimates of ability. The SIGI-PLUS program invites participants to pit one value against another in their career planning to help them clarify and rank order their work-related values. A third measure of work values, the Minnesota Importance Questionnaire (Rounds, Henly, Dawis, Lofquist, & Weiss, 1981), assesses 20 work-related values and needs for adults.

Multiple Roles and Career Assessment for Women

During the 1980s several measures, in addition to those assessing interests, skills, and values, were developed to help women with their career planning. These newer measures took into account the likelihood that many working women would be juggling the multiple roles of worker, homemaker, parent, and leisurite. These newer measures assessed the importance of various life roles for the client, the potential for conflict between life roles such as family and work, and the readiness of the client to plan for these life roles in ways that would reduce stress and conflict. Hackett and Lonborg (1994) have commented on the importance of addressing these issues in career counseling for women.

Research and assessment of life-role importance was studied by Greenhaus (1971) and Super evolved a career rainbow describing the changing importance of various life roles throughout the lifespan (Super, 1990). Super and Nevill developed the Role Salience Inventory (RSI), a measure that has proved useful for counseling women about their multiple roles (Nevill & Super, 1986a; Super, 1990). The RSI assesses the relative importance of six life roles and may help women as well as men to see how their investment in various roles may change over time. Amatea, Cross, Clark, and Bobby (1986) developed a measure to assess work- and family-role expectations of career-oriented women and men, called the Life Role Salience Scales. Farmer (1984) developed a measure of Home-Career Conflict (Beere, 1990; Tipping & Farmer, 1991) to assess the extent of conflict between home and career roles that a woman experiences. Weitzman (1994) and Weitzman and Fitzgerald (1996) designed a measure to assess multiple-role realism. This measure has four scales that assess independence, involvement, commitment to multiple roles, and knowledge/certainty about combining roles. These measures are intended to assist dual-worker couples with long-range career planning that takes into account the couple's priorities for other life roles. Farmer et al. (1997) noted that awareness of not only the current importance of various life roles, but also how the future may change that importance, may encourage some women to begin long-range career planning earlier than they normally would. Tinsley (1997) edited a special issue of the *Journal of Vocational Behavior* on work and family balance, which provides articles relevant to career-planning assessment and to career counseling for women and men who are currently employed.

Career-Counseling Assessment for Women:
The Work Environment

Career planning requires not only a knowledge of the self, but also a knowledge of the requirements of various occupations and the kind of work environments available for women. For example, knowing the degree to which there is discrimination against women in general, women of color, and lesbian and bisexual women is important for women in making a career choice. Evidence of sexual harassment in a work environment is also important. Astin (1984) referred to a positive perception of "the structure of opportunity" within the work environment as an important motivator for women in choosing higher level, challenging careers. In the 1970s the U.S. Department of Labor, Women's Bureau (1972) published a series of myths and related realities about the work environment for women that provided evidence that many beliefs were unfounded. This set of myths was developed into a measure by Farmer (1985) and her research team to assess the strength of a woman's belief in these myths. This measure, called Support for Women Working, has proved useful in research studies, indicating that women who are more career oriented and have higher motivation to achieve in a career also reject these myths (Farmer, 1985, 1997). Fitzgerald (1990) developed a measure of sexual harassment in the workplace that has proved useful in helping women recognize their beliefs and feelings about sexual harassment.

CAREER COUNSELING FOR WOMEN:
PREVENTIVE INTERVENTIONS

Both Mitchell and Krumboltz (1996) and Gottfredson (1981, 1996) noted the importance of career education in the early school grades. The relative lack of career education in today's public school system leaves a serious gap in the career development of young children and adolescents.

Elementary School

The federal-level legislation in the 1970s growing out of sex equity legislation requirements provided funds for career education at both the elementary and secondary school levels (Farmer & Seliger, 1985). Families were found to be the most powerful influence on the career development of young people by Altman (1997), but because many gifted young people have parents who lack a college education, the federal government stepped in to help optimize the career potential of such gifted young people. Special semester- or year-long classes were provided for students to learn about career possibilities in order to broaden the range of occupations children of both sexes considered. However, all schools did not benefit equally from this federal support. When funding for career education dried up in the 1980s very few of the demonstration schools continued the programs they had established under federal funding (Farmer & Seliger, 1985).

Although more funds were also available for sex equity in career education and counseling for the nation's high school students in the 1970s, there is research evidence to show that high school students did not give their teachers high marks for helping them with planning for their future careers in this decade (Farmer, 1985). High school counselors received even less credit for helping high school students, girls or boys, with their career planning in the 1970s (Farmer, 1985). Reports continue to appear critical of the nation's high schools for failing to achieve gender equity (National Coalition for Women and Girls in Education, 2002; Sattler, 1998). However, at least three sources of federal funding have remained strong during the past 20 years: funding from NSF to increase girls' interest and competency in science and technology careers (NSF, 1997); funding from Title IX related to vocational education to reduce high school dropouts, smooth the path from school to work, and encourage girls to train in nontraditional occupations such as plumber, electrician, and carpenter; and funding from the Women's Educational Equity Act (2000) for the development of curricula for increasing gender equity in schools.

In addition to the career development and planning needs of the typical middle-class adolescent White girl are urgent career-related needs for girls who come from poor families and ethnic minority backgrounds (Bingham & Ward, 1994). The high school dropout rate of Hispanics is the highest in the nation, followed closely by that of Blacks (Cohn, 1997; NSF, 2000). Many of these girls are alienated from school and have not developed a sense of their own potential. Fassinger (1996) also suggested that girls struggling with their sexual identity may be so distracted by this issue that their career development needs are ignored.

Some career education classes have used computer-assisted help with teaching planning and decision-making skills. SIGI-PLUS (Educational Testing Service, 1985) and DISCOVER (Sampson, Reardon, & Ryan-Jones, 1992; Walsh & Betz, 2001) provide experiences that help build decision-making skills and career-planning skills for high school and college students, and out-of-school adults. Additional computer-assisted systems were evaluated in a special issue of the *Journal of Career Development* (Sampson & Reardon, 1990).

The Women's Educational Equity Act (WEEA, 1974) provided federal funding for the development of program materials that address the career development needs of girls with disabilities and girls from different cultural backgrounds, including recent immigrants. The WEEA catalogue (2000) lists publications that address ethnic identity issues, especially for African American and Hispanic girls. Examples include: Bingham and Ward (1994) which provides many suggestions for facilitating the career development needs of ethnic minority girls; and EQUALS, an in-service program for high school teachers, administrators, and counselors developed by staff at the University of California, Berkeley, that helps these professionals use materials to promote the participation of minority women and women in general in science and math careers (see Conwell, 1990; Kaseberg, Kreinberg, & Downie, 1980; NSF, 1997).

Preventive and Remedial Career Counseling for Adult Women: College and Work Settings

Theorists generally agree (Betz, 1994; Farmer et al., 1997; Gilbert, 1994; Hackett & Lonborg, 1994) that career counseling for women in college or employed settings should include some form of "feminist consciousness raising," and whether it uses a method such as gender-role analysis (Brooks & Forrest, 1994) or group counseling methods, the goal is the same: to highlight for women clients prior learning experiences that may be hindering their full self-actualization. Bingham and Ward (1994) provided a series of important suggestions for career counselors working with minority women. They stressed the importance of training counselors in cultural sensitivity, familiarity with cross-cultural knowledge and the sociopolitical strengths of ethnic groups, receptivity to the client as a cultural teacher, awareness of their own worldview, and racial identity development, including attitudes of privilege and entitlement. For lesbian and bisexual women, sexual identity management in the workplace is a critical issue that career counselors need to attend to (Fassinger, 1996). In addition, Bingham and Ward and Fassinger noted that discrimination in the workplace and in higher education settings affecting women of color and LGB persons needs to be addressed in career counseling with these women.

Techniques for career counseling with various subgroups of women are discussed in some detail in the chapters that follow. Early in the 1970s career counseling for women typically emphasized procedures that were uniquely for women. However, career-counseling procedures now apply increasingly to both men and women as the career needs of various subgroups have come to the fore. Thus career counselors provide help with planning for multiple roles to both men and women, help with surfacing the client's history of victimization and discrimination for both women and men, and so forth. There are some career problems that are still unique to women (e.g., sexual harassment, underrepresentation in science and technology careers), but there are more career problems that are unique to the poor, persons of color, LGB persons, and new immigrants that apply to both men and women.

Theorists also generally agree that career counseling for women should include a social change agenda in order to reduce barriers to women's optimal career development (Betz & Fitzgerald, 1987; Farmer, 1976, 1985, 1997; Fitzgerald, 2003; Hackett & Lonborg, 1994; Hansen, 1978; Harmon, 1970; Harmon & Meara, 1994; Psathas, 1968). These authors stress family-friendly employer policies, improved and increased child-care facilities, strengthened sanctions against sexual harassment in education and employment, and support for affirmative action initiatives in higher education student bodies and faculty.

CONCLUSION

Researchers and practitioners engaged in career counseling for women are making strides in the direction of integrating the dominant themes of the past 30 years into theory and practice. Although many of the issues that emerged apply to the career-counseling needs of both women and men, there are still needs that remain unique to women today. Globalization of our economy and our increasing interrelatedness as a world community will likely refocus career counseling for women once again. We will grapple with issues of poverty, diversity, and justice in new ways that we can only begin to imagine.

REFERENCES

Altman, J. (1997). Career development in the context of family experiences. In H. Farmer, J. Altman, A. Carter, J. Cohn, R. Conrad, S. Giurleo, et al., *Diversity and women's career development: From adolescence to adulthood* (pp. 229–242). Thousand Oaks, CA: Sage.

Amatea, E., Cross, E., Clark, J., & Bobby, C. (1986). Assessing the work and family role expectations of career-oriented men and women: The Life Role Salience Scales. *Journal of Marriage and the Family, 48,* 831–838.

American Educational Research Association, American Psychological Association, & National Council on Measurement in Education. (1985). *Joint technical standards for educational and psychological testing.* Washington, DC: Author.

American Educational Research Association, American Psychological Association, & National Council on Measurement in Education. (1999). *Standards for educational and psychological testing.* Washington, DC: Author.

American Psychological Association. (1993). Guidelines for providers of psychological services to ethnic, linguistic, and culturally diverse populations. *American Psychologist, 48,* 45–48.

American Psychological Association. (1995). *Lesbian and gay parenting: A resource for psychologists.* Washington, DC: Author.

American Psychological Association. (1998). Appropriate therapeutic responses to sexual orientation: In the proceedings of the APA, Incorporated, for the legislative year 1997. *American Psychologist, 53,* 882–939.

American Psychological Association. (2000). Guidelines for psychotherapy with lesbian, gay, and bisexual clients. *American Psychologist, 55,* 1440–1451.

American Psychological Association. (2002). Ethical principles of psychologists and code of conduct. *American Psychologist, 57,* 1060–1073.

American Psychological Association. (2003a). Guidelines on multicultural education, training, research, practice, and organizational change for psychologists (2003). *American Psychologist, 58,* 377–402.

American Psychological Association. (2003b). *Policy statement on legal benefits for same sex couples.* Retrieved August 18, 2003, from http://www.apa.org/pi/igbc/reslbssc.html

American Psychological Association, Division 17 Ad Hoc Committee on Women. (1979). Principles concerning the counseling and therapy of women. *The Counseling Psychologist, 8,* 21.

Americans with Disabilities Act, 42 U.S.C. § 12101 (1990).

Arredondo, P. (2002). Counseling individuals from specialized, marginalized, and underserved groups. In P. Pedersen, J. Draguns, W. Lonner, & J. Trimble (Eds.), *Counseling across cultures* (5th ed., pp. 241–250). Thousand Oaks, CA: Sage.

Association of American Colleges. (1972). *Federal laws and regulations concerning sex discrimination in educational institutions.* Washington, DC: Project on the Status and Education of Women, Association of American Colleges.

Astin, H. (1984). The meaning of work in women's lives: A socio-psychological model of career choice and work behavior. *The Counseling Psychologist, 12,* 117–126.

Bandura, A. (1969). Social-learning theory of identificatory processes. In D. A. Goslin (Ed.), *Handbook of socialization theory and research* (pp. 213–262). Chicago: Rand McNally.

Bandura, A. (1977). *Social learning theory.* Englewood Cliffs, NJ: Prentice Hall.

Bandura, A. (1989). Human agency in social cognitive theory. *American Psychologist, 44,* 1175–1184.

Bandura, A. (1997). *Self efficacy: The exercise of control.* New York: Freeman.

Barnett, R., & Hyde, J. (2001). Women, men, work, and family: An expansionist theory. *American Psychologist, 56,* 781–796.

Beere, C. (Ed.). (1990). *Gender roles: A handbook of tests and measures.* Westport, CT: Greenwood Press.

Bem, S. (1981). *Bem Sex Role Inventory: Professional manual.* Palo Alto, CA: Consulting Psychologists Press.

Betz, N. (1994). Basic issues and concepts in career counseling for women. In B. Walsh & S. Osipow (Eds.), *Career counseling for women* (pp. 1–41). Hillsdale, NJ: Lawrence Erlbaum Associates.

Betz, N. (2002). The 2001 Leona Tyler Award address: Women's career development: Weaving personal themes and theoretical constructs. *The Counseling Psychologist, 30,* 467–481.

Betz, N., Borgen, F., & Harmon, L. (1996). *Skills Confidence Inventory: Applications and technical guide.* Palo Alto, CA: Consulting Psychologists Press.

Betz, N., & Fitzgerald, L. (1987). *The career psychology of women.* New York: Academic Press.

Betz, N., & Hackett, G. (1997). Applications of self-efficacy theory to the career assessment of women. *Journal of Career Assessment, 5,* 383–402.

Bingham, R., & Ward, C. (1994). Career counseling with ethnic minority women. In B. Walsh & S. Osipow (Eds.), *Career counseling for women* (pp. 165–195). Hillsdale, NJ: Lawrence Erlbaum Associates.

Birk, J., & Tanney, M. (Eds.). (1976). Counseling women II [Special issue]. *The Counseling Psychologist, 6,* 2–63.

Bowman, S., & Tinsley, H. (1991). The development of vocational realism in Black American college students. *Career Development Quarterly, 39,* 240–249.

Brooks, L., & Forrest, L. (1994). Feminism and career counseling. In B. Walsh & S. Osipow (Eds.), *Career counseling for women* (pp. 87–134). Hillsdale, NJ: Lawrence Erlbaum Associates.

Broverman, I., Vogel, S., Broverman, D., Carlson, R., & Rosenkranz, P. (1972). Sex-role stereotypes: A current appraisal. *Journal of Social Issues, 28,* 59–78.

Brown, D. (1996). Brown's values based holistic model of career and life-role choices and satisfactions. In D. Brown, L. Brooks, H. Borow, S. Brown, A. Collin, R. Dawis, et al., *Career choice and development* (3rd ed., pp. 337–372). San Francisco, CA: Jossey-Bass.

Brown, D., Brooks, L., Borow, H., Brown, S., Collin, A., Dawis, R., et al. (1996). *Career choice and development* (3rd ed.). San Francisco, CA: Jossey-Bass.

Brown, L. S. (1990). Taking gender into account in the clinical assessment interview. *Professional Psychology, 21,* 12–17.

Brown v. Board of Educ., 347 U.S. 483 (1954).

Campbell, D. P., Hyne, S. A., & Nilsen, D. L. (1992). *Manual for the Campbell Interest and Skill Survey.* Minneapolis, MN: National Computer Systems.

Chung, Y. B. (2003). Ethical and professional issues in career assessment with lesbian, gay, and bisexual persons. *Journal of Career Assessment, 11,* 96–112.

Civil Rights Act, 42 U.S.C. § 2000e-12 (1964).

Cohn, J. (1997). The effects of racial and ethnic discrimination on the career development of minority persons. In H. Farmer, J. Altman, A. Carter, J. Cohn, R. Conrad, S. Giurleo, et al., *Diversity and women's career development: From adolescence to adulthood* (pp. 161–171). Thousand Oaks, CA: Sage.

Cole, N. (1973). On measuring the vocational interests of women. *Journal of Counseling Psychology, 20,* 105–112.

Conger, J. J. (1975). Proceedings of the American Psychological Association, Incorporated, for the year 1974: Minutes of the Annual Meeting of the Council of Representatives. *American Psychologist, 30,* 620–651.

Conwell, C. (1990). *Science equals success.* Swickley, PA: Women's Educational Equity Act, Education Development Center.

Cook, E. P., Heppner, M. J., & O'Brien, K. M. (2002). Career development of women of color and white women: Assumptions, conceptualizations, and interventions from an ecological perspective. *Career Development Quarterly, 50,* 291–304.

Crawford, N. (2003). Helping women beat the odds. *Monitor on Psychology, 34,* 86–87.

Croteau, J. M., & Bieschke, K. J. (1996a). Beyond pioneering: An introduction to the special issue on the vocational issues of lesbian women and gay men. *Journal of Vocational Behavior, 48,* 119–124.

Croteau, J. M., & Bieschke, K. (Eds.). (1996b). Vocational issues of lesbian women and gay men [Special issue]. *Journal of Vocational Behavior, 48*(2).

Dawis, R. (1991). Vocational interests, values, and preferences. In M. D. Dunette & L. M. Howe (Eds.), *Handbook of industrial and organizational psychology* (2nd ed., Vol. 2, pp. 833–872). Palo Alto, CA: Consulting Psychologists Press.

De Beauvoir, S. (1953). *The second sex* (H. M. Parshley, Trans.). New York: Knopf. (Original work published 1949)

Diamond, E. (Ed.). (1975). *Issues of sex bias in interest measurement.* Washington, DC: U.S. Government Printing Office.

Dittman, M. (2003). Sexual harassment too often leads to humiliation for victims. *Monitor on Psychology, 34,* 24.

Driscoll, J., Kelley, F., & Fassinger, R. (1996). Lesbian identity and disclosure in the workplace: Relation to occupational stress and satisfaction. *Journal of Vocational Behavior, 48,* 229–242.

Dunkle, J. H. (1996). Toward an integration of gay and lesbian identity development and Super's life-span approach. *Journal of Vocational Behavior, 48,* 149–159.

Educational Testing Service. (1985). *SIGI PLUS.* Princeton, NJ: Author.

Exec. Order No. 11246, 30 F.R. 12319 (1965).

Exec. Order No. 11375, 32 F.R. 14303 (1968).

Farmer, H. (1971). Helping women to resolve the home-career conflict. *Personnel and Guidance Journal, 49,* 795–801.

Farmer, H. (1976). What inhibits achievement and career motivation in women? *The Counseling Psychologist, 6,* 12–15.

Farmer, H. (1984). Development of a measure of home-career conflict related to career motivation in college women. *Sex Roles, 10,* 663–676.

Farmer, H. (1985). A model of career and achievement motivation for women and men. *Journal of Counseling Psychology, 32,* 363–390.

Farmer, H. (1997). Women's motivation related to mastery, career salience, and career aspiration: A multivariate model focusing on the effects of sex role socialization. *Journal of Career Assessment, 5,* 355–381.

Farmer, H. (2002). Legacies and traditions: Focus on Division 17's Committee on Women/ Section for the Advancement of Women (SAW) 1970–2030: Achievements and challenges. *The Counseling Psychologist, 30,* 417–440.

Farmer, H., Altman, J., Carter, A., Cohn, J., Conrad, R., Giurleo, S., et al. (1997). *Diversity and women's career development: From adolescence to adulthood.* Thousand Oaks, CA: Sage.

Farmer, H., & Backer, T. (1977). *New career options for women: A counselor's sourcebook.* New York: Human Sciences Press.

Farmer, H., & Bohn, M. (1970). Home-career conflict reduction and the level of career interest in women. *Journal of Counseling Psychology, 17,* 228–232.

Farmer, H., Rotella, S., Anderson, C., & Wardrop, J. (1998). Gender differences in science, math, and technology careers: Prestige level and Holland type. *Journal of Vocational Behavior, 53,* 73–96.

Farmer, H., & Seliger, J. (1985). Sex equity in career and vocational education. In S. Klein (Ed.), *Handbook for achieving sex equity through education* (pp. 338–359). Baltimore, MD: Johns Hopkins University Press.

Farmer, H., Wardrop, J., Anderson, M., & Risinger, R. (1995). Women's career choices: Focus on science, math and technology careers. *Journal of Counseling Psychology, 42,* 155–170.

Fassinger, R. (1996). Notes from the margins: Integrating lesbian experience into the vocational psychology of women. *Journal of Vocational Behavior, 48,* 160–175.

Fassinger, R. (2000). Diversity at work: Research issues in vocational development. In D. Pope-Davis & H. Coleman (Eds.), *The intersection of race, class, and gender in multicultural counseling* (pp. 267–288). Thousand Oaks, CA: Sage.

Fitzgerald, Laurine, & Harmon, L. (Eds.). (1973). Counseling women [Special issue]. *The Counseling Psychologist, 4*(1).

Fitzgerald, Louise. (1990). Sexual harassment: The definition and measurement of a construct. In M. Paludi (Ed.), *Ivory power: Sexual harassment on campus* (pp. 21–44). Albany: State University of New York Press.

Fitzgerald, Louise. (1993, February). *The last great open secret: The sexual harassment of women in the workplace and academia.* Paper presented at the Science and Public Policy Seminar, Federation of Behavioral Psychological and Cognitive Sciences, Washington, DC.

Fitzgerald, Louise. (2003). Sexual harassment and social justice: Reflections on the distance yet to go. *American Psychologist, 58,* 915–924.

Fitzgerald, Louise, & Crites, J. (1980). Toward a career psychology of women: What do we know? What do we need to know? *Journal of Counseling Psychology, 27,* 44–62.

Fitzgerald, Louise, Fassinger, R., & Betz, N. (1995). Theoretical developments in women's career development. In W. B. Walsh & S. Osipow (Eds.), *Handbook of vocational psychology* (2nd ed., pp. 67–109). Hillsdale, NJ: Lawrence Erlbaum Associates.

Fitzgerald, Louise, & Nutt, R. (1986). The Division 17 Principles concerning the counseling/ psychotherapy of women: Rationale and implementation. *The Counseling Psychologist, 14,* 180–216.

Flores, L., Spanierman, L., & Obasi, E. (2003). Ethical and professional issues in career assessment with diverse racial and ethnic groups. *Journal of Career Assessment, 11*, 76–95.

Freeman, J. (1979). How to discriminate against women without really trying. In J. Freeman (Ed.), *Women: A feminist perspective* (2nd ed., pp. 194–208). Palo Alto, CA: Mayfield.

Friedan, B. (1963). *The feminine mystique.* New York: Norton.

Garnetts, L., Hancock, K. A., Cochran, S. D., Goodchilds, J., & Peplau, L. A. (1991). Issues in psychotherapy with lesbians and gay men: A survey of psychologists. *American Psychologist, 46*, 964–972.

Gilbert, L. (Ed.). (1987). Dual-career families in perspective [Special issue]. *The Counseling Psychologist, 15*(1).

Gilbert, L. (1994). Reclaiming and returning gender to context: Examples from studies of heterosexual dual-earner families. *Psychology of Women Quarterly, 18*, 539–558.

Gilbert, L., Hallett, M., & Eldridge, N. (1994). Gender and dual-career families: Implication and applications for the career counseling of women. In B. Walsh & S. Osipow (Eds.), *Career counseling for women* (pp. 135–164). Hillsdale, NJ: Lawrence Erlbaum Associates.

Gilligan, C. (1977). In a different voice: Women's conception of the self and of morality. *Harvard Education Review, 47*, 481–517.

Ginsberg, E., Berg, I., Brown, C., Herma, J., Yohalem, A., & Gorelick, S. (1966). *Life styles of educated women.* New York: Columbia University Press.

Ginsberg, E., Ginsberg, S. W., Axelrod, J., & Herma, J. L. (1951). *Occupational choice: An approach to a general theory.* New York: Columbia University Press.

Gottfredson, L. (1981). Circumscription and compromise: A developmental theory of occupational aspirations. *Journal of Counseling Psychology, 28*, 545–579.

Gottfredson, L. (1996). Gottfredson's theory of circumscription and compromise. In D. Brown & L. Brooks (Eds.), *Career choice and development* (3rd ed., pp. 179–232). San Francisco, CA: Jossey-Bass.

Gratz v. Bollinger, 537 U.S. 1044 (2003).

Greenhaus, H. (1971). An investigation of the role of career salience in vocational behavior. *Journal of Vocational Behavior, 1*, 209–216.

Gump, J., & Rivers, L. (1975). The consideration of race in efforts to end sex bias. In E. Diamond (Ed.), *Issues of sex bias and sex fairness in career interest measurement* (pp. 123–139). Washington, DC: U.S. Government Printing Office.

Gyspers, N., Johnston, J., & Gust, T. (1968). Characteristics of homemaker and career-oriented women. *Journal of Counseling Psychology, 15*, 541–546.

Hackett, G., & Betz, N. (1981). A self-efficacy approach to the career development of women. *Journal of Vocational Behavior, 18*, 326–339.

Hackett, G., & Betz, N. (1992). Self-efficacy perceptions and the career-related choices of college students. In D. H. Schrunk & J. L. Meece (Eds.), *Students' perceptions in the classroom: Causes and consequences* (pp. 229–246). Hillsdale, NJ: Lawrence Erlbaum Associates.

Hackett, G., Esposito, D., & O'Halloran, M. S. (1989). The relationship of role model influence to the career salience and educational and career plans of college women. *Journal of Vocational Behavior, 35*, 164–180.

Hackett, G., & Lonborg, S. (1994). Career assessment and counseling for women. In B. Walsh & S. Osipow (Eds.), *Career counseling for women* (pp. 43–85). Hillsdale, NJ: Lawrence Erlbaum Associates.

Hall, C. S., & Lindzey, G. (1978). *Theories of personality* (3rd ed.). New York: Wiley.

Hall, D. (1972). A model of coping with role conflict: The role behavior of college educated women. *Administrative Science Quarterly, 17*, 471–486.

Hansen, L. S. (1978). Promoting female growth through a career development curriculum. In L. S. Hansen & R. S. Rapoza (Eds.), *Career development and counseling of women* (pp. 425–442). Springfield, IL: Thomas.

Hansen, L. S., & Rapoza, R. S. (Eds.). (1978). *Career development and counseling of women.* Springfield, IL: Thomas.

Hansen, N. D. (2005). Society of Counseling Psychology, APA Division 17: Minutes of the Executive Board Meeting, San Diego, CA, February 5, 2004. *The Counseling Psychologist, 33*(1), 123–133.

Harmon, L. (1970). Anatomy of career commitment. *Journal of Counseling Psychology, 17,* 77–80.

Harmon, L. (1984). What's new? A response to Astin. *The Counseling Psychologist, 12,* 127–128.

Harmon, L. (1997). Do gender differences necessitate separate career development theories and measures? *Journal of Career Assessment, 5,* 463–470.

Harmon, L., & Campbell, D. (1968). The use of interest inventories with non-professional women. *Journal of Counseling Psychology, 15,* 17–22.

Harmon, L., Hansen, J. I., Borgen, F., & Hammer, A. (1994). *Strong Interest Inventory: Applications and technical guide.* Palo Alto, CA: Consulting Psychologists Press.

Harmon, L., & Meara, N. (1994). Contemporary developments in women's career counseling: Themes of the past, puzzles for the future. In B. Walsh & S. Osipow (Eds.), *Career counseling for women* (pp. 355–368). Hillsdale, NJ: Lawrence Erlbaum Associates.

Helms, J. (1984). Toward a theoretical explanation of the effects of race on counseling: A Black and White model. *The Counseling Psychologist, 12,* 153–165.

Helms, J. (1990). *Black and White racial identity: Theory, research and practice.* Westport, CT: Greenwood Press.

Hertzberg, H. (2003, July 7). Northern light. *New Yorker,* July 7, 23–24.

Hill, C., Birk, J., Blimline, C., Leonard, M., Hoffman, M., & Tanney, M. F. (Eds.). (1979). Counseling women III [Special issue]. *The Counseling Psychologist, 8*(1).

Holland, J. (1959). A theory of vocational choice. *Journal of Counseling Psychology, 6,* 35–45.

Holland, J. (1997). *Making vocational choices: A theory of vocational personalities and work environments* (3rd ed.). Odessa, FL: Psychological Assessment Resources.

Holland, J., Fritzsche, B., & Powell, A. (1994). *Self-directed search: Technical manual.* Odessa, FL: Psychological Assessment Resources.

Hooker, E. (1957). The adjustment of the male overt homosexual. *Journal of Projective Techniques, 21,* 18–31.

Horner, M. S. (1969). Bright women. *Psychology Today, 3,* 36–41.

Horney, K. (1926). Flight from womanhood. *International Journal of Psychoanalysis, 7,* 324–339.

Horney, K. (1945). *Our inner conflicts.* New York: Norton.

Hotchkiss, L., & Borow, H. (1996). Sociological perspective on work and career development. In D. Brown & L. Brooks (Eds.), *Career choice and development* (3rd ed., pp. 281–334). San Francisco, CA: Jossey-Bass.

Hoyt, D., & Kennedy, C. (1958). Interest and personality correlates of career-motivated and homemaking-motivated college women. *Journal of Counseling Psychology, 5,* 44–49.

Hyde, J. (1995). Women and maternity leave: Empirical data and public policy. *Psychology of Women Quarterly, 19,* 257–298.

Kaseberg, A., Kreinberg, N., & Downie, D. (1980). *Use EQUALS to promote the participation of women in mathematics.* Berkeley: University of California, Lawrence Hall of Science.

Katz, M. (1975). *SIGI: A computer-based system of interactive guidance and information.* Princeton, NJ: Educational Testing Service.

Keith-Spiegel, P., & Koocher, G. (1985). *Ethics in psychology: Professional standards and cases.* New York: Random House.

Kingdon, M. (1979). Lesbians. *The Counseling Psychologist, 8,* 44–45.

Kinsey, A. C., Pomeroy, W. B., & Martin, C. E. (1948). *Sexual behavior in the human male.* Philadelphia, PA: Saunders.

Kinsey, A. C., Pomeroy, W. B., Martin, C. E., & Gebhard, P. H. (1953). *Sexual behavior in the human female.* Philadelphia, PA: Saunders.

Klein, S. (1985). *Handbook for achieving sex equity through education.* Baltimore, MD: Johns Hopkins University Press.

Kohlberg, L. (1966). A cognitive-developmental analysis of children's sex-role concepts and attitudes. In E. Maccoby (Ed.), *The development of sex differences.* Palo Alto, CA: Stanford University Press.

Krumboltz, J., Mitchell, A. M., & Jones, G. B. (1976). A social learning theory of career selection. *The Counseling Psychologist, 6,* 71–81.

La Fromboise, T., & Howard-Pitney, B. (1995). The Zuni life skills development curriculum. *Journal of Counseling Psychology, 42,* 479–486.

La Fromboise, T. D., & Jackson, M. (1996). MCT theory and Native-American populations. In D. Sue, A. Ivey, & P. Pedersen (Eds.), *A theory of multicultural counseling and therapy* (pp. 192–203). Pacific Grove, CA: Brooks/Cole.

Lent, R., Brown, S. D., & Hackett, G. (1994). Toward a unifying social cognitive theory of career and academic interest, choice, and performance. *Journal of Vocational Behavior, 45,* 79–122.

Lockheed, M. (1975). Female motive to avoid success: A psychological barrier or a response to deviancy? *Sex Roles, 1,* 41–50.

Mitchell, L., & Krumboltz, J. (1996). Krumboltz' learning theory of career choice and counseling. In D. Brown, L. Brooks, H. Borow, S. Brown, A. Collin, R. Dawis, et al., *Career choice and development* (3rd ed., pp. 233–280). San Francisco: Jossey-Bass.

Mobley, M., & Slaney, R. (1996). Holland's theory: Its relevance for lesbian women and gay men. *Journal of Vocational Behavior, 48,* 125–135.

Morgan, K. S., & Brown, L. S. (1991). Lesbian career development, work behavior, and vocational counseling. *The Counseling Psychologist, 19,* 273–291.

Morin, S., & Rothblum, E. (1991). Removing the stigma: Fifteen years of progress. *American Psychologist, 46,* 947–949.

Morrow, S., Gore, P., & Campbell, B. (1996). The application of a socio-cognitive framework to the career development of lesbian women and gay men. *Journal of Vocational Behavior, 48,* 136–148.

National Coalition for Women and Girls in Education. (2002). *Title IX at 30: Report card on gender equity.* Washington, DC: Author.

National Science Foundation. (1997). *Women and science: Celebrating achievements, charting challenges.* Arlington, VA: Author.

National Science Foundation. (2000). *Women, minorities, and persons with disabilities in science and engineering: 2000.* Arlington, VA: Author.

Nevill, D., & Super, D. (1986a). *Manual for the Salience Inventory: Theory, application, and research.* Palo Alto, CA: Consulting Psychologists Press.

Nevill, D., & Super, D. (1986b). *The Values Inventory.* Palo Alto, CA: Consulting Psychologists Press.

Neville, D., Lilly, R., Duran, G., Lee, R., & Browne, L. (2000). Construction and initial validation of the color-blind racial attitudes scale (CoBAS). *Journal of Counseling Psychology, 47,* 59–70.

Osipow, S. (1983). The career development of women. In S. Osipow (Ed.), *Theories of career development* (3rd ed., pp. 254–274). Englewood Cliffs, NJ: Prentice Hall.

Osipow, S., & Fitzgerald, L. (1996). *Theories of career development* (4th ed.). Boston: Allyn & Bacon.

Patterson, C. H. (1966). *Theories of counseling and psychotherapy.* New York: Harper & Row.

Pedersen, P. B. (2000). *A handbook for developing multicultural awareness* (5th ed.). Alexandria, VA: American Counseling Association.

Pedersen, P. B., Draguns, J., Lonner, W., & Trimble, J. (Eds.). (2002). *Counseling across cultures* (5th ed.). Thousand Oaks, CA: Sage.

Ponterotto, J., Casas, J., Suzuki, L., & Alexander, C. (Eds.). (2001). *Handbook of multicultural counseling* (2nd ed.). Thousand Oaks, CA: Sage.

Prediger, D., & Swaney, K. B. (1995). Using UNIACT in a comprehensive approach for career planning. *Journal of Career Assessment, 3,* 429–452.

Psathas, G. (1968). Toward a theory of occupational choice for women. *Sociology and Social Research, 52,* 253–268.

Quinn, S. (1987). *A mind of her own: The life of Karen Horney.* New York: Addison-Wesley.

Rapoport, R., & Rapoport, R. N. (1969). The dual-career family. *Human Relations, 22,* 3–30.

Raymond, J. (1974). *Unisex Interest Inventory (UNIACT).* Ames, IA: American College Testing Program.

Riger, S. (1991). Gender dilemmas in sexual harassment policies and procedures. *American Psychologist, 46,* 497–505.

Roe v. Wade, 410 U.S. 113 (1973).

Rounds, J., Henly, G., Dawis, R., Lofquist, L., & Weiss, D. (1981). *Manual for the Minnesota Importance Questionnaire.* Minneapolis: University of Minnesota, Department of Psychology.

Sampson, J. P., Jr., & Reardon, R. C. (Eds.). (1990). Evaluating computer-assisted career guidance systems [Special issue]. *Journal of Career Development, 17*(2).

Sampson, J. P., Jr., Reardon, R., & Ryan-Jones, R. (1992). *Computer-assisted career guidance: DISCOVER.* Tallahassee: Florida State University.

Sattler, C. (1998). *Gender gaps: Where schools still fail our children.* Washington, DC: American Association of University Women.

Sekaran, U. (1986). *Dual-career families.* San Francisco: Jossey-Bass.

Sells, L. (1975). *Sex, ethnic, and field differences in doctoral outcomes.* Unpublished doctoral dissertation, University of California, Berkeley.

Sewell, W. H., & Shaw, V. P. (1968). Social class, parental encouragement, and educational aspirations. *American Journal of Sociology, 73,* 559–572.

Smith, E. J. (1983). Issues in racial minorities' career behavior. In W. B. Walsh & S. H. Osipow (Eds.), *Handbook of vocational psychology: Vol. 1. Foundations* (pp. 161–222). Hillsdale, NJ: Lawrence Erlbaum Associates.

Spence, J., & Helmreich, R. (1978). *Masculinity and femininity: Their psychological dimensions, correlates, and antecedents.* Austin: University of Texas Press.

Stone, G. (Ed.). (1994). Multicultural training [Special issue]. *The Counseling Psychologist, 22*(2).

Strong, E. K. (1927). Vocational Interest Test. *Educational Record, 8,* 107–121.

Strong, E. K. (1933). *Strong Vocational Interest Blank for Women.* Stanford, CA: Stanford University Press.

Sue, D. W. (1975). Asian Americans: Social-psychological forces affecting their life styles. In S. Picou & R. Campbell (Eds.), *Career behavior of special groups* (pp. 97–121). Columbus, OH: Merrill.

Sue, D. W. (1981). *Counseling the culturally different.* New York: Wiley.

Sue, D. W., & Sue, D. (2003). *Counseling the culturally diverse.* New York: Wiley.

Super, D. (1957). *The psychology of careers.* New York: Harper & Row.

Super, D. (1990). A life-span, life-space approach to career development. In D. Brown & L. Brooks (Eds.), *Career choice and development* (2nd ed., pp. 197–261). San Francisco: Jossey-Bass.

Super, D., Starishevsky, R., Matlin, N., & Jordaan, J. P. (1963). *Career development: Self-concept theory.* New York: College Entrance Examination Board.

Thompson, N. L., McCandless, B. R., & Strickland, B. R. (1971). *Loving boldly: Issues facing lesbians.* New York: Haworth Press.

Tiedeman, D., & O'Hara, R. P. (1963). *Career development: Choice and adjustment.* New York: College Entrance Examination Board.

Tinsley, H. E. (Ed.). (1994). Racial identity and vocational behavior [Special issue]. *Journal of Vocational Behavior, 44*(2).

Tinsley, H. E. (Ed.). (1997). Work and family balance [Special issue]. *Journal of Vocational Behavior, 50*(2).

Tinsley, H. E., & Stockdale, M. S. (Eds.). (1993). Sexual harassment in the workplace [Special issue]. *Journal of Vocational Behavior, 42*(1).

Tipping, L. (1997). Work and family roles: Finding a new equilibrium. In H. Farmer, J. Altman, A. Carter, J. Cohn, B. Conrad, S. Giurleo, et al., *Diversity and women's career development: From adolescence to adulthood* (pp. 243–270). Thousand Oaks, CA: Sage.

Tipping, L., & Farmer, H. (1991). A home-career conflict measure: Career counseling implications. *Measurement and Evaluation in Counseling and Development, 24*(3), 111–118.

Tittle, C., & Zytowski, D. (Eds.). (1978). *Sex-fair interest measurement: Research and implications.* Washington, DC: National Institute of Education.

U.S. Bureau of the Census. (2001). *Population profile of the United States.* Washington, DC: U.S. Government Printing Office.

U.S. Department of Labor, Women's Bureau. (1969). *Handbook on women workers* (Bulletin No. 294). Washington, DC: U.S. Government Printing Office.

U.S. Department of Labor, Women's Bureau. (1972). *The myth and the reality.* Washington, DC: U.S. Government Printing Office.

U.S. Equal Employment Opportunity Commission. (1980). Final amendment to guidelines on discrimination because of sex under Title VII of the Civil Rights Act of 1964, as amended (29 C.F.R. pt. 1604). *Federal Register, 45,* 74675–74677.

Unger, R., & Crawford, M. (1992). *Women and gender: A feminist psychology.* New York: McGraw-Hill.

Vasquez, M. (1998). Distinctive traits of Hispanic students. *The Prevention Researcher, 5,* 1–2.

Vetter, L. (1973). Career counseling for women. *The Counseling Psychologist, 4,* 54–66.

Walsh, W. B. (Ed.). (1997). Career assessment for women: Theory into practice [Special issue]. *Journal of Career Assessment, 5,* 355–474.

Walsh, W. B., & Betz, N. (2001). *Tests and assessment* (4th ed.). Englewood Cliffs, NJ: Prentice Hall.

Walsh, W. B., & Osipow, S. H. (1994). *Career counseling for women.* Hillsdale, NJ: Lawrence Erlbaum Associates.

Ward, C. M., & Bingham, R. P. (1993). Career assessment of ethnic minority women. *Journal of Career Assessment, 1,* 246–257.

Weitzman, L. M. (1994). Multiple role realism: A theoretical framework for women's attitudes toward multiple role planning. *Journal of Applied and Preventive Psychology, 3,* 15–26.

Weitzman, L. M., & Fitzgerald, L. F. (1996). The development and initial validation of scales to assess attitudes toward multiple role planning. *Journal of Career Assessment, 4,* 269–284.

Whiteley, J. (Ed.). (1984). Career development of women [Special issue]. *The Counseling Psychologist, 12*(4).

Women's Educational Equity Act, Public Law 93-380 (1974).

Women's Educational Equity Act (WEEA). Equity Resource Center at EDC. (2000). *Practical tools and supports for equity fair learning.* Sewickley, PA: Education Development Center.

Zytowski, D. (1969). Toward a theory of career development for women. *Personnel and Guidance Journal, 47,* 660–664.

Zytowski, D. (1999). *Kuder career search: Manual.* Adel, IA: National Career Assessment Service.

APPENDIX
Events Affecting Women's Career Development

Decade	Event
1920s	Women's suffrage
	Karen Horney publishes *Flight From Womanhood* (1926) criticizing Freud
1930s	Planned Parenthood Federation established by Margaret Sanger
	E. K. Strong (1933) publishes women's form of Strong Vocational Interest Blank
1940s	Women work in factories during WWII: Rosie the Riveter
1950s	Ginsberg et al. (1951) and Super (1957) publish theories of women's career choices and career patterns
	Kinsey et al. (1953) publish *Sexual Behavior in the Human Female*
	In *Brown v. Board of Education* (1954), the Supreme Court supports the decision desegregating the nation's schools
	De Beauvoir's (1949/1953) book *The Second Sex* appears in English translation advocating economic independence for women
	Automated household equipment widely available for household chores
	Hooker (1957) publishes "The Adjustment of the Male Overt Homosexual"
	Hoyt and Kennedy (1958) publish "Interest and Personality Correlates of Career-Motivated and Homemaking-Motivated College Women"
1960s	Betty Friedan (1963) publishes *The Feminine Mystique*
	Contraceptive pill available
	The Civil Rights Act (1964) is passed
	Executive orders No. 11246 (1965) and No. 11375 (1968) on affirmative action issued
	War on Poverty and Head Start initiated
	National Organization for Women (NOW) established
	U.S. Equal Employment Opportunity Commission established
	Harmon and Campbell (1968) publish "The Use of Interest Inventories With Non-Professional Women"
	Gyspers et al. (1968) publish "Characteristics of Homemakers and Career-Oriented Women"
	Zytowski (1969) publishes "Toward a Theory of Career Development for Women"
	Horner (1969) publishes "Bright Women," which introduces theory of female fear of success
	Psathas (1969) publishes "Toward a Theory of Occupational Choice for Women"
	Rapoport and Rapoport (1969) publish "The Dual-Career Family"
	U.S. Department of Labor, Women's Bureau established in 1969
1970s	Harmon (1970) publishes "Anatomy of Career Commitment"
	Farmer and Bohn (1970) publish "Home-Career Conflict Reduction and the Level of Career Interest in Women"
	Amendments to civil right and higher education legislation in 1972, including Title VII and Title IX related to sex equity
	Broverman et al. (1972) publish "Sex-Role Stereotypes: A Current Appraisal"
	Fitzgerald and Harmon (1973) publish "Counseling Women"

(Continued)

Decade	Event
	Vetter (1973) publishes "Career Counseling for Women"
	Cole (1973) publishes "On Measuring the Vocational Interests of Women"
	Supreme Court decision in *Roe v. Wade* (1973) supports legalizing abortions
	Women's Educational Equity Act passed by federal government (1974)
	Raymond (1974) publishes *Unisex Interest Inventory (UNIACT)*
	Conger (1975): APA declares homosexuality is not a mental illness
	Diamond (1975) publishes federal guidelines to reduce bias in interest measurement
	Gump and Rivers (1975) publish "The Consideration of Race in Efforts to End Sex Bias"
	Sells (1975) publishes "High School Mathematics as the Critical Filter in the Job Market"
	Birk and Tanney (1976) publish "Counseling Women II"
	Farmer and Backer (1977) publish *New Career Options for Women: A Counselor's Sourcebook*
	Gilligan (1977) publishes "In a Different Voice: Women's Conception of the Self and of Morality"
	Hansen and Rapoza (1978) publish *Career Development and Counseling of Women*
	Spence and Helmreich (1978) publish *Masculinity and Femininity: Their Psychological Dimensions, Correlates, and Antecedents*
	APA, Division 17 Ad Hoc Committee on Women (1979) publishes "Principles Concerning the Counseling and Therapy of Women"
	Freeman (1979) publishes "How to Discriminate Against Women Without Really Trying"
	Hill, Birk, Blimline, Leonard, Hoffman, and Tanney (1979) publish "Counseling Women III"
1980s	Federal guidelines published for reducing sexual harassment in employment (1980)
	Fitzgerald and Crites (1980) publish "Toward a Career Psychology of Women"
	APA, Division 44 formed: Lesbian, Gay and Bisexual Issues
	APA, Division 45 formed: Ethnic and Minority Issues
	Gottfredson (1981) publishes "Circumscription and Compromise: A Developmental Theory of Occupational Aspirations"
	Hackett and Betz (1981) publish "A Self-Efficacy Approach to the Career Development of Women"
	Bem (1981) publishes the *Bem Sex-Role Inventory*
	Sue (1981) publishes *Counseling the Culturally Different*
	Smith (1983) publishes "Issues in Racial Minorities' Career Behavior"
	Whiteley (1984) publishes "Career Development of Women"
	Astin (1984) publishes "The Meaning of Work in Women's Lives"
	Helms (1984) publishes "Toward a Theoretical Explanation of the Effects of Race on Counseling"

(Continued)

Decade	Event
	American Educational Research Association, APA, and National Council on Measurement in Education (1985) publish *Joint Technical Standards for Educational and Psychological Testing*
	Farmer (1985) publishes "A Model of Career and Achievement Motivation for Women and Men"
	Fitzgerald and Nutt (1986) publish "The Division 17 Principles Concerning the Counseling/Psychotherapy of Women: Rationale and Implementation"
	Nevill and Super (1986a) publish the *Manual for the Salience Inventory*
	Betz and Fitzgerald (1987) publish *The Career Psychology of Women*
	Gilbert (1987) publishes "Dual-Career Families in Perspective"
1990s	Americans with Disabilities Act passed in 1990: a civil rights amendment
	Lesbian and gay persons included in Civil Rights Act
	Fitzgerald (1990) publishes "Sexual Harassment: The Definition and Measurement of a Construct"
	Tinsley and Stockdale (1993) publish "Sexual Harassment in the Workplace"
	Tinsley (1994) publishes "Racial Identity and Vocational Behavior"
	Stone (1994) edits special issue of *The Counseling Psychologist* on multicultural issues
	Walsh and Osipow (1994) publish *Career Counseling for Women*
	APA (1995) publishes "Guidelines for Providers of Psychological Services to Ethnic, Linguistic, and Culturally Diverse Populations"
	Croteau and Bieschke (1996b) publish "Vocational Issues of Lesbian Women and Gay Men"
	Fassinger (1996) publishes "Notes From the Margins: Integrating Lesbian Experience Into the Vocational Psychology of Women"
	Tinsley (1997) publishes "Work and Family Balance"
	Walsh (1997) publishes special issue of the *Journal of Career Assessment* on career assessment for women
	Farmer, Altman, Carter, Cohn, Conrad, Giurleo, et al. (1997) publish *Diversity and Women's Career Development: From Adolescence to Adulthood*
	APA (1998) publishes "Appropriate Therapeutic Responses to Sexual Orientation"
2000s	APA (2000) publishes "Guidelines for Psychotherapy With Lesbian, Gay, and Bisexual Clients"
	APA (2003a) publishes "Guidelines on Multicultural Education, Training, Research, Practice, and Organizational Change for Psychologists"
	Chung (2003) publishes "Ethical and Professional Issues in Career Assessment With Lesbian, Gay, and Bisexual Persons"
	Supreme Court decision supports the removal of state laws against sodomy

Chapter 2

Basic Issues and Concepts in the Career Development and Counseling of Women

Nancy Betz
The Ohio State University

Although the focus of this book is on career counseling for women, it presumes that the reader has a basic, working knowledge of the major theories of and approaches to career development and career counseling. The field of vocational psychology is nearly 100 years old, if Frank Parsons' groundbreaking work, *Choosing a Vocation* (1909), can be considered its birth. Since then we have built a rich tradition of theory, research, and counseling methods, including methods of vocational and career assessment. Accordingly, I assume a familiarity with the theories of Super (see Super, Savickas, & Super, 1996), Holland (see Spokane & Cruza-Guet, 2005), Dawis and Lofquist (Dawis, 2005), Gottfredson (Gottfredson, 2005), Krumboltz' social learning approach (Mitchell & Krumboltz, 1996), and Lent, Brown, and Hackett's (1994, 2000; Lent, 2005) social cognitive theory and with traditional methods of career assessment in the areas of abilities and aptitudes, vocational interests, and vocational needs and values. Readers who wish to expand or review their knowledge in these areas may consult such resources as Brown and Lent's (2005) *Career Development and Counseling*, Osipow and Fitzgerald's classic text *Theories of Career Development* (1996), the *Handbook of Vocational Psychology* (Walsh & Osipow, 1995), the *Handbook of Counseling Psychology* (Brown & Lent, 2000), Swanson and Fouad's (1999) *Career Theory and Practice*, Spokane's (1991) *Career Intervention*, and Luzzo's (2000) *Career Counseling With College Students*.

Given basic knowledge of the field of vocational behavior and career development, this chapter is designed to set the stage for a volume on career counseling of women. In order to set this stage it is necessary to outline some issues that make women's career development different from that of men. There are a number of unique issues faced by women that make it necessary to question the particular relevance of our traditional theories and assessment methods. In the section to follow I begin by discussing why careers are important to women. I then review the state of women's career development in terms of both the extent and nature of women's labor force participation. I discuss barriers to and supports of women's career choices, achievements, and satisfaction and end with some general suggestions for career counseling. This chapter is intended to set the stage for the more detailed and targeted chapters to follow, for example, those concerning the needs of ethnic minority women (Bingham, Ward, & Butler, chap. 7), lesbian women (Bieschke & Toepfer-Hendey, chap. 11), women in management (Russell, chap. 14), and women in science and engineering (Fassinger & Asay, chap. 13) to name only a few.

OVERVIEW OF ISSUES AND ASSUMPTIONS

Although it used to be assumed that women's careers were not as important as men's because they occupied only short periods of the adult woman's life span, societal changes over the last 40 or 50 years have led to women's work, and women's careers, being a critically important part of most women's lives and, thus, a critically important focus for career psychology and career counseling. Current data on the nature, extent, and importance of women's labor force participation are reviewed in this section.

The Nature of Women's Labor Force Participation

Women now constitute a significant portion of the labor force and the vast majority of U.S. women work outside the home. In the year 2000, three fifths of women were employed. Of those ages 25 to 44, 75% were employed. Sixty percent of women with children under the age of 1 year are employed (U.S. Department of Labor, Bureau of Labor Statistics, 2003). The odds that a woman will work outside the home during her adult life are over 90%. What this adds up to is that paid employment (vs. work inside the home) is now the rule rather than the exception. There is no category of women in which the majority is not employed outside the home.

Not surprisingly, the most common family lifestyle today is the dual-earner family (Gilbert, 2002; Gilbert & Kearney, chap. 6, this volume). As described by Gilbert and by Barnett and Hyde (2001), we now have work–family role convergence where both work and family are considered important in the lives of both women and men, and where many if not most workers like the two roles equally. Thus, as career psychologists and counselors it is now essential to understand the issues facing women at work and the reality that both work and family roles are salient in the lives of contemporary women and men.

WHY CAREERS ARE IMPORTANT TO WOMEN

Women, like men, need a variety of major sources of satisfaction in their lives. As once stated by Freud (cited in Erickson, 1950), the psychologically well-adjusted human being is able "to love and to work" effectively. Both women and men need the satisfaction of interpersonal relationships with family or friends, but also the satisfaction of achievement in the outside world. As stated by Baruch and Barnett (1980):

> It is almost a cliche now for people who work long hours at demanding jobs, aware of what they are missing in terms of time with family, long talks with friends, concerts, all kinds of opportunities for leisure, to express the sentiment that "there is more to life than work." The problem is that life *without* productive work is terrible. We assume this for men in thinking about their unemployment and retirement, but we do not think about the situation of women in this way. (p. 244)

In addition to the overall importance of love and work, there are several other reasons, documented by research, that work is important to women's mental health. There are the problems of underutilization of abilities and talents and the beneficial effects of multiple roles.

Underutilization of Abilities

Research has shown that the fulfillment of individual potential for achievement is vitally important. Although the roles of homemaker and mother are important and often very satisfying, they do not allow most women to fully develop their unique abilities and talents. These, rather, must be fulfilled through career pursuits or volunteer and avocational activities, just as they are for men. This is not to discount the importance of childrearing, but only its insufficiency as a lifelong answer to the issue of self-realization. Even if a woman spends a number of years creatively rearing children, these children inevitably grow up and begin their own lives, lives that must necessarily be increasingly independent from the parental home.

The evidence is strong that homemakers who do not have other outlets for achievement and productivity are highly susceptible to psychological distress, particularly as children grow and leave home. For example, in the

Terman studies of gifted children (Terman & Oden, 1959), when followed up in their 60s (Sears & Barbie, 1977), the women who reported the highest levels of life satisfaction were the employed women. Least satisfied were those who had been housewives all of their adult lives. The most psychologically disturbed women were those with exceptionally high IQs (above 170) who had not worked outside the home. It seems fairly clear that intellectually talented women who did not pursue meaningful careers outside the home suffered psychological consequences. Other studies found that underutilization of skills is related to psychological distress for both men and women (Barnett & Brennan, 1997).

More generally, there is strong evidence for the beneficial effects of working outside the home on a woman's psychological adjustment, regardless of her marital status. Early research on the relationship between marital status and psychological health concluded that the healthiest individuals were the married men and the single women, whereas married women were at particularly high risk for psychological distress (Radloff, 1975). However, it does not seem to be marriage per se that is detrimental to women's psychological adjustment, but rather the lack of meaningful paid employment. In the studies mentioned, the women who were not employed accounted for the surplus of psychological distress among the married women.

Beneficial Effects of Multiple Roles

Although a full discussion of dual-career families can be found in chapter 6 (Gilbert & Kearney), a few observations are made here. There is strong evidence that multiple roles, that is, those of both worker and family member, are important to women's mental and physical health (Barnett & Hyde, 2001). Most research finds that even though multiple roles are time consuming, they are protective against depression (Crosby, 1991) and facilitate positive mental health. There are several hypotheses about why multiple roles are beneficial for women (Barnett & Hyde). First, when more than one role is important in a person's life, stress or disappointment in one domain can be buffered by success or satisfaction in another role. Second, the added income of a second job or career can reduce the stress of being the sole breadwinner and can in fact provide an economic lifeline when one spouse or partner becomes unemployed—in difficult economic times characterized by high unemployment and corporate downsizing or collapse, two incomes can be virtually lifesaving. Third, jobs provide an additional source of social support, which increases well-being (Barnett & Hyde). For example, Greenberger and O'Neil (1993) found that whereas men's well-being was related most significantly to social support from their wives, women's well-being was related to support from neighbors, supervisors, and coworkers, as well as from husbands. It should be noted that social support at work is useful only if the women feel integrated into some social network. For example, a woman of color may feel left out of a predominantly White social group, or if a woman is a token female in an all or mostly male work environment, social support may be lacking.

Finally, the benefits of multiple roles seem to be connected with role quality and satisfaction. In studies by Hyde, Klein, Essex, and Clark (1995) and Klein, Hyde, Essex, and Clark (1998) higher levels of perceived rewards from work were related to lower levels of depressive symptoms, and a sense of work-role overload was related to higher levels of depressive symptoms.

Interestingly, multiple roles seem to benefit the physical and psychological health of men as well as women (Barnett, Marshall, & Pleck, 1992; Gore & Mangione, 1983). Men's well-being benefits from involvement in spouse and parent as well as employee roles. Stereotypes that men are not family oriented seem as incorrect as those that women are not career oriented. Studies of single-parent fathers show that they are as caring and nurturing as mothers (Coltrane, 1996); in their behavior as parents, single fathers resemble mothers more than they do other fathers. Thoits (1992) found that men ranked their family roles higher in salience than their supposed primary role of paid employee, and other studies have shown the centrality of the parental role for men's well-being. There is evidence to contradict the myth that women's career commitment will have a negative effect on their marriage and family. It seems that more equitable sharing of breadwinning may increase marital satisfaction in both spouses, but especially husbands (Wilke, Ferree, & Ratcliff, 1998). Also interesting is data showing that the two roles are not contradictory but may in fact have a mutually catalytic effect: Studies of the relationship between work commitment and family commitment show a modest positive correlation between the two (Marks & MacDermid, 1996). Thus, women should not have to choose between work and home and family.

In considering women's career development and multiple roles it should be noted that traditional married couples with children no longer constitute a majority of U.S. citizens. There are 12 million single parents in this country, most of them women (Gilbert, 2002). There are also an increasing number of people who choose to remain single, as well as an increasing number of committed gay and lesbian couples, many of whom are now choosing to have children either biologically or through adoption. Thus, although the satisfaction of heterosexual dual-career couples will be of interest to the majority of young women planning careers, the options of remaining single or in a committed same-sex or nonmarital partnership should also be considered viable in life planning (see Farmer, 1997). It goes without saying that the issues of combining work and parenthood are different for single people who usually carry sole responsibility for home and parenting, and for those in same-sex partnerships for whom there is no obvious assignment of roles and responsibilities based on gender. But regardless of the precise nature of the family unit, helping people to have and manage multiple roles may be beneficial.

Problems in Women's Labor Force Participation

Although women now work in overwhelming numbers, the nature of their work continues to be focused in traditionally female occupations, and they continue to be paid less than men. Even though women have made much progress in entering traditionally male-dominated professions such as medicine and law, where half the entering students are now women, the occupational world still has many areas of extreme sex segregation. For example, over 90% of preschool and kindergarten teachers, dental hygienists, secretaries, child-care workers, cleaners and servants, nurses, occupational and speech therapists, and teacher's aides are women (U.S. Department of Labor, Bureau of Labor Statistics, 2003). Just 9% of teachers in elementary and middle schools are men, down from 18% in 1981.

In contrast, women remain seriously underrepresented in scientific and technical careers and high-level positions in business, government, education, and the military. For example, women earn fewer than 20% of the bachelor's degrees in fields such as engineering and physics and fewer than 10% of the graduate degrees in engineering (Kuh, 1998). High technology offers one of the fastest growing and best paid occupational fields, yet women represent only about 10% of engineers, 30% of computer systems analysts, and 25% of computer programmers (U.S. Department of Labor, Bureau of Labor Statistics, 2003). Women were 8% of physicists and astronomers, 7% of air traffic controllers, 5% of truck drivers, 4% of pilots, and 3% of firefighters. Even within a given field, women are found in lower prestige occupations. For example, Farmer (1997) discussed the career choices of young women and men interested in the sciences: Women's choices were clustered in the health sciences such as nursing and medical technician (46% of women vs. 4% of men) whereas men's were clustered in engineering (35% of men vs. 3% of women). Women remain only a small proportion of workers in the generally well-paid skilled trades and protective service occupations like police officer and firefighter—men are nine times as likely as women to be employed in these occupations.

Women continue to be paid less for full-time employment in this country. Overall, women earn 72.7% of what men earn, when both are employed full time. Women make most compared to men when they work in the District of Columbia (89.2%) and least when they work in Wyoming (64.4%) and Louisiana (65.2%). The income gap is greater for middle-aged and older workers than for young workers and is greater for White women compared to African American or Hispanic women.

In considering women's lower income it is essential to note that women cannot assure they will be taken care of by a husband. Today the average marriage lasts 7 years (Harvey & Pauwels, 1999), and 20% of children live in a single-parent home. There are 12 million single-parent households, most of them headed by women. Women are much more likely to be both single or widowed than men, and women represent 75% of the elderly poor, a percentage much greater than their representation (59%) among the elderly population. The odds that a woman will have to care for herself financially during adult life are high, and failure to prepare her for this likelihood with high-quality education or training can have tragic consequences.

In summary, career pursuits will play a major role in most women's lives, so it is imperative that career counselors help them make career choices that they find fulfilling, satisfying, and economically sufficient work. Yet the data I have described suggest that women are still choosing a smaller range of traditionally female, lower paid careers and are making substantially less money than men, even when employed full time. In the sections to follow I discuss barriers to choice and barriers to equity, but following each discussion of barriers I also discuss supportive factors. This organization follows the distinction of career barriers and supports used in social-cognitive career theory (Lent et al., 2000; see also Lent, 2005) and as originated in the writings of Farmer (1976) and Harmon (1977) in their pioneering work on women's career development. Facilitating women's career development depends in part on managing or eliminating barriers and finding ways to increase their access to supportive factors and conditions.

BARRIERS TO WOMEN'S CAREER CHOICES

Some of these are socialized barriers, that is, socialized belief systems or behavior patterns that lead women themselves to avoid certain career fields. Factors that are discussed here are math anxiety and avoidance, low self-efficacy, gender and occupational stereotypes, and a restricted range of vocational interests. Problems with our educational system, the concept of the null educational environment, and multiple-role concerns are other barriers to women's career development. These are not all of the possible barriers to women, but rather some of the most pervasive ones.

Math: The Critical Filter

The critical importance of a mathematics background for entrance to many of the best career opportunities in our society, such as engineering, scientific and medical careers, computer science, business, and the skilled trades—is now generally recognized (Chipman & Wilson, 1985), and lack of math background constitutes one of the major barriers to women's career development. Sells (1982) elaborated the vital importance of math preparation for both career options and future earnings. Four full years of high school math are vital to surviving the standard freshman calculus course, now required for most undergraduate majors in business administration, economics, agriculture, engineering forestry, resource management and conservation, health sciences, nutrition, food and consumer sciences, and natural, physical, and computer sciences. Only the arts and humanities do not now require a math background. Furthermore, Sells showed a strong and direct relationship between college calculus background and both starting salaries and employers' willingness to interview a student for a given job. Mathematics is important even for non-college-degree technical occupations; the U.S. Department of Labor's *Occupational Outlook Handbook* (2000) showed that high school math and science are "strongly recommended" for technical and trades occupations. As so well stated by Sells, "Mastery of mathematics and science has become essential for full participation in the world of employment in an increasingly technological society" (p. 7).

Given the importance of math background to career options rather than to choices by default, females' tendency to avoid math coursework becomes one of the most serious barriers to their career development. Furthermore, it is fairly clear now that it is lack of math background, rather than lack of innate ability, that is to blame for females' poorer performance on quantitative aptitude and mathematics achievement tests (e.g., Chipman & Wilson, 1985; Eccles & Jacobs, 1986). Thus, a critical issue is females' avoidance of math. Educational and counseling interventions capable of helping young women to be full participants in an increasingly technological society may be among the most crucial strategies in attempts to broaden women's career choices.

Self-Efficacy and Outcome Expectations

Self-efficacy is one of the central concepts of the Lent et al. (1994, 2000) social-cognitive theory. Self-efficacy expectations (Bandura, 1977, 1997) refer to our beliefs that we can successfully complete specific tasks or behaviors. For example, individuals may perceive themselves as able (or unable) to solve algebraic equations, fix a flat tire, or care for an infant.

Self-efficacy expectations were postulated by Bandura (1977, 1997) to have at least three behavioral consequences: (a) approach versus avoidance behavior, (b) quality of performance of behaviors in the target domain, and (c) persistence in the face of obstacles or disconfirming experiences. Thus, low self-efficacy expectations regarding a behavior or behavioral domain are postulated to lead to avoidance of those behaviors, poorer performance, and a tendency to give up when faced with discouragement or failure.

The concept of approach versus avoidance behavior is one of the simplest in psychology, yet one of the most profound in its impact. In the context of career development in particular, approach behavior describes what we will try, whereas avoidance behavior refers to things we will not try. It thus encompasses both the content of career choice, that is, the types of educational majors and careers we will attempt, and the process of career choice, that is, the career-exploratory and decision-making behaviors essential to making good choices.

The effects of self-efficacy expectations on performance can refer to effects such as performance on the tests necessary to complete college coursework or the requirements of a job training program. Finally, the effects of self-efficacy on persistence are essential for long-term pursuit of one's goals in the face of obstacles, occasional failures, and dissuading messages from the environment, for example, gender- or race-based discrimination or harassment.

There is now over 20 years of research (Betz & Hackett, 1997) allowing some generalities about career-related self-efficacy expectations in women. In educational or job content domains, college women tend to score lower than college men on domains having to do with math, science, computer science and using technology, mechanical activities, and outdoor and physical activities. Women tend to score higher on self-efficacy in social domains of activity. Note that these differences are consistent with stereotypic patterns of gender socialization. For example, Betz and Hackett (1981) asked college women and men to report whether they felt themselves capable of completing various educational majors. Even though the men and women as a group did not differ in their tested abilities, they differed significantly in their self-perceived abilities. These differences were especially striking with occupations involving mathematics: 59% of college men versus 41% of college women believed themselves able to complete a degree in that field. Seventy-four percent of men, versus 59% of women, believed they could be accountants. Most dramatically, 70% of college men but only 30% of women believed themselves able to complete a degree in engineering.

Betz and Hackett (1981) also found that this lower self-efficacy was related to lower likelihoods of considering a nontraditional (male-dominated) career, and that self-efficacy for mathematics influences choice of a science career (Betz & Hackett, 1983; Hackett, 1985). Other studies have shown that self-efficacy beliefs are related to performance and persistence. For example, Lent, Brown, and Larkin (1984, 1986) showed that efficacy beliefs regarding the educational requirements of scientific and technical occupations were related to both the performance and persistence of students enrolled in engineering programs.

Thus, low self-efficacy, especially in relationship to male-dominated careers and careers requiring mathematical or technical expertise, may reduce the self-perceived career options of women. Also important for women are outcome expectations, the beliefs that desired outcomes will follow from successful behaviors. Given continuing discrimination in the workforce it would not be surprising if women felt that competent work behavior might not be rewarded. Women of color may have particularly low outcome, as well as self-efficacy, expectations (Byars & Hackett, 1998).

Occupational and Gender Stereotypes

These stereotypes detrimentally affect the development of girls and women in at least two ways. Stereotypes regarding gender roles may lead girls to believe that they should prioritize homemaking and childrearing roles and de-emphasize their own educational achievements. One manifestation of this stereotyping is a progressive decrease in the aspirations of girls.

Numerous studies suggest that although boys and girls start out with equally high aspirations, girls reduce theirs over time (Farmer, 1997). For example, the high school boys and girls studied in Project Talent and the High School and Beyond Study reported that although they initially aspired to relatively similar levels of career prestige, as adults women selected less prestigious majors and ended up in lower level career fields. For men, but not women, persisting in science was related to high aspirations when young; women's youthful aspirations faded as they matured. In Arnold and Denny's (Arnold, 1995) sample of high school valedictorians, the girls but not the boys showed steady decrements in aspirations and also in self-esteem after college. The stronger the home-family priorities were, the more precipitous the decline in both aspirations and self-esteem.

In addition to stereotypes about women's roles are stereotypes about occupations best suited for males and females. Although beliefs that some occupations are more appropriate for men versus women may have lessened somewhat, they still exist, as shown by research. For example, in an illuminating study, Nelson, Acke, and Manis (1996) found that college students assumed that men were majoring in engineering and women in nursing even when information contrary to that was provided. For example, a 20-year-old male described as having worked in a day-care center was assumed to be majoring in engineering, whereas a 20-year-old female who had had considerable outdoor and mechanical experience was assumed to be majoring in nursing.

Children are susceptible to these stereotypes, and begin to use them to guide choice. Early studies (see Betz & Fitzgerald, 1987, for a review) showed that people consistently rate many occupations as either masculine or feminine. For example, Shinar (1975) showed that miner, federal judge,

engineer, physicist, and heavy-equipment operator were judged highly masculine, whereas nurse, receptionist, elementary school teacher, and dieti-
tian were judged highly feminine. Children learn these stereotypes at ages
as young as 2 to 3 and tend to make stereotypic choices for themselves while
in elementary school. Restricting one's choices based on sex typing of occupations is consistent with postulates of Gottfredson's (1981, 1996) vocational theory.

Restricted Vocational Interests

The use of ability and interest measures in career assessment and counseling derived from the matching or trait-factor approach to vocational psychology, as originated by Parsons and furthered by Lofquist and Dawis,
among others (see Dawis, 1996; Lofquist & Dawis, 1991). Simply stated, the
bases of this approach are that: (a) individuals differ in their job-related
abilities and interests, (b) job or occupational environments differ in their
requirements and in the kinds of interests they appeal to, and (c) a congruence (or fit) between an individual's characteristics and the characteristics
of the job is an important consideration in making good career choices.
Among the important variables to consider are abilities and aptitudes as included, for example, in the theory of work adjustment (Lofquist & Dawis)
and vocational interests, for example, as included in Holland's (1997) theory. From this perspective, the purpose of assessment is to assist counselor
and client in generating educational or career options that constitute congruent or realistic (Fitzgerald & Crites, 1980) career choices.

Although the matching model has been supported by much empirical
research, in the last 20 to 30 years we have also come to realize that this
model oversimplifies the career choice process for some groups of people.
With regard to women, for example, research over the past several decades
has indicated that the career choices of women are unrealistic in that
women tend to underutilize their abilities in selecting careers (Betz & Fitzgerald, 1987; Fitzgerald & Crites, 1980). Furthermore, women's overrepre-
sentation in traditionally female careers and underrepresentation in many
male-dominated careers may in part be due to restrictions in how vocational interests have developed.

Girls and women respond differently from men to vocational interest
items. For example, women are more likely to endorse the item "I like babies" and men are more likely to endorse the item "I enjoy repairing automobiles." Although such item-level differences are not themselves important, they can lead to very different overall scores on vocational interest
inventories. These score differences can in turn result in very different occupational suggestions being given to men and women.

Using Holland's (1997) vocational theory as an example, women score lower on realistic and higher on social than men when raw scores are used (Lunneborg, 1979; Prediger, 1980). The realistic theme includes activities involving technical, outdoor, hands-on activities, the kinds of skills often taught in high school shop, electronics, and trades courses or under the tutelage of a parent comfortable with home and automobile repair. The realistic theme is one central component for pursuit of careers in engineering and technology; when realistic interests and confidence accompany Holland's investigative (scientific) theme, a large array of engineering and technical specialties becomes viable for career exploration. For example, all of the engineering occupations listed in the Occupations Finder for Holland's (1996) *Self-Directed Search* have either *RI* or *IR* as the first two letters of their Holland code. The *Strong Interest Inventory* (Harmon, Hansen, Borgen, & Hammer, 1994) includes the occupational scales of engineer (RI) and systems analyst (IR). Women have reported consistently lower levels of realistic interests (Lunneborg). In contrast, women's higher scores on social theme would disproportionately suggest traditionally female occupations such as teacher and social worker.

There is strong evidence that these interest differences are in part due to stereotypic gender socialization: Boys and girls are exposed to different types of learning opportunities growing up. Because of gender-stereotypic socialization, neither gender learns all the skills necessary for adaptive functioning and responding (see Bem, 1974; Stake, 1997). For example, in a landmark study, Bem showed that traditionally socialized (gender-typed) men and women were unwilling to perform a non-gender-stereotypic task (ironing or nurturance as stereotypic feminine tasks and carpentry or independence as stereotypic masculine behaviors) even when they were offered money to do so. Educational and career options are also likely to be restricted because of restricted learning opportunities rather than inadequate ability or potential. Thus, restricted interest development can restrict women's career options.

Multiple-Role Concerns

Fitzgerald, Fassinger, and Betz (1995) noted that "the history of women's traditional roles as homemaker and mother continues to influence every aspect of their career choice and adjustment" (p. 72), typically in the direction of placing limits on what can be achieved. Women today may not be viewing this as an either-or choice but they often do plan careers mindful of how they will integrate these with home and family. In contrast, most men plan their careers without needing to sacrifice levels of achievement to accommodate home and families.

One unfortunate implication of the perceived overload caused by career and family priorities is that women for whom husband and children are a high priority tend to downscale their career aspirations, relative to other women and to men. (Men, of course, have not had to downscale their career aspirations in order to have a family.) The research of Arnold and Denny (see Arnold, 1995) following the lives of Illinois valedictorians and discussed earlier in this chapter provides a particularly vivid illustration of such downscaling in a group of intellectually superior female high school students. Farmer (1997), describing her longitudinal study of Midwestern high school students into adulthood, noted that a large number of young women who were interested in science chose to pursue nursing because they thought it would fit well with having and rearing children or with being a single or divorced head of household. Men made no such compromises. In Farmer's sample of women (high school students in 1980), career motivation was inversely related to homemaking commitment. As concluded by Gerson (1986), women's choices about work continue to be inextricably linked with their decisions about family, and thus family-role considerations limit women's investment in the occupational world. Ironically, family involvement has probably served to increase and facilitate men's career involvements because it gives them a strong rationale for achievement-related behavior.

Although the relationship of marital or familial status to women's career development has been weakening as we have witnessed tremendous increases in workforce participation among women in all marital and parental categories, the relationship of marital or parental status to career attainment, commitment, and innovation is still very strong. Studies have shown inverse relationships between being married or number of children and every measurable criterion of career involvement and achievement (see Betz & Fitzgerald, 1987, for a comprehensive review). This inverse relationship is not true among men: Highly achieving men are at least as likely as (if not more than) their less highly achieving male counterparts to be married and to have one or more children. In other words, men do not have to choose or downscale their aspirations. Women, like men, deserve to have, or at least try for, it all.

Barriers in the Educational System

It is probably difficult to overestimate the importance of education to career development and achievement. The nature and level of obtained education are importantly related to subsequent career achievements and to adult socioeconomic status and lifestyle. For example, an undergraduate degree is now a necessary minimum requirement for the pursuit of many occupations, and graduate or professional education is the only route to careers in many professions. All workers, men and women, earn more with increasing levels of education. For example, Latinos with a college education earn 82% more than do Latinos with a high school diploma (National Center for Education Statistics, 2002). Education is crucial for economic power (Wycott, 1996) and independence (Cardoza, 1991). In general, appropriate educational preparation is a major gate for occupational entrance. Education creates options, whereas lack of education closes them; without options, the concept of choice itself has no real meaning. Thus, the decisions individuals make concerning their education, both the level and the major areas of study, are among their most important career decisions. Furthermore, success and survival in the educational programs chosen will be critical to the successful implementation of these career decisions.

Studies commissioned by the American Association of University Women (1992, 1999) and major reviews done by Sadker and Sadker (1994) documented the continuing disadvantaged position of girls in our educational system. Researchers concluded that girls receive less attention from teachers than boys. African American girls receive less attention than White girls. Gender harassment in schools is increasing, and curriculum and texts ignore or marginalize the contributions of girls and women. This research and that by Brody (1997) have convincingly documented a decline in self-esteem among girls, but not boys, from elementary to middle and high school. For example, 55% of elementary school girls agreed with the statement "I am good at a lot of things," but this percentage declined to 29% in middle school and 23% in high school. Interestingly, girls who pursued math and science courses and who participated in sports maintained their self-esteem over this time period (American Association of University Women, 1992). These characteristics of our schools, including higher education, have been dubbed the "chilly educational climate" for girls and women (Sandler & Hall, 1996).

By the time girls enter college they can expect to encounter an educational environment that may continue to be chilly. Sexual harassment, being discouraged from classroom participation, and lack of support and mentoring can affect women in any major, but these and other subtle or direct messages that women do not belong are particularly true in male-dominated fields such as engineering and the physical sciences (see the discussion of the experiences of token women in the section on barriers to equity). Ehrhart and Sandler (1987) documented other types of differential treatment of women in higher education, including disparaging women's intellectual capabilities or professional potential, using sexist humor, advising women to lower their academic and career goals, responding with surprise when women express demanding career goals, and not actively encouraging women to apply for fellowships, grants, and awards. As stated by Pearson, Shavlik, and Touchton (1988), "The present record of higher education, in spite of some significant efforts, is not particularly good. Female students, on the whole, still experience a loss of personal and career confidence over the period they spend in higher education, even when they make very high grades. For men, the reverse is true" (p. 46). Bernard (1988) characterized the effects of such continuing discrimination on women as the "inferiority curriculum," causing even the most capable women depression, frustration, and damaged self-esteem.

Higher Education for Women: The Null Environment

One of the most basic and most important concepts summarizing the difficulties faced by women in higher education is Freeman's (1979) concept of the null educational environment. A null environment, as discussed by Betz (1989) and Freeman, is an environment that neither encourages nor discourages individuals—it simply ignores them. Its effect is to leave individuals at the mercy of whatever environmental or personal resources to which they have access. The effects of null environments on women were first postulated by Freeman following her study of students at the University of Chicago, who were asked to describe the sources and extent of environmental support they received for their educational and career goals. Although both male and female students reported being ignored by faculty, thus experiencing what Freeman called a null educational environment, male students reported more encouragement and support from others in their environments, for example, parents, friends, relatives, and significant others.

When added to the greater occurrence of negative messages regarding women's roles and, in particular, regarding women's pursuit of careers in fields traditionally dominated by men, the overall effect of the faculty's simply ignoring women students was a form of passive discrimination, of discrimination through failure to act. As stated by Freeman (1979, p. 221), "An academic situation that neither encourages nor discourages students of either sex is inherently discriminatory against women because it fails to take into account the differentiating external environments from which women and men students come," where external environments refer to differences in familial, peer, and societal support for career pursuits. In other words, professors do not have to overtly discourage or discriminate against female students. Society has already placed countless negative marks on the female student's ballot, so a passive approach, a laissez-faire attitude, may contribute to her failure. Career-oriented female students, to survive, must do without much support from their environments (Betz, 1989).

Thus, discrimination can result from errors of omission as well as of commission, and both have negative effects on females' progress and success in higher education. The critical aspect of this concept for educators, counselors, and parents is that if we are not actively supporting and encouraging women, we are in effect leaving them at the mercy of gender-role and occupational stereotypes. Eccles (1987) also stated it well: "Given the omnipresence of gender-role prescriptions regarding appropriate female life choices, there is little basis for females to develop non-traditional goals if their parents, peers, teachers, and counselors do not encourage them to consider these options" (p. 164). Failure to support her may not be an error of commission, like overt discrimination or sexual harassment, but it is an error of omission because its ultimate effects are the same, that is, limitations in her ability to fully develop and utilize her abilities and talents in educational and career pursuits. The null environment is a crucial concept to remember when doing career counseling.

SUPPORTS TO CAREER CHOICES

Among the factors that have been found to facilitate women's career achievements, including perceiving a broader array of career options, are a number of variables that, by their absence, also serve as barriers. For example, just as unsupportive environments can serve as barriers, supportive environments can be very helpful. One of the most crucial areas of support is that from families, especially parents and older relatives, and this has been found to be true for women of all racial and ethnic groups. Studies by Fisher and Padmawidjaja (1999), Flores and O'Brien (2002), Pearson and Bieschke (2001), and Juntunen et al. (2001) found parental support and availability to be very important in the career aspirations and achievements of Mexican American, African American, Native American, and White women.

Selkow (1984) found that girls with employed mothers chose a broader variety of occupations and more masculine occupations than did the daughters of homemakers. Zuckerman (1981) reported that female nontraditional career plans were related to mothers' nontraditional occupations, and Steele and Barling (1996) reported that female undergraduates with nontraditional career goals had mothers with nontraditional gender-role beliefs. Gomez et al. (2001) found that although Latina high achievers came from families where traditional gender roles were emphasized, most also had nontraditional female role models; for example, their mothers were nontraditionally employed or, if homemakers, held leadership roles in community organizations. Their mothers endorsed traditional roles in front of their husbands, but lived nontraditional roles. On the other hand, Hackett, Esposito, and O'Halloran (1989) and Weishaar, Green, and Craighead (1981) reported findings suggesting the importance of support from a male family member in girls' pursuit of nontraditional career fields. Many women pursuing nontraditional career fields relied heavily on male mentors (Betz, 2002) because no female mentors were available in the environment.

FACILITATIVE PERSONALITY FACTORS

Much previous research has shown the importance of personality factors such as instrumentality, internal locus of control, high self-esteem, and a feminist orientation on women's career achievements (Betz & Fitzgerald, 1987; Farmer, 1997; Fassinger, 1990; O'Brien & Fassinger, 1993). Instrumentality refers to a constellation of traits that were previously called "masculinity" but were seen to in actuality reflect a collection of characteristics having to do with independence, self-sufficiency, and the feeling that one was in control of one's life. It has also been described as "agency" and has much in common with self-efficacy (Bandura, 1997; Lent et al., 2000).

The possession of instrumental traits does not mean that one cannot also possess the most traditionally feminine traits of nurturance and sensitivity to others; these characteristics are now referred to as "expressiveness" or "communion" when balanced with agency and together form the androgynous person, thought to be desirable for both women and men. Thus, positive factors related to support and mentoring from others and a personality characterized by high self-esteem and self-efficacy and a sense of self-sufficiency and independence can help women reach their career goals.

WOMEN OF COLOR: SPECIAL CONCERNS

Just as research and theory developed with men in mind cannot be assumed to apply to women, research on women cannot be assumed to apply to all women, because much of it was done with White, middle-class women as participants. More complete discussions of career development with women of color (Bingham et al., chap. 7), immigrant women (Yakushko, chap. 12), lower socioeconomic status women (Heppner & O'Brien, chap. 3), and lesbian women (Bieschke & Toepfer-Hendey, chap. 11) provide information about the needs of these groups of women. I have tried to integrate research on women of color where relevant throughout this chapter, but a few more general issues and factors should be mentioned.

The disadvantages facing women in the labor force are accentuated for women of color, who have often been described as facing the "double jeopardy" (Beale, 1970; see also Gomez et al., 2001) of both gender and ethnic discrimination. Women of color are employed at rates comparable to those of White women, but they earn less than either White women or minority men. The wage gaps in comparison to White men are as follows: 71%, 64%, and 53% for White, African American, and Latina women (versus 76% and 63% for African American and Latino men, respectively). Lesbians and physically disabled women also earn less than heterosexual White women (Yoder, 1999). Interestingly, this gender gap is much smaller in many Western and African countries: Women make 90% of what men do in the countries of Iceland, France, Australia, and Tanzania.

African American women have achieved higher educational and occupational levels than have African American men, but at the same time they continue to earn substantially less than African American men. African American women are found in menial jobs such as maids and nannies more often than White women (DeVaney & Hughey, 2000). Latinos currently represent the largest minority group in the United States, 32.8 million or 12.5% in the 2000 census. The achievement of Latinas at both educational and occupational levels lags well behind that of other U.S. minorities except for Native Americans (Arbona & Novy, 1991). Mexican American women are behind other women of Hispanic ethnicity in college-completion rates, and are even behind Latino men who earned poorer grades in college.

Asian American women are somewhat more likely than other groups of women to be found in occupations emphasizing math or technology, but they are still predominantly found in traditionally female fields and, like other groups of women, earn less money than men. Finally, Native American women, including Native Hawaiians, are almost entirely invisible (Bowman, 1998) and are the most occupationally disadvantaged and most likely unemployed of any group of women. Clearly, the career development needs of women of color must receive more of our attention.

In addition to the fact of double jeopardy, another important way in which the career development of women of color may differ from that of White women is in their gender-role socialization, which differs in different cultures. There is, for example, some evidence that African American women may be less traditionally socialized, because traditional gender roles and household duties are less gender based. Many if not most African American women expect to work and to support themselves rather than relying on men (Bowman, 1998; DeVaney & Hughey, 2000). Betz and Fitzgerald (1987) summarized a number of studies supporting the benefits of an androgynous upbringing to career achievement in women, and to the extent that African American women are raised to be more androgynous this may be beneficial for their career development.

On the other hand there is evidence that African Americans raised to value academic achievement and success may be affected by perceptions of structural inequalities and discrimination causing them to doubt that they could actually succeed or to attribute their success to luck or random factors. Thus, their outcome expectations may be lower than those of White women. "Stereotype threat" has been found to impair the actual performance of both African Americans and women (Steele, 1997), so African American women may be susceptible to a double dose of such expectations.

Latinas are in general particularly well socialized in the traditional role of women, and they tend to aspire to traditionally female occupations in Holland's social and conventional areas (Arbona & Novy, 1991; Rivera, Anderson, & Middleton, 1999). Gomez et al. (2001), in a study of highly achieving Latinas, found that these women were raised with stricter gender roles than other groups of women and were encouraged to pursue traditionally female occupations. Yet they typically also had nontraditional female role models who helped them broaden their views of what women could do. Most felt enormous conflict when forced to choose between career and family responsibilities.

Asian American women also tend to be traditionally socialized and are generally taught to prioritize family and home responsibilities. DeVaney and Hughey (2000) discussed the tendency of Asian American women to seek traditional occupations, operate from an external locus of control, and have a dependent decision-making style. Asian American women may feel considerable conflict if their career aspirations are culturally inappropriate or appear to conflict with traditionally female role expectations. On the other hand, Asian American women, as well as men, are taught to value education as the route to success, because other means of mobility (e.g., business success, rising in a White-dominated business or other institution such as the military or government) may be perceived as limited (see Byars & Hackett, 1998). Asian American women are more likely to pursue math and science careers than other groups of women, perhaps consonant with expectations among many Asians that all their children, female as well as male, become competent in mathematics and science. Finally, Native American women have different experiences with gender-role socialization depending on tribal customs and values, but overall are likely to have low self-efficacy and outcome expectations even in comparison to other women.

EXTERNAL BARRIERS TO EQUITY

The barriers of discrimination and sexual harassment have long been discussed as crucial in women's attempts to attain equity in the workplace (see Fassinger, 2002; Phillips & Imhoff, 1997). Although outright gender discrimination is against the law, informal discrimination continues to exist (Fitzgerald & Harmon, 2001). For example, although women may be allowed to enter a male-dominated workplace, it may be made clear to them, overtly or subtly, that they are not welcome. Messages from overt verbal harassment to simply being ignored and receiving no social support from colleagues can make a work environment very unpleasant, and less obvious forms of discrimination in pay, promotions, and perquisites of the job continue as well (Fitzgerald & Harmon).

The importance of promotions is related to the continuing existence of the glass ceiling, which refers to the very small number of women at top levels of management (Yoder, 1999). The glass ceiling refers to artificial barriers, based on attitudinal or organizational bias, that prevent some groups of people from advancing in an organization. In 1995 the Department of Labor appointed a Federal Glass Ceiling Commission, which concluded that there still existed a corporate ceiling in that only 3% to 5% of senior corporate leadership positions are held by women, far fewer than their proportionate representation in the labor force. In addition, however, the commission reported that although the notion of a glass ceiling implies subtlety, the ceiling for women of color is by no means subtle and is better called a "concrete wall" (Federal Glass Ceiling Commission, 1995, pp. 68–69).

Another barrier to women in nontraditional careers is that of being a "token." First described by Kanter (1977), tokens are people who in gender or ethnicity (or both) constitute less than 15% of their work group. Tokens experience stress, social isolation, heightened visibility, and accusations of role violations (i.e., "You don't belong here"). African American women firefighters, who are double tokens, faced insufficient instruction, coworker hostility, silence, overly close and punitive supervision, lack of support, and stereotyping—an unwavering message of exclusion and a hope that they would fail (Yoder & Aniakudo, 1997). More generally, studies of African American firefighters (Yoder & Aniakudo), police officers (Martin, 1994), and elite Black leaders (Jackson, Thois, & Taylor, 1995) showed that both ethnicity and gender are barriers to these women's satisfaction and success. As one African American firefighter put it, "Being a black female—it was like two things needed to be proven" (Yoder & Aniakudo, p. 336).

Sexual harassment also continues to be a major problem in the workplace, with serious consequences for both women and organizations. Sexual harassment was described in detail by authors such as Fitzgerald (1993) and Norton (2002). Research now distinguishes two categories of sexual harassment: quid pro quo harassment and hostile environment harassment. Quid pro quo harassment refers to situations in which an employee is asked to give in to a supervisor's sexual demands in exchange for pay, a promotion, or continued employment, with the implied threat of loss of raise or promotion, or loss of employment, if the employee refuses to comply. Hostile environment harassment refers to instances where the employee is subject to sexual innuendo, sexist or sexually oriented comments, physical touching, or sexually oriented posters or cartoons placed in the work area. The issue here is making women workers sex objects at work—they are there to make a living and advance their careers, and sexual harassment can seriously interfere with those aims.

Although sexual harassment is not limited to men harassing women—women can harass men, and same-sex harassment can also occur—the vast majority (90%) of complaints involve men harassing women. Fitzgerald (1993) estimated on the basis of large-scale surveys of working women that one of every two will be harassed during their work lives. Women of color may be even more vulnerable: Gutek (1985) reported even greater likelihoods of harassment for Hispanic and African American women (possibly because they are often paid less so have even fewer resources to fall back on if they lose their jobs).

Although responses to sexual harassment are beyond the scope of this chapter, it suffices to say that this is a major barrier to women's equity in the workplace. Research has shown decreases in job satisfaction and organizational commitment, job withdrawal, increased symptoms of anxiety and depression, and higher levels of stress-related illness as responses to sexual harassment. We should also consider the consequences for job performance, not to mention job satisfaction—a woman cannot be expected to perform her best, and thus receive adequate pay and deserved promotions, if she is sexually harassed at work (Norton, 2002).

OVERLOAD

One of the persistent conditions affecting women's equity in the workplace is that although their workforce participation has increased dramatically, their work at home has not decreased. Women are now expected to cope with two full-time jobs, one outside and the other inside the home. Instead of "having it all," women are "doing it all" (Fitzgerald & Harmon, 2001, p. 215).

Early research on women's career development used the term *home-career conflict*, but that term communicates the need to choose between home and career. Most young women now plan on both. But few men view parenting and homemaking as their responsibility—they are primarily available to help out (Farmer, 1997). Yoder (1999) summarized data showing that women in married couples do 33 hours of household chores weekly, compared to 14 for their husbands—this constitutes 70% of the workload for women and 30% for men, and does not even include child care. With child care, these women are working one full-time job at home, in addition to what they are doing at work. Interestingly, these figures describe African American and Latino couples as well. Supreme Court Justice Ruth Bader Ginsburg noted that there could be no equity in the workplace until men assume equal sharing of homemaking and parenting roles (Farmer).

Related to this is the lack of organizational structures and support systems for employees with families. Options like subsidized child or elder care, paid family leave, flextime, job sharing, and telecommuting can greatly ease the burdens of managing home, family, and careers, burdens carried mostly by women (Fitzgerald & Harmon, 2001). We are still the only developed country in the world without a national child-care policy and one that has no systematic means of addressing the serious problems of elder care (Fitzgerald & Harmon).

SUPPORTS FOR CAREER ADJUSTMENT

Richie et al. (1997) titled their study of highly achieving African American and White women "Persistence, Connection, and Passion" (p. 133), and this title well summarizes some of the supports for women's achievement of their career goals. These might also be viewed as strengths of women that carry them through or enable them to surmount the barriers they confront. These strengths have been shown in a number of studies of highly achieving women (Gomez et al., 2001; Reddin, 1997; Richie et al.).

Persistence is critical to succeeding in the face of obstacles, and strong self-efficacy expectations, self-esteem, and a strong sense of purpose are essential in this. The characteristics of instrumentality discussed previously, that is, the sense of being in control of one's own life and destiny, of being agentic, able to act on one's own behalf, are also important to persistence.

Related to both self-efficacy and instrumentality is coping efficacy, which plays an increasingly important role in Lent et al.'s (2000) social-cognitive career theory. As Lent et al. stated, "When confronted with adverse contextual conditions, persons with a strong sense of coping efficacy (beliefs regarding one's capabilities to negotiate particular environmental obstacles) may be more likely to persevere toward their goals" (p. 76). Gomez et al. (2001) found coping strategies especially important to their highly achieving Latinas, as did Richie et al. (1997) with highly achieving African Americans and White women—they listed "flexibility, creativity, reframing and redefining challenges, barriers, or mistakes, maintaining a balanced perspective in understanding how racism and sexism may affect careers, developing support networks, and developing bicultural skills where applicable" (Gomez et al., 2001, p. 298).

Connection refers to the absolutely essential part played by familial and peer or friend support in persisting in one's goals. There is ample literature documenting the importance of family, including spouse and children, friends both at work and outside work, and mentors. And this importance has been demonstrated for women of color as well as for White women. For example, Gilbert (1994) and Gomez et al. (2001) discussed the crucial role of a supportive spouse in managing both career and home and family responsibilities. Gomez et al. reported that supportive families were crucial in maintaining career commitment after the birth of children. Richie et al. (1997) emphasized the importance of interconnectness with others in the continuing high achievement of both African American and White women.

Connection may also be facilitated by a feminist orientation, which gives women a sense of a female community beyond themselves. Feminist orientation has consistently been shown to be a facilitative factor in women's career achievements.

Finally, passion is for some women loving what they do, and for others feeling that they made a difference in the world (Gomez et al., 2001). For some women, this is the sense of a life's calling. Although not all people, women or men, are lucky enough to have such a passion in their work, helping people make choices that increase the possibility of achieving this passion is a worthy goal of the career counselor.

SUMMARY AND IMPLICATIONS FOR COUNSELING

The preceding review was designed to provide a general overview of issues and concepts important in the study of women's career development. I tried to address the problematic aspects of women's career development and both the barriers to and facilitators of that development. One facilitator not yet mentioned though is that of counseling itself. Because the chapters to follow cover specific target groups of women or specific aspects of career-counseling techniques (e.g., assessment, feminist applications) my recommendations for career counseling itself are brief and somewhat general. I recommend that career counseling for women focus on: (a) restoring their options to them, (b) convincing them that they, like men, not only can but deserve to have it all, and (c) helping them gain the personal and structural resources to cope effectively with external barriers such as discrimination and sexual harassment and to deal with the serious consequences of role overload.

Because a sexist society and stereotypic socialization have often stood in the way of matching for women, leading them to choose down, I recommend overt attempts to restore options that society has taken away. In other words, I urge counselors and psychologists to remain aware of the possible impact of sexism and stereotyping in concert with null environments and to accept and act on their role as options restorers. More specifically, I suggest that we: (a) encourage obtaining high-quality education or technical training so that even if a woman does not wish to support herself, she can if she has to; (b) encourage women to stay in math coursework as long as possible because math background opens options and prevents others from being eliminated by default; (c) encourage decisions that eliminate the fewest options (staying in school and staying in math do this); (d) use same-sex norms in interpreting vocational interest inventories so that women can see where their interests may develop further if given new opportunities; (e) help women explore new learning experiences so that they can fully develop all their capabilities, including those not reinforced by traditional gender stereotyping; (f) help women explore their outcome expectations and concerns about barriers to their goal pursuits with the idea of helping them develop coping mechanisms and coping self-efficacy; (g) remember that all it takes is one supportive counselor to enrich the null environment; (h) assess the role of culture and ethnicity in women's planning; and (i) use traditional career theories and assessment methods, but always ask whether women's gender, ethnicity, social class, sexual orientation, or any other individual differences variable may affect a particular method's utility for the client or the counselor's effectiveness.

For employed women, concerns usually fall in the areas of success, performance, and satisfaction. As I indicated earlier, discrimination, sexual harassment, tokenism, lack of support, and sheer overload from two full-time jobs (for women taking full responsibility for family and housework) are major causes of decrements in both performance and satisfaction. Counselors should focus on: (a) helping women at work develop support systems; (b) helping to change the system, or helping clients change the system, as it pertains to flexible work schedules and family-leave policies (which ideally allow leave for adoption as well as for childbearing and elder care, and which assume that men are as willing to be responsible for those they love as are women); (c) helping token women (especially women of color) find support, often by broadening the net that is cast (e.g., creating a support group of all the women in the college of sciences vs. just the two in chemistry); (d) teaching women to expect full participation in homemaking and childrearing from their husbands or partners and teaching men that it is their responsibility, and also to their benefit, to participate fully in home and family life and work; and (e) helping women develop effective cognitive and behavioral coping strategies, as discussed earlier in the section on supports for career adjustment.

For adult women considering career change or advancement, the counselor should help them to explore areas of behavior where they feel their skills are holding them back or preventing them from pursuing desired options. In many fields, technical expertise is necessary but not sufficient to the pursuit of managerial or supervisory roles in those areas. If a woman wishes to make such a move, her self-efficacy beliefs regarding her managerial or leadership skills may be highly relevant to her perceived options. Other assessment questions might be "What new skills would really increase your options or satisfaction?" and "What is stopping you from developing these new skills?" In many cases the counselor will hear perceived self-efficacy: self-doubts about competence and ability to move in a new direction.

There also may be cases where, due to inadequate career counseling (or none) when a woman first selected an occupation, she is in an occupation with poor fit in terms of either ability or interest, or both. Given that women often choose down initially or make decisions based on factors other than their individual characteristics, the chances that a woman has in fact made a choice that fits her poorly are high. In such cases, going back to the beginning—doing a comprehensive assessment of her abilities, interests, values, and self-perceptions in relationship to careers—may be the best place to start.

Organizational and Structural Change

We in psychology and counseling also have a responsibility to work for organizational, legal, and societal changes that will reduce sexism, stereotyping, discrimination, and harassment, and that will create more flexible and family-friendly workplaces. Meara (1997) noted that we must also work to change the structure of the workplace. Current structures, especially in high-prestige professional occupations, make it extremely difficult to have strong community bonds to care for children and elders, and to have balanced and healthy lifestyles.

On the other hand, Harmon (1997) noted that in our focus on facilitating women's career development we may have shortchanged the other side of the coin—that is, how to facilitate men's development in homemaking and childrearing roles. For example, as counselors provide support for women's working and help them gain self-efficacy for nontraditional careers, we should also support men's pursuits of nurturing roles and help them gain self-efficacy with respect to nurturing and multiple-role management. If we only focus on women's needs in broadening their roles, we continue to foster traditional gender roles by allowing men not to broaden their roles. Gilbert (1994) argued similarly that we have made role conflict a women's issue. It is time to move on to theories that conceptualize career development and family life in a more interactive way and the roles of men and women as interactive within the natural setting of work and family life (Harmon, p. 466).

Summary

This chapter was designed to serve as a general introduction to issues and factors counselors should be aware of when working with women clients on issues that include or involve their career development. The remaining chapters in the book expand on and refine these issues as they pertain to specific groups of women and with reference to more specific aspects of the counseling process.

REFERENCES

American Association of University Women. (1992). *The AAUW Report: How schools shortchange girls.* Washington, DC: Author.

American Association of University Women. (1999). *Gender gaps: Where schools still fail our children.* New York: Marlowe.

Arbona, C., & Novy, D. M. (1991). Career aspirations and the expectations of black, Mexican American, and White students. *Career Development Quarterly, 39,* 231–239.

Arnold, K. D. (1995). *Lives of promise: What becomes of high school valedictorians.* San Francisco: Jossey-Bass.

Bandura, A. (1977). Self-efficacy: Toward a unifying theory of behavioral change. *Psychological Review, 84,* 191–215.

Bandura, A. (1997). *Self-efficacy: The exercise of control.* New York: Freeman.

Barnett, R. C., & Brennan, R. T. (1997). Change in job conditions, changes in psychological distress, and gender. *Journal of Organizational Behavior, 18,* 253–274.

Barnett, R. C., & Hyde, J. S. (2001). Women, men, work, and family: An expansionist theory. *American Psychologist, 56,* 781–796.

Barnett, R., Marshall, N., & Pleck, J. (1992). Men's multiple roles and their relationship to men's psychological distress. *Journal of Marriage and the Family, 54,* 350–367.

Baruch, G. K., & Barnett, R. C. (1980). On the well-being of adult women. In L. A. Bond & J. C. Rosen (Eds.), *Competence and coping during adulthood* (pp. 240–257). Hanover, NH: University Press of New England.

Beale, F. (1970). Double jeopardy: To be black and female. In T. Cade (Ed.), *The black woman: An anthology* (pp. 90–100). New York: New American Library.

Bem, S. L. (1974). The measurement of psychological androgyny. *Journal of Consulting and Clinical Psychology, 42,* 155–162.

Bernard, J. (1988). The inferiority curriculum. *Psychology of Women Quarterly, 12,* 261–268.

Betz, N. E. (1989). The null environment and women's career development. *The Counseling Psychologist, 17,* 136–144.

Betz, N. E. (2002). Women's career development: Weaving personal themes and theoretical constructs. *The Counseling Psychologist, 30,* 467–481.

Betz, N. E., & Fitzgerald, L. F. (1987). *The career psychology of women.* New York: Academic Press.

Betz, N. E., & Hackett, G. (1981). The relationship of career-related self-efficacy expectations to perceived career options in college women and men. *Journal of Counseling Psychology, 28,* 399–410.

Betz, N. E., & Hackett, G. (1983). The relationship of mathematics self-efficacy expectations to the selection of science-based college majors. *Journal of Vocational Behavior, 23,* 328–345.

Betz, N., & Hackett, G. (1997). Applications of self-efficacy theory to the career development of women. *Journal of Career Assessment, 5,* 383–402.

Bowman, S. L. (1998). Minority women and career adjustment. *Journal of Career Assessment, 6,* 417–431.

Brody, J. E. (1997, November 4). Girls and puberty: The crisis years. *The New York Times,* p. B8.

Brown, S. D., & Lent, R. W. (2000). *Handbook of counseling psychology* (3rd ed.). New York: Wiley.

Brown, S. D., & Lent, R. W. (Eds.). (2005). *Career development and counseling.* New York: Wiley.

Byars, A., & Hackett, G. (1998). Applications of social cognitive theory to the career development of women of color. *Applied and Preventive Psychology, 7,* 266–267.

Cardoza, D. (1991). College attendance and persistence among Hispanic women: An examination of some contributing factors. *Sex Roles, 24,* 133–147.

Chipman, S. F., & Wilson, D. M. (1985). Understanding mathematics course enrollment and mathematics achievement: A synthesis of the research. In S. F. Chipman, L. R. Brush, &

D. M. Wilson (Eds.), *Women and mathematics: Balancing the equation* (pp. 275–328). Hillsdale, NJ: Lawrence Erlbaum Associates.

Coltrane, S. (1996). *Family man: Fatherhood, housework and gender equity.* New York: Oxford University Press.

Crosby, F. J. (1991). *Juggling: The unexpected advantages of balancing home and family.* New York: Free Press.

Dawis, R. V. (2005). The theory of work adjustment and person-environment correspondence counseling. In S. Brown & R. Lent (Eds.), *Career development and counseling* (pp. 3–23). New York: Wiley.

DeVaney, S. B., & Hughey, A. W. (2000). Career development of ethnic minority students. In D. A. Luzzo (Ed.), *Career counseling with college students* (pp. 233–252). Washington, DC: American Psychological Association.

Eccles, J. (1987). Gender roles and women's achievement-related decisions. *Psychology of Women Quarterly, 11,* 135–172.

Eccles, J. S., & Jacobs, J. (1986). Social forces shape math participation. *Signs, 11,* 367–380.

Ehrhart, J. K., & Sandler, B. R. (1987). *Looking for more than a few good women in traditionally male fields.* Washington, DC: Project on the Status and Education of Women.

Erickson, E. (1950). *Childhood and society.* New York: Norton.

Farmer, H. S. (1976). What inhibits achievement and career motivation in women? *The Counseling Psychologist, 6,* 12–14.

Farmer, H. S. (1997). *Diversity and women's career development.* Thousand Oaks, CA: Sage.

Fassinger, R. E. (1990). Causal models of career choice in two samples of college women. *Journal of Vocational Behavior, 36,* 225–240.

Fassinger, R. E. (2002). Hitting the ceiling: Gendered barriers to occupational entry, advancement, and achievement. In L. Diamant & J. Lee (Eds.), *The psychology of sex, gender, and jobs* (pp. 21–46). Westport, CT: Praeger.

Federal Glass Ceiling Commission. (1995). *Report on the glass ceiling for women.* Washington, DC: U.S. Department of Labor.

Fisher, T. A., & Padmawidjaja, L. (1999). Parental influences on career development perceived by African American and Mexican American college students. *Journal of Multicultural Counseling and Development, 27,* 136–152.

Fitzgerald, L. F. (1993). Sexual harassment: Violence against women in the workplace. *American Psychologist, 48,* 1070–1076.

Fitzgerald, L. F., & Crites, J. O. (1980). Toward a career psychology of women. *Journal of Counseling Psychology, 27,* 44–62.

Fitzgerald, L. F., Fassinger, R. E., & Betz, N. (1995). Theoretical advances in the study of women's career development. In W. B. Walsh & S. H. Osipow (Eds.), *Handbook of vocational psychology* (2nd ed., pp. 67–110). Hillsdale, NJ: Lawrence Erlbaum Associates.

Fitzgerald, L. F., & Harmon, L. W. (2001). Women's career development: A postmodern update. In F. L. T. Leong & A. Barak (Eds.), *Contemporary models in vocational psychology* (pp. 207–230). Mahwah, NJ: Lawrence Erlbaum Associates.

Flores, L., & O'Brien, K. (2002). The career development of Mexican-American adolescent women. *Journal of Counseling Psychology, 49,* 14–27.

Freeman, J. (1979). How to discriminate against women without really trying. In J. Freeman (Ed.), *Women: A feminist perspective* (2nd ed., pp. 217–232). Palo Alto, CA: Mayfield.

Gerson, K. (1986). *Hard choices: How women decide about work, career, and motherhood.* Berkeley: University of California Press.

Gilbert, L. (1994). Current perspectives on dual career families. *Current Directions in Psychological Science, 3,* 101–104.

Gilbert, L. A. (2002, August). *Changing roles of work and family.* Paper presented at the meeting of the American Psychological Association, Chicago.

Gomez, M. J., Fassinger, R. E., Prosser, J., Cooke, K., Mejia, B., & Luna, J. (2001). Voices abriendo caminos (Voices forging paths): A qualitative study of the career development of notable Latinos. *Journal of Counseling Psychology, 48,* 286–300.

Gore, S., & Mangione, T. W. (1983). Social roles, sex roles, and psychological distress. *Journal of Health and Social Behavior, 24,* 300–312.

Gottfredson, L. S. (1981). Circumscription and compromise: A development theory of occupational aspirations. *Journal of Counseling Psychology, 28,* 545–579.

Gottfredson, L. S. (2005). Applying Gottfredson's theory of circumscription and compromise in career guidance and counseling. In S. D. Brown & R. W. Lent (Eds.), *Career development and counseling* (pp. 71–100). New York: Wiley.

Greenberger, E., & O'Neil, R. (1993). Spouse, parent, worker: Role commitments and role-related experiences in the construction of adults' well-being. *Developmental Psychology, 29,* 181–197.

Gutek, B. (1985). *Sex and the workplace.* San Francisco: Jossey-Bass.

Hackett, G. (1985). The role of mathematics self-efficacy in the choice of math-related majors of college women and men: A path analysis. *Journal of Counseling Psychology, 32,* 47–56.

Hackett, G., Esposito, D., & O'Halloran, M. S. (1989). The relationship of role model influences to the career salience and educational and career plans of college women. *Journal of Vocational Behavior, 35,* 164–180.

Harmon, L. W. (1977). Career counseling of women. In E. Rawlings & D. Carter (Eds.), *Psychotherapy for women* (pp. 197–206). Springfield, IL: Thomas.

Harmon, L. W. (1997). Do gender differences necessitate separate career development theories and measures? *Journal of Career Assessment, 5,* 463–470.

Harmon, L., Hansen, J., Borgen, F., & Hammer, A. (1994). *Manual for the Strong Interest Inventory.* Palo Alto, CA: Consulting Psychologists Press.

Harvey, J. H., & Pauwels, B. G. (1999). Recent developments in close relationships. *Current Directions in Psychological Science, 8,* 93–95.

Holland, J. L. (1996). *The Self-Directed-Search (SDS) Form E* (4th ed.). Odessa, FL: Psychological Assessment Resources.

Holland, J. L. (1997). *Making vocational choices: A theory of vocational personalities and work environments.* Odessa, FL: Psychological Assessment Resources.

Hyde, I. S., Klein, M., Essex, M. J., & Clark, R. (1995). Maternity leave and women's mental health. *Psychology of Women Quarterly, 19,* 257–285.

Jackson, P. B., Thois, P. A., & Taylor, H. F. (1995). Composition of the workplace and psychological well-being: The effects of tokenism on America's black elite. *Social Forces, 74,* 543–557.

Juntunen, C. L., Barraclough, D. J., Broneck, C. L., Seibel, G. A., Winlow, S. A., & Morin, P. M. (2001). American Indian perspectives on the career journey. *Journal of Counseling Psychology, 48,* 274–285.

Kanter, R. M. (1977). *Men and women of the corporation.* New York: Basic Books.

Klein, M. H., Hyde, J. S., Essex, M. J., & Clark, R. (1998). Maternity leave, role quality, work involvement and mental health one year after delivery. *Psychology of Women Quarterly, 22,* 239–266.

Kuh, C. V. (1998, November). *Data on women doctoral level scientists and universities.* Paper presented at National Invitational Conference on Women in Research Universities, Cambridge, MA.

Lent, R. W. (2005). A social cognitive view of career development and counseling. In S. D. Brown & R. W. Lent (Eds.), *Career development and counseling* (pp. 101–130). New York: Wiley.

Lent, R. W., Brown, S. D., & Hackett, G. (1994). Toward a unifying social cognitive theory of career and academic interest, choice, and performance. *Journal of Vocational Behavior, 45,* 79–122.

Lent, R. W., Brown, S. D., & Hackett, G. (2000). Contextual supports and barriers to career choice: A social cognitive analysis. *Journal of Counseling Psychology, 47*, 36–59.

Lent, R. W., Brown, S. D., & Larkin, K. (1984). Relation of self-efficacy expectations to academic achievement and persistence. *Journal of Counseling Psychology, 31*, 356–362.

Lent, R. W., Brown, S. D., & Larkin, K. (1986). Self-efficacy in the prediction of academic success and perceived career options. *Journal of Counseling Psychology, 33*, 265–269.

Lofquist, L., & Dawis, R. (1991). *Essentials of person-environment correspondence counseling.* Minneapolis: University of Minnesota Press.

Lunneborg, P. (1979). Service vs. technical interest: Biggest sex difference of all? *Vocational Guidance Quarterly, 28*, 146–153.

Luzzo, D. A. (Ed.). (2000). *Career counseling of college students.* Washington, DC: American Psychological Association.

Marks, S. R., & MacDermid, S. M. (1996). Multiple roles and the self: A theory of role balance. *Journal of Marriage and the Family, 58*, 417–432.

Martin, S. E. (1994). "Outsider within" the station house: The impact of race and gender on black women police. *Social Problems, 41*, 383–400.

Meara, N. M. (1997). Changing the structure of work. *Journal of Career Assessment, 5*, 471–474.

Mitchell, L., & Krumboltz, J. (1996). Krumboltz' learning theory of career choice and counseling. In D. Brown & L. Brooks (Eds.), *Career choice and development* (3rd ed., pp. 233–280). San Francisco: Jossey-Bass.

National Center for Education Statistics. (2002). *The condition of education 2002* (NCES Publication No. 2000-025). Washington, DC: U.S. Government Printing Office.

Nelson, T. E., Acke, M., & Manis, M. (1996). Irrepressible stereotypes. *Journal of Experimental Social Psychology, 32*, 13–38.

Norton, S. (2002). Women exposed: Sexual harassment and female vulnerability. In L. Diamant & J. Lee (Eds.), *The psychology of sex, gender, and jobs* (pp. 82–103). Westport, CT: Praeger.

O'Brien, K. M., & Fassinger, R. E. (1993). A causal model of the career orientation and career choice of adolescent women. *Journal of Counseling Psychology, 40*, 1–14.

Osipow, S., & Fitzgerald, L. F. (1996). *Theories of career development* (4th ed.). Boston: Allyn & Bacon.

Parsons, F. (1909). *Choosing a vocation.* Boston: Houghton Mifflin.

Pearson, C., Shavlik, D., & Touchton, J. (Eds.). (1988). *Prospectus for educating the majority: How women are changing higher education.* Washington, DC: American Council on Education.

Pearson, S. M., & Bieschke, K. (2001). Succeeding against the odds: An examination of familial influences on the career development of professional African American women. *Journal of Counseling Psychology, 48*, 301–309.

Phillips, S., & Imhoff, A. R. (1997). Women and career development: A decade of research. *Annual Review of Psychology, 48*, 31–59.

Prediger, D. (1980). The determination of Holland types characterizing occupational groups. *Journal of Vocational Behavior, 16*, 33–42.

Radloff, L. (1975). Sex differences in depression: The effects of occupation and marital status. *Sex Roles, 1*, 249–265.

Reddin, J. (1997). Highly achieving women: Career development patterns. In H. S. Farmer (Ed.), *Diversity and women's career development* (pp. 95–126). Thousand Oaks, CA: Sage.

Richie, B. S., Fassinger, R. E., Lenn, S. G., Johnson, J., Prosser, J., & Robinson, S. (1997). Persistence, connection, and passion: A qualitative study of the career development of highly achieving African-American Black and White women. *Journal of Counseling Psychology, 44*, 133–148.

Rivera, A. A., Anderson, S. K., & Middleton, V. A. (1999). A career development model for Mexican American women. *Journal of Career Development, 26*, 91–106.

74
BETZ

Sadker, M., & Sadker, D. (1994). *Failing at fairness: How our schools cheat girls.* New York: Touchstone.

Sandler, B. R., & Hall, R. M. (1996). *The chilly classroom climate: A guide to improve the education of women.* Washington, DC: National Association for Women in Education.

Sears, P. S., & Barbie, A. H. (1977). Career and life satisfaction among Terman's gifted women. In J. C. Stanley, W. George, & C. Solano (Eds.), *The gifted and caretive: Fifty year perspective* (pp. 72–106). Baltimore: Johns Hopkins University Press.

Selkow, P. (1984). Effects of maternal employment on kindergarten and first-grade children's vocational aspirations. *Sex Roles, 11,* 677–690.

Sells, L. (1982). Leverage of equal opportunity through mastery of mathematics. In S. M. Humphreys (Ed.), *Women and minorities in science* (pp. 7–26). Boulder, CO: Westview Press.

Shinar, E. H. (1975). Sexual stereotypes of occupations. *Journal of Vocational Behavior, 7,* 99–111.

Spokane, A. R. (1991). *Career intervention.* Englewood Cliffs, NJ: Prentice Hall.

Spokane, A. R., & Cruza-Guet (2005). Holland's theory. In S. Brown & R. Lent (Eds.), *Career choice and development* (pp. 24–41). New York: Wiley.

Stake, J. (1997). Integrating expressiveness and instrumentality in real life settings: A new perspective on benefits of androgyny. *Sex Roles, 37,* 541–564.

Steele, C. M. (1997). A threat in the air: How stereotypes shape the intellectual identities and performance of women and African Americans. *American Psychologist, 52,* 613–629.

Steele, J., & Barling, J. (1996). Influence of maternal gender role beliefs and role satisfaction on daughters' vocational interests. *Sex Roles, 34,* 637–648.

Super, D., Savickas, M., & Super, C. (1996). The life-span life-space approach to careers. In D. Brown & L. Brooks (Eds.), *Career choice and development* (3rd ed., pp. 79–232). San Francisco: Jossey-Bass.

Swanson, J. L., & Fouad, N. A. (1999). *Career theory and practice: Learning through case studies.* Thousand Oaks, CA: Sage.

Terman, L. M., & Oden, M. H. (1959). *Genetic studies of genius: Vol. 5. The gifted group at midlife.* Stanford, CA: Stanford University Press.

Thoits, P. A. (1992). Identity structures and psychological well-being. *Social Psychology Quarterly, 55,* 236–256.

U.S. Department of Labor. (2000). *Occupational outlook handbook.* Washington, DC: U.S. Government Printing Office.

U.S. Department of Labor, Bureau of Labor Statistics. (2003). *Facts on women workers.* Washington, DC: Author.

Walsh, W. B., & Osipow, S. H. (1995). *Handbook of vocational psychology* (2nd ed.). Hillsdale, NJ: Lawrence Erlbaum Associates.

Weishaar, M. E., Green, G. J., & Craighead, L. W. (1981). Primary influences of initial vocational choices for college women. *Journal of Vocational Behavior, 34,* 289–298.

Wilke, J. R., Ferree, M. M., & Ratcliff, K. (1998). Gender and fairness: Marital satisfaction in two-earner couples. *Journal of Marriage and the Family, 60,* 577–594.

Wycott, S. E. M. (1996). Academic performance of Mexican American women: Sources of support that serve as motivating variables. *Journal of Multicultural Counseling and Development, 24,* 146–155.

Yoder, J. (1999). *Women and gender: Transforming psychology.* Upper Saddle River, NJ: Prentice Hall.

Yoder, J., & Aniakudo, P. (1997). "Outsider within" the firehouse. *Gender and Society, 11,* 324–341.

Zuckerman, D. M. (1981). Family background, sex-role attitudes, and the goals of technical college and university students. *Sex Roles, 7,* 1109–1126.

Chapter 3

Women and Poverty:
A Holistic Approach
to Vocational Interventions

Mary J. Heppner
University of Missouri–Columbia

Karen M. O'Brien
University of Maryland

> *It is common, among the non-poor, to think of poverty as a sustainable condition—austere, perhaps, but they get by somehow, don't they? They are "always with us." What is harder for the non-poor to see is poverty as acute distress: The lunch that consists of Doritos or hot dog rolls, leading to faintness before the end of the shift. The "home" that is also a car or van. The illness or injury that must be "worked through," with gritted teeth, because there's no sick pay or health insurance and the loss of one day's pay will mean no groceries for the next. These experiences are not part of a sustainable lifestyle. . . . They are, by almost any standard of subsistence, emergency situations. And that is how we should see the poverty of so many millions of low-wage Americans—as a state of emergency.*
> —Ehrenreich (2001, p. 214)

Poverty is a gender issue. Those bearing the heaviest brunt of the impact of poverty are unquestionably women and their children. The gender-based occupational structure and subsequent low wages in traditionally female occupations have been major contributors to making poor women poor. Despite the interest among vocational psychologists in the career development of people of color and women, the effects of poverty on the career paths of many of these individuals have gone virtually unstudied. Vocational psychology, and psychology in general, have been slow to focus research on, and develop interventions for, low-income women. The overarching goals of this chapter are to begin to discuss issues related to how poverty affects the vocational development of women and to make several recommendations for how vocational psychologists might work effectively with low-income women.

75

Specifically, after providing general statistics, the first purpose of this chapter is to describe several factors contributing to the large numbers of women living in poverty. We then discuss the impact of poverty on the lives of women and their children. Next, we present several hypotheses that might assist in understanding the reluctance of researchers and clinicians to advance knowledge regarding the poor. We address the disinterest in studying those whose lives are different from our own, the lack of congruence between the tenets of career development and the needs of women living in poverty, and the notion of classism being an acceptable "ism." Next we propose three key areas that we believe to be of particular importance to career counselors working with women in poverty, which include: (a) recognizing and working on our biases and tendencies toward cognitive distancing, (b) framing our work using the ecological model of career development thereby recognizing the systems and subsystems of an individual's context and how they influence career development, and (c) reinforcing strengths and building resiliency in clients with whom we work. Finally, this chapter concludes with suggestions for becoming more knowledgeable about research, services, and programs that maximize effective interventions with women in poverty.

HOW MANY WOMEN ARE POOR?

There are currently 34.6 million Americans living in poverty (U.S. Bureau of the Census, 2003), which represents an increase of 1.7 million from the previous year. According to the U.S. Bureau of the Census, individuals are considered to live in poverty if they earn less than $18,392 for a family of four, $14,348 for a family of three, and $11,756 for a family of two. Of the people living in poverty in the United States, 57% (or 19.8 million) are women (U.S. Bureau of the Census). Factors contributing to the high prevalence of women living in poverty include the low wages associated with traditional women's work, educational attainment disparity, divorce, domestic violence, racial prejudice and discrimination, and responsibility for children and aging relatives. Moreover, factors associated with living in poverty (such as physical and mental illnesses) also contribute to low socioeconomic status (SES) and high levels of underemployment among women. The focus of this chapter is on women who live in poverty and are employable. Due to the myriad challenges facing the poorest of the poor, this chapter does not address vocational interventions for these individuals.

Although many believe that our economy is on the mend, the experiences of low-income women are not improving. The dramatic gap between rich and poor has continued to widen over the last 20 years in the United States, with the average income of the poorest 20% of the population decreasing by 6% and the average income of the wealthiest 20% increasing by 30% (Bernstein, McNichol, Mishel, & Zahradnik, 2000). As Blustein et al. (2002) emphasized, "The United States is becoming a nation of two classes—one with resources and access to the opportunity structure and one without. . . . Wealth is becoming increasingly concentrated in the upper strata of society, which is impacting the vocational trajectories of many poor and working class individuals" (p. 311). Yet as Rice (2001) pointed out, we continue to focus on the "welfare crisis" as opposed to examining the way that money and resources are unequally, perhaps unfairly, distributed in our society. Moreover, although in absolute numbers there are more White people living in poverty than any other racial or ethnic group in the United States, the overall percentage of poor Whites is relatively low at 8%. Racial and ethnic minority groups are overrepresented among those living in poverty (i.e., 10% of Asian and Pacific Islanders, 21.8% of Latinos, and 23.9% of African Americans live below the poverty level; U.S. Bureau of the Census, 2003).

WHAT FACTORS CONTRIBUTE TO WOMEN BEING POOR?

A critical review of the literature related to women living in poverty revealed salient antecedents to the low SES of many women including sexism, racism, divorce, care for children and aging parents, and violence. One study of over 400 homeless and low-income women determined that higher levels of education and positive parental role models contributed to the employability of these women (Brooks & Buckner, 1996). Other positive factors included delaying motherhood and receiving income from a partner. In the next section, we outline several contributing factors to women's continued segregation in low-paying, low-status jobs. Although several barriers that are present in the lives of low-income women are discussed, in reality, their lives are filled with countless obstacles that impinge on their ability to remain employed in adequately paying jobs.

Disparity in the Occupational Pay Structure

One salient barrier to women's full and equal participation in the workforce relates to job earnings. Although we are now five decades into the second wave of feminism, our society continues to operate in a patriarchial manner that affects the ability of many women to achieve economic self-sufficiency. Women continue to earn less money than men (for comparable work), and they are less likely to obtain advanced education in their fields of study. In fact, the average woman earns only 73% of the pay that is earned by her male counterpart (Thomas, 2000). Even after decades of programs aimed at helping women obtain higher paying nontraditional jobs, the vast majority of women have not become part of the skilled trades and have not become union workers benefiting from higher wage structures. Low-income women often work in food service, retail, secretarial, and cleaning occupations. Often, non-poverty-wage occupations require postsecondary education or training, which typically are not available to poor women. Interestingly, women who receive welfare assistance are more likely to escape poverty if they obtain jobs that include participation in a union (Spalter-Roth, Burr, Hartmann, & Shaw, 1995).

Moreover, the American Psychological Association (APA, 1998) reported that the hourly wages of the lowest paid employees have declined over time, with women in 1995 earning an average hourly wage of $4.84 (a decline from $5.82 in 1979). These trends have also continued in higher level positions. For example, a recent study of 2,000 managers in 500 companies found that women managers earn significantly lower salaries than male managers (Ostroff & Atwater, 2003). Moreover, the researchers revealed that managers whose employees are predominantly female earn less than those individuals who manage male employees, reflecting the interplay of sexism and SES.

Racism

For women of color, racism in the form of discrimination in hiring and promotion contributes to poverty. Women of color continue to be concentrated in low-status and low-paid positions. For example, Latinas have particularly high rates of poverty, with over 25% of Latina households being headed by single moms who often fall below the poverty line (U.S. Bureau of the Census, 2002). Moreover, a study of older adults found minority women to be at a double disadvantage with regard to the risk of living in poverty due to both racial and gender discrimination (Hardy & Hazelrigg, 1995). These high rates of poverty are influenced by a history of racism and discrimination that has resulted in occupational segregation in extremely low-wage positions. Similarly, immigrant women consistently are overrepresented in low-wage positions (Ben-Sira, 1997), even when they come to the United States with prestigious credentials from their countries of origin. Immigrant women may face not only sexism and racism, but also xenophobia as they seek to become productive U.S. citizens.

Divorce

One major negative consequence of divorce for many women is the loss of significant financial resources. The U.S. Bureau of the Census (2001) reported that 21% of recently divorced women live below the poverty line (compared to only 9% of divorced men). In many states, women are not enti-tled to half of the family's earnings or compensation for their contributions to raising children or caring for the home in a divorce (Crittenden, 2001). Crittenden indicated that many mothers have a much lower earning poten-tial after divorce than they did prior to having children. In addition, 40% of women who are divorced turn to welfare benefits for financial assistance.

Responsibility for Children

Women historically (and currently) have primary responsibility for the care of children and the welfare of the home. Not surprisingly, the majority of poor families with children have a female head of household and an aver-age income of $9,211 (Lott & Bullock, 2001). Low-income women often are raising their children without emotional or financial support from family members. They often live in unsafe neighborhoods where their children are at risk for harm, involvement in unhealthy behaviors, and even death. The demands of caring for children can create problems for achieving in the workplace, one significant contributor to this being the lack of afford-able and quality child care. According to the APA (1998), many women feel they are unable to seek employment because of the lack of availability and the tremendous expense associated with quality child care. Furthermore, single mothers are at a greater risk of living in poverty in old age: A recent study found that women who raised children on their own for 10 or more years were 55% more likely to live in poverty when they reached age 65 than women who were married while they raised their children (Johnson & Favreault, 2004).

Donna McDonald, a counseling psychologist who has worked with many low-income women, believes that sole responsibility for children greatly de-tracts from women's ability to remain employed (personal communication, February 10, 2004). She stated, "Imagine raising two or three children with-out a partner, with little or no family support, and without a car. Now, try to get yourself to work and your children to child care. More than likely, your work involves physical activity or standing for long periods of time. You come home, cook dinner, deal with the kids, and still try to figure out how you will pay your rent because your job doesn't pay well. Even the task of try-ing to look for work can be challenging."

Caring for Aging Relatives

An additional contributor to women living in poverty are the employment difficulties faced by high numbers of women because they are caring for ag-ing parents and relatives. The National Alliance for Caregiving (1997) re-ported that 73% of the primary caregivers for elderly people are women.

Many of these women (41%) are also caring for children at the same time. The time and energy spent assisting ailing relatives greatly impacts the ability of women to focus on work outside the home.

Violence Against Women

Research also suggests that a large percentage of homeless and poor women are victims of domestic violence. In fact, a study of over 300 low-income and homeless women found that almost 60% of the women reported being physically assaulted by their partners and over 80% reported being physically or sexually abused during their lifetime (Bassuk et al., 1996). Victims of domestic violence often struggle to succeed in jobs, with the abuse often leading to tardiness, absenteeism, and disruption at work. Kenney and Brown (1997) suggested that batterers may attempt to sabotage their partners' efforts at economic self-sufficiency through physical beatings or refusal to provide child care during their working hours.

Relatedly, many low-income women are forced to live in unsafe neighborhoods due to the cost of housing. One study of low-income African American women revealed that 25% of the women sampled had family members who had been murdered (McDonald, 1998). Their grief, ongoing fear regarding their safety and that of their family members, and efforts to keep their children safe often interfere with their ability to remain in their jobs.

WHAT ARE THE EFFECTS OF POVERTY ON WOMEN AND CHILDREN?

Poverty exerts deleterious effects on the lives of women and children. Many women living in poverty were poor as children and their adult lives have been negatively affected by socioeconomic disadvantage. Poverty influences physical and mental health as well as academic, vocational, social, relational, and parental functioning. A lifetime of living in poverty can have devastating effects on the long-term productivity of individuals (Hill & Sandfort, 1995).

Effects of Poverty on Women

The physical health of women is compromised as low SES correlates with higher death rates and a number of serious illnesses (e.g., coronary heart disease, hypertension, cervical cancer, AIDS/HIV; Adler & Coriell, 1997). Women living in poverty are more likely to have physical disabilities (Falik & Collins, 1996; Olson & Pavetti, 1996) and lack access to health insurance and adequate medical care (National Center for Health Statistics, 1995).

When medical care is available, low-income women often experience long waits to see doctors and may receive substandard care. The costs of prescription medicines and needed tests may be prohibitive for many poor women. In addition, low-income women also often lack the time, energy, and cooking materials to prepare healthy meals at home, thus leading to consumption of fast food and nutritionally lacking meals. Moreover, many jobs held by low-income women are physically demanding, requiring much physical exertion or long periods of standing.

Poverty also affects the psychological health of women, with those living in poverty much more likely to experience mental illness than those in higher socioeconomic groups. In fact, higher incidents of depression, PTSD, and substance abuse have been documented among low-income women and homeless women (APA, 1998). Access to mental health services is also limited by poverty (McGrath, Keita, Strickland, & Russo, 1990). The APA noted that poor women face a "double whammy" of poverty as they are at greater risk to experience depression due to stressors and consequences of being poor, and their low SES makes it very difficult to overcome obstacles to obtain treatment and medication.

Poverty affects women's ability to parent their children effectively. Because so many poor women were born into poverty (see the next section for effects of poverty on children), they often did not receive adequate parenting due to myriad stressors and the need to focus on survival experienced by low-income parents. As stated earlier, parenting is challenging when little or no emotional or financial support is available, when parents are working multiple jobs to survive, and when their living conditions are dangerous and inconsistent over time.

In addition, the effects of poverty may influence a client's ability to maximize the services available from a career counselor. Christel Nichols, executive director of House of Ruth in Washington, DC (a program that seeks to enable those women in greatest need to live stable and independent lives), indicated that many of their clients have unrealistic expectations for counseling and for their performance on the job (personal communication, January 26, 2004). Some women who have experienced poverty, violence, addictions, or mental illness may have difficulty trusting others, regulating their affect, and responding to the responsibilities and demands of many work environments.

Effects of Poverty on Children

Over 12.1 million individuals living in poverty are children under the age of 18 (U.S. Bureau of the Census, 2003). In fact, one in six children is poor, which is the highest level of childhood poverty in the industrialized world. Children living in poverty often receive inadequate nutrition, live in fear,

and experience chronic stress and unpredictability—conditions antitheti-
cal to focusing and succeeding in school. Many adults who are poor grew
up in poverty, thus the following effects of poverty on children can assist in
understanding the challenges faced by many low-income women to obtain
and remain employed in jobs that pay well.

Poverty is associated with deficits in children's socioemotional, cognitive,
and verbal skills (Evans, 2004; Korenman, Miller, & Sjaastad, 1995) and
children and adolescents' academic achievement (Conger, Conger, & Elder, 1997; Evans). Researchers have hypothesized that inadequate prenatal
care, premature birth, exposure to alcohol, drugs, or nicotine, and low maternal age contribute to the problems that children in poverty experience
(McLoyd, 1998). Furthermore, McLoyd pointed out that children born
into poverty rarely have the resources needed to lessen the effects of harmful perinatal conditions. For example, children born of poor women tend
to receive less cognitive stimulation in the home. Their schools are substandard and often lack basic instructional resources such as books. Teachers
have lowered expectations for the performance of poor children, which
can contribute to lowered motivation to achieve. Also, parents are often less
able to be involved in the school lives of children due to having to work
many jobs just to survive. Moreover, during summers, when school is not
meeting, poor parents are rarely able to provide enrichment activities or
even adequate supervision of their children. Finally, poor children often receive harsh and inconsistent parenting that some researchers attribute to
the myriad stressors in parents' lives (McLoyd).

McLoyd (1998) also noted that children living in poverty are affected
strongly by the lack of affordable housing and crime-ridden neighborhoods. The substandard housing in which poor children live is not only
structurally unsound but also may contain dangerous levels of lead, which
can cause cognitive deficits in children. Many poor neighborhoods are dangerous, and children living in poor neighborhoods report chronic stressors
including exposure to domestic and street violence (Attar, Guerra, &
Tolan, 1994). Recent research showed that poor families who moved to affluent neighborhoods reported significant increases in job experiences for
the parents and improved social and academic functioning for the children
(DeAngelis, 2001). Other researchers found that neighborhoods can exert
a positive influence on children's lives through shared resources, modeling
parenting skills, and the presence of a strong social network (Wandersman
& Nation, 1998); such neighborhoods are not often accessible to low-
income families.

It appears that although any one of these individual predictors can be
damaging to children, it is their cumulative impact that leads to the most severe effects. In his recent critical review article on the effects of childhood
poverty, Evans (2004) concluded that "the confluence of multiple demands

from the psychosocial and physical environment appears to be a powerful force leading to physical and psychological morbidity among low income children" (p. 88).

ATTENTION TO POVERTY AMONG CAREER COUNSELORS

We turn to vocational psychology for direction, as it would seem that the primary means to escape the cycle of poverty may be through gainful employment at a wage that can support the individual woman and her family. However, to date, with some notable recent exceptions within the field of counseling psychology (e.g., Blustein et al., 2002; Blustein, Juntunen, & Worthington, 2000; Brown, Fukunaga, Umemoto, & Wicker, 1996; Flores & O'Brien, 2002; Fouad & Brown, 2000; Kenny, Blustein, Chaves, Grossman, & Gallagher, 2003; Liu, 2001; O'Brien, Dukstein, Jackson, Tomlinson, & Kamatuka, 1999; Phillips, Blustein, Jobin-Davis, & White, 2002; Savickas, 1999), we find minimal research and even fewer clinical writings directed at low-income individuals. We acknowledge that many career counselors may have little experience with low-income clients because these clients are not likely to have the time or financial resources to be seen in therapy offices or on college campuses. We examine several contributing factors to the lack of empirical research and clinical focus on poverty among vocational psychologists and career counselors. Included in this discussion are: (a) a reluctance to study those we view as different from ourselves, (b) the lack of congruence between the tenets of career development and the needs of the poor, and (c) the proposition that classism may still be an acceptable "ism."

Our Reluctance to Study Lives Different From Our Own

The exclusion and silencing of the poor from our research and practice is not unique to vocational psychologists, but also has occurred throughout the field of psychology. In her seminal article in the *American Psychologist* on cognitive distancing, Lott (2002) argued that psychologists have operated as if the United States is a classless society, thus rendering those who are not in the middle class invisible. Lott suggested that psychologists have seemingly little interest in those from whom their lives differ. She concluded that psychological theories largely reflect the lives of those who have constructed the theories (primarily White middle-class individuals); this tenet can also be applied to the theories of career development. In trying to understand why psychologists have begun attending to gender, race, and disability issues, but not issues of class, Lott concluded:

Although those who are middle class or affluent can experience the negative consequences of racism, sexism, ageism, and heterosexism or the stigma and exclusion associated with disability, they do not personally experience the stigma and exclusion associated with being poor. A sizable minority within the discipline of psychology may come from low-income or working class backgrounds, but it is clearly not a salient feature of their current lives. (p. 101)

A continued lack of focus on those with "lives different from our own" (Reid, 1993, p. 134) may impact negatively our ability to effectively train students, work with clients, and advance knowledge regarding this salient population.

The Incongruity Between the Tenets of Career Development and the Needs of the Poor

The basic tenets of career development espouse autonomous choice, the goal of self-realization, and the beliefs that work is psychologically central to life and that individuals can achieve what they work to achieve. It is a field whose beginnings were based in democratic, pluralistic, and individualistic values (Gysbers, Heppner, & Johnston, 2003), although, interestingly, the founder of vocational psychology, Frank Parsons, provided many early vocational interventions for those living in poverty (O'Brien, 2001). However, for millions of people in the United States today, the basic tenets advanced by vocational psychology have little or no relevance. The goal of economic survival becomes more salient for women living in poverty than the "self-actualization through work" philosophy that has been advanced by vocational psychology. Much of our research reflects this significant error as we continue to focus our studies on the lives of middle-class individuals in high schools, colleges, or the workforce, with exceedingly rare focus on those living in poverty, who constitute a large but seemingly invisible underclass.

It seems important to acknowledge that vocational research and theory development have become more inclusive in the past decade. However, we still know most about the career patterns of middle-class, White, heterosexual, male individuals, and far less about women, racial and ethnic minority individuals, lesbian, gay, bisexual, and transgendered individuals, the disabled, and those living in poverty. For many people living in poverty, career counseling is less relevant or irrelevant as their focus is on the here and now, that is, finding and keeping a job to ensure survival, rather that considering several possible life career paths. Moreover, career as a construct is more applicable to people with money, formal education, and resources. Many low-income individuals do not have the luxury of exploring interests and matching them to potential careers. Work, as noted by Richardson

(1993), is a more salient construct than career choice. The choices of those in poverty are limited greatly by the nature of their lives and the obstacles that they face to ongoing employment. Recently, Blustein, McWhirter, and Perry (2005) proposed a framework to more explicitly and intentionally endorse social justice goals with vocational psychology. This framework offers promise for altering vocational theory practice and research to better address the needs of people who are able to have little volition in their choice of work.

Classism: Still a Socially Acceptable "Ism"?

Although gender and racial stereotyping are no longer considered acceptable, Lott and Bullock (2001) proposed that many people feel comfortable verbalizing negative stereotypes about those living in poverty. According to social-psychological research, people believe that individuals are in the socioeconomic class in which they deserve to be, and their placement is largely due to their own effort or lack thereof (Hill, 1996). Thus, socioeconomic class continues to be seen as something people choose and, thus, something they can change. In a recent review of the literature on the attributions related to poverty, researchers concluded that "most of the studies find that Americans believe that there are multiple determinants of poverty but that individualistic or 'internal' causes (e.g., lack of effort, being lazy, low in intelligence, being on drugs) tend to be more important than societal or 'external' ones (e.g., being a victim of discrimination, low wages, being forced to attend bad schools)" (Cozzarelli, Wilkinson, & Tagler, 2001, p. 209).

Moreover, attitudes toward the poor have been shown in both foundational and recent studies to be highly related to core American values such as a "belief in a just world" and the Protestant work ethic (Cozzarelli et al., 2001). That is, research consistently has indicated that those who have a stronger belief in the Protestant work ethic, and in the belief that getting ahead is possible for anyone who is willing to work hard enough for it, tend to blame the victims more for their life dilemmas. Similarly, negative attitudes toward individuals living in poverty are related to beliefs in a just world, where, in effect, people get what they deserve (Kluegel & Smith, 1986). These beliefs reflect a tendency toward and some comfort in holding individuals living in poverty completely responsible for their fates, comparable to a blame-the-victim mentality. A prime example of the intense feeling directed at those living in poverty is research on attitudes toward welfare recipients. Researchers found that welfare recipients were the only group they studied who were both disliked and disrespected and seen as lacking in both competence and warmth (Bullock, Wyche, & Williams, 2001; Fiske, Xu, Cuddy, & Glick, 1999).

Some career counselors may struggle with guilt about the many opportunities that they have received, especially in comparison to low-income clients. These feelings of guilt have the potential to negatively influence the development of a working alliance with the client (as clients rarely want their life situations to evoke guilt in their service providers) and lessen interventions designed to empower low-income clients to make changes in their lives (as guilty counselors may be overactive in sessions to alleviate their guilt). Similar to the work done in multicultural counseling related to race and ethnicity, career counselors should seek to understand how their SES affects their work, including an analysis of their resources and the barriers they confront in their career paths.

ENHANCING EFFECTIVENESS WHEN WORKING WITH WOMEN IN POVERTY

The following three sections provide recommendations that might enhance the effectiveness of vocational interventions when working with women who are living in poverty. First, career counselors are encouraged to examine their beliefs and attitudes about poverty and how these thoughts might impact their work. Second, we propose that conceptualizing clients from an ecological perspective that recognizes the multiple systems and subsystems operating on the individual might assist career counselors in providing a comprehensive and holistic approach to their interventions. Third, as counseling psychologists, we recommend recognizing and reinforcing the strengths of our clients and maximizing resiliency in the lives of women who are poor.

Examining Our Own Classism: The Mechanism of Cognitive Distancing

Career counselors are encouraged to examine their biases, feelings, and attitudes toward those living in poverty. Unfortunately, few training programs address the importance of examining these attitudes and few models exist for reflecting on preconceived notions and stereotypes about people from lower socioeconomic classes. In addition, the terminology used by some scholars writing about poverty often reflects distance from those who live in poverty (e.g., using terms like *these people* to refer to individuals who are poor). Lott (2002) proposed that "cognitive distancing" occurs among psychologists when they are confronted with issues related to poverty: "Treating poor people as other as and less than oneself is central to the concept and practice of classism. Through cognitive distancing and institutional and interpersonal discrimination, the non-poor succeed in separating from the poor in excluding, discounting, discrediting and disenabling them" (p. 102). As Lott contended, the dominant response to poor people by those who are not poor is that of distancing, and this distancing generally takes the form of stereotyping of the poor.

As described earlier, much of this stereotyping conceptualizes the problem of poverty from a micro (or lying within the individual), rather than macro (or having social or economic roots) perspective. Similarly, if career counselors are viewing poverty as resulting from the effort, ability, and personal initiative of the individual, then vocational interventions are focused on changing (and in many cases blaming) the individual rather than challenging the system that promulgates poverty. This perspective (i.e., unrecognized classism) may negatively influence the provision of services to those who struggle with poverty through paternalistic and distancing counselors whose interventions are based in a deficit and pathological model. The examination of our thoughts and feelings about poverty can help to ensure that interventions are provided by counselors who are aware of their biases and working to reduce the negative affects of classism on the counseling process.

Examining Poverty Within the Ecological Model

An ecological model of career development has been proposed to provide a structure for understanding the systems and subsystems that influence a person's life (Cook, Heppner, & O'Brien, 2002a, 2002b, 2004, in press) and may be helpful when intervening in the lives of women who struggle with poverty. Ecological models stress that human behavior is the result of a multitude of factors at the individual, interpersonal, and broader sociocultural levels. Vocational behavior must be understood as an "act-in-context" (Landrine, 1995, p. 5), where the context is essential to the naming and meaningfulness of the individual's behavior. For example, a woman who consistently obtains jobs but fails to attend training sessions must be conceptualized in light of the larger context of her life (e.g., no reliable transportation, difficulty securing quality child care, a partner who becomes abusive when the woman moves toward economic self-sufficiency).

To further understand an ecological approach to career development, we turn to Bronfenbrenner (1977), who first identified four major subsystems affecting an individual's life or ecosystem. First, the microsystem includes the interpersonal interactions within a given environment such as home, school, or work settings. Second, the mesosystem consists of interactions between two or more microsystems, such as the relationship between a woman's school and her home environment. Third, the exosystem is represented by linkages between subsystems that indirectly influence the individual, such as the individual's neighborhood or the media. And finally, the macrosystem is comprised of ideological components of a given society, including norms and values.

The ecological model of career development proposed by Cook et al. (2004) recognized that humans live interactionally in a social environment and that factors such as gender, race, and class decisively shape the work life of all individuals. Implicit in the model is the knowledge that interrelationships occur simultaneously on multiple levels so that a focus on any one level is by definition a limited picture of the dynamics shaping the career behaviors of the individual. For example, in applying the ecological model to low-income women it is clear that the larger culture operates as a macrosystem that perpetuates myths and stereotypes about the poor and institutionalizes inaccurate beliefs (e.g., the belief in a meritocracy, a just world, and the ability to remove oneself from poverty if so desired). Macrosystem values are then internalized by the individual (internalized classism) and influence how others treat people who are living in poverty and how those living in poverty think of themselves (internalized classism).

One of the more important aspects of an ecological perspective is the much broader purview provided to the career counselor. For example, the model calls on counselors to advocate for societal changes that may lessen the incidence of poverty. In addition, the model requires a range of skills not typically required in traditional counseling interventions. Although the interventions that are appropriate for any particular career counselor and client depend very much on the unique circumstances of the individual's situation, some examples of interventions at the individual and micro, meso, and macro levels may be helpful.

Examples of Individual- and Micro-Level Interventions. At the micro level, there are a host of practical suggestions to inform work with women who are living in poverty. For example, knowledge of community resources is central for helping clients to obtain and retain employment. Often, the United Way provides a phone information service that can link clients with needed resources in their communities. Clients may need assistance with clothing for job interviews and for the workplace (many cities have services directed specifically for these needs; Turner-Bowker, 2001). Many women living in poverty may not have ever considered or had access to role models of women working in nontraditional jobs. Exposure to role models in the skilled trades can increase a woman's self-efficacy that she can find employment that is more likely to raise her and her children out of poverty.

In addition, many women living in poverty are also victims of domestic violence. Assessment of the presence of violence in the woman's life is critical, and referrals to safe shelters and domestic violence programs could assist her in leaving the violent situation. Given the sheer magnitude of the issues that women living in poverty face, career counselors may need to be more active and directive and willing to initially assume the role of an advocate and ally. Assisting women in building support systems as they try to make the changes necessary to move out of poverty is also critical. Providing a network of peers who can give and receive assistance can reduce isolation and enhance motivation for change.

Although much of the actual work within career counseling will take place at the individual and micro levels, it seems important that both the counselor and client conceptualize the client's problems within the larger ecological context that contributes to the situation. Explaining the many barriers present at the macro level can assist clients in understanding how societal factors may contribute additional obstacles to their success. Often the macro-level issues of classism, racism, and sexism may seem overwhelming to the counselor. However, career counselors can also advocate for an end to these "isms" in their own ecosystems. For example, counselors can work to understand how macro-level forces (e.g., classism, racism, sexism, discrimination) impact their work and the lives of clients and communicate this understanding to clients in ways that normalize their situations and limit self-blame.

Examples of Mesosystem Interventions.   According to McDonald (personal communication, February 10, 2004), the mesosystem may be the most important to examine with regard to low-income women. She indicated that "it is the careful and positive mixing/interactions of microsystem resources (supports, transportation, work environment, children's schools and childcare) that allow low-income women to be employed successfully." For example, the House of Ruth in Washington, DC operates a therapeutic child-care center for children who have experienced poverty, homelessness, and domestic violence. In addition to the individual counseling, speech and language therapy, and educative interventions provided to the children at this center, staff members work to ensure that mothers receive safe housing at the affiliated battered women's shelter, legal services, counseling for alcohol and drug addictions, transportation vouchers, parenting skills training, and vocational assistance. This holistic approach to child care provides low-income women with the support they need to move toward economic self-sufficiency.

Examples of Macro-Level Interventions.   Myriad interventions are possible at the macro level for career counselors. For example, the APA Resolution on Poverty and Socioeconomic Status (2000) provided suggestions for how the APA could address poverty (e.g., advocating for more research that examines the causes and impacts of poverty as well as disseminating these findings). In addition, the resolution called for changes in graduate and postgraduate training to better respond to the needs of the poor and to facilitate cultural competency among those who work with people living in poverty. The resolution also supported advances in public policy related to education, child care, family-friendly jobs, and medical and mental health insurance coverage to assist families in escaping poverty.

In addition, Rice (2001) articulated nine macro-level change recommendations that are supported by research and that address systemic antecedents of women's poverty:

(a) Equal pay for equal work reduces poverty by 50%, (b) union membership increases the chances of women moving out of poverty by 40%, (c) requiring mandatory prorated benefits for part-time and contingent work will benefit the economic status of women, (d) one year of postsecondary education reduces the poverty rate of minority women by 50%, (e) protection from violence increases the chances of poor women becoming financially independent and escaping poverty, (f) universal health care insurance and preventive health services for women will significantly decrease disparities in access to health care related to income and poverty, (g) universal access to quality, publicly funded, full-day childcare for all preschool children positively affects the welfare of children as well as the employment of women, (h) enforcement of all child support laws and the enactment of an assured child support benefit would reduce the poverty gap for single parent families by 25–33% and that (i) paying caregiver allowances to parents to raise young children gives a living wage to all. (pp. 264–269)

Given the complexity and enormity of efforts needed to end poverty, working on organized efforts to affect change through large professional organizations (e.g., the APA or American Counseling Association), labor unions, and legislative organizations is encouraged. Becoming knowledgeable of the potential impact these structural changes can have for those women living in poverty is a critical first step. Readers are referred to both the APA (2000) and Rice's (2001) excellent review as starting points for such information gathering.

Reinforcing Strengths and Building Resiliency

Most importantly, career counselors can reinforce strengths and facilitate resiliency among clients living in poverty. Women living in poverty often have had to demonstrate initiative, courage, and innovative thinking just to survive. Helping to assess and reinforce strengths through careful and systematic interviewing helps bolster self-esteem and provides a foundation for the development of other skills. Research has shown that even when individuals have lived through extremely difficult life circumstances of poverty and abuse, a high percentage still manifest the characteristic of resiliency (Bernard, 1995). Moreover, one study of 50 low-income African American women found that the absence of problematic social ties and the presence of downward social comparisons of others contributed significantly to the prediction of resilience in their lives (Todd & Worell, 2000).

The word *resiliency* comes from the Latin term meaning "to jump or bounce back." The term connotes elasticity and buoyancy and one's ability to function when challenged, to recover even when confronted with trauma or intense misfortune. Writers within the social sciences (Bernard, 1995) contend that we are born with the capacity for resilience and that this capacity allows us to develop five key skills and attitudes: social competence, problem-solving skills, critical consciousness, autonomy, and a sense of purpose. Helping clients develop these skills and attitudes may facilitate resiliency among low-income women and children. Briefly, Bernard defined these five key skills as follows:

> *Social competence* includes qualities such as responsiveness, especially the ability to elicit positive responses from others; flexibility, including the ability to move between different cultures; empathy; communication skills; and a sense of humor. *Problem-solving skills* encompass the ability to plan; to be resourceful in seeking help from others; and to think critically, creatively, and reflectively. In the development of a *critical consciousness*, a reflective awareness of the structures of oppression (be it from an alcoholic parent, an insensitive school, or a racist society) and creating strategies for overcoming them has been key. *Autonomy* is having a sense of one's own identity and an ability to act independently and to exert some control over one's environment, including a sense of task mastery, internal locus of control, and self-efficacy. The development of resistance (refusing to accept negative messages about oneself) and of detachment (distancing oneself from dysfunction) serves as a powerful protector of autonomy. Lastly, resilience is manifested in having a *sense of purpose* and a belief in a bright future, including goal direction, educational aspirations, achievement motivation, persistence, hopefulness, optimism, and spiritual connectedness. (p. 1)

BECOMING KNOWLEDGEABLE ABOUT RESEARCH, PROGRAMS, RESOURCES, AND SERVICES

To conclude this chapter, we highlight research articles, web sites, a successful vocational training program, and a summary of the best practices associated with welfare-to-work programs for women. These resources provide a starting point for career counselors who are interested in learning more about working effectively with women in poverty.

Research Articles

In 1997, Meara, Davis, and Robinson wrote a seminal article providing specific suggestions for vocational interventions with low-income women. First, they identified some of the ways in which current theories fail to fit the experiences of this population (e.g., poor women rarely follow a planned path to vocational development). Second, they offered suggestions for assessment with women living in poverty. Specifically, they provided many salient and specific suggestions on how to build a working alliance with clients who are living in poverty. They outlined the use of "possible selves" interview strategies and interventions in career counseling. They also encouraged counselors to exercise caution when using assessment materials not previously tested or validated on populations living in poverty. Throughout their article, they highlighted the complex issues and multilevel barriers facing women who are poor and unemployed and they articulated one important point especially well: "No matter how much the counselor wishes to emphasize freedom of choice for every client, at times it is not realistic to do so" (Meara et al., p. 124).

In 1998, Weinger wrote an article addressing the effects of living in poverty on children's perceptions of vocational opportunities. Children in low-income families perceived limited future career options and exhibited hopelessness regarding attaining economic self-sufficiency. She concluded that social workers need to become politically active to advocate for the creation of more jobs with adequate salaries. She also called for a movement to build communities to provide role models of working adults and to provide services to keep children safe (e.g., after-school child care). Moreover, she argued that youth must be exposed to activities outside of their neighborhood and to career development in school curricula.

More recently, a special issue of the *Journal of Social Issues* entitled "Listening to the Voices of Poor Women" was published (2001). The issue editors (Lott & Bullock) combined a series of articles that addressed attitudes toward the poor and attributions of poverty as well as media images of those living in poverty. The articles discussed the experiences of women on public assistance, housing concerns for low-income women, issues related to the public school system, and providing appropriate work clothing for the poor. In a section on applied research in community agencies, researchers described building relationships with underserved communities and negotiating partnerships with community-based agencies. The issue concluded with an article that further examined the macro-level changes needed in social policy and the impact of poverty, welfare, and patriarchy. This special issue represents cutting-edge research and practice on poverty and is helpful reading for career counselors.

Lott (2002) also published an article on cognitive distancing and the poor in the *American Psychologist* that provides salient information for career counselors. In this article, Lott discussed the many ways in which individuals act to distance themselves from those living in poverty. She indicated that many societal institutions provide few resources for poor people (e.g., educational settings, housing opportunities, mental and medical health care). According to Lott, psychologists often act in a discriminatory manner toward the poor as evidenced by the lack of research and theory addressing the experience of poverty. She pointed out that even multicultural theories often neglect to address the role that SES plays in individuals' lives.

Web Resources for Career Counselors Working With Low-Income Women

Several web sites and a brief description of their content can be found in the Appendix at the end of this chapter. We have included both resources for career counselors who are interested in learning more about poverty and resources for low-income women. Also included are web sites that could be helpful to clients who are seeking employment or career-related information.

A Successful Vocational Intervention for Low-Income Women: Women Entrepreneurs of Baltimore

One example of a successful vocational intervention for women living in poverty was developed by Women Entrepreneurs of Baltimore (WEB), an organization founded to help women escape poverty and become economically self-sufficient by obtaining the training and resources needed for self-employment (Servon, 1998). The WEB staff members provide an intensive 12-week training course in which small groups of mostly low-income women (about 30) meet three times a week for 3 hours. All participants meet individually with the staff twice during the training (and more often if necessary). The goal of the training is to assist women in beginning their own business by helping them develop skills and apply for business loans. Evaluation of their program outcomes indicated a graduation rate of 76%. Graduates have access to a network of professionals (e.g., lawyers, accountants) who provide periodic assistance on a pro bono basis.

Interestingly, and a testament to the difficulty of providing interventions for poor women, Servon (1998) reported that although initially WEB services were targeted to assist the poorest women in Baltimore, the program experienced difficulty recruiting and retaining women who lived in extreme poverty. Their services are now open to women living below the poverty line and low-income women and a small number of women who do not qualify as being poor.

Welfare-to-Work Programs for Women in Poverty

Career counselors might also learn about effective vocational interventions for poor women from a survey identifying the best practices associated with welfare-to-work programs. In August of 1996, legislation was passed to replace the previous welfare program (i.e., Aid to Families with Dependent Children) with the Temporary Assistance for Needy Families (TANF) program. Unlike the previous program, TANF severely restricted the amount of time during which individuals were able to receive financial assistance and focused on moving individuals from receiving welfare to obtaining work. Welfare-to-work programs were initiated to address the needs of those who were no longer eligible for financial assistance from the government.

The fundamental goal of the welfare-to-work grants program was "to promote the long-term economic self-sufficiency of individuals who have serious employment difficulties" (Nightingale, Pindus, & Trutko, 2002, p. ix). Most of the recipients of the welfare-to-work grant programs were women living in poverty and experiencing multiple barriers to employment (e.g., substance abuse, mental or physical disabilities; Nightingale et al.). A call for feedback was issued by the U.S. Department of Labor to assess the best practices associated with these welfare-to-work programs. Twenty-eight papers were received and many of the suggestions provided can be applied to the development of career-counseling programs for women living in poverty.

Best Practices Suggestions From Welfare-to-Work Grant Programs.   According to the U.S. Department of Labor (2003), increasing the range of educational and training options available to those living in poverty is necessary. A whole-family approach is needed whereby certain members of the family can be targeted for an intervention, but all must receive services simultaneously for the best possible outcomes. In addition, service providers should take an interdisciplinary-interagency approach to the provision of services and partner with other community agencies and supports (e.g., schools, child support enforcement, churches, employers, nonprofit social service agencies) to provide comprehensive services to families living in poverty. Programs must be innovative and longitudinal, and supportive services including quality child care, affordable and safe housing, and reliable transportation are needed. In addition, Turner-Bowker (2001) pointed to the importance of helping women on welfare to obtain work-appropriate clothing at discount prices to facilitate their obtaining and retaining work.

Moreover, providers must recognize special needs and barriers faced by individuals seeking employment. Specifically, "learning/developmental/physical disabilities and mental health, substance abuse, English as a second language, and domestic violence issues are the most common and most challenging barriers among the TANF/WtW populations" (U.S. Department of Labor, 2003, p. 3). Given these barriers, successful welfare-to-work programs were comprehensive and intensive (Nightingale et al., 2002). Individual case-management services, accompanied by coaching, training, education, and job-transition assistance, are needed. Preemployment interventions are necessary, but not sufficient.

According to Christel Nichols, executive director of a comprehensive nonprofit agency serving hundreds of women in crisis daily in Washington, DC, many of their clients lack the ability to keep jobs once they obtain them (personal communication, September 17, 2003). They need assistance developing skills to interact with others in a professional setting, help with meeting basic dependability and reliability requirements of work, and on-the-job training and support. Nichols maintained that keeping the job (rather than obtaining a job) is the most salient challenge for most of their clients. Thus, career counselors would need to go beyond training and testing of career interests and abilities to either providing or facilitating the provision of support services postemployment.

Finally, the recommendations issued by the U.S. Department of Labor (2003) also indicated that empirical research on the efficacy of the interventions is necessary to ensure the effectiveness of the services provided. Vocational intervention services provided to women living in poverty must be evaluated to determine whether they meet the desired outcomes, and which components of the program are contributing to economic self-sufficiency for the clients. Brodsky (2001) offered suggestions for building research relationships with underserved members of the community and Reid and Vianna (2001) emphasized the importance of common goals, respect for cultural differences, and collaboration with community members in interpreting the findings of evaluation studies.

It is important to note that as a result of changes in legislation, many women (and their children) are experiencing more extreme poverty because they have gone from receiving welfare to working at substandard wages (Rice, 2001). Many jobs available to the women pay below-poverty wages and are not stable over time. Some women who previously received welfare benefits have been forced to leave college or training programs to obtain jobs that have little promise of enabling their families to escape poverty. Rice pointed out that the lack of safe and affordable child care, the discrepancy in salaries between women and men, the presence of violence and abuse in women's lives, and the absence of health care and health insurance all contribute to a devastating cycle of poverty for millions of women and children.

RECOMMENDATIONS FOR COUNSELORS WORKING WITH LOW-INCOME WOMEN

We conclude our chapter by highlighting four recommendations regarding vocational interventions with low-income women. First, career counselors must recognize the myriad barriers, obstacles, and challenges to successful employment of women living in poverty. Due to space considerations, it is impossible to detail all of the obstacles encountered by these women. However, it is our hope that career counselors recognize, appreciate, and communicate to the clients an understanding of the overwhelming obstacles to successful employment that are faced by low-income women, especially women with children.

Second, we stress the importance of a holistic approach to vocational interventions with women living in poverty. Providing individual counseling that focuses on testing, interpretation, matching interests, and characteristics of the world of work, in isolation, is not appropriate for low-income women. Effective counseling must go beyond individual and microsystem interventions to assist women in mobilizing resources at the meso-, exo-, and macrosystem levels. Career counselors must connect low-income women with support and resources from reputable community agencies. They should view themselves as one tool among many that are needed to empower women in their movement toward economic self-sufficiency. Moreover, focused attention and resources are needed to ensure that children living in poverty have the opportunity to complete high school and attain college degrees, one possible solution for ending the devastating intergenerational cycle of poverty. Clearly, career counselors must work on a host of levels, using a much more holistic approach than is typical, to ameliorate the problems of women and children living in poverty.

Third, even a holistic approach to developing women's skills in job searching, exposing them to nontraditional higher wage positions, and helping them obtain necessary training, though critically important, does little to address the structural issues of discrimination, racism, sexism, and classism that perpetuate poverty in America. As Rice (2001) argued, macrolevel approaches are critically important: "Macro level changes that address these issues include equal pay and benefits, non-sex segregated job structure, access to higher education, guaranteed child support, national child care, and protection from violence and abuse" (p. 264). For example, in addressing equal-pay issues alone, the Institute for Women's Policy Research (1999) and the AFL-CIO conducted the Equal Pay for Working Families study, which concluded:

> [The] average family loses nearly $4,300 annually because of wage discrimination and the poverty rates would drop by more than 50% if women received equal pay for equal work. Although all groups of women would experience significant drops in poverty if they were paid wages equal to men's wages, the poverty rate for single working mothers would drop the most, from more than 25% to 12.6%. (cited in Rice, 2001, p. 365)

Thus, a holistic perspective that addresses the critical macro issues of women living in poverty is needed.

Finally, we embrace the recommendation of the APA (2000) Resolution on Poverty and Socioeconomic Status that proposed that graduate education include material on the causes and effects of poverty as well as on interventions that may assist low-income individuals. Thus, educators of career counselors are encouraged to include written materials and experiential exercises in their courses to assist students in learning about vocational interventions with low-income women. We refer readers to a series of case studies that apply the ecological model of career counseling to work with a variety of women, several of whom struggle with poverty or reduced opportunities (Cook et al., 2002a). In addition, based on our experience in two counselor-training programs at the University of Missouri–Columbia and the University of Maryland, we wanted to share examples of training opportunities for master's and doctoral students to provide career interventions with low-income individuals in both rural and urban settings.

At the University of Missouri–Columbia, students provide career counseling to adults in the community from a variety of socioeconomic classes who for many reasons are faced with unemployment. They focus on assisting these adults in successfully navigating their career transitions. Students at the University of Missouri–Columbia also have participated in vocational interventions for farmers who, because of economic hardships, lost their family farms and had to consider alternative means of employment (Heppner, Cook, Strozier, & Heppner, 1991; Heppner, Johnston, & Brinkhoff, 1988).

At the University of Maryland, students enrolled in the doctoral course on career counseling provide vocational interventions to women living in poverty in addition to the more typical clients encountered at the university counseling center. Each student is asked to work with one career client from the House of Ruth in Washington, DC. These clients have experienced poverty, homelessness, domestic violence, alcohol or drug addictions, or mental illness. Students learn to provide nontraditional, holistic career interventions to their career clients. At the conclusion of their experience, students often comment that this experience has broadened their understanding of career counseling and encouraged them to develop creative and innovative approaches to clinical work.

A CALL TO ACTION

Vocational psychologists are uniquely positioned to make a difference in the lives of low-income women and children. With our skills and robust knowledge base, we can first look within to examine our preconceived notions about poverty and, second, as Blustein et al. (2002) stated, "learn a great deal by listening to the voices of those who have been on the margins of our scholarly attention" (p. 311). Then, to ameliorate the influences of poverty on the lives of women, counseling psychologists can venture beyond their offices to advocate for social change (Fassinger & O'Brien, 2002; Meara et al., 1997; Weinger, 1998). Together, we can work with existing programs to develop innovative and holistic interventions to reduce, and some day end, the devastating effects of poverty in women's lives.

ACKNOWLEDGMENTS

The authors express their appreciation to the following individuals, who contributed many thoughtful ideas and helpful comments regarding this chapter: Lisa Flores, Donna McDonald, Christel Nichols, Nora O'Brien, and David Petersen.

REFERENCES

Adler, N. E., & Coriell, M. (1997). Socioeconomic status and women's health. In S. J. Gallant, G. P. Keita, & R. Royak-Schaler (Eds.), *Health care for women: Psychological, social, and behavioral influences* (pp. 11–23). Washington, DC: American Psychological Association.

American Psychological Association. (1998). *Making "welfare to work" really work: Report from the Division 35 Public Task Force on Women, Poverty, and Public Assistance.* Retrieved October 22, 2003, from http://www.apa.org/pi/publicat.html

American Psychological Association. (2000). *Resolution on poverty and socioeconomic status.* Washington, DC: Author.

Attar, B. K., Guerra, N. G., & Tolan, P. H. (1994). Neighborhood disadvantage, stressful life events, and adjustment in urban elementary-school children. *Journal of Clinical Child Psychology, 23,* 391–400.

Bassuk, E. L., Weinreb, L. F., Buckner, J. C., Browne, A., Salomon, A., & Bassuk, S. S. (1996). The characteristics and needs of sheltered homeless and low-income housed mothers. *Journal of the American Medical Association, 276,* 640–646.

Ben-Sira, Z. (1997). *Immigration, stress, and readjustment.* Westport, CT: Praeger.

Bernard, B. (1995). *Fostering resilience in children.* Champaign: University of Illinois, ERIC Clearinghouse on Elementary and Early Childhood Education.

Bernstein, J., McNichol, E. C., Mishel, L., & Zahradnik, R. (2000). *Pulling apart: A state-by-state analysis of income trends.* Washington, DC: Center on Budget and Policy Priorities, Economic Policy Institute.

Blustein, D. L., Chaves, A. P., Diemer, M. A., Gallagher, L. A., Marshall, K. G., Sirin, S., et al. (2002). Voices of the forgotten half: The role of social class in the school-to-work transition. *Journal of Counseling Psychology, 49,* 311–323.

Blustein, D. L., Juntunen, C. L., & Worthington, R. L. (2000). The school-to-work transition: Adjustment challenges of the forgotten half. In S. D. Brown & R. W. Lent (Eds.), *Handbook of counseling psychology* (pp. 435–470). New York: Wiley.

Blustein, D. L., McWhirter, E. H., & Perry, J. C. (2005). An emancipatory communitarian approach to vocational development theory, research, and practice. *The Counseling Psychologist, 33,* 141–179.

Brodsky, A. E. (2001). More than epistemology: Relationships in applied research with underserved communities. *Journal of Social Issues, 57,* 323–335.

Bronfenbrenner, U. (1977). Toward an experimental ecology of human development. *American Psychologist, 32,* 513–531.

Brooks, M. G., & Buckner, J. C. (1996). Work and welfare: Job histories, barriers to employment, and predictors of work among low-income single mothers. *American Journal of Orthopsychiatry, 66,* 526–537.

Brown, M. T., Fukunaga, C., Umemoto, D., & Wicker, L. (1996). Annual review 1990–1996: Social class, work, and retirement behavior. *Journal of Vocational Behavior, 49,* 159–189.

Bullock, H., Wyche, K., & Williams, W. (2001). Media images of the poor. *Journal of Social Issues, 57,* 229–246.

Conger, R. D., Conger, K. J., & Elder, G. H. (1997). Family economic hardship and adolescent adjustment: Mediating and moderating processes. In G. J. Duncan & J. Brooks-Gunn (Eds.), *Consequences of growing up poor* (pp. 288–310). New York: Russell Sage Foundation.

Cook, E. P., Heppner, M. J., & O'Brien, K. M. (2002a). Career development of women of color and White women: Assumptions, conceptualization and interventions from an ecological perspective. *Career Development Quarterly, 50,* 291–305.

Cook, E. P., Heppner, M. J., & O'Brien, K. M. (2002b). Multicultural and gender influences in women's career development: An ecological perspective. In S. Niles (Ed.), *Adult career development: Concepts, issues and practices* (pp. 169–189). Alexandria, VA: National Career Development Association.

Cook, E. P., Heppner, M. J., & O'Brien, K. M. (2004). Career counseling from an ecological perspective. In R. K. Conyne & E. P. Cook (Eds.), *Ecological counseling: An innovative approach to conceptualizing person-environment interaction* (pp. 219–242). Alexandria, VA: American Counseling Association.

Cook, E. P., Heppner, M. J., & O'Brien, K. M. (in press). Understanding diversity within women's career development: An ecological perspective. *Journal of Multicultural Counseling and Development.*

Cozzarelli, C., Wilkinson, A. V., & Tagler, M. J. (2001). Attitudes toward the poor and attributions for poverty. *Journal of Social Issues, 57,* 207–227.

Crittenden, A. (2001). *Commentary: Mothers pay price for nurturing human capital.* Retrieved November 19, 2003, from http://www.now.org/eNews/feb2001/022101raisingchildren.html

DeAngelis, T. (2001). Movin' on up? *American Psychological Association Monitor, 32,* 70–73.

Ehrenreich, B. (2001). *Nickel and dimed: On (not) getting by in America.* New York: Holt.

Evans, G. W. (2004). The environment of childhood poverty. *American Psychologist, 59,* 77–92.

Falik, M. M., & Collins, K. S. (1996). *Women and health: The Commonwealth Fund Survey.* Baltimore: Johns Hopkins University Press.

Fassinger, R. E., & O'Brien, K. M. (2002). Career counseling with college women: A scientist-practitioner-advocate model of intervention. In D. A. Luzzo (Ed.), *Career counseling of college students: An empirical guide to strategies that work* (pp. 253–265). Washington, DC: American Psychological Association.

Fiske, S. T., Xu, J., Cuddy, A. C., & Glick, P. (1999). (Dis)respecting versus (dis)liking: Status and interdependence predict ambivalent stereotypes of competence and warmth. *Journal of Social Issues, 55,* 473–490.

Flores, L. Y., & O'Brien, K. M. (2002). The career development of Mexican American adolescent women: A test of social cognitive theory. *Journal of Counseling Psychology, 49,* 14–27.

Fouad, N. A., & Brown, M. T. (2000). The role of race and class in development: Implications for counseling psychology. In S. D. Brown & R. W. Lent (Eds.), *Handbook of counseling psychology* (3rd ed., pp. 379–408). New York: Wiley.

Gysbers, N. C., Heppner, M. J., & Johnston, J. A. (2003). *Career counseling: Process, issues, and techniques.* Boston: Allyn & Bacon.

Hardy, M. A., & Hazelrigg, L. E. (1995). Gender, race/ethnicity, and poverty in later life. *Journal of Aging Studies, 9,* 43–63.

Heppner, M. J., Johnston, J. A., & Brinkhoff, J. (1988). Creating a career hotline for rural residents. *Journal of Counseling and Development, 66,* 340–341.

Heppner, P. P., Cook, S. W., Strozier, A. L., & Heppner, M. J. (1991). An investigation of coping styles and gender differences with farmers in career transition. *Journal of Counseling Psychology, 38,* 167–174.

Hill, M. (1996). We can't afford it: Confusions and silences on the topic of class. In M. Hill & E. D. Rothblum (Eds.), *Classism and feminist therapy: Counting costs* (pp. 1–6). New York: Haworth Press.

Hill, M. S., & Sandfort, J. R. (1995). Effects of childhood poverty on productivity later in life: Implications for public policy. *Children and Youth Services Review, 17,* 91–126.

Institute for Women's Policy Research. (1999). *Equal pay for equal working families.* Washington, DC: Author.

Johnson, R. W., & Favreault, M. M. (2004). *Economic status in later life among women who raised children outside of marriage.* Washington, DC: Urban Institute.

Kluegel, J. R., & Smith, E. R. (1986). *Beliefs about inequality: Americans' views of what is and what ought to be.* New York: de Gruyter.

Korenman, S., Miller, J., & Sjaastad, J. (1995). Long-term poverty and child development in the United States: Results from the NLSY. *Children and Youth Services Review, 17,* 127–155.

Landrine, H. (1995). *Bringing cultural diversity to feminist psychology: Theory, research, and practice.* Washington, DC: American Psychological Association.

Liu, W. M. (2001). Expanding our understanding of multiculturalism: Developing a social class world view model. In D. B. Pope-Davis & H. L. K. Coleman (Eds.), *The intersection of race, class, and gender in counseling psychology* (pp. 127–170). Thousand Oaks, CA: Sage.

Lott, B. (2002). Cognitive and behavioral distancing from the poor. *American Psychologist, 57,* 100–110.

Lott, B., & Bullock, H. E. (2001). Who are the poor? *Journal of Social Issues, 57,* 189–206.

McDonald, D. L. (1998). *A qualitative comparison of employed and unemployed low-income African-American single mothers.* Unpublished doctoral dissertation, Michigan State University, Lansing.

McGrath, E., Keita, G. P., Strickland, B. R., & Russo, N. F. (Eds.). (1990). *Women and depression: Risk factors and treatment issues: Final report of the American Psychological Association's National Task Force on Women and Depression.* Washington, DC: American Psychological Association.

McLoyd, V. C. (1998). Socioeconomic disadvantage and child development. *American Psychologist, 53,* 185–204.

Meara, N. M., Davis, K. L., & Robinson, B. S. (1997). The working lives of women from lower socioeconomic backgrounds: Assessing prospects, enabling success. *Journal of Career Assessment, 5,* 115–135.

National Alliance for Caregiving. (1997). *Family caregiving in the U.S.: Findings from a national survey.* Bethesda, MD: Author.

National Center for Health Statistics. (1995). *Health: United States.* Hyattsville, MD: U.S. Public Health Service.

Nightingale, D. S., Pindus, N., & Trutko, J. (2002). *The implementation of the Welfare-to-Work grants program* (Contract No. 100-98-0009). Washington, DC: Department of Health and Human Services.

O'Brien, K. M. (2001). The legacy of Parsons: Career counselors and vocational psychologists as agents of social change. *Career Development Quarterly, 50,* 66–76.

O'Brien, K. M., Dukstein, R. D., Jackson, S. L., Tomlinson, M. J., & Kamatuka, N. A. (1999). Broadening career horizons for students in at-risk environments. *Career Development Quarterly, 47,* 215–229.

Olson, K., & Pavetti, L. (1996). *Personal and family challenges to the successful transition from welfare to work.* Washington, DC: Urban Institute.

Ostroff, C., & Atwater, L. E. (2003). Does whom you work with matter? Effects of referent group gender and age composition on managers' compensation. *Journal of Applied Psychology, 88,* 725–740.

Phillips, S. D., Blustein, D. L., Jobin-Davis, K., & White, S. F. (2002). Preparation for the school-to-work transition: The views of high school students. *Journal of Vocational Behavior, 61,* 202–216.

Reid, P. T. (1993). Poor women in psychological research: Shut up and shut out. *Psychology of Women Quarterly, 17,* 133–150.

Reid, P. T., & Vianna, E. (2001). Negotiating partnerships in research on poverty with community-based agencies. *Journal of Social Issues, 57,* 337–354.

Rice, J. K. (2001). Poverty, welfare, and patriarchy: How macro-level changes in social policy can help low-income women. *Journal of Social Issues, 57,* 355–374.

Richardson, M. S. (1993). Work in peoples' lives: A location for counseling psychologists. *Journal of Counseling Psychology, 40,* 425–433.

Savickas, M. L. (1999). The transition from school to work: A developmental perspective. *Career Development Quarterly, 47,* 326–336.

Servon, L. J. (1998, December). Women Entrepreneurs of Baltimore. In *Microenterprise development as an economic adjustment strategy* (pp. 117–137). Washington, DC: U.S. Department of Commerce Economic Development Administration.

Spalter-Roth, R., Burr, B., Hartmann, H., & Shaw, L. (1995). *Welfare that works: The working lives of AFDC recipients.* Washington, DC: Institute for Women's Policy Research.

Thomas, L. (2000). *Women, pay equity and housing.* Retrieved November 19, 2003, from http://www.mcauley.org/payequity.pdf

Todd, J. L., & Worell, J. (2000). Resilience in low-income, employed, African American women. *Psychology of Women Quarterly, 24,* 119–128.

Turner-Bowker, D. M. (2001). How can you pull yourself up by your bootstraps, if you don't have boots? Work-appropriate clothing for poor women. *Journal of Social Issues, 57,* 311–322.

U.S. Bureau of the Census. (2001). *Poverty in the United Sates.* Washington, DC: U.S. Department of Commerce.

U.S. Bureau of the Census. (2002). *The Hispanic population in the United States: 2002.* Retrieved November 7, 2003, from http://www.census.gov/population/www/socdemo/hispanic/ppl-165.html

U.S. Bureau of the Census. (2003). *Current population survey: 2003 annual social and economic supplement.* Washington, DC: U.S. Department of Commerce.

U.S. Department of Labor. (2003). *Welfare-to-work lessons learned for TANF and WIA reauthorization.* Retrieved September 29, 2003, from http://www.doleta.gov/documents/lessons.asp

Wandersman, A., & Nation, M. (1998). Urban neighborhoods and mental health: Psychological contributions to understanding toxicity, resilience, and interventions. *American Psychologist, 53,* 647–656.

Weinger, S. (1998). Children living in poverty: Their perception of career opportunities. *Families in Society, 79*(3), 320–330.

APPENDIX

Web Resources for Low-Income Women and Their Career Counselors

Organization	Web Address	Description of Resources Available on the Web Site
American Psychological Association	www.apa.org/pi/urban/powres.html	The Resolution on Poverty and Socioeconomic Status (APA, 2000) provides numerous citations for research, legislation, and programs related to providing services to those living in poverty.
Children's Defense Fund	www.childrensdefense.org	Founded by Marian Wright Edelman, this private, nonprofit organization seeks to ensure safety, good health, and quality education for all children in the U.S., especially poor children, children of color, and children with disabilities.
Michigan Program on Poverty and Social Welfare Policy	www.fordschool.umich.edu/poverty	This Program "promotes interdisciplinary applied research on poverty and social welfare policy and works to translate research findings for public policy decision makers." They provide links to other web sites related to poverty.
National Committee on Pay Equity	www.pay-equity.org	The National Committee on Pay Equity is a nonprofit organization that seeks to educate the public regarding pay equity issues affecting workers in the United States. Their web site provides information about policy and legal issues, lawsuits involving discrimination, and research on the wage gap between women and men.
National Organization for Women	www.now.org	The National Organization for Women advocates for changes in U.S. society to ensure economic, legal, political and social equality for women.
Northwestern University/University of Chicago Joint Center on Poverty Research	www.jcpr.org	This Joint Center describes itself as "a national and interdisciplinary academic research center that seeks to advance our understanding of what it means to be poor in America." They publish working papers, policy briefs, and other research. They provide a list of conferences and events related to poverty.
Southern Poverty Law Center	www.tolerance.org/	The Center has the goal of "dismantling bigotry and creating, in hate's stead, communities that value diversity." Included are news about groups that are working for tolerance, guidebooks for adults and youth on topics like 101 Tools for Tolerance, practical resources for parents and teachers that are relevant for career counselors, and tests to help uncover hidden biases in beliefs and attitudes.
Urban Institute	www.urban.org	The Urban Institute describes itself as "a nonpartisan economic and social policy research organization." They publish research, reports and books related to poverty.
Women Work! The National Network for Women's Employment	www.womenwork.org/	This organization provides support for women moving toward economic self-sufficiency and was originally founded to help displaced homemakers find employment. The web site offers many resources for women who seek to prepare themselves for jobs and/or training for work.

Chapter 4

Career Assessment and Counseling for Women

Susan D. Lonborg
Central Washington University

Gail Hackett
Arizona State University

Given the "vigorous and exciting" research on women's career development in recent decades (Fassinger & O'Brien, 2000; Fitzgerald, Fassinger, & Betz, 1995), the reader may rightfully question the continued need for a chapter on assessment issues specifically for female clients. Many of the issues addressed in the now quite extensive literature on career assessment certainly apply equally to women and men, yet there are some issues unique to women in that broader literature that continue to be cause for concern among career counselors and their female clients. The sex-bias debates in assessment are only the tip of the iceberg. More fundamentally, we must consider how gender influences women's career development, and therefore how gender is addressed in the context of assessment in career counseling. In doing so, it is helpful to examine the implications of contemporary career theory and research for career assessment and counseling with women.

Betz (chap. 2, this volume) examined the internal and external limitations on women's career choices that result in women occupying a disadvantaged place in the workforce. Unfortunately, testing and assessment procedures have too often reinforced existing constraints and barriers (Betz, 1992, 1993; Lent, Brown, & Hackett, 1996). Given that 60.2% of women ages 18 and older and 71.8% of women with children under 18 are currently employed outside the home (U.S. Bureau of Labor Statistics, 2004), it is essential that career counselors be prepared to address the unique concerns of working women. The question addressed in this chapter, then, is: How can career counselors approach assessment in their work with female clients in a way that facilitates confrontation and surmounting of limits, rather than in a manner that perpetuates the status quo? This question becomes particularly salient when we consider 21st-century changes in the nature of both work and the workplace (Chartrand & Walsh, 2001; Fitzgerald & Harmon, 2001; Höpfl & Atkinson, 2000). Consequently, our discussion of assessment issues must take place in the context of the broader issues of the goals, purposes, and theories guiding career counseling today.

We cannot proceed, however, without the usual disclaimers about space and scope. We assume that readers of this chapter: (a) are conversant with basic psychometric concepts, (b) have a knowledge of test-user guidelines regarding competent and ethical use of assessment procedures, (c) possess a working knowledge of career assessment, and (d) have at least some familiarity with the career development of women. Useful resources on testing include Anastasi and Urbina's (1997) *Psychological Testing* and Walsh and Betz's (2001) *Tests and Assessment*. Likewise, the American Psychological Association's *Ethical Principles* (APA, 2002), the National Career Development Association's *Career Counseling Competencies* (NCDA, 1997), and *Standards for Educational and Psychological Testing* (American Educational Research Association, APA, & National Council on Measurement in Education, 1999) are germane. Several recent publications addressing assessment in counseling and career counseling are also useful, particularly Watkins and Campbell's (2000) *Testing in Counseling Practice* and Zunker and Osborn's (2002) *Using Assessment Results for Career Development*. For an informative review of issues concerning the career development of women, we recommend Betz's (1992) chapter in the second edition of the *Handbook of Counseling Psychology* and Fitzgerald and Harmon's (2001) chapter in *Contemporary Models in Vocational Psychology*. Finally, although we discuss specific career tests and inventories, the reader needs to consult the appropriate technical manuals and test reviews for complete information on administration and interpretation of these assessments (e.g., Hood & Johnson, 2002; Kapes & Whitfield, 2002).

ASSESSMENT WITHIN CAREER COUNSELING FOR WOMEN

When assessment takes place, it occurs within the context of the counselor's theoretical assumptions about and general approach to counseling. The goals of career counseling have expanded considerably since the publication of Parsons' (1909) famous prescription for career guidance. With the increasing acknowledge of life-role perspectives on career development, career counseling is now viewed as a much more complex enterprise than the old notions of simple choice that have been manifested in matching models (Brown & Brooks, 1991). Contemporary models of career development call for greater attention to these life-role concerns, but also to other contextual influences on career decision making (e.g., Lent et al., 1996; Young, Valach, & Collin, 1996). Perhaps a very general goal that would fit most approaches to career counseling would be that career counselors attempt to promote and facilitate satisfying and realistic decision making and career adjustment through the life span. Thus, goals for career counseling must necessarily encompass assisting clients with acquiring the knowledge and developing the skills needed to make and implement career decisions, adjust to work circumstances, and negotiate work and other life roles. Although these overall goals are compatible with the goals of career counseling with women, they do not necessarily lead to specific counselor behaviors that promote effective career assessment and counseling with women. As we review the extant literature on career assessment and counseling with women, several important themes will likely emerge.

CAREER COUNSELING FOR WOMEN

Fitzgerald and Crites (1980) noted some time ago that women's career development is not so much different from men's as it is more complex. We echo this statement and extend it to career counseling. Career counseling (and assessment) with women is similar to and more complicated than career counseling (and assessment) with men. For ethical and effective career counseling with female clients, counselors must not only be good career counselors, but their counseling and assessment practices must be informed by the extensive literature on the career psychology of women (see Betz, chap. 2, this volume) and principles for counseling women (see Kopala & Keitel, 2003). The APA ethical principles (APA, 2002) concerning assessment techniques and competence underscore this point, that is, the necessity of recognizing differences among people such as those associated with sex, ethnicity, socioeconomic status (SES), and sexual orientation. Fortunately, there is a growing body of literature concerning the career development of ethnic and racial minorities (e.g., Betz & Fitzgerald, 1995; Bingham & Ward, 2001; Constantine, 2001; Fouad, 1995; Leong & Brown, 1995; Ward & Bingham, 2001), immigrants (e.g., Yakushko, chap. 12, this volume), gay, lesbian, and bisexual individuals (e.g., Bieschke & Toepfer-Hendey, chap. 11, this volume; Croteau, Anderson, DiStefano, & Kampa-Kokesch, 2000; Fukuyama & Ferguson, 2000; Reynolds, 2003), clients with disabilities (e.g., Alston, Bell, & Hampton, 2002; Enright, Conyers, & Szymanski, 1996; Farley, Johnson, & Parkerson, 1999; Noonan et al.,

2004), and those living in poverty (e.g., Heppner & O'Brien, chap. 3, this volume). We encourage counselors working with diverse groups of women to become familiar with this literature.

More fundamentally, we as career counselors need, at the very least, to adopt some variants of gender-sensitive and multiculturally competent counseling if we are to work equitably with all of our clients, but particularly with female clients. Counselors who treat female clients in a gender-blind manner often merely serve to perpetuate or reinforce the gender-role stereotyping that has already occurred and continues throughout clients' lives (Betz, 1993; Brown & Brooks, 1991). Even when no active bias on the part of counselors is perceived, that is, when clients report being treated in a sex-fair manner by their counselors, errors of omission are still common. For example, in a survey of former clients, participants reported that counselors often inadvertently promoted acceptance of the status quo, failed to actively explore gender roles, and missed issues of victimization (Sesan, 1988). All of these problems reflect the failure of counselors to adequately assess important gender-related aspects of clients' concerns, thereby overlooking important guidelines for psychological practice with girls and women (Kopala & Keitel, 2003).

We recommend Good, Gilbert, and Scher's (1990) guidelines for gender-aware therapy as a useful guide for incorporating gender in assessment in counseling. In their view, effective counseling requires: (a) regarding conceptions of gender as integral aspects of counseling and mental health (to which we would add career development), (b) considering client concepts within their societal context (see Betz, chap. 2, this volume), (c) actively addressing gender injustices, (d) collaborative therapeutic relationships, and (e) respect for the client's freedom to choose. To this we also add the importance of respect for other forms of diversity and the development of multicultural counseling competencies (e.g., Atkinson, 2004; Smith, 2004; Sue & Sue, 1999), including those specific to multicultural career counseling (e.g., Bingham, Ward, & Butler, chap. 7, this volume; Bingham & Ward, 1996; Constantine, Greer, & Kindaichi, 2003; Spokane, Fouad, & Swanson, 2003). These assumptions are reflected throughout the rest of this chapter.

GENDER ISSUES IN THEORY AND ASSESSMENT

The influence of gender and gender-role socialization on assessment in counseling is apparent at many levels. Although the problem of sex bias in testing comes readily to mind, there are some underlying issues, embedded in many of the fundamental assumptions of counselors that surface at different points in counseling (Brown, 1990; Jackson, Tal, & Sullivan, 2003).

Gender-aware counseling is not a theory of counseling per se, but rather an approach to conceptualizing and working with client problems applicable across theoretical perspectives. We must therefore examine the possible gender issues embedded in the broadest of our conceptual frameworks, that is, our theoretical models of counseling.

Theory-Based Career Assessment

Career assessment and intervention are always guided by some conceptual framework, and often by a formal theory of career counseling. Each of the major theories of career counseling contains clear implications for diagnosis and assessment; however, historically, it was rare to see any attention to gender issues in the more established trait-factor and developmental career-counseling theories. In contrast, some of the emerging theories of career development emphasize contextual factors, of which gender is an important one. As we consider both the established and more contemporary theories of career development, we offer a few illustrations of the potential strengths and limitations of each of these major theoretical models in guiding assessment of women's career concerns.

Individual Differences Perspective

Within the individual differences perspective (including trait-factor and person-environment or P-E fit theories), assessment occupies a prominent place. Exploration of aptitudes, abilities, interests, personality, needs, and values is considered crucial to informed decision making. An ongoing problem in assessment within the individual differences or P-E fit approaches to career counseling is the relative absence of consideration of two very basic dimensions of individual differences, namely, gender and ethnicity (Betz, 1992; Fassinger & O'Brien, 2000). The individual differences perspective may therefore be useful in understanding the career development of men and nontraditional women, but is probably inadequate in attempts to understand the majority of women unless these contextual factors are explicitly addressed (Betz, 1993; Fassinger & O'Brien).

Specific diagnostic categories used within the individual differences perspective present some dilemmas for career counselors working with female clients. One of the major foci of diagnosis within this tradition has been the concept of career choice realism (Crites, 1981). *Realistic* choices refer to those demonstrating congruence between level of ability, interests, and the requirements of the chosen occupation. When women choose careers that are clearly incongruent with their interests and measured ability levels, they are diagnosed as having made "unrealistic" career choices. Unrealistic career choices may reflect a choice that is significantly below a woman's ability levels (labeled "unfulfilled"), or "coerced" choices, reflecting appropriate ability levels for the job but an incongruence in interests (Crites). However, vocational choice realism is only part of the issue for most women (Fitzgerald & Weitzman, 1992). Many women are primarily responsible for childrearing, and therefore women's occupational choices, narrowly considered, may be unrealistic. In addition, the challenges associated with managing single-parent households and the related geographic constraints imposed by child custody arrangements may further constrain women's occupational choices. Consequently, in the context of a woman's other life roles, plans, and priorities, these so-called unrealistic choices might be very appropriate. That is, decontextualizing women's career issues from the rest of their lives results in assessment of only a few narrow aspects of the overall picture.

Fitzgerald and Weitzman (1992) suggested reconceptualizing career choice realism for women, and proposed two alternate concepts to explain the choice process of women seeking to negotiate both work and family roles: *satisficing*, or making choices that are "good enough," and *optimization*, or actively seeking to maximize outcomes in both family roles and careers. Ideally, career counselors ought to explore optimizing choices with their female clients. However, in keeping with the Good et al. (1990) principle of respect for the client's choice, satisficing options might also be explored. The question of how far the career counselor should pursue the issue of women's settling or satisficing is a thorny one (see Betz, chap. 2, this volume). In reflecting on Holland's (1985) typology model, Spokane (1996, p. 64) also noted that it is not sufficient to merely help clients identify their personality types and corresponding work environments; rather, counselors must help clients "mobilize the behaviors and attitudes required to implement that choice" as well as to identify internal and external factors that affect such decisions.

Whereas P-E fit conceptions include consideration of both the person and the work environment, little attention has been devoted to possible gender differences in subjective perspectives of work environments, or to the assessment of work environments. Research indicates that gender influences observer evaluations of work performance (Betz & Fitzgerald, 1987). How then might scores on an instrument such as the Minnesota Satisfactoriness Scales (Dawis & Lofquist, 1984), based on observer ratings of employee job performance, be influenced by the gender of the rater and the employee? Could there be gender differences in the experience of the same work environment, particularly for women entering male-dominated occupations or job settings? Furthermore, might there also be specific gender-role expectations for women in a particular workplace? How might such factors affect assessments of the potential for P-E fit?

P-E fit theory, formerly known as the theory of work adjustment (Dawis, 1996; Dawis & Lofquist, 1984), presents a number of variables that might

prove useful to counselors working with women on issues of career implementation and adjustment. These variables include: (a) personality structure (i.e., abilities, values), (b) personality style (i.e., celerity, pace, rhythm,
endurance), and (c) adjustment style (i.e., flexibility, activeness, reactive-
ness, perseverance). Correspondence (or discorrespondence) between a
client's personality style and the environment style is posited to be related
to satisfaction and satisfactoriness and, therefore, to work adjustment; consequently, developing clients' self-knowledge and occupational knowledge
is an important component of the P-E fit approach to career planning.
However, in keeping with its emphasis on work adjustment, it is also important for counselors to obtain information about an individual's adjustment
style, that is, understanding the extent to which the client is active or reactive, flexible, and willing to persevere in the face of discorrespondence. According to Dawis, adjustment style may be an important predictor of the client's future work-adjustment behavior. Interestingly, consistent with more
feminist counseling ideals, these theorists suggest that counseling interventions may also be directed toward empowering clients to make efforts to
change their work environments, perhaps by developing clients' skills in effective confrontation and negotiation (Dawis).

The Developmental Perspective

Within the developmental perspective the goal of career counseling is to
develop a dynamic description of the client's career through various
means, including a mixture of directive and nondirective interview techniques as well as qualitative and quantitative methods (Crites, 1981; Jepsen,
1990; Super, Savickas, & Super, 1996). Despite the relative absence of specific attention to gender, developmental career counseling does have much
in common with feminist notions of assessment and testing in counseling
female clients. For example, Good et al. (1990) recommended a collaborative relationship between counselor and client along with respect for a client's freedom to choose, seeing these as critical elements of gender-aware
counseling. Within developmental career counseling, the client is intimately involved in the assessment process, including the selection of any instruments, and assessment procedures are geared to the client's developmental level (Jepsen). Moreover, current developmental approaches to
career counseling reflect developmental theory's concern with the various
life roles of the client (Jepsen; Super et al.). Super's (1990) life-span, life-
space model is one of the few views of career development that actually addresses the intersection of roles that must be considered in career decision
making, an extremely important consideration for most female clients. In
addition, Super et al. recommended that career researchers and counselors
also focus on how individuals negotiate these roles in an effort to assist clients in learning to manage role overload and role conflict.

Although the developmental perspective offers much in guiding assessment with female clients, for the most part it does not specifically address gender roles or internal and external barriers. Equal treatment of the life roles of males and females, without consideration of how those roles play out differentially by gender, can be problematic (Betz & Fitzgerald, 1987). Can anyone truly accept that the homemaker role is considered an equally viable choice for most men and women in our society? Or that a combination of parenting and worker roles is experienced similarly by men and women? For women, the worker role is usually added on to the home and family roles and parenting responsibilities are rarely shared equally (Betz & Fitzgerald; Gilbert & Rader, 2001); in addition, a growing number of single, divorced, and widowed women are multiple job holders (U.S. Bureau of Labor Statistics, 2004). Research indicates that role conflict and role overload are critical issues in the lives of many employed women (Gilbert, 1987; Gilbert & Brownson, 1998; Gilbert & Rader), and may be particularly challenging for the growing number of women heading single-parent households (Woollett & Marshall, 2001). Thus, developmental career assessment must be expanded substantially to be considered appropriate for women. Although her model is not well supported by empirical data, Gottfredson's (1996) concepts of circumscription and compromise may nonetheless pose interesting questions about the ways in which some women narrow their zone of acceptable career alternatives or compromise occupational choices due to multiple-role or accessibility issues.

The Values-Based Perspective

According to Brown (1996), satisfying career choices are invariably linked to expected outcomes that are, in turn, prioritized according to one's values. Thus, values serve as an important determinant of career choice and behavior and are developed through an interaction of inheritance and experience. Although this model does not explicitly hypothesize about contextual influences on career decision making, Brown readily acknowledged that cultural background, gender, and SES will likely influence both social interactions and opportunities, thereby affecting career choice and other life-role concerns. Unfortunately, this theory is of limited practical value for career counseling with diverse groups of women, given its lack of attention to ways in which gender-role socialization, restricted academic and work experiences, internal and external barriers, and opportunity structures serve to limit clients' perceived career options. Brown did, however, acknowledge that the dominant values of the power elite in organizations will significantly influence an individual's experiences in the work environment. This suggests that women should be encouraged to anticipate and prepare for potential difficulties in the workplace, particularly when there is discorrespondence between their personal values and the value system of the work environment. This becomes particularly important for those women whose options for career change are limited by financial, geographic, or ability concerns.

The Social Learning Perspective

Although the social learning perspectives on career counseling account for their influence on learning experiences (Krumboltz & Nichols, 1990; Mitchell & Krumboltz, 1996), gender and ethnicity are viewed as background variables, rather than as integral factors influencing ongoing learning experiences. The social learning view of vocational interests and learned preferences is one aspect of the model that is particularly advantageous in working with women. A central issue in career assessment has been the restriction of women's career interests due to limited exposure to and experience with nontraditional activities (Betz, chap. 2, this volume; Fitzgerald et al., 1995). Adoption of a learning perspective on the development of interests provides theoretical guidance for understanding, assessing, and providing appropriate corrective experiences to encourage the development of nascent but unexplored preferences. This framework suggests that career counselors explore with women opportunities for both direct and vicarious experiences related to the development of nontraditional career interests.

Specific gender influences on career-related cognitions also remain relatively unexplored within the social learning tradition. Nevertheless, the literature on the career development of women is replete with examples of gender differences in cognitions and related cognitive processes (Betz & Fitzgerald, 1987; Fitzgerald et al., 1995; O'Brien, 2003). The internal, psychological barriers to women's career development discussed by Betz (chap. 2, this volume) reflect, to a great degree, the limiting nature of gender-circumscribed cognitions and point to ways in which a social learning perspective on assessment might be expanded to more thoroughly address gender dynamics. Career counselors may find a number of the social learning constructs (e.g., instrumental and associative learning experiences, task approach skills, self-observation generalizations, worldview generalizations) particularly useful when exploring with female clients their career-related experiences and aspirations; however, specific attention to and inclusion of issues of gender will undoubtedly enhance the career-assessment and counseling process.

The Social-Cognitive Perspective

In an effort to build conceptual bridges linking constructs from several prominent career theories, social-cognitive career theory (SCCT) was developed, in part, to address the ways in which contextual variables (e.g., gender, culture, health status, sociostructural considerations) can affect the development of career-related cognitions, interests, and career choice behavior (Lent et al., 1996). In particular, SCCT is concerned with specific cognitive factors that mediate the learning experiences guiding career behavior; the interrelationships of interests, abilities, and values; the paths by which contextual and individual factors influence career choice and behavior; and the processes by which individuals exercise personal agency (Lent et al.).

Three central variables are of interest to SCCT researchers and have important implications for career counseling with women: self-efficacy expectations, outcome expectations, and personal goals. *Self-efficacy expectations* are an individual's beliefs about his or her abilities to "organize and execute courses of action required to attain designed types of performances" (Bandura, 1986, p. 391) or, stated more simply, a person's estimates of her or his ability to successfully carry out certain tasks. *Outcome expectations* refer to an individual's beliefs about the consequences associated with performing specific behaviors. According to Lent et al. (1996, p. 381), "Whereas self-efficacy beliefs are concerned with one's capabilities (Can I do this?), outcome expectations involve the imagined consequences of performing given behavior (*If* I do this, what will happen?)." In other words, career counselors should not only consider their female clients' self-efficacy expectations with respect to traditional and nontraditional skill domains, they must also carefully examine the ways in which their clients' outcome expectations potentially limit career choices and behavior. This suggests that one potentially useful intervention with female clients is to help them identify positive, intrinsic outcomes (e.g., pride in oneself, enjoyment in performing tasks) associated with nontraditional career choices, rather than focusing exclusively on potential negative and external outcomes (e.g., negative feedback from significant others).

In the SCCT model, personal goals play an important role in organizing, guiding, and sustaining career behavior. Not surprisingly, the fully bidirectional, causal nature of this model suggests "a complex interplay between goals, self-efficacy, and outcome expectations in the self-regulation of behavior" (Lent et al., 1996, p. 381). In other words, career counselors must assess carefully the ways in which a client's career goals reflect the influence of self-efficacy and outcome expectations, as well as the ways in which current goals and academic or career behavior may serve to reinforce these career-related cognitions.

Although a number of career theorists (e.g., Holland, 1985) have suggested that interests play a prominent role in career choice, SCCT notes that interests are more likely to influence career choice when optimal conditions exist. However, SCCT also posits that self-efficacy and outcome expectations are likely to shape interest patterns, suggesting that counselors carefully consider the possibility that women's traditional career interests, at least in part, reflect gender-related patterns of self-efficacy and outcome expectations. One strategy for addressing the limiting effects of self-efficacy on interests is to target for further exploration those occupational titles suggested by aptitude and values assessment data that are not also generated by interest inventories (Lent et al., 1996).

Finally, proponents of SCCT recognize that clients may be unwilling or unable to move from occupational interests to vocational goals and actions because of perceived barriers to their career success. Consequently, counselors are encouraged to assist clients in identifying and analyzing such barriers as well as to strategize internal and external methods for preventing or managing those barriers that are most likely to threaten career implementation or work adjustment (Lent et al., 1996).

The Cognitive Information-Processing Perspective

The cognitive information-processing (CIP) model outlines three important domains in career decision making and problem solving: self-knowledge, occupational knowledge, and decision skills. The goal of CIP is to assist clients in becoming independent and responsible career problem solvers by teaching them a five-step problem-solving sequence and facilitating the growth of clients' information-processing skills (Peterson, Sampson, Reardon, & Lenz, 1996). In addition, clients are encouraged to explore ways that this career decision-making model might generalize to other areas of their lives. Although there is little discussion of contextual factors (e.g., gender, culture, health status) in this model, it nonetheless offers some useful ideas for career assessment and counseling with women. Most notably, counselors are encouraged to not only help clients expand their knowledge of self and occupations, but also to develop specific skills in problem analysis, generation and evaluation of options, and implementation of solutions. In addition, counselors may enhance a woman's problem-solving skills by encouraging self-monitoring through each phase of the decision-making cycle, with the option to backtrack and reexamine options as needed. Finally, as part of the career decision-making and problem-solving process, clients are encouraged to identify self-talk that serves to facilitate or inhibit progress toward solutions (Peterson et al.). This recommendation is certainly in keeping with the extant literature on the effects of self-efficacy and outcome expectations on career decision making.

Summary

Clearly, each of the major models of career development has something to offer counselors working with girls and women, despite the potential limitations of some theories in addressing contextual factors such as gender, ethnicity, and social class. Tables 4.1 and 4.2 provide a summary of the ways

TABLE 4.1

Implications of Established Career Development Theories for Career Assessment With Women

Theory	Assessment	Counseling/Intervention
Holland's Typology Theory	• Primary assessment activities include assessment of the individual's vocational personality and assessment of occupational environments with the goal of good person-environment fit. • Gender role, culture, and career-related cognitions (e.g., self-efficacy) may influence the projection of the client's personality onto occupational titles, and consequently the assessment feedback she receives during that process. • Once this feedback is given, the projection process may continue to affirm *and* disaffirm the woman's career and life decisions, thus restricting the range of career options.	• It is not enough to merely assist a client in learning about her personality type and related occupational environments; instead, clients may need assistance mobilizing the behaviors and career-related attitudes necessary for the implementation of their career choices. • Both career decision making and the implementation of career choices may be affected by internal and external factors.
Person-Environment Correspondence (or Theory of Work Adjustment)	• Women and minority group workers have not been afforded the same opportunities as majority workers; consequently, they may not have developed the full range of skills required in the world of work. • This restricted range of experiences may also limit awareness of their work needs and available reinforcers in the work environment. • Career assessment should include exploration of *personality structure* (i.e., abilities and values), *personality style* (i.e., celerity, pace, rhythm, and endurance) and *adjustment style* (i.e., flexibility, activeness, reactiveness, and perseverance).	• Career interventions should provide clients with a "conceptual framework" (i.e., satisfaction and satisfactoriness) with which to understand career choice and work adjustment, particularly given the likelihood of career changes throughout the lifespan. • Counseling interventions for work adjustment should include assessment of the individual as well as the susceptibility of the work environment to change in order to increase satisfaction and satisfactoriness. • Counseling interventions may also focus on empowering clients to effect change in their work environments.
Life-Span, Life-Space	• Career assessment should include consideration of women's "life space" and role salience as well as traditional elements of vocational identity (i.e., interests, aptitudes, values). • Important to consider how women negotiate multiple roles and manage the demands associated with these roles.	• Counseling interventions can be helpful in clarifying sources of interrole conflicts for women, as well as the ways in which multiple roles provide opportunities for the personal fulfillment. • Career counseling may also be helpful to women whose circumstances (e.g., divorce) necessitate "life redesign."

TABLE 4.2

Implications of Contemporary Career Development Theories for Career Assessment With Women

Theory	Assessment	Counseling/Intervention
Social Learning Theory of Career Decision Making	• Important to assess genetic endowments and special abilities, environmental conditions and events, instrumental and associative learning experiences, and task approach skills (including work habits and career-related cognitions) that influence a woman's career path. • Given that people often repeat behaviors for which they have been reinforced, counselors should assess the extent to which a restricted range of vocational interests is the result of limited experiences.	• Counseling interventions should focus on: (a) stimulating new learning in clients; (b) helping clients cope with a constantly changing work world; and (c) assisting clients in the process of creating satisfying lives. • In order to do this, counselors may need to assist women in expanding their capabilities and interests rather than basing decisions on existing information about themselves. • Career counselors should prepare clients to learn to develop skills on an ongoing basis given anticipated changes in the world of work and in their own criteria for vocational satisfaction.
Social Cognitive Career Theory (SCCT)	• When traditional assessment methods are used, counselors should target for further exploration those occupations that are suggested on the basis of aptitude and needs/values data but that are not identified by interest data. • Occupational card sorts may be useful in helping women explore the ways in which self-efficacy and outcome expectations have constrained their range of career options.	• Counselors must assess women's career-related self-efficacy, outcome expectations, goals, and behavior with attention to the complex interaction of these and other contextual factors (e.g., gender, ethnicity) in determining career interest, choice, and performance. • Counseling interventions should assist women in expanding their occupational options by helping to identify opportunities for increasing career-related self-efficacy in nontraditional domains. • Counselors should also assist clients in identifying and analyzing potential barriers to their career success, as well as helping them to develop strategies for preventing or overcoming these barriers.

(Continued)

TABLE 4.2
(Continued)

Theory	Assessment	Counseling/Intervention
Cognitive Information Processing (CIP) Theory	• Counselors should assess the extent of clients' self-knowledge and occupational knowledge, as well as executive functions (i.e., metacognition) such as self-talk, self-awareness, and monitoring/control.	• CIP interventions can teach women not only the steps required for career decision making and problem solving, but also generic skills that may be useful in other problem-solving contexts.
Values-Based Theory	• Clients should be assisted in identifying their career-related values through use of both quantitative and qualitative measures. • Cultural background, gender, and socioeconomic status may affect an individual's values; therefore these influences should also be assessed.	• Because mood can impact an individual's ability to make good decisions, career interventions should not take place until mood problems (e.g., anxiety, depression) can be addressed. • Assessment and counseling strategies may vary depending on whether clients have planned or unplanned career decisions or changes, and whether psychological, physical, or ability issues are potentially limiting the range of a woman's career options.

in which the assumptions and theoretical constructs embedded in these models may be useful in career assessment and counseling with girls and women.

Gender Issues in Approaches to Assessment

Gender issues arise not only within a counselor's theory or conceptual model of career counseling, but also within the approaches used to gather information across theoretical perspectives. Therefore, we now turn to considerations of gender issues that may arise in a career counselor's views of the purposes of career assessment, and in the specific approaches used to gather information.

Purposes of Career Assessment

The primary purpose of any type of assessment within the context of counseling is to gather information to understand and address the client's concerns (Hood & Johnson, 2002). Put simply, "psychological assessment is a process of understanding and helping people cope with problems. In this process, tests are frequently used to collect meaningful information about the person and his or her environment" (Walsh & Betz, 2001, p. 10). Yet many writers attest to other uses of test and assessment information. For example, according to Campbell (1990), assessment information can: serve as a source of feedback, provide new perspective, teach or present new ideas, and serve as a stimulus for discussion. Finally, Hood and Johnson identified an additional purpose of career assessment, that is, evaluating the effectiveness of career interventions.

Essentially, assessment serves to advance counseling most simply through its informational function, but information itself can serve to create new awareness and redefine goals and directions. Moreover, a number of writers have discussed assessment procedures, particularly self-guided interest inventories and qualitative assessment methods as career interventions (Goldman, 1990; Slaney & MacKinnon-Slaney, 1990, 2000; Spokane, 1990, 1991; Subich & Billingsley, 1995). For example, assessment can be used to unearth conflicts or problems that may impede the progress of career counseling, can be employed to motivate clients to engage in career behaviors, and is sometimes useful in providing clients with cognitive structures for evaluating career alternatives (Chartrand & Walsh, 2001; Spokane, 1991). Goldman argued that qualitative assessment methods provide a closer link between assessment and counseling than standardized test procedures.

Although the general purposes of assessment revolve primarily around information gathering, the specific procedures to be employed with individual clients depend on the nature of the problem, the issues to be addressed, and the type of information needed. Put another way, "The business of assessment—of any variety—is essentially directed toward collecting observations on some dimension of interest" (Phillips & Pazienza, 1988, p. 1). However, specification of these "dimensions of interest" within the context of career counseling is heavily influenced by the conceptual framework and approach of the counselor. That is, a career counselor's basic assumptions about the nature of the individual, along with the counselor's theoretical views about career development and counseling, will determine what is considered important or salient given similar client concerns, and, in fact, what is attended to as relevant to assessment and counseling. Fortunately, counselors are beginning to give greater consideration to contextual factors (e.g., gender, culture, sexual orientation, health status, socioeconomic level) as dimensions of interest in career assessment (e.g., Chartrand & Walsh, 2001; Subich & Billingsley, 1995; Whiston & Bouwkamp, 2003).

It is also important to note that the scope of career assessment is expanding to include factors associated with the "transfiguration of work and the workforce" (Chartrand & Walsh, 2001, p. 234). As economic and technological factors change the nature of work and the workplace itself, employers have become increasingly interested in evaluating workers' characteristics such as flexibility, adaptability, cognitive style (e.g., creativity, problem solving), and self-management skills. These characteristics will likely become an important focus of career assessment in the future (Chartrand & Walsh; Fitzgerald & Harmon, 2001).

Major Approaches to Assessment

After examining their theoretical and conceptual views and their views of the purposes and goals of career counseling, career counselors must also address gender issues that may arise within their approach to assessment. We focus next on the general procedures employed by counselors to assess client concerns, that is, interviewing techniques, tests and inventories, cognitive and behavioral assessment techniques, and qualitative assessment.

The Interview.   Assessment in career counseling begins, and may sometimes end, with the interview. Person-centered career counselors often use only this (Crites, 1981), but all counselors rely to a greater or lesser degree on the information obtained in the counseling interview (Walsh & Betz, 2001). At a minimum, the counseling interview serves as a vehicle for clarifying the presenting concern, establishing rapport, and exploring the client's frame of reference and perspectives on presenting concerns (Zunker, 2002). However, skilled counselors can also gather much information about individual differences, career development, and the cognitions, skills, and aspirations of clients via interviewing (Brown & Brooks, 1991).

More generally, the information gathered in the early stages of the counseling interview serves to inform decision making about the desirability of other types of assessment information that may be necessary, as well as planning for interventions. If gender and other individual difference issues fail to be considered in these early stages, the counselor's developing picture of the client, her concerns, and her personal circumstances will be sorely flawed if not outright inaccurate. Integration of gender into the assessment interview is particularly important in career counseling, in that lack of attention to gender issues will cause the counselor to miss crucial information about life-role considerations, sources of stress and strain, and possible gender influences on the consideration of occupational alternatives and career directions (Betz, chap. 2, this volume; Subich & Billingsley, 1995).

Brown (1990) lamented the lack of attention to gender issues in the clinical assessment interview; her comments are as relevant to career counseling as they are to counseling for personal or interpersonal concerns. Sex per se is of far less importance than gender, which has been defined as the socially constructed attributions, assumptions, and expectations assigned to individuals on the basis of their biological sex (Unger, 1979). In addition to considering the dynamics of gender, counselors must also address the influence of gender role, gender stereotyping, and potential gender-role conflict to develop a genuine understanding of the client and her concerns (for further discussion see Brown & Brooks, 1991). Equally important, however, is the career counselor's awareness and consideration of the counselor's own gender issues, that is, basic values and assumptions that might be affected by societal attitudes about gender and appropriate gender-role behavior (Brown, 1986, 1990). Consequently, counselors must consider gender at various stages of the counseling interview, beginning before a counselor ever sees clients (Brown, 1990). Such considerations of gender encompass an ongoing examination of the counselor's "conscious and nonconscious biases and expectations regarding gender" (Brown, 1990, p. 14), as well as continuing efforts by counselors to educate themselves about the career psychology of women (Betz & Fitzgerald, 1987; Fitzgerald et al., 1995; Jackson et al., 2003).

Within the counseling session the career counselor might actively pursue the meaning of gender in clients' lives, within their family and cultural circumstances, as well as in the broader societal context in which clients find themselves (Brown, 1990). Issues surrounding acquiescence to or deviation from internal or externally imposed gender stereotypes and expectations must also be addressed, and are of particular importance in considering clients' career options. Brown and Brooks (1991) provided several examples of specific lines of inquiry in career counseling reflecting attention to gender, for example, asking female clients about the meaning of achievement and career success or failure as a woman, or exploring expectations about life roles and the influence of gender socialization on such expectancies. Gender-role analysis—discussed more extensively in a subsequent section—can be an effective strategy for exploring the possible costs and benefits of adherence to or noncompliance with gender-role expectations or pressures (Brown, 1986; Subich & Billingsley, 1995).

Although we are focusing specifically on gender issues in this chapter, we would be remiss not to discuss cultural bias. Creation of a contextually sensitive picture of the client and her career-related concerns includes assessment of the specifics of a client's family culture and current circumstances; this is important for the Anglo or Caucasian client, but particularly vital for women of color (Betz & Fitzgerald, 1995; Brown, 1986; Fouad, Helledy, & Metz, 2003; Smith, 1983; Ward & Bingham, 2001). The career counselor might explore contextual information such as: "Age cohort, religions raised in and currently practicing . . . family history with regard to ethnicity and participation in ethnic culture, generation from immigration (where appropriate), languages spoken in the home . . . family roles of men and women, class background and education of parents" (Brown, p. 246). Although such an extensive exploration of background may not be necessary or possible for every client, at least some attention to these and related matters is, Brown argued, necessary to providing "the sociological framework for the phenomenological inquiry into what meaning gender membership gave to life experiences, [and] what was normal and useful for women and men in the world of this individual" (p. 246). Certainly, race, class, and culture influence career decision-making and vocational behavior in profound and complex ways, and some consideration of the interaction between gender and ethnicity is fundamental to understanding the career concerns of women of color (Betz & Fitzgerald; Bingham & Ward, 1996; Fitzgerald & Weitzman, 1992). Several important articles and chapters addressing the career development of women of color have been published recently (e.g., Betz & Fitzgerald; Bingham & Ward; Constantine et al., 2003; Fouad, 1995; Fukuyama & Ferguson, 2000; Subich, 1996); we refer the reader to these for a more complete discussion.

Finally, there is a growing recognition that cross-cultural counseling competencies encompass not only appropriate beliefs and attitudes equipping one with a sensitivity to, and appreciation for, other cultures and specific knowledge and information about cultural differences, but also cross-culturally appropriate skills (Atkinson, 2004; Smith, 2004; Sue & Sue, 1999; Trevino, 1996). For example, some interviewing methods may be less appropriate than others in counseling women from varying cultural backgrounds. The competent cross-cultural counselor must be able to begin to understand clients' differing worldviews (e.g., Trevino) as well as generate culturally sensitive verbal and nonverbal responses (Atkinson, Morten, & Sue, 1989; Sue & Sue, 1999). Strong culturally sensitive interviewing skills are particularly important at the assessment stage, and crucial to gaining an adequate understanding of women of color and their career concerns.

Tests and Inventories. Issues of race and sex bias in standardized tests and inventories have been raised and debated extensively over the years, prompting revisions in the most commonly used instruments for career counseling (Betz, 1990; Lewin & Wild, 1991; Selkow, 1984; Walsh & Betz, 2001). Improvements in the technical quality of tests and inventories have not, however, totally resolved the widespread concern about bias in testing. Two interrelated issues have surfaced in the literature addressing fairness in testing: the technical qualities of the test and the social policy issues about the use and impact of testing. Attention to the first issue, technical quality, has resulted in improvements in the validity of the instruments we use (e.g., interest inventories); research has documented the absence of widespread, blatant bias (Walsh & Betz). Technical quality reflects the question: "Is the test a good measure of what it purports to assess?" Attention to the psychometric properties of tests cannot, however, address the underlying value issues that arise from the adverse impact test results may have on certain groups in our society, for example, women and people of color. Social policy concerns reflect the question: "Should a test, even if it is valid, be used?" (Cole, 1981).

Career counselors must first be concerned with the technical quality of the tests and inventories they use. Cultural and sex bias in testing are manifested psychometrically in a number of ways: content bias, bias in internal structure, and selection or predictive bias (Cole, 1981; Walsh & Betz, 2001). All three reflect concern about different aspects of the validity of an instrument. All tests are culture bound in that they have been developed within the context of the norms, values, assumptions, and experiences of a particular culture. More specifically, most of our psychological tests are developed within the context of the dominant White, middle-class culture, and thus may not be entirely suitable across different cultural groups within the United States (Walsh & Betz). Understandably, many researchers and practitioners have continued to call for greater attention to issues of diversity in the development of standardized tests and inventories.

Content bias refers to words, examples, or the content of questions that may be more familiar to one group than another, and is a concern for women as well as for people of color. Content bias may occur at the item level, or at the overall test score level. For example, items on interest inventories about auto mechanics, plumbing, or other stereotypically masculine activities are likely to be foreign to many women (Walsh & Betz, 2001). Sexist occupational titles (e.g., mailman) are another example of sex bias in interest inventory content. Gender differences in mathematics do not appear on problems requiring symbolic manipulation (e.g., computation), but do appear for story-based word problems. Research evidence suggests that differential familiarity with sex-typed word problem content accounts for these observed gender differences in math performance (Chipman, Marshall, & Scott, 1991). Cultural content bias on achievement tests may also result from differential familiarity of problem content, for example, problems requiring knowledge of farm animals that may be disadvantageous to inner-city African American children (Walsh & Betz). Content bias may also arise from cross-cultural or gender differences in the values or perceptions of the appropriateness of different behaviors. For example, women tend to view achievement differently from men, and cultural differences in perspectives on cooperation and competition have been identified (Betz & Fitzgerald, 1987; Mednick & Thomas, 1993; Walsh & Betz). Experts in the field agree that offensive, biased, or stereotypical item content ought to be modified for the sake of equity and the general social welfare, as well as to reduce the possibility of inadvertent cultural or gender bias (Cole, 1981). Fortunately, most test developers have made considerable strides, particularly with vocational interest inventories and achievement tests, in eliminating facial bias in content (Cole). For example, test developers are now including experts representing diverse groups in the process of developing and refining items for such tests (Walsh & Betz).

Sex and cultural bias may also be evident in the internal structure of tests. If the scores of different groups (e.g., men vs. women) yield different relationships, or the factor structures for the groups are different, then a test is considered to be biased (i.e., invalid). Traditional psychometric procedures such as examination of item difficulties, item total correlations, and factor analyses are used to explore the internal structure of tests for bias (Walsh & Betz, 2001). Most career-assessment instruments either have been revised to address concerns about bias in internal structure or have not shown problems on this dimension (Cole, 1981; Walsh & Betz). However, it is essential that developers of new career-assessment instruments continue to monitor these issues of internal structure.

Selection bias, however, has been of concern to career researchers and counselors. If a test score is differentially predictive across groups, selection bias is operating. A vast amount of research has been conducted exploring selection bias in intelligence, ability, and achievement tests. The consensus in the literature is that achievement and aptitude tests predict about as well for people of color as for Anglos (Anastasi & Urbina, 1997; Cole, 1981; Walsh & Betz, 2001). For women, however, there is some evidence for selection bias in that achievement test scores (e.g., SATs, GREs) underpredict women's college and graduate school performance compared to men's (Betz, 1990; Walsh & Betz). Career counselors must be mindful of this trend when forming their picture of a client's abilities.

Attempts to address bias in testing have taken several forms. All of the major interest inventories and most standardized ability, aptitude, and achievement tests have been revised to minimize content bias. Teams of expert raters are often used to identify culture-bound and sex-typed items and questions (Cole, 1981). Selection bias due to differential predictive validity has been addressed through methods such as changing the selection procedures of universities and employers (Betz, 1990; Fitzgerald et al., 1995). However, as mentioned previously, improvements in the psychometric adequacy of tests do not necessarily produce fairness in the use of these tests. Thus, test developers have revised not only their instruments but also their interpretative materials, and professional organizations have developed extensive guidelines to promote fairness in testing (e.g., AERA/APA/NCME *Joint Technical Standards for Educational and Psychological Testing* [1999]; APA's *Code of Fair Testing Practices in Education* [2004]). In addition to being familiar with professional ethical and technical guidelines, career counselors must consider test scores as only one piece of evidence about their client's abilities, aptitudes, and interests. Numerous factors aside from the characteristic being measured may influence test scores. Lack of motivation, lack of experience in taking standardized tests, and poor educational preparation are concerns for all test takers, whereas for women of color there is the additional possibility of alienation due to cultural bias; all are important considerations in evaluating the accuracy of aptitude and achievement test scores (Walsh & Betz, 2001). Alternative explanations for a client's scores should be carefully considered before accepting such scores as evidence of specific characteristics or skills (Walsh & Betz, 2001). A case in point is the issue of sex restrictiveness in interest inventories.

As most career counselors know, in the past many of the major interest inventories employed separate forms for men and women (Hansen, 1986). All of the major interest inventories now have merged forms for use with women and men, prompted by concerns about sex bias (Borgen, 1986; Hansen; Walsh & Betz, 2001). Yet women and men continue to respond differently to inventory items, resulting in gender differences in the overall patterns of occupational interests. Women tend to express interests congruent with the traditional female gender role (e.g., social, artistic, child welfare), whereas men express more interest in traditionally masculine domains such as scientific, technical, and mechanical activities (Walsh & Betz). The end result is that the use of interest inventories with female clients may result in reinforcement of traditional feminine socialization rather than facilitating exploration of viable options (Betz, chap. 2, this volume; Betz & Fitzgerald, 1987; Lent et al., 1996).

The thorny problem of sex restrictiveness in vocational interest inventories is not caused by vocational interest inventories, but uninformed use of inventories that reinforce traditional gender-role socialization can perpetuate the internal and structural pressures detrimental to women. Due to continuing occupational segregation in the workforce, the percentage of women and men in different occupational fields persists, with women overrepresented in lower paying, lower status jobs across a circumscribed range of fields (Betz & Fitzgerald, 1987; Fitzgerald et al., 1995; Fitzgerald & Harmon, 2001; Jackson et al., 2003). This occupational segregation continues to be of concern, particularly in light of the fact that the fastest growing occupations in the next decade are largely computer related and require what are thought of as traditionally masculine skills and interests (U.S. Bureau of Labor Statistics, 2004). Differential gender-role socialization and consequent gender differences in life experiences from early childhood influence the gender differences in interest patterns reflected in responses to interest inventories (Betz & Fitzgerald). Thus, women's interest patterns may be more indicative of experiences, or the lack thereof, than of genuine interests (Lent et al., 1996). Some researchers have also suggested that these interest patterns may reflect, in part, the influence of career-related self-efficacy expectations (e.g., Hackett & Betz, 1981; Lent et al.). The fact of gender differences in interest inventory results is generally accepted. The debate revolves around what to do about it (Walsh & Betz, 2001). Is it the career counselor's job to explore what is? Holland (1982) argued that it is unethical to tamper with gender-role socialization, and therefore concluded that interest inventories should be interpreted straightforwardly. We argue that career counselors who fail to consider the adverse impact of gender-role socialization and differential life experiences in the interpretation of interest inventories and tests are merely unwitting accomplices of the status quo.

The controversy surrounding sex restrictiveness has resulted in several approaches to the selection, use, and interpretation of vocational interest inventories. Although most of the major interest inventories use raw scores or combined-sex norms, we agree with Walsh and Betz (2001) that career counselors should use at least one of two alternatives: same-sex norms, or interest inventories with sex-balanced items. If same-sex norms are used to interpret scores, women's raw scores are compared to the patterns of scores of other women. Thus, women who have some nontraditional interests may be more readily identified. The counselor may then explore the impact of gender-role orientation, beliefs about women's roles, and lack of experience and exposure to nontraditional activities, in an effort to promote active examination and exploration of options. Alternatively, there are several interest inventories that have been developed to minimize gender differences in responses at the item level, most notably, the revised version of the Vocational Interest Inventory (VII; Lunneborg, 1981) and the Unisex version of the ACT-IV (UNIACT; Lamb & Prediger, 1981). The VII and the UNIACT include an even balance of items typical of both feminine and masculine gender-role socialization so that few gender differences result at the item level. Both of the recommended approaches (use of same-sex norms or sex-balanced items) are aimed at identifying interests that female clients have developed despite their socialization experiences (Walsh & Betz).

Cognitive and Behavioral Assessment. Behavioral and cognitive assessment procedures were developed in reaction to traditional psychometric assessment, and rest on fundamentally distinct conceptual assumptions. Traditional psychometric assessment attempts to measure intrinsic traits, whereas cognitive and behavioral assessment procedures focus on discrete, situational thoughts or behaviors (Glass & Merluzzi, 2000; Groth-Marnat, 2003; Merluzzi & Boltwood, 1990; Merluzzi, Glass, & Genest, 1981). Although there are distinctions between behavioral and cognitive assessment, both focus on obtaining samples of performance (i.e., behaviors or thoughts).

The sine qua non of behavioral assessment is direct observation of performance (Groth-Marnat, 2003; Merluzzi & Boltwood, 1990). In career counseling, for example, observation of live or simulated job interviewing behavior provides information not available from retrospective reports of interview performance. Behavioral assessment methods have been expanded to include behavioral interviews, self-report questionnaires, self-monitoring, and psychophysiological assessment (Groth-Marnat; Merluzzi & Boltwood). The unique contribution of behavioral assessment rests in its focus on behavior per se. Behavioral self-report methods, for example, focus on tallying the frequency of behavior, along with antecedent conditions and consequences, to analyze functional relationships of behavior and situational influences (Groth-Marnat; MacDonald, 1984).

Because of the emphasis on observable behavior, behaviorists have assumed that their assessment methods are valid, unbiased, and equally applicable to women and men (MacDonald, 1984). Thus, the literature on gender bias within the behavioral assessment tradition is scant, and does not compare to that which exists within the psychometric tradition. In fact, "there has been essentially no attention to feminist issues in the behavioral assessment literature" (MacDonald, p. 60). Nevertheless, MacDonald criticized behavioral assessment methods, recommending attention to many of the gender issues we have already discussed in this chapter. To assess women's behavior in context, the sociopolitical realities and gender-related experiences and influences on behavior must be examined, or else any functional analysis will be invalid or misleading (MacDonald). The research on assertion is an example of some of the problems resulting from ignoring gender in behavioral assessment. Constraints on space prevent us from a fuller exploration of gender issues in behavioral assessment; however, the interested reader is referred to an earlier discussion of gender and assertion (Hackett & Lonborg, 1994).

Cognitive assessment is actually a hybrid, evolving out of cognitive-behavioral assessment procedures, but also influenced by other perspectives, including social-cognitive theory, information-processing models, and personal construct theory (Glass & Merluzzi, 2000; Merluzzi et al., 1981). Cognitions may include self-statements and self-talk, attributions or explanatory style, imagery, beliefs, efficacy and outcome expectations, and cognitive style, depending on one's theoretical perspective (Segal & Shaw, 1988). Cognitive assessment procedures include thought listing and think-aloud methods, prompted recall, and self-report questionnaires assessing attributions, self-efficacy, and beliefs (Glass & Merluzzi; Groth-Marnat, 2003). In the career literature, Krumboltz's *Career Beliefs Inventory* (Krumboltz, 1991), Sampson and associates' *Career Thoughts Inventory* (Sampson, Peterson, Lenz, Reardon, & Saunders, 1996), and career self-efficacy measures (Betz, 2001; Lent & Hackett, 1987; O'Brien, 2003) are examples of cognitive assessment.

Gender issues have received somewhat more attention in the cognitive assessment literature than in the behavioral literature. In practice, counselors generally adopt a combined cognitive-behavioral approach to assessment, so many of the issues mentioned in the context of behavioral assessment with women may well apply to cognitive assessment. The example of assertion is also relevant here; clearly, the role of gender-related beliefs and expectations, in combination with the very real social consequences for women acting assertively, underscore the need for assessing gender, cognitions, behaviors, and affect in interaction to understand the complexity of gender issues in social situations (Gervasio & Crawford, 1989). Although gender differences in irrational beliefs about assertive behavior have received some attention (Jakubowski, 1977), little attention has been devoted to the appropriateness of irrational beliefs per se as a focus of cognitive assessment for women. To extend the assertion example, women's choices to refrain from actively assertively under certain conditions may actually be quite rational, reflecting acknowledgement of unacceptable social consequences of assertion and the associated negative outcome expectations. Nor have gender issues in the assessment of career cognitions (e.g., Krumboltz, 1991; Mitchell & Krumboltz, 1996) been examined to any great extent, save for the growing body of literature on gender and career self-efficacy (e.g., Betz, 2001; Hackett & Betz, 1992; Hackett & Lent, 1992; O'Brien, 2003). However, there has been some work done in identifying the cognitive themes salient for women at different stages of career development (Richman, 1988); this work is a starting point for cognitive career assessment in a developmental context.

Computer-Assisted Career Assessment. Major advances in information technology have also influenced new development in career assessment, namely, the increasing use of computer work stations (e.g., desktop computers) and the Internet in career assessment and counseling. Not surprisingly, numerous practical and ethical issues concerning such use have emerged (NCDA, 1998). In a recent review, Sampson, Lumsden, and Carr (2002) identified three major role issues in computer-based career assessment: role of the computer, role of the counselor, and role of the client or individual. Clearly, it is important for those recommending the use of computer- and Internet-based assessment to consider carefully the ways in which these technologies may positively and negatively affect the delivery of career-assessment and counseling services. For example, how might the role of the counselor change when test administration, scoring, and interpretation are provided by a software program? Are clients or other consumers readily able to interpret and apply the results of Internet-based assessments obtained independently of a career-counseling professional? To what extent are the cultural contexts (e.g., gender, ethnicity, sexual orientation, multiple-role issues) in career development fully explored when clients, consumers, and counselors rely heavily on computer-based assessment and interventions? What do we know about the reliability and validity of paper-and-pencil career measures when implemented in a different format (e.g., the Internet)? Career counselors considering computer-based approaches to service delivery should become familiar with the growing body of career literature devoted to the advantages and limitations of these methods (e.g., Oliver & Chartrand, 2000; Oliver & Zack, 1999; Reile & Harris-Bowlsbey, 2000; Sampson et al., 2002) as well as the professional and ethical standards for the delivery of Web-based counseling (e.g., National Board for Certified Counselors, 2001; NCDA, 1997).

Other Assessment Methods. A number of alternate approaches to career assessment may be roughly termed "qualitative" (Goldman, 1990). A wide range of methods fit under the qualitative assessment rubric, and are characterized more by what they are not (i.e., standardized tests and inventories) than by what they are (Goldman). Goldman cited several examples of qualitative career assessment, including vocational card sorts, values-clarification exercises, the vocational lifeline exercise, work samples, and observation. To this list we would add the various career-exploration exercises described elsewhere in the literature (e.g., Brown & Brooks, 1991), such as vocational autobiographies, genograms, fantasy and imagery techniques (e.g., occupational daydreams and the ideal-future day exercise), and gender-role analysis (Brown & Brooks; Spokane, 1991). Qualitative career-assessment techniques may be used to explore interests, values, personality, abilities, functional skills, and gender issues—indeed, every aspect of career decision making and adjustment. It is important to note, however, that the use of these informal assessment strategies also requires an awareness of and sensitivity to gender issues and ethical practices in assessment (Whiston & Bouwkamp, 2003).

The advantages of qualitative assessment in career counseling for women are several: They encourage the active participation of clients in assessment, they tend to promote a holistic and integrated view of career concerns, and they make it easier to incorporate cultural and gender issues at a very fundamental level (Goldman, 1990). Many of the qualitative career-assessment techniques are, in fact, interventions as well (e.g., career lifeline, fantasy, and values-clarification exercises), facilitating the intimate connection between career assessment and counseling that is so crucial (Goldman). Furthermore, "in practice, a comprehensive and meaningful psychological assessment is based on information that emerges from both qualitative and quantitative methods of assessment" (Walsh & Betz, 2001, p. 262). Qualitative career-assessment methods can be used alone, but may be more effective in combination with standardized assessment tools. Although the use of qualitative career-assessment methods facilitates attention to gender and cultural issues, it does not guarantee their incorporation. In the section of this chapter devoted to specific techniques, we show that even the rise of a nonsexist vocational card sort may be insufficient in promoting gender-aware counseling.

GENDER ISSUES IN CAREER-ASSESSMENT METHODS

In this section we focus primarily on gender issues in the use and interpretation of tests, inventories, and techniques. Only the most commonly used tests and inventories are highlighted, and selected alternate methods particularly useful for career assessment with women are explored. The reader is referred to other sources for detailed technical and interpretational information (e.g., Anastasi & Urbina, 1997; Kapes & Whitfield, 2002; Walsh & Betz, 2001; Watkins & Campbell, 2000; Zunker & Osborn, 2002).

Assessment of Individual Differences

Interest Assessment

Super and Crites (1949) described four types of interests: (a) *expressed* interests, or what people say when asked about their likes, dislikes, or preferences; (b) *manifest* interests, or assessments based on observations of people's behavior across different situations; (c) *tested* interests, or inferences based on people's knowledge of special information about a topic; and (d) *inventoried* interests, or people's reports of likes, dislikes, and preferences among a list of items. Of these, the inventory method of assessing interests is probably the most widely used (Walsh & Betz, 2001), and receives the most attention here. However, Borgen (1986) reminded us that expressed interests "are at least as predictive of future career behavior as inventory results" (p. 112). We highly recommend that the reader consider interest assessment via the interview and other qualitative methods in exploring women's vocational preferences. At the very least, interpretation of interest inventory results should occur in conjunction with exploration of expressed interests.

The Big Three Interest Inventories. Borgen (1986) characterized the Strong Interest Inventory (SII), the Kuder inventories (e.g., the Kuder Occupational Interest Scale, KOIS), and Holland's measures (especially the Self-Directed Search, or SDS) as the "Big Three" of interest assessment. Of these, the SII and the KOIS are true interest inventories, whereas the SDS is a self-administered and self-scored assessment procedure. Some gender-related issues in use and interpretation are shared by all three (and other methods as well), whereas some are instrument specific.

In considering the use of any interest inventory with female clients, at least four issues are salient: the basic assumptions underlying the development of interest inventories in general, questions about what the inventory is actually measuring (or construct validity), issues about how sex restrictiveness in vocational interests is addressed (e.g., the use of single-sex or combined-sex norms, or sex-balanced items), and concern about the validity—or hit rates—of the instrument when examining the career choices of people of color.

Most of the major interest inventories rest on the assumption that responses to unfamiliar as well as familiar items are equally indicative of basic interests (Hansen, 1990). Yet we have seen that women's gender-role socialization often results in traditional patterns of interests that may reflect differential experience much more so than fundamental preferences (see Lent et al., 1996). Although the same argument holds for men who have been traditionally socialized, the circumscription of career options is more serious for women than men. Betz (2000) suggested that, when interpreting interest inventories, counselors should consider issues of opportunity dominance and socialization dominance. Furthermore, Betz (1992) suggested that "interpretation of low scores on interest scales as indicative of lack of interest should be deferred until alternative explanations, such as lack of background exposure to a particular area, have been considered" (p. 461).

Of the major interest inventories, the SII has the longest continuous history (Hansen, 1990). The current edition of the SII utilizes same-sex norms for the occupational scales in an effort to reduce sex bias (Hansen, 2000; Harmon, Hansen, Borgen, & Hammer, 1994). The 1994 version of the SII was also designed to address issues of both inclusion and balance by "including more and different kinds of people in the research and development phase" and by including occupations representing both innovation and tradition (Walsh & Betz, 2001, p. 238). Despite continuing debates about the most effective manner in which to address sex restrictiveness in interest inventories, the use of single-sex occupational scales on the SII offers some advantages. First, female clients' scores on the occupational scales can be compared to separate male and female criterion samples, thus allowing a female career client to examine the ways in which her scores are similar and dissimilar to both occupational reference groups. Second, women can compare their scores to those of other women. According to Hansen (1990), "Interpretation based on the client's own sex typically provides the most valid and reliable information and the most options for exploration of interests in areas considered non-traditional for one sex or the other" (p. 181). Finally, comparisons between a woman's own interests and the interests of men dominating a particular field of work may be especially helpful for women considering nontraditional occupations. Knowing the extent to which their broad patterns of interests resemble the interest patterns of their potential colleagues may assist women in anticipating issues of choice implementation and occupational adjustment.

Whereas there is ample evidence of the predictive validity of the occupational scales, Hood and Johnson (1997) encouraged counselors to exercise caution when interpreting the personal style scales for clients. More specifically, the authors noted that these scales lack the established validity enjoyed by the other SII scales.

In addition to familiarizing themselves with issues of sex bias, users of the SII should also be aware of the results of available research on the appropriateness of the SII for use with people of color. Results of recent research suggest there are few, if any, significant differences in general occupational themes (i.e., Holland types) among racial groups (Davison Aviles & Spokane, 1999; Lattimore & Borgen, 1999). Although Hansen (1990) concluded that the inventory may be used "with a variety of special populations, such as cross-ethnic or international populations, disabled clients, and culturally disadvantaged clients" (p. 179), most of the validity data on this instrument have been gathered with college-educated populations. In addition, more than 99% of individuals in the current general reference sample finished high school; a majority of the sample also completed 4 years of college (Harmon et al., 1994). Consequently, the interpretation of SII profiles for non-college-age women of color must be made with caution. Counselors must also consider acculturation issues when working with women of color. The client's degree of familiarity with the dominant culture helps provide a larger context in which to interpret her interest inventory results.

The KOIS, Form DD differs from the SII in the construction and scoring of occupational scales. Rather than constructing scales based on differences in the patterns of responses of a general reference sample and members of an occupational criterion group, Kuder chose to examine differences in the proportions of two occupational groups endorsing responses to the occupational interest inventory items (Diamond, 1990). The subsequent use of Cleman's lambda coefficient allows for comparison of a client's scores directly to those of the criterion (i.e., occupational) groups. An individual's scores are also rank ordered separately, by gender, for occupational and college-major scales.

As is the case with other major interest inventories, gender differences in patterns of scores have been found. Thus, clients should be encouraged to compare their rankings on the KOIS for same- and other-sex samples (Diamond & Zytowski, 2000; Zytowski & Kuder, 1986). On the KOIS women tend to score lower than men on the mechanical and science vocational interest estimates (VIE) scales, whereas men score lower than women on the social service and art VIE scales. Research on the predictive validity of the separate-sex scales on the KOIS has demonstrated roughly equivalent predictive validity of the two sets of norms (Zytowski & Laing, 1978).

The major advantages associated with the use of the KOIS with women include provision of same-sex and other-sex scale rankings and a broader range of occupations than most of the other major interest inventories. The KOIS also appears relatively equal to other interest inventories in predicting occupational membership (Kelly, 2002). However, there are also several limitations to the KOIS. First, the KOIS contains an imbalance in the number of male-dominated versus female-dominated occupations and college majors included in the inventory. The 1985 version of the KOIS contains only 29 out of 104 occupational scales and 17 out of 39 college-major scales that have been developed with female samples (Diamond, 1990). In deciding whether to use the KOIS, counselors may need to consider whether the limited range of options related to female occupations and college majors will hinder a client's exploration of a variety of traditional and nontraditional occupations. The absence of some type of occupational clustering of scores (such as the Holland codes for the SII) and the lack of male and female general reference samples must also be considered. On the other hand, Zytowski and Kuder (1986) argued that Holland codes may mask subtle differences in work environments, a factor that may be problematic for women. Thus, ranked listings of occupations and college majors on the KOIS might, in fact, be useful in encouraging female clients to develop their own meanings for the results. One final limitation of the KOIS concerns the criterion groups used in the development of this inventory. Most of these groups were originally sampled more than 30 years ago; consequently, KOIS feedback to clients is based on research done with individuals employed in the 1950s, 1960s, and 1970s. Similarly, because the KOIS has not been updated recently, it will not provide clients with feedback about occupational interests associated with new and emerging career fields (Kelly). Given these limitations, counselors should exercise caution when using the KOIS with female clients.

The SDS (Holland, Fritzsche, & Powell, 1997) is the major self-administered, self-scoring, self-interpreting career interest inventory (Spokane, 1990). As such, it presents some unique advantages but also idiosyncratic problems in career assessment with women. First, the absence of same-sex norms flies in the face of guidelines for eliminating sex bias in interest assessment (Betz, 1992). An equally important problem concerns the construct validity of the measure. Although two of the four sections of the assessment booklet ask the client to assess her interests, the remaining two sections ask for estimates of ability or competence. However, scores for all four sections are combined in order to identify the client's three-digit Holland code (Holland et al., 1997). In turn, the Holland codes identified by the SDS are used in selecting occupations for further exploration. When interest assessments are combined with estimates of competence or ability, what do these combined scores actually represent? The problem is further complicated when we consider the research data that suggest that women tend to report lower self-efficacy or confidence in their abilities than men with respect to traditionally male-dominated activities and occupations (Betz, 1999, 2001; Hackett & Betz, 1992, 1995; O'Brien, 2003). One likely outcome of combining women's ability and interest estimates on the SDS is that female clients may find themselves with sex-stereotypical Holland codes; in fact, women do score higher on artistic and social themes and lower than men on the realistic theme (Spokane & Catalano, 2000). To circumvent possible limitations in the use of the SDS, counselors may find it beneficial to actively work with female clients in interpreting SDS results, rather than relying on a completely self-guided process.

Despite the drawbacks, there are several benefits in using the SDS with women. The SDS has the advantage of providing immediate feedback to the client about her occupational interests, self-estimates, and Holland codes, and may engender a greater sense of involvement in the career-assessment process (Spokane, 1990; Spokane & Catalano, 2000). The accompanying occupations finder (Holland, 1996) now includes a vast range of occupational titles serving to expose women to a wide range of occupations (Spokane & Catalano). Similarly, the educational opportunities finder (Rosen, Holmberg, & Holland, 1997) may prove useful in helping female students explore postsecondary fields of study. The unscored "Occupational Daydreams" section of the SDS assessment booklet may provide a rough measure of the degree to which a female client's expressed interests are sex typed (Holland, 1985a). Similarly, an inspection of a client's responses to the sections of the assessment booklet requiring self-estimates of ability or competence may provide both client and counselor with specific information about the areas in which the client feels particularly competent, providing a rough screening of the client's career-related self-efficacy. Finally, the SDS has been shown to have positive effects on clients (Reardon, 1996; Walsh & Betz, 2001) and thus enjoys tremendous popularity as a self-guided interest inventory.

Other Interest Inventories.   Alternatives to the Big Three are briefly mentioned here as illustrative of other issues for career counselors to consider. The current edition of the Vocational Preference Inventory (VPI; Holland, 1985b) incorporates revisions eliminating sex-biased occupational titles. Unfortunately, no new reliability or normative data have been provided, despite changes in the item content of the inventory. Several reviewers (e.g., Drummond, 1986; Rounds, 1985) have expressed concern about the lack of evidence for the reliability and validity of this version. Reliability data provided in the 1985 manual indicate that VPI scores appear somewhat less stable for women than for men. Thus, although prima facie sex bias appears to have been reduced in the VPI, questions remain about the technical validity of this instrument.

Career counselors considering using the VPI with female clients should also consider the extent to which there is evidence for the interpretations provided in the manual. For example, the source of the validity data used in developing the empirical summary for the masculinity–femininity (M-F) scale of the VPI is unclear. Because the clinical interpretation of this scale makes reference to preferences for traditionally male and female careers, interpretation of the M-F scale with clients should proceed cautiously.

The Kuder Career Search With Person Match (Zytowski, n.d., 2001) is a relatively new, untimed survey designed to measure Kuder's traditional 10 vocational interest scales. Given the newness of this instrument, its psychometric properties are largely unknown at this time (Walsh & Betz, 2001); therefore, counselors should exercise caution when using it with female clients.

Several interest inventories have been developed for use with noncollege populations. The Career Assessment Inventory (CAI; Johansson, 1996), patterned after the SII, was originally designed for individuals who are seeking immediate entry into an occupation, or who wish to pursue technical or business school training. An enhanced version of the CAI is also available; this new measure focuses on careers requiring up to 4 years of college (Walsh & Betz, 2001). The CAI relies on the use of combined-sex occupational scales, eliminating sex bias at the item level. Drawbacks include the lack of same-sex normative data, little supporting research, outdated item content, and the absence of predictive validity data (Miner & Sellers, 2002).

Two other major interest inventories, the Vocational Interest Inventory–Revised (VII-R; Lunneborg, 1993) and the Unisex edition of the ACT Interest Inventory–Revised (UNIACT-R; Lamb & Prediger, 1981; Swaney, 1995) employ homogenous interest scales. The VII-R is intended to produce sex-balanced suggestions of occupational alternatives, but questions about its success have arisen. Efforts to eliminate gender differences at the item level on the VII-R have not been entirely effective, in that differences between men and women are still observed on some of the scales (Schafer, 2002). The VII-R is probably most useful in promoting career exploration and predicting college-major choice, whereas disadvantages include the absence of empirically keyed occupational interest scores (Krumboltz, 1988) and concern that the geographic and racial homogeneity of the normative sample leads to questions about the predictive validity of the instrument for some groups (Schafer). For example, Blacks and Hispanics are underrepresented in the normative sample, whereas college-bound students are overrepresented. Nonetheless, the fact that VII-R results correlated with both students' intended majors and selected educational programs provides some evidence for the predictive validity of the instrument.

The UNIACT-R (Swaney, 1995) is one part of the ACT assessment program; it is used nationally and its impact is extensive (Borgen, 1986). On the whole, the UNIACT-R and the VII-R appear comparable in eliminating sex bias in item content, but the UNIACT-R has the edge in predictive validity (Johnson, 1985; Kifer, 1985). Decided advantages of the UNIACT-R are the use of Holland's classification system, and the additional keying of interests to the data-people-things orientation used to classify occupations in the Dictionary of Occupational Titles (DOT; U.S. Department of Labor, Employment and Training Administration, 1977). The new online O*NET system (National O*Net Consortium, 2004) provides counselors and clients easy access to a system for translating DOT codes into specific information about job families and occupations.

One additional interest inventory employing gender-neutral norms has recently become available. The Campbell Interest and Skill Survey (CISS; Campbell, Hyne, & Nilsen, 1992) is a measure of self-reported interests and skills designed to assist individuals in understanding the ways in which interests and skills mesh into the world of work. Rather than using the traditional Holland coding system, the CISS provides results for seven orientation scales as well for basic interest, skills, and occupational scales (Campbell et al.). Advantages of the CISS include the availability of parallel skill scales for every basic interest scale as well as ease in interpreting four interest and skill patterns (e.g., pursue, develop, explore, and avoid). Counselors should note, however, that the CISS skill scales should be considered self-estimates of perceived ability. This provides yet another potential use of the CISS with clients who have also taken ability or aptitude tests; that is, clients' CISS skill scores may be compared with the results of ability tests in order to better understand the relation of perceived and measured ability (Boggs, 2002). Such a comparison may prove particularly helpful to counselors working with female clients reporting low self-efficacy for traditionally masculine educational and occupational domains.

Vocational Card Sorts.   More than 40 years after Tyler (1961) outlined an occupational card sort procedure, there are numerous commercially available vocational card sorts, most preserving her basic ideas. Although there are advantages to norm-based assessment methods (e.g., interest inventories), vocational card sorts can offer much in the assessment of the unique ways in which individual women approach the task of career decision making. Vocational card sorts can also serve as a structured method for assessing clients' gender-role beliefs, values, interests, occupational stereotypes, and self-perceptions.

As the client is asked to sort occupations into piles such as "might choose," "would not choose," and "in question," and to identify common reasons for these decisions, both the counselor and client have an opportunity to explore the kinds of perceptions and experiences that may limit or expand the client's perceptions of her career options. The opportunity for women to collaborate with counselors in the career-assessment process may be particularly empowering for those women who have typically relied on the feedback and expertise of significant others in their lives. Career counselors who wish to explore gender-role stereotyping can modify card sort procedures to include a step in which clients sort the occupations as if they were a member of the opposite sex, thus facilitating discussion of the client's perceptions of their options as a female (Slaney & MacKinnon-Slaney, 2000). Cultural influences might also be explored through modifying card sort procedures.

The main disadvantage of the vocational card sort technique is the absence of normative and psychometric data. Two lines of argument have been pursued to address the psychometric issue: (a) data supportive of the predictive validity of expressed interests (e.g., Dolliver, 1969) have been marshaled as evidence for the predictive validity of card sorts, and (b) card sort techniques have been conceptualized as interventions rather than assessment methods (e.g., Goldman, 1983; Slaney & MacKinnon-Slaney, 2000). Whether an assessment tool, an intervention, or (in our view) both, card sort procedures are clearly a useful tool for career counseling with women, offering definite advantages over alternative interest-assessment methods (Slaney & MacKinnon-Slaney).

At present, several different vocational card sorts are commercially available, for example, the Non-Sexist Vocational Card Sort (NSVCS; Dewey, 1974), the Missouri Occupational Card Sort (Krieshok, Hansen, & Johnston, 1982), the Occ-U-Sort (Jones, 1979), the Missouri Occupational Preference Inventory (MOPI; Moore & Gysbers, 1980), and Slaney's (1978) Vocational Card Sort.

Dewey's NSVCS is often mentioned as a nonsexist approach to assessing women's (and men's) vocational choices. Gender-neutral terms in occupational titles are used, and the interactive process of the technique allows the counselor and client to explore issues related to gender-role stereotyping and sex bias. Unfortunately, the use of the term *nonsexist* in the label may lead some career counselors to believe that the nonsexist approach is inherent in the technique itself. On the contrary, as with any other assessment tool, gender bias may enter into the administration and interpretation of the NSVCS. For example, the occupations represented in the NSVCS are not equally distributed across the six Holland codes; in fact, the frequencies range from a low of 9 occupations in the conventional category to a high of 21 in the social category. The fact that 28% of the occupations in the card sort are in the class (social) in which traditionally female occupations predominate raises some concerns about the extent to which this technique will stimulate consideration of nontraditional occupational alternatives. The other card sorts available differ too in their representation of field, level, and gender relatedness of the occupations represented, as well as in the quality of the interpretational materials available. Counselors interested in using a vocational card sort that explores the Holland codes, basic interest scales, and occupations contained in the SII might do well to consider Slaney's (1978) version of this technique when working with female clients (see Slaney & MacKinnon-Slaney, 2000).

Ability and Aptitude Assessment

Concerns about the assessment of women's career-related aptitudes and abilities usually reflect issues in interpretation rather than in the technical adequacy of aptitude and ability tests. Commonly used aptitude batteries such as the Differential Aptitude Tests (DAT) or the General Aptitude Test Battery (GATB) are probably about as useful for women as for men. Career counselors must, however, keep in mind that so-called aptitude tests are in reality measures of developed abilities. Abilities develop from combined experience and exposure as well as from innate aptitude. Thus, career counselors must exercise caution in interpreting women's low aptitude test scores as indicative as inherent ability deficits, particularly in traditionally masculine domains such as science, mathematics, and mechanical reasoning (Betz, 1992; Walsh & Betz, 2001).

Likewise, mathematics test scores on scholastic achievement tests such as the ACTs, SATs, and GREs must be viewed holistically. Sex bias in item content does seem to be a problem on math achievement tests (Chipman et al., 1991), but other factors such as math anxiety, low math self-efficacy, and lack of experience and background in mathematics have all been identified as contributing to findings of gender differences in math achievement (Betz & Fitzgerald, 1987). In fact, many of the factors contributing to lowered math performance are open to remediation. As previously mentioned, the career counselor must consider the tendency of achievement tests to underpredict women's academic achievement (Betz, 1992; Walsh & Betz, 2001). Finally, in the course of most career counseling, ability assessment is based primarily on clients' self-reports. Yet significant gender differences in self-confidence in abilities (or self-efficacy) have been consistently found, especially with respect to gender-typed tasks, behaviors, and activities (Betz, 2001; Hackett & Betz, 1995). Thus the counselor is encouraged to consider abilities and self-efficacy jointly when attempting to assess ability.

One final caution concerning the use of aptitude tests with female clients relates to the increasing availability of the Armed Services Vocational Aptitude Battery (ASVAB) to high schools. The newest ASVAB is described as a career-exploration program (CEP) designed to provide students with guidance concerning both military and civilian occupations by providing materials useful in integrating information about aptitudes, interests, work values, and personal and educational goals. Despite its widespread availability and successful use in military settings, many reviewers have expressed concern about the ASVAB's predictive validity for civilian occupations and for the career choices of students of color (see Rogers, 2002). Consequently, school counselors should carefully consider the appropriateness of the ASVAB CEP in their comprehensive, developmental school guidance program.

Work Values, Needs, and Career Salience

Values and Needs.   In the career literature, the terms *values, needs,* and *preferences* are often defined quite differently, yet the empirical literature indicates that the various work values, needs, and worker preference inventories measure much the same thing (Betz, 1992). Essentially, the scales described in this section all tap into "the kinds of things people look for in satisfying work" (Betz, p. 464). Unlike some of the other career-assessment techniques, work values scales often have direct roots in theory; both the individual differences and development perspectives emphasize the role of needs and values in career assessment. Problems with blatant sex bias are not of major concern with these inventories.

The Work Values Inventory (WVI; Super, 1973) is most appropriate as a career-exploration tool for high school and college students, although it has been used with adult workers as well. Scores are reported for 15 work values that may be divided into three categories: intrinsic work values, extrinsic work values, and extrinsic rewards. Norms for both sexes are available, but the norm groups have predominantly been high school students, limiting the usefulness of the WVI with adult workers. As with many other vocational measures, further research investigating the psychometric properties of this inventory is needed (Walsh & Betz, 2001).

Nevill and Super (1989) have constructed a relatively new measure, the Values Scale (VS), which has great potential for career assessment with women. Developed as part of the Work Importance Study, the VS contains 21 scales measuring both work-related and general values. The VS is particularly useful with female clients as it taps multiple ways in which values may be met, that is, through work as well as other life roles. It appears to have cross-cultural applicability with extensive normative data drawn from ethnically diverse samples in a number of different countries (Schoenrade, 2002). Nonetheless, it is important for career counselors to interpret scores from the VS in the context of what is known about the client's life situation and goals (Nevill & Super; Schoenrade). The major drawback of the VS is that it is still relatively new; consequently, more information about the reliability and validity of the instrument with both student and adult populations is needed.

The Minnesota Importance Questionnaire (MIQ; Rounds, Henly, Dawis, Lofquist, & Weiss, 1981), developed in the context of research on the theory of work adjustment, has been widely used in research. Its major advantage, aside from psychometric adequacy, is that the MIQ was designed for use with adult workers. In addition to scores for 20 worker needs, the MIQ profile also includes measures of correlation between the test taker's needs profile and that of needs satisfied in occupational settings (called "Occupational Reinforcer Patterns" or ORPs). It is therefore useful not only in assessment for career choice, but also in counseling for career adjustment. A disadvantage in assessing women's work-related needs is the absence of specific attention to gender issues; however, extensive norms on both male and female workers are available.

Career and Work Salience.   People vary not only in what they look for in satisfactory work, but also in the degree to which work is important. The issue of career salience is of special importance to women (Betz & Fitzgerald, 1987) and is a neglected dimension in assessment in career counseling. Greenhaus' (1971) Career Salience Inventory has been the most visible measure of work-role salience in the research literature, but has not been widely used in career counseling. More recently, Nevill and Super (1986) introduced the Salience Inventory (SI), a measure of the "participation, commitment, and values expectations for five roles: Studying, working, community service, home and family, and leisure" (Zytowski, 1988, p. 151). As with the VS, the SI was constructed as part of the Work Importance Study, and reflects Super's theoretical statements about life roles (Super et al., 1996). Hansen (1994) proposed that the SI may be used to help clients see the relative importance they place on work when compared to other life roles, as well as to assist clients in understanding values specific to each role. Nevill and Calvert (1996) also suggested that the SI may prove useful in facilitating career conversations about gender and multicultural concerns; as such, counselors are encouraged to consider using the SI for this purpose.

Given the importance of issues of role salience and role conflict in women's career development, we predict increasing use of the SI and like measures.

Personality Assessment

There are a number of objective personality instruments that have been used as an adjunct to career assessment (Zunker & Osborn, 2002). Among the more commonly used is the Myers-Briggs Type Indicator (MBTI; Myers, McCaulley, Quenk, & Hammer, 1998). Other measures of "normal" personality have been used for career assessment, but their use in this context is arguable. Although a number of career development theories address personality factors, few inventories have been developed to specifically address career theory-based dimensions of personality. Zunker and Osborn (p. 114) recommended that personality measures "should be used as a means of evaluating support for or opposition to a career under consideration" rather than a sole predictor of success or failure in an occupation. In career counseling with women, a drawback in the use of personality assessment is that attention to individual dynamics may be reinforced to the neglect of environmental barriers and challenges known to complicate women's career development. Possible sex bias in personality measurement must also be considered; test developers have not responded to the feminist critique to the extent to which developers of vocational assessment procedures have (Lewin & Wild, 1991; Rosewater, 1985). Nonetheless, personality assessment has been employed in career counseling as a self-awareness tool, to clarify worker roles and activity preferences, and to examine sources of job dissatisfaction (Brown & Brooks, 1991).

MBTI. The MBTI was developed to measure four dimensions of Jung's theory of personality types (McCaulley, 2000; Myers & McCaulley, 1985) and was most recently revised in 1998 (Myers et al., 1998). Scores obtained on the MBTI across the four Jungian dimensions or functions can be combined to form 16 types; one's type can then be used to explore personal strengths (Hood & Johnson, 2002). What makes the instrument particularly attractive to career counselors is the extensive work that has been done in delineating the 16 types and correlating these with various occupational demands (McCaulley, 1990). Thus, in career assessment and counseling, data about a client's type can be used to understand and explore preferences for work activities, promoting both self and occupational exploration (Healy, 2002; Hood & Johnson, 2002; McCaulley, 2000; Willis & Ham, 1988).

The MBTI test manual (Myers et al., 1998) and available supporting materials offer the career counselor a great deal of information to guide use of this inventory (Hood & Johnson, 2002). There is some research to support the linkages between types and career preferences (McCaulley, 2000), and norms are available for both men and women. Little guidance is provided for exploring gender issues in Jungian type development, a surprising trend given Jung's original theory. Still, the MBTI does not appear to suffer unduly from sex bias. If used in the context of a thorough career assessment with female clients, the instrument has decided advantages over many of the alternatives. It is important to note, however, that some reviewers have urged caution in use of the MBTI given concerns about criterion-related validity for some settings and the potential for overly rigid interpretation of results (Healy, 2002; Hood & Johnson).

Other Personality Measures. The Sixteen Personality Factor Questionnaire (16PF) was intended as an objective test of 16 "source traits" of personality (Cattell, Eber, & Tatsuoka, 1970). The attractiveness of the instrument for career counselors is that personality patterns derived from 16PF scores can be related to important career-exploration issues, for example, problem solving and preferences for career activities (Vansickle, 2002; Wholeben, 1988). Furthermore, computer-generated expert reports based on the 16PF (i.e., the 16PF Career Development Profile) are now commercially available for use in career counseling (Vansickle). Counselors who are considering use of the 16PF with female clients should attend to several cautions associated with this instrument. First, the terminology employed in naming and describing the 16PF scales appear to have some inherent biases; there is ample opportunity for misinterpreting scale scores given the colloquial meaning of many of the terms used in describing the scales (e.g., emotional stability, tough-mindedness). Second, some of the bipolar scales used in the 16PF may produce sex-stereotypical interpretations. For example, emotional sensitivity, a traditionally feminine trait, and self-reliance, a traditionally masculine attribute, are presented as polar opposites, reinforcing dichotomous notions of gender roles. Third, significant gender differences have been found for the 16PF. And fourth, there is a long history of controversy about the technical adequacy of the instrument for any use (Anastasi & Urbina, 1997; Butcher, 1985; Zuckerman, 1985); however, counselors are encouraged to examine the current *16PF Technical Manual* (Conn & Rieke, 1994) and recent test reviews (e.g., Hood & Johnson, 2002; Schuerger, 2000; Vansickle) for more information about the psychometric properties of the current version.

An alternative to the 16PF is the California Psychological Inventory (CPI; Gough, 1957). The CPI was designed to assess everyday normal human attributes or qualities referred to as "folk concepts." Folk concepts are described as widely recognizable human attributes. Known as the "sane person's MMPI," the CPI actually contains a large number of items drawn from the MMPI, but item content is generally less objectionable (Hood & Johnson, 2002). The most recent version of the CPI appears to be applicable for use in career and occupational exploration (Wegner, 1988) with reported utility in predicting choice and success in some educational and occupational domains (Gough, 2000; Hood & Johnson). Overall, the CPI compares favorably with alternative personality measures, being fairly easy to interpret and having acceptable reliability and validity (Walsh & Betz, 2001). There is also some evidence that the CPI might be fairly appropriate for cross-cultural use (Gough, 1990). On the other hand, the M-F scale presents some interpretational problems for use with female career clients (Beere, 1990; Gough, 1990). Baucom (1980) introduced procedures whereby the CPI's bipolar M-F scale can be transformed into two unipolar scales reflecting instrumentality and expressiveness.

Recently, the Big Five personality model and the NEO Personality Inventory–Revised (NEO PI-R; Costa & McCrae, 1995) have garnered increased attention as a potentially useful method for assessing personality in career counseling (Borgen, 1999; Zunker & Osborn, 2002). The NEO PI-R is designed to assess the Big Five domains of personality including neuroticism, extraversion, openness, agreeableness, and conscientiousness. Career counselors may wish to consider the NEO PI-R as an alternative method of assessing normal adult personality. Continued research investigating the relationship between the NEO PI-R and educational and career choice and adjustment is likely and may prove useful in illuminating the implications of the Big Five model for career counseling.

Assessment of Career Process Variables

One of the most commonly expressed goals of career counseling is vocational choice. Despite the seeming simplicity of this outcome, there has been considerable debate about definitions and measurement of career indecision (Savickas, 2000; Slaney, 1988). Furthermore, developmental perspectives require attention to the process of decision making, not just choice content. In this section we review assessment tools for measuring constructs emanating from developmental theory and focusing on career process variables. Attention to career indecision allows for differential diagnosis of decision-making problems and issues, whereas career maturity measures contribute to developmental assessments of client functioning (Savickas). Finally, career-related cognitions (e.g., career self-efficacy, dysfunctional career beliefs) compose an important new area for assessment of career process (e.g., Krumboltz, 1991; Sampson et al., 1996).

Career Decision Making

Career indecision seems to be multidimensional, but the literature remains unclear about the specific nature and number of the dimensions of indecision (Betz, 1992; Savickas, 2000). Total scores on career indecision scales may thus reflect aspects of the decision-making process such as clarity and certainty as well as indecision (Betz). Distinctions have also been made between developmentally normal undecidedness (or simple indecision) and indecisive, or chronically undecided, individuals (Betz); determinations of developmental versus chronic undecidedness have important implications for intervention.

Several measures have been found useful in understanding the career decision status of clients and identifying sources of career indecision. The Career Decision Scale (CDS; Osipow, 1987) is widely used, psychometrically sound, and useful for working with women. The CDS provides a measure of undecidedness and information about specific sources of indecision (Osipow). When using the CDS with women, same-sex norms should be used, and information from the scale about the specific antecedents of indecision may need to be fully explored to check on the extent to which gender is an issue.

Holland, Daiger, and Power's (1980) My Vocational Situation (MVS) was designed to provide information about indecision and the type of vocational assistance needed. Scores for the vocational identity (i.e., clarity and stability of one's career-related attributes), lack of information, and perceptions of barriers are provided. The MVS has potential as an instrument to assist in exploring perceptions of environmental obstacles and barriers; however, it has been criticized for failing to include a broader range of important barriers to career development, particularly for women and persons of color (Lunneborg, 1985). Research support for the use of the MVS as a diagnostic tool is limited (Lunneborg; Westbrook, 1988), therefore the instrument is better viewed as a checklist for counseling rather than as a formal scale (Walsh & Betz, 2001).

In an effort to more fully assess factors that interfere with career choice and implementation, Swanson and Tokar (1991) developed the 70-item Career Barriers Inventory (CBI). The CBI scales represent a variety of barriers to career development (e.g., race and sex discrimination, role conflict); as such, the instrument has potential in identifying factors contributing to women's (and men's) career indecision. Reviewers, although calling for more research on the psychometric properties of the instrument, appear cautiously optimistic about its usefulness in career counseling (Walsh & Betz, 2001).

Two other measures of career decision making might also be considered when working with female career clients. The Career Factors Inventory (CFI; Chartrand, Robbins, Morrill, & Boggs, 1990) is a brief, 21-item measure designed to assess antecedents of career indecision. The four CFI scales include career choice anxiety, generalized indecisiveness, perceived need for career information, and perceived need for self-knowledge; to date, the inventory has been validated with both students and employed adults

(Luzzo, 2002). It is also important to note that no significant gender and ethnic differences have been observed on the four CFI scales. According to Luzzo, the CFI "can be useful in ascertaining the degree to which a client or groups of clients are ready to engage in the career decision-making process . . . it can also help individuals uncover the source of their indecision" (p. 333). In contrast to the MVS, the CFI has the advantage of assessing multiple antecedents of career indecision. Finally, counselors interested in assessing their female clients' decision-making styles (e.g., rational, intuitive, dependent) may want to consider using Harren's (1979) Assessment of Career Decision Making (ACDM) scale. For more information about the current version (Buck & Daniels, 1985) the counselor is referred to a review by Hood and Johnson (2002).

Career Maturity and Adjustment

Career Maturity. Crites' (1978) Career Maturity Inventory (CMI) is a measure of the attitudes and competencies indicative of career maturity in adolescence. The most recent version, the CMI–Revised (CMI-R), is designed for use with adults as well as adolescents; it was also revised to reduce ethnic, racial, and gender bias at the item level. The CMI-R is accompanied by an instructional program called the Career Developer, which may be helpful in teaching clients the process of career decision making. Although reviewers continue to express concern about the reliability of the CMI, and construct validity is an issue for all of the measures of career maturity, the CMI is widely used (Betz, 1988; McDivitt, 2002; Walsh & Betz, 2001). We have previously addressed concerns about how well career maturity scores predict choice realism for women. Because of the complex issues related to definitions of the construct, the career counselor must be cautious in making assumptions derived from CMI-R scores about women's career status. Betz's (1988) model of career maturity suggested that antecedents such as intelligence and school performance, career-related experiences, and cultural values must be considered in interpreting the meaning of the results of career maturity measures. The appropriate consequences of career maturity, in her view, are "realistic career decisions; consistency of choices over time, field, and level (outcome variables in Crites' theory of career maturity); and later, indicators of vocational success and satisfaction" (Betz, 1992, p. 467). Recognizing the potential value of the CMI-R for career counseling, Walsh and Betz called for further research investigating the psychometric properties of the revised instrument.

The Career Development Inventory (CDI; Super, Thompson, Lindeman, Jordaan, & Myers, 1984), like the CMI-R, contains both attitude and knowledge scales. Reviewers are largely in agreement that the CDI represents the type of theory-based measure rarely found in the career literature

(Savickas, 1990), but the CDI shares with the CMI-R problems with reliability and construct validity (Betz, 1992) as well as a need for more research on criterion-related validity (Savickas, 2000). Nonetheless, following their comprehensive review of the CDI, Savickas and Hartung (1996) suggested that research "strongly supports the sensitivity and specificity of the inventory as a measure of readiness to make educational choices, vocational choices, or both" (p. 185). Counselors using the CDI with female clients, however, are urged to use caution when interpreting CDI subscales, given ongoing questions about internal consistency (Walsh & Betz, 2001).

Adult Career Adjustment. Adult workers have different concerns and issues from adolescents and young adults, yet until recently measures of adult career adjustment were unavailable. Several new measures will be reviewed here, including those designed to assess adult career concerns, adult career attitudes and strategies, career-transition issues, and occupational stress and strain.

The Adult Career Concerns Inventory (ACCI; Super, Thompson, & Lindeman, 1988) measures career issues in the later stages of career development. Likewise, the Career Mastery Inventory (CMAS; Crites, 1990) assesses "mastery of six developmental tasks postulated to be important in the Establishment stage of career development" (Betz, 1992, p. 468). Widespread use of either instrument awaits further research; more specifically, reviewers have noted the need for more reliability, validity, and normative data (e.g., Manuele-Adkins, 1995).

The Career Attitudes and Strategies Inventory (CASI; Holland & Gottfredson, 1994) was designed to measure nine aspects of work adaptation. Reviewers suggest that the CASI should be used in conjunction with career counseling, thereby enabling the client to receive assistance from the counselor in addressing issues or problems identified by the inventory (Walsh & Betz, 2001). Although some of the CASI scales (e.g., interpersonal abuse) may, on the face of things, appear useful in career counseling with women, at least one reviewer questioned whether some scales have practical value given the heterogeneity of issues contained within the scale (Kinnier, 1998). Furthermore, the measure may prove more useful in counseling when counselors rely on an ipsative rather than normative approach to scale interpretation; this recommendation is in keeping with concerns about the current psychometric quality of the instrument (Brown, 2002). We also agree with the suggestion of Walsh and Betz that interpretations should occur primarily in the context of individual scale content.

One promising new scale for career counseling with adults is the Career Transitions Inventory (CTI; Heppner, 1998), which was designed for use with those clients who are contemplating or in the middle of career changes. As Hesketh (2000) noted, "All transitions involve changed requirements of the individual, and often disrupt the use of expectations and well-automated skills" (p. 476), thus we note the importance of finding ways to assess these important career-transition issues, particularly given the complex issues involved in the career development of women. Although more research is needed on norms, reliability, and validity, recent reviews suggest the CTI shows promise for career counseling and research (Drummond, 2003; Kirnan, 2003).

Of immediate use in career assessment is Campbell and Cellini's (1981) diagnostic taxonomy of adult career problems. Their diagnostic classification includes attention to problems in career decision making, implementing career plans, and organizational and institutional performance and adaptation. Included in this taxonomy are some of the career adjustment issues widely experienced by women, for example, sexual harassment (e.g., Fitzgerald & Ormerod, 1993; Gutek & Done, 2001). Other common career concerns of women are included under more general problems that are not totally descriptive. For example, role conflict seems to be subsumed under "adverse off-the-job personal circumstances or stressors" (Campbell & Cellini, p. 180). When using this taxonomy with women, the career counselor may need to supplement it by additional exploration of concerns such as discrimination, role conflict, workplace incivility, and sexual harassment.

Other measures useful in the assessment of career adjustment include measures of the work environment (Spokane, 1991), particularly the Occupational Stress Inventory–Revised (OSI-R; Osipow, 1998). Occupational stress, role strain, and personal coping resources are measured on the OSI-R in a manner that allows for analyses of the sources of stress and, of course, the identification of sources of occupational stress has clear treatment implications. The OSI-R is based on the assumption that stress in the workplace is a function of the interaction of external stressors, personal affective reactions, and lack of appropriate coping resources. As such, it offers much in work with women. The current version provides updated norms for both occupational categories and gender. For more complete reviews see Freitag (2001) and Wall (2001).

Career-Related Cognitions

Many writers have argued for the importance of assessing career-related cognitions in exploring the process of career development (Betz, 1992). Brown and Brooks (1991) devoted considerable attention to the assessment of cognitive clarity; Spokane (1991) spoke to the need for acquiring a cognitive structure to evaluate career alternatives; Rounds and Tracey (1990) argued for an information-processing approach to career assessment and counseling; Neimeyer (1988) proposed cognitive vocational schema as important; and cognitive problem-solving and decision-making abilities have long been considered crucial to career development (Brooks & Brown, 1996). In reviewing the career development literature from the last decade it is clear that both theorists and researchers have heeded the call for greater attention to the role of career-related cognitions in career assessment and counseling. Two major types of career cognitions have received enough attention to warrant routine consideration in career assessment with women: career beliefs and career-related self-efficacy.

Career Beliefs. Several measures of irrational beliefs have been developed, but Krumboltz's (1991) Career Beliefs Inventory (CBI) measures specific cognitions that interfere with career decision making. The manual for the CBI contains helpful suggestions for its use in career counseling, but the inventory itself contains no items specifically addressing gender-role beliefs. Potentially quite useful in counseling with women, the CBI will nonetheless need to be augmented by gender-role assessment to produce a comprehensive understanding of women's "private rules about the self" (Mitchell & Krumboltz, 1990) that interfere with career decision making. Such a discussion of gender-role issues would certainly be consistent with Krumboltz's (1999) suggestion that the instrument be viewed as a stimulus for discussion in counseling. This suggestion is also supported by reviewers who urge caution in the use of the CBI for selection or classification purposes, given questions about the psychometric properties of the instrument (Hall & Rayman, 2002; Hood & Johnson, 2002).

The Career Thoughts Inventory (CTI; Sampson et al., 1996) was also designed to assess dysfunctional career thoughts in high school students, college students, and adults. The CTI provides both a total score and scores on three scales: decision-making confusion, commitment anxiety, and external conflict. One potential benefit of the CTI is that it is accompanied by a workbook designed to assist clients with career decision making and planning (Reardon & Wright, 1999). Recent reviews of the CTI suggest it "is a well developed inventory with good reliability and validity that does a good job of doing what it says it does" (Feller & Daly, 2002, p. 347). Nonetheless, counselors should consider the potential limitations of a self-administered, self-scoring instrument in addressing the complex issues often faced by female career clients; from this perspective, the CTI may be a useful adjunct to the career-counseling process.

Career Self-Efficacy. Considerable evidence now exists that significant gender differences in career self-efficacy (SE), or confidence in one's career-related abilities, are related to gender differences in educational and career choice (Betz, 1999, 2001; Hackett & Betz, 1992; O'Brien, 2003; Tracey, 1997). Career counselors are advised to routinely assess women's SE expectations hand in hand with abilities, especially with reference to traditionally masculine-typed activities, tasks, and occupations. Within the interview, career SE can be assessed through questions that tap the client's confidence in her ability to succeed in a domain. Qualitative assessment procedures such as the vocational card sort can also provide opportunities for exploration of the role SE expectations play in limiting perceived career options. A number of assessment instruments are now available in the research literature, some of which may prove useful in counseling. For example, Rooney and Osipow's (1992) Occupational Self-Efficacy Scale (OSES) was developed with a counseling use in mind. The OSES provides information about task-specific self-efficacy; thus, it might be particularly helpful in identifying sources of low self-efficacy, and may be more generally useful than some of the other measures.

The Career Decision Self-Efficacy Scale (CDSE; Taylor & Betz, 1983) was designed to measure individuals' confidence in their ability to make effective career-related decisions (Betz & Taylor, 1994; Hood & Johnson, 2002). Although the CDSE can produce five scale scores related to self-appraisal, occupational information, goal selection, future plans, and problem solving, factor analytic research suggests that counselors simply interpret the total score as a global index of self-efficacy expectations concerning career decision making (Hood & Johnson; Luzzo, 1996). A short form of the CDSE is also available (Betz, Klein, & Taylor, 1996); career counselors may find this a helpful adjunct to the career intake, or screening, process.

Counselors using the SII with female clients may also find it beneficial to include the Skills Confidence Inventory (SCI; Betz, Borgen, & Harmon, 1996) as part of the assessment process. The SCI, a 60-item measure, provides confidence scores corresponding to the six general occupational themes (GOTs) included on the SII. SCI results are provided on a profile form that facilitates comparison of the client's perceived skills or capabilities with expressed interests in each of the GOTs. According to Betz (1999), "In a general sense the career assessment should lead to some type of cross classification of levels of interest (e.g., high, medium, and low) with levels of confidence (high, medium, low) with concomitant counseling implications" (p. 333). Counselors using the SCI as a companion to the SII should keep in mind, however, that the client's confidence in a particular area does not necessarily reflect her actual ability or aptitude in that domain (Vacc & Newsome, 2002).

Research instruments have been developed to assess SE with respect to Holland themes, occupational choices, mathematics, science, academic milestones, and home–career conflict (see Betz, 2001; Hackett & Betz, 1995; O'Brien, 2003). Although there are a number of unresolved issues in the measurement of career self-efficacy, overall the internal consistency and predictive validity data are decent for most measures (Betz, 2001; Gwilliam & Betz, 2001; Lent & Hackett, 1987), although there have been recent calls for greater research attention to the psychometric properties of SE measures when used with diverse samples (O'Brien, 2003). Aside from their nascent state of development, a disadvantage of using career SE measures, and a point of confusion for many, is the need for SE to be assessed with reference to some specific set of behaviors or tasks. SE is not, conceptually, a stable personality trait. SE is more accurately defined as a cognitive appraisal of one's capabilities (Hackett & Lent, 1992). There is no one SE measure, but rather multiple measures; the career counselor must select the measure most appropriate for a particular client's concerns. However, SE assessments are easily tailored to suit the specific needs of clients and are amenable to assessment within the counseling interview. The research literature is replete with suggestions for how to integrate career SE assessment with other important career issues (Betz, 1999, 2001; Hackett & Betz; O'Brien). Because "studies on gender-role and career self-efficacy support the Hackett and Betz (1981) contention that gender differences in self-efficacy are related to the different socialization experiences of women and men" (Hackett & Betz, p. 270), we now turn our attention to the assessment of gender-role issues.

Assessment of Gender-Role Issues

It is evident by now that we recommend considering gender issues centrally in any career assessment with female clients. Yet too often counselors mistake awareness of gender differences per se for understanding gender dynamics. In this section we review inventories and assessment techniques specifically designed to promote a greater appreciation for the dynamics of gender. All have the potential for serving as career interventions as well as assessment tools. Unfortunately, most of the gender-role measures have been developed for research purposes rather than for use in counseling. With this caveat, we begin our discussion with gender-role analysis because of its potential for stimulating a comprehensive career assessment with women.

Gender-Role Analysis

Gender-role analysis is an extremely useful assessment tool in developing an accurate understanding of the female client in her sociocultural context. We assume that the career counselor will routinely take issues of gender and culture into account in the context of career assessment. However, gender-role analysis, a structure technique for examining the meaning of influence and gender in a client's life, is a useful adjunct to standard interview procedures. Introduced as the major technique of feminist (or gender-aware) counseling and therapy (Brodsky, 1975), gender-role analysis assists the client in analyzing the potential costs and benefits of traditional and nontraditional gender-role behavior—an analysis, by the way, that can be equally useful for male and female clients (Rawlings & Carter, 1977). For example, a counselor might help a woman in clarifying the potential costs and benefits that may accrue from traditionally feminine behaviors such as nurturance, dependence on others, living through and for others, and passivity. Additionally, the counselor might explore the benefits of nontraditional feminine gender-role behavior, such as psychological and economic autonomy and development of a full range of interpersonal competencies and behaviors, along with perceived costs. The gender-role analysis would thus serve to bring unconscious assumptions and limits to the forefront of consciousness, assist clients in evaluating their self-imposed gender-role constraints, and facilitate informed decision making about gender-role-related choices and behaviors. Gender-role analysis can easily be extended to the evaluation of career options. Fitzgerald (1985) offered specific illustrations of a gender-role analysis of the consequences of the homemaker role versus traditional and nontraditional career options.

Measures of Gender Role

Attitudes Toward Women. Perhaps the most widely used measure of attitudes toward women and women's roles has been Spence and Helmreich's (1972) Attitudes Toward Women Scale (ATW). Consequently, the reliability and predictive validity of the various versions of the ATW are acceptable, and the research literature is quite extensive (Beere, 1990). Betz and Fitzgerald (1987) reported that "liberated" sex-role values, of the type tapped by the ATW, are facilitators of women's career development. Use of the ATW may therefore assist career counselors in identifying and exploring the specific attitudes toward women and beliefs about women's roles that may serve as barriers to informed career choice. A drawback of the ATW is that the scale "tops out," failing to discriminate among individuals who have fairly liberated attitudes. In cases where this may be an issue—for example, with feminist clients—the counselor might consider the use of an Attitudes Toward Feminism Scale (see Beere).

Another alternative to the ATW is the Feminist Identity Development Scale (FID; McNamara & Rickard, 1989). This and other FID scales are somewhat recent developments, based conceptually on Downing and Roush's (1985) model, and describing the developmental stages women pass through in their efforts to come to terms with sexism in our culture. Women in the earliest stages of feminist identity development, that is, passive or unconscious acceptance, often need help in becoming aware of gender influences on their lives. Women in the early stages of awareness of sexism may need to express anger, whereas women in the later stages of feminist identity development may require other types of assistance in coming to terms with sexism in their lives (McNamara & Rickard). Although FID measures are still in the developmental stage and thus not ideally suited for counseling use, career counselors can pursue feminist identity via interviewing procedures.

An interesting new area for measurement with implications for women's career development is that of "subtle sexism" (see Kite, 2001). One such instrument, the Modern Sexism Scale (MS; Swim, Aiken, Hall, & Hunter, 1995) is designed to assess the ways in which subtly sexist behaviors can exist, even in those who support women's rights. Other instruments designed to measure these subtle forms of sexism include the Ambivalent Sexism Inventory (ASI; Glick & Fiske, 1996) and the Neosexism Scale (NS; Tougas, Brown, Beaton, & Joly, 1995). Kite suggested that each of these measures of subtle sexism demonstrates excellent reliability and validity. When working with female clients, counselors may find it helpful to assess the ways in which subtle or ambivalent sexism serves to constrain clients' career options or produce barriers to successful career implementation and adjustment.

Gender-Role Orientation. Better known than any other gender-role measure is Bem's (1981a) Sex Role Inventory (BSRI). Originally developed to assess androgyny, the BSRI was reconceptualized by Bem (1981b) as a measure of gender schema. The 60-item scale produces two scores, a masculinity score and a femininity score, each representing the degree to which individuals characterize themselves in terms of stereotypically masculine or stereotypically feminine adjectives. In the past, the two scores have been combined to produce a fourfold classification: masculine or feminine sex typed, androgynous, or undifferentiated. Current usage varies considerably, but our recommendation for career counselors is congruent with Gilbert's (1985): Masculinity and femininity scores on the BSRI and similar inventories should be viewed as indicators of only limited aspects of the masculine and feminine gender roles. Specifically, masculinity scores actually reflect instrumental characteristics such as independence and self-assertiveness, whereas femininity scores tap the dimension of expressiveness or nurturance. High instrumentality scores have been found to be predictive of achievement-related behavior and nontraditional career choices (Betz & Fitzgerald, 1987).

Bem's (1981b) work on gender schema theory incorporates important constructs in cognitive psychology. In this view, BSRI scores are seen as reflections of the degree to which an individual processes information in gender-stereotypical ways; sex typing is viewed as a result of gender-schematic processing. Women who score in a sex-typed manner on the BSRI would, theoretically, tend to see potential occupational choices as gender appropriate or gender inappropriate, rather than view occupational alternatives in the context of their unique interests, needs, and values. Gender schema theory offers the career counselor a conceptual base and accompanying techniques for determining which clients might require more active confrontation of gender-restricting beliefs and perceptions. As noted previously in this chapter, career researchers have begun to explore more vigorously the role of cognitive structures, vocational schemas, and career-related cognitions in career decision making (Krumboltz, 1991; Neimeyer, 1988; Sampson et al., 1996).

Role Conflict

Vocational researchers have been increasingly attentive to what career counselors have long known—that career choice occurs in the context of other life roles. We have already discussed career and role salience measures as important to understanding women's career development. But there are alternative measures constructed to assess dimensions of role conflict untapped by the Career Salience Scale and the SI. Interventions aimed at decreasing or resolving role conflict and role strain depend on a careful assessment of the origins of the personal, interpersonal, and environmental pressures women experience in coping with multiple roles. Farmer's (1984) Home–Career (H-C) Conflict Scale, for example, provides a measure of the extent of conflict experienced by women who value both work and family roles but perceive them as incompatible. High scores on this scale have been found to be predictive of lowered career motivation (Farmer). For counseling purposes, the H-C measure has the potential for identifying sources of psychological distress in female clients. Beere (1990) described numerous measures for assessing job and home demands, role strain, role overload, and role conflict. Choosing an appropriate assessment tool clearly requires knowledge of the multiple-role literature (Betz & Fitzgerald, 1987).

SUMMARY

We briefly summarize here our recommendations for career assessment with women. Counselors must be intimately familiar with the literature on the career psychology of women and with career-assessment procedures, including the technical aspects of test construction, as well as the issues of bias in testing. Assessment in career counseling is best viewed as an integral component of intervention rather than as a discrete activity; thus, career counselors need to examine the conceptual underpinnings of their approach to career counseling, being aware of the possibilities for bias. In assessment, the career counselor should routinely view female clients within a sociocultural context, adopting some variants of gender-aware and multicultural counseling and utilizing gender-role analysis as an integral part of the career-assessment process. Career counselors should routinely make use of, where possible, qualitative alternatives to standardized testing such as vocational card sorts. When quantitative career-assessment measures are used, counselors should carefully consider whether there are alternative explanations (e.g., lack of experience, low self-efficacy) for female clients' test results. We as counselors must also continually examine and work on our own gender-related issues if we are to be maximally effective and ethically responsible in delivering career services. We also recognize that many of the recommendations contained in this chapter and summarized in Table 4.3 require a substantial investment of

TABLE 4.3

Summary Observations and Recommendations for Career Assessment and Counseling With Women

Observation	Recommendation
• The majority of women continue to work outside the home even while raising very young children	• Educators must prepare girls for employment outside the home, with particular attention to expanding their range of career options. Greater attention to the school-to-work transition is needed for non-college-bound girls.
• Contemporary career theories emphasize contextual factors (e.g., gender, ethnicity, family status) instead of or in addition to traditional measures of vocational identity	• Career counselors must carefully assess the ways in which individual differences (e.g., gender, ethnicity, sexual orientation, disability) among women influence their career-related experiences, aspirations, and perceptions of barriers to and facilitators of career development.
	• 21st-century career counselors should possess strong multicultural counseling skills, including expertise in the delivery of gender-aware therapy or other forms of nonsexist counseling.
• Vocational sex segregation of women into jobs that are low in status, pay, and opportunity for advancement suggests the continued underutilization of women's abilities and talents	• Educators and counselors must assist girls and women in expanding the range of their academic and vocational experiences in order to build marketable work skills, increase self-efficacy in nontraditional career areas, and identify new career options.

- Career researchers and practitioners are giving greater recognition to the social and cognitive processes governing career choice, implementation, and adjustment

- Multiple role considerations are clearly instrumental in shaping most women's career-related decisions

- Limited experiences can restrict the range of women's vocational interests, values, and work skills as well as their awareness of work environments and work-related reinforcers

- The 21st-century workplace is very different than that of the last century; successful work adjustment is no longer defined primarily in terms of job tenure, but rather in terms of an individual's ability to adapt to a changing work environment and to successful transfer work skills to new projects and assignments

- Career counselors must assist clients in identifying and evaluating the self-efficacy and outcome expectations that may serve to restrict a woman's occupational aspirations and range of career options.

- Counselors should assist women in developing strategies for identifying and overcoming perceived barriers to their career development.

- Female career clients will likely benefit from gender-role analyses, as well as careful exploration of the multiple role issues that may serve to constrain their career choices or increase role-related stress.

- Given that the fastest growing occupations are in service and computer-related occupations, women seeking opportunities for advancement and greater financial security are well advised to develop strong skills in math and science.

- In order to prepare girls and women for computer-related occupations, counselors may need to assist them in expanding their range of school and work experiences, thus aiding them in developing strong math skills and self-efficacy.

- Career education and counseling must prepare girls and women for a rapidly changing workforce in which successful workers will possess transferable skills and the ability to adapt to changes in job descriptions and requirements.

- Career counselors should prepare clients to learn to develop or improve skills on an ongoing basis given these anticipated changes in the world of work.

- Career interventions should also focus on developing clients' task approach skills, enhancing career-related self-efficacy, and managing multiple role demands.

time on the part of both counselors and clients. Given pressures to more effectively facilitate school-to-work transitions for all students and to provide cost-effective services to unemployed and underemployed individuals, we argue for continuing efforts to develop short-term group interventions that will provide clients with self and occupational knowledge, while also addressing these important contextual issues (e.g., gender, culture) in career development. Finally, we support individual efforts and ecological interventions (e.g., Heppner, Davidson, & Scott, 2003) to effect change in the broader institutional and societal contexts in order to facilitate more fully the career development of girls and women.

REFERENCES

Alston, R. J., Bell, T. J., & Hampton, J. L. (2002). Learning disability and career entry into the sciences: A critical analysis of attitudinal factors. *Journal of Career Development, 28*, 263–275.

American Educational Research Association, American Psychological Association, and National Council on Measurement in Education. (1999). *Joint technical standards for educational and psychological testing.* Washington, DC: Author.

American Psychological Association. (2002). Ethical principles of psychologists and code of conduct. *American Psychologist, 57*, 1060–1073.

Anastasi, A., & Urbina, S. (1997). *Psychological testing* (7th ed.). Upper Saddle River, NJ: Prentice Hall.

Atkinson, D. R. (2004). *Counseling American minorities* (6th ed.). New York: McGraw-Hill.

Atkinson, D. R., Morten, G., & Sue, D. W. (1989). *Counseling American minorities: A cross-cultural perspective* (3rd ed.). Dubuque, IA: Brown.

Bandura, A. (1986). *Social foundations of thought and action: A social cognitive theory.* Englewood Cliffs, NJ: Prentice Hall.

Baucom, D. H. (1980). Independent CPI masculinity and femininity scales: Psychological correlates and a sex-role typology. *Journal of Personality Assessment, 44*, 262–271.

Beere, C. (1990). *Gender roles: A handbook of tests and measures.* Westport, CT: Greenwood Press.

Bem, S. L. (1981a). *Bem Sex-Role Inventory: Professional manual.* Palo Alto, CA: Consulting Psychologists Press.

Bem, S. L. (1981b). Gender schema theory: A cognitive account of sex-typing. *Psychological Review, 88*, 354–364.

Betz, N. E. (1988). The assessment of career development and maturity. In W. B. Walsh & S. H. Osipow (Eds.), *Career decision making* (pp. 77–136). Hillsdale, NJ: Lawrence Erlbaum Associates.

Betz, N. E. (1990). Contemporary issues in testing use. In C. E. Watkins, Jr. & V. L. Campbell (Eds.), *Testing in counseling practice* (pp. 419–450). Hillsdale, NJ: Lawrence Erlbaum Associates.

Betz, N. E. (1992). Career assessment: A review of critical issues. In S. D. Brown & R. W. Lent (Eds.), *Handbook of counseling psychology* (2nd ed., pp. 453–484). New York: Wiley.

Betz, N. E. (1993). Women's career development. In F. L. Denmark & M. A. Paludi (Eds.), *Psychology of women: A handbook of issues and theories* (pp. 627–684). Westport, CT: Greenwood Press.

Betz, N. E. (1999). Getting clients to act on their interests: Self-efficacy as a mediator of the implementation of vocational interests. In M. L. Savickas & A. R. Spokane (Eds.), *Vocational interests: Meaning, measurement and counseling use* (pp. 327–344). Palo Alto, CA: Davies-Black.

Betz, N. E. (2000). Contemporary issues in testing use. In C. E. Watkins & V. L. Campbell (Eds.), *Testing and assessment in counseling practice* (2nd ed., pp. 481–516). Mahwah, NJ: Lawrence Erlbaum Associates.

Betz, N. E. (2001). Career self-efficacy. In F. T. L. Leong & A. Barak (Eds.), *Contemporary models in vocational psychology: A volume in honor of Samuel H. Osipow* (pp. 55–77). Mahwah, NJ: Lawrence Erlbaum Associates.

Betz, N. E., Borgen, F., & Harmon, L. (1996). *Skills Confidence Inventory applications and technical guide*. Palo Alto, CA: Consulting Psychologists Press.

Betz, N. E., & Fitzgerald, L. F. (1987). *The career psychology of women*. San Diego, CA: Academic Press.

Betz, N. E., & Fitzgerald, L. F. (1995). Career assessment and intervention with racial and ethnic minorities. In F. T. L. Leong (Ed.), *Career development and vocational behavior of racial and ethnic minorities* (pp. 263–279). Hillsdale, NJ: Lawrence Erlbaum Associates.

Betz, N. E., Klein, K. L., & Taylor, K. M. (1996). Evaluation of a short form of the Career Decision-Making Self-Efficacy Scale. *Journal of Career Assessment, 4*, 47–57.

Betz, N. E., & Taylor, K. M. (1994). *Manual for the Career Decision-Making Self-Efficacy Scale*. Columbus, OH: The Ohio State University, Department of Psychology.

Bingham, R. P., & Ward, C. M. (1996). Practical applications of career counseling with ethnic minority women. In M. L. Savickas & W. B. Walsh (Eds.), *Handbook of career counseling theory and practice* (pp. 291–313). Palo Alto, CA: Davies-Black.

Bingham, R. P., & Ward, C. M. (2001). Career counseling with African American males and females. In W. B. Walsh, R. P. Bingham, M. T. Brown, & C. M. Ward (Eds.), *Career counseling for African Americans* (pp. 49–75). Mahwah, NJ: Lawrence Erlbaum Associates.

Boggs, K. R. (2002). Campbell Interest and Skill Survey. In J. T. Kapes & E. A. Whitfield (Eds.), *A counselor's guide to career assessment instruments* (4th ed., pp. 194–201). Tulsa, OK: National Career Development Association.

Borgen, F. H. (1986). New approaches to the assessment of interests. In W. B. Walsh & S. H. Osipow (Eds.), *The assessment of interests* (pp. 83–126). Hillsdale, NJ: Lawrence Erlbaum Associates.

Borgen, F. H. (1999). New horizons in interest theory and measurement: Toward expanded meaning. In M. L. Savickas & A. R. Spokane (Eds.), *Vocational interests: Meaning, measurement and counseling use* (pp. 383–411). Palo Alto, CA: Davies-Black.

Brodsky, A. M. (1975, March). *Is there a feminist therapy?* Paper presented at the annual meeting of the Southeastern Psychological Association, Atlanta.

Brown, D. (1996). Brown's values-based, holistic model of career and life-role choices and satisfaction. In D. Brown & L. Brooks (Eds.), *Career choice and development* (3rd ed., pp. 337–372). San Francisco: Jossey-Bass.

Brown, D., & Brooks, L. (1991). *Career counseling techniques*. Boston: Allyn & Bacon.

Brown, D., & Brooks, L. (Eds.). (1996). *Career choice and development* (3rd ed.). San Francisco: Jossey-Bass.

Brown, L. S. (1986). Gender-role analysis: A neglected component of psychological assessment. *Psychotherapy, 23*, 243–248.

Brown, L. S. (1990). Taking gender into account in the clinical assessment interview. *Professional Psychology, 21*, 12–17.

Brown, M. T. (2002). Career Attitudes and Strategies Inventory (CASI). In J. T. Kapes & E. A. Whitfield (Eds.), *A counselor's guide to career assessment instruments* (4th ed., pp. 310–315). Tulsa, OK: National Career Development Association.

Buck, J. N., & Daniels, M. H. (1985). *Assessment of Career Decision Making manual*. Los Angeles: Western Psychological Services.

Butcher, J. N. (1985). Review of the Sixteen Personality Factor Questionnaire. In J. V. Mitchell, Jr. (Ed.), *The ninth mental measurements yearbook* (Vol. 2, pp. 1391–1392). Lincoln, NE: Buros Institute of Mental Measurements.

Campbell, D. P., Hyne, S. A., & Nilsen, D. L. (1992). *Manual for the Campbell Interest and Skill Survey*. Minneapolis, MN: National Computer Systems.

Campbell, R. E., & Cellini, J. V. (1981). A diagnostic taxonomy of adult career development problems. *Journal of Vocational Behavior, 19*, 175–190.

Campbell, V. L. (1990). A model for using tests in counseling. In C. E. Watkins, Jr. & V. L. Campbell (Eds.), *Testing in counseling practice* (pp. 1–7). Hillsdale, NJ: Lawrence Erlbaum Associates.

Cattell, R. B., Eber, H. W., & Tatsuoka, M. M. (1970). *Handbook for the Sixteen Personality Factor Questionnaire (16PF)*. Champaign, IL: Institute for Personality and Ability Testing.

Chartrand, J. M., Robbins, S. B., Morrill, W. H., & Boggs, K. R. (1990). Development and validation of the Career Factors Inventory. *Journal of Counseling Psychology, 37*, 491–501.

Chartrand, J. M., & Walsh, W. B. (2001). Career assessment: Changes and trends. In F. T. L. Leong & A. Barak (Eds.), *Contemporary models in vocational psychology: A volume in honor of Samuel H. Osipow* (pp. 231–255). Mahwah, NJ: Lawrence Erlbaum Associates.

Chipman, S. F., Marshall, S. P., & Scott, P. A. (1991). Content effects on word problem performance: A possible source of test bias? *American Educational Research Journal, 28*, 897–915.

Code of Fair Testing Practices in Education. (2004). Washington, DC: Joint Committee on Testing Practices.

Cole, N. S. (1981). Bias in testing. *American Psychologist, 36*, 1067–1077.

Conn, S. R., & Rieke, M. L. (1994). *16PF fifth edition technical manual*. Champaign, IL: Institute for Personality and Ability Testing.

Constantine, M. G. (2001). Addressing the career transition issues of African American women: Vocational and personal considerations. In W. B. Walsh, R. P. Bingham, M. T. Brown, & C. M. Ward (Eds.), *Career counseling for African Americans* (pp. 99–112). Mahwah, NJ: Lawrence Erlbaum Associates.

Constantine, M. G., Greer, T. M., & Kindaichi, M. M. (2003). Theoretical and cultural considerations in counseling women of color. In M. Kopala & M. A. Keitel (Eds.), *Handbook of counseling women* (pp. 40–52). Thousand Oaks, CA: Sage.

Costa, P. T., & McCrae, R. R. (1995). *NEO Personality Inventory–Revised*. Lutz, FL: Psychological Assessment Resources.

Crites, J. O. (1978). *Theory and research handbook for the Career Maturity Inventory*. Monterey, CA: McGraw-Hill.

Crites, J. O. (1981). *Career counseling*. New York: McGraw-Hill.

Crites, J. O. (1990). *Career Mastery Inventory*. Boulder, CO: Crites Career Consultants.

Croteau, J. M., Anderson, M. Z., DiStefano, T. M., & Kampa-Kokesch, S. (2000). Lesbian, gay, and bisexual vocational psychology: Reviewing foundations and planning construction. In R. M. Perez, K. A. DeBord, & K. J. Bieschke (Eds.), *Handbook of counseling and psychotherapy with lesbian, gay, and bisexual clients* (pp. 383–408). Washington, DC: American Psychological Association.

Davison Aviles, R. M., & Spokane, A. R. (1999). The vocational interests of Hispanic, African American, and White middle school students. *Measurement and Evaluation in Counseling and Development, 32*, 138–148.

Dawis, R. V. (1996). Vocational psychology, vocational adjustment, and the workforce: Some familiar and unanticipated consequences. *Psychology, Public Policy, and Law, 2*, 229–248.

Dawis, R. V., & Lofquist, L. (1984). *A psychological theory of work adjustment*. Minneapolis: University of Minnesota Press.

Dewey, C. R. (1974). Exploring interests: A non-sexist method. *Personnel and Guidance Journal, 52*, 311–315.

Diamond, E. E. (1990). The Kuder Occupational Interest Survey. In C. E. Watkins, Jr. & V. L. Campbell (Eds.), *Testing in counseling practice* (pp. 211–239). Hillsdale, NJ: Lawrence Erlbaum Associates.

Diamond, E. E., & Zytowski, D. G. (2000). The Kuder Occupational Interest Survey. In C. E. Watkins & V. L. Campbell (Eds.), *Testing and assessment in counseling practice* (2nd ed., pp. 263–294). Mahwah, NJ: Lawrence Erlbaum Associates.

Dolliver, R. H. (1969). Strong Vocational Interest Blank versus expressed vocational interests: A review. *Psychological Bulletin, 72,* 95–107.

Downing, N. E., & Roush, K. L. (1985). From passive acceptance to active commitment: A model of feminist identity development for women. *Counseling Psychologist, 13,* 695–709.

Drummond, R. J. (1986). Vocational Preference Inventory. In D. J. Keyser & R. C. Sweetland (Eds.), *Test critiques* (Vol. 5, pp. 545–548). Kansas City, MO: Test Corporation of America.

Drummond, R. J. (2003). Career Transitions Inventory. In B. S. Plake, J. C. Impara, & R. Spies (Eds.), *The fifteenth mental measurements yearbook* (pp. 165–166). Lincoln, NE: Buros Institute of Mental Measurements.

Enright, M. S., Conyers, L. M., & Szymanski, E. M. (1996). Career and career-related educational concerns of college students with disabilities. *Journal of Counseling and Development, 75,* 103–114.

Farley, R. C., Johnson, V. A., & Parkerson, S. S. (1999). Effects of a career assessment and planning intervention on the vocational development of secondary students with disabilities: A pilot study. *Vocational Evaluation and Work Adjustment Journal, 32,* 15–21.

Farmer, H. S. (1984). Development of a measure of home-career conflict related to career motivation in college women. *Sex Roles, 10,* 663–675.

Fassinger, R. E., & O'Brien, K. M. (2000). Career counseling with college women: A scientist-practitioner-advocate model of intervention. In D. A. Luzzo (Ed.), *Career counseling of college students: An empirical guide to strategies that work* (pp. 253–265). Washington, DC: American Psychological Association.

Feller, R., & Daly, J. (2002). Career Thoughts Inventory (CTI). In J. T. Kapes & E. A. Whitfield (Eds.), *A counselor's guide to career assessment instruments* (4th ed., pp. 343–348). Tulsa, OK: National Career Development Association.

Fitzgerald, L. F. (1985). Career counseling with women. In Z. Leibowitz & D. Lea (Eds.), *Adult career development* (pp. 116–131). Alexandria, VA: American Association for Counseling and Development.

Fitzgerald, L. F., Fassinger, R. E., & Betz, N. E. (1995). Theoretical advances in the study of women's career development. In W. B. Walsh & S. H. Osipow (Eds.), *Handbook of vocational psychology: Theory, research, and practice* (2nd ed., pp. 67–109). Hillsdale, NJ: Lawrence Erlbaum Associates.

Fitzgerald, L. F., & Harmon, L. W. (2001). Women's career development: A postmodern update. In F. T. L. Leong & A. Barak (Eds.), *Contemporary models in vocational psychology: A volume in honor of Samuel H. Osipow* (pp. 207–230). Mahwah, NJ: Lawrence Erlbaum Associates.

Fitzgerald, L. F., & Ormerod, A. J. (1993). Breaking silence: The sexual harassment of women in academic and the workplace. In F. L. Denmark & M. A. Paludi (Eds.), *Psychology of women: A handbook of issues and theories* (pp. 553–581). Westport, CT: Greenwood Press.

Fitzgerald, L. F., & Weitzman, L. M. (1992). Women's career development: Theory and practice from a feminist perspective. In Z. Leibowitz & D. Lea (Eds.), *Adult career development: Concepts, issues, and practices* (pp. 125–157). Alexandria, VA: National Career Development Association.

Fouad, N. A. (1995). Career behavior of Hispanics: Assessment and career intervention. In F. T. L. Leong (Ed.), *Career development and vocational behavior of racial and ethnic minorities* (pp. 165–191). Hillsdale, NJ: Lawrence Erlbaum Associates.

Fouad, N. A., Helledy, K. I., & Metz, A. J. (2003). Effective strategies for career counseling with women. In M. Kopala & M. A. Keitel (Eds.), *Handbook of counseling women* (pp. 131–151). Thousand Oaks, CA: Sage.

Freitag, P. K. (2001). Occupational Stress Inventory–revised edition. In B. S. Plake & J. C. Impara (Eds.), *The fourteenth mental measurements yearbook* (pp. 844–846). Lincoln, NE: Buros Institute of Mental Measurements.

Fukuyama, M. A., & Ferguson, A. D. (2000). Lesbian, gay, and bisexual people of color: Understanding cultural complexity and managing multiple oppressions. In R. M. Perez, K. A. DeBord, & K. J. Bieschke (Eds.), *Handbook of counseling and psychotherapy with lesbian, gay, and bisexual clients* (pp. 81–105). Washington, DC: American Psychological Association.

Gervasio, A. H., & Crawford, M. (1989). Social evaluations of assertiveness. *Psychology of Women Quarterly, 13,* 1–25.

Gilbert, L. A. (1985). Measures of psychological masculinity and femininity: A comment on Gaddy, Glass, and Arnkoff. *Journal of Counseling Psychology, 32,* 163–166.

Gilbert, L. A. (Ed.). (1987). Dual career families in perspective [Special issue]. *Counseling Psychologist, 15*(2).

Gilbert, L. A., & Brownson, C. (1998). Current perspectives on women's multiple roles. *Journal of Career Assessment, 6,* 433–448.

Gilbert, L. A., & Rader, J. (2001). Current perspectives on women's adult roles: Work, family, and life. In R. K. Unger (Ed.), *Handbook of the psychology of women and gender* (pp. 156–169). New York: Wiley.

Glass, C. R., & Merluzzi, T. V. (2000). Cognitive and behavioral assessment. In C. E. Watkins & V. L. Campbell (Eds.), *Testing and assessment in counseling practice* (2nd ed., pp. 175–224). Mahwah, NJ: Lawrence Erlbaum Associates.

Glick, P., & Fiske, S. T. (1996). The ambivalent sexism inventory: Differentiating hostile and benevolent sexism. *Journal of Personality and Social Psychology, 70,* 491–512.

Goldman, L. (1983). The Vocational Card Sort technique: A different view. *Measurement and Evaluation in Guidance, 16,* 107–109.

Goldman, L. (1990). Qualitative assessment. *The Counseling Psychologist, 18,* 205–213.

Good, G. E., Gilbert, L. A., & Scher, M. (1990). Gender aware therapy: A synthesis of feminist therapy and knowledge about gender. *Journal of Counseling and Development, 68,* 376–380.

Gottfredson, L. S. (1996). Gottfredson's theory of circumscription and compromise. In D. Brown & L. Brooks (Eds.), *Career choice and development* (3rd ed., pp. 179–232). San Francisco: Jossey-Bass.

Gough, H. G. (1957). *Manual for the California Psychological Inventory.* Palo Alto, CA: Consulting Psychologists Press.

Gough, H. G. (1990). The California Psychological Inventory. In C. E. Watkins & V. L. Campbell (Eds.), *Testing in counseling practice* (pp. 37–62). Hillsdale, NJ: Lawrence Erlbaum Associates.

Gough, H. G. (2000). The California Psychological Inventory. In C. E. Watkins & V. L. Campbell (Eds.), *Testing and assessment in counseling practice* (2nd ed., pp. 45–71). Mahwah, NJ: Lawrence Erlbaum Associates.

Greenhaus, J. H. (1971). An investigation of the role of career salience in vocational behavior. *Journal of Vocational Behavior, 18,* 326–336.

Groth-Marnat, G. (2003). *Handbook of psychological assessment* (4th ed.). Hoboken, NJ: Wiley.

Gutek, B. A., & Done, R. S. (2001). Sexual harassment. In R. K. Unger (Ed.), *Handbook of the psychology of women and gender* (pp. 367–387). New York: Wiley.

Gwilliam, L. R., & Betz, N. E. (2001). Validity of measures of math- and science-related self-efficacy for African Americans and European Americans. *Journal of Career Assessment, 9,* 261–281.

Hackett, G., & Betz, N. E. (1981). A self-efficacy approach to the career development of women. *Journal of Vocational Behavior, 18,* 326–336.

Hackett, G., & Betz, N. E. (1992). Self-efficacy perceptions and the career-related choices of college students. In D. H. Schunk & J. L. Meece (Eds.), *Student perceptions in the classroom: Causes and consequences* (pp. 229–246). Hillsdale, NJ: Lawrence Erlbaum Associates.

Hackett, G., & Betz, N. E. (1995). Career choice and development. In J. E. Maddux (Ed.), *Self-efficacy, adaptation, and adjustment: Theory, research, and application* (pp. 249–280). New York: Plenum Press.

Hackett, G., & Lent, R. W. (1992). Theoretical advances and current inquiry in career psychology. In S. D. Brown & R. W. Lent (Eds.), *Handbook of counseling psychology* (2nd ed., pp. 419–451). New York: Wiley.

Hackett, G., & Lonborg, S. D. (1994). Career assessment and counseling for women. In W. B. Walsh & S. H. Osipow (Eds.), *Career counseling for women* (pp. 43–85). Hillsdale, NJ: Lawrence Erlbaum Associates.

Hall, M. E., & Rayman, J. R. (2002). Career Beliefs Inventory (CBI). In J. T. Kapes & E. A. Whitfield (Eds.), *A counselor's guide to career assessment instruments* (4th ed., pp. 316–322). Tulsa, OK: National Career Development Association.

Hansen, J. C. (1986). Strong Vocational Interest Blank/Strong–Campbell Interest Inventory. In W. B. Walsh & S. H. Osipow (Eds.), *The assessment of interests* (pp. 1–30). Hillsdale, NJ: Lawrence Erlbaum Associates.

Hansen, J. C. (1990). Interpretation of the Strong Interest Inventory. In C. E. Watkins, Jr. & V. L. Campbell (Eds.), *Testing in counseling practice* (pp. 177–209). Hillsdale, NJ: Lawrence Erlbaum Associates.

Hansen, J. C. (1994). Salience Inventory. In J. T. Kapes, M. M. Mastie, & E. A. Whitfield (Eds.), *A counselor's guide to career assessment instruments* (pp. 231–235). Alexandria, VA: National Career Development Association.

Hansen, J. C. (2000). Interpretation of the Strong Interest Inventory. In C. E. Watkins & V. L. Campbell (Eds.), *Testing and assessment in counseling practice* (2nd ed., pp. 227–262). Mahwah, NJ: Lawrence Erlbaum Associates.

Harmon, L. W., Hansen, J. C., Borgen, F. H., & Hammer, A. L. (1994). *Strong Interest Inventory application and technical guide.* Palo Alto, CA: Consulting Psychologists Press.

Harren, V. A. (1979). A model of career decision making for college students. *Journal of Vocational Behavior, 14,* 119–133.

Healy, C. C. (2002). Myers–Briggs Type Indicator (MBTI). In J. T. Kapes & E. A. Whitfield (Eds.), *A counselor's guide to career assessment instruments* (4th ed., pp. 363–368). Tulsa, OK: National Career Development Association.

Heppner, M. J. (1998). The Career Transitions Inventory: Measuring internal resources in adulthood. *Journal of Career Assessment, 6,* 135–145.

Heppner, M. J., Davidson, M. M., & Scott, A. B. (2003). The ecology of women's career barriers. In M. Kopala & M. A. Keitel (Eds.), *Handbook of counseling women* (pp. 173–184). Thousand Oaks, CA: Sage.

Hesketh, B. (2000). Prevention and development in the workplace. In S. D. Brown & R. W. Lent (Eds.), *Handbook of counseling psychology* (3rd ed., pp. 471–498). New York: Wiley.

Holland, J. L. (1982). The SDS helps both females and males: A comment. *Vocational Guidance Quarterly, 30,* 195–197.

Holland, J. L. (1985a). *The self-directed search: Professional manual.* Odessa, FL: Psychological Assessment Resources.

Holland, J. L. (1985b). *Vocational Preference Inventory professional manual.* Lutz, FL: Psychological Assessment Resources.

Holland, J. L. (1996). *The occupations finder.* Lutz, FL: Psychological Assessment Resources.

Holland, J. L., Daiger, D. C., & Power, P. G. (1980). *My vocational situation.* Palo Alto, CA: Consulting Psychologists Press.

Holland, J. L., Fritzsche, B. A., & Powell, A. B. (1997). *Self-Directed Search technical manual.* Lutz, FL: Psychological Assessment Resources.

Holland, J. L., & Gottfredson, G. D. (1994). *Career Attitudes and Strategies Inventory: An inventory for understanding adult careers.* Lutz, FL: Psychological Assessment Resources.

Hood, A. B., & Johnson, R. W. (1997). *Assessment in counseling: A guide to the use of psychological assessment procedures* (2nd ed.). Alexandria, VA: American Counseling Association.

Hood, A. B., & Johnson, R. W. (2002). *Assessment in counseling: A guide to the use of psychological assessment procedures* (3rd ed.). Alexandria, VA: American Counseling Association.

Höpfl, H., & Atkinson, P. H. (2000). The future of women's career. In A. Collin & R. A. Young (Eds.), *The future of career* (pp. 130–143). Cambridge, UK: Cambridge University Press.

Jackson, M. A., Tal, A. I., & Sullivan, T. R. (2003). Hidden biases in counseling women: Balancing work and family concerns. In M. Kopala & M. A. Keitel (Eds.), *Handbook of counseling women* (pp. 152–172). Thousand Oaks, CA: Sage.

Jakubowski, P. A. (1977). Self-assertion training procedures for women. In E. I. Rawlings & D. K. Carter (Eds.), *Psychotherapy for women: Treatment toward equality* (pp. 168–190). Springfield, IL: Thomas.

Jepsen, D. A. (1990). Developmental career counseling. In W. B. Walsh & S. H. Osipow (Eds.), *Career counseling* (pp. 117–158). Hillsdale, NJ: Lawrence Erlbaum Associates.

Johansson, C. B. (1996). *Career Assessment Inventory: The enhanced version.* Minneapolis, MN: National Computer Systems.

Johnson, R. W. (1985). Review of the Vocational Interest Inventory. In J. V. Mitchell (Ed.), *The ninth mental measurements yearbook* (Vol. 2, pp. 1678–1679). Lincoln, NE: Buros Institute of Mental Measurements.

Jones, L. K. (1979). Occ-U-Sort: Development and evaluation of an occupational card sort system. *Vocational Guidance Quarterly, 28,* 56–62.

Kapes, J. T., & Whitfield, E. A. (Eds.). (2002). *A counselor's guide to career assessment instruments* (4th ed.). Tulsa, OK: National Career Development Association.

Kelly, K. R. (2002). Kuder Occupational Interest Survey, Form DD (KOIS-DD) and Kuder Career Search with Person Match (KCS). In J. T. Kapes & E. A. Whitfield (Eds.), *A counselor's guide to career assessment instruments* (4th ed., pp. 265–275). Tulsa, OK: National Career Development Association.

Kifer, E. (1985). Review of the ACT assessment program. In J. V. Mitchell (Ed.), *The ninth mental measurements yearbook* (Vol. 1, pp. 31–36). Lincoln, NE: Buros Institute of Mental Measurements.

Kinnier, R. T. (1998). Career Attitudes and Strategies Inventory. In J. C. Impara & B. S. Plake (Eds.), *The thirteenth mental measurements yearbook* (pp. 184–185). Lincoln, NE: Buros Institute of Mental Measurements.

Kirnan, J. P. (2003). Career Transitions Inventory. In B. S. Plake, J. C. Impara, & R. A. Spies (Eds.), *The fifteenth mental measurements yearbook* (pp. 166–168). Lincoln, NE: Buros Institute of Mental Measurements.

Kite, M. E. (2001). Changing times, changing gender roles: Who do we want women and men to be? In R. K. Unger (Ed.), *Handbook of the psychology of women and gender* (pp. 215–227). New York: Wiley.

Kopala, M., & Keitel, M. A. (Eds.). (2003). *Handbook of counseling women.* Thousand Oaks, CA: Sage.

Krieshok, T. S., Hansen, R. N., & Johnston, J. A. (1982). *Missouri Occupational Card Sort manual (college form).* (Available from the Career Planning and Placement Center, 100 Noyes Hall, University of Missouri–Columbia, Columbia, MO 65211)

Krumboltz, J. D. (1988). Review of the Vocational Interest Inventory. In J. T. Kapes & M. M. Mastie (Eds.), *A counselor's guide to career assessment instruments* (2nd ed., pp. 137–142). Alexandria, VA: National Career Development Association.

Krumboltz, J. D. (1991). *Manual for the Career Beliefs Inventory.* Palo Alto, CA: Consulting Psychologists Press.

Krumboltz, J. D. (1999). *Career Beliefs Inventory applications and technical guide.* Palo Alto, CA: Consulting Psychologists Press.

Krumboltz, J. D., & Nichols, C. W. (1990). Integrating the social learning theory of career decision making. In W. B. Walsh & S. H. Osipow (Eds.), *Career counseling: Contemporary topics in vocational psychology* (pp. 159–192). Hillsdale, NJ: Lawrence Erlbaum Associates.

Lamb, R. R., & Prediger, D. J. (1981). *Technical report for the unisex edition of the ACT Interest Inventory (UNIACT).* Iowa City, IA: American College Testing Program.

Lattimore, R. R., & Borgen, F. H. (1999). Validity of the 1994 Strong Interest Inventory with racial and ethnic groups in the United States. *Journal of Counseling Psychology, 46*, 185–195.

Lent, R. W., Brown, S. D., & Hackett, G. (1996). Career development from a social cognitive perspective. In D. Brown & L. Brooks (Eds.), *Career choice and development* (3rd ed., pp. 373–421). San Francisco: Jossey-Bass.

Lent, R. W., & Hackett, G. (1987). Career self-efficacy: Empirical status and future directions [Monograph]. *Journal of Vocational Behavior, 30*, 347–382.

Leong, F. T. L., & Brown, M. T. (1995). Theoretical issues in cross-cultural career development: Cultural validity and cultural specificity. In W. B. Walsh & S. H. Osipow (Eds.), *Handbook of vocational psychology: Theory, research, and practice* (2nd ed., pp. 143–180). Hillsdale, NJ: Lawrence Erlbaum Associates.

Lewin, M., & Wild, C. L. (1991). The impact of the feminist critique on tests, assessment, and methodology. *Psychology of Women Quarterly, 15*, 581–596.

Lunneborg, P. W. (1981). *The Vocational Interest Inventory manual.* Los Angeles: Western Psychological Services.

Lunneborg, P. W. (1985). My vocational situation. In J. V. Mitchell (Ed.), *The ninth mental measurements yearbook* (Vol. 2, pp. 1026–1027). Lincoln, NE: Buros Institute of Mental Measurements.

Lunneborg, P. W. (1993). *The Vocational Interest Inventory–Revised.* Los Angeles: Western Psychological Services.

Luzzo, D. A. (1996). A psychometric evaluation of the Career Decision-Making Self-Efficacy Scale. *Journal of Counseling and Development, 74*, 276–279.

Luzzo, D. A. (2002). Career Factors Inventory (CFI). In J. T. Kapes & E. A. Whitfield (Eds.), *A counselor's guide to career assessment instruments* (4th ed., pp. 331–335). Tulsa, OK: National Career Development Association.

MacDonald, M. L. (1984). Behavioral assessment of women clients. In E. A. Blechman (Ed.), *Behavior modification with women* (pp. 60–93). New York: Guilford Press.

Manuele-Adkins, C. (1995). Adult Career Concerns Inventory. In J. C. Conoley & J. C. Impara (Eds.), *The twelfth mental measurements yearbook* (pp. 48–50). Lincoln, NE: Buros Institute of Mental Measurements.

McCaulley, M. H. (1990). The Myers–Briggs indicator: A measure of individuals and groups. *Measurement and Evaluation in Counseling and Development, 22*, 181–195.

McCaulley, M. H. (2000). The Myers–Briggs Type Indicator in counseling. In C. E. Watkins & V. L. Campbell (Eds.), *Testing and assessment in counseling practice* (2nd ed., pp. 111–173). Mahwah, NJ: Lawrence Erlbaum Associates.

McDivitt, P. J. (2002). Career Maturity Inventory (CMI). In J. T. Kapes & E. A. Whitfield (Eds.), *A counselor's guide to career assessment instruments* (4th ed., pp. 336–342). Tulsa, OK: National Career Development Association.

McNamara, K., & Rickard, K. M. (1989). Feminist identity development: Implications of feminist therapy with women. *Journal of Counseling and Development, 68*, 184–189.

Mednick, M. T., & Thomas, V. G. (1993). Women and the psychology of achievement: A view from the eighties. In F. L. Denmark & M. A. Paludi (Eds.), *Psychology of women: A handbook of issues and theories* (pp. 585–626). Westport, CT: Greenwood Press.

Merluzzi, T. V., & Boltwood, M. D. (1990). Cognitive and behavioral assessment. In C. E. Watkins, Jr. & V. L. Campbell (Eds.), *Testing in counseling practice* (pp. 135–176). Hillsdale, NJ: Lawrence Erlbaum Associates.

Merluzzi, T. V., Glass, C. R., & Genest, M. (Eds.). (1981). *Cognitive assessment.* New York: Guilford Press.

Miner, C. V., & Sellers, S. M. (2002). Career Assessment Inventory (CAI). In J. T. Kapes & E. A. Whitfield (Eds.), *A counselor's guide to career assessment instruments* (4th ed., pp. 202–209). Tulsa, OK: National Career Development Association.

Mitchell, L. K., & Krumboltz, J. D. (1990). Social learning approach to career decision making: Krumboltz's theory. In D. Brown & L. Brooks (Eds.), *Career choice and development* (2nd ed., pp. 145–196). San Francisco: Jossey-Bass.

Mitchell, L. K., & Krumboltz, J. D. (1996). Krumboltz's learning theory of career choice and counseling. In D. Brown & L. Brooks (Eds.), *Career choice and development* (3rd ed., pp. 233–280). San Francisco: Jossey-Bass.

Moore, E. J., & Gysbers, N. L. (1980). *Missouri Occupational Preference Inventory.* Columbia, MO: Human Systems Consultants.

Myers, I. B., & McCaulley, M. H. (1985). *Manual: A guide to the development and use of the Myers–Briggs Type Indicator.* Palo Alto, CA: Consulting Psychologists Press.

Myers, I. B., McCaulley, M. H., Quenk, N. L., & Hammer, A. L. (1998). *MBTI manual: A guide to the development and use of the Myers–Briggs Type Indicator* (3rd ed.). Palo Alto, CA: Consulting Psychologists Press.

National Board for Certified Counselors. (2001). *The practice of Internet counseling.* Greensboro, NC: Author.

National Career Development Association. (1997). *Career counseling competencies.* Retrieved February 14, 2004, from http://www.ncda.org/pdf/counselingcompetencies.pdf

National Career Development Association. (1998). *Guidelines for the use of the Internet for provision of career information and planning services.* Columbus, OH: Author.

National O*Net Consortium. (2004). *Occupational Information Network O*Net Online.* Retrieved March 26, 2004, from http://online.onetcenter.org/

Neimeyer, G. J. (1988). Cognitive integration and differentiation in vocational behavior. *The Counseling Psychologist, 16,* 440–475.

Nevill, D. D., & Calvert, P. D. (1996). Career assessment and the Salience Inventory. *Journal of Career Assessment, 4,* 399–412.

Nevill, D. D., & Super, D. E. (1986). *Manual for the Salience Inventory: Theory, application, and research.* Palo Alto, CA: Consulting Psychologists Press.

Nevill, D. D., & Super, D. E. (1989). *Manual for the Values Scale* (2nd ed.). Palo Alto, CA: Consulting Psychologists Press.

Noonan, B. M., Gallor, S. M., Hensler-McGinnis, N. F., Fassinger, R. E., Wang, S., & Goodman, J. (2004). Challenge and success: A qualitative study of the career development of highly achieving women with physical and sensory disabilities. *Journal of Counseling Psychology, 51,* 68–80.

O'Brien, K. M. (2003). Measuring career self-efficacy: Promoting confidence and happiness at work. In S. J. Lopez & C. R. Snyder (Eds.), *Positive psychological assessment: A handbook of models and measures* (pp. 109–126). Washington, DC: American Psychological Association.

Oliver, L. W., & Chartrand, J. M. (2000). Strategies for career assessment research on the Internet. *Journal of Career Assessment, 8,* 95–103.

Oliver, L. W., & Zack, J. S. (1999). Career assessment on the Internet: An exploratory study. *Journal of Career Assessment, 7,* 323–356.

Osipow, S. H. (1987). *Career Decision Scale: Manual.* Odessa, FL: Psychological Assessment Resources.

Osipow, S. H. (1998). *Occupational Stress Inventory Revised Edition (OSI-R) professional manual.* Lutz, FL: Psychological Assessment Resources.

Parsons, F. (1909). *Choosing a vocation.* Boston: Houghton Mifflin.

Peterson, G. W., Sampson, J. P., Reardon, R. C., & Lenz, J. G. (1996). A cognitive information processing approach to career problem solving and decision making. In D. Brown & L. Brooks (Eds.), *Career choice and development* (3rd ed., pp. 423–475). San Francisco: Jossey-Bass.

Phillips, S. D., & Pazienza, N. J. (1988). History and theory of the assessment of career development and decision making. In W. B. Walsh & S. H. Osipow (Eds.), *Career decision making* (pp. 1–31). Hillsdale, NJ: Lawrence Erlbaum Associates.

Rawlings, E. I., & Carter, D. K. (1977). *Psychotherapy for women*. Springfield, IL: Thomas.

Reardon, R. (1996). A program and cost analysis of a self-directed career decision-making program in a university career center. *Journal of Counseling and Development, 74*, 280–285.

Reardon, R. C., & Wright, L. K. (1999). The case of Mandy: Applying Holland's theory and cognitive information processing theory. *Career Development Quarterly, 47*, 195–203.

Reile, D. M., & Harris-Bowlsbey, J. (2000). Using the Internet in career planning and assessment. *Journal of Career Assessment, 8*, 69–84.

Reynolds, A. L. (2003). Counseling issues for lesbian and bisexual women. In M. Kopala & M. A. Keitel (Eds.), *Handbook of counseling women* (pp. 53–73). Thousand Oaks, CA: Sage.

Richman, D. R. (1988). Cognitive career counseling for women. *Journal of Rational Emotive and Cognitive Behavior Therapy, 6*, 50–65.

Rogers, J. E. (2002). Armed Services Vocational Aptitude Battery Career Exploration Program. In J. T. Kapes & E. A. Whitfield (Eds.), *A counselor's guide to career assessment instruments* (4th ed., pp. 93–101). Tulsa, OK: National Career Development Association.

Rooney, R. A., & Osipow, S. H. (1992). Task-Specific Occupational Self-Efficacy Scale. *Journal of Vocational Behavior, 40*, 14–32.

Rosen, D., Holmberg, K., & Holland, J. L. (1997). *The educational opportunities finder*. Lutz, FL: Psychological Assessment Resources.

Rosewater, L. B. (1985). Feminist interpretation of traditional testing. In L. B. Rosewater & L. E. Walker (Eds.), *Handbook of feminist therapy* (pp. 266–273). New York: Springer.

Rounds, J. B. (1985). Vocational Preference Inventory. In J. V. Mitchell, Jr. (Ed.), *The ninth mental measurements yearbook* (Vol. 2, pp. 1683–1684). Lincoln, NE: Buros Institute of Mental Measurements.

Rounds, J. B., Henly, G. A., Dawis, R. V., Lofquist, L. H., & Weiss, D. J. (1981). *Manual for the Minnesota Importance Questionnaire*. Minneapolis: University of Minnesota, Vocational Psychology Research.

Rounds, J. B., & Tracey, T. J. (1990). From trait-factor to person-environment fit counseling: Theory and process. In W. B. Walsh & S. H. Osipow (Eds.), *Career counseling: Contemporary topics in vocational psychology* (pp. 1–44). Hillsdale, NJ: Lawrence Erlbaum Associates.

Sampson, J. P., Lumsden, J. A., & Carr, D. L. (2002). Computer-assisted career assessment. In J. T. Kapes & E. A. Whitfield (Eds.), *A counselor's guide to career assessment instruments* (4th ed., pp. 47–63). Tulsa, OK: National Career Development Association.

Sampson, J. P., Peterson, G. W., Lenz, J. G., Reardon, R. C., & Saunders, D. E. (1996). *Career Thoughts Inventory: Professional manual*. Lutz, FL: Psychological Assessment Resources.

Savickas, M. L. (1990). The use of career choice process scales in counseling practice. In C. E. Watkins, Jr. & V. L. Campbell (Eds.), *Testing in counseling practice* (pp. 373–418). Hillsdale, NJ: Lawrence Erlbaum Associates.

Savickas, M. L. (2000). Assessing career decision making. In C. E. Watkins & V. L. Campbell (Eds.), *Testing and assessment in counseling practice* (2nd ed., pp. 429–477). Mahwah, NJ: Lawrence Erlbaum Associates.

Savickas, M. L., & Hartung, P. (1996). The Career Development Inventory in review: Psychometric and research findings. *Journal of Career Assessment, 4*, 171–188.

Schafer, W. D. (2002). Vocational Interest Inventory, Revised (VII-R). In J. T. Kapes & E. A. Whitfield (Eds.), *A counselor's guide to career assessment instruments* (4th ed., pp. 303–307). Tulsa, OK: National Career Development Association.

Schoenrade, P. (2002). Values Scale (VS). In J. T. Kapes & E. A. Whitfield (Eds.), *A counselor's guide to career assessment instruments* (4th ed., pp. 298–302). Tulsa, OK: National Career Development Association.

Schuerger, J. M. (2000). The Sixteen Personality Factor Questionnaire (16PF). In C. E. Watkins & V. L. Campbell (Eds.), *Testing and assessment in counseling practice* (2nd ed., pp. 73–110). Mahwah, NJ: Lawrence Erlbaum Associates.

Segal, Z. V., & Shaw, B. F. (1988). Cognitive assessment: Issues and methods. In K. S. Dobson (Ed.), *Handbook of cognitive-behavioral therapies* (pp. 39–81). New York: Guilford Press.

Selkow, P. (1984). *Assessing sex bias in testing.* Westport, CT: Greenwood Press.

Sesan, R. (1988). Sex bias and sex-role stereotyping in psychotherapy with women: Survey results. *Psychotherapy, 25*, 107–116.

Slaney, R. B. (1978). Expressed and inventoried vocational interests: A comparison of instruments. *Journal of Counseling Psychology, 25*, 520–529.

Slaney, R. B. (1988). The assessment of career decision making. In W. B. Walsh & S. H. Osipow (Eds.), *Career decision making* (pp. 33–76). Hillsdale, NJ: Lawrence Erlbaum Associates.

Slaney, R. B., & MacKinnon-Slaney, R. (1990). The use of vocational card sorts in career counseling. In C. E. Watkins, Jr. & V. L. Campbell (Eds.), *Testing in counseling practice* (pp. 317–371). Hillsdale, NJ: Lawrence Erlbaum Associates.

Slaney, R. B., & MacKinnon-Slaney, F. (2000). Using vocational card sorts in career counseling. In C. E. Watkins, Jr. & V. L. Campbell (Eds.), *Testing and assessment in counseling practice* (2nd ed., pp. 371–428). Mahwah, NJ: Lawrence Erlbaum Associates.

Smith, E. J. (1983). Issues in racial minorities' career behavior. In W. B. Walsh & S. H. Osipow (Eds.), *Handbook of vocational psychology: Foundations* (Vol. 1, pp. 161–222). Hillsdale, NJ: Lawrence Erlbaum Associates.

Smith, T. B. (Ed.). (2004). *Practicing multiculturalism: Affirming diversity in counseling and psychotherapy.* Boston: Pearson Education.

Spence, J. T., & Helmreich, R. L. (1972). The Attitudes Toward Women Scale: An objective instrument to measure attitudes toward the rights and roles of women in contemporary society [Ms. No. 153]. *JSAS Catalog of Selected Documents in Psychology, 2*, 66.

Spokane, A. R. (1990). Self-guided interest inventories and career interventions. In C. E. Watkins, Jr. & V. L. Campbell (Eds.), *Testing in counseling practice* (pp. 285–316). Hillsdale, NJ: Lawrence Erlbaum Associates.

Spokane, A. R. (1991). *Career intervention.* Englewood Cliffs, NJ: Prentice Hall.

Spokane, A. R. (1996). Holland's theory. In D. Brown & L. Brooks (Eds.), *Career choice and development* (3rd ed., pp. 33–74). San Francisco: Jossey-Bass.

Spokane, A. R., & Catalano, M. (2000). The Self-Directed Search: A theory-driven array of self-guiding career interventions. In C. E. Watkins & V. L. Campbell (Eds.), *Testing and assessment in counseling practice* (2nd ed., pp. 339–370). Mahwah, NJ: Lawrence Erlbaum Associates.

Spokane, A. R., Fouad, N. A., & Swanson, J. L. (2003). Culture-centered career intervention. *Journal of Vocational Behavior, 62*, 453–458.

Subich, L. M. (1996). Addressing diversity in the process of career assessment. In M. L. Savickas & W. B. Walsh (Eds.), *Handbook of career counseling theory and practice* (pp. 277–289). Palo Alto, CA: Davies-Black.

Subich, L. M., & Billingsley, K. D. (1995). Integrating career assessment into counseling. In W. B. Walsh & S. H. Osipow (Eds.), *Handbook of vocational psychology: Theory, research, and practice* (2nd ed., pp. 261–293). Hillsdale, NJ: Lawrence Erlbaum Associates.

Sue, D. W., & Sue, D. (1999). *Counseling the culturally different: Theory and practice* (3rd ed.). New York: Wiley.

Super, D. E. (1970). *Work Values Inventory manual.* Chicago: Riverside.

Super, D. E. (1973). The work values inventory. In D. G. Zytowski (Ed.), *Contemporary approaches in interest measurement* (pp. 189–205). Minneapolis: University of Minnesota Press.

Super, D. E. (1990). A life-span, life-space approach to career development. In D. Brown & L. Brooks (Eds.), *Career choice and development: Applying contemporary theories to practice* (2nd ed., pp. 197–261). San Francisco: Jossey-Bass.

Super, D. E., & Crites, J. O. (1949). *Appraising vocational fitness.* New York: Harper & Row.

Super, D. E., Savickas, M. L., & Super, C. M. (1996). The life-span, life-space approach to careers. In D. Brown & L. Brooks (Eds.), *Career choice and development* (3rd ed., pp. 121–178). San Francisco: Jossey-Bass.

Super, D. E., Thompson, A. S., & Lindeman, R. H. (1988). *Adult Career Concerns Inventory: Manual for research and exploratory use in career counseling.* Palo Alto, CA: Consulting Psychologists Press.

Super, D. E., Thompson, A. S., Lindeman, R. H., Jordaan, J. P., & Myers, R. A. (1984). *Technical manual for the Career Development Inventory.* Palo Alto, CA: Consulting Psychologists Press.

Swaney, K. B. (1995). *Technical manual: Revised Unisex Edition of the ACT Interest Inventory (UNIACT).* Iowa City, IA: American College Testing.

Swanson, J. L., & Tokar, D. M. (1991). Development and initial validation of the Career Barriers Inventory. *Journal of Vocational Behavior, 39,* 344–361.

Swim, J. K., Aiken, K. J., Hall, W. S., & Hunter, B. A. (1995). Sexism and racism: Old-fashioned and modern prejudices. *Journal of Personality and Social Psychology, 68,* 199–214.

Taylor, K. M., & Betz, N. E. (1983). Applications of self-efficacy theory to the understanding and treatment of career indecision. *Journal of Vocational Behavior, 22,* 63–81.

Tougas, F., Brown, R., Beaton, A. M., & Joly, S. (1995). Neosexism: Plus ça change, plus c'est pareil. *Personality and Social Psychology Bulletin, 21,* 842–849.

Tracey, T. J. G. (1997). The structure of interests and self-efficacy expectations: An expanded examination of the spherical model of interests. *Journal of Counseling Psychology, 44,* 32–43.

Trevino, J. G. (1996). Worldview and change in cross-cultural counseling. *The Counseling Psychologist, 24,* 198–215.

Tyler, L. E. (1961). Research explorations in the realm of choice. *Journal of Counseling Psychology, 8,* 195–201.

Unger, R. K. (1979). Toward a redefinition of sex and gender. *American Psychologist, 34,* 1085–1094.

U.S. Bureau of Labor Statistics. (2004). *Current population survey.* Retrieved February 14, 2004, from http://www.bls.gov/cps/#overview

U.S. Department of Labor, Employment and Training Administration. (1977). *Dictionary of Occupational Titles* (4th ed.). Washington, DC: U.S. Government Printing Office.

Vacc, N. A., & Newsome, D. W. (2002). Strong Interest Inventory (SII) and Skills Confidence Inventory (SCI). In J. T. Kapes & E. A. Whitfield (Eds.), *A counselor's guide to career assessment instruments* (4th ed., pp. 288–297). Tulsa, OK: National Career Development Association.

Vansickle, T. R. (2002). Sixteen Personality Factor (16PF) Questionnaire. In J. T. Kapes & E. A. Whitfield (Eds.), *A counselor's guide to career assessment instruments* (4th ed., pp. 369–376). Tulsa, OK: National Career Development Association.

Wall, R. (2001). Occupational Stress Inventory–revised edition. In B. S. Plake & J. C. Impara (Eds.), *The fourteenth mental measurements yearbook* (p. 846). Lincoln, NE: Buros Institute of Mental Measurements.

Walsh, W. B., & Betz, N. E. (2001). *Tests and assessments* (4th ed.). Upper Saddle River, NJ: Prentice Hall.

Ward, C. M., & Bingham, R. P. (2001). Career assessment for African Americans. In W. B. Walsh, R. P. Bingham, M. T. Brown, & C. M. Ward (Eds.), *Career counseling for African Americans* (pp. 27–48). Mahwah, NJ: Lawrence Erlbaum Associates.

Watkins, C. E., Jr. & Campbell, V. L. (Eds.). (2000). *Testing and assessment in counseling practice* (2nd ed.). Mahwah, NJ: Lawrence Erlbaum Associates.

Wegner, K. W. (1988). Review of the California Personality Inventory, 1987 revised edition. In D. J. Keyser & R. C. Sweetland (Eds.), *Test critiques* (Vol. 7, pp. 66–75). Kansas City, MO: Test Corporation of America.

Westbrook, B. W. (1988). My vocational situation. In J. T. Kapes & M. M. Mastie (Eds.), *A counselor's guide to career assessment instruments* (2nd ed., pp. 187–190). Alexandria, VA: National Career Development Association.

Whiston, S. C., & Bouwkamp, J. C. (2003). Ethical implications of career assessment with women. *Journal of Career Assessment, 11,* 59–75.

Wholeben, B. E. (1988). Sixteen PF Career Development Profile. In J. T. Kapes & M. M. Mastie (Eds.), *A counselor's guide to career assessment instruments* (2nd ed., pp. 238–242). Alexandria, VA: National Career Development Association.

Willis, C. G., & Ham, T. L. (1988). The Myers–Briggs Type Indicator. In J. T. Kapes & M. M. Mastie (Eds.), *A counselor's guide to career assessment instruments* (2nd ed., pp. 230–233). Alexandria, VA: National Career Development Association.

Woollett, A., & Marshall, H. (2001). Motherhood and mothering. In R. K. Unger (Ed.), *Handbook of the psychology of women and gender* (pp. 170–182). New York: Wiley.

Young, R. A., Valach, L., & Collin, A. (1996). A contextual explanation of career. In D. Brown & L. Brooks (Eds.), *Career choice and development* (3rd ed., pp. 477–512). San Francisco: Jossey-Bass.

Zuckerman, M. (1985). Review of the 16 Personality Factor Questionnaire. In J. V. Mitchell, Jr. (Ed.), *The ninth mental measurements yearbook* (Vol. 2, pp. 1392–1394). Lincoln, NE: Buros Institute of Mental Measurements.

Zunker, V. G. (2002). *Career counseling: Applied concepts of life planning* (6th ed.). Pacific Grove, CA: Brooks/Cole.

Zunker, V. G., & Osborn, D. S. (2002). *Using assessment results for career development* (6th ed.). Pacific Grove, CA: Brooks/Cole.

Zytowski, D. G. (1988). Review of the Salience Inventory. In J. T. Kapes & M. M. Mastie (Eds.), *A counselor's guide to career assessment instruments* (2nd ed., pp. 151–154). Alexandria, VA: National Career Development Association.

Zytowski, D. G. (2001). Kuder Career Search With Person Match: Career assessment for the 21st century. *Journal of Career Assessment, 9,* 229–242.

Zytowski, D. G. (n.d.). *Kuder Career Search With Person Match user manual.* Retrieved March 26, 2004, from http://www.kuder.com/custom/user_manual/

Zytowski, D. G., & Kuder, F. (1986). Advances in the Kuder Occupational Interest Survey. In W. B. Walsh & S. H. Osipow (Eds.), *Advances in vocational psychology: Vol. 1. The assessment of interests* (pp. 31–54). Hillsdale, NJ: Lawrence Erlbaum Associates.

Zytowski, D. G., & Laing, L. (1978). Validity of other-gender-normed scales on the KOIS. *Journal of Counseling Psychology, 25,* 205–209.

Chapter 5

A Critical Feminist Approach
to Career Counseling With Women

Krista M. Chronister
Ellen Hawley McWhirter
Linda Forrest
University of Oregon

The purpose of this chapter is to describe a critical feminist approach to career counseling with women. The feminist approach we describe utilizes primary feminist principles and an empowerment model (McWhirter, 1994) to address the intersection of gender, race, class, and other social variables in career counseling with women. Our focus is on working with women of color, immigrant women, and women from lower socioeconomic backgrounds, populations that historically received limited attention in the career-counseling literature. Due to space constrictions, we assume that the reader has fundamental knowledge of career-counseling theory, research, and practice. We first provide a brief overview of the development of feminist theories and therapies as well as their strengths and limitations. Second, we describe an empowerment model for counseling and how this model complements and expands on feminist theories and therapies. Third, we use two women's stories to illustrate the application of a critical feminist approach to career counseling with women of color.

INTRODUCTION TO FEMINIST THEORY

Feminist theory and therapy modalities were first developed in the 1970s in response to the sexist and oppressive nature of traditional psychotherapies (Chesler, 1972; Tennov, 1975; Weisstein, 1972) and the exclusion of women's issues in theory development and research (Cox, 1976; Fitzgerald

& Harmon, 1973; Franks & Burtle, 1974; Hill et al., 1979; Miller, 1976; Rawlings & Carter, 1977). Early feminist criticism of psychotherapy focused on the androcentric nature of psychological theory and the consequences for women clients. Early critiques asserted that therapists' sexist attitudes and practices created a double standard for mental health of women clients (Broverman, Broverman, Clarkson, Rosenkrantz, & Vogel, 1970). Feminist theories and therapies also have addressed the heterosexual bias inherent in traditional theories and therapies by articulating the need for women's financial independence from men (Greenspan, 1983; Sturdivant, 1980) and the right of women to choose to live alone or with another woman as a life companion (Brown, 1992; Millet, 1969).

Although there are different feminist positions regarding the source of women's oppression and the solutions for achieving equality for women, there are shared principles among most feminist theories and therapy modalities (Brooks & Forrest, 1994; Enns, 1993, 1997; Enns & Forrest, 2005; Gilbert & Scher, 1999; Worell & Johnson, 1997; Worell & Remer, 1992). Feminist theories assert that sociocultural conditions are the primary source of women's psychological problems. Women's experiences of depression, low self-efficacy, negative body image, and violence, for example, and the presenting problems they bring to therapy are conceptualized as originating from socially defined and oppressive sex roles. Feminist therapists view their clients' presenting problems as normal responses and healthy attempts to cope with restrictive societal roles for women rather than as pathology or symptoms that need to be eliminated. Feminist therapists seek to help women clients understand their psychological symptoms in the larger societal context that relies on, yet undervalues, women's relational strengths and at the same time judges women for being too independent or assertive.

Second, feminist theory purports that the personal is political, that is, the experiences of individual women are linked directly to the collective condition of women in society, and for this reason feminist theory conceptualizes women's experiences within a social context. Also, solutions to women's psychological concerns are not solvable solely by individuals because they are embedded in larger social structures and systems that require social, political, and institutional change. Thus, the goal of therapy is not to adapt to current social circumstances, but to change the restrictive forces that confine and limit all women's choices.

Third, feminist therapies are built on egalitarian relationships between clients and counselors. Therapists acknowledge the power differential between themselves and their clients, but work to minimize power differences through collaboration and power-sharing strategies (e.g., jointly setting therapeutic goals, therapists' self-disclosures, fully transparent informed consent that views the client as an educated consumer, fee negotiation, encouraging client feedback to the therapist). Feminist therapists view clients as having expertise about their own life experiences (Sturdivant, 1980). Additionally, feminist therapists remain open to feedback and explore and validate clients' reactions to therapists, rather than dismiss clients' reactions only as transference.

Fourth, feminist therapy is a "consciousness-raising, woman-valuing, and self-validating process" (Worrell & Remer, 1992, p. 22). Feminist therapists help women clients to trust their own experiences and intuition, value and nurture themselves as women, and value their relationships with other women. Feminist therapy modalities "reject social conformity in favor of personal self definition and self determination" (Brooks & Forrest, 1994, p. 114). Feminist therapy modalities also encourage women to identify, develop, and utilize their strengths for their benefit and the benefit of all women (Espín, 1994; Williams, McCandies, & Dunlap, 2002; Worrell & Remer).

From the beginning, scholars have criticized feminist theory and feminist therapies for addressing only the experiences of middle-class, European American women (Anzaldúa, 1990; Espín, 1994; Glenn, 1991; Mays & Comas-Díaz, 1988; Williams et al., 2002). Traditional feminist approaches have incorrectly assumed that women's gender-based experiences of oppression were the most salient for all women, and ignored the oppression experienced by ethnic minority women and immigrant women of color that was based on their race, ethnicity, or nationality. Furthermore, feminist approaches have assumed that ethnic minority and immigrant women of color share a stronger bond with European American women than they might with ethnic minority and immigrant men of color (Kanuha, 1994; Mays & Comas-Díaz; Williams et al.).

Feminist theories and conceptual frameworks also have been criticized for their inattention to class. Feminist theories of career development, in particular, have focused on important issues related to women who experience careers, including women's career adjustment, satisfaction, and achievement of career potential (Betz & Fitzgerald, 1987; Fitzgerald & Weitzman, 1992). This focus fails to include women who do not have the necessary resources to experience work as a volitional process of choosing from among a broad range of career options (Blustein, McWhirter, & Perry, 2004; Cook, Heppner, & O'Brien, 2002; Meara, Davis, & Robinson, 1997). For many women, work is not a source of personal meaning or fulfillment; it simply enables them to provide for their families (Heppner & O'Brien, chap. 3, this volume; Richardson, 1993).

Feminist theories and frameworks that do address the intersection of gender, race, and class conceptualize women's oppression as a product of two interacting social systems: patriarchy and capitalism (Boyd, Mulvihill, & Myles, 1995; Glenn, 1991). As a hierarchical system of power, patriarchy enables men to have power over women. Additionally, colonial labor systems characterized by "a segmented labor market, discriminatory barriers, and separate wage scales ensure that people of color are given the worst jobs (i.e., insecure, low-paying, dangerous, dirty, and dead-end)" (Glenn, p. 174). This oppression is even more severe for immigrant women who face the triple jeopardy of oppression based on their gender, class, and nationality, ethnicity, or race (Glenn). The application of these frameworks to therapeutic and career-counseling practice, however, has been slow and inadequately defined (Constantine, 2002).

Even with these criticisms, psychologists and counselors recognize the potential of feminist theory to empower all women and facilitate social change (Brown, 1991, 1994; Enns, 1997; Espín, 1994; Glenn, 1991; Mays & Comas-Díaz, 1988; Worrell & Remer, 1992). More recent developments in feminist theory and therapy modalities address issues of power and oppression related to a broad range of multicultural factors (Sparks & Park, 2000), such as race, gender, sexual orientation, nationality, age, and class. Espín noted that feminist theory reaffirms ethnic minority women's right to control their bodies, validates their anger, and encourages them to utilize anger as a source of strength in the face of oppression. In addition, the identification of social change as a significant part of promoting the well-being of all women is a powerful and inclusive tenet of feminist theory and therapy (Brooks & Forrest, 1994; Brown, 1994; Enns, 1993).

We believe that a feminist approach can therefore provide a career-counseling experience that is empowering for all women. To apply feminist approaches to career counseling with women, however, psychologists and counselors must think critically about the strengths and limitations of feminist principles, particularly when applying them to the experiences of poor women and women of color. Moreover, counselors must increase their critical awareness of their beliefs and values, and how they challenge and maintain the status quo for all women. In the next section, we describe McWhirter's (1994, 2001) and Chronister and McWhirter's (2003) counseling for empowerment model and a critical feminist approach to career counseling with women.

COUNSELING FOR EMPOWERMENT MODEL

McWhirter (1994) defined empowerment as "the process by which people, organizations, or groups who are powerless or marginalized (a) become aware of the power dynamics at work in their life context, (b) develop the skills and capacity for gaining some reasonable control over their lives, (c) which they exercise, (d) without infringing on the rights of others, and (e) which coincides with actively supporting the empowerment of others in their community" (p. 12). Career counseling for the empowerment of women, therefore, includes facilitating awareness and critical reflection of the power dynamics operating in women's lives, enhancing women's abilities to recognize their existing skills and supports, developing additional career-related skills and supports, and enhancing women's ability to gain support and contribute to the empowerment of others (Chronister & McWhirter, 2003).

The empowerment model underscores primary feminist principles and provides a framework by which counselors can systematically examine the influence of individual and larger contextual influences on women's career development. Our use of the term *critical* means that we support a feminist approach to career counseling that acknowledges the strengths and limitations of feminist theories and therapy modalities, and uses an empowerment model to systematically address the multiple and overlapping contexts of women's lives. To better understand the contributions of McWhirter's empowerment model to a critical feminist approach to career counseling with women, we describe the five *C*s of empowerment: collaboration, competence, context, critical consciousness, and community (McWhirter, 1997, 2001).

Collaboration refers to the dynamic relationship between the counselor and client in which both are expected to play an active role. The counseling relationship is characterized by mutual definition of the client's problem(s) and collaborative development of interventions and strategies for change. The power differential is minimized, but not negated.

The second component is *competence*. Competence is crucial to building a collaborative relationship because it refers to recognizing and drawing on the many skills, resources, and experiences that women possess and that may contribute to the achievement of their counseling goals (McWhirter, 1997). Competence also refers to facilitating the development of new skills and refining existing skills in a manner consistent with the client's goals and values.

The third component is *context* and refers to understanding women clients' lives within a dynamic ecology. Elements of that ecology include families, work environments, sociopolitical histories, cultures, educational environments, the socioeconomic conditions within the home, neighborhood, larger community, and the nation, as well as factors such as exposure to role models, and gender-role expectations in the immediate environments in which women are raised. The dynamics of power and privilege are also important elements of the context that influence women's career development and work lives (Cook et al., 2002; Harley, Jolivette, McCormick, & Tice, 2002; Heppner & O'Brien, chap. 3, this volume). Women have experienced oppressive power and privilege such as violence and discrimination based on gender, sexual orientation, nationality, and ethnicity. At the same time, each woman possesses power and privilege that might be related to her membership in a majority group. For example, a woman may have experienced horrifying discrimination and have little power and privilege in many contexts because she is a lesbian, and she may posses some power and privilege because she is college educated and able-bodied. Understanding context is essential to understanding the short- and long-term career goals and needs of women and the sociocultural factors that shape those needs.

The fourth component of counseling for empowerment, *critical consciousness*, is a concept introduced by Latin American scholar Paulo Freire (1970). Drawing on his work and that of Ignacio Martín-Baró (1994), McWhirter (1997, 2001) described critical consciousness as involving the dual processes of power analysis, or identifying how power is manifested and expressed in a woman's life context, and critical self-reflection, which generates awareness of how women can transform those dynamics. Counselors' critical consciousness is crucial to prevent fostering oppressive power dynamics in the counseling relationship (McWhirter, 1994). Counselors increase their critical consciousness by identifying how their values, beliefs, and assumptions influence their career counseling with women (Prilleltensky, 1997; Prilleltensky & Nelson, 2002). Counselors may facilitate their critical consciousness by educating themselves with multicultural literature (American Psychological Association [APA], 2003), cross-cultural experiences, difficult dialogues with peers and different communities, and intense self-exploration. Facilitating critical consciousness requires counselors to take risks, open themselves to different worldviews and change, and hear feedback from others.

The fifth component is *community*. The empowerment process ultimately requires engagement with some form of community, both as a source of support and as a means of contributing to the empowerment of others. Women's communities are individually defined and may consist of other women, members of a support group, or a community defined by ethnicity, religious affiliation, family ties, or another social identity. A supportive and challenging community also is critical in facilitating counselors' critical consciousness.

McWhirter's (1994) empowerment model and five *C*s of empowerment (McWhirter, 1994, 1997) underscore feminist values and principles in significant ways. First, McWhirter's empowerment definition encourages counselors and clients to address power dynamics related to gender, class, race, ability, sexual orientation, and age. Examining such diverse power dynamics captures the complex interrelationships among women's social identities and contexts (Constantine, 2002; Cook et al., 2002; Harley et al., 2002). Considering power dynamics associated with multiple social identities also places issues of diversity at the center of feminist career counseling.

Second, McWhirter's (1994) empowerment model considers the influence of power dynamics across a broad range of contexts in which women live and work. Women of color and poor women, in particular, may conceptualize work as related to a larger network of family and community (Bingham, Ward, & Butler, chap. 7, this volume; Heppner & O'Brien, chap. 3, this volume), which underscores the feminist principle of the importance of relationships in all aspects of women's lives, including their work lives (Forrest & Mikolaitis, 1986). For example, economic dependence is often bidirectional for ethnic minority and immigrant families (Glenn, 1991). A woman contributes financially to her family and community and, in turn, the family and community support the woman's economic needs. For these reasons, work performance and career choice for many women of color cannot be considered separately from their families and communities.

Third, McWhirter (1994) emphasized the feminist principle of utilizing the strengths and resources of women's communities as part of the empowerment process. Many ethnic minority women and immigrant women of color are part of a community to which they are connected in numerous ways: through church, organization of community events, and caring for children (Cook et al., 2002; Glenn, 1991). Career counseling and interventions with women of color, as well as with women who may be members of other minority groups (i.e., women who identify as lesbian or bisexual, women with disabilities), therefore, must address how communities contribute to women's resilience and can facilitate their empowerment. Although significant community and larger cultural barriers that hinder women's career development have been identified (Astin, 1984; Carter & Cook, 1992; Cook et al.), there is limited research on the identification and utilization of community supports for the empowerment of women (Chronister & McWhirter, 2003; Harley et al., 2002; Lent, Brown, & Hackett, 2000).

Finally, McWhirter (1994) explicitly defined empowerment as a process that includes efforts to support and promote the empowerment of others. This aspect of empowerment often occurs later in the process but is nonetheless a critical element distinguishing empowerment from individualistic definitions of betterment. Defining empowerment as a process of individual and community empowerment underscores the notion of career counseling as a process of creating social change and advancing social justice for all (Bingham, 2002; Blustein et al., 2004; Chronister, Wettersten, & Brown, 2004; DeBell, 2002; Gore, Leuwerke, & Krumboltz, 2002; Heppner & Davidson, 2002; Krieshok & Pelsma, 2002; O'Brien, 2001). Because many of the barriers that women face in their career development are rooted in social arrangements that benefit those with privilege (Cook et al., 2002; Harley et al., 2002), we view the responsibilities of career counselors as multifaceted and including social change advocacy. We view career counseling as a political act because the career counselor must decide how and when to address the process of creating social change and advancing justice as part of the career-counseling process. We elaborate on this notion through-out the chapter.

In this chapter we focus on career counseling with ethnic minority women, immigrant women of color, and women from lower socioeconomic backgrounds, for whom career choices often are severely limited. Extant theoretical, practical, and research literature, for the most part, does not bear directly on the concerns of these groups (Constantine, 2002; Cook et al., 2002, Meara et al., 1997). As such, we present two women's stories to il-lustrate using the empowerment framework to apply a critical feminist ap-proach to career counseling with women of color.

RAQUELA'S STORY

Raquela is an 18-year-old Mexican American high school senior who lives in West Phoenix with her younger siblings, mother, and father. For three gen-erations, her family has run a small Mexican restaurant, and Raquela and her siblings have participated in running the business "since we could carry a paper sack." Her five siblings range in age from 4 to 16, and she also has a brother, Amado, who died in a traffic accident several years ago. Her 16-year-old brother, Rafael, lives one block away with Raquela's grandmother and aunt. Rafael does the physical chores for them and he is available to her grandmother when her aunt is working at the restaurant.

Raquela's father, Reynaldo, dropped out of high school to help his fa-ther run the restaurant, but earned his GED by age 21. Her mother, Cristina, completed high school and has worked as a waitress, cook, dish-washer, cashier, accountant, and manager at the restaurant at various times, with her roles and hours varying as a function of restaurant needs and fam-ily demands. Since Amado's death, Cristina has withdrawn from her in-volvement in the restaurant and from the family. She is less warm and re-sponsive to her children. Raquela is worried about her mother, but Cristina insists that she is fine. Over the past 3 years, with her mother less active and available, Raquela has taken on more responsibilities at the restaurant and at home. She seems relatively content with this, especially since her closest girlfriend began working at the restaurant a year ago. Raquela's primary so-cial outlet is through her family and social network at the restaurant. Even the family gatherings that occur every few weeks take place at the restau-rant. The combination of working and socializing has been a constant rhythm of Raquela's life.

Both of Raquela's parents have emphasized the importance of finishing high school. She has obtained good grades throughout her schooling and as a senior has a B+ average. She has never considered dropping out. Her plans beyond high school, however, are not decided. One of the regular customers at the family restaurant is a Latina social worker and family friend. She has been asking Raquela what she plans to do after high school, and although Raquela has been evasive, Reynaldo insists that Raquela will go to night school and get a business degree. After several unsuccessful attempts to get Raquela to talk, the social worker convinced Raquela and her father that Raquela should talk with one of the student counselors at the high school. These counselors (counseling psychology graduate students completing an advanced practicum) know how to pursue a business degree, find scholarships, and test Raquela's abilities, according to the social worker. In the next several paragraphs we describe how Raquela's practicum student counselor might utilize the five Cs of empowerment to provide Raquela with critical feminist career counseling.

Collaboration

One of the challenges in establishing a collaborative counseling relationship may have to do with the manner by which Raquela was referred. That is, she may be following the recommendation of a family friend without any personal interest or investment in the process. If Raquela views the first counseling session as a one-time obligation, the counselor will need to provide her with a realistic perspective of the benefits of counseling in that first meeting. In addition, communicating clearly about Raquela's role as an active participant in the counseling process will be important in establishing a collaborative relationship. The counselor will have to negotiate between reinforcing a passive role (e.g., one-way communication that provides information) and setting Raquela up to feel inadequate or unmotivated to participate (i.e., by asking her to respond to a situation that clearly has norms for behavior, but without providing information about those norms). If the counselor asks a series of open-ended questions such as "What do you want to do with your life?" before Raquela has a sense of what counseling might offer, the experience of the first session may create anxiety and frustration. If the counselor is White, a member of an ethnic group other than Mexican American, or (perceived to be) of a higher social class background even if Mexican American, Raquela may assume that the counselor will not value her family obligations, will not understand or respect her culture, will consider her incapable of higher education, or will deliver a blanket recommendation that she attend a university. A question from Raquela about the counselor's family and the counselor's educational background might be interpreted as that of an informed consumer, but could also be designed to establish that the counselor left his or her family behind and therefore is too dissimilar to be helpful, or to test whether working together is actually a two-way process. The counselor is challenged to establish rapport and engage Raquela in a relationship that is collaborative at the outset. Perhaps the most essential elements for the counselor to communicate (through language and action) are the following: what career counseling typically involves, what resources and information are available, what the process and roles of the counselor and Raquela might look like, possibilities for how career counseling might be useful to Raquela, and the fact that Raquela's values, interests, and goals will be the guiding force of the process rather than the counselor's values or a prescribed set of goals.

Context

Raquela's career counselor has numerous contextual factors and dynamics to consider. The socioeconomic status (SES) of Raquela's family has implications for the real and perceived opportunities of each family member, as well as their worldviews, expectations, and self-concepts (Fouad & Brown, 2000; Heppner & O'Brien, chap. 3, this volume; Liu, 2001; Liu et al., 2004; Liu, Soleck, Hopps, Dunston, & Pickett, 2004). Raquela's views of the nature of work, and the close linkages between work, family, and community, emerge from her family's experience of running a restaurant for three generations. Choices about Raquela's future role relative to the restaurant are inexorably choices about loyalty, fidelity, legacy, and identity. Furthermore, they are choices that have far greater daily and long-term implications for her family members than the career choices of many 18-year-olds. The counselor's respect for these contextual dimensions will be conveyed via phrasing, timing, and nuance. For example, the counselor's response to Raquela's sense of obligation to the family business may convey that it is an obstacle to be overcome, a regrettable source of pressure that is "understandable," or a valuable dimension of her decision-making process.

Another aspect of context is that Latino high school seniors, similar to White seniors, are frequently very poorly informed about post–high school options and the steps required to pursue those options (Immerwahr, 2003). In his report, *With Diploma in Hand: Hispanic High School Seniors Talk About Their Future,* Immerwahr noted that Latino high school seniors who are considering college frequently identified obstacles such as lack of guidance from teachers, lack of information from family, and misinformation about higher education, and they frequently made choices that inadvertently limited their possibilities for college attendance (e.g., curriculum). The counselor should be aware of the career-planning resources within Raquela's school and the extent to which career education has been embedded within the curriculum, while simultaneously being aware that students receive differential treatment from teachers and guidance counselors even when the curriculum is standard. For example, Latino students and students from lower socioeconomic backgrounds often experience differential treatment in the form of lower expectations, less initiation and promotion of discussions about higher education, and less consideration as "college material" (Blustein et al., 2002; Ginorio & Huston, 2001; Immerwahr; Padrón, Waxman, & Rivera, 2002; Sadker & Sadker, 1994). Although Latino parents typically have high educational aspirations for their children (Arbona, 1990; Azmitia, 1994; Clayton, 1992; Griggs, 1992; Immerwahr; Levine & Trickett, 2000), the counselor cannot make assumptions about Reynaldo and Cristina. Reynaldo may actually hope that Raquela will graduate from a university, but believe that she will do better if she starts at community college. Cristina may believe that Raquela should stay home and work so that her younger siblings can pursue higher education.

Critical Consciousness

Exploring power dynamics in Raquela's life could include examination of family and work dynamics, the school context, gender-role socialization, racism, and classism. For example, the counselor might explore with Raquela her attitudes toward and perceptions of people with different levels of education, attending to downward, upward, and lateral classism (Liu, 2001; Liu et al., 2004), as well as how Raquela views her own family. If she has global perceptions that university-educated Latinos look down on their families, for example, the counselor can help her explore and test the validity of those perceptions, and to distinguish between what some Latinos convey versus what she herself can choose to convey. Because Raquela would be a first-generation college student if she pursues that path, a discussion of the variety of experiences, challenges, and assets of first-generation Latino college students may be useful. We note that exploration of gender-role socialization from a critical feminist perspective does not mean that the counselor advocates for a particular arrangement of gender roles. Rather, the counselor would explore Raquela's beliefs and those of her family members, and explore the function and usefulness of those beliefs. In many Latino families, differences in acculturation levels occur by generation, leading to conflict in areas such as gender-role expectations. Raquela may or may not have expectations that differ from those of her parents. Similarly, differences in acculturation may influence Raquela's ability to fully explore her sexual orientation and its relationship to her future job or career options (Bieschke & Toepfer-Hendey, chap. 11, this volume). Internal confusion, intrafamily disruptions, or the potential loss of family and friends' support created by Raquela's coming out might disrupt or delay her ability to explore her work and career options (Boatwright, Gilbert, Forrest, & Ketzenberger, 1996; Fassinger, 1995). Critical consciousness of the larger economic consequences of Raquela's decision making also seems important. Although the short-term family benefits of working at the restaurant may be evident, the long-term consequences relative to other vocational and educational options also should be examined. Potential for employment with benefits, earning potential of various degrees, and other dimensions are important considerations for Raquela given her family commitment.

Another important area to explore is the effects of Amado's death on the family, particularly on Cristina and Raquela, and how this has influenced Raquela's experience of the restaurant, the availability of support, and the roles and tasks that Raquela has assumed. She may make attributions that are inaccurate. For example, she may associate her mother's withdrawal with the difficulty of running the restaurant rather than Amado's death. Of course the counselor does not know "the truth" about these dynamics, but might encourage Raquela to explore them if it appears that Raquela is making important decisions based on her attributions.

Raquela was evasive with the social worker when asked about her postsecondary goals. We offer here a number of possibilities that might underlie her reticence, as a means of highlighting the need for critical consciousness: (a) Raquela does not want to go to business school but does not want to disappoint her father, (b) Raquela is unsure of what she wants to do, but trusts her father's plan, (c) Raquela has a well-developed plan for her future that she has not yet brought to her father's attention, and she does not want to discuss it publicly until she has spoken with him about it, (d) Raquela has fallen in love, and all of her future thinking is focused on this relationship and how to tell her parents, whom she fears will not approve of the relationship, (e) Raquela is deeply conflicted about what to do because her value system is in conflict with her interests—she actually wants to be a social worker, but doing so would leave her family in a difficult situation with respect to the restaurant, and she is not sure she wants to give up the identity, role security, and socialization benefits of working at the restaurant, or (f) Raquela wants to get a business degree and work in the restaurant, but at the same time, she does not want to bring her children up in a restaurant even though she views her own childhood as very positive.

Further examination of any of these possible explanations (or countless others) will be beneficial, and critical self-reflection will assist Raquela in exploring her options for maintaining or transforming the dynamics around her. The counselor must invite her out of silence and discover Raquela's hopes, goals, and ambitions to be sure that they are represented in the decision-making process (Iglesias & Cormier, 2002). We have not identified particular dynamics that would lead us to characterize Raquela as oppressed. At the same time, the juxtaposition of her lower SES with being a young woman, and a young woman of color, places her at risk in a society that is permeated with the dynamics of racism, sexism, and classism. It is beyond question that her life is affected by these social forces (Constantine, 2002; Harley et al., 2002). The extent to which she perceives, ignores, yields to, resists, or otherwise incorporates them into her ambitions needs illumination (Iglesias & Cormier). This illumination process also requires counselors to be critically aware of their beliefs about Raquela and her family and their values for specific educational and occupational pursuits, individual and collective decisions, and expectations of Raquela as a "good" client. The importance of a collaborative relationship is essential. Raising critical questions and unconsidered possibilities can easily be experienced as judgments or criticisms, and instead of liberating may constrict options.

Competence

Raquela is an 18-year-old woman with a great deal of work and life experience. An important dimension of counseling will be investigating Raquela's awareness and evaluation of her skills and resources, and increasing the realism of those perceptions if needed. It may be that Raquela minimizes her skills and experiences because "anybody could do that" or "that's not a skill, it's just something I know how to do." Raquela may not be aware, for example, that her ability to assume responsibility for complex household-management and restaurant tasks is a valuable worker asset, and one that would also serve her well in higher education settings. She may employ a wide variety of what Iglesias and Cormier (2002) referred to as "resistance strategies" that counter the effects of sexism, racism, and classism in her life. Enhancing her recognition of her skills, however, may violate her values around humility or noncompetition with family members who work beside her. The process of accessing and incorporating Raquela's competencies into the counseling process, and into exploring her future options, will be hampered if the counselor is not sensitive to these possibilities.

Some of the skills and resources that Raquela is likely to possess and that warrant exploration include: a positive attitude about hard work, her understanding of the complexity of running a business, her understanding of the relationship between the local economy and the family business (e.g., unemployment rates, cost of health insurance, recession, availability of workers, food regulations, number of customers, and profits), interpersonal skills, numeric and literacy skills, bilingualism, academic aptitude, family support, a broader support network in the customer community, money management, and multiple-role management (negotiating rapid switching between her many roles: daughter, worker, student, niece, big sister, etc.). Raquela may need to develop skills in gathering vocational and educational information beyond that obtained through her personal networks. Another potential area for skill development is linking her existing skills with settings, that is, understanding the relationships between the skills she exercises in her daily life and those demanded in settings such as business school.

Community

Raquela has a rich community network. The community component of empowerment pertains to helping clients identify and connect with or enhance their involvement in communities. In community, clients can find a source of identity, strength, hope, history, resources and opportunities, support and challenge, interaction, and contribution. Raquela's community includes her extended family network, coworkers at the restaurant, the circle of neighbors and friends who frequent the restaurant, and her peer group at school. Raquela may or may not experience her school context as a community. The counselor should explore whether Raquela participates in or identifies with a particular faith-based community, as this also may be a resource. Within her various communities, Raquela clearly is already receiving and providing support, role modeling, and assistance. Her family and the restaurant community provide a strong sense of family identity. The closeness of her extended family provides opportunities to know her Mexican American culture and history from varying political, social, and values perspectives. Her ethnic, family, and work identities are intertwined and mutually support each other.

Casting this network of relationships in community terminology should not be interpreted as an assumption of perfect harmony and absence of conflict. Within every community, there will be the uncle or aunt who drinks or the cousin with a mental illness. In Raquela's family we have some evidence that her mother is depressed, and there may be conflicts of turf, status, methodology, and personality manifested within the restaurant. All communities have conflicts. Our point is that Raquela has a rich community, and therefore, in this domain, the counselor may focus on enriching the resources of the community itself. For example, there may be a lack of information about career and educational planning and opportunities across Raquela's communities. The counselor may share with Reynaldo and Cristina the report "College Knowledge: What Latino Parents Need to Know and Why They Don't Know It" (Tornatzky, Cutler, & Lee, 2002), which has the potential to benefit Raquela and her siblings, cousins, and other family members. If Raquela decides to pursue higher education, she also may benefit from developing additional community support with people who have experience with and knowledge of higher education settings and negotiating those settings as a first-generation and ethnic minority student. Given Raquela's relationship with her parents and the cultural and social contexts of her life, as well as the importance of parent support in the vocational pursuits of all young people, inclusion of Raquela's parents in various aspects of the career-counseling process seems optimal.

TERESA'S STORY

Teresa is a 26-year-old Filipino woman who immigrated to the United States 5 years ago after she married Clark, an American citizen and military serviceman stationed in the Philippines. Shortly after getting married in the Catholic church in which she grew up, Teresa returned with Clark to the United States. Initially, Teresa was excited about earning more money in the United States and sending some back to her family. She also was excited about expanded opportunities (e.g., community colleges, financial aid options) to pursue an accounting career. When they arrived in the United States, Clark and Teresa lived in a modest one-bedroom apartment and Clark worked at his brother's large appliance store. Teresa did not seek employment because Clark expressed a desire to have children immediately. Ten months after arriving in the United States, Teresa gave birth to their son, Clark Jr. Teresa was filled with joy, but she also felt sad and lonely. She cried most nights because she felt guilty for leaving her family and for preventing them from seeing their grandson. Teresa also longed for the familiarity and comforts of home and to have her mother by her side. Teresa felt especially cramped in the apartment because she did not know how to drive, and although she spoke English, she did not feel confident initiating many conversations with Americans other than Clark and her neighbors, Jim and Ethel.

During the next 3 years, Clark and Teresa argued more often and more intensely. Clark did not seem to understand Teresa's sad moods and sometimes shouted, "Snap out of it and grow up! I'm your family now. Don't I make you happy?" Teresa felt confused and guilty for not adjusting better to her life in the United States. She tried harder to hide her sad feelings and to appear happy. One day, Clark returned from work and announced to Teresa that he was leaving her for another woman. He told Teresa that she was not fun and did not devote enough time to him anymore. Clark packed his things, leaving Teresa with enough money for food, and left to live with his girlfriend. He kept an apartment key so that he could visit Clark Jr. when he wanted.

Teresa became very depressed and spent more of her time isolated in her apartment. She was afraid to tell her family what happened because she felt ashamed and confused about Clark not wanting to be with her. She also did not want to worry her mother. Teresa was frightened about her future and Clark Jr.'s future, and she understood that she needed to get a job that provided for them both. During this difficult time, Teresa grew close with her neighbors, Jim and Ethel, who reminded Teresa of her parents. Jim and Ethel encouraged Teresa to see a counselor at the free counseling clinic downtown, but she refused. Instead, Teresa asked her priest for help. The priest gave Teresa enough money to pay rent that month and asked two parishioners to drive Teresa to the state employment agency office. With much encouragement from her priest, Teresa also agreed to visit with a counselor (who was an advanced counseling psychology doctoral student completing a year-long practicum) at least one time. In the following sections, we use the five *C*s of empowerment to illustrate a critical feminist approach to career counseling with Teresa.

Collaboration

Toward the development of a collaborative relationship, the counselor must acknowledge and address Teresa's fears and expectations about counseling. Teresa has expressed hesitation about visiting with a counselor and indicated her preference for turning to her priest and church for help. Teresa may fear that the counselor is going to blame her for her current difficulties, fail to understand her cultural and spiritual beliefs and attitudes about her situation, share what she says in session with her husband, take away her son, or create difficulties with immigration services by interfering with her U.S. citizenship application. Teresa also may fear that she will not be able to communicate effectively in English and that the counselor will negatively judge her based on her English skills (i.e., less intelligent, less competent). A critical point for the counselor is to acknowledge and accept Teresa's fears to build a relationship that allows her to voice her feelings, experiences, and goals.

A collaborative and egalitarian relationship is also characterized by flexibility. Early in the therapeutic relationship, the counselor may focus too narrowly on Teresa's emotional well-being and fail to address her immediate economic needs (e.g., finding a job, paying for day care, food, and rent) or the opposite (i.e., focusing exclusively on Teresa's immediate financial and day-care needs without acknowledging her feelings of loss, fear, and depression). Without a trusting relationship, a counselor's narrow and inflexible focus on Teresa's self-esteem, family of origin, or marriage may elicit feelings of shame, guilt, and distrust of the counselor. The counselor is challenged to acknowledge and discuss Teresa's emotional well-being as well as attend to her more immediate and financial needs. The counselor may create such a balance by helping Teresa identify charities, businesses, and social service agencies that can help her secure employment and pay for food, rent, day care, and utilities for the next month.

Counselors also must expand clients' future planning in times of crisis and immediate need. To expand clients' future planning requires counselors to carefully assess clients' emotional and cognitive states as well as provide consistent attention to clients' future decisions, and the possible consequences of those decisions. Teresa may not be thinking in detail about longer term goals, needs, and consequences because she is scared, stressed, and overwhelmed with recent life changes. She needs money and she may be focused only on getting a job that is immediately available, which typically includes job positions that are temporary, low paying, or exclude health benefits (Chronister & McWhirter, 2003; Heppner & O'Brien, chap. 3, this volume). Such work may not allow Teresa to support herself and her son in the long term, or provide her with a work environment that contributes to her emotional, mental, and physical well-being. Additionally, Teresa may no longer be considering her educational and career pursuits in accounting as viable opportunities. The counselor may dialogue with Teresa over time about longer term career goals and planning by identifying career and educational interests and opportunities that match Teresa's potential and provide longer term career satisfaction. The counselor may work with Teresa to create a plan for how she can pursue these longer term goals when she is ready and able. This plan might include identifying government financial assistance and vocational training opportunities, meeting with college career counselors, or conducting informational interviews with community professionals. Teresa and the counselor also may discuss the influence of larger contextual issues such as whether Teresa wants to stay in the United States and obtain citizenship, what her expectations and hopes are for her marriage, and how child custody arrangements might be made.

Context

Understanding the multiple sociocultural and ecological factors exerting influence on clients' lives is critical to accurately understanding their emotional, physical, mental, economic, career, and spiritual needs. Important contextual influences include culture, family structure (e.g., children in the home), religious or spiritual beliefs, economic situation, support networks, and characteristics of the surrounding community, such as demographic makeup, political climate, and educational resources (Chronister & McWhirter, 2004). We find Bronfenbrenner's (1979) ecological model, in particular, to be a useful framework for examining the influence of multiple sociocultural contexts.

Considering the influence of Teresa's ethnic and national identities is important. The counselor may clarify Teresa's feelings about living in the United States and gather information about her experiences as an immigrant and immigrant woman of color (Yakushko, chap. 12, this volume). Direct questioning of Teresa's immigration status and experiences may help build trust between the counselor and client, and at the same time, Teresa may perceive direct questioning as threatening and fear that the counselor is seeking information that will later be used against her. The critical consciousness of the counselor allows the counselor to observe and assess Teresa's response to the therapeutic process, and make adjustments accordingly.

Teresa's ethnic and national identities also may have changed due to acculturation processes and she may identify significant resources and stressors resulting from her biculturalism (Falicov, 1998). It is possible that Teresa's experiences in the United States have resulted in internalized racism toward Filipino or other ethnic minority cultures, and have fostered negative feelings toward her home country, culture, family, and self. Teresa's identity as an immigrant woman of color may have decreased her self-efficacy and outcome expectations for achieving her career goals. These expectations may further be reinforced because Teresa has seen few immigrant role models who have come to the United States and achieved their career goals and she has seen negative attitudes expressed toward immigrants living in the United States. The fact that the Philippines is a country that was colonized by the United States may influence Teresa's response to living here. Teresa's perceptions and experiences of racism and U.S. culture may be positively or negatively influenced by her experiences with Americans in the Philippines, her understanding of the stories that her parents and grandparents shared about American colonization, and the information she learned in school about the United States. For example, Teresa may feel more comfortable with an American identity and feel more familiar with certain aspects of American culture so that she does not perceive or experience much racism.

The counselor also should explore how ethnic cultural, religious, and family (Clark, Clark Jr., parents, extended family) values and expectations influence Teresa's perceptions of contextual barriers and supports and conceptualizations of gender roles, parenting, and the meaning of work. Many of Teresa's values and beliefs may have changed since living in America and it is important to explore why and how these beliefs have changed (Yakushko, chap. 12, this volume). For example, Teresa may consider it selfish or indulgent to take time to further her education or vocational training at this time because she may have to reduce her work hours and will make less money to send back to her parents. We encourage the counselor to help Teresa identify and weigh the short- and long-term consequences of her decisions. A counselor may validate and communicate respect for Teresa's concerns and priorities, and at the same time clarify that going back to school or receiving additional vocational training may take away money from her family in the short term, but also may better provide for them financially in the long term. The counselor and Teresa may engage in a dialogue of all of her options, that is, Teresa may not have to choose whether to further her education, but rather to make an informed decision about when she will return to school.

A final component of attending to context is the counselor's knowledge of the current political climate and available government and community resources, including a general understanding of immigration laws and information about immigration resources, emergency state funds for single parents and immigrant women, and mental health, financial, and community resources that may provide Teresa with short- and long-term support. Past and present relationships between the United States and the Philippines as well as the current feelings of Americans toward immigrants are important contextual factors to consider. Depending on current U.S. policy and American culture, Americans may react with hostility toward immigrants who are "stealing" American jobs and overloading educational and social service systems (Brettell, 2002; Foner, 2002; Law, 2002; Yakushko, chap. 12, this volume). Such political factors may significantly influence Teresa's access to essential resources.

Community

Since leaving her home country, Teresa has expressed feeling lonely and isolated. Part of the empowerment process and a key component of a feminist approach to career counseling is building women's communities. Teresa and her counselor may work collaboratively to identify communities that will provide Teresa with a greater sense of support and connection. Teresa may be interested in connecting with other Filipino Americans or immigrants, becoming more intimately involved in her church, or meeting other women who are part of a career-counseling or parenting group. A counselor also may facilitate Teresa's community connections to professionals and role models in different educational and occupational settings. These connections will give Teresa the opportunity to build supportive relationships, observe role models, learn more about different career options, and receive feedback on her abilities. Furthermore, the counselor and Teresa may work together to utilize the strengths of Teresa's community. The counselor may encourage Teresa to recognize and use the supportive relationships that she has with Jim and Ethel and with church parishioners. Jim and Ethel may be able to provide Teresa with transportation and church parishioners may be able to provide Teresa with information about employment opportunities and quality day-care services. Community can be a significant source of strength and validation that furthers the principles of increasing consciousness, woman valuing, and self-validation (Chronister & McWhirter, 2003; Worell & Remer, 1992; Yakushko, chap. 12, this volume).

Competence

A feminist approach to career counseling includes facilitating Teresa's ability to recognize her competencies and value herself. The counselor must carefully assess Teresa's career-related self-efficacy, skills, and achievements because she may not be able, or willing, to identify her skills and achievements when asked directly. A counselor may help Teresa recognize her skills by dialoguing with her about her lived experiences. Through Teresa's stories, the counselor may identify Teresa's secretarial and family budgeting skills, her accomplishments related to attaining professional secretarial certification in the Philippines, learning to play the piano, raising her son, caring for the elderly (e.g., her parents, Jim and Ethel), and keeping donation records for her parish. Teresa may not recognize these skills and accomplishments because she feels so much shame related to Clark's abandonment, or it may be that her self-efficacy has decreased significantly over time because of difficulties related to immigration and adjustment experiences. Thus, it may be important to identify similarities and differences in Teresa's career-related self-efficacy when she lived in the Philippines and since living in the United States. This dialogue may help increase Teresa's critical consciousness of the influences on her career-related self-efficacy as well as how her self-efficacy has changed over time due to her immigration experience. Additionally, Teresa's counselor must be careful not to assume that a successful therapeutic outcome would be for Teresa to speak openly and comfortably about her skills and accomplishments. Teresa's hesitancy to speak about her skills may not be because she does not recognize them, but because speaking openly about herself is incongruent with her value for humility. An alternative outcome may be whether Teresa identifies and utilizes her skills to advance toward her life goals and manage challenging life situations.

Equally importantly, the counselor needs to facilitate Teresa's development and utilization of new skills, which is intimately linked with being connected to supportive communities. For example, Teresa may ask Jim and Ethel to help her learn to drive, teach her how to use the public transportation system, assist with completing citizenship and job-related paperwork, or practicing her interview skills. The counselor and Teresa also may focus their initial work on completing job applications, role playing job interviews, and practicing Teresa's English so that she feels more confident speaking. Teresa also may want to enroll in postsecondary and vocational training courses or English classes. The counselor's role is to help Teresa identify strategies for minimizing emotional and physical stress (e.g., relaxation techniques, communication skills) so that her job-search experiences are manageable, and even serve to increase her self-efficacy.

Critical Consciousness

Facilitating Teresa's critical consciousness of the difficulties associated with immigration and adjustment to a new country and culture is important. Stressors related to migration may include grief and loss, posttraumatic stress, culture shock, uprootedness, loneliness, decline in self-esteem, strain and fatigue from cognitive overload, and perceptions that one cannot function competently in the new culture (Espín, 1997, 1999; Garza-Guerrero, 1974; Rumbaut, 1991; Yakushko, chap. 12, this volume). Providing Teresa with information about the range of immigrants' experiences of migration and acculturation may be validating and help reduce her feelings of guilt and blame for her husband leaving. The counselor also may want to gather information about the circumstances under which Teresa came to the United States. For example, did she and Clark decide together that they would live here, did Teresa feel forced to come, or did Teresa see the move as full of opportunities and have few reservations about immigrating? These initial conditions and power dynamics are important to discuss as they may affect Teresa's future decisions about living in the United States. The counselor also might dialogue with Teresa about how living in the United States may or may not have impacted her ethnic, racial, and national identities, and in turn, how changes in these identities may have impacted her relationships and experiences here, including her roles with her husband and son (Serdarevic & Chronister, 2005). For example, many immigrant women experience significant pressure to keep their families together and take care of their families' emotional and physical well-being after transitioning to a new country (Espín, 1999; Narayan, 1997; Simons, 1999; Yakushko), often resulting in the neglect of women's needs. Moreover, the counselor and Teresa may dialogue about her gender-role and marriage ideals and expectations as well as what female role models she has observed throughout her lifetime. It is important to distinguish between what kind of woman Teresa believes that she should be and what she wants to be. These distinctions increase Teresa's critical consciousness of the contextual influences affecting her identity development and interpersonal relationships, and consequently, Teresa will be better able to make life decisions that are congruent with her aspirations.

Teresa's Catholic values also may influence her beliefs about her relationship with her husband and their marriage. Specifically, Teresa may not believe in separation or divorce, and as a result, she may feel spiritually disheartened and her primary goal may be to work on her marriage. Teresa also may feel great shame because her husband left and her family's reputation has been tarnished. The counselor may clarify Teresa's hopes and expectations for her marriage as well as facilitate Teresa's critical thinking about how her expectations and beliefs have been influenced by larger sociocultural factors, including Filipino and American cultures, gender-role expectations, and religious values. Moreover, the counselor should discuss with Teresa how differences in Clark's and her nationalities, genders, and ethnic identities may have impacted their marriage, such as distribution of power and control to make decisions related to intimacy, finances, work, and parenting.

Some counselors may find it difficult to support Teresa's goal of trying to make her marriage work. Pursuit of this option may not seem to support Teresa's autonomy and empowerment. Part of the critical-consciousness process and a critical feminist approach to career counseling, however, involves counselors thinking critically about their own cultural and racial ethnic background, areas of privilege and power, and how these factors influence their definitions of feminism, empowerment, autonomy, and strength. A critical feminist approach to career counseling involves facilitating Teresa's valuing of herself so that she is able to make decisions that are congruent with her multiple cultural identities (e.g., ethnicity, gender, class, sexual orientation) and advance her empowerment, as she defines it.

CONCLUSION

A critical feminist approach to career counseling with Raquela and Teresa meets them in the context of their lives; provides and elicits information, ideas, possibilities, and strategies; explores options and consequences; and affirms both women's active roles in constructing their future within the values, goals, and relationships that they identify as important. A critical feminist approach raises questions about assumptions and practices, acknowledges the values and assumptions that guide the questions, and refrains from imposing those values and assumptions on the client. How does this approach differ from good career counseling? It does not. We are not advocating a radical new approach, and in fact there is nothing new about what we are recommending. Rather, we offer a critical feminist conceptualization of career counseling that highlights certain processes and dynamics within a heuristic that we hope is useful for guiding the career-counseling process with women.

REFERENCES

American Psychological Association. (2003). Guidelines on multicultural education, training, research, practice, and organizational change for psychologists. *American Psychologist, 58*, 377–402.

Anzaldúa, G. (Ed.). (1990). *Making face, making soul, haciendo caras: Creative and critical perspectives by feminists of color.* San Francisco: Aunt Lute Books.

Arbona, C. (1990). Career counseling research and Hispanics: A review of the literature. *The Counseling Psychologist, 18,* 300–323.

Astin, H. S. (1984). The meaning of work in women's lives: A sociopsychological model of career choice and work behavior. *The Counseling Psychologist, 12,* 117–126.

Azmitia, M. (1994). *Links between home and school among low-income Mexican-American and European-American families.* Santa Cruz, CA: National Center for Research on Cultural Diversity and Second Language Learning. (ERIC Document Reproduction Service No. ED370757)

Betz, N. E., & Fitzgerald, L. (1987). *The career psychology of women.* Orlando, FL: Academic Press.

Bingham, R. P. (2002). The issue may be the integration of personal and career issues. *The Counseling Psychologist, 30,* 885–890.

Blustein, D. L., Chaves, A. P., Diemer, M. A., Gallagher, L. A., Marshall, K. G., Sirin, S., et al. (2002). Voices of the forgotten half: The role of social class in the school-to-work transition. *Journal of Counseling Psychology, 49,* 311–323.

Blustein, D. L., McWhirter, E. H., & Perry, J. C. (2005). An emancipatory communitarian approach to vocational development theory, research, and practice. *The Counseling Psychologist, 33*(2), 141–179.

Boatwright, K. J., Gilbert, M. S., Forrest, L., & Ketzenberger, K. (1996). Impact of identity development on career trajectory: Listening to the voices of lesbian women. *Journal of Vocational Behavior, 48,* 210–228.

Boyd, M., Mulvihill, M. A., & Myles, J. (1995). Gender, power, and post-industrialism. In J. A. Jacobs (Ed.), *Gender inequality* (pp. 178–206). Thousand Oaks, CA: Sage.

Brettell, C. B. (2002). From Ellis Island to JFK: Comparison in anthropology and history. *Journal of American Ethnic History, 21,* 68–73.

Bronfenbrenner, U. (1979). *The ecology of human development.* Cambridge, MA: Harvard University Press.

Brooks, L., & Forrest, L. (1994). Feminism and career counseling. In B. Walsh & S. Osipow (Eds.), *Career counseling for women* (pp. 87–143). Hillsdale, NJ: Lawrence Erlbaum Associates.

Broverman, I. K., Broverman, D. M., Clarkson, F., Rosenkrantz, P., & Vogel, S. (1970). Sex role stereotyping and clinical judgments of mental health. *Journal of Consulting and Clinical Psychology, 45,* 250–256.

Brown, L. S. (1991). Antiracism as an ethical imperative: An example from feminist therapy. *Ethics and Behavior, 1,* 113–127.

Brown, L. S. (1992). While waiting for the revolution: The case for a lesbian feminist psychotherapy. *Feminism and Psychology, 2,* 239–253.

Brown, L. S. (1994). *Subversive dialogues: Theory in feminist therapy.* New York: Basic Books.

Carter, R. T., & Cook, D. A. (1992). A culturally relevant perspective for understanding the career paths of visible racial/ethnic group people. In H. D. Lea & Z. B. Leibowitz (Eds.), *Adult career development: Concepts, issues, and practices* (2nd ed., pp. 192–217). Alexandria, VA: National Career Development Association.

Chesler, P. (1972). *Women and madness.* New York: Doubleday.

Chronister, K. M., & McWhirter, E. H. (2003). Women, domestic violence, and career counseling: An application of social cognitive career theory. *Journal of Counseling and Development, 81,* 418–425.

Chronister, K. M., & McWhirter, E. H. (2004). Ethnic differences in career supports and barriers for battered women: A pilot study. *Journal of Career Assessment, 12,* 169–187.

Chronister, K. M., Wettersten, K., & Brown, C. (2004). Vocational psychology research for the liberation of battered women. *The Counseling Psychologist, 32*(6), 900–922.

Clayton, K. K. (1992). *The role of family in the educational decisions of Mexican Americans.* Berkeley, CA: National Center for Research in Vocational Education. (ERIC Document Reproduction Service No. ED357270)

Constantine, M. (2002). The intersection of race, ethnicity, gender, and social class in counseling: Examining selves in cultural contexts. *Journal of Multicultural Counseling and Development, 30,* 210–215.

Cook, E. P., Heppner, M. J., & O'Brien, K. M. (2002). Career development of women of color and white women: Assumptions, conceptualization, and interventions from an ecological perspective. *Career Development Quarterly, 50,* 291–305.

Cox, S. (Ed.). (1976). *Female psychology: The emerging self.* Chicago: Science Research Associates.

DeBell, C. (2002). Practice for a paradigm shift: A complete model for an integrative course. *The Counseling Psychologist, 30,* 858–877.

Enns, C. Z. (1993). Twenty years of feminist counseling and therapy: From naming biases to implementing multifaceted practice. *The Counseling Psychologist, 21,* 3–87.

Enns, C. Z. (1997). *Feminist theories and feminist psychotherapies: Origins, themes, and variations.* New York: Haworth Press.

Enns, C. Z., & Forrest, L. (2005). Toward defining and integration multicultural and feminist pedagogies. In C. Z. Enns & A. Sinacore (Eds.), *Teaching and social justice: Integrating multicultural and feminist theories in the classroom.* Washington, DC: American Psychological Association.

Espín, O. M. (1994). Feminist approaches. In L. Comas-Díaz & B. Greene (Eds.), *Women of color: Integrating ethnic and gender identities in psychotherapy* (pp. 265–286). New York: Guilford Press.

Espín, O. M. (1997). *Latina realities: Essays on healing, migration, and sexuality.* Boulder, CO: Westview Press.

Espín, O. M. (1999). *Women crossing boundaries: A psychology of immigration and transformation of sexuality.* New York: Routledge.

Falicov, C. J. (1998). *Latino families in therapy: A guide to a multicultural practice.* New York: Guilford Press.

Fassinger, R. E. (1995). From invisibility to integration: Lesbian identity in the workplace. *Career Development Quarterly, 44,* 148–167.

Fitzgerald, L. F., & Harmon, L. W. (Eds.). (1973). Counseling women [Special issue]. *The Counseling Psychologist, 4*(1).

Fitzgerald, L. F., & Weitzman, L. M. (1992). Women's career development: Theory and practice from a feminist perspective. In H. D. Lea & Z. B. Leibowitz (Eds.), *Adult career development: Concepts, issues, and practices* (2nd ed., pp. 124–160). Alexandria, VA: National Career Development Association.

Foner, N. (2002). Response. *Journal of American Ethnic History, 21,* 102–119.

Forrest, L., & Mikolaitis, N. (1986). The relational component of identity: An expansion of career development theory. *Career Development Quarterly, 35,* 76–88.

Fouad, N. A., & Brown, M. T. (2000). The role of race and class in development: Implications for counseling psychology. In S. D. Brown & R. W. Lent (Eds.), *Handbook of counseling psychology* (3rd ed., pp. 379–408). New York: Wiley.

Franks, V., & Burtle, V. (Eds.). (1974). *Women in therapy.* New York: Brunner/Mazel.

Freire, P. (1970). *Pedagogy of the oppressed.* New York: Continuum.

Garza-Guerrero, A. C. (1974). Culture shock: Its mourning and the vicissitudes of identity. *Journal of the American Psychoanalytic Association, 22,* 408–429.

Gilbert, L. A., & Scher, M. (1999). *Gender and sex in counseling and psychotherapy.* Boston: Allyn & Bacon.

Ginorio, A., & Huston, M. (2001). *¡Sí se Puede! Yes, We Can!: Latinas in school.* Washington, DC: American Association of University Women Educational Foundation.

Glenn, E. N. (1991). Racial ethnic women's labor: The intersection of race, gender, and class oppression. In R. L. Blumberg (Ed.), *Gender, family, and economy: The triple overlap* (pp. 173–200). London: Sage.

Gore, P. A., Leuwerke, W. C., & Krumboltz, J. D. (2002). Technologically enriched and boundaryless lives: Time for a paradigm upgrade. *The Counseling Psychologist, 30*, 847–857.

Greenspan, M. (1983). *A new approach to women and therapy: How psychotherapy fails women and what they can do about it.* Blue Ridge Summit, PA: Tab Books.

Griggs, M. B. (1992). *Factors that influence the academic and vocational development of African American and Latino youth.* Berkeley, CA: National Center for Research in Vocational Education. (ERIC Document Reproduction Service No. ED351566)

Harley, D., Jolivette, K., McCormick, K., & Tice, K. (2002). Race, class, and gender: A constellation of *positionalities* with implications for counseling. *Journal of Multicultural Counseling and Development, 30*, 216–238.

Heppner, M. J., & Davidson, M. M. (2002). Be careful what we wish for: The integration of career psychology. *The Counseling Psychologist, 30*, 878–884.

Hill, C. E., Birk, J. M., Blimline, C. A., Leonard, M. M., Hoffman, M. A., & Tanney, M. F. (Eds.). (1979). Counseling women III [Special issue]. *The Counseling Psychologist, 8*(1).

Iglesias, E., & Cormier, S. (2002). The transformation of girls to women: Finding voice and developing strategies for liberation. *Journal of Multicultural Counseling and Development, 30*, 259–271.

Immerwahr, J. (2003). *With diploma in hand: Hispanic high school seniors talk about their future* (Report No. 03-2). San Jose, CA: National Center for Public Policy and Higher Education Public Agenda.

Kanuha, V. (1994). Women of color in battering relationships. In L. G. Comas-Diaz & B. Greene (Eds.), *Women of color: Integrating ethnic and gender identities in psychotherapy* (pp. 428–454). New York: Guilford Press.

Krieshok, T. S., & Pelsma, D. M. (2002). The soul of work: Using case studies in the teaching of vocational psychology. *The Counseling Psychologist, 30*, 833–846.

Law, A. O. (2002). The diversity visa lottery: A cycle of unintended consequences in United States immigration policy. *Journal of American Ethnic History, 21*, 3–27.

Lent, R. W., Brown, S. D., & Hackett, G. (2000). Contextual supports and barriers to career choice: A social cognitive analysis. *Journal of Counseling Psychology, 47*, 36–49.

Levine, E. B., & Trickett, E. J. (2000). Toward a model of Latino parent advocacy for educational change. *Journal of Prevention and Intervention in the Community, 20*, 121–137.

Liu, W. M. (2001). Expanding our understanding of multiculturalism: Developing a social class worldview model. In D. B. Pope-Davis & H. L. K. Coleman (Eds.), *The intersection of race, class, and gender in counseling psychology* (pp. 127–170). Thousand Oaks, CA: Sage.

Liu, W. M., Ali, S. R., Soleck, G., Hopps, J., Dunston, K., & Pickett, T. (2004). Using social class in counseling psychology research. *Journal of Counseling Psychology, 51*, 3–18.

Liu, W., Soleck, G., Hopps, J., Dunston, K., & Pickett, T. (2004). A new framework to understand social class in counseling: The social class worldview model and modern classism theory. *Journal of Multicultural Counseling and Development, 32*(2), 95–122.

Martín-Baró, I. (1994). *Writings for a liberation psychology.* Cambridge, MA: Harvard University Press.

Mays, V. M., & Comas-Díaz, L. (1988). Feminist therapy with ethnic minority populations: A closer look at Blacks and Hispanics. In M. A. Dutton-Douglas & L. E. A. Walker (Eds.), *Feminist psychotherapies: Integration of therapeutic and feminist systems* (pp. 228–251). Norwood, NJ: Ablex.

McWhirter, E. H. (1994). *Counseling for empowerment.* Alexandria, VA: American Counseling Association Press.

McWhirter, E. H. (1997). Empowerment, social activism, and counseling. *Counseling and Human Development, 29*, 1–11.

McWhirter, E. H. (2001, March). *Social action at the individual level: In pursuit of critical conscious-ness.* Paper presented at the 5th biennial conference of the Society for Vocational Psychol-ogy, Houston, TX.

Meara, N. M., Davis, K. L., & Robinson, B. S. (1997). The working lives of women from lower socioeconomic backgrounds: Assessing prospects, enabling success. *Journal of Career Assess-ment, 5,* 115–135.

Miller, J. B. (1976). *Toward a new psychology of women.* Boston, MA: Beacon Press.

Millet, K. (1969). *Sexual politics.* New York: Avon Books.

Narayan, U. (1997). *Dislocating cultures: Identities, traditions, and Third World feminism.* New York: Routledge.

O'Brien, K. M. (2001). The legacy of Parsons: Career counselors and vocational psychologists as agents of social change. *Career Development Quarterly, 50,* 66–76.

Padrón, Y. N., Waxman, H. C., & Rivera, H. H. (2002). *Educating Hispanic students: Obstacles and avenues to improved academic achievement* (Educational Practice Report No. 8). Santa Cruz, CA: Center for Research on Education, Diversity, and Excellence.

Prilleltensky, I. (1997). Values, assumptions, and practices: Assessing the moral implications of psychological discourse and action. *American Psychologist, 52,* 517–535.

Prilleltensky, I., & Nelson, G. (2002). *Doing psychology critically: Making a difference in diverse set-tings.* New York: Palgrave Macmillan.

Rawlings, E. I., & Carter, D. K. (Eds.). (1977). *Psychotherapy for women.* Springfield, IL: Thomas.

Richardson, M. S. (1993). Work in people's lives: A location for counseling psychologists. *Jour-nal of Counseling Psychology, 40,* 425–433.

Rumbaut, R. G. (1991). The agony of exile: A study of the migration and adaptation of Indochinese refugee adults and children. In F. L. Ahearn & J. L. Athey (Eds.), *Refugee chil-dren: Theory, research, and services* (pp. 53–91). Baltimore: Johns Hopkins University Press.

Sadker, M., & Sadker, D. (1994). *Failing at fairness: How America's schools cheat girls.* New York: Scribner's.

Serdarevic, M., & Chronister, K. M. (2005). Research with immigrant populations: The appli-cation of an ecological framework to mental health research with immigrant populations. *The International Journal of Mental Health Promotion, 7*(2), 24–34.

Simons, L. (1999). Mail order brides: The legal framework and possibilities for change. In G. A. Kelson & D. L. DeLaet (Eds.), *Gender and immigration* (pp. 127–143). New York: New York University Press.

Sparks, E. E., & Park, A. H. (2000). The integration of feminism and multiculturalism: Ethical dilemmas at the border. In M. M. Brabeck (Ed.), *Practicing feminist ethics in psychology* (pp. 203–224). Washington, DC: American Psychological Association.

Sturdivant, S. (1980). *Therapy with women: A feminist philosophy of treatment.* New York: Springer.

Tennov, D. (1975). *Psychotherapy: The hazardous cure.* New York: Abelard-Schuman.

Tornatzky, L. G., Cutler, R., & Lee, J. (2002). *College knowledge: What Latino parents need to know and why they don't know it.* Claremont, CA: Tomas Rivera Policy Institute.

Weisstein, N. (1972). Psychology constructs the female. In V. Gornick & B. Morin (Eds.), *Woman in sexist society* (pp. 207–224). New York: New American Library.

Williams, M. K., McCandies, T., & Dunlap, M. R. (2002). Women of color and feminist psychol-ogy: Moving from criticism and critique to integration and application. In L. H. Collins, M. R. Dunlap, & J. C. Chrisler (Eds.), *Charting a new course for feminist psychology* (pp. 65–90). Westport, CT: Praeger.

Worell, J., & Johnson, N. (Eds.). (1997). *Shaping the future of feminist psychology: Education, re-search, and practice.* Washington, DC: American Psychological Association.

Worell, J., & Remer, P. (1992). *Feminist perspectives in therapy: An empowerment model for women.* New York: Wiley.

Chapter 6

Sex, Gender, and Dual-Earner Families: Implications and Applications for Career Counseling for Women

Lucia Albino Gilbert
Lisa K. Kearney
The University of Texas at Austin

> *Controversy, like a magician, often misdirects our attention from the real action. In this case, the real action lies in the rise of dual-earner families, not in imagined fears of the death of the family, loss of masculinity, or domination by women. The story that needs to be told involves a different kind of drama, one that centers on the development of new patterns of relationships among individuals, families, workplaces, and the larger social context.*
>
> —Hertz and Marshall (2001, p. 1)

Most women today, just like most men, are engaged in paid employment through much of their lives. Similarly, most women today, just like most men, are involved in family life with a partner and children during most of this same period in their lives (Gutek, 2001). This is the case for both working-class and middle-class families. The modal family form in the United States is the dual-earner family (Stebbins, 2001).

Dual-earner families are a diverse group and include heterosexual and same-sex partners with and without children in the home. The term *dual earner* also includes the subset of families described in the research literature as dual-career families. We have chosen to focus our chapter on the broader, more diverse group of dual-earner families for several reasons.

The recognition and naming of the dual-career family as a family form in the late 1960s marked a significant shift in views of women's roles in the United States (Rapoport & Rapoport, 1969). It recognized women as engaging in influential occupational positions, undertaken or engaged in as a life work, which had historically only been open to men. Also significant was that the dual-career family form assumed women who prepared themselves for careers did not necessarily leave their careers for marriage and children. Because the dual-career family form signaled profound social change, a good deal of research in the 1970s and 1980s studied the women and men in these families, a population that is quite educated, well-off economically, and, in the United States, largely White.

As women in the 1980s and 1990s were increasingly recognized as economic providers for their families, and as desiring equitable employment, studies of dual-career families broadened to studies of dual-wage or dual-earner families, and thus to more diverse populations. This shift in focus reflected the broader range and variation in women's continuous employment, from jobs to careers. Historically, in comparison to careers, jobs involved less commitment to the work involved, required less training, paid less, and were more likely to lack clear developmental stages and accumulation of experience. In addition, the distinction between what constitutes jobs and careers has become more fluid. Today, jobs and careers are not necessarily differentiated by demands, commitments, and responsibilities. Moreover, how a person views her or his involvement in a career or job may or may not reflect that person's self-concept and life goals.

Our chapter first describes the historical context of dual-earner families and how it differs from the context for today's dual-earner families, and what generally characterizes contemporary dual-earner work and family life. Gender theories and processes are described next as they are central to the contemporary dual-earner story and provide the overarching theoretical framework for the chapter. We then describe factors of particular importance for women's career development and for successful dual-earner family life. The chapter concludes with a section on important factors in career counseling.

WHAT ARE DUAL-EARNER FAMILIES?

The contemporary dual-earner family emerged in the second half of the 20th century in the context of women's changing status and educational and employment opportunities. Although it is not a new family form, the dual-earner family continues to evolve as women's and men's traditional sex-specialized roles converge. It is important for young women today to understand this history and how their current experiences are informed and shaped by the many societal changes that have occurred, and still are needed, to accommodate what has become the modal family form in the United States.

Historical Overview of Dual-Earner Families

The industrial revolution in the late 19th century was pivotal in transforming the meaning of work and its relationship to the family in the United States (Stebbins, 2001). By 1910, farm work was performed by less than 30% of the labor force, down from 60% in 1860. With increased employment in factories, work became physically separated from the home. Married women who worked in factories mostly did so because their families were poor. They worked, most often in low-paying jobs, moving in and out of the workplace, rearing children, and caring for their families. Little societal attention was given to their work–family conflict, their career development, or who was caring for their children.

Societal views of working women at that time did not challenge traditional assumptions about a woman's place, and thus did not call for any structural changes related to work and family. Work defined men socially and economically, but did not define women, who worked only to benefit the family. Women had limited power over their own destiny, and were defined socially by their husband's (or father's) occupation and socioeconomic standing (Bernard, 1975).

This situation slowly changed in the 20th century. Women received the right to vote in 1921, and for the first time were in a position to influence the social and legal policies affecting them. Especially important to the changing societal views of women's work was their extensive participation in the labor force during World War II, and the subsequent women's movement of the 1960s. The women's movement of the 1960s largely concentrated on employment—how to provide increased and more equitable educational and job opportunities for women in comparison to men. By the 1980s, the women's movement had expanded its focus on employment to include the culture of work and changes needed to accommodate work and family life. Over the past 25 years there has been an enormous increase in the work-life programs that respond to the work and family needs of employees (Galinsky & Bond, 1998; Stebbins, 2001). Another important change has to do with male spouses' behaviors in the home (Gilbert, 1985). By the 1990s, national time surveys began to document a significant shift toward more sharing of housework and child care between spouses (Coltrane & Adams, 2001).

Thus, contemporary views of working women in dual-earner families are built on very different assumptions about work and family than was the case at the turn of the 19th century. The single most important change influencing the relationship between work and family today is not women's increased involvement in paid work per se, but that increased involvement coupled with women's increased access to education, good job opportunities, laws to protect them from discriminatory practices, and a status and meaning separate from their affiliations with men.

As we begin the 21st century, less than 5% of American families with children living in the home are traditional in the sense of having a single-wage father and a full-time homemaker mother. More than 60% of married women with preschool-age children are currently employed outside the home, compared with 19% in 1960; and approximately 75% of married women with school-age children are employed. Moreover, women now constitute nearly half of the professional labor force, compared with 26% in 1960. The large majority of these women are married and most have children (U.S. Bureau of the Census, 2002).

Women today have more opportunities for education and career placement and advancement than in the past. Currently women and men graduate from high school and college in about the same proportion. Approximately 84% of both women and men are high school graduates, and 28% are college graduates (U.S. Bureau of the Census, 2001). Women are entering college and graduating with advanced degrees from fields such as law, medicine, life sciences, and business administration at a rate similar to men. However, this is less true in the physical sciences, computer sciences, and engineering, where significantly fewer women receive advanced degrees (Smallwood, 2003). Forty percent of college-educated women earn as much or more than their spouses (Stebbins, 2001), and married women on average provide 40% of their families' income. Finally, for both women and men, age of first marriage is increasing, and the number of children in families is decreasing (Bachu & O'Connell, 2001; Hertz & Marshall, 2001). This begins the story of where we are today.

General Characteristics of Contemporary Dual-Earner Families

The story of today's dual-earner family is one in which work and family are important components of both women's and men's identity and well-being. We are witnessing a work–family convergence in which employment and involvement with family are recognized as an appropriate, normative, healthy, and intrinsically rewarding aspect of women's and men's adult lives (Barnett & Hyde, 2001). Among dual-earner families, and across various ethnic groups, both spouses are employed full time in three fourths of families (Bond, Galinsky, & Swanberg, 1998).

Much can be said based on the large body of empirical studies that have been conducted. We identify six key characteristics and provide further detail on these in later sections of the chapter, especially as they relate to sex and gender. In all these areas, sex and gender can play a significant role in women's career development, psychological health, and marital satisfaction:

1. There are many variations of dual-earner families, from quite egalitarian to quite traditional. There are many ways partners can integrate and balance their employment and home roles. These variations depend to a large degree on partners' attitudes and values, personal needs, educational and career preparation, incomes, and employment situation (e.g., Barnett & Rivers, 1996; Coltrane, 2000; Gilbert, 1993; Goodnow & Bowes, 1994; Stebbins, 2001). Studies indicate that at least one third of heterosexual two-career families have established egalitarian role-sharing arrangements, although many families who are not role sharing describe their situation as equitable in the context of their work and family situation (Gerson, 1993). Same-sex dual-earner families, although less studied than heterosexual partners, are reported to be quite egalitarian in their role patterns (e.g., Eldridge & Gilbert, 1990).

2. The context of work and family issues differs along dimensions of race, ethnicity, socioeconomic status, and sexual orientation. The needs and challenges of dual-earner families are not the same for all women or for all men. African American women, for example, have traditionally had a high labor force participation, both prior to and during marriage, and societal views of male economic success and power have extended to a lesser extent to African American men than to White men (Osipow, Walsh, & Bingham, 2000). Partners in same-sex families or the biological children of same-sex partners often are not entitled to the same health benefits as heterosexual partners; and lower income dual-earner families have fewer resources to cover the costs of child care and health care.

3. Families engage in their various roles within the context of institutional and workplace practices and policies. The implicit and actual practices of employers and the educational, government, and corporate institutions they represent, as well as the structure of occupational work and careers and opportunity all greatly determine how partners live out their private lives despite their individual or family preferences (Bailyn, 1993; Okin, 1989). For example, how success is defined in an occupational field, and whether a field has work-life options available, significantly impact partners' choices and career paths. Women and men pursuing academic careers, for instance, need to achieve tenure within a set time frame. For many women, the tenure clock ticks simultaneously with their biological clock resulting in women more than men not having children or changing career paths (Armenti, 2004; Ward & Wolf-Wendel, 2004). A similar situation occurs in other professional fields (Valian, 1999).

4. Work–family issues are similar for women and men—they are life issues. Fathers and mothers both experience conflict between their work and family roles and desire more flexibility in their work schedules and more time with their families (Bond et al., 1998; Brownson & Gilbert, 2002; Thoits, 1992). Although household work and parenting remain unevenly

divided in many marriages, the distribution of income and participation in family roles is more equitable than in past decades (Stebbins, 2001). Husbands' participation in housework increases when wives earn more of the family income (Stebbins) and when husbands participate more in the care and nurturing of their children (Coltrane & Adams, 2001). Approximately 20% of spouses in dual-earner families work different shifts in order to share childrearing (Smith, 2000).

5. Work and family are compatible and mutually enhancing. The evidence is overwhelming and undeniable that, under most circumstances, engaging in both family and work roles is beneficial to women and men, as reflected in indices of physical health, mental health, and relational health (Barnett & Hyde, 2001). Many studies support this expansionist perspective on work and family. Theories that assumed marital stability arises from participation in specialized, segregated roles tied to biological sex are inconsistent with research data and the behavior of most women and men.

6. Gender matters. The personal lives of individuals are always played out within the constraints of societal norms and values and social institutions, and these remain influenced by conventional notions of sex and gender, the topic we next address. Indeed, if any one factor potentially affects women's career development it would be assumptions and processes associated with sex and gender.

SEX, GENDER, AND GENDER PROCESSES

In this chapter the term *sex* refers to whether a person is biologically male or female, and to characteristics determined by that biology. For example, the female sex has the capacity to bear children, and the male sex has the capacity to fertilize eggs. The term *gender*, in contrast, acknowledges the broader meaning typically associated with being born biologically female or male. Gender refers to the psychological, social, and cultural features and characteristics that have become strongly associated with the biological categories of female and male (Deaux, 1985). For example, women and men in our society are equally likely to become parents (i.e., biologically, conception requires a female and a male), but disproportionately more women than men are involved in the day-to-day care of children (i.e., culturally, women rear children). From a gender perspective, women typically rear children, not because men are less nurturing than women by nature, but because societal expectations associated with sex prescribe that women more than men should engage in nurturing activities.

Individuals are not born with gender, but rather learn to be women (or men) within the context of their historical and cultural circumstances, including race, ethnicity, and other sources of social identities. That is, their gender identities are negotiated and developed over time. In the words of Deaux and Stewart (2001), "We *do* gender, and it is in the doing of gender that identities are shaped and altered" (p. 94). According to gender theory, many of the traits and behaviors traditionally assumed to be determined by biological sex have become "constructed by the social reality" of individual women and men (Hare-Mustin & Marecek, 1990, p. 28). Moreover, gender is experienced through race and class. The experience of being a woman may be different for an African American and an Asian American, for example, because womanhood may be defined and socially constructed differently for the two groups. Thus, gender pertains to what we assume is true or will be true of someone who is born biologically female or male. It concerns personal and societal beliefs, stereotypes, and ingrained views about the fundamental nature of women and men. Such views are created and maintained through interpersonal interactions, formal and informal institutional practices, and other complex processes within the societal and cultural environment (Deaux & LaFrance, 1999). We give particular attention to gender because career counseling with women in dual-earner families requires understanding the "gendered" context of their lives.

Gilbert and Scher (1999) identified several "faces of gender" that actively work to shape the developmental process of all individuals. These include gender as difference, gender as language and discourse, gender as interactive process, and gender as structurer or organizer. These conceptualizations help illuminate how gender processes influence women's development and life choices.

Gender Operating as Difference

Gender as difference refers to the deeply ingrained but erroneous assumption that one set of characteristics, abilities, and interests belongs to one sex, and that another complementary set belongs to the other, or opposite, sex. The idea that "men are from Mars, women are from Venus" permeates our culture despite all evidence to the contrary. Examples of these stereotypic assumptions include such attributes as dependence and nurturance, which supposedly characterize women, and not men. However, many women are less dependent than many men, and many men are more dependent than many women. The same is true for the attribute of nurturance. Many men are more nurturing than many women, and many women are less nurturing than many men. Indeed there is always a greater difference within each sex on cognitive variables and personal attributes than between the sexes (Gilbert & Scher, 1999). That is, women and men as a group differ more among themselves than they do compared to the other sex.

The gender-as-difference lens perpetuates the stereotypic notion that because women and men differ biologically, they are opposite sexes. Women and men are not opposite psychologically, cognitively, or behaviorally, and in fact are more similar than dissimilar (Hyde, 1994). Gender operating as difference distorts perceptions of women's and men's abilities, capacities, and opportunities.

Gender Operating as Language and Discourse

Gender as language and discourse refers to how conventional views of male and female differences are embedded and reproduced in everyday language. For example, the term *working mother* is commonly used to recognize the fact that many women are parents and are employed. The term *working father* is used far less, obscuring the fact that many men are parents and are employed. In 1995, there were 24 million employed fathers in the United States with a child under 18 living in their home (Levine & Pittinsky, 1997). Another example is the prevalent discourse that depicts the computer world as an essentially male domain (Margolis & Fisher, 2002), a topic we revisit at several points later in the chapter.

Gender Operating as an Interactive Process

Gender as interactive process refers to the active aspects of gender. Contrary to conventional thinking, gender is not static; it is a verb, not a noun: "We do gender" (Deaux & Stewart, 2001, p. 94). As mentioned earlier, a person is not born with gender; instead, a person's gender is constructed on a daily basis through interactive processes associated with that person's biological sex. This doing or constructing of gender occurs through individuals being encouraged and rewarded in daily interactions, in multiple settings, to act in accordance with what is expected for a person of their biological sex. To return to our example of the computer culture, research indicates that interactions within many environments create and sustain the view that boys and men belong to the computer culture, and girls and women do not (American Association of University Women [AAUW], 2000).

Shields' (1994) observation in *The Stone Diaries* illustrates the formidable pressure to do gender by conforming to gender roles that seem polarized, arbitrary, and contrived. Her main character says:

> Our wont is to put up with things, with the notion that men behave in one manner, and women in another. You might say it is a little side show we put on for ourselves, a way of squinting at human behavior, a form of complicity. Only think of how we go around grinning and winking and nodding resignedly or shrugging with frank wonderment! Oh well, we say with a knowing lilt in our voice, that's a man for you. Or that's just the way women are. (Shields, p. 121)

This pressure to conform to gender proscriptions is normative in our culture and is a largely unconscious process for men and women.

Gender Operating as a Structural and Organizing Factor

Gender as organizer and structurer refers to how conventional views of female and male differences extend beyond individual women and men and their socialization to the social structures and principles of organizations and to societal institutions, laws, and policies (Sherif, 1982; Zuckerman, Cole, & Bruer, 1991). Historical examples include not allowing women to vote, barring women from an advanced education or from entering certain professional fields, and requiring women to leave their places of employment when they become pregnant. These laws and policies were consistent with views of male prerogative in the workplace, and women's place in the home.

Gender as organizer continues in today's educational and occupational world. For example, the fields of study that represent the fastest growing and best paying occupations include computer and information sciences. In 1998, approximately one half of men, but only one fourth of women, majored in a field closely linked with these high-growth occupations (AAUW, 2003). Moreover, women were less likely to major in computer science and related high-growth fields in 1998 than they were in 1990 (Margolis & Fisher, 2002).

The areas and challenges we discuss in the next section on dual-earner family life are associated with conventional cultural norms and gender roles. In particular, they relate to the concepts of gender as difference, discourse, or interactive process (e.g., participation in family work, decision making within families) and gender as structure (e.g., implicit and explicit policies for salary increases, promotions, and work-life benefits).

GENDER AND DUAL-EARNER FAMILY LIFE

The majority of working women in the United States anticipate being in long-term romantic relationships that include children (Gutek, 2001; Okin, 1989). Women need to be informed about factors that will help or hinder achieving the kinds of dual-earner relationships they envision and be prepared for the daily realities and possible obstacles to achieving their goals. Career counselors working with women must be knowledgeable about how these factors influence both home and family life, and strive to increase women's awareness at earlier stages in their career and job planning. This section first describes factors associated with gender ideology that can influence women's career development and then describes factors that facilitate

role convergence in dual-earner families. Finally, recommendations for career counseling are presented.

Continuing Challenges for Dual-Earner Families Associated With Conventional Cultural Norms and Gender-Role Ideology

Women in dual-earner families face challenges and possible roadblocks in
their pursuit of both family- and work-related life goals. Many of these challenges are tied to cultural norms and beliefs about women's and men's
roles, which have been internalized from childhood and reinforced over
time. Cultural norms define what is acceptable and unacceptable behavior
and thus influence the work- and family-role aspirations and practices for
both women and men (Barnett & Hyde, 2001).

Although cultural norms reflect the values and social practices of particular historical periods, they are often slow to change as social conditions alter. Unlike previous generations, most women today assume that they will
be involved in paid employment for most of their life span and that they
can choose from a wide range of occupations (Gutek, 2001). Despite this
significant change in women's lives, traditional gender-role norms continue to influence their aspirations, decisions, and perceived choices.

We address several challenges for women that are associated with conventional cultural norms and beliefs. Although we divide them into sociopsychological factors and structural factors, this division is somewhat artificial. Much of one's internal sociopsychological world is influenced by and
takes place within one's external structural environments, and vice versa.
Nevertheless, the division is useful in examining these factors in a systematic manner. These factors are summarized in Table 6.1.

Sociopsychological Factors

Prioritization of Men's and Women's Careers.   Historically women have
been expected to accommodate their occupational aspirations to men's careers with the assumption that home and family responsibilities would fall

TABLE 6.1
Continuing Challenges for Dual-Earner Families Associated
With Conventional Cultural Norms and Gender-Role Ideology

Sociopsychological Factors	*Structural Factors*
Prioritization of men's and women's careers	Occupational sex segregation
Views of motherhood and fatherhood	Gender gaps in salary
Views of women's and men's abilities	Sexual harassment and other forms of dis-crimination

more to them than to their spouses (Bernard, 1981; Friedman & Greenhaus, 2000). This deference to the careers of male spouses and the associated increases in family responsibilities for wives often slows the career advancement of women (Valian, 1999). To accommodate, depending on the circumstances, women may work fewer hours, transfer to less demanding positions, or accept part-time employment (Stebbins, 2001).

For some women, the prioritization of the male career over their own begins during their educational years. Women more than men pursue fields of study or career paths they view as consistent with their future responsibilities as parents and spouses, such as choosing a career as a teacher in order to have the same schedules as school-age children (Okin, 1989). Women in less traditional fields such as the sciences or engineering may choose tracks that will allow them greater flexibility to balance work and family responsibilities to a greater extent than men do (Valian, 1999; Ward & Wolf-Wendel, 2004; Zuckerman et al., 1991). In contrast, relatively fewer men consciously plan their occupational aspirations to fit with their future views of family life (Cleveland, Stockdale, & Murphy, 2000).

For some women and men, this prioritization comes later, often with the birth of the first child. Becker and Moen (1999), for example, reported that young women empowered by newer cultural values of equality and opportunity for both sexes may begin with high career expectations. However, once they are confronted with marital and parental responsibilities, usually around the time of the birth of a first child, young women may begin to follow a "job track" rather than a "career trajectory." As noted by Gutek (2001), although it appears that women may make these choices "freely," they are not made in a vacuum, but rather reflect subtle gender processes within the marital relationship and society at large that define the ways in which women are expected to change their occupational aspirations to accommodate their spouse's work and fulfill responsibilities for children.

Views of Motherhood and Fatherhood.   Culturally, mothering is still viewed as more important than fathering, despite the greater involvement of men in parenting since the 1980s (Levine & Pittinsky, 1997; Silverstein, 1996). Increasing numbers of men actively participate in parenting and are the primary caregivers of young children (Christiansen & Palkovitz, 2001; Coley, 2001; Pleck, 1997). Nonetheless, women more than men are culturally expected to be actively involved with and available to their children and responsible for their care.

Some working women exhibit a form of internalized guilt as a result of their choice to be employed. Because many middle-class women in dual-earner families were reared by mothers who were not employed in the workplace, their own pictures of what motherhood should look like may not match their present life experience, and may cause them to feel they are failing their children and families in some way (Barnett & Rivers, 1996). In addition, cultural pressures that give greater importance to mothering than to fathering not only heighten possible feelings of guilt but also increase barriers to men's involvement in parenting.

Views of Women's and Men's Abilities.   Early socialization emphasizing the superiority of men's abilities in certain areas can result in girls' internalization of the belief that they are less capable and less likely to succeed than their male counterparts (Barnett & Rivers, 1996). A case in point is math ability. Compared to men, women have less confidence in their abilities, especially in areas that are stereotyped as male (Barnett & Hyde, 2001). Recent studies on "stereotype threat" with regard to math ability provided evidence for the effect of internalized gendered beliefs about mathematics achievement. When instructions to participants indicated that males usually scored higher on the math SAT test, males outperformed females. However, when instructions indicated that scores on the test were similar for women and men, female and male participants performed equally well (Spencer, Steele, & Quinn, 1999).

A second example relates to the previously mentioned view of technology as a "male domain" (AAUW, 2000). Girls enrolled in advanced computer courses reported feeling isolated and teased about their appearance and their technology competence by both girls and boys, reinforcing the cultural assumption that boys are better with computers than girls (Margolis & Fisher, 2002). These patterns of behavior are supported by societal norms, discourses, and practices that place girls interested in technology in a position of risking peer acceptance if they pursue these interests (Davidson & Schofield, 2002). A woman's occupational aspirations and career choices are thereby frequently shaped, from an early age, by cultural assumptions related to gender and ability.

Structural Factors

Women may encounter structural factors in the workplace, which influence the ways in which they can integrate their work and family lives. Several of these structural factors are illuminated in this section.

Occupational Sex Segregation.   Women and men are still found in quite different occupations, with many women still concentrated in occupations that were historically female dominated (AAUW, 2003). Today the highest proportion of women with a college education are primary and secondary school teachers and registered nurses; neither of these occupations appears among the 10 most common occupations for college-educated men (AAUW). Overall, men have a wider base of power and easier access to valuable resources, and women on average continue to earn significantly less than men, although a significant proportion of women earn more than their spouses (Stebbins, 2001). Men still predominantly hold more positions of power and leadership in business organizations and academic institutions, and the structures of career participation, which require individuals to be single-minded in their pursuits in order to be successful, have not changed appreciably (Zuckerman et al., 1991). Although there have been continuing challenges to the long-held assumptions of what defines success at work, traditional views continue to prevail (Strober & Chan, 1999). Current employment benefits and policies enable women more than men to ask for and receive the accommodations necessary for combining work and family responsibilities (e.g., maternity leaves, flexible schedules).

Gender Gaps in Salary. Approximately half of all working women are employed in fields that are more than 75% female (Cleveland et al., 2000). This is of particular importance as the proportion of women in a particular field has been found to be one of the best predictors of status and pay level (Cleveland et al.). Earning differences for women and men have decreased from the $0.59 for every $1.00 men earned in the period from 1960 to 1980, but they still persist.

Women and men between the ages of 16 and 24 tend to have similar earnings, with a wage gap occurring for older women and men. Among Black and Hispanic women and men, women earn approximately 88% of what men earn; among White women and men it is 75% (U.S. Bureau of the Census, 2002). The reasons for this gap are complex but subtle discrimination is likely a significant contributor (Stebbins, 2001). A much discussed report on the status of women faculty at the Massachusetts Institute of Technology (MIT) concluded that "gender discrimination in the 1990s is subtle but pervasive, and stems largely from unconscious ways of thinking that have been socialized into all of us, men and women alike" (MIT, 1999, p. 6). The report noted that the consequences of these more subtle forms of discrimination are as demoralizing to women as were the blatant inequities and intimidation of former decades. Among other indices of inequity, women at MIT earned less than what men earned in comparable positions.

The gender gap in wages impacts women's careers and how they combine their work and family roles. As long as men continue to earn significantly more than women, it will continue to be more financially sound for the female partners to move to part-time work, reduce their hours, or take additional leave to care for children, thereby altering their own career paths and chances for advancement (Gilbert & Rader, 2001). Moreover, the continued presence of a glass ceiling further limits women's career opportunities and adds to possible psychological stress (Barnett & Rivers, 1996; Cleveland et al., 2000; Gutek, 2001).

Sexual Harassment and Other Forms of Discrimination.   Despite changes in
the law, working women still face discriminatory practices, in both subtle
and blatant ways. In addition, lesbian women may face additional discrimination based on their sexual orientation. Workplace heterosexism and
unsupportive social interactions at work due to heterosexism are related to
negative psychological health outcomes for employed lesbian, gay, and bisexual individuals (Smith & Ingram, 2004). Being "out" on the job can have
negative repercussions for career advancement. Choosing to "be discreet"
can have great personal costs in terms of feeling isolated, compartmental-
ized, and invisible.

    Discrimination becomes more blatant when exhibited in the form of sex-
ual harassment, another method of impeding the advancement of women
in the workplace. Gutek (2001) reported that sexual harassment is still a
pervasive problem in the workplace. Sexual harassment is used as a method
of reinforcing traditional power differentials between men and women by
reminding women of their place in society as sexualized objects. Harassment can take many forms from sexualized innuendoes to overt sexual
comments and sexual coercion. Regardless of its form, harassment demor-
alizes women in the workplace and may cause professional and psychological distress impacting long-term career outcomes with losses of job opportunities or promotions, choices to switch positions to avoid harassers, and
reprisal for reporting (Gutek, 1986; Schneider, Swan, & Fitzgerald, 1997).

Succeeding as a Dual-Earner Family

Although dual-earner families face a number of unique challenges, research has provided useful information about how these families succeed
and flourish. A number of factors have been identified in the research literature as important to the success of dual-earner families. We divide these
into internal factors and external factors. The internal factors are associated with partner behaviors within the family and include flexibility; communication, mutuality, and spousal support; and balance. The external factors reside outside the family and include social support and family-friendly
work environments (see Table 6.2).

Internal, Family Factors

Flexibility.   Two types of flexibility are important: ideological and behavioral on the part of family members and work–family options in the workplace (Jacobs & Gerson, 2001; Lee & Duxbury, 1998). The flexibility of
gender-role beliefs and behaviors are central to partners' abilities to successfully balance work and family life (Barnett & Hyde, 2001; Lee & Duxbury). Both men and women must be able to move outside traditional gen-

TABLE 6.2
Succeeding as a Dual-Earner Family

Internal, Family Factors	*External, Societal Factors*
Flexibility (gender roles, scheduling, responsibilities)	Family-friendly work environment (family-friendly benefits, investment in employees, mentoring)
Communication, mutuality, and spousal support (partner appreciation, scheduling fit, parenting)	Social support (family, friends, coworkers)
Balance (work-home, self-care, family-care)	

der-role norms and become comfortable with creating new norms for their unique situations.

For example, fathers may need to become accustomed to changing diapers, preparing lunches, and managing carpools. Partners may use this flexibility to create their own work–family adaptive strategy (Moen & Wethington, 1992) to meet their unique family's needs. At times, one partner may be able to take time off work to spend extra time at home, enabling the other to work later. Partners must strike a balance in several areas, including child-care responsibilities, household work, and emotion work, to increase family-life satisfaction and create a partnership based in equality and role sharing (Barnett & Rivers, 1996; Haddock, Zimmerman, Ziemba, & Current, 2001; Stevens, Kiger, & Riley, 2001). This balance will most likely be achieved if partners commit to frequent times together focused on communication about such issues.

Communication, Mutuality, and Spousal Support. Of vital importance to the success of dual-earner families are both the quality of the communication between partners and their ability to communicate in areas central to the relationship. Partners must create time together as a couple to increase communication (Barnett & Rivers, 1996; Zimmerman, Haddock, Current, & Ziemba, 2003). Dual-earner partners often struggle to make this time for one another, especially when children arrive in the picture. Even when both partners are home at the same time, they are likely distracted with the daily tasks of keeping a household running (e.g., cooking meals, mowing the lawn, child care), with very little time available to focus exclusively on their relationship with one another. Valuing time with one another, and striving to keep that time a priority, gives partners the opportunity to show their mutual respect and appreciation (Zimmerman et al.). Relationships are benefited when partners communicate care and interest in the other's professional activities and respect for their capabilities in their career, in addition to praising family involvement and support (Stevens et al., 2001; Zimmerman et al.).

Communication is also necessary for partners to express when they are feeling imbalanced, giving the other partner a chance to offer assistance and discuss possible solutions. Of continued importance is communicating about a "schedule fit" in which each partner's work hours and home responsibilities meets their own, the other partner's, and the children's needs. If a good schedule fit is achieved, a better quality of life is accomplished within the partnership, decreasing the amount of stress in each individual's life (Barnett, Brennan, & Gareis, 1999; Moen & Wethington, 1992). Stevens et al. (2001) found that it was not the particular division of time and labor that affected marital satisfaction, but whether both partners were satisfied with the unique arrangement they had made together as a couple, which underscores the importance of communicating about each other's needs and desires. Perceived equity in relationships has been found to be a critical factor in relationship satisfaction, for both lesbian and heterosexual partners in dual-earner relationships (Gilbert, 1993; Savoy, 2004; Steil, 2001).

Additional important areas of communication are whether to have a child, when to have a first child, and whether or when to have additional children. Partners can explore how having a child will affect their relationship and their careers and how they will address these changes. The timing of the first child can also influence the timeline for having a larger family. Relevant to these discussions is the availability of work flexibility at both partners' places of employment, discussing if a male partner's company provides paternity leave or if there is freedom in decreasing workloads or changing work hours at either workplace (Lero, Brockman, Pence, Goelman, & Johnson, 1993).

Communication about parenting responsibilities is still another important area. Although the role of mother is still extensively emphasized in parenting (Hays, 1997), fathers are also actively involved in the daily lives of their children (Barnett & Rivers, 1996). Simple tasks must be discussed, including who will change diapers, wake up for early morning feedings, and take off work to take children to the doctor when they are ill. Also critical is the discussion of child-care possibilities, as partners may have very different viewpoints about what type of child care is best. Is an extended leave possible for father or mother during the first year? Does the budget allow for in-home care of the infant? Is child care available at either partner's workplace? A discussion of one's values and desires is necessary in exploring child-care options, even before the birth of a child.

Balance. Couples need to be able to identify when they are feeling out of balance either at work or at home. Too much time at work can cause harm to either personal or family welfare, whereas too little time dedicated to one's work may endanger a family's economic security (Jacobs & Gerson, 2001). Although many studies have shown the benefits of multiple roles, balance is essential in identifying when role demands have become excessive (e.g., working 80 or more hours the week after the birth of a child; Barnett & Hyde, 2001). Both partners must discipline themselves to uphold boundaries around their work, taking responsibility to not work excessive hours or let their work lives negatively impact their home lives (Haddock et al., 2001).

As mentioned earlier, the extent to which partners in heterosexual dual-earner families hold traditional or nontraditional attitudes about the appropriate roles of women and men moderates how partners accomplish and share in household work and parenting. Although husbands and fathers in these families have increased their involvement in housework and parenting, women on average do proportionally more than their spouses (Stebbins, 2001). An important part of achieving balance involves how partners manage their multiple roles and whether participation in home roles is consistent with each partner's values and expectations. For example, a husband who is an involved father, but views household duties as a woman's job, may cause stress, resentment, and a lack of balance if his wife holds egalitarian views (Gilbert, 1993; Hoffman, 1989).

Dual-earner families can often be stretched for time with family members juggling multiple roles. Because of this, self-care and family care have the tendency to be shortchanged due to time restraints, yet giving attention to both family and partnership building and to self-care is vital to the success of dual-earner families. Partners and children are wise to spend time each week dedicated to such self-care activities as personal hobbies, athletic activities, time with friends, or quiet time alone to reflect, read, or rest (Zimmerman et al., 2003). Family care includes setting aside time for the family to simply be together as a family, apart from running errands and doing chores of the daily household (Haddock et al., 2001). Some families have weekly family nights that include game nights, cooking a fun meal together, or field trips to different activities around the town. Others may have more informal methods of accomplishing the same tasks (e.g., time throughout the week spent taking walks together, tossing a softball, cooking together).

Balance also includes a financial component, wherein families limit "competitive materialism," which may lead to partners working excessively to meet greater demands at home (Stevens et al., 2001). Focusing on the valuing of family and taking pride in accomplishments as a dual-earner family may bring greater fulfillment in life than increased financial status (Haddock et al., 2001).

External, Societal Factors

The success of a dual-earner family is not only dependent on the changes made within the family and by partners, but is also affected by the larger influences associated with cultural norms, workplace practices, and support networks.

Family-Friendly Work Environments. A large factor in successful dual-earner families is a family-supportive work environment (Jacobs & Gerson, 2001). Workplaces that provide flexibility on the job are associated with happier and more productive employees (Jacobs & Gerson). The following family-friendly benefits for both women and men provide much-needed support for dual-earner families: extended maternity or paternity leaves, option of working part time, flexible work hours, workplace child care, family-responsibility leave, job sharing, opportunities to work from home, and fewer work hours (Lee & Duxbury, 1998; Lero et al., 1993).

Family-friendly benefits are offered by most employers (Galinsky & Bond, 1998). Many employers allow flextime schedules and many offer dependent-care assistance programs that help employees pay for child care with pretax dollars. Under the Family and Medical Leave Act, companies with 50 or more employees are required to provide 12 weeks of unpaid leave for childbirth, adoption, and other family-related situations. More supportive family-friendly workplaces are associated with higher levels of job satisfaction among employees and more commitment to company success.

Both men and women should be encouraged to use these benefits. Fewer men than women use family benefits (Levine & Pittinsky, 1997; Pleck, 1996) because of either societal views that they should fulfill the provider role (Hyde, Essex, & Horton, 1993) or employers' negative attitudes toward men who take leave (Pleck, 1988; Wayne & Cordeiro, 2003). Either implicitly or explicitly, men are often discouraged from making use of these benefits, leaving greater family responsibilities to women, and causing a negative impact on their early and mid-career development.

Workplaces also support the success of dual-earner families by providing positions that are personally meaningful and by being invested in the development of individualized career goals (Haddock et al., 2001). Feeling invested in one's career and feeling that one is being a productive contributor to society brings individuals fulfillment, benefiting the family as a whole. When a partner is in an emotionally draining position at work, with long hours and little personal fulfillment, family members are often negatively impacted. This underscores the importance of finding a job that is both family friendly and personally fulfilling.

Mentoring can also have benefits for women in the workplace by providing knowledge of how to advance in their career and further develop their strengths and improve their weaknesses. Mentoring has been consistently associated with career and organizational advancement (Gutek, 2001). Working women benefit from gaining advice and encouragement from other women who have faced such factors as discrimination, glass ceilings, and traditional gender-role beliefs in the workplace, as well as observing someone who has successfully combined work and home responsibilities. Yet fewer role models exist for professional women than for men, and women have a greater difficulty obtaining a mentor than men do (Gutek), making this buffer an unlikely presence for most women in the working world.

Social Support. Dual-earner families may find support in a number of locations, including friends, neighbors, family, coworkers, supervisors, and counselors. Friends, family, and neighbors, especially those who share their value systems and lifestyle, often provide the most tangible support, providing meals and child care when parents wish to have a night out, and emotional support. Yet they may also be a source of criticism if such individuals do not support the concept of dual-earner families and hold more traditional views of a working husband and stay-at-home mother. Deutsch and Saxon (1998), for example, reported that women and men holding more traditional views of gender roles criticized other women for working outside the home too much and other men for lacking dedication to employment and devoting too much time at home.

Social support networks in the workplace have also been found to be a positive influence on working parents, with greater support being associated with lower anxiety and depression levels (Polasky & Holahan, 1998). Workplaces that have family-friendly policies and view employees in a holistic context, which includes their roles as spouses, parents, family members, and employees, facilitate employees' psychological health and productivity (Barnett & Rivers, 1996; Lee & Duxbury, 1998).

Social support has also been found to be a key factor in relationship satisfaction for dual-earner lesbian couples (Savoy, 2004). Lesbian partners may benefit from additional social support, especially as they face discriminatory practices discussed earlier in the chapter, in addition to the unique challenges faced by all women in dual-earner relationships.

CAREER COUNSELING DUAL-EARNER PARTNERS

The previous sections provided counselors with information about the unique challenges faced by women in dual-earner families as well as factors associated with the success of women in these families. This section provides further information about specific areas career counselors may wish to address with women in dual-earner families.

Avoiding Common Pitfalls

In a recent study of marriage and family therapists, Haddock and Bowling (2001) found that when presented with a vignette of a dual-earner couple struggling with family-work balance, 73% of therapists did not attempt to increase partners' sharing of household and child-care tasks, even when this was stated as a problem by one of the partners. The majority of therapists suggested that the woman reduce her hours at work, rather than working with the couple to find a more equitable balance of work load in the home. Career counselors will need to examine ways in which they may reinforce traditional gender norms and assumptions within their own counseling and strive to alter such practices before working with women planning or involved in dual-earner relationships.

Educating Clients About Normative Issues in Dual-Earner Families

The majority of individuals in the United States marry at some point in their lives and have children (Gutek, 2001), an obvious factor many young people overlook as they plan their careers. Educating young people on the upcoming responsibilities they may undertake in dual-earner families will help them make better informed decisions about their futures. By assisting women in thinking early on about their possible lives in dual-earner families, career counselors can prepare women for the challenges they will likely face at work and at home. Career counselors may wish to ask young women questions about their views regarding dual-earner families, their expectations about role divisions within their future families, and value conflicts that exist between their own desires and their partners' or the ways in which they were raised. Career counselors can raise awareness in young men of the issues of dual-earner families, rather than confirming assumptions that their career trajectory has a fixed path. Counselors working with young people in relationships possibly leading to long-term partnerships would assist them greatly by bringing these issues to the table at an early point, rather than focusing exclusively on the individual's own career pathway.

Counseling for Both Family and Work Life

Beyond work decisions, therapists should address the balance of domestic labor in the home, which includes three dimensions: household tasks, emotion work, and status-enhancement work (Stevens et al., 2001). All three dimensions have been associated with marital satisfaction. Household tasks include both chores around the house and organizational responsibility (e.g., making a grocery list and meal plan for the week, arranging the child care, packing lunches, organizing carpool). Emotion work includes increasing family communication, family warmth, and cohesiveness (e.g., having a family meeting to discuss problems, making weekly family fun nights). Status-enhancement work includes those factors that promote both partners' careers and includes expressing appreciation and respect for each other's jobs and what they bring to the family, assisting in family tasks to free up a partner for job-related duties (e.g., picking up a child after school so the other can attend a late-night work event), and being supportive about job possibilities and projects. When working with dual-earner families, counselors should consider bringing questions about such issues into the discussions, as these will impact their clients' career fulfillment and home life in reciprocal ways.

Considering Joint Sessions for Dual-Earner Partners

Counseling individuals in committed partnerships with children provides the opportunity for more in-depth counseling about dual-earner issues. For example, when working with one partner in a couple, it may be beneficial to invite the other partner for a few joint sessions to address job decisions that may be affecting the family as a whole. Other possible topics for joint sessions include achieving equality within the marital relationship, discussing how such equality benefits the individual and the family (Zimmerman et al., 2003), improving communication (Barnett & Rivers, 1996), and increasing role flexibility. All these areas are associated with greater marital happiness among dual-earner couples.

Becker and Moen (1999) proposed three keys to success in a dual-earner family: scaling back, placing limits, and trading off. Scaling back involves the possible limiting of the number of children, reducing housework expectations, and reducing social commitments while families are young and require more time commitment. Placing limits refers to limiting hours worked, reducing long-term expectations regarding career advancement in order to increase family time, and choosing not to take jobs or promotions that negatively impact children or the spouse's career. Finally, trading off involves partners alternating the implementation of these strategies so that one partner is not the only individual scaling back and placing limits, which in the past has typically been the female partner. Discussing these strategies with clients can broaden their usual ways of approaching decision making as well as their typical coping strategies.

CONCLUSION

At the beginning of the 20th century, the industrial revolution was influential in transforming work and family when the economy shifted from agriculture to industry. As we begin the 21st century, we are on the threshold of another significant change—this time to a global and technological economy (Hertz & Marshall, 2001). The career counseling of women in dual-earner families, the modal family form in the United States today, must address the changing sociocultural contexts of work and family life and take into account the cultural norms, gender-role values, and unique challenges faced by partners in these families. Rather than viewing multiple-role occupancy as a problem for marriages, counselors are in a position to work effectively with partners to understand the structures (i.e., employer attitudes and policies) that prohibit or inhibit the beneficial integration and convergence of roles once thought to be mutually exclusive, and assist them in finding solutions that fit this modern and healthy role convergence (Barnett & Hyde, 2001).

By understanding the real story of today's dual-earner families, career counselors will be better able to assist women, as well as men, to create fulfilling lives for themselves, both at work and at home. Career counselors thereby play a critical role in helping women succeed in these areas by assisting them with strategies of balance, communication, and flexibility in their personal and work lives.

REFERENCES

American Association of University Women. (2000). *Tech-savvy: Educating girls in the new computer age.* Washington, DC: American Association of University Women Educational Foundation.

American Association of University Women. (2003). *Women at work.* Washington, DC: American Association of University Women Educational Foundation.

Armenti, C. (2004). May babies and posttenure babies: Maternal decisions of women professors. *Review of Higher Education, 27,* 211–231.

Bachu, A., & O'Connell, M. (2001). *Fertility of American women: June 2000* (Current Population Report No. P20-543RV). Washington, DC: U.S. Bureau of the Census.

Bailyn, L. (1993). *Breaking the mold: Women, men, and time in the new corporate world.* New York: Free Press.

Barnett, R. C., Brennan, R. T., & Gareis, K. C. (1999). A closer look at the measurement of burnout. *Journal of Applied Biobehavioral Research, 4,* 65–78.

Barnett, R. C., & Hyde, J. S. (2001). Women, men, work, and family: An expansionist theory. *American Psychologist, 56,* 781–796.

Barnett, R. C., & Rivers, C. (1996). *She works, he works: How two income families are happier, healthier, and better off.* San Francisco: Harper.

Becker, P. E., & Moen, P. (1999). Scaling back: Dual-earner couples' work-family strategies. *Journal of Marriage and the Family, 61,* 995–1007.

Bernard, J. (1975). *Women, wives, and mothers.* Chicago: Aldine.

Bernard, J. (1981). The good provider role: Its rise and fall. *American Psychologist, 36,* 3–12.

Bond, J. T., Galinsky, E., & Swanberg, J. E. (1998). *The 1997 national study of the changing workforce.* New York: Families and Work Institute.

Brownson, C., & Gilbert, L. A. (2002). The development of the Discourses about Fathers Inventory: Measuring fathers' perceptions of their exposure to discourses. *Psychology of Men and Masculinity, 3,* 97–106.

Christiansen, S. L., & Palkovitz, R. (2001). Why the "good provider" role still matters. *Journal of Family Issues, 22,* 84–106.

Cleveland, J. N., Stockdale, M., & Murphy, K. R. (2000). *Women and men in organizations: Sex and gender issues at work.* Mahwah, NJ: Lawrence Erlbaum Associates.

Coley, R. L. (2001). (In)visible men: Emerging research on low-income, unmarried, and minority fathers. *American Psychologist, 56,* 743–753.

Coltrane, S. (2000). Research on household labor: Modeling and measuring the social embeddedness of routine family work. *Journal of Marriage and the Family, 62,* 363–389.

Coltrane, S., & Adams, M. (2001). Men's family work: Child-centered fathering and the sharing of domestic labor. In R. Hertz & N. L. Marshall (Eds.), *Working families: The transformation of the American home* (pp. 72–102). Berkeley: University of California Press.

Davidson, A. L., & Schofield, J. W. (2002). Female voices in virtual reality: Drawing young girls into an on-line world. In K. A. Renninger & W. Schumar (Eds.), *Learning and change in cyberspace* (pp. 34–59). New York: Cambridge University Press.

Deaux, K. (1985). Sex and gender. In L. Porter & M. Rosenzeig (Eds.), *Annual review of psychology, 1985* (Vol. 36, pp. 49–81). Palo Alto, CA: Annual Reviews.

Deaux, K., & LaFrance, M. (1999). Gender. In D. Gilbert, S. T. Fiske, & G. Lindzey (Eds.), *Handbook of social psychology* (Vol. 1, pp. 788–827). New York: McGraw-Hill.

Deaux, K., & Stewart, A. J. (2001). Framing gendered identities. In R. K. Unger (Ed.), *Handbook of the psychology of women and gender* (pp. 84–100). New York: Wiley.

Deutsch, F., & Saxon, S. (1998). The double standard of praise and criticism for mothers and fathers. *Psychology of Women Quarterly, 22,* 665–683.

Eldridge, N. S., & Gilbert, L. A. (1990). Correlates of relationship satisfaction in lesbian couples. *Psychology of Women Quarterly, 14,* 43–62.

Friedman, S. D., & Greenhaus, J. H. (2000). *Work and family: Allies or enemies?* New York: Oxford University Press.

Galinsky, E., & Bond, J. T. (1998). *1998 business work-life study: A sourcebook.* New York: Families and Work Institute.

Gerson, K. (1993). *No man's land: Men's changing commitments to family and work.* New York: Basic Books.

Gilbert, L. A. (1985). *Men in dual-career families.* Hillsdale, NJ: Lawrence Erlbaum Associates.

Gilbert, L. A. (1993). *Two careers/One family.* Newbury Park, CA: Sage.

Gilbert, L. A., & Rader, J. (2001). Current perspectives on women's adult roles: Work, family, and life. In R. K. Unger (Ed.), *Handbook of the psychology of women and gender* (pp. 156–169). New York: Wiley.

Gilbert, L. A., & Scher, M. (1999). *Gender and sex in counseling and psychotherapy.* Boston: Allyn & Bacon.

Goodnow, J. J., & Bowes, J. M. (1994). *Men, women, and household work.* New York: Oxford University Press.

Gutek, B. A. (1986). *Sex and the workplace.* San Francisco: Jossey-Bass.

Gutek, B. A. (2001). Women and paid work. *Psychology of Women Quarterly, 25,* 379–393.

Haddock, S. A., & Bowling, S. (2001). Therapists' approaches to the normative challenges of dual-earner couples: Negotiating outdated societal ideologies. *Journal of Feminist Family Therapy, 13,* 91–120.

Haddock, S. A., Zimmerman, T. S., Ziemba, S., & Current, L. (2001). Ten adaptive strategies for work and family balance: Advice from successful dual earners. *Journal of Marital and Family Therapy, 27,* 445–458.

Hare-Mustin, R. T., & Marecek, J. (Eds.). (1990). *Making a difference: Psychology and the construction of gender.* New Haven, CT: Yale University Press.

Hays, S. (1997). *The cultural contradictions of motherhood.* New Haven, CT: Yale University Press.

Hertz, R., & Marshall, N. L. (2001). *Working families: The transformation of the American home.* Berkeley: University of California Press.

Hoffman, L. W. (1989). Effects of maternal employment in the two-parent family. *American Psychologist, 44,* 349–359.

Hyde, J. S. (1994). Can meta-analysis make feminist transformations in psychology? *Psychology of Women Quarterly, 18,* 451–462.

Hyde, J. S., Essex, M. J., & Horton, F. (1993). Fathers and parental leave: Attitudes and experiences. *Journal of Family Issues, 14,* 616–638.

Jacobs, J. A., & Gerson, K. (2001). Overworked individuals or overworked families? Explaining trends in work, leisure, and family time. *Work and Occupations, 28,* 40–63.

Lee, C. M., & Duxbury, L. (1998). Employed parents' support from partners, employers, and friends. *Journal of Social Psychology, 138,* 303–322.

Lero, D. S., Brockman, L. M., Pence, A. R., Goelman, H., & Johnson, K. L. (1993). *Workplace benefits and flexibility: A perspective on parents' experiences.* Ottawa, Canada: Statistics Canada.

Levine, J. A., & Pittinsky, T. L. (1997). *Working fathers: New strategies for balancing work and family.* Reading, MA: Addison-Wesley.

Margolis, J., & Fisher, A. (2002). *Unlocking the clubhouse: Women in computing.* Cambridge, MA: MIT Press.

Massachusetts Institute of Technology. (1999, March). A study on the status of women faculty in science at MIT. *MIT Faculty Newsletter, 9*(4). Retrieved November 22, 2003, from http://web.mit.edu/fnl/women/women.html

Moen, P., & Wethington, E. (1992). The concept of family adaptive strategies. *Annual Review of Sociology, 18,* 233–251.

Okin, S. M. (1989). *Justice, gender, and the family.* New York: Basic Books.

Osipow, S., Walsh, B., & Bingham, R. (Eds.). (2000). *Career counseling for African Americans.* Mahwah, NJ: Lawrence Erlbaum Associates.

Pleck, J. H. (1988). Fathers and infant care leave. In E. F. Zigler & M. Frank (Eds.), *The parental leave crisis: Toward a national policy* (pp. 177–191). New Haven, CT: Yale University Press.

Pleck, J. H. (1996, June). *Paternal involvement: Levels, sources, and consequences.* Paper presented at the Co-Parenting Roundtable of Fathers and Families, Boston.

Pleck, J. H. (1997). Paternal involvement: Levels, sources, and consequences. In M. E. Lamb (Ed.), *The role of the father in child development* (pp. 66–103). New York: Wiley.

Polasky, L. J., & Holahan, C. K. (1998). Maternal self-discrepancies, interrole conflict, and negative affect among married professional women with children. *Journal of Family Psychology, 12,* 388–401.

Rapoport, R. L., & Rapoport, R. N. (1969). The dual-career family. *Human Relations, 22,* 3–30.

Savoy, H. B. (2004). *Dual-earner couples: Predicting relationship satisfaction among women with male or female partners.* Unpublished doctoral dissertation, University of Missouri, Columbia.

Schneider, K. T., Swan, S., & Fitzgerald, L. F. (1997). Job-related and psychological effects of sexual harassment in the workplace: Empirical evidence from two organizations. *Journal of Applied Psychology, 82,* 401–415.

Sherif, C. W. (1982). Needed concepts in the study of gender identity. *Psychology of Women Quarterly, 6,* 375–398.

Shields, C. (1994). *The stone diaries.* New York: Penguin Books.

Silverstein, L. B. (1996). Fathering is a feminist issue. *Psychology of Women Quarterly, 20,* 3–37.

Smallwood, S. (2003, December 12). American woman surpass men in earning doctorates. *The Chronicle of Higher Education,* p. A10.

Smith, K. (2000). *Who's minding the kids? Child care arrangements: Fall 1995* (Current Population Report No. P70-70). Washington, DC: U.S. Bureau of the Census.

Smith, N. G., & Ingram, K. M. (2004). Workplace heterosexism and adjustment among lesbian, gay, and bisexual individuals: The role of unsupportive social interactions. *Journal of Counseling Psychology, 51,* 57–67.

Spencer, S. J., Steele, C. M., & Quinn, D. M. (1999). Stereotype threat and women's math performance. *Journal of Experimental Social Psychology, 35,* 4–28.

Stebbins, L. F. (2001). *Work and family in America: A reference handbook.* Santa Barbara, CA: ABC-CLIO.

Steil, J. M. (2001). Family forms and member well-being: A research agenda for the decade of behavior. *Psychology of Women Quarterly, 25,* 344–363.

Stevens, D., Kiger, G., & Riley, P. J. (2001). Working hard and hardly working: Domestic labor and marital satisfaction among dual-earner couples. *Journal of Marriage and Family, 63,* 514–526.

Strober, M. H., & Chan, A. M. K. (1999). *The road winds uphill all the way: Gender, work, and family in the United States and Japan.* Cambridge, MA: MIT Press.

Thoits, P. A. (1992). Identity structures and psychological well-being: Gender and marital status comparisons. *Social Psychological Quarterly, 55,* 236–256.

U.S. Bureau of the Census. (2001). *Women in the United States: 2000* (Current Population Report No. PPL-121). Washington, DC: Author.

U.S. Bureau of the Census. (2002). *Highlights of women's earnings in 2001* (Report No. 960). Washington, DC: Author.

Valian, V. (1999). *Why so slow: The advancement of women.* Cambridge, MA: MIT Press.

Ward, K., & Wolf-Wendel, L. (2004). Academic motherhood: Managing complex roles in research universities. *Review of Higher Education, 27,* 233–257.

Wayne, J. H., & Cordeiro, B. L. (2003). Who is a good organizational citizen? Social perception of male and female employees who use family leave. *Sex Roles, 49,* 233–246.

Zimmerman, T. S., Haddock, S. A., Current, L. R., & Ziemba, S. (2003). Intimate partnership: Foundation to the successful balance of family and work. *American Journal of Family Therapy, 31,* 107–124.

Zuckerman, H., Cole, J. R., & Bruer, J. T. (Eds.). (1991). *The outer circle: Women in the scientific community.* New York: Norton.

Chapter 7

Career Counseling With African American Women

Rosie Phillips Bingham
The University of Memphis

Connie M. Ward
Private Practice, Jonesboro, Georgia

Melissa McGhee Butler
The University of Memphis

At the dawn of the 21st century, African American women's parity with other Americans in the United States in earnings and career advancement remains almost as elusive as it did in the 20th century. Findings from a study conducted to investigate the deterioration of Black women's earnings throughout the 1980s showed that although some African American women returned to school and continued to make advancements in work over the decade, this was offset by the negative effects of changing family structure, lack of metropolitan residence, and occupational redistribution (Newsome & Dodoo, 2002). In addition, it was found that there was an increase in the number of African American women who were at the lower end of the earnings distribution. In the summer of 2002, the unemployment rate was 4.9% for White women and 9.8% for African American women (U.S. Department of Labor, Bureau of Labor Statistics, 2002). African American women continue to face barriers to advancement within private-sector management, in that subtle racism prevents some African American women from receiving promotions (Dresser, 1995). Apparently glass ceilings and sticky floors (Fassinger, 2001) are all too common for this racial group of women, many of whom may be blocked from access to mentors, information, or advancement opportunities.

Although corporations have expanded their public support for diversity in the workplace, we are still left to wonder why African American women are not equal participants in the career and vocational advancement process. It is clear that systems need to open doors so that African American women can have access. It would be beneficial if counselors and psychologists could help to ensure that these women have the information and skills they need to take advantage of such access. If career counselors are trained with appropriate skills and knowledge, then it is our contention that career counselors can help these women successfully advance and attain their job and career goals. In this chapter we describe a method to enhance the training of psychologists and counselors who are interested in providing more effective career counseling to African American women. The method includes three steps. First, trainees must acquire the general knowledge implied by the set of assumptions listed later and the "Guidelines on Multicultural Education, Training, Research, Practice, and Organizational Change for Psychologists" (hereafter referred to as the multicultural guidelines) that were adopted as American Psychological Association (APA) policy in 2002 (APA, 2003). The next step is to decide on a career-counseling model or theory that includes the unique needs and considerations of African American women. Such models or theories build on the foundation of the multicultural guidelines. We subscribe to models described in the work of Bingham, Fouad, and Ward (Bingham, 2000; Bingham & Ward, 1994, 1996; Fouad & Bingham, 1995; Ward & Bingham, 1993). Finally, it is important to select a training technique that will enhance the counselor's intervention skills. We submit that using a think-aloud protocol (Johns, Lenski, & Elish-Piper, 2002) will enhance career-counseling effectiveness with African American women regardless of the theory or model a counselor chooses.

First, in order to understand our training method, we detail our assumptions about the career counselor and the career-counseling process. Next, we summarize the multicultural guidelines; we believe that any work we do must seek to reach the aspirations set forth in these guidelines. We then provide some examples of general knowledge contained or implied in the assumptions and the multicultural guidelines. Next we provide a critique of the culturally specific models for career counseling that have potential applications with African American women. We then present a think-aloud protocol or method that allows readers a glimpse into the thinking process of two different counselors working with two different African American women clients in scenarios derived from real-life composites of African American females. We end the chapter with recommendations for education, training, practice, and research.

GENERAL KNOWLEDGE

Assumptions

We make several assumptions about the type of career-counseling experience for which the information in this chapter would be appropriate.

These assumptions are based on our collective experience providing career counseling to women of color. The assumptions are as follows:

1. Career counselors are familiar with theories of counseling, career development, adult development, and multicultural guidelines.

2. Career counselors are open to developing sensitivity to and understanding of how a client's worldview is shaped by culture, ethnicity, race, and gender. Counselors are aware of within-group differences among African American women.

3. Career counselors are open to acquiring the sensitivity to and understanding of how their career-counseling orientation, values, and beliefs are shaped by their own culture, ethnicity, race, and gender.

4. The career-counseling length is at least two to six sessions. The emphasis is on developing an interview style that allows counselors to gain access to information about clients and helps clients see the variety of factors that impact their career decisions.

5. Career counselors recognize and acknowledge the social, political, and economic realities of this nation at a given time in history. This assumption asks career counselors to acknowledge the present realities of the world of work.

6. Career counselors are open to being challenged in ways that go beyond the learning of the technology of assessment instruments and familiarity with career resources.

7. Career counselors understand that a career decision will impact all parts of the client's life and see career counseling as an educational and lifelong process.

8. Career counselors are willing to learn and use a career-counseling model or theory that accommodates the unique needs and experiences of African American women.

9. Career counselors are open to being challenged to look differently at expanding the tasks involved in career counseling and providing career services to African American women.

10. All clients will be treated with respect, dignity, and humanity because ultimately it is the clients who have answers to their own questions. Career counselors have the expertise to facilitate clients finding those answers.

Although these 10 assumptions serve as a framework for our thinking about career counseling with African American women, the multicultural guidelines serve as the official aspirational test for our further conceptualization and application of career-counseling methods and models.

Multicultural Guidelines

The multicultural guidelines were approved as policy of the APA in 2002 (APA, 2003) to help clinicians and researchers meet the needs of people who have been historically marginalized because of their ethnicity or race and social group identity or membership. The guidelines' goals are to "provide psychologists with (a) the rationale and needs for addressing multiculturalism and diversity in education, training, research, practice, and organizational change; (b) basic information, relevant terminology, current empirical research from psychology and related disciplines, and other data that support the proposed guidelines and underscore their importance; (c) references to enhance on-going education, training, research, practice, and organizational change methodologies; and (d) paradigms that broaden the purview of psychology as a profession" (APA, p. 1).

The guidelines that we believe are most relevant to the focus of this chapter in addressing career counseling with African American women are:

1. Psychologists are encouraged to be aware of the attitudes and beliefs they may hold about individuals who are ethnically and racially different from themselves.
2. Psychologists are encouraged to be aware of the importance of multicultural sensitivity, knowledge, and understanding about ethnically and racially diverse individuals.
3. Psychologists are encouraged to apply culturally appropriate skills in clinical and other applied psychological practices.

When working with African American women requesting career counseling, the counselor will need to consider various factors in order to be effective. Sociopolitical factors affecting African American women, the role of changing demographics in the United States, the individuals' experience along with their worldview, and the multicultural guidelines all need to be taken into consideration when working with this population. These women's experiences vary, and it is up to counselors to prepare themselves to have a good, working knowledge of how to work with and assist these women.

Related Literature

General knowledge about African American women needs to include: information about the employment environment for African American women; their view on the role of sexism and racism in their occupational life; and the role of education and the impact of their worldview and racial identity development. The review that follows summarizes some of the related literature in all of these areas.

The employment environment for African American women has changed substantively since 1986 when the earnings gap between Black and White women widened. In 2000 Black women's participation rate in the labor market was 63.2% compared to 59.8% for White women. Yet in 2002 White women's earnings were 15.8% higher than Black women and 33.4% of White women were likely to be managers compared with 24.8% of Black women. Some of these differences might be explained by the gap in educational achievement of Black and White women. In 2000, 54.6% of Black women over 25 years old had more than a high school diploma, compared with a 60% rate for White women (U.S. Department of Labor, Bureau of Labor Statistics, 2002).

Although education is likely to account for some of the difference in selection of occupations and subsequent earnings, some of the difference may be explained by worldviews, socialization, and other psychological factors. These following factors appear to remain consonant in women's career choice and career development: (a) balance between work and family, (b) socialization around the role of women, (c) barriers and challenges presented by sexism and racism, (d) role of and access to mentors, and (e) information about the world of work.

Richie et al. (1997) found that African American women who are high achieving and prominent still report the oppression they face as a result of sexism and racism. The women in Richie et al.'s study reported outright discrimination, prejudice, and lack of opportunity. The women discussed the importance of support from family and friends and yet highlighted the lack of role models and mentors. The women in the study did report feelings of connection to the African American community and to an interest in making a difference in the world.

Such research findings may lend some support to the impact of worldviews on the career development and the career-counseling process for African American women. The definition of worldview generally includes references to individual perceptions of the world around them; a worldview can be described as a cultural lens or frame of reference. It includes the views (of a defined group of people) shaped by culture, mores, values, and attitudes of majority and minority groups. Over the past 30 years Sue (1981), Nobles (1976), and Pederson (1976) provided seminal definitions of worldviews that have been used by many writers of the multicultural literature. Nobles and Pederson, respectively, outlined the differences in worldviews in terms that subscribe to either a collectivistic or individualistic view of the world. Sue, on the other hand, added the concept of the sense of internal versus external control of one's life.

For African American women these theories may have salience because such ways of viewing the world could influence career choice and career progression. For example, if an African American woman has a collectivistic worldview, she may believe that her career choice must positively affect her entire racial or ethnic group. Such a view may compel her to succeed beyond her even originally conceived limits because she is working for the success of her entire racial group. Or it could be that she feels such responsibility for the group that she dare not venture beyond certain restricted borders because her failure would be the group's failure. Nobles and Goddard (1993) would speculate that such individuals have a collectivistic or African worldview and would therefore value the needs of the group over the needs of the individual. According to Bingham (2000) and Akbar (1991), these women would have strong needs for relationships and affiliation. A career counselor would need to understand the woman's worldview because her career indecision could be related to her views about herself in relation to her racial group, rather than to a lack of information about the world of work. Or the career indecision could be more related to the worldview definition espoused by Sue (1981), who described a worldview based on Rotter's theory of internal and external locus of control (Rotter, 1955). According to Sue, ethnic minority individuals could have a sense of internal control and believe that whatever happens to them and their careers is controlled by their own behavior regardless of what is happening in the external world. These individuals would believe that their success is not determined by the "structure of opportunity" (Lent, Brown, & Hackett, 1994) in a dominant group environment. Or they could believe that their career decisions are almost entirely controlled by external forces such as racism, regardless of what they believe about themselves and their abilities. So the level of stress experienced by an African American woman as she makes a career decision could be influenced by her beliefs about her internal and external sense of control. If she believes that racism will determine her vocational progress then she may believe that she essentially has few career choices.

In an interesting comparative case study of the college enrollment of African American women from poor communities, Matthews-Armstead (2002) found that the college-going women saw themselves as independent, self-reliant, competent, and empowered. They saw themselves as connected to their families and to their communities. They also expressed a belief in a need to make the world different and better. Their families were a source of support and the women saw themselves as strongly connected to their race.

Shaw and Coleman (2000) reported on the importance of powerful Black mentors in the lives of African American females as they made decisions about attending college. The authors also talked about the tension that arose in families when the women seemed to put college above family. These two researchers, along with Matthews-Armstead (2002), may lend some support to the importance of racial identity development in the career-counseling and development process for African American women. The differences found in these two studies certainly highlight the fact that African American women are not monolithic and that identification with race is important.

Cross (1971) asserted that Black individuals evolve through a racial identity process that begins with a state of being anti-Black and pro-White and could continue through a state of internalization in which the individual is pro-Black and pro all other ethnic groups. Cross' original conceptions were refined and operationalized through the work of Helms (1990) and her colleagues. In recent years, researchers (Cokley, 2002; Vandiver, Cross, Worrell, & Fhagan-Smith, 2002) have further refined the racial identity development theories and demonstrated the soundness of the model. Equally important has been the work on the development of a White racial identity model. Readers are referred to works by Helms as well as Ponterotto (1989) for extensive discussions of these models.

Recently, there have been other researchers (Sellers, Smith, Shelton, Rowley, & Chavous, 1998) who have conceptualized racial identity somewhat differently from Cross (1971) and Helms (1990) and have concluded that there are two approaches to African American racial identity: mainstream and underground. The mainstream approach of African American identity has historically focused only on the stigma associated with being African American, as opposed to the qualitative meanings and cultural influences of the African American experience. The underground approach recognizes that African American identity is influenced by more factors than racism and incorporates African Americans' historical and contemporary experiences in America and Africa in its definition of African American identity. The multidimensional model of racial identity (Sellers et al.) is a fusion of both approaches and of the existing theories on group identity and its four assumptions are that: (a) identities are situationally influenced as well as stable properties within the person, (b) individuals have different identities that are hierarchically ordered, (c) individuals' perception of their racial identity is the most valid indicator of their identity, and (d) there is concern for status of an individual's racial identity rather than its development.

Ward and Bingham (1993) and Fouad and Bingham (1995) maintained that racial identity development is important in the career-counseling process with African American women. Bingham and Ward (1994) stated that the racial identity of both the client and the counselor could be important in a career-counseling encounter. (See Bingham & Ward, 1996, for a practical example demonstrating the role of racial identity development in the career-counseling process.) Alfred (2001) maintained that one must simultaneously study race and career development along with culture and identity in order to provide effective interventions. Alfred further asserted that

African American women maintain a "double consciousness" as a result of being a Black female worker in a White world and that identity is dynamic and situational. These contentions mirror the recent research and theoretical conceptualizations regarding the racial identity development process. Parham (1989) and Vandiver et al. (2002) stated that the racial identity development process is cyclical, thus supporting Alfred's notion that identity is dynamic.

If the previous assertions are true, one can easily see the importance of the first two multicultural guidelines. Counselors must be continually sensitive to the changing dynamic affiliated with being cultural beings and the need for "multicultural sensitivity to knowledge of, and understanding about ethnically and racially different individuals" (APA, 2003, p. 385). It is also clear that any theory or model of counseling with African American women will rest on the foundation provided by the multicultural guidelines, will be culturally sensitive, and will pay particular attention to issues of worldview, racial identity development, and culturally appropriate interventions.

MODELS AND THEORIES OF CAREER COUNSELING WITH AFRICAN AMERICAN WOMEN

Over the last decade numerous writers have reported on the applicability of major career-counseling theories to the career development of people of color in general and specifically to African American women (Bingham & Ward, 1994; Bowman, 1993; Brown, 1995; Constantine & Parker, 2001; Fouad & Arbona, 1994; Walsh, Bingham, Brown, & Ward, 2001). There is general consensus that the major career theories have some application to counseling with African Americans, but there is not enough research to be definitive about how to apply those theories.

Within the past few years, there have been two new approaches (social-cognitive theory and ecological perspective) that propose to attend to career development and career barriers in racially and ethnically diverse populations. However, when applied to African American women and compared against the multicultural guidelines, neither approach seems to completely embody the spirit of these guidelines. For instance, Lent, Brown, and Hackett (2000) discussed using the social-cognitive theory (SCT) as a framework in which to explain academic and career behavior among individuals. This model concentrates on cognitive-person variables (self-efficacy, outcome expectations, and goals) and their interaction with personal characteristics and personal environment (gender, ethnicity, social supports, and barriers) in order to shape career development. Much of the research and practice to originate from this theory has only attended to the cognitive-person variables and failed to acknowledge the environmental factors that also affect career behavior. Although Lent et al. (1994) postulated in Hypothesis 1G of SCT that "gender and racial/ethnic differences in interests and in interest-goal relations arise largely through differential access to opportunities, supports, and socialization process" (p. 108), little research afterward addressed this area. However, there has been a surge in the career literature on career barriers (e.g., sex and race discrimination) and career supports (e.g., mentors, family, friends).

Although this theory has generated an abundance of research, in terms of providing career counseling for African American women, it only addresses one of the three multicultural guidelines we presented. In a broad way, it encourages psychologists to be aware of the importance of multicultural sensitivity, knowledge, and understanding about ethnically and racially diverse people, in that membership in a racially diverse social group may also bring with it career barriers and supports that are idiosyncratic to that membership group. In addition, Lent et al.'s (1994) concentric model of environmental influences has similar features to that of Fouad and Bingham's (1995) cultural variables spheres of influence model. However, SCT does not encourage psychologists to be aware of the attitudes and beliefs they may hold about those who are racially or ethnically different from themselves. Nor does it encourage psychologists to use culturally appropriate skills in clinical practice.

Cook, Heppner, and O'Brien's (2002) ecological approach emphasizes the relationship between women and their environment. The authors assert that the female client's career behavior is and will be influenced by factors germane to her environment or ecosystem. The authors maintain that clarifying and affirming women's life options, managing time demands of multiple roles, obtaining quality child care, creating healthy working environments, improving access to role models and mentors, and equalizing salaries are all interventions with which career counselors can assist their women of color clients. This model did address two of the three guidelines we highlighted for this chapter. It does encourage career counselors to be aware of the importance of knowledge and understanding about ethnically and racially diverse individuals and how that information may differ from that of the majority culture. The authors even provide examples of what some of those differences may look like in relation to the major subsystems of an ecological model. This approach also encourages career counselors to apply culturally appropriate interventions when working with women of color. However, this approach does not encourage psychologists to be aware of attitudes and beliefs they may have about people who are racially and ethnically different from themselves. This is an important omission from both approaches.

Ward maintained that any effective career-counseling process must "begin with the end in mind" (cited in Covey, 1989, p. 98). Thus the end of the career-counseling process is that the career client will have asked, explored, and answered the questions that most inform, influence, and impact her ability to implement her career decision or choice. The process would have looked at expectations, aspirations, self-efficacy, ability, perceived limitations, fears, and self-imposed restrictions. The multicultural guidelines provide parameters by which counselors internally prepare themselves to guide and educate clients through the process by first looking at worldview and racial identity issues. We therefore found that the most effective conceptualization for doing career counseling with African American women was a summary of three overlapping models: steps to career counseling with minority females (Bingham & Ward, 1994), culturally appropriate career counseling model (Fouad & Bingham, 1995), and steps to multicultural career assessment (Bingham, 2000). In fact, multicultural guidelines numbers 1, 2, and 5 are consistent with the phases of the career-counseling process with ethnic minority women as proposed by Bingham and Ward. They called the first phase "counselor preparation" and it involved the counselor being: culturally sensitive, familiar with the sociopolitical strengths of ethnic groups, familiar with a body of cross-cultural information, receptive to the client as cultural teacher, and knowing the counselor's worldview and the counselor's racial identity development. Ward and Bingham (1993) developed an instrument, the Multicultural Career Counseling Checklist (MCCC), that can help guide the counselor through the preparation phase. The MCCC helps the counselor focus in depth on potential client issues and even the process for the client and counselor to agree on the central issues and the process for working on those issues. In 1990 Ward and Tate (Ward & Bingham) developed an instrument, the Career Counseling Checklist, to help with the second phase of the career-counseling process that helps the client to focus on issues related to worldview, family issues, race, class concerns, career daydreams, and so on. In the third phase the counselor and client negotiate and come to a consensus about what will be the focus in the counseling sessions. The fourth phase is a culturally appropriate intervention and follow-up.

Fouad and Bingham (1995) described a seven-step culturally appropriate career-counseling model that builds on and overlaps with the Bingham and Ward (1994) model. The culturally appropriate model begins with establishing a culturally appropriate relationship, then moves to the assessment of career issues and cultural variables. Then the counselor and client must establish a culturally appropriate counseling process, as well as goals and interventions. The model ends with decision making, intervention, and follow-up.

Bingham (2000) proposed that counselors begin with assessing cultural variables that might have an impact on a woman of color in career decision making, followed by assessment of gender variables, and then efficacy issues. Finally the counselor can examine more traditional career factors. Such a method is consistent with the model proposed by Ward and Bingham (1993) and would make the counseling process that much more effective. These models are consistent with the multicultural guidelines in that they very specifically encourage multicultural sensitivity, knowledge, and understanding; they ask counselors to be aware of their own attitudes and beliefs about the client and counselors are specifically encouraged to only apply culturally appropriate interventions. (For an in-depth description and discussion of those instruments and models, see Bingham & Ward, 1994; Ward & Bingham.)

From the previous works we have derived seven components to a potential model for career counseling with African American women: counselor and client preparation for counseling, establishment of a culturally appropriate relationship, multicultural career assessment, setting culturally appropriate counseling goals or processes, determining and implementing culturally appropriate interventions, decision making, and follow-up. Although this suggested format and the works by Bingham, Fouad, and Ward rest on a foundation of the multicultural guidelines and the assumptions presented in this chapter, these works (Bingham, 2000; Bingham & Ward, 1994, 1996; Fouad & Bingham, 1995; Ward & Bingham, 1993) suffer from lack of research.

THINK ALOUD

Even when counselors clearly understand multicultural career-counseling models and theories and even when they believe that there is a difference in the counseling process for African American clients and White clients, the counselors will sometimes declare that the counseling process looks the same. It is our contention that if counselors are using the multicultural guidelines then their thinking process about their clients will be different. The question is how can we get a glimpse into that thinking process? We propose a think-aloud protocol.

For this chapter we thought it would be useful to explore the actual process of counseling in two specific cases. To this end we are aware that the actual counseling process between an African American female counselor with an African American female client, when compared to that of a White female counselor and an African American female client, might look and sound fairly similar if the two counselors have had some multicultural career-counseling training. And yet, we believe that the thinking process that shapes the questions for the client and the hypotheses that lead the counselor to the questions may be different for the two counselors. We further believe that if we can expose some of the thinking behind the Black female counselor's questions, we can benefit the educational process for counselor trainees. In other words, if we can more clearly delineate the metacognition process or the think-aloud counseling process (adapted from Johns et al., 2002), then we can more ably demonstrate the kinds of questions that might be useful to think about when the counselor sits down with an African American female client. These questions may never be asked of the client, but the think-aloud questions help to shape the hypotheses that will be formed and the subsequent questions that will be asked of the client. In what follows, we summarize the case scenario. Then we describe the first set of questions that came to the counselor's mind. Next we examine the issues or questions behind the questions or the thinking out loud. This process allows the counselor trainee a unique opportunity to look into the mind of a more seasoned counselor as she works with an African American client.

CAREER-COUNSELING CASE STUDIES

Case 1

Sylvia is a 28-year-old African American female who is currently in a doctoral program studying to become a psychologist. She has come to career counseling because she is not sure what type of employment she would like to pursue with her doctorate. She feels that she has many possibilities and is excited by that prospect, but she also feels overwhelmed by the number of choices she can make and comes in for counseling to help narrow her choices.

Sylvia comes from an African American, middle-class, two-parent family in the South. She has two siblings: an older brother and a younger sister. Her mother has a college education but her father served in the military and has vocational school training. Education has always been stressed in her family, especially by her father. Sylvia excelled in school and although she has always been aware of being a female and an African American, she has never thought of her race or gender hindering her in realizing her career aspirations.

Sylvia attended a historically Black college-university as an undergraduate and then a predominantly White institution to obtain her master's degree. Although she was the only Black person in her master's program, she did not feel excluded because of her race and felt it necessary to offer opinions she had about a subject if diversity had not been considered. In her current doctoral program, she feels the same way. She is once again the only Black person in her program and feels that her race and position put her in a unique situation to challenge stereotypes her colleagues may have about race and ethnicity, culture, institutionalized racism, or oppression.

Sylvia would like a career counselor who will be empathic and knowledgeable about her cultural background, but who does not assume to know

Sylvia's experience. Sylvia would like the opportunity to tell her own story and not have it contrived through stereotypes and past knowledge about African Americans without taking her individual experience into account.

Think Aloud.   Counselor preparation: These are my initial thoughts that I may or may not share with Sylvia, but they would inform my line of questioning. Here are my first thoughts before I meet this client. She is an African American client. I need to watch for transference and countertransference. She is in a psychology doctoral program. What do I know about the history, politics, gender, and racial breakdowns of this department? I am conscious of the possible impact of my race on this client.

Is she single or married? Does she have a partner or someone else's opinions to consider? I wonder where she is developmentally. In which particular program in the department is she enrolled? I am surprised at her choice of words, "type of employment," rather than talking about a career path. I wonder why she is really here. What makes her excited? Why is she feeling overwhelmed? Where are her mentors? Where is her advisor? Why did she decide to pursue being a psychologist? Is this client naive or just unaware of the opportunities and information that should be available to her from her department?

I note that she is the middle child. What jobs or careers have the other siblings pursued? I see that she grew up in the South and wonder whether in an urban, suburban, or rural setting. Was her mother employed outside the home? How long was her father in the military? What type of vocational training did her father complete? What type of employment? How was education stressed by her father? Was it in words, examples, expectations, or aspirations? Was race or gender considered? Has the impact been considered even if race is not a hindrance? "Sylvia excelled in school and although she has always been aware of being a female and an African American, she has never thought of her race or gender hindering her in realizing her career aspirations?" How aware is the client of racial and gender issues? Where is she in her racial identity development?

What did she take from that experience at a historically Black college-university as an undergraduate? Who were her mentors? Who was influential? What did she take from her master's experience? Who were her mentors or influential people? "Although she was the only Black person in her master's program, she did not feel excluded because of her race and felt it necessary to offer opinions she had about a subject if diversity had not been considered. In her current doctoral program, she feels the same way." It seems like a different program, same experience. Had she expected to feel excluded? "She is once again the only Black person in her program and feels that her race and position put her in a unique situation to challenge stereotypes her colleagues may have about race and ethnicity, culture, institutionalized racism, or oppression." This seems like a double-edged-sword role. Has she felt supported, understood, acknowledged? I wonder about the burden she feels to provide the "diversity" opinion?

Why would Sylvia not expect to be treated as a unique client? What has been Sylvia's experience that led her to believe a career counselor would assume to know her experience? This sounds either defensive or weary of feeling like she has to continually educate others. How does she want to tell her story? Has she been interfered with before? It seems to me that Sylvia is trying to serve two roles in the program: (a) "I'm just like everyone else" and (b) "I'm the diversity conscious-barometer for my colleagues." How is that balance working for her? Did she take that role on willingly or by default? How does this person make decisions? Can she let someone help her, given her fears? Why has she really come here today?

Information provided by Sylvia and her answers to my questions would allow me to make decisions about additional information I might need or data gaps that Sylvia might be challenged to fill. It is likely that in addition to information about employment in Sylvia's chosen field, she may need help with assertion, negotiation skills, and raising her expectations of the help she can expect from her department.

Summary.   The reader can easily see in the think aloud that the counselor is constantly raising questions about issues of race and racism as she thinks through the client statements and problems. Clearly the counselor's questions are shaped by her own experience with race and racism in the United States. That is part of the reason that the multicultural guidelines are so important and that the steps to career counseling with women of color are equally important. Each counselor is shaped by culture and brings that culture into the counseling session.

As we prepared this chapter on career counseling with African American women we found that the steps to multicultural career assessment (Bingham, 2000) continue to be appropriate. The counselor must first resolve matters of race and culture, then issues around gender, next matters of self-efficacy, and then traditional vocational problems that might involve the administration of a career inventory such as the Strong Interest Inventory. Although it is unlikely that the steps to career counseling with African American women will ever follow such a precise order, it is clear that until our society changes we will always need to be very cognizant of race matters.

Case 2

Bernita is a 48-year-old African American woman who is currently the assistant director of human resources for the Southeast U.S. regional division of a large multinational bank. Bernita comes to career counseling because she feels she is at a crossroads in her career. Bernita is presently on medical leave from her job for emergency surgery. During that hospitalization she was also diagnosed with diabetes, having had a blood sugar reading of 575. She was in the hospital for 3 weeks and now is at home recuperating.

Bernita comes from an African American, lower socioeconomic status, two-parent family in the lower Midwest. Two parents, who are from the rural South, raised her. Bernita is the fifth of nine children. She has five brothers and three sisters. Mother, grandmother, and one sister have died from complications from diabetes. Her sister died at age 40. Both of Bernita's parents have eighth-grade educations. Her father worked as a laborer and her mother was a stay-at-home mom who babysat for extra money. One brother and one sister finished college in addition to Bernita, who also completed an MBA at night school after 4 years. Bernita has been married for 8 years. This is her first marriage and her husband's second marriage. They do not have children. Bernita's husband is 10 years older than she is and has taken an early retirement package from his employer. They both have invested and have paid into 401k plans and have been financially successful.

Bernita has progressed through the ranks at work since joining the bank after graduation from a predominantly White Midwestern university. Her MBA was completed at a predominantly White state university in the Southeast. Bernita has felt a responsibility, as one of two African Americans at her level in the organization, to mentor and be available to others, especially African Americans and other minorities. Bernita has found herself having difficulty saying "no" even during lunch, when she should be going home, and while at home.

Bernita's boss, the director of human resources, is set to retire in 9 months. He has been grooming Bernita to take over his job. She has even held this job temporarily when her boss was out for 3 months on medical leave. She received good reviews from the vice president and the president. Bernita went to the regional directors' meeting where she was the only African American. She reports feeling a great deal of responsibility and isolation because everyone acted as if it was downtime and she felt on guard the whole time.

Bernita has been told she has to change her lifestyle because of the diabetes. She experienced near death at the hospital and is very serious about these changes. She comes to career counseling to request help with deciding what to do in her career, how to integrate this health issue into her career path, and how to balance her work and personal life. She wants help with setting boundaries, saying "no," and dealing with the impact of this life-changing event.

Think Aloud.   First as an African American counselor I am always conscious of race—my race and that of the client. I wonder on the front end what, if any, are the client's issues, concerns, and questions about her race and about my race. Bernita—I notice her name. Social class questions and generation questions come to mind because in certain geographical locations in the United States the naming of children tends to follow a pattern. The pattern of names will sometimes provide clues to the client's social class and historical context. For example, beginning in the 1970s there was a move to give African-affiliated names to children. That movement tended to begin with young African Americans who attended college. Bernita's name suggests that she is not a part of that cohort. Next I am aware of the client's age and I wonder why someone who is 48 is seeking career counseling, especially given her position with a large multinational bank. I am already wondering if I will see issues related to a potential job promotion that might be connected to race.

Because Bernita has trouble saying "no," I wonder if that difficulty comes from responsibilities she may feel because of her race, gender, family values, worldview, or personality. I would note the age difference between Bernita and her husband, the length of the marriage, and the apparent financial stability. I wonder about the husband's support of Bernita's career because of the role expectations each brings to the marriage. Diabetes is fairly common among African American families. Because Bernita's sister died from complications with diabetes I will listen to determine if family and illness questions or fears prompted the client to seek counseling.

I take note that Bernita's boss is "grooming her to take his position." I wonder about the boss' race and what their relationship in the workplace might be like. If he is White does this provide some insight about Bernita's comfort level and how she might interact with a particular kind of White male? Because Bernita is on guard and feels very responsible at a conference I wonder more about the role of race, family dynamics, and her personality. Her sense of isolation makes me wonder about her comfort in a racial group in which she is the only African American. Will these feelings enter into whatever is her career-counseling question? At this point I have begun to consciously call on my own racial experience to help me understand what it is like to be an "only" African American in a group of White professionals. My experience and feelings whether like Bernita's or not will inform the questions and hypotheses I will develop as I work with this client.

I really want to know what Bernita means by "deciding what to do in her career." I need to understand if she is questioning whether she wants a promotion or to take another route. What influence does her health have on her career? What role will her husband play in her decision? Does Bernita have any questions or worries about herself as an African American woman role model for her family members, mentees, and "others, especially African

Americans and other minorities"? This question leads me to wonder about Bernita's worldview, her awareness of that worldview, and my role in helping her to understand that conceptualization. I wonder if an understanding of worldviews will help her to understand more about how to set boundaries.

My alternate hypothesis has to do with exploring more traditional developmental issues, generativity, and fears about life and death. Bernita could be concerned with how much time she has left to live and she may want to decide how to come to terms with what is really important to her. My next set of questions to myself have to do with how the issues of race and worldview intersect with more traditional developmental career and life questions.

Summary.   This case represents the complexity of issues a counselor might face when an African American woman walks through the door with a simple career-counseling question. The counseling interaction might look the same as a counseling interaction with a European American woman were one to view the sessions on videotape. However, we hope the reader can see that if we examine the thinking behind the visible interaction, the counselor's internal thinking process must be very different. In this case example the counselor tended to follow the steps to multicultural career assessment (Bingham, 2000).

The counselor started with thinking about questions that had to do with race and its impact on the client's thinking, career goals, and the structure of opportunity. Comingled with the race questions were family questions. The counselor's thinking process demonstrates that there is not a definitive line or order to the steps in career counseling with African American women. Sometimes family is more salient than gender. That is part of the reason why it is so important for trainers to help trainees to think through all of the steps to career counseling with this population of women.

The think-aloud method in this chapter can allow trainers and trainees to look at the kinds of questions that might be raised in cases like the two presented. Individuals could begin with an examination of the steps to multicultural career assessment. Just examining those steps could help them to begin the metacognition process. Then counselors can add an instrument like the Career Counseling Checklist or the MCCC. If a counselor has not had the life experience or in-depth training to develop the internal questions or hypotheses in a career-counseling context with African American women, these instruments will prove quite valuable.

CONCLUSION

The common omission we noticed in reviewing multicultural career-counseling theories is that career counselors are not explicitly encouraged to be conscious of the attitudes and beliefs they may hold about the particular racial or ethnic group with whom they are working. These attitudes and beliefs are important because they will guide the work counselors do with clients. They will also be used to generate hypotheses about what is important in the client's life, as well as what the major issues are. Recognizing their own biases and beliefs is an important first step when counselors are working with any client, but particularly when working with someone who is racially or ethnically different from themselves. Career counselors are never fully able to comprehend the importance of being culturally sensitive or to apply culturally appropriate skills if they are not first aware of their own attitudes about clients' racial or ethnic group and about how it will impact their work together. The think-aloud process can help counselors acknowledge their attitudes and beliefs about clients' racial or ethnic group.

We believe that this chapter can be of benefit to counselor trainees and those who are interested in developing their counseling skills with African American clients and offer the following recommendations:

1. Become more familiar with metacognition methods or thinking aloud about counseling. More on the procedure can be found in the field of reading (Johns et al., 2002). This method is consistent with the counselor-preparation phase of career counseling with African Americans (Bingham & Ward, 1994) and demonstrates how to shape preview questions before the actual session begins with the client.

2. Become familiar with the multicultural guidelines; train where deficient.

3. Become familiar with models and theories for doing career counseling with African American women.

4. Become familiar with the MCCC for assistance with counselor preparation.

5. Remember that the interface between worldview and racial identity development makes for a myriad of complexity of within-group differences in African American women.

6. Remain open to the possibility that your view of the world of work may be different from your client's view, let the client inform you and then try to educate around any misconceptions.

7. Design more research studies to examine the existing theories on multicultural career counseling that have been advanced in the last decade.

The think-aloud protocol can be used in a number of research studies to examine the thinking processes of counselors by race, gender, or level of training. Counselors of different races or ethnicities could be given the same client scenario. The counselors would be asked to write their thoughts and questions after reading the case. Raters could examine the counselors' products for themes and trends. The researcher could look for differences by race or ethnicity. In another example the think-aloud products could be correlated with client outcomes in live settings. Researchers could explore correlations between various variables, including multicultural training, gender, race, or even socioeconomic status. As the reader can see, the think-aloud technique lends itself to various research designs that can be consistent with the multicultural guidelines and can produce knowledge that will impact education, training, and the practice of career counseling with African American women.

Multicultural career counseling is not as easy as it first appears because there are so many potential complicating factors such as self-efficacy and the structure of opportunity in a society that still has to cope with sexism, racism, ageism, and individual personalities. The counseling process is sometimes easy to read about and even easy to talk about, yet it is more complex than that. We encourage counselors to think beyond the obvious and, as they begin work with a client, to start with the end in mind.

REFERENCES

Akbar, N. (1991). *Chains and images of psychological slavery.* Jersey City, NJ: New Mind Productions.

Alfred, M. (2001). Expanding theories of career development: Adding the voices of African American women in the White academy. *Adult Education Quarterly, 51,* 108–127.

American Psychological Association. (2003). Guidelines on multicultural education, training, research, practice, and organizational change for psychologists. *American Psychologist, 58,* 377–402.

Bingham, R. P. (2000). Multicultural career counseling: Awareness, knowledge and skills for the changing workplace. In J. M. Kummerow (Ed.), *New directions in career planning and the workplace* (pp. 247–272). Palo Alto, CA: Davies-Black.

Bingham, R. P., & Ward, C. M. (1994). Career counseling with ethnic minority women. In W. B. Walsh & S. H. Osipow (Eds.), *Career counseling for women* (pp. 165–196). Hillsdale, NJ: Lawrence Erlbaum Associates.

Bingham, R. P., & Ward, C. M. (1996). Practical application with ethnic minority women. In M. L. Savickas & W. B. Walsh (Eds.), *The handbook of career counseling: Theory and practice* (pp. 291–314). Palo Alto, CA: Davies-Black.

Bowman, S. L. (1993). Career intervention strategies for ethnic minorities. *Career Development Quarterly, 42,* 14–25.

Brown, M. T. (1995). The career development of African Americans: Theoretical and empirical issues. In F. T. L. Leong (Ed.), *Career development and vocational behavior of racial and ethnic minorities* (pp. 7–36). Hillsdale, NJ: Lawrence Erlbaum Associates.

Cokley, K. O. (2002). Testing Cross's revised racial identity model: An examination of the relationship between racial identity and internalized racism. *Journal of Counseling Psychology, 49,* 476–483.

Constantine, M. G., & Parker, V. F. (2001). Addressing the career transition issues of African American women: Vocational and personal considerations. In W. B. Walsh, R. P. Bingham,

M. T. Brown, & C. M. Ward (Eds.), *Career counseling for African Americans* (pp. 99–112). Mahwah, NJ: Lawrence Erlbaum Associates.

Cook, E. P., Heppner, M. J., & O'Brien, K. M. (2002). Career development of women of color and White women: Assumptions, conceptualization, and interventions from an ecological perspective. *Career Development Quarterly, 50,* 291–305.

Covey, S. R. (1989). *The 7 habits of highly effective people: Restoring the character ethic.* New York: Simon & Schuster.

Cross, W. E., Jr. (1971). The Negro-to-Black conversion experience. *Black World, 20*(9), 13–27.

Dresser, L. (1995). To be young, Black, and female: Falling further behind in the shifting economy. *Dollars and Sense, 199,* 32–34.

Fassinger, R. E. (2001, March). *On remodeling the master's house: Tools for dismantling sticky floors and glass ceilings.* Paper presented at the fifth biennial conference of the Society of Vocational Psychology, Houston, TX.

Fouad, N. A., & Arbona, C. (1994). Careers in a cultural context. *Career Development Quarterly, 43,* 96–104.

Fouad, N. A., & Bingham, R. P. (1995). Career counseling with racial/ethnic minorities. In W. B. Walsh & S. H. Osipow (Eds.), *Handbook of vocational psychology* (2nd ed., pp. 331–366). Hillsdale, NJ: Lawrence Erlbaum Associates.

Helms, J. E. (1990). An overview of Black racial identity theory. In J. E. Helms (Ed.), *Black and White racial identity: Theory, research, and practice* (pp. 9–47). New York: Greenwood Press.

Johns, J. L., Lenski, S. D., & Elish-Piper, L. (2002). *Teaching beginning readers: Linking assessment and instruction* (2nd ed.). Dubuque, IA: Kendall/Hunt.

Lent, R. W., Brown, S. D., & Hackett, G. (1994). Toward a unifying social cognitive theory of career and academic interest, choice, and performance. *Journal of Vocational Behavior, 45,* 79–122.

Lent, R. W., Brown, S. D., & Hackett, G. (2000). Contextual supports and barriers to career choice: A social cognitive analysis. *Journal of Counseling Psychology, 47,* 36–49.

Matthews-Armstead, E. (2002). And still they rise: College enrollment of African American women from poor communities. *Journal of Black Studies, 33,* 44–65.

Newsome, Y. D., & Dodoo, F. N. (2002). Reversal of fortune: Explaining the decline in Black women's earnings. *Gender and Society, 16,* 442–464.

Nobles, W. W. (1976). Extended self: Rethinking the Negro self concept. *Journal of Black Psychology, 2,* 15–24.

Nobles, W. W., & Goddard, L. L. (1993). An African centered model of prevention for African-American youth at high risk. In L. L. Goddard (Ed.), *An African centered model of prevention for African American youth at high risk* (Center for Substance Abuse Prevention Report No. 6, pp. 115–128). Rockville, MD: U.S. Department of Health and Human Services.

Parham, T. (1989). Cycles of psychological nigrescence. *The Counseling Psychologist, 17,* 187–226.

Pederson, P. B. (1976). The field of intercultural counseling. In P. Pederson, W. J. Lonner, & J. G. Dragus (Eds.), *Counseling across cultures* (pp. 17–41). Honolulu: University of Hawaii Press.

Ponterotto, J. G. (1989). Expanding directions for racial identity research. *The Counseling Psychologist, 17,* 204–272.

Richie, B. S., Fassinger, R. E., Linn, S. G., Johnson, J., Robinson, S., & Prosser, J. (1997). Persistence, connection, and passion: A qualitative study of the career development of highly achieving African American-Black and White women. *Journal of Counseling Psychology, 44,* 133–148.

Rotter, J. B. (1955). The role of the psychological situation in determining the direction of human behavior. In M. R. Jones (Ed.), *Nebraska symposium on motivation* (pp. 245–268). Lincoln: University of Nebraska Press.

Sellers, R. M., Smith, M. A., Shelton, J. N., Rowley, S. A. J., & Chavous, T. M. (1998). Multidimensional model of racial identity: A reconceptualization of African American racial identity. *Personality and Social Psychology Review, 2,* 18–39.

Shaw, K. M., & Coleman, A. B. (2000). Humble on Sundays: Family, friends, and faculty in the upward mobility experiences of African American females. *Anthropology and Education Quarterly, 3,* 449–470.

Sue, D. W. (1981). *Counseling the culturally different: Theory and practice.* New York: Wiley.

U.S. Department of Labor, Bureau of Labor Statistics. (2000). *Employment and unemployment* [Data file]. Available from the Bureau of Labor Statistics Web site, http://www.bls.gov

U.S. Department of Labor, Bureau of Labor Statistics. (2002). *Wages, earnings, and benefits* [Data file]. Available from the Bureau of Labor Statistics Web site, http://www.bls.gov

Vandiver, B., Cross, W. E., Worrell, F. C., & Fhagan-Smith, P. E. (2002). Validating the Cross Identity Scale. *Journal of Counseling Psychology, 49,* 71–85.

Walsh, W. B., Bingham, R. P., Brown, M. T., & Ward, C. M. (2001). *Career counseling for African Americans.* Mahwah, NJ: Lawrence Erlbaum Associates.

Ward, C. M., & Bingham, R. P. (1993). Career assessment of ethnic minority women. *Journal of Career Assessment, 1,* 246–257.

Chapter 8

Career Counseling for Asian Women

Saba Rasheed Ali
Samuel Z. Lewis
Riddhi Sandil
University of Iowa

Asians make up approximately 60% of the world population and over 50% of this population is female (Population Resource Center, n.d.). The rate of female labor force participation has shown a great deal of variation across the different Asian countries, but in general there has been an increased trend in female labor participation over the last century (Sethuraman, 1998). According to the U.S. Equal Employment Opportunity Commission (2002), Asian women make up approximately 2.1% of the private sector workforce in the United States, an increase of 0.8% since 1990. Despite these trends, very little attention has been paid to the career development and counseling issues of Asian women. Perhaps this is due to the complexity of the concept of "being Asian." Asia is a large continent with people from over 40 countries who speak numerous languages and dialects and subscribe to a variety of different religious and spiritual traditions. The racial-ethnic category of "Asian" is complicated by within-group differences and adherence to multiple identities. To this date most of the literature pertaining to Asian or Asian American career concerns has focused on those individuals from East Asia (i.e., China, Korea, Vietnam, Japan; e.g., Tang, Fouad, & Smith, 1999; Yang, 1991), although more recently, attempts have been made to understand the career development of South Asian women and Israelis (e.g., Balagopal, 1999; Rachman-Moore & Danziger, 1998). Yet, this literature still excludes a huge number of individuals such as those from the Muslim Middle East, former Soviet Union (e.g., Uzbekistan, Tajikistan), and the Pacific islands such as the Philippines and Indonesia.

In this chapter we discuss the career development and counseling issues of Asian women with an emphasis on Asian women living and working in the United States. Because a discussion of the specific career development and counseling of Asian women from each of the various nationalities within Asia is beyond the scope of this chapter, we focus on the application of specific theories that can address the contextual and complex identity issues related to the career development of Asian women regardless of their country of origin. We also focus on the application of recent models of career counseling and assessment techniques that have been developed specifically for working with individuals from racial-ethnic minorities. In the following section we provide a brief overview of the demographic characteristics of Asian women in the national workforce.

ASIAN IMMIGRATION TO THE UNITED STATES

A number of authors (Bradshaw, 1994; Foo, 2002; Sue & Sue, 2002) have outlined the immigration history of Asians to the United States, which like that of most immigrants, is based on capitalism and labor needs. In the mid-1800s Chinese laborers were brought to the United States by the U.S. government to help construct the Trans-Continental Railroad. Anti-Chinese sentiments against the influx of Chinese immigrants during the recessions of that period led Congress to pass the Chinese Exclusion Act in 1882. This was the first racially based act passed and prevented all Chinese persons from becoming U.S. citizens. Thus, laborers from other Asian nations such as Japan, India, the Philippines, and Korea began arriving in the United States in the late 1880s. Most of these laborers settled in California and Hawaii. Bradshaw suggested that "the technique of importing diverse groups of Asians [to the United States] could be used to control the immigrant Asian workforce, and these groups could also be pitted against the immigrant White workforce in the manner of an 'industrial reserve army' " (p. 74). This technique led to growing resentment of Asian workers and resulted in the "gentleman's agreement" designed to stop immigration of Asians to the United States and the Alien Land Law of 1913 (as cited in Sue & Sue, 1999) passed in California that forbade aliens to own land. Filipinos and Koreans were brought as a source of labor to Hawaii to work on the sugar plantations, but due to the anti-Asian immigration laws and acts, Filipinos were also deemed a cheap source of labor that lowered the standard of living for White workers and plantation owners were forced to stop hiring Filipinos and find another source of labor.

More recently, the newer waves of immigration resulted in the birth of the "model minority" myth, which is particularly salient to the career development of Asians. This myth is largely based on the characteristics of the second wave of immigration of Asians (Foo, 2002). In this wave, large numbers of Asians began immigrating to the United States after anti-Asian exclusion laws were repealed and the passage of the 1965 Immigration Act (as cited in Foo, 2002) lifted quotas based on national origin. Therefore, between 1960 and 1970, immigration from Asia rose to over 10% of total immigration. The wave of immigrants from the 1965 Immigration Act consisted of large numbers of professionals from South and Southeast Asia and Foo (2002) stated that this led "publications such as *The New York Times* and *U.S. News and World Report* to contrast their skill level and work ethics with those of African Americans" (p. 9). The contrast led to the myth that Asians are brighter and work harder than other minority groups in the United States. Foo concluded: "This was the birth of the 'model minority' myth that endures to this day" (p. 9).

Foo (2002) also described later waves of immigration, which included in the early 1970s large numbers of Cambodians, Laotians, and Vietnamese, who were displaced by the ravages of the Indo-China wars. According to Foo:

> They were accepted as "boat people" but dispersed throughout the country with the hopes that they would soon blend in and assimilate. This wave of immigration included large numbers of women and children. In addition, a significant number of middle class persons from all over Asia began arriving in 1970's with their working class counterparts arriving in large numbers in the 1980's. Once settled, the family members of immigrants also made the move from Asia. In all, some 4.5 million Asians immigrated to the US between 1970 and 1990. (p. 9)

ASIAN WOMEN IN THE U.S. WORKFORCE

The earliest immigration of Asian women to the United States were Chinese women who were lured or sold into sexual servitude. Typically, these women were indentured as prostitutes for 4 or 5 years without wages. After the period of servitude was over they generally took jobs as seamstresses, domestic service workers, or other laborers (Bradshaw, 1994). Today, U.S. labor statistics support the idea of the model minority myth among Asian women. For example, the U.S. Equal Employment Opportunity Commission (2001) reported that the top-ranked industry for the employment of Asian women is computer and electronic product manufacturing; an estimated 2.3% of Asian women are employed within this industry. Additionally, Asian women tend to be overrepresented in the professional, technical, and clerical industries, whereas they are underrepresented in craft worker and service positions. Asian and Pacific Islander women are more likely than women of other races to achieve higher levels of education. Approximately 41% of Asian and Pacific Islander women had a bachelor's degree or above in 2000 compared to 25.5% of non-Hispanic White women, and 17% of non-Hispanic Black women (U.S. Equal Employment Opportunity Commission, 2001).

Although these figures may suggest that Asian women are faring well in the American workforce, they do not address the gap between affluent Asians and those living in poverty. As Foo (2002) explained:

> Though the Census Bureau has not released details, its March 1999 Current Population Reports states that while one-third of Asian families have incomes of $75,000 or more, one-fifth have incomes of less than $25,000. Asians are more likely than Whites to have earned a college degree and to have less than a ninth-grade education. Asian Americans occupy the extreme spectrums: from wealth to poverty, entrepreneurial success to marginal daily survival, advanced education to illiteracy. Research and data concerning Asian Americans often are not disaggregated for different subgroups. For example, Census 2000 reports an overall poverty rate of 10.7%, the lowest poverty rate the Census Bureau ever measured for Asian Americans when certain Asian ethnic subgroups have had poverty rates as high as 63%. The result is a picture that portrays Asian Americans as a "model minority" and hides the human and civil rights violations suffered by Asian American women at the bottom of the economic ladder. (p. 10)

An example of one of the significant issues that plague Asian women living in poverty is welfare reform and its impact on immigrant Asian women. Welfare reform acts that were implemented during the 1990s impacted immigrants greatly, especially immigrant women (Foo, 2002). Welfare for immigrants was replaced with Temporary Assistance for Needy Families (TANF), which limits to 5 the number of years that a woman can receive assistance, after which recipients are required to find a job. With limited English proficiency and lack of job skills, many Asian immigrant women were forced to take low-paying jobs in which earnings were below the federal poverty level (Foo). The majority of these women were also denied welfare-to-work services that would enable them to receive the training necessary to find higher paying jobs. Foo concluded, "Without job training, ESL, and vocational ESL classes, Asian immigrant women will be tracked into low wage jobs that lack health benefits. When they reach their lifetime cap in 2002, working full time at the minimum wage of $5.15 per hour or less, Asian immigrant women will have to work the equivalent of 60 to 80 hour weeks or two or three jobs just to move out of poverty" (p. 20).

FUTURE IMMIGRATION TRENDS

By the year 2020 it is projected that the Asian population in the United States will reach 20 million (Sue & Sue, 1999), with women making up half of this population. The majority of these will be first- and second-generation immigrants and will represent a wide variety of national origins, languages, and religious affiliations. Therefore, it important that career counselors have a comprehensive understanding of Asian female clients that addresses the complexity of issues that Asian women face. The next section will focus on defining cultural values that are important to consider in Asian women's career development process. Additionally, we outline career development theories that can be applied to the career-counseling process with Asian women.

ASIAN WOMEN'S CAREER DEVELOPMENT

Cultural Values and Asian Women's Career Development

As mentioned previously, there is a great deal of cultural heterogeneity among Asian women and therefore they cannot be portrayed as having one specific cultural identity. However, there are certain values that are shared across many Asian cultures and nationalities (Sue & Sue, 2003). These values may impact the career development of Asian women and it is thus important for career counselors to have knowledge of these values. Additionally, career counselors should also consider how these may interact with other contextual factors such as socialization, acculturation, identity, and political and social forces to impact career development and counseling. The following section highlights five cultural values that can have a significant impact on the career development process and career-counseling needs of Asian women.

Collectivism. Collectivism refers to placing the family or group's well-being before oneself, making decisions that may fulfill the needs of a group as opposed to concentrating on one's own needs, and believing that personal achievement is reflective of the achievement of the entire family or group (Kim, Atkinson, & Umemoto, 2001). Therefore, family expectations and community influences can be an important component of identity development for Asian individuals and much of identity development is based on social influences, family obligations, and the importance of maintaining the family's status in the community. Yee, Huang, and Lew (1998) noted that this collectivistic identity is the reason that individuals from Asian cultures are likely to take into account or even rely on external influences when making important decisions such as choosing a career. For example, Leong (1991) found that Asian American college students appeared to have developed less career maturity than their European American counterparts because they often relied on the opinions of their parents and family elders when making career decisions. Although more research is needed in this area, it can be assumed that career theories and interventions that rely on a Western individualistic perspective, and that do not take into account the social construction of identity for Asian women, may not match the needs of many Asian women. Therefore, it may be helpful for career theorists and counselors to acknowledge the social aspects of career identity when writing about or working with Asian women. In subsequent sections we address the specific ways that counselors may be able to incorporate family and contextual issues into career assessment and counseling with Asian women.

Filial Piety.   Filial piety is a cultural value that is directly related to the value of collectivism. According to Wong and Ujimoto (1998), "The norm [of filial piety] involves the expectation that children have successful careers to honor their parents and ancestors. It is also expected that a married son and wife support and serve the needs and wishes of the husband's parents" (pp. 180–181). Kim et al. (2001) described filial piety as a value characterized by honor, respect, fidelity, devotion, dutifulness, and sacrifice on the part of children for their parents. Therefore, filial piety brings with it an obligation and responsibility to achieve career success and financial stability in order to demonstrate respect and care for one's parents. Although there is literally no research or literature that describes exactly how filial piety might impact the career development of Asian women, it can be assumed that this value would have a considerable effect on the types of career decisions made by Asian women. Asian women who are married might need to work outside of the home to contribute to the family income. However, a woman may choose or be expected to provide care at home for the husband's elderly parents. Therefore, it might be difficult for Asian women to choose a career that requires them to be away from home for extended periods of time. It is also possible that many Asian women may have personal interests and goals that interfere with family obligations and therefore may seek assistance from career counselors to find a workable solution. Career counseling and interventions can assist Asian women in finding a balance between their family obligations and personal interests. However, career counselors need to be sensitive to the collectivistic identity of their clients. Asian female clients with a strong sense of filial piety and collectivism may benefit from career counseling if the counselor can help them to make career choices that are consistent with their cultural values.

Conformity to Norms.   Kim et al. (2001) noted that "conforming to familial and societal norms is important; one should not deviate from these norms. It is important to follow and conform to the expectations of one's family and the society has for one. Individuals should not make waves and should avoid disrupting the status quo" (p. 576). In terms of career development, conformity to norms can be seen in the types of career choices that Asian individuals make. Asians often report choosing a particular career path because they have witnessed other Asian individuals succeeding in that field (Leong & Serafica, 1995). Therefore, counselors may find themselves in a difficult situation when they ask a client to consider nontraditional career roles that might contradict the norms set forth by her culture. This may be especially important in the case of Asian women, as there are certain careers that may be perceived as masculine by the community and pursuing those careers might be detrimental to the cultural and gender identity of an Asian female. Yang (1991) noted that this is particularly true of Chinese American women who are trying to "live simultaneously in two patriarchal societies: the traditional Chinese family system and the work world of the United States. When they lose the moral support of one society, they may not be equipped to succeed in the other" (p. 356).

Emotional Self-Control.   Uba (1994) acknowledged that traditional Asian culture discourages the expression of emotions and values the ability to control one's emotions. Many Asians and Asian Americans are taught emotional self-control and are actively discouraged from expressing strong emotions. Within a career-counseling situation this value can manifest itself in different ways. Asian women may be reluctant to express strong emotions about career choices and may not state their ideas and opinions assertively. Thus, a counselor might feel that the client is unenthusiastic or disinterested in a particular idea, although the client might be responding in a manner that is acceptable in her culture.

Educational and Occupational Achievement.   As stated previously, in most Asian cultures there is a high value placed on educational and occupational achievement in order to fulfill family and societal expectations. In a study conducted by Kim, Atkinson, and Yang (1999) 14 dimensions were identified as key for Asian Americans. One of these was the emphasis on working hard to become academically and occupationally successful. Leong and Serafica (1995) acknowledged that often parents of Asians and Asian Americans encourage their children to pursue professions that are respected and autonomous (physicians, engineers) because they have witnessed other Asians succeeding in these professions and they believe that their children will face less discrimination within these occupations. There is virtually no existing literature that outlines the impact of this value on the career development process of Asian women. However, it can be assumed that this value may interact with multiple contextual and individual factors to impact the way in which Asian women achieve career and educational success. For example, although there may be a high value for educational and occupational success within an Asian community, there may also be an emphasis on traditional gender roles that may cause conflict for some Asian women who are trying to achieve occupationally while at the same time fulfilling gender-role expectations.

The cultural factors outlined in this section do not encompass the entire spectrum of cultural, social, and political forces that can impact the career development of Asian women. In the next section we discuss how career development theories can better assist us in understanding the impact of contextual factors on Asian women's career beliefs and decisions.

CURRENT THEORIES APPLIED TO THE CAREER DEVELOPMENT OF ASIAN WOMEN

Several authors have discussed the career development of Asian Americans (Leong, 1991; Leong & Chou, 1994; Leung, Ivey, & Suzuki, 1994; Tang et al., 1999; Yang, 1991), but there is still a great deal of research and literature required to address the unique needs of this diverse population. Leong and Serafica (1995) discussed the application of Holland's (1985) theory of vocational choice and behavior, Super's (1990) life-span career development theory, Lofquist and Dawis' (1969) theory of work adjustment, and Krumboltz's (1979) social learning theory in an effort to describe Asian Americans' career development. However, these theories do not specifically address the contextual and political issues that Asian women face in their career development. We believe that Asian women's career development might be better understood as an amalgamation of several theories that consider social, individual, and political factors acting to enable or inhibit various career trajectories. Because discussing Asian women's career development from the perspective of all of the career development theories is beyond the scope of this chapter, we have decided to include three theories that we believe highlight important contextual and individual considerations. These include Lent, Brown, and Hackett's (1994) social-cognitive career theory, the developmental contextual model, and feminist perspectives. These models cannot possibly address each aspect of the career development process for Asian women, but they do address some of the important social, political, and historical factors that need to be considered. In the following sections we outline these theories and discuss ways in which they can be applied to Asian women's career development processes.

Social-Cognitive Career Theory

Lent, Brown, and Hackett (1994) developed social-cognitive career theory (SCCT), which has groundwork in Bandura's (1986) social-cognitive theory, but emphasizes cognitive processes that moderate or regulate one's career aspirations and actions. SCCT postulates that prior learning experiences affect career choice through several elements: self-efficacy, outcome expectations, personal goals, choices, and environmental factors. Specifically, self-efficacy beliefs are defined as an individual's "judgments about his or her capabilities to organize and execute courses of action required to attain designated performances" (Bandura, p. 391). By better understanding an individual's self-efficacy beliefs, one may make inferences with regard to an individual's exploration of interests, career and educational choice, performance, and perseverance.

Outcome expectations, as described by Bandura (1997), are expectations of what may happen in response to given circumstances, whereas self-efficacy refers to individuals' confidence in their abilities to handle such circumstances. Outcome expectations refer to individuals' beliefs about probable outcomes of their actions related to their careers. Depending on the situation, either self-efficacy beliefs or outcome expectations may present as the more forceful element in vocational or other choice considerations, and may be related to the incorporation of goals that the individual has set. Goals refer to attainment and aspirational considerations and the drive an individual has in reaching the standards they have set for themselves. For instance, a person may feel efficacious in a particular task and perform the task well quite regularly. This confidence engenders further interest in the particular task and also likely contributes to the development of a deeper interest in the activity. This may contribute to longevity, satisfaction, and eventual vocational type selection. Confidence is generally considered a product of several years of development and must consider numerous contextual factors that influence the construction of self-efficacy beliefs. The individual interacts with the environment to formulate an appropriate fit for the individual in regard to vocational development.

Bandura (1986) proposed that interests are reinforced by successes or failures in activities that are related to the interest in question. Expanding on this principle, Lent et al. (1994) suggested that people tend to develop interest and skills in activities in which they feel efficacious. These interests in turn affect goal formation and the actions that an individual will take to realize those goals. The outcomes of such goals can reinforce or diminish an individual's efficacy beliefs and outcome expectations. Self-efficacy and outcome expectations affect interests, goals, and actions in response to goals to determine performance and career attainment. However, a crucial mediating variable in this model, especially in considerations of Asian women, is that of contextual factors.

Contextual factors influence all the stages of vocational development in the SCCT model. These contextual factors are generally outside of the control of the individual, and include barriers and support systems in a number of facets (Lent, Brown, & Hackett, 2000). For instance, barriers could include real or perceived discrimination, social expectations, and the persistence of expected gender roles. Contextual supports could include family support and encouragement, financial stability and availability, and educational attainment, access, and advantages. These contextual factors could potentially influence goal formation, efficacy beliefs, and attainment if they are powerful enough to discourage some vocational choices while encouraging others. Contextual factors may be particularly salient to minorities and women in their vocational development. Hackett and Betz (1981) described some contextual challenges women face in the environment, such as being socialized away from certain fields and educational subjects (math, science). Part of the challenge for career counselors working from an SCCT perspective is to assist women in understanding that their efficacy beliefs are in large part formulated by society's views, pressures, and expectations.

Tang et al. (1999) found Lent et al.'s (1994) model to be a useful framework for understanding career choice of Asian American college students. Findings from this study indicated that Asian Americans' career choices were more influenced by acculturation, family background, and self-efficacy than by interests. Therefore, many Asian women might not choose to pursue a career in their field of interest for a variety of reasons such as financial considerations, lack of confidence about success, and parental discouragement. Tang et al. suggested that SCCT might be the theory that best explains Asian Americans' career development because it examines the influence of family expectations, role models, successful experiences, and other contextual factors such as tradition. However, the findings from this study cannot necessarily be generalized to all Asian women. The majority of participants (57.1%) had parents who held a college degree. Asian Americans and Asian immigrants with limited resources may face additional challenges in their career development process.

Barriers and Support Systems.   Contextual and political factors of immigration or refugee status may play an important role in the types of occupations in which Asian women can be employed and can therefore limit their career options. These contextual factors can also function as barriers to career success. In the case of refugees, being raised in one environment (country of origin) and then being transplanted to another country (United States) with a different set of languages, customs, and possibly different types of occupations can have a great impact on the types of jobs for which they are employable. For example, a woman who holds a bachelor's degree in psychology from a university in Vietnam cannot directly transfer this degree to the United States because psychological issues here may differ from issues in Vietnam, rendering this degree useless to her. Root (1995) acknowledged that this type of change in status can result in psychological distress or loss of self-esteem for many immigrant Asian women. Similarly, a non-English-speaking immigrant with no transferable skills, little social support, and no governmental support may experience a lack of ability to translate any career-related interests into career goals or performance accomplishments. Yang (1991) discussed the lack of available role models for Chinese American women as another major barrier to the career success of these women and suggested that lack of role models prevents vicarious learning opportunities for Chinese American women. According to SCCT, lack of vicarious learning or role modeling can result in low self-efficacy beliefs and outcome expectations, thus affecting the translation of interests into career goals.

On the other hand, support systems that provide verbal encouragement can function to increase self-efficacy beliefs and outcome expectations (Lent et al., 2000). As stated previously, one of the strengths of most Asian cultures is the adherence to a collectivistic mentality that may serve as a source of financial and emotional support for Asian women in their career development process. Furthermore, within most Asian cultures there is a strong value for educational and occupational achievement. Therefore, some Asian and Asian American women can draw on these sources of support to pursue career goals and interests. More research in the area of support for career goals and overcoming barriers is needed to better understand the career development of Asian women.

The SCCT model is a useful framework that can help career counselors to work with Asian women and provide some understanding of how contextual factors may influence career beliefs and outcomes. The following section outlines the application of the developmental-contextual model to the career development of Asian women and further explicates the role of contextual factors in the career choice process of Asian women.

Developmental-Contextual Approach

Patton and McMahon (1999) described the development-contextual (D-C) approach to career development as a movement away from the formulaic and stage-dependent theories of vocational development. The D-C model developed by Lerner (1979) can be seen as a merging of the developmental organic perspective and the environmental perspective. Vondracek, Lerner, and Schulenberg (1986) adapted this model to describe career development and it is one of the first approaches to integrate the individual and contextual factors with regard to career development. Vondracek et al. (1986) recognized that development could not be simply mapped on a continuum or in a prescribed fashion because this is at odds with the inherent complexity of vocational development. Patton and MacMahon stated, "There has been an overemphasis on within-person factors such as values, abilities, and interests in career choice, at the expense of contextual issues, such as family-of-origin issues, labor market changes, and organizational constraints" (p. 68). Therefore, D-C theory proposes that individuals are capable of interacting with their environment and contexts to create a basis for their own vocational development. The term *contextual affordance* was coined to describe the individual's ability to recognize and use personal characteristics and translate them into career futures. This concept allows for changing contexts to interact with the individual, thus providing a basis for the individual's own development. Vondracek, Lerner, and Schulenberg (1983) identified three key elements in vocational development: the individual, context, and the relationship between the two. Vocational development can be seen as the interplay between these factors, of the individual interacting and acting on the constantly changing environment. The model allows for the individual and contextual factors to evolve over time and vocational decisions may follow.

Embeddedness is a term used to describe psychological, biological, social, and cultural and community levels of influence in life. The D-C perspective postulates that at a given time any combination of these factors may be influencing the individual's experiences. These influences have the ability to effect change in other factors (e.g., contextual) and thus may open doors for vocational interventions. Additionally, change in one level likely affects change in another because the levels are considered to be integrated. Change occurs across contexts, time, and person–environment interactions. For instance, changes in one's physical health may affect changes in one's mental health and may affect career outcomes. Recent revisions to the theory posited by Vondracek and Kawasaki (1995) include in the model the integration of career development stages with information that takes into account the subjective nature of the individual. This has provided a framework for understanding the person, functioning in context. The applicability of the D-C model, then, can be particularly effective with diverse populations. For instance, Vondracek and Fouad (1994) proposed that this model can account for how changes in the socioeconomic and cultural environment influence an individual's career development, which is often relevant for minorities.

Social and Cultural Factors. Contextual factors encompass consideration of family influences, acculturation, and cultural emphasis with regard to the individual's role in the family and society. As previously noted, Asian women can be greatly influenced by their traditional cultures, which are often reflective of a collectivist sociological viewpoint, deference to elders and authority, conformity with social norms, and obligation to the family and the family's well-being. Tang et al. (1999) suggested that Asian Americans may see career choice as a process that involves both the individual's and the family's interests, and that Asian Americans may feel pressure to carry on family traditions and may choose careers based in family interests. Finally, educational and vocational achievement is considered an individual's top priorities.

There is scant literature on the career development of Asian women with regard to interactions between the individual and the aforementioned contextual factors. It is possible that these factors may be magnified considerably for those women in double-jeopardy circumstances such as being a woman and minority, as the individual will have to face a larger degree of differentiation from the majority norms. It is likely that Asian women must face considerable conflict between their familial culture and the norms of American work society. These family-of-origin concerns may be represented in the types of jobs that a family supports for a woman. Additionally, the family may discourage traditionally masculine educational aspirations, interests, and careers, while maintaining pressure to succeed in high-prestige vocations and education. Whereas some Asian American families maintain a cultural interest in the sons' continuing the family business, this opportunity may be frowned on for Asian women. As suggested by Leong and Serafica (1995), for Asian Americans reared in the traditional manner, social roles are crucial elements in the development of a career trajectory, such as is filial piety and overarching obligations to the family. Asian American women may be pressured further into doing what is "right for the family" rather than pursuing their individual desires. This may be carried out in such a way that Asian American women may show more interest in advancement and success because of the related honor it bestows on the family rather than for individual success. This attitude must be accounted for in career-counseling formulations, particularly because it differs from the individualistic nature of American society and the structure of many of the Western models of career development.

Cultural influences such as the need to maintain harmony and placing others' needs above one's own are emphasized within most Asian cultures, while avoiding family shame is of the utmost importance. Self-effacement is expected; one should be humble, modest, and not boastful. It is considered inappropriate to draw attention to oneself and individuals are discouraged from talking about personal accomplishments. For Asian women this may create a particularly difficult situation in the workplace as female Asian workers may be labeled passive and unassertive and therefore passed over for leadership positions. However, hard work in school and on the job is considered a virtue and Asian women may also be seen by coworkers as diligent and steadfast. Asian women may feel pressure to have both home and work life "under control," denying the stressors, not asking for personal time, and taking on additional work-related tasks when already overburdened.

Logically, the degree to which Asian Americans have become acculturated into American culture moderates the degree to which individuals subscribe to the aforementioned contextual factors. For example, recently immigrated Asian woman may feel more pressure to engage in self-effacing behaviors than Asian Americans that have become more accustomed to the individualistic atmosphere of American culture. Leong and Tata (1990) found that acculturation level affects occupational values of Asian Americans. As individuals become more acculturated, they adopt more mainstream cultural values. The continuum of acculturation suggests that higher degrees of acculturation encourage an understanding of multiple cultures and the ability to see strengths and weaknesses of each, whereas low acculturation may perpetuate the perceptions of discrimination and occupational stereotyping that affect Asian Americans attempting to enter the American workforce (Leong & Chou, 1994).

Political and Environmental Factors. Other contextual factors of relevance include changes in the labor market, technology, laws, economic conditions, post-9-11 political climate, and job opportunities. As noted previously, the labor needs in American history and at present have impacted on the immigration rates. In considering this, one may assert that the opportunity and labor market contextual factors may be influenced by the needs of the American economy and also the expectations of the Asian woman, as she may be expecting to fill a particular type of job according to demand in the market. The D-C developmental model would suggest that an Asian woman may interpret the contextual needs of the market and modify her own interests so that they are in line with the current labor needs of the market. For example, the technological boom of the 1990s coincided with a rise in the number of Asian women employed in this industry. This might be due to Asian women's perception that jobs in this area would provide economic security and stability and therefore many Asian women may have modified their career interests in order to take advantage of these opportunities. More research needs to be conducted that investigates this hypothesis.

Environmental factors such as discrimination may also be factors that lead Asian women to alter their career behavior. For example, Asian women may have to contend with the expected contextual barriers of racism, sexism, and possible glass ceilings in occupational attainment. Their degree of acculturation may mediate the effects these barriers have on their attainment beliefs, as will their perceptions of minority status. Leong and Chou (1994) discussed the ways in which ethnic identity and acculturation level interact with aspects of Asian Americans' vocational behavior. They proposed that less acculturated individuals are more vulnerable to occupational stereotyping, segregation, and discrimination; that they are less likely to choose a career based on their own interests and desire; and that they are more likely to have higher aspirations but lower expectations. These variables may also affect Asian women's beliefs about the degree to which they are in control of their own destiny, that is, even if they work hard and are well educated they may be discriminated against due to minority status or cultural beliefs.

These difficulties may be further complicated by sexual orientation and disability status. In these cases Asian women may be in triple jeopardy for job discrimination. An Asian woman who is also a member of these groups will almost certainly face further social oppression from the larger American society. Her career development may be limited in terms of how much she may rely on support systems such as friends and family, while also attempting to enter a working culture that generally marginalizes people with disabilities and sexual orientations other than heterosexual.

Contextual factors such as racism prompted by recent political events (e.g., the recent Gulf War) are also a prevalent issue that impacts the career development of Asian women. McWhirter, Torres, and Rasheed (1998) discussed the case of a Pakistani Muslim American woman who faced discrimination at her workplace due to her decision to wear the *hijab* (traditional headscarf worn by many Muslim women). The post-9-11 political climate has caused many Muslim women to be concerned about their appearance and the reactions that they receive from others (Ali, Liu, & Humedian, 2004). These types of environmental influences may hinder or present obstacles to Asian Muslim women as they formulate career goals or try to advance within their chosen career.

Although there has been very limited discussion of racism related to Asian women, there is even less research and literature that discusses issues of social class and classism related to this group. There is a significant gap in the literature on career issues of Asian women from low socioeconomic backgrounds. As mentioned previously, Foo (2002) noted the two extremes of Asian communities: the highly affluent and those who live in desperate poverty. Consequently, socioeconomic status (SES) can be a major factor in the determination of work goals and decisions for Asian women. Asian women who are recent immigrants or refugees are limited to the type and amount of governmental assistance they receive and are often relegated to low-paying jobs earning wages that are at or below the federal poverty line (Foo). With no skills and significant language barriers, it is difficult for these women to find higher paying jobs or advance in their current positions. On the other hand, Bradshaw (1994) discussed the issues surrounding the affluent Asian population. According to Bradshaw, images of affluent Asians create disdain in the American public and lead to socioeconomic stereotyping, a stereotyping that is associated with Asian immorality (e.g., Imelda Marcos) and fear of "being overrun by outsiders (e.g. Japan bashing)" (Bradshaw, p. 88). Bradshaw further stated that this stereotyping can have important consequences for Asians and Asian Americans, such as: (a) the failure to distinguish those whose families have resided in the United States for generations, (2) preserving the image of Asian Americans as perpetual foreigners with no allegiance to the United States, and (3) encouraging fears of affluence among new Asian immigrants perpetuating the idea that this influx of immigrants threatens the American way of life or White American job security, which further justifies racism and job discrimination. It is quite possible that this type of socioeconomic stereotyping may interact with Asian cultural factors such as the need for harmony and conformity, causing Asian women to internalize racist attitudes that could potentially impact their career development process and career adjustment. More research in this area is needed in order to determine the specific ways that socioeconomic stereotypes and racism interact to influence the career development of Asian women.

The D-C perspective addresses important contextual influences that impact the career development of Asian women. Although this theory outlines the specific influences and their impact on the career development process, it does not necessarily provide a framework for intervention. We turn next to the feminist perspectives that are able to offer a system of intervention.

Feminist Perspectives

Another useful theory that may help career counselors to understand the career development process of Asian women is feminist theory. Feminist theories developed since the 1960s hold that power inequalities and individuals' expectations are formed through gender-role socialization and political, economic, and social processes (Enns, 1993; Sturdivant, 1980). This process starts at a young age and is continually reinforced and ingrained as an individual continues to grow in society's framework. The theory posits that the gender-role socialization process may have detrimental effects for both men and women, but focuses on the challenges a woman faces in a patriarchical society. Feminist theories suggest that challenging sexist attitudes, beliefs, and practices is a crucial element of healthy psychological and social adjustment. It is our position that understanding the influences that society places on women may clarify numerous obstacles in the path of the optimal career development of Asian women. Thus, a feminist perspective allows us to better conceptualize the barriers society places on Asian women through role socialization and contextual factors.

Feminists believe it is crucial to challenge sexist attitudes, pressures, and beliefs in society, and to empower women to set and accomplish goals while overcoming debilitating societal expectations. Consideration is paid to an individual's experience of oppression, and hopes to engender freedom of choice and power. The concept of the "personal is political" is the central component of the feminist perspective. Essentially, this belief assumes that the problems women encounter are connected to the social and political climate in which they live (Enns, 1997). The major goals of feminist therapy are that individuals benefit from self-acceptance, self-efficacy, and empowerment. Relationships are seen as crucial elements of daily life and improving the number and quality of these relationships relates to an individual's adjustment in society. In evaluating an individual through the feminist perspective, considerable analysis is done on gender roles and the degree to which the individual subscribes to them, and how the individual is affected by contextual factors such as political structures, laws, and social norms. Advocacy of the self and of the oppressed group as a whole plays a crucial part in attempting to eliminate social barriers and expectations that work against women's decision-making processes (Enns, 1993).

Women's Career Socialization.   Brooks and Forrest (1994) suggested that women are oppressed and restricted in life roles due to prescribed gender roles. The nature of these roles in the United States creates an environment that results in women occupying a very limited range of work and achievement roles. From a feminist standpoint, career choice and problems or limitations are viewed as a result of societal and political issues, not necessarily those of the individual. Helping women to make decisions outside of these learned and very limiting roles, and encouraging the development of an understanding of the cultural, political, and societal implications that make it difficult for women to feel at ease in the American workforce are the major foci of change in vocational development. Interpreting and reformulating the individual's analysis of her role, while focusing on present conditions in an individual's life is a pivotal element of developing healthy vocational outlooks. Furthermore, Brooks and Forrest suggested that occupational sex segregation still exists in the U.S. workforce despite gains made in the last 40 years. Women get paid less for doing the same job as men, and most of the jobs women are concentrated in tend to be low paying and low status with little advancement opportunity. Societal occupational stereotyping is the most prominent barrier to women's vocational freedom. Walsh and Osipow (1995) noted that the common practice of the male in a relationship focusing on career duties while the female focuses on the needs of the family and home is reinforced by numerous areas of society, in school, in the home, and in the media.

Incorporating the feminist perspective into an examination of vocational development for Asian women relies on investigating the environmental, social, and political forces that influence Asian women's choice capabilities.

Historically, feminist perspectives have been criticized for ignoring the issues of women of color (Enns, 1997), but more recently attempts have been made to integrate the experiences of diverse women into the feminist perspective. For example, Worell and Remer (2003) discussed the importance of having an "understanding of the sociopolitical system's operation in the dominant culture with respect to its treatment of minorities" (p. 34) and an awareness of and sensitivity to the cultural heritage of the client. Therefore, a feminist perspective applied to the career development of Asian women would call for an examination of the social and cultural perceptions of Asian women's roles and the ways that these may be interfering with their career success. For example, Asian women are not only affected by gender roles prevalent in the United States, but are also likely influenced by those of their culture of origin. Yang (1991) described the challenges of career counseling with Chinese American women. Chinese women are encultured in a subordinate role, and to alter such a role is to upset the structure and integrity of the family and kinship. This creates a challenging situation for Asian women, as they attempt to gain ground in the vocational realm while simultaneously nurturing family expectations of their educational and vocational attainment. Fouad and Bingham (1995) also recognized the collectivist nature of Asian American culture as being at odds with the White American ideology of "pulling oneself up by the bootstraps" and making individual vocational choices. Balancing the desires and interests of an Asian female client with cultural expectations is an important part of a feminist career perspective.

Career Counseling From a Feminist Perspective.   Worell and Remer (2003) suggested that feminist career counseling should: (a) address both external and internal factors affecting career development, (b) teach strategies for dealing with oppression, (c) include strategies for bringing about changes in economic and occupational structures, (d) account for the interaction between the individual's choices and environmental opportunities and barriers, as well as allowing for changes in both, and (e) challenge restrictions placed on women's potential by gender-role socialization and internalized SEARCH (sexism, ethnocentrism, ableism and ageism, racism, classism, and heterosexism) factors.

Feminist therapists and researchers are still in the process of incorporating feminism and diverse perspectives. There is considerably more work to be done in this area. However, the feminist values of grassroots advocacy and providing information and understanding of social barriers to equality are principles that can benefit Asian women. Given that many Asian immigrant women are in need of assistance in understanding their rights as immigrants and the impact of cultural pressure on their career choices, the incorporation of feminist career-counseling techniques used to empower Asian women might prove to be quite useful to career counselors.

CAREER COUNSELING AND ASSESSMENT WITH ASIAN WOMEN

Career Assessment

The process of career counseling with Asian American women requires careful consideration of the specific needs of this group. Although career counselors have access to hundreds of published vocational and career interest measures in the United States, very few of these measures specifically address the needs of Asian women. Often, counselors are forced to mix and match measures of occupational interest with acculturation and similar measures to gain a picture of the vocational concerns of this population. Of the many measures available, there currently exist measures for individuals with disabilities, and people from varying age groups, but minority-status-specific measures are difficult to find and are not likely to be empirically grounded. The situation reflects the somewhat exclusionary nature of past vocational research and initiatives. As a result, counselors face a daunting task of providing competent services to a population for which a paucity of directional research exists. In fact, Leong and Gim-Chung (1995) indicated that there are only three studies focusing specifically on the career development of Asian American women, two of which are over three decades old. The problem is exacerbated by the fact that the more popular measures that have been developed for career exploration are often lacking in relevance for Asian Americans, let alone Asian American women. Despite these limitations, there are some potential benefits to using career assessment with Asian women. The following section attempts to address some of the assessment tools and strategies that can be employed in career interventions and counseling with Asian women.

Cultural Values. As previously discussed, Asian women's adherence to culture-of-origin values may play an important role in the provision of culturally relevant career services. However, Asian cultural values have been difficult to assess due to the lack of instruments that measure ethnic cultural values. Recently, Kim et al. (1999) developed the Asian Values Scale (AVS), which has four subscales measuring conformity to norms, family recognition through achievement, emotional self-control, and collectivism. The AVS might have some promise for providing information to career counselors about Asian females' adherence to Asian values and therefore counselors may be able to alter career interventions based on this information. However, this instrument has not been validated on a variety of Asian ethnic subgroups and there is more research to be done regarding the role of the AVS in the counseling process.

Acculturation.   One acculturation scale that has been used in research to better understand the acculturation process for Asians and Asian Americans is the Suinn-Lew Asian Self-Identity Scale (SL-ASIA; Suinn, Rickard-Figueroa, Lew, & Vigil, 1987). This instrument measures the degree to which an individual has embraced Western cultural values. Topics include language preference, ethnic identity, ethnicity of friends, cultural behaviors, generational and geographic background, and attitudes toward cultures. Similar to the AVS, this measure has been used primarily for research purposes, but may have some promise for use in career counseling with Asian women. However, this tool should also be used in conjunction with interviewing and discussion about issues of gender-role socialization and adherence to traditional female roles and responsibilities.

Interest Inventories.   Some of the more commonly used and recognized measures for vocational interest are the Strong Interest Inventory (SII), Campbell Interest and Skills Inventory (CISS), and Self-Directed Search (SDS). Over decades of use, many vocational interest measures have undergone several revisions to reduce language, gender, and cultural biases. These measures continue, however, to pose a challenge to practitioners hoping to use them with Asian women. The SII, one of the most popular vocational exploration measures, is a self-report measure, and like many others, it asks the examinee to report affinities or dislikes for various activities and occupational situations. The premise behind vocational interest measures is that a pattern of responses emerges that can be compared with occupational codes, interests, and the responses of others. For instance, individuals may complete the SII and be presented with themes from Holland's (1985) hexagonal model. These themes can then be compared with specific occupations that correspond with the items endorsed, but can also be compared with the response patterns of other people in various careers. In this manner, individuals can consider career options that match their endorsements, and can also determine the fields in which people with similar responses are working. This process has been well established in traditional vocational counseling and there is evidence to suggest that interest inventories are an appropriate assessment tool for Asians and Asian Americans (Fouad, 2002).

One potential problem in using interest inventories with Asian women is that often the interpretation provided for the client ignores the client's cultural context. For instance, duty to family roles, traditions, and expectations may take priority over personal interests. It is possible that expressing individualistic aspirations may be against Asian women's cultural expectations.

Therefore, it is important when using interest inventories with Asian women to consider their adherence to traditional values and acculturation level in the interpretation of their results.

The use of career assessment in career counseling can be a potentially informative and useful tool when working with Asian women. However, it is important that the counselor choose assessment instruments that have been validated for Asian women. It is equally important that career counselors use culturally appropriate models of career counseling that appropriately integrate assessment techniques. Fouad and Bingham (1995) developed a culturally appropriate model of career counseling that includes a seven-step career-counseling process. This approach, along with an integration of SCCT, D-C, and feminist theories, is applied specifically to the career counseling of Asian women in the following section. A case example is used to illustrate the application of these models.

Culturally Appropriate Career-Counseling Model

Fouad and Bingham (1995) asserted that "cultural is a critical variable in career counseling, enters into every part of the counseling process, and may modify counseling. We also propose that the assessment of the effect of cultural is a very specific step" (p. 344). The culturally appropriate career-counseling model includes the following seven steps: establishing a culturally appropriate relationship (Step 1), identifying the career issues that the client brings (Step 2), assessing the impact of cultural variables of those career issues (Step 3), setting culturally appropriate processes and goals (Step 4), determining and implementing a culturally appropriate intervention (Step 5), helping the client make a culturally appropriate decision (Step 6), and implementing the client's plans and follow-up plans (Step 7). We further propose that within each of these steps the career counselor must attend to the client's need for advocacy when negotiating systems that might assist or prevent her from reaching her career or occupational goals.

Counselor Preparation. Fouad and Bingham (1995) suggested that an important part of successful career counseling is counselor preparation. Drawing from Sue et al.'s (1992) three-by-three model, Fouad and Bingham suggested that counselors should have awareness, knowledge, and skills about their own culture, others' culture, and a variety of counseling techniques. In previous sections we outlined the cultural values that are salient when working with Asian women. In this section we highlight some general career-counseling and assessment techniques that might prepare counselors to work with Asian women, but encourage counselors to modify counseling techniques according to the unique needs of their clients.

Preference for Counseling Style. Kim et al. (2001) acknowledged that Asians and Asian Americans with traditional values may be more comfortable seeking assistance with career and educational concerns than with personal or family problems. Additionally, because of the emphasis of many Asian cultures on hierarchical relationships, Asians and Asian Americans often expect their counselor to be an authority figure and directly guide them to a right career choice (Leong, 1993). A counselor who tries to establish an egalitarian relationship with a Asian client who has a strong adherence to traditional values may be perceived as less credible than a counselor who can provide a directive, task-oriented approach to counseling (Kim et al.). Therefore, depending on the needs and acculturation of the client, it might be helpful for career counselors to take a more directive and task-oriented approach with Asian female clients, especially in the early sessions. This may help an Asian woman to feel more comfortable with the process and possibly help her feel safe to divulge information about her contextual and social history.

Counselor Biases.   According to Fouad and Bingham (1995), counselors should also be aware of their own biases and cultural attitudes. A counselor might possess stereotypes of Asian women that can interfere with the career-counseling process. This can be more often seen in counselors who deal with clients not fluent in English (Leong, 1993). Counselors might become frustrated with difficulties in communication and consequently give up on their clients (Leong). Stereotypes of Asian women as passive and unassertive can also be potentially damaging if counselors are unaware of their biases. They can lead a career counselor to suggest certain occupations that would steer a client away from positions of leadership or management.

Another factor that might cloud a counselor's perspective is occupational stereotyping. The counselor might be inclined to suggest that the client consider a particular career choice because of the previous success of Asians in that field (Leong, 1993; Leong & Serafica, 1995). Therefore, counselors may want to be careful about their suggestions and the way they are made. In these cases it may actually be helpful for career counselors to use self-report interest inventories in order to integrate the interests of the client, as well as openly discuss how occupational stereotypes may affect the client's interests.

Openness to a woman's experiences, competence, and strengths is an important component in combating stereotypes and biases. The experiences of Asian women may include survival of difficult circumstances such as immigration or fleeing their home country. Second-generation Asian American women may have oral traditions or histories that contain important lessons. For example, many second- and third-generation Japanese Americans whose families were interned during World War II might teach their children to be overly humble and not draw attention to themselves for fear that they may be targeted. It is important for the counselor to be open to learning about these family traditions and cultural attitudes from their client. This type of preparation for career counseling might improve the quality of the relationship and effectiveness of the career-counseling process.

Case Example

In order to illustrate the use of the culturally appropriate career-counseling model with an Asian female client, we use the case of Thüc. Thüc is a 40-year-old woman who currently lives with her mother, father, sister, brother-in-law, and younger brother. Thüc's family fled Vietnam when she was 9 years old and relocated to the United States. When Thüc first arrived in the United States she and her family stayed in a refugee camp until they obtained sponsorship from a Catholic community in Los Angeles and then relocated there. Thüc graduated from high school and immediately went to work in a Vietnamese grocery store. Thüc is a major contributor to the family's income and has been since she first started working. Her parents are unable to work due to their limited English skills. Thüc and her brother provide the main source of income for their family. Recently, the grocery store where Thüc was the store manager went out of business. She has come to the local community mental health center to deal with feelings of anxiety and depression related to her concerns about her job situation. During the intake she requested assistance in finding a new job. Thüc was assigned to see Shelia who is an African American counselor at the community mental health center. Shelia, having some experience with the Vietnamese population in Los Angeles, felt comfortable working with Thüc. Shelia immediately realized the predominant source of Thüc's presenting problems were due to her unemployment status and decided to approach counseling from a career- or employment-counseling perspective.

Step 1: Establishment of Rapport (Culturally Appropriate Relationship). During Shelia and Thüc's first meeting Shelia asked Thüc about her priorities for counseling. Thüc stated that her first priority was to deal with her current unemployment situation and that she needed to find a job as soon as possible in order to support her family. Shelia demonstrated empathy and understanding of Thüc's need to support her family, but also explained to Thüc that the process of finding a job might take some time. Shelia asked Thüc about the family's current financial situation. Thüc explained that her brother did have a "good job" and that this job would be able to sustain the family for about 2 months. Thüc and Shelia agreed to work together for 10 sessions to establish her career-counseling needs and goals as well as to determine the types of occupations for which Thüc would be qualified. Shelia had experience working with Vietnamese clients from Thúc's community and was aware that the majority of these clients preferred a directive, problem-solving approach to counseling. Therefore, Shelia asked Thúc if she would feel more comfortable if they had a general plan for each session in order to make progress toward the goal of employment. Thúc stated that she appreciated this approach and that it would help her to feel that she was working toward her goals. Shelia was also aware of her own collective orientation and strong community affiliation. She did not choose to disclose this to Thúc at the time, but was aware of how her own values might affect the counseling process.

Step 2: Identification of Career and Employment Issues.   During the next session, the goal included understanding the career issue and finding out about Thúc's employment history. Thúc explained that she had worked at the Vietnamese grocery store for about 22 years. After high school she started working as a cashier and after 5 years was promoted to assistant manager. After 6 years she was promoted to manager and was employed in this position until recently when the owner was forced to close the store due to recent loss of revenue. Thúc's manager position entailed employee scheduling and training, maintaining and ordering stock, monitoring the financial aspects, and bookkeeping. However, as Shelia asked more directive questions about Thúc's workday she also learned that Thúc provided an essential service to the Vietnamese community. She not only managed the store, but she also provided customers with services such as English translation, assisting them with their finances, and negotiating governmental systems. Often the customers would bring their tax forms and other financial or government documents to Thúc, who would provide explanation and assistance in completing these forms. On occasion she would accompany the customers to the social security office or other agencies in order to provide translation services. The store owner was extremely supportive of Thúc's advocacy efforts and Thúc admitted to Shelia that this was the most important and enjoyable aspect of her job. Since the store closed she has been volunteering at the Vietnamese Catholic church providing the same types of services. Thus, Shelia learned that one of Thúc's core values was to assist her community. Shelia also learned that Thúc was committed to continuing to support her family. Her sister and brother-in-law were both pursuing master's degrees in public health and she wanted to ensure that they would be able to complete their studies. She revealed that her contributions to the family income would ensure that her sister and brother-in-law would be able to continue their studies without interruption. Shelia asked Thúc if she was aware that she was eligible for unemployment benefits. Thúc responded that she was not aware of this and Shelia also made an appointment for Thúc with the agency's unemployment benefit specialist to help Thúc navigate that system.

Step 3: Assessment of Effects of Cultural Variables. Shelia had already gathered some information about Thüc's cultural worldview on the impact of her career-employment concerns. She understood Thüc's value of contributing to her family's income and providing social services to her community. Thüc is the eldest of the three children in the family and believes that it is her duty to provide for the family. She also stated that she had decided not to pursue marriage or family life because she believed it would interfere with this duty. From Shelia's assessment of Thüc's acculturation level she realized that Thüc was able to integrate into the dominant society fairly easily and that she had high self-efficacy for dealing with the government and business systems. This was clear from her advocacy work, as was the fact that her core values were social collectivist in nature and that duty and honor to family were of the utmost importance to Thüc. Shelia broached the subject of Thüc's individual needs for her career (i.e., pursuing education or training) and Thüc responded that she had been interested at one point in obtaining an associate's degree in social work so that she could provide services to her community on a regular basis.

Shelia's assessment of Thüc's cultural values made clear the importance of Thüc finding employment quickly given her family's situation. Shelia was aware that had she and Thüc been given more time she would have explored Thüc's educational and occupational aspirations in more detail. However, given the circumstances she decided that she would help Thüc to explore some of her own interests while concentrating on helping her to find a job.

Step 4: Setting of Counseling Goals. Shelia and Thüc established the following goals for their remaining sessions: clarifying skills and interests, matching these skills and interests to available job opportunities, discussing possible barriers to employment, resume writing, practicing interview skills, and discussing more about Thüc's advocacy work and how she might continue this with a new job. Shelia asked Thüc if she felt these goals were appropriate and consistent with cultural expectations and Thüc agreed that the goals were consistent with her cultural values and beliefs.

Step 5: Culturally Appropriate Counseling Interventions. Because Thüc's main goal was employment, Shelia asked Thüc to complete the Work Skills Inventory (WSI) so that they could identify the transferable skills that Thüc possessed. Shelia also explained to Thüc that completing the WSI would assist Thüc in writing a resume listing her different skills. Shelia decided that an interest inventory was a culturally inappropriate invention because most interest inventories are focused on exploration. As Shelia and Thüc developed a resume from her past experiences and information gathered from the WSI, they also identified job opportunities from Internet, newspaper, and employment listings. For each job they identified possible barriers to gaining employment in that area and also discussed Thüc's level of interest in each of the positions. Throughout the assessment and intervention, Shelia learned more about Thüc's background and skills. One of the skills that Thüc possessed that seemed desirable in the job market was that she was fluent in both Vietnamese and English. Several of the employment opportunities that were available involved bilingual social services such as smoking cessation hotline language services and Asian social services caseworkers. However, Thüc did not have the necessary education or training for these positions. Shelia and Thüc identified lack of education as a potential barrier for these positions. Shelia and Thüc also discussed and practiced interview skills. Shelia chose to use interventions focused on helping Thüc find employment and steered away from career exploration due to Thüc's financial and family situation.

Step 6: Decision Making.   Thüc applied to several of the social service positions and was able to secure three interviews. Two of the interviewers discussed her lack of education and training as a problem, but one suggested that she receive training through the local community college while she worked. Thüc discussed her options with Shelia and decided to pursue an associate's degree in social work while working at the Asian social services. Shelia informed her that she could apply for student loans to help her cover the cost of the tuition. Shelia assisted Thüc with the necessary student loan paperwork and provided guidance on how to register for classes and buy books.

Step 7: Implementation and Follow-Up.   Thüc finished her first semester at the community college with good grades. She reported feeling satisfied and happy with her new employment and educational opportunities. Her new job required her to provide many of the same services that she had been providing at the Vietnamese grocery store. Her sister and brother-in-law were able to continue their graduate studies and she felt that her income was enough to contribute to her family's financial resources. Thüc reported that the counseling she received was directive and helpful in fulfilling her need for employment and appreciated the practical nature of counseling.

CONCLUSION

The case of Thüc provides an example of culturally appropriate career counseling with an Asian female with limited education and resources. In this case traditional career counseling that included lengthy exploration of interests and values was not appropriate. Instead Thüc benefited from

Shelia's focus on employment counseling and assessment of skills. Shelia also provided referrals and advocacy in the form of assistance in finding sources of funding for community college and unemployment benefits. Counselors who are aware of these types of resources can assist clients who are unfamiliar with financial aid programs to navigate the systems and find the assistance they need.

There is very little research that explores the career issues and concerns of Asian women. Fouad and Bingham (1995) suggested that "the discussion of cultural variables is too easily interpreted as overgeneralizing about members of various racial and ethnic groups" (p. 360). We argue that the same is true for Asian women. The literature that does exist generally does not focus on the study of within-group differences among Asian women. More research that focuses on these differences in relation to career development is sorely needed. It is very likely that a Vietnamese woman and an Asian Indian woman will have different a different career development process and thus have different career-counseling needs.

In addition, the majority of the research and literature ignores socioeconomic status (SES) as a factor in the career development and counseling of Asian women. Because there is a bimodal distribution of SES in the Asian community (i.e., those who are affluent and those that are below or at the poverty line), SES can be a crucial contextual factor that can inhibit or enhance the career opportunities that are available to Asian women. More research on how SES impacts the career development of Asian women is needed. Contextual factors such as religious affiliation, sexual orientation, disability status, and generational status also need to be considered and investigated in relation to the career development of Asian women. These types of investigations could provide information regarding the ways that various contextual factors interact to impact the career development process of Asian women.

Finally, having more information about the career development of Asian women is necessary to build culturally appropriate and sensitive career interventions. Without information on the career development process of Asian women from various ethnic groups, it is virtually impossible to address the career-counseling needs of this diverse population. Investigations that utilize existing career development theories such as SCCT, D-C, and feminist career-counseling perspectives applied to the career development of Asian women could provide information about which of these career theories or combinations of theories best explain the career development of Asian women. Career-counseling models like the culturally appropriate model also have promise for providing culturally appropriate career services to Asian women, but would benefit from quantitative and qualitative studies that investigate their effectiveness with this population. Research on the career development and counseling of Asian women would greatly add to our ability to better understand the diverse needs of this population and therefore provide better career services.

REFERENCES

Ali, S. R., Liu, W., & Humedian, M. (2004). Islam 101: Understanding the religion and therapy implications. *Professional Psychology: Research and Practice, 35,* 635–642.

Balagopal, S. S. (1999). The case of the brown memsahib: Issues that confront working South Asian wives and mothers. In S. R. Gupta (Ed.), *Emerging voices: South Asian American women redefine self, family, and community* (pp. 146–168). Walnut Creek, CA: Altamira Press.

Bandura, A. (1986). *Social foundations of thought and action: A social cognitive theory.* Englewood Cliffs, NJ: Prentice Hall.

Bandura, A. (1997). *Self-efficacy: The exercise of control.* San Francisco: Freeman.

Bradshaw, C. K. (1994). Asian and Asian American women: Historical and political considerations in psychotherapy. In L. Comas-Díaz & B. Greene (Eds.), *Women of color: Integrating ethnic and gender identities in psychotherapy* (pp. 72–113). New York: Guilford Press.

Brooks, L., & Forrest, L. (1994). Feminism and career counseling. In B. W. Walsh & S. H. Osipow (Eds.), *Career counseling for women: Contemporary topics in vocational psychology* (pp. 87–134). Hillsdale, NJ: Lawrence Erlbaum Associates.

Enns, C. Z. (1993). Twenty years of feminist counseling and therapy: From naming biases to implementing multifaceted practice. *The Counseling Psychologist, 21,* 3–87.

Enns, C. Z. (1997). *Feminist theories and feminist psychotherapies: Origins, themes, and variations.* New York: Harrington Park Press.

Foo, L. J. (2002). *Asian American women: Issues, concerns, and responsive human civil rights advocacy.* Retrieved December 4, 2003, from http://www.fordfound.org/publications/recent_articles/asian_american_women.cfm

Fouad, N. A. (2002). Cross-cultural differences in vocational interests: Between-group differences on the Strong Interest Inventory. *Journal of Counseling Psychology, 49,* 282–289.

Fouad, N. A., & Bingham, R. P. (1995). Career counseling with racial ethnic minorities. In W. B. Walsh & S. H. Osipow (Eds.), *Handbook of vocational psychology: Theory, research, and practice* (2nd ed., pp. 331–365). Hillsdale, NJ: Lawrence Erlbaum Associates.

Hackett, G., & Betz, N. E. (1981). A self-efficacy approach to the career development of women. *Journal of Vocational Behavior, 18,* 326–339.

Holland, J. L. (1985). *Making vocational choices: A theory of careers.* Englewood Cliffs, NJ: Prentice Hall.

Kim, B. S., Atkinson, D. R., & Umemoto, D. (2001). Asian cultural values and the counseling process: Current knowledge and directions for future research. *The Counseling Psychologist, 29,* 570–603.

Kim, B. S., Atkinson, D. R., & Yang, P. H. (1999). The Asian Values Scale: Development, factor analysis, validation, and reliability. *Journal of Counseling Psychology, 46,* 342–352.

Krumboltz, J. D. (1979). A social learning theory of career decision making. In A. M. Mitchell, G. B. Jones, & J. D. Krumboltz (Eds.), *Social learning and career decision making* (pp. 19–49). Cranston, RI: Carroll.

Lent, R. W., Brown, S. D., & Hackett, G. (1994). Toward a unified social cognitive theory of career and academic interest, choice, and performance. *Journal of Vocational Behavior, 45,* 79–122.

Lent, R. W., Brown, S. D., & Hackett, G. (2000). Contextual supports and barriers to career choice: A social cognitive analysis. *Journal of Counseling Psychology, 47,* 36–49.

Leong, F. T. (1991). Career development attributes and occupational values of Asian American and White American college students. *Career Development Quarterly, 39,* 221–230.

Leong, F. T. (1993). The career counseling process with racial-ethnic minorities: The case of Asian Americans. *Career Development Quarterly, 42,* 26–40.

Leong, F. T., & Chou, E. L. (1994). The role of ethnic identity and acculturation in the vocational behavior of Asian Americans: An integrative review. *Journal of Vocational Behavior, 44,* 155–172.

Leong, F. T., & Gim-Chung, R. H. (1995). Career development and vocational behavior of racial and ethnic minorities. In F. T. Leong (Ed.), *Career assessment and intervention with Asian Americans* (pp. 193–227). Hillsdale, NJ: Lawrence Erlbaum Associates.

Leong, F. T., & Serafica, F. C. (1995). Career development of Asian Americans: A research area in need of a good theory. In F. T. Leong (Ed.), *Career development and vocational behavior of racial and ethnic minorities* (pp. 67–102). Hillsdale, NJ: Lawrence Erlbaum Associates.

Leong, F. T., & Tata, S. P. (1990). Sex and acculturation differences in occupational values among Chinese-American children. *Journal of Counseling Psychology, 37,* 208–212.

Lerner, R. M. (1979). A dynamic interactional concept of individual and social relationship development. In R. L. Burgess & T. L. Huston (Eds.), *Social change in developing relationships* (pp. 271–305). New York: Academic Press.

Leung, S. A., Ivey, D., & Suzuki, L. (1994). Factors affecting the career aspirations of Asian Americans. *Journal of Counseling and Development, 4,* 404–410.

Lofquist, L. H., & Dawis, R. V. (1969). *Adjustment to work.* New York: Appleton-Century-Crofts.

McWhirter, E. H., Torres, D. M., & Rasheed, S. (1998). Assessing barriers to women's career adjustment. *Journal of Career Assessment, 6,* 449–479.

Patton, W., & McMahon, M. (1999). *Career development and systems theory.* Pacific Grove, CA: Brooks/Cole.

Population Resource Center. (n.d.). *Executive summary: World population trends.* Retrieved April 6, 2005, from http://www.prcdc.org/summaries/worldpopupdate02/worldpopupdate02.html

Rachman-Moore, D., & Danziger, N. (1998). Gender differences in early career attainment of business school graduates. *Megamot, 40,* 262–279.

Root, M. P. P. (1995). The psychology of Asian American women. In H. Landrine (Ed.), *Bringing cultural diversity to feminist psychology: Research, theory, and practice* (pp. 265–301). Washington, DC: American Psychological Association.

Sethuraman, S. V. (1998). *Gender, informality and poverty: Gender bias in female informal employment and incomes in developing countries.* Retrieved December 4, 2003, from http://www.wiego.org/papers/sethcontents.html

Sturdivant, S. (1980). *Therapy with women: A feminist philosophy of treatment.* New York: Springer.

Sue, D. W., Bernier, J. E., Durran, A., Feinbert, L., Pedersen, P., Smith, E., & Vasquez-Nuttal, E. (1992). Position paper: Cross-cultural counseling competencies. *The Counseling Psychologist, 10,* 45–52.

Sue, D. W., & Sue, D. (1999). *Counseling the culturally different* (3rd ed.). New York: Wiley.

Sue, D. W., & Sue, D. (2002). *Counseling the culturally different* (4th ed.). New York: Wiley.

Sue, D. W., & Sue, D. (2003). *Counseling the culturally diverse: Theory and practice.* New York: Wiley.

Suinn, R. M., Rickard-Figueroa, K., Lew, S., & Vigil, P. (1987). Suinn-Lew Asian Self-Identity Acculturation Scale: An initial report. *Educational and Psychological Measurement, 7,* 401–407.

Super, D. E. (1990). A life span, life-space approach to career development. In D. Brown & L. Brooks (Eds.), *Career choice and development* (2nd ed., pp. 197–261). San Francisco: Jossey-Bass.

Tang, M., Fouad, N. A., & Smith, P. L. (1999). Asian Americans' career choices: A path model to examine factors influencing their career choices. *Journal of Vocational Behavior, 54,* 142–157.

Uba, L. (1994). *Asian Americans: Personality patterns, identity, and mental health.* New York: Guilford Press.

U.S. Equal Employment Opportunity Commission. (2001). *Women of color: Their employment in the private sector.* Retrieved December 3, 2003, from http://www.ilo.org/public/english/bureau/inf/pr/1996/1.htm

U.S. Equal Employment Opportunity Commission. (2002). *Job patterns for minorities and women in private industry (EEO-1).* Retrieved April 6, 2005, from http://www.eeoc.gov/stats/jobpat/jobpat.html

Vondracek, F. W., & Fouad, N. A. (1994). Developmental contextualism: An integrative framework for theory and practice. In M. L. Savickas & R. W. Lent (Eds.), *Convergence in career development theories: Implications for science and practice* (pp. 207–214). Hillsdale, NJ: Lawrence Erlbaum Associates.

Vondracek, F. W., & Kawasaki, T. (1995). Toward a comprehensive framework for adult career development theory and intervention. In W. B. Walsh & S. H. Osipow (Eds.), *Handbook of vocational psychology* (2nd ed., pp. 111–141). Hillsdale, NJ: Lawrence Erlbaum Associates.

Vondracek, F. W., Lerner, R. M., & Schulenberg, J. E. (1983). The concept of development in vocational theory and intervention. *Journal of Vocational Behavior, 23,* 179–202.

Vondracek, F. W., Lerner, R. M., & Schulenberg, J. E. (1986). *Career development: A life-span developmental approach.* Hillsdale, NJ: Lawrence Erlbaum Associates.

Walsh, W. B., & Osipow, S. H. (1995). Introduction: Career counseling for women. In W. B. Walsh & S. H. Osipow (Eds.), *Career counseling for women* (pp. ix–xvii). Hillsdale, NJ: Lawrence Erlbaum Associates.

Wong, P. T. P., & Ujimoto, K. V. (1998). The elderly: Their stress, coping, and mental health. In L. C. Lee & W. S. Z. Nolan (Eds.), *Handbook of Asian American psychology* (pp. 165–209). Thousand Oaks, CA: Sage.

Worell, J., & Remer, P. (2003). *Feminist perspectives in therapy: Empowering diverse women.* Hoboken, NJ: Wiley.

Yang, J. (1991). Career counseling of Chinese American women: Are they in limbo? *Career Development Quarterly, 39,* 350–359.

Yee, B. W., Huang, L. N., & Lew, A. (1998). Families: Life-span socialization in a cultural context. In L. C. Lee & W. S. Z. Nolan (Eds.), *Handbook of Asian American psychology* (pp. 83–135). Thousand Oaks, CA: Sage.

Chapter 9

Career Counseling With Latinas

Lisa Y. Flores
Rachel L. Navarro
Lizette Ojeda
University of Missouri-Columbia

Women's career development in the United States has gained prominence in the career literature in the past several decades. Researchers have identified salient issues that influence women's career development, such as gender-role socialization, multiple-role management, and sexism. Although many of these experiences are relevant to many women in the United States, there are aspects to the career process of women from diverse racial and ethnic groups that are influenced by culture. Due to their experiences as members of culturally oppressed groups, women of color share some common experiences, however, their career processes are further differentiated by their distinctive cultural backgrounds. In this chapter, we highlight career development issues among Latinas in the United States. Before we address the career literature on Latinas, we provide a brief introduction on the Latino/a culture and Latinas' educational and vocational patterns.

There are numerous terms that are critical to understanding Latino/a culture. Therefore, in the first part of this chapter we present these constructs and their implications for career counselors. Within the social science literature, the term *Hispanic* initially was used to describe descendants from countries that had Spanish roots (Arbona, 1995). Because this term was imposed by the Office of Management and Budget (Federal Register, 1978, as cited in McNeill et al., 2001), many people of Spanish descent have rejected its use (Albert, 1996). Instead, people began to use terms that specifically described their country of origin (e.g., *Mexican, Puerto Rican,* and *Cuban*) or a combination of their roots and political ideology (e.g., *Chicano/*

a). The term *Latino* (short for *Latino Americano*) was adopted because it re-affirmed their native, pre-Hispanic identity (Falicov, 1998). In recent years, the terms *Hispanic* and *Latino* have been used interchangeably; however, the prevalence of and preference for the term *Latino* has increased substantially within and outside of the social sciences (McNeill et al., 2001). Thus, the term *Latina* will be used throughout this chapter to refer to women of Mexican, Puerto Rican, Cuban, and Central and South American descent who are residing in the United States, *Latino* will refer to men from these backgrounds, and *Latina/o* will refer to both women and men. It is important to note that the definition of Latina/os that we use does not include people from Spain due to their European background and because of this country's history of oppression in the Americas.

INTRODUCTION TO LATINAS

Who Are Latinas?

Before highlighting some of the cultural group characteristics of Latinas in the United States, it is important to note that there is much diversity within this group. Although Latinas have a common cultural background, Latinas may differ along several dimensions. Aspects of these differences that ca-reer counselors should consider in their work with and assessment of Latina clients include: race, acculturation level, and ethnic or racial iden-tity. Each of these areas may play a significant role in the career develop-ment of their Latina clients.

Race. Latinas can be White, Black, Asian, indigenous (native groups from their country), or a combination of these. Discriminatory practices continue to occur today based on a person's race-group categorization, phenotype, and skin color. As such, a Latina's career development may be differentially affected depending on her racial group affiliation, physical features, and skin color.

Acculturation. Acculturation refers to the process of change resulting from contact between two different cultures (Berry, Trimble, & Olmedo, 1986). Changes can occur along multiple dimensions, including attitudinal and behavioral changes, and at either the group or individual level. Con-trary to early conceptions that acculturation was a unidimensional, linear process whereby individuals were believed to be either highly acculturated into the dominant culture (and to shed attitudes and behaviors common to their culture) or highly acculturated into their original culture (and to re-ject the attitudes and values of the host culture), recent conceptualizations of acculturation have advanced a multidimensional approach to assessment. In the latter approach, acculturation is assessed separately along two dimensions: acculturation into the mainstream culture and acculturation into one's own culture of origin, such that one can be highly acculturated into two cultures simultaneously. Due to both the increasing numbers of Latina/os in the United States and the proximity of the United States to Mexico and other Spanish-speaking countries, it is not uncommon to find Latinas who are bicultural, as well as those who are strongly acculturated to either the White American or Latina/o culture.

Ethnic and Racial Identity.　　Ethnic or racial identity refers to "a sense of group or collective identity based on one's *perception* that he or she shares a common racial [ethnic] heritage with a particular racial [ethnic] group" (Helms, 1993, p. 3). Although Latinas may be designated to the same racial group category based on their physical characteristics, the extent to which they identify with both their racial group and ethnic group may vary; thus, assessment of a Latina client's ethnic and racial group identity and its relation to the client's perception of her career and educational progression may provide a career counselor with important information to understand differences among Latinas. According to ethnic and racial identity models (Helms; Phinney, 1989), identity is a dynamic process that is subject to change as individuals come to understand their ethnic group affiliation and the meaning they attribute to their ethnic background. Identity is hypothesized to range from unawareness of society's racial dynamics and an internalization of the negative messages regarding an individual's ethnic or racial group, to the integration of a positive reference-group identity.

Demographic Information on Latinas.　　According to the U.S. Bureau of the Census (2002d), over 1 million Latinas reside in the United States, representing 7% of the total U.S. population and slightly more than half of the total U.S. Latina/o population. In 2050, Latinas are projected to represent approximately 12.24% of the total U.S. population, making them one of the fastest growing and youngest racial ethnic groups (U.S. Bureau of the Census, 2002b). Slightly over a third of Latinas are under the age of 18, and Latinas have a median age of 26.3 years (U.S. Bureau of the Census, 2002a).

Together, Latinas represent a diverse, heterogeneous population of U.S.-born and immigrant women whose ancestry stems from over 20 different Latin American countries including Mexico, Puerto Rico, Cuba, and Central and South American countries (Giachello, 1996). Most have ancestry from Mexico (67%), followed by Central or South America (15%), Puerto Rico (8%), Cuba (4%), and a combination thereof (7%) (U.S. Bureau of the Census, 2002a). Presently, slightly over half of Latinas in the United States were born in another country (U.S. Bureau of the Census).

Furthermore, Latinas are geographically concentrated in different parts of the United States, with Mexican American women in the West (e.g., California, Arizona, New Mexico, Texas), Puerto Rican women in the Northeast (e.g., New Jersey, New York), Cuban women in Southeast (e.g., Florida), and Central and South American women spread evenly throughout the geographical regions (U.S. Bureau of the Census). These figures, however, may be underestimations given the number of undocumented Latina immigrants living in the country.

Latinas and their families have their own unique reasons for leaving their home countries and immigrating to the United States (Falicov, 1998; Marin & Marin, 1991; Rogler, 1994). Bases for immigration include the search for political stability (e.g., Cuba, El Salvador, and Colombia), the pursuit of increased economic opportunities (e.g., Mexico, Puerto Rico, and Central and South America), the preservation of economic resources and lifestyles (e.g., Cuba), and the quest for improved educational opportunities (e.g., Central and South America). Immigration factors may influence the differential social and occupational experiences of Latinas.

Latinas' Educational Trends.   All Latinas in the United States experience double jeopardy due to their gender and racial and ethnic minority status, and many experience additional oppression as members of lower socioeconomic groups (Gloria, 2001; Ortiz, 1994). In general, these external barriers may be related to their long history of unfavorable outcomes in their educational and occupational status. According to the findings of a White House task force, Latina student achievement is negatively affected by a range of factors including poverty, lack of participation in preschool programs, poor school attendance, and limited English proficiency (*Latinos in Education*, 1999). Disparities in educational achievement between Latina students and others begin in kindergarten and remain constant through high school, college, and graduate school. For example, by the age of 9, Latinas perform far below their non-Latina peers in reading, mathematics, and science (*Latinos in Education*).

Although Latinas' high school completion rates have increased from 34.2% in 1970 to 57.5% in 2000, Latinas still lag behind the current national high school completion rate of 84.4% (U.S. Bureau of the Census, 2000). Indeed, the gap between Latinas and their White female and male peers is approximately 30%. Differences between Latina subgroups also are evident; Mexican American women have the lowest high school completion rates (51.5%) of all Latina ethnic groups, whereas Cuban American women have the highest rates (71.0%) (U.S. Bureau of the Census, 2002a). Women of Puerto Rican and Central and South American descent are in between, with high school graduate rates of 66.3% and 65.5%, respectively (U.S. Bureau of the Census, 2002a). Latinas and their Latino peers have relatively equal high school graduation rates (U.S. Bureau of the Census, 2002a).

Latinas' representation at each progressive step of the educational system is lower than that of their White peers (U.S. Bureau of the Census, 2002d). Latinas lag behind White men and women in the attainment of postsecondary degrees by approximately 24% and 12%, respectively. Whereas the national average for college graduation rates increased by 14% between 1970 and 2000, Latinas' college graduation rate increased by 6.3%, from 4.3% to 10.6% (U.S. Bureau of the Census, 2000). Currently, 7.3% of Latinas earn a bachelor's degree, 2.2% earn a master's degree, and 1% earn a doctorate (0.4%) or professional (0.7%) degree (U.S. Bureau of the Census, 2002d).

Again, differences in the attainment of postsecondary degrees exist between the various Latina ethnic groups. Similar to high school completion rates, women of Mexican descent have the lowest postsecondary graduation rates (7.5%) and women of Cuban descent have the highest (20.2%), with women of Puerto Rican descent (13.2%) and Central and South American descent (17.7%) in the middle (U.S. Bureau of the Census, 2002a). Although college graduation rates of Latinas (10.6%) and Latinos (10.7%) are not significantly different, trends demonstrate that Latinas are less likely to earn bachelor's (7.31% vs. 8.59%), professional (0.67% vs. 0.70%), and doctorate (0.38% vs. 0.74%) degrees and more likely to earn master's degrees (2.24% vs. 2.04%) than their Latino peers (U.S. Bureau of the Census, 2002d).

In light of these statistics, research is greatly needed to assess the degree to which sociopolitical and sociocultural variables influence Latinas' educational achievement. More longitudinal and cross-sectional studies are recommended to determine long-term and generational effects. Such research can aid in the creation of effective educational interventions for Latinas.

Latinas' Earning Power and Employment Characteristics. Historically, Latinas have had higher unemployment rates and lower labor force participation rates than their Latino and White female counterparts (U.S. Bureau of the Census, 2002c). A quarter of all Latina/o families are headed by single mothers whose underemployment is related to many of these Latina-headed families living below the poverty line (36.4%). These rates are higher in comparison to all Latina/o and U.S. families living in poverty, respectively (U.S. Bureau of the Census, 2002d). In addition, Latina/o families tend to be larger than White families (U.S. Bureau of the Census, 2002d), suggesting that relatively more Latina/o than White children are living below the poverty line.

There are differences among Latinas from various countries of origin in unemployment, labor force participation, and poverty. In terms of unemployment, women of Mexican descent have the highest unemployment rates (8.1%), closely followed by Puerto Rican (7.6%), Cuban (7.2%), and Central and South American (7.0%) women (U.S. Bureau of the Census, 2002a). However, women of Central and South American descent have the highest labor force participation rates (63.3%), followed by Mexican (57.0%), Puerto Rican (55.4%), and Cuban (49.8%) women (U.S. Bureau of the Census). Furthermore, women of Puerto Rican descent are more likely to head households living below the poverty line (43.6%) than Cuban (38.7%), Mexican (38.4%), and Central and South American (25.7%) women (U.S. Bureau of the Census).

The high rate of Latina family poverty is undoubtedly related to Latinas' low earning potential. According to the U.S. Bureau of the Census (2000), in 1999, Latinas earned $18,187 per year on average compared to the national average of $32,356. In fact, Latinas earned only 43%, 77%, and 72% of the yearly income of their White male, White female, and Latino peers, respectively. Latinas' earning potential increases with each advancement in education (U.S. Bureau of the Census, 2002d), indicating that efforts to improve their educational attainment may simultaneously improve their socioeconomic status. Latinas with a high school, college, or master's degree earned approximately 90%, 90%, and 98%, respectively, of their White female peers' annual salaries at corresponding levels of education. However, regardless of educational attainment, Latinas continue to earn approximately 70% of their Latino peers' salaries and approximately 55% of their White male peers' salaries. Comparisons between Latinas, Latinos, and Whites who have earned professional degrees or doctorates could not be made due to the relatively few Latinas who have earned those degrees (U.S. Bureau of the Census, 2002d).

Historically, Latinas have experienced occupational segregation in the U.S. labor market, which still persists today (U.S. Bureau of the Census, 2000). Latinas are underrepresented in occupations classified as managerial and overrepresented in service occupations (U.S. Bureau of the Census, 2002a) compared to women in general. At the same time, differences between Latina ethnic groups exist in other occupations. For example, whereas women of Puerto Rican and Cuban descent are overrepresented in technical occupations and underrepresented in farming occupations, women of Mexican descent are overrepresented in factory-operating and farming jobs. Additionally, women of Central and South American descent are overrepresented in manufacturing and factory occupations. Latinas continue to earn less income than their Latino and White peers across all occupational categories, excluding farming, where Latinas earn more than White women (U.S. Bureau of the Census, 2000). In conclusion, it is important to note that many Latinas work in low-paying service occupations, which may also contribute to their high poverty levels.

Influence of Latino Cultural Values on Latinas' Career Development and Career Counseling

The career behavior of Latinas may be explained and predicted by the degree of their adherence to overarching Latina/o cultural values (Fouad, 1994, 1995). According to Marin and Marin (1991), the Latina/o culture can be distinguished from other cultures based on a shared set of cultural values. These cultural values were transmitted throughout Latin America via Spanish colonization and were integrated with the indigenous cultures of each Latin American country to create a unique blending of Latino/a and indigenous values. Common cultural values have endured across Latin American countries and their inhabitants (Falicov, 1998; Marin & Marin). Understanding the potential influence of these shared cultural values on Latinas' career development is key in the provision of culturally sensitive and effective career counseling to this population (see Table 9.1 for examples of how cultural values may be related to Latinas' career decision making). At the same time, Latinas' adherence to these shared cultural values may differ based on their acculturation level, educational attainment, immigrant or generational status, race, and ethnic or racial identity (Falicov; Fouad, 1994, 1995). There-

TABLE 9.1
Examples of Latina/o Cultural Values
and Their Relation to Latinas' Career Beliefs

Cultural Value	Statements Reflecting Cultural Beliefs Related to Career
Familismo	It is important to my parents that I attend college close to home so that I can live at home. I would like to find a job in this area to stay close to my family.
Personalismo	I would rather attend a community college than a university because I will be able to develop closer relationships with both students and faculty. This job is more appealing to me because the people at work seem to get along well with each other.
Allocentrism	In consideration of my family, I will delay my education so that I can work to help improve our financial situation.
Simpatía	Although I feel that I deserve the promotion more than my coworker, I will remain silent to avoid confrontation.
Respeto	The career counselor is a professional, and thus knows what career path is best for me. Out of respect, I will not disagree with my advisor's suggestions even though I feel they are not right for me.
Time orientation	It is important that I find work immediately to start earning an income. Making money for the family today is most important.
Marianismo	It is not necessary that I pursue more education when I plan on raising children.
Fatalismo	If it is God's will, then I will get the job promotion. I will put this decision about my career in God's hands.

fore, it is important to avoid generalizing these values and their influence to all Latinas. Instead, career counselors should assess both the degree of adherence to and the influence of these shared cultural values on career behaviors for each Latina career client. Individualized career-counseling interventions based on this assessment can be developed accordingly.

Familismo (Familialism).   The value placed on the family is one of the most important and central characteristics of the Latino/a culture. For Latinas, their everyday actions and decisions may be geared so that they benefit the family, and the needs of the family are prioritized over individual needs (Falicov, 1998; Santiago-Rivera, Arredondo, & Gallardo-Cooper, 2002). The cultural value of *familismo* reflects this priority via the emphasis on family interdependence, loyalty, cooperation, affiliation, and responsibility (Falicov; McNeill et al., 2001; Santiago-Rivera et al.). According to Falicov, *familismo* includes the extension of kinship relationships beyond the boundaries of the nuclear family to comprise extended family members, important family friends, *padrinos* (godparents), and religious leaders, all of whom may be involved in family decision making (Falicov; McNeill et al.; Santiago-Rivera et al.). This strong familial orientation is related to the tendency to settle and remain in geographic proximity to other family members (McNeill et al.; Santiago-Rivera et al.). Thus, Latinas' career decisions may be based on availability of jobs within specific geographic regions and on the need of supporting their families financially and emotionally, all of which may result in a limited range of career options.

Familismo lends itself to group career decision making and thus the inclusion of the family in the career-counseling process may be essential. However, seeking help outside the family often is frowned on and may even be insulting to other family members (Altarriba & Bauer, 1998; Fouad, 1994). Thus, career counselors who are working with traditional Latinas should approach the career-counseling process with the utmost respect for the role and influence of the family in their career development. In working with Latinas who adhere to *familismo*, career counselors also should be aware that geographical relocation may not be a viable option given the need to financially and emotionally support their families (Fouad, 1994, 1995; Hurtado, 1995). Additionally, Latinas may make career decisions that allow them to support their families financially in the present and may not give credence to long-term financial gain from educational pursuits (Fouad, 1994, 1995). For Latinas from lower socioeconomic groups, this may mean foregoing a college education and working to provide financially for the family. On the other hand, it can also serve to the advantage of Latina clients' educational and career pursuits when their performance and behaviors in those arenas are perceived to bring honor and respect to the family. Given the emphasis on family in the Latina/o culture, the family can either serve as an important social support or a source of stress depending on the amount of support or discouragement a Latina receives from her family members for pursuing career opportunities. Career counselors should highlight and build on this support when working with Latina clients.

Allocentrism. Latinas often are described as having interpersonal relationships that are marked by mutuality, reciprocity, and interdependence (Altarriba & Bauer, 1998; Arredondo, 1996; Zea, Garcia, Belgrave, & Quezada, 1997). This cultural value has been termed *allocentrism* (Marin & Marin, 1991) and is believed to promote a stronger sense of group identity over individual identity (Arredondo). Given the importance of the group, Latinas may undertake a process of career decision making in consideration of others (Fouad, 1994, 1995). In addition, Latinas may consider occupations that benefit their communities or family but are of little interest to them personally. Furthermore, in work settings, Latinas may stress the accomplishments of the work team as a whole rather than their own individual contributions.

When working with Latinas who hold the traditional cultural value of allocentrism, the involvement of family members and close friends in the career-counseling process may be warranted (Fouad, 1994, 1995). Such involvement may include asking for the opinions of family members, close friends, and community leaders as well as facilitating group discussion and evaluation of how Latina career clients can help meet the group's needs and wishes. In this process, career counselors also may be able to help the group broaden their ideas of acceptable and helpful occupations that Latinas can consider and pursue to benefit the group more fully. In addition, career counselors may assist traditional Latinas in their search for work environments that value their group orientation, and reward these behaviors through promotions and raises. Furthermore, career counselors may aid traditional Latinas in the presentation of their previous accomplishments through the resume or curriculum vitae in a manner that does not devalue their group identity or earlier workplace contributions.

On the other hand, career counselors who are working with less traditional Latinas should be aware that such women may make individual career decisions that are counter to the group's needs and wishes (Fouad, 1994, 1995). In this situation, career counselors can help Latinas to determine the consequences for their personal decision making (e.g., parental disapproval, lack of support), their willingness to encounter such consequences, and ways to cope with the consequences.

Personalismo (Personalism). Many Latinas value, develop, and maintain interpersonal relationships characterized by a strong emotional investment and mutual dependency (Santiago-Rivera et al., 2002). Thus, preference is given to personal contacts rather than impersonal or institutional ones (McNeill et al., 2001). In addition, Latinas may gauge their willingness to engage in relationships based on their own personal subjective sense of a person rather than that person's objective social status (Comas-Diaz, 1997). Taken together, these interpersonal tendencies define the Latino cultural value of *personalismo*, which often is demonstrated through nonverbal expressions that result in less physical distance in interpersonal interactions and more physical touching (McNeill et al.). Although personal relationships are valued within the Latina/o culture, *personalismo* does not overshadow the importance placed on respect and authority in interpersonal relationships. Thus, whereas personal contacts are preferred, such contacts are not always viewed as informal (Comas-Diaz; McNeill et al.).

Based on their degree of adherence to *personalismo*, Latinas may find it difficult to trust and develop a relationship with career counselors who approach the counseling process in an impersonal and sterile manner (Altarriba & Bauer, 1998). Hence, career counselors should attempt to develop a personal, albeit professional, relationship with their Latina clients. In addition, adherence to *personalismo* may make it difficult for Latina clients to ask unknown individuals who are working in a particular career of interest for occupational information and mentoring. Thus, career counselors can assist traditional Latina clients in the career-exploration process by personally introducing them to such persons. Formal mentoring programs also may assist in establishing needed mentor-mentee relationships for Latina clients.

Simpatía (Congeniality).   Great importance is placed on interpersonal relationships that are smooth and conflict-free, and reflects the Latina/o cultural value termed s*impatía* (Altarriba & Bauer, 1998; Fouad, 1994; Santiago-Rivera et al., 2002). Behaviors that promote a pleasant demeanor and agreement are highly valued and rewarded (Comas-Diaz, 1997; McNeill et al., 2001). Adherence to *simpatía* often produces the avoidance of direct confrontations in both personal and professional relationships (Comas-Diaz; Santiago-Rivera et al.). Much like *personalismo, simpatía* may result in a preference for personal networking over approaching unfamiliar persons for occupational information or opportunities (Fouad). Taken together, *simpatía* and *personalismo* may make Latinas popular colleagues; however, these same characteristics may lead to problems in educational and work settings when Latinas appear unassertive, conflict avoidant, and indirect in their communication (Comas-Diaz).

In designing and implementing interventions for Latina clients, it is essential that career counselors take into account the potential influence of *simpatía* on the counseling process, therapeutic relationship, and the clients' prior work experiences. First, as in other personal and professional relationships, traditional Latinas may avoid conflicts or disagreements with career counselors resulting in socially desirable responses to counseling interventions during session (Fouad, 1994; Marin & Marin, 1991), and perhaps leading to little follow-through outside of session. Thus, it is important to explore Latinas' responses to interventions and their willingness to engage in certain activities in more depth. In terms of previous work experiences, it is important to assess the potential positive and negative effects of *simpatía* on traditional Latinas' professional relationships and record of promotion and pay raises. Through this exploration, career counselors may be called on to help Latina clients develop appropriate ways of addressing conflicts in work and educational settings while still remaining true to this value.

Respeto (Respect).   The meaning and internalization of this cultural value are different for Latinas and for members of other racial or ethnic groups. Within mainstream American culture, *respect* denotes a detached sense of mutual admiration and esteem; however, in Latina/o culture, *respeto* refers to the appropriate deference paid to the power of authority figures (Falicov, 1998). Such deference manifests itself through sensitivity to the power of an individual's gender, generation, and position of authority within the family (Falicov; Fouad, 1994; Santiago-Rivera et al., 2002). For example, men are afforded more respect than women, parents more than children, and elders more than all. Deference to authority figures also manifests itself in the use of language, which serves to reinforce relational boundaries (Santiago-Rivera et al.).

The influences of *respeto* on career development and career counseling can be numerous. To begin, like *familismo, respeto* may result in career decisions based on the suggestions of family members, particularly the parents. For some Latinas, parents represent unquestioned authority figures who have the final say on their personal and professional behaviors (Falicov, 1998). Such parental authority may result in limited career options or early foreclosure on a career decision. Again, parental involvement in the career-counseling process may prove beneficial to both Latina clients and their families via the provision of occupational information and the opportunity to demonstrate the importance of education to occupational and financial success. In addition, it is important for career counselors to carefully balance the role of children in the counseling process if working with parents who have limited English-speaking abilities and if children are the main translators (Fouad, 1994). In such situations, appropriate respect for the parents is crucial, given that the power of information flow is held by the children. Finally, akin to *simpatía, respeto* may lead to socially desirable responses to career-counseling interventions from Latina clients given the amount of respect imparted to the role of counselor or professional

(Fouad, 1994, 1995). Thus, assessing Latina clients' true sense of commitment and willingness to engage in career-counseling activities is essential.

Time Orientation.   Collectivist and individualistic cultures have very distinct time orientations (Sue & Sue, 2003). More specifically, collectivist cultures tend to stress the importance of tradition (i.e., past orientation), while simultaneously focusing on their present circumstances (i.e., present orientation). On the other hand, individualistic cultures tend to be focused on future gains (i.e., future orientation). Given that the Latina/o culture is relatively collectivistic, Latinas may be focused on both the past and the present. Thus, Latinas may act in ways to preserve tradition and to meet their families' immediate, daily needs (Zea et al., 1997). Indeed, Latinas' focus on immediate needs may impede long-term career planning; however, the extent of this potential impediment may depend on socioeconomic status (SES). For example, Latinas from middle-, upper-middle-, and upper-class statuses will have more opportunities to focus on their future career development (i.e., continuing postsecondary education) without having to work to meet immediate financial needs of the family than Latinas from lower socioeconomic groups.

Because traditional career-counseling theories and interventions are clearly embedded in the mainstream, individualistic American culture, career counselors may need to make significant shifts in their case conceptualizations and interventions with Latina clients. More specifically, career counselors will need to refrain from viewing Latina clients who arrive late for appointments due to other family and work commitments as lazy, uninvested in the counseling process, or unwilling to better their current social and economic situations. In addition, career counselors need to help Latina clients make connections between long-term career goals and more immediate, daily needs (Zea et al., 1997). For example, career counselors can facilitate greater awareness of the career ladder within specific occupations and how certain steps can help meet the Latina's family's immediate daily needs. Because the pursuit of education undoubtedly is a major aspect in gaining class status, career counselors can assist Latina clients in developing ways to balance school and work responsibilities. Furthermore, career counselors can aid Latina clients in applying for and acquiring financial aid, scholarships, and fellowships to assist in meeting both educational bills and immediate financial needs.

Marianismo (Female Gender Role).   Traditional Latina/o culture has been described as patriarchal. Recently, suggestions that the Latina/o culture is truly matriarchal have been made such that Latina women are perceived to be the silent power within the family given their responsibility for the emotional welfare of the children and maintenance of the household (Santiago-

Rivera et al., 2002). In addition, others have argued that Latina gender roles are changing due to their increased rates of employment outside of the house (Altarriba & Bauer, 1998), perhaps resulting in more egalitarian relationships. Despite these changes, traditional views of appropriate gender behavior can vary based on educational level, SES, family constellation, sexual orientation, acculturation, and ethnic identity (Quinoñes, 2000). Therefore, a discussion of Latina gender-role socialization and its potential influence on career development and career counseling is warranted.

In the past and in highly traditional families, Latinas were socialized to be gentle, nurturing, intuitive, dependent, submissive, impulsive, and docile (McNeill et al., 2001; Santiago-Rivera et al., 2002). In addition, they were expected to be virtuous and humble, yet spiritually stronger than their male peers (McNeill et al.; Santiago-Rivera et al.; Sue, Ivey, & Pedersen, 1996). These characteristics represent the traditional Latina gender role of *marianismo*, which is related to the Latino culture's strong tie to Catholicism and calls for Latinas to model their behavior after the Virgin Mary. Thus, Latinas were expected to be virginal until marriage. In traditional families, unmarried Latinas may be allowed to date only if accompanied by a family member or close friend to protect their chastity, which is strongly tied to the family's honor (Altarriba & Bauer, 1998). During marriage, Latinas were expected to honor their husbands and nurture their children through self-sacrifice (McNeill et al.). Ultimately, motherhood is revered as the ultimate role for Latinas (Sue et al.).

When working with Latina clients, career counselors first need to assess the degree to which their clients adhere to traditional gender roles. This assessment will prevent career counselors from erroneously assuming that all Latinas adhere to traditional gender-role characteristics to the same degree (Fouad, 1994, 1995). This is especially true with Latina clients who identify as lesbian or bisexual. Given the traditional values within this culture and the strong association between the *marianismo* gender role and heterosexuality, it may be particularly difficult for lesbian and bisexual Latinas to come out to their families and to understand how their sexual orientation may influence their career choices. Moreover, career counselors need to be aware of their own views of gender roles and egalitarian relationships so as not impose those views on Latina clients (Fouad, 1994, 1995). Career counselors who are working with traditional Latina clients can intervene by introducing these women to a wider range of traditional and nontraditional career options, particularly given the tendency for Latinas to perceive few acceptable career possibilities (Fouad, 1994, 1995). In addition, traditional Latinas may need help developing strategies for balancing work and family. Given the priority placed on the welfare of children, career counselors can help Latina mothers find part-time careers or careers that fit their children's school schedules. On the other hand, career counselors can also help nontraditional Latina women increase their awareness of career options by focusing on ways to cope with the potential lack of support from family and friends who disagree with nontraditional career decisions.

Fatalismo (Fatalism).   The cultural value of *fatalismo* is reflective of religious beliefs that one's fate in life is predetermined or left to the will of a higher power. Common sayings in Spanish reflect this cultural belief, such as *Uno propone y Dios dispone* (One proposes, but God disposes), *Hay que aceptar lo que Dios manda* (We have to accept what God sends), and *Sera lo que Dios quiere* (It will be what God wants).

Adherence to these *fatalismo* spiritual beliefs may influence the career decision-making process for Latinas. Specifically, Latinas who believe in *fatalismo* may be more likely to believe that their career and life path is external to their control rather than under their personal control. As such, adherence to this cultural belief may hinder Latinas from engaging in actions that will advance them in their careers because they may believe career outcomes occur regardless of their efforts. These Latinas may be less likely to actively participate in their career development process and may leave major career decisions to chance or to others, or look for signs from a higher being as to the direction they should take. Similarly, Latinas who ascribe to this belief may attribute success or accomplishments in their career to good fortune or to God's graces. Indeed, many of the Latina professionals in one study believed that their career success had been serendipitous and attributed their success purely to luck (Pesquera, 1991). Conversely, hardships that Latinas may experience in life and in their careers may also be attributed to God's plan for their life, or to the belief that they are not more deserving.

Overview of Chapter

In the remaining sections of this chapter, we provide an overview of the vocational psychology literature pertaining to Latinas. Specifically, we summarize the career research with Latinas in the following areas: theoretical applications; educational and career supports and barriers; educational attainment; career interests, choices, and commitment; vocational assessment; and educational and career interventions. Next, we address career-counseling services with Latinas and provide suggestions for facilitating their educational and career development. Finally, we conclude by discussing various implications for career-counseling training to develop effective skills for facilitating Latinas' career development.

It is important to note that most of the studies cited in the following section pertain solely to Latinas' career development. In those instances where a specific subgroup was investigated, we identify the ethnic group affiliation. Furthermore, we use the general term *Latina/o* to refer to studies that included both men and women.

REVIEW OF CAREER DEVELOPMENT RESEARCH WITH LATINAS

Theoretical Applications

Scholars have recently begun to question the cross-cultural validity of vocational theories (e.g., Leong & Brown, 1995) and have encouraged researchers to empirically test whether these theories are applicable to non-White samples. Vocational theories have been criticized for reflecting values and tenets that are highly associated with European American culture and experiences. Specifically, Gysbers, Heppner, and Johnston (2003) identified five tenets that have served as the foundation for much of the career theory and research in the United States, including importance of the individual and autonomy, affluence, belief that opportunities are available to all who work hard, work or career is central to one's life, and belief that career development occurs in a linear, rational process. In the next section, we highlight studies that have validated propositions of traditional vocational theories with Latinas and those that have developed original theoretical explanations for Latinas' career development.

Person-Environment Theory. The applicability of Holland's (1985) theory of vocational choice has been examined with Latina samples and studies have provided mixed support for Holland's theory with Latinas. Specifically, these studies have tested whether the data fit the circular pattern (sequential ordering of R-I-A-S-E-C) and the hexagonal structure (equal distances between themes). Day and Rounds (1998) found support for Holland's circular structure of interests and a three-dimensional solution with a large, nationwide sample of college-bound Mexican American women. Day, Rounds, and Swaney (1998) found similar patterns of interest for their non-college-bound counterparts. In a meta-analytic study examining the structural validity of Holland's theory with international and U.S. ethnic samples, Rounds and Tracey (1996) reported that data from four studies using three mixed gender samples of Latina/os and one Latina sample had a good fit to the Holland's circular structure.

A study of mostly educated, employed Latinas found support for the circular pattern but not for the hexagonal model (Fouad, Harmon, & Borgen, 1997). Both the Realistic and Investigative themes and Social and Enterprising themes were perceived to be more similar for the Latinas in this study than predicted by Holland's theory. Moreover, these researchers found support for one-, two-, and three-dimensional solutions for Latinas.

Another study examined these questions with a sample of Latina college students who were primarily of Mexican origin (Hansen, Sarma, & Collins, 1999). The ordering of the RIASEC types differed for Latinas and, similar to those findings reported by Fouad and her colleagues, the hexagonal solution did not fit the hypothesized structure. Specifically, data supported a circular ordering of R-I-A-E-S-C (note that S and E are reversed), and the realistic type fell closer to the center of the hypothesized hexagonal structure. Findings from this study also supported a two-dimensional solution. Results differed from a comparable sample of Latino students.

In a study of Mexican American high school students, Flores, Spanierman, Armstrong, and Velez (in press) found that the hypothesized RIASEC order was supported among females for general occupational theme scores of the Strong Interest Inventory (Harmon, Hansen, Borgen, & Hammer, 1994) but not for general confidence theme scores of the Skills Confidence Inventory (Betz, Borgen, & Harmon, 1996). Moreover, the hexagonal model fit for both measures was poor among the Mexican American high school women when compared to results obtained with reference samples.

These studies suggest that: (a) the circular structure generally fits with samples of Latinas, (b) the distance between themes is not equal, as some themes are perceived by Latinas to be more similar than hypothesized by Holland, and (c) one- to three-dimensional solutions are possible for Latinas. Additionally, preliminary evidence indicates that Latinas' interest structures are similar regardless of educational attainment, yet different from their male counterparts. The latter findings suggest that Latinas and Latinos may perceive the world of work quite differently based on their differential gender-role socialization within Latina/o families. For example, there is greater differentiation in how Latinos perceive careers based on the RIASEC pattern than Latinas (Fouad et al., 1997). When using career assessments based on Holland's structure with Latina clients, career counselors should consider realistic and investigative careers and enterprising and social careers to be similar to one another.

Developmental Theory. Researchers have explored the applicability of developmental theory and its related constructs to the career development of Latina/o adolescents. In a study with academically at-risk high school students (comprised of 42% Latina/os and 44% females), career maturity attitudes were most strongly influenced by a component of career beliefs addressing overcoming obstacles (Schnorr & Ware, 2001). Career counselors working with Mexican American adolescents who are at risk of academic achievement may consider interventions to increase their skills in dealing with obstacles to their careers.

In a qualitative study of four Mexican American high school students (two girls) with interests in attending college, Bullington and Arbona (2001) reported that the students were engaged in developmentally age-appropriate vocational tasks as described in Super's (1984) developmental theory, such as specifying an occupational choice, awareness of barriers that might affect career goals, awareness of present behaviors to future plans, understanding of the role of interests and values in career choices, and planning for occupational entry. Additionally, students were strongly identified with their Mexican American ethnicity and described ways in which their ethnic background could both facilitate and hinder their career plans. Results of this study, though the sample size was very small, suggest that Super's theory may be helpful in understanding and guiding the career development process of Mexican American adolescent women when career counselors also take into account the perceived roles of ethnicity and family in their career planning.

Social-Cognitive and Social Learning Theory.   Several studies have assessed the relationship of social-cognitive variables to Latinas' career development. Specifically, studies have tested both Hackett and Betz's (1981) career self-efficacy theory and portions of Lent, Brown, and Hackett's (1994) social-cognitive career theory (SCCT) with adolescent and adult Latinas.

Researchers have examined gender, SES, and ethnic comparisons in self-efficacy beliefs, and results indicated that men and women reported greater self-efficacy for occupations dominated by their gender group (Church, Teresa, Rosebrook, & Szendre, 1992; Lauver & Jones, 1991), upper SES students reported greater career self-efficacy than students of lower SES (Lauver & Jones), and European Americans reported higher career self-efficacy than Latinos and Native Americans (Lauver & Jones).

Specifically focusing on Latina/o students in their sample, Lauver and Jones (1991) found that sources of self-efficacy beliefs for predominantly female occupations included range of female careers considered, self-esteem, gender (female), and SES, whereas range of male careers considered, self-esteem, and SES predicted self-efficacy beliefs for predominantly male careers. In addition, using a sample of predominantly Latina/o high school equivalency students, Church et al. (1992) reported that self-efficacy was related to interests, perceived positive outcomes for occupations, and occupational consideration, yet aptitude was not related to self-efficacy. Church et al. suggested that high school and career counselors working with Latina/o high school equivalency students should examine the "accuracy and realism of students' self-efficacy beliefs, while keeping in mind the possible limited predictive validity of aptitude tests for these students" (p. 507).

Variables that influence the development of self-efficacy beliefs have been explored with solely Latina samples as well as with mixed-gender and mixed-ethnicity samples including Latinas. One study reported that neither gender nor acculturation level was related to college self-efficacy or college outcome expectations among Mexican American men and women high school students (Flores & Dewitz, 2001). Social support predicted college self-efficacy, and family members with a college education influenced college outcome expectations for this group. Hernandez (1995) found no improvements in self-efficacy beliefs following an intervention exposing a group of Latina high school students to successful Latina role models. In another study, using a smaller group of Latinas participating in the same program, results indicated that encouragement and support from mothers were related to higher levels of academic aspirations (Hernandez, Vargas-Lew, & Martinez, 1994).

Using a sample of Latina/o urban and inner-city adolescents (mostly Mexican American and female), Chin and Kameoka (2002) investigated the influences of previous performance, vicarious experience, and social persuasion and two contextual factors (neighborhood resources and neighborhood safety) to educational and occupational self-efficacy beliefs. They reported that the strongest predictor of both educational and occupational self-efficacy beliefs was social persuasion. Previous academic performance influenced educational self-efficacy, but not occupational self-efficacy. Additionally, neither gender, nor vicarious experiences, nor contextual factors related to income were predictive of educational or occupational self-efficacy.

In an investigation of college students in engineering, significant gender and ethnic differences were reported on academic and occupational self-efficacy (Hackett, Betz, Casas, & Rocha-Singh, 1992). Specifically, Mexican American women (along with their European American counterparts) reported that they received less encouragement from faculty than their male peers. Gender and ethnicity were not predictive of students' academic performance; however, ethnicity influenced self-efficacy beliefs, with Mexican American students reporting lower academic and occupational self-efficacy than their European American counterparts.

Social-cognitive theory has been applied to samples of Latinas in early adolescence, late adolescence, and adulthood. Fouad and Smith (1996) tested this model with a middle school sample that was predominantly Latina/o and female. In this study, the researchers reported that neither gender nor age influenced math-science self-efficacy or math-science outcome expectations. In addition, math self-efficacy and math outcome expectations directly predicted math-science interests, and all three influenced math-science intentions.

Three studies examined tenets of SCCT with Latina/o high school students. In one study with Mexican American women seniors, results indicated that acculturation level, feminist attitudes, mother's educational level, and mother's occupational traditionality did not predict nontraditional career self-efficacy (Flores & O'Brien, 2002). As predicted, nontraditional career self-efficacy influenced nontraditional career interests; however, nontraditional career interests were not predictive of Mexican American adolescent women's career choice prestige, career choice traditionality, or career aspirations. Nontraditional career self-efficacy influenced career choice prestige and career choice traditionality, but not career aspirations. Finally, parental support influenced both career choice prestige and career aspirations, and perceived barriers predicted career choice prestige. Data suggested that acculturation level directly predicted career choice prestige and career choice traditionality, whereas feminist attitudes exerted a direct influence on career choice traditionality and career aspirations. In the other study with 11th-grade students attending parochial schools (35% of the sample were Latinas), ethnic identity and standardized test scores were predictive of math self-efficacy beliefs, yet gender and family income were not predictive of math self-efficacy (O'Brien, Kopala, & Martinez-Pons, 1999). Math self-efficacy and gender directly influenced career interests in math and science. Finally, Flores and Dewitz (2001) found that higher educational plans were influenced by positive college outcome expectations, higher acculturation levels, fewer family members with college education, and fewer perceived barriers among a sample of Mexican American high school women and men.

In the final SCCT study, Rivera and Chen (2001) examined the influence of role models, acculturation level, and perceived barriers on nontraditional career self-efficacy, and the influence of nontraditional career self-efficacy on nontraditional career consideration. Using a sample of Latinas (primarily Dominican and Puerto Rican) living in a large urban setting, results indicated that the data fit the model, however, the variables did not predict as hypothesized by SCCT. Nontraditional career self-efficacy predicted nontraditional career consideration. Contrary to expectations, barriers, role-model influence, and acculturation did not have a direct influence on nontraditional career self-efficacy, and role-model influence and barriers did not predict career consideration.

Findings from these SCCT-related studies suggest that: (a) the social-cognitive variable of self-efficacy may be minimally influenced by personal and background contextual factors, (b) of the four sources of influence to self-efficacy proposed by Bandura (1977), vicarious experiences (operationalized through modeling in the studies) may not be as important in the development of career-related self-efficacy beliefs for Latinas, while evidence indicates that social persuasion is significant, (c) background contextual variables may exert a direct influence on Latinas' educational and career goals, and (d) acculturation, perceived barriers, and interests may have a differential influence on career choice depending on the age group of Latina clients.

New Theoretical Advancements.   Recent developments in the career literature have introduced career theories or models to describe the career development process of Mexican American women (Rivera, Anderson, & Middleton, 1999) and Latinas (Gomez & Fassinger, 1994; Gomez et al., 2001).

Rivera et al. (1999) proposed a culture-specific career decision-making model to describe Mexican American women's career development. They hypothesized that the career decision process is initiated with a career opportunity or transition, and values, social issues, culture, and self-efficacy exert an influence on the career decision making of Mexican American women. The foundation of the model consists of the individual's values, social issues relevant to the Mexican American community, and aspects of Mexican American culture, all of which are hypothesized to influence the career choice process for Mexican American women. Bandura's (1977) self-efficacy theory is an additional component to the career decision-making process for Mexican American women. Rivera et al. hypothesized that Mexican American women's self-efficacy will influence their decision to accept job offers, undergo transitions in their career, or turn down these opportunities. Career transitions may contribute to changes in the foundational structure of the model, whereas no change in the Mexican American woman's career process may serve to maintain personal and cultural values. Rivera et al. recommended that career counselors working with Mexican American women structure their interview questions according to the three foundational components of values, social issues, and culture, to better understand the internal cognitions that may direct the Latina client's decisions.

Researchers used grounded theory to explore the career development of 20 high-achieving Latinas in the United States (Gomez et al., 2001). The theoretical model that emerged from this qualitative investigation described Latinas' career development as a nonlinear process influenced by a series of four interactive concentric circles consisting of the self; culture, family and personal background; the immediate context; and the sociopolitical conditions. Each component of the model consists of various dimensions that help to shape the individual's career life path. Thus, according to Gomez et al., a Latina's career development is conceptualized as an interaction of the person's identity, values and life goals, her cultural and gender-role socialization, her family's aspirations for her career life path, the opportunities, barriers, and resources within her immediate environment, and the historical context in which her career life path is taking shape. Although the Gomez et al. model overlaps with other career development models for high-achieving women, the environments in which Latinas' career paths emerge operate differently from those of women from other cultures. Thus, Latina/o cultural norms, limited role models for success within Latina/o communities, and differential experiences of members of various Latina/o subgroups may have a unique influence on Latinas' career progression.

Career Supports and Barriers

Because Latinas/os are less likely to exhibit help-seeking behaviors than Asian Americans, Native Americans, and Whites (Perrone, Sedlacek, & Alexander, 2001), career counselors may not be cognizant of the barriers that may hinder Latinas from achieving their academic and career goals. Various factors that impede or facilitate the educational and vocational development of Latinas have been discussed in the literature and will be highlighted in this section. It is important to note that several of these variables can serve as either a support or a barrier to success, and career counselors are urged to assist their Latina clients in developing the tools to overcome the barriers they experience. See Table 9.2 for examples of supports and barriers in Latinas' career development.

Financial Concerns. Financial issues for Latinas, particularly those from lower socioeconomic backgrounds, can significantly encumber their presence in higher education. Experiencing financial hardship is related to Latina/o college students' perception of barriers to their career goals (Perrone et al., 2001). In instances where Latinas are first-generation college students, family members may not be able to adequately inform them

TABLE 9.2
Supports and Barriers to Latinas' Career Development

Supports	*Barriers*
Availability of financial resources	Need to contribute financially to family
Parental encouragement to attend college	Lack of financial resources for college tuition
Collectivism	Negative family attitudes toward education
Liberal attitudes about women's roles	Adherence to *marianismo* values
Social support of teachers, peers	Lack of mentors or mentoring relationships
High confidence or self-efficacy about intellectual abilities	Self-doubt or low self-efficacy about intellectual abilities
Relative ease in functioning between two different cultures	Experiencing stress or conflict between own culture versus dominant culture
Ethnic and gender composition of students and employees	Few students or employees who are women and members of diverse racial-ethnic groups
Environment that is open to and values diversity	Experiences of racial and gender discrimination
Presence of successful Latina role models	Absence or lack of Latina role models

of financial aid opportunities, and Latinas may be at risk of missing out on options that would make their lives as college students easier (i.e., not working). Additionally, Latina college students who must work to help support their family financially may find balancing the roles of family provider and student stressful and burdensome. Career counselors, particularly those working in high schools, must inform Latina students about financial aid options and may provide support for completing these applications.

Family and Social Support.   Because *la familia* is of great importance and significance in the Latina/o culture, familial support is a critical factor for the educational advancement and career development of Latinas. Unfortunately, Mexican American high school girls are more likely than their White counterparts to experience negative family attitudes about attending college (McWhirter, 1997), which may discourage them from attending. In addition, socioeconomic background was related to perceived parental support for education and career among Mexican American girls, with those from lower class backgrounds perceiving less support from their parents (McWhirter, Hackett, & Bandalas, 1998). Another study of Latina college students reported that over half received the least amount of support from their fathers compared to support received from their mothers and spouses (Wycoff, 1996).

Family attitudes about college attendance can influence Latinas' academic decision making, adjustment to college, and persistence in college. The absence of positive family regard and support for attending college can often result in Latinas' restricting their choice of college or university to one that is closer to home (Wycoff, 1996) or deciding not to pursue higher education at all. Latinas attending college mentioned that receiving emotional support, especially from their mothers, was an important influence in their academic achievement (Wycoff). Lack of social support was related to an increase in college maladjustment (Solberg, Valdez, & Villarreal, 1994) and academic stress for Latina/o students (Solberg et al.; Solberg & Villarreal, 1997). Finally, the adverse effects of negative family regard also have been found to relate to the academic nonpersistence decisions of Chicana college students (Gloria, 1997). Interestingly, encouragement and support from parents was not related to Latinas' career commitment (Caldera, Robitschek, Frame, & Pannell, 2003).

In addition to family support, Latinas' perception of academic support from other significant adults is also important. McWhirter et al. (1998) posited that the reason Mexican American high school girls' perceived educational and career barriers did not influence their educational plans or career expectations may have been due to the students' high perception of teacher support.

Career counselors should assess the amount of support for educational goals their Latina clients perceive from individual family members as well as the family as a whole, particularly for those clients from lower socioeconomic backgrounds. Career counselors may consider connecting those students with little support from their family to mentoring programs and other individuals on campus who can support and encourage their educational pursuits.

Self-Confidence.   Latinas who experienced feelings of self-doubt, lack of confidence in intellectual abilities (McWhirter, 1997), and lack of self-efficacy (Torres & Solberg, 2001) are more likely to experience academic and career barriers. Research demonstrates that Mexican American girls are more likely than White adolescent girls to believe that they are not smart enough to be in college (McWhirter). These negative self-beliefs may serve to prevent Latinas from taking risks and selecting career paths that may be perceived as challenging. As such, it is important that career counselors design interventions to promote the self-esteem, self-confidence, and self-efficacy of Latinas in the hopes of producing positive educational outcomes.

Bicultural Stress.   The stress that Latinas experience as members of two cultures may serve as a barrier to their career development. This may occur when Latinas feel "stuck" between their culture and mainstream society (Wycoff, 1996), which results in conflict between their cultural values, traditions, and beliefs and mainstream, institutionalized values and beliefs. The tension that is brought on by the conflicting expectations between these two distinct cultures can feel overwhelming and consume unnecessary emotional energy, which may impede their academic or career performance (Wycoff).

Latinas may also experience pressure from their families to prove that an education is beneficial. Many first-generation Latina college students often report experiencing additional academic stress because they are the first in their family to attend college, and therefore feel vigilantly watched by their family members to see the effects of higher education (Wycoff, 1996). Such stress can leave Latina college students with a tremendous amount of pressure to excel academically so that college attendance can be a continuing trend within their family (Wycoff).

Academic and Work Environment.   The ethnic and gender composition of students or employees in the academic or work environment may also serve as a support or barrier to Latinas' career development. Attending a university with a small enrollment of Latina/os may contribute to Latinas' feelings of isolation and alienation. Negative perceptions of the campus climate can make it challenging for Latinas to progress academically and may lead to academic nonpersistence decisions (Gloria, 1997). Research suggests that

Latinas who attended a predominantly Mexican American university received social support from extended relatives and immediate family, had fewer negative academic experiences, and were more involved in extracurricular activities on campus (Garza, 1998). Conversely, Latinas who attended predominantly White female or coeducational universities received most of their familial support from mothers and were more likely to express feelings of alienation and isolation on campus (Garza).

Gender-Role Attitudes.   Gender-role attitudes also play an important role in the academic and career pursuits of Latinas. The presence of more liberal gender-role attitudes is stronger in Latinas than Latinos (Valenzuela, 1993), and these attitudes seem to placate the negative effects of perceived barriers on Mexican American girls' educational plans and career expectations (McWhirter et al., 1998).

Liberal gender-role attitudes were associated with academic achievement more strongly than educational aspirations or parent education level for middle school Mexican American girls (Valenzuela, 1993). Latinas who chose a more liberal gender role were more likely to enroll and persevere in college (Cardoza, 1991). Finally, a study of Puerto Rican women employed in settings of higher education indicated that they felt pressured to conform to cultural expectations and norms such as compromising their career aspirations and assuring that their career development did not surpass the importance of their husband's or that of other significant male family members (Hernandez & Morales, 1999). These studies suggest that Latinas who adhere to liberal gender roles may have higher academic achievement and persistence rates than those with traditional gender roles, yet they may also experience pressure to be "less successful" than their Latino partners, boyfriends, or potential mates.

Role Modeling.   Research findings are limited regarding the influence of role modeling on Latinas' career development. One study reported that the occupation of Latina mothers was not related to the amount of support from mothers perceived by Latinas (Garza, 1998). Another study found that Puerto Rican women attributed the scarcity of role models within higher education to feelings of alienation in their jobs (Hernandez & Morales, 1999).

Discrimination.   Experiences of racial, ethnic, and gender discrimination can also take its toll on Latinas' career progress. Their status as double minorities can make them the targets of negative events related to their visible reference-group identities. Indeed, one study reported that the anticipated discrimination in future careers is present in high school, as Mexican American high school girls were more likely than their White female counterparts to expect to encounter both ethnic and sex discrimination as a barrier to their future careers (McWhirter, 1997). Unfortunately, racial-ethnic minority women may experience feelings of marginalization within their careers (Wyche & Graves, 1992), and accusations that their efforts are evaluated based primarily on their gender and ethnicity as opposed to their true merit may contribute to unnecessary concern and questioning on the part of Latinas.

The importance of being in an environment that values Latinas is also critical at the professional level. For instance, Puerto Rican women employed in higher education reported feeling limited in their roles because of their ethnicity and gender (Hernandez & Morales, 1999). These Latinas felt constrained to succeed based on employers' beliefs of roles reserved for women or racial-ethnic minorities, such as addressing only minority-related issues and working with minority students.

Educational Attainment

A review of the literature on Latinas' educational development reveals inconsistencies between their achievements and aspirations. Census data indicate that Latinas' educational achievement rates lag behind those of other major racial-ethnic groups and to their Latino male counterparts. In spite of these dismal education rates, studies have revealed that parents have high expectations for their Latina daughters regardless of the parents' education level (Garza, 1998), and Mexican American girls aspire both to careers that require a college degree and to obtaining a postsecondary education (Hernandez et al., 1994; Valenzuela, 1993). The difference between Latinas' educational aspirations and their actual achievements suggest that these women are not realizing their educational dreams. Understanding the factors that either inhibit or facilitate the educational goals of Latinas is needed in order for career counselors to intervene and successfully promote their educational aspirations. In the following section, we review the empirical research that has been conducted to identify the variables that influence Latinas' educational achievement.

Personal characteristics associated with Latinas' academic achievement have been described. A qualitative study with Mexican American college students revealed the following characteristics germane to participants' academic success: optimistic outlook, persistence, and strong ethnic identification (Arellano & Padilla, 1996). A sample of Mexican American women in their final year of college ranked responsibility and persistence as the two most important personal attributes, and interest in getting a better job or earning a higher income and interest in pursuing further studies in the major area of specialization as the two most important motivational variables related to their academic achievement (Valencia, 1994).

Finally, academic motivation (Hernandez, 2000; Waxman, Huang, & Padron, 1997), a positive view of one's intellectual skills (Alva, 1991), and personal responsibility (Alva; Hernandez) were related the academic performance of samples of Latina/o middle school students and 10th-grade Mexican American students.

In addition to these personal qualities, other influential variables on Latinas' educational decision making include social support, family members' educational attainment, acculturation, prior academic achievement, and undergraduate education. Specifically, studies have reported that parents greatly influenced Mexican American high school and Latina/o college students' educational aspirations and persistence (Arrellano & Padilla, 1996; Hernandez, 2000; Ramos & Sanchez, 1995), and Latina college students' decision to attend college and choice of college major (Morales, 1996). Moreover, Mexican American women in graduate school indicated that their mothers were their strongest supporters in their decision to pursue graduate study, and the majority felt that their education was important to their family (Lango, 1995). Those Latinas who pursue higher education may encounter many stressors and experience psychological distress when they do so against the support of their family, particularly the encouragement of their parents (Niemann, 2001), and may seek guidance from career counselors as they attempt to negotiate their educational and career aspirations with their family's plans and their cultural values.

Social support of peers, teachers, and mentors can also help Latinas in their academic pursuits. Latina/o college students identified the importance of mentors and role models (Arrellano & Padilla, 1996), friends and peer support (Hernandez, 2000), and faculty and staff relationships (Hernandez) in their academic success and persistence. In addition, Latinas attending college cited relationships with other Latinas in their academic environment as protective factors in their educational experiences (Barajas & Pierce, 2001). The guidance and support for attending college that Latinas receive from their peers and mentors may be critical to their persistence and success in college.

Having other family members who have graduated from high school or attended college is positively associated with Latinas' educational attainment. These individuals may be in a better position to impart advice and guidance to their children about college because of their prior experiences. Indeed, a study of Mexican American children in elementary school reported that those with older siblings who were making satisfactory academic progress had higher expectations for completing high school and attended school more regularly than children with older siblings who had dropped out of school (Hess & D'Amato, 1996). Another study reported that Mexican American parents with more academic experience were better able to provide educational guidance to their children than parents with less academic experience (Delgado-Gaitan, 1992). Mothers' education influenced Latina college students' attendance and persistence in college (Cardoza, 1991) and Mexican American students' college attendance (Hurtado & Gauvin, 1997). Interestingly, fathers' education was not related to Mexican American students' college attendance (Hurtado & Gauvin).

Lack of education in the family may motivate Latinas to excel academically to avoid the struggles their parents have experienced. Indeed, Caldera et al. (2003) reported that Mexican American girls wanted to surpass their parents' educational level more than White girls. Additionally, these Latinas reported feeling a lack of connectedness and identification with their parents' education (Caldera et al.). Conversely, if family members with higher levels of education have had negative experiences in college or certain work environments, Latinas may learn to avoid these settings. This may partly explain the inverse association reported between having family members with a college education and Mexican American high school students' educational plans (Flores & Dewitz, 2001).

McWhirter et al. (1998) noted that acculturation was the only variable in their study that accounted for significant variance in the educational aspirations of Mexican American high school girls. Other researchers also documented that acculturation was positively related to educational aspirations (Flores & Dewitz, 2001; Ramos & Sanchez, 1995), college attendance (Hurtado & Gauvin, 1997), and achievement styles (Gomez & Fassinger, 1994) among Latina/o high school and college students. Contrary to these findings, Hurtado and Gauvin reported that acculturation was not related to Mexican American students' desire to attend college or engage in college-planning behaviors.

Prior academic achievement and college attendance are other factors that have been tied to Latinas' educational goals. Specifically, Ramos and Sanchez (1995) reported that prior academic success contributed to Mexican American high school students' educational aspirations. Latinas' educational attainment has also been associated with their undergraduate education. An examination of the origins of Mexican American women who received doctorates in the social sciences between 1980 and 1990 indicated that many began their postsecondary education in small colleges with large enrollments of Latina/o students (Solorzano, 1995). Interestingly, these postsecondary institutions are classified according to the Carnegie classifications as Comprehensive I and II, and tend to be less prestigious, less selective in their admissions, and less research oriented. Thus, Latinas attending these colleges may have limited opportunities for developing research skills that are appealing to graduate programs.

Other studies have reported that academic self-concept and fewer hours working were related to academic achievement or time to complete college (Rodriguez, 1996; Waxman et al., 1997; Young, 1992) for both Latina/o

middle school and Mexican American college students. For their high
school peers, both sense of belonging to school (Gonzalez & Padilla, 1997)
and supportive network of teachers and friends (Alva, 1991) were related to
high school grade point average. Academically successful Mexican American high school students (who were primarily girls) scored higher than
their academically unsuccessful peers on supportive academic environment
(i.e., family and peer support, teacher feedback) and sense of belonging to
school (i.e., positive ties to school and teacher, value placed on school, and
peer-group belonging; Gonzalez & Padilla).

Achievement Styles.   An investigation of undergraduate Latinas explored
the relation between acculturation, nationality, and race on achievement
style preferences (Gomez & Fassinger, 1994). Participants in the study attended a large Eastern state university and were primarily Puerto Rican,
White, or bi- or multiracial, and upper or upper middle class. Their most
preferred achieving style was intrinsic-direct, and social-instrumental and
competitive-direct were their least preferred styles. Acculturation to the
Hispanic culture was related to the contributory-relational achievement
style, and acculturation to the American culture was related to the competitive-direct and social-instrumental achievement styles. Nationality differences indicated that Central Americans used more contributory-relational
styles than South Americans, and Caribbeans used competitive-direct style
more than Central Americans.

Career Selection

Latina girls and women have high career aspirations. Studies revealed that
Mexican American girls aspired to careers that required a college degree
(Valenzuela, 1993), and the majority of Mexican American 10th-grade girls
in another study aspired to nontraditional or male-dominated careers
(Reyes, Kobus, & Gillock, 1999). As described earlier, their educational aspirations and attainment are greatly influenced by their family (Caldera et
al., 2003), gender-role attitudes (Valenzuela), acculturation (McWhirter et
al., 1998), and environment. These same variables may also exert an influence on Latinas' career aspirations and selection.

   The career choices of Latina children have been examined in several
studies. Mexican American girls aspired to traditional careers (e.g.,
teacher, nurse; Day, Borkowski, Punzo, & Howsepian, 1994), however,
older girls tended to select from a wide variety of careers, including nontraditional occupations (Bobo, Hildreth, & Durodoye, 1998). Even though a
broader selection of careers is positively correlated with age, Latina students in middle school are still more likely to choose conventional careers
than Latino males as well as African American and White male and female

counterparts (Davison Aviles & Spokane, 1999). School counselors could still work to broaden young Latina students' knowledge and familiarity with diverse types of occupations within the early years of their education.

The career options of Latinas in high school and college appear to narrow during these developmental periods. Lauver and Jones (1991) found that both gender and self-efficacy beliefs were directly related to range of perceived career options among Latina/o high school students, with Latinas reporting higher perceived options for predominantly female occupations and lower perceived options for predominantly male occupations than their Latino peers. The types of jobs that Latinas in college aspire to also appear to follow traditional careers for women. According to the Holland typology, Mexican American college women were less likely to enter realistic, investigative, and enterprising jobs than Mexican American men, African Americans, and Caucasians (Arbona & Novy, 1991). These women were more likely to enter social- and conventional-type occupations. These studies suggest that career options considered by Latinas may increase during late childhood and early adolescence, and begin to narrow to traditional careers in high school and college.

The roles of family, culture, and gender-role socialization are important factors that may influence Latinas' career goals and aspirations. In traditional homes, Latinas may be socialized to be subordinate to males, to serve as caregivers, and to focus on their family's needs before their own. This socialization to women's roles in the culture may influence the type of careers Latinas are interested in and pursue. Growing up in an environment that socializes Latinas to believe that work and other roles are secondary to the roles within the family may influence their decision to select careers that are more family friendly.

One study examining the attitudes toward family and career roles of Mexican Americans found that females held more liberal gender-role attitudes regarding career and family than males (Gowan & Trevino, 1998). Two additional studies examined Latinas' perceptions of work and family. Specifically, Segura (1991) examined differences between Mexican-born women and Chicanas (Mexican American women) concerning motherhood and employment. Mexican-born women's major motivation to work was the improvement of their family's financial situation. Their job choice tended to be one that consisted of labor-intense work, which they believed they would continue to do until they became disabled or were laid off, or when their husband's income alone became sufficient for the family. Although both groups identified motherhood as their most important role, Chicanas felt more compelled to quit their employment for the sake of taking care of their children and felt more ambivalent about their dual roles of mother and employee. Additionally, Chicanas felt more obligated to remain subordinate to their husbands in terms of job status than Mexican-born women.

In a separate study, Pesquera (1991) examined the work commitment and identity of Latinas. Latinas in this study felt obligated to give more priority to their domestic role than to their work role and reported feeling tension between their work identity and family values. This tension was particularly salient for Latinas in professional occupations. Results indicated that Latinas' commitment to work was substantially influenced by family financial difficulties and a strong work ethic, professional women had a stronger work identity than clerical or blue collar workers, and regardless of their occupation, all Latinas reported gaining much personal satisfaction through employment, including independence, pride, confidence, and a sense of self-identity.

The conflict Latinas experience between work and family may demonstrate the influence of acculturation on Latinas' career development. Career counselors may want to assess the presence of this conflict with Latina clients, and should be aware of within-group differences that may be related to higher conflict (e.g., generational status, acculturation level).

Vocational Assessment

Previous scholars have proposed a career-counseling model with women of color (Bingham & Ward, 1994), which was later extended to include career counseling with culturally diverse populations (Fouad & Bingham, 1995). A central feature of most career-counseling models is assessment as an important part of the process. These models highlight the importance of assessing individual differences variables and cultural variables to understand how they may influence the career development of culturally diverse clients.

Models that specifically address career assessment with women of color (Bingham & Ward, 1997; Ward & Bingham, 1993) offer practical tools for career counselors, such as assessments (i.e., Career Checklist for clients; Multicultural Career Counseling Checklist for counselors), a decision-making model, and ways to organize career assessment information. Their assessment model focuses on obtaining information on culture, gender, self-efficacy, and traditional career constructs. Other important contributions to multicultural career assessment have identified psychometric concerns that career counselors should be aware of, such as language equivalence, conceptual equivalence, and normative reference data (Fouad, 1993, 1995; Leong & Hartung, 1997; Marsella & Leong, 1995; Subich, 1996).

Several studies have established normative data, examined the validity of career instruments with Latina samples, or developed career-related measures to understand the career process of Latinas and their male counterparts. The studies reviewed earlier in the section on person-environment theory suggest that career assessments based on Holland's theory (i.e., Strong Interest Inventory, Self-Directed Search) can be used to assess interests for college-educated Latinas. However, career counselors need to carefully assess both how Latinas perceive the world of work and the relations among their reported interests to reap the full benefit, from the results of these assessments.

Morales (1996) reported validity information on a measure of vocational identity, My Vocational Situation (Holland, Daiger, & Power, 1980), with a sample Latina/o college students (most were Latinas and identified as Mexican American). Participants in this study reported average vocational identity scores that were comparable to those of other college students. Vocational identity was negatively related to acculturation (though the strength of the relationship was quite small), and positively associated with age, influence by peers to attend college, and involvement of parents in selection of college major. Although this study suggests that Latina clients who are more acculturated to the Latina/o culture have a less clear picture of their career interests and goals, career counselors are urged to consider the weak relationship between these variables. Career counselors may consider how cultural variables (in addition to acculturation) may effect the vocational identity of their Latina clients, while keeping in mind that this study found that few background and family variables were associated with Latina students' vocational identity.

The Career Aspiration Scale (O'Brien, 1996), a measure to assess the value attached to having a career, was validated with a sample of Mexican American high school women (Carrubba, 2003). Carrubba reported significant gender, age, and racial group differences and found a two-factor solution for the scale representing a leadership factor and a status quo factor. Participants in this study scored higher than their Mexican American male peers and a sample of White junior high girls, and lower than samples of White women in high school and college.

Two studies have reported validity information for measures relevant to Latina college students' academic persistence and retention. A measure to assess students' self-efficacy in performing behaviors and tasks common to college students was validated with Latina/o college students who were mostly women and who primarily identified as Mexican (Solberg, O'Brien, Villareal, Kennel, & Davis, 1993). Results indicated a three-factor structure, representing efficacy across performance in courses, dealing with roommates, and social situations. High internal reliability coefficient alphas were reported for the full scale and its three subscales, and findings suggested that the scale was related to adjustment rather than nonadjustment measures. Gloria and Robinson Kurpius (1996) provided scale development and validity information for the Cultural Congruity Scale and the University Environment Scale. The scales assessed students' perceptions of cultural fit in the university setting and concerns about the university environment, respectively. The authors provided normative data for the scales, and reported that both scales evidenced good internal consistency reliability and predictive validity for academic persistence. Career counselors and university student-services personnel working to improve the academic retention of Latina college students may consider using these scales to assess students' college self-efficacy and cultural concerns about the university environment.

Career maturity, as assessed by the Career Development Inventory (CDI; Super, Thompson, Lindeman, Jordaan, & Myers, 1981), has been applied to Latina samples in two studies. Normative data for the CDI and Salience Inventory (SI; Nevill & Super, 1986) were provided for a sample of Latina first-year academically at-risk college students (Jackson & Healy, 1996). Results indicated that Latinas' scores on the CDI career exploration were above the norm reference group, and both the CDI decision making and CDI world of work were below the norm reference group. SI scores were not different from those of the norm group of other women. Data were combined to include peers of Latinos and African American men and women, and gender differences (but no ethnic or interaction effects) were reported for both the CDI and SI scores. Specifically, women scored higher than men on the knowledge-of-work and decision-making scales of the CDI, and participation in the home-family role and valuing of the home-family role of the SI. These findings suggest that gender may have a larger effect on career maturity measures than race-ethnicity.

Differences between a sample of Mexican American (53% female) and Anglo American 9th-grade students were found on both of the cognitive-related subscales related to career maturity, the decision-making and world-of-work information scales of the CDI (Lundberg, Osborne, & Miner, 1997). No differences were reported for the career-planning and career-exploration subscales of the CDI between the Mexican American and Anglo American students. Additionally, there were differences between these groups on three of the four types assessed on the Myers-Briggs Type Indicator, with Mexican Americans scoring higher on sensing and thinking and Anglo American students scoring higher on intuition and feeling. Both favored the extraversion end of the extraversion-introversion scale and the perceiving end of the judging-perceiving scale, with Anglo American students scoring higher on this end than their Mexican American peers. Lundberg et al. indicated that career counselors may consider the personality differences in Mexican American adolescents to inform their career interventions such that approaches based on "giving information, stressing personal logic, and accepting decisions more conclusively" (p. 211) may be more appropriate when working with Mexican American youth.

Educational and Career Intervention Programs

The development and implementation of career and educational programs targeted to Latinas are crucial. More research is needed to understand the components of intervention programs that are most successful in increasing Latinas' educational achievement and broadening their career choices. Effective strategies suggested for career development programs for adolescent females include: (a) encouragement from teachers and school administrators, (b) collaboration between schools, universities, and community agencies (e.g., Girl Scouts, science museum), (c) accurate career information, (d) encouragement to pursue nontraditional female careers, (e) improvement of coping skills for dealing with gender and ethnic oppression, (f) exposure to role models of similar backgrounds, and (g) practical, hands-on experiences to develop skills (Weiler, 1997).

An intervention program was created for Mexican American elementary school children that centered on the notion of possible selves, which includes the hopes, fears, and expectations individuals for their future (Markus & Nurius, 1986). Children who participated in the program became more aware of the importance of education for achieving occupational goals and hoped for more prestigious careers than children who did not participate (Day et al., 1994). Because children are exposed to gender stereotyping for careers at a very young age, the establishment of intervention programs for Latina elementary school students is critical to counteract the effects of gender-role socialization on their career options as children.

Capello (1994) found that the college experiences of Puerto Rican and Dominican women were viewed more positively as a result of their participation in a Latina support group. These women expressed multiple hardships in college, including time management, establishing adequate study habits, feelings of alienation from nonminority classmates, perceptions of devaluation, lack of *respeto* from other students and instructors, and a sense of low self-worth. Students who participated in this support group indicated a need for the presence of more Latina leaders and role models. Aspects of the support group attributing to its success included: learning about the Latina/o culture and its traditions and practices, learning firsthand about the experiences of a successful Latina, and learning to cope with the cultural stereotypes of Latinas such as early pregnancies, single parenting, and the triple-oppression status that many Latinas face. These women stated that being in an environment where other Latinas were also dealing with similar issues instilled encouragement in them, diminished isolation, and was important to their well-being (Capello).

When establishing educational and career intervention programs, it is necessary to introduce Latina students to role models to instill empowerment and inspiration. Because many Latinas are the first in their families to attend a higher education institution, they may have had limited opportunities to associate with other Latinas who have achieved academic success. Such association allows students to realize that other Latinas also have struggled in the academic and occupational domains, but have overcome some of the same difficulties they may be experiencing. In addition, intervention programs should emphasize the importance of cultural issues (e.g., family, gender roles, religion) and how these values may influence Latinas' educational and vocational aspirations.

CAREER-COUNSELING PRACTICE WITH LATINAS

Due to the increasing diversity in our society today, career counselors must develop effective cross-cultural career-counseling skills to work with all of their clients. In addition, career counselors should be sensitive to the internal and external barriers that may limit the educational and career options of Latinas, and work with their clients to help them understand how socialization processes may affect their career development so that they are making fully informed and well-planned decisions about school and work. Specifically, helping Latina clients to explore and understand how environmental and background factors may have influenced their career decisions to date can assist these clients in making decisions about their future that are not solely bound by the limited societal expectations for Latinas.

To work effectively in facilitating the educational and career decision making of their Latina clients, it is important that career counselors assess their racial and ethnic attitudes and biases regarding Latinas and their roles in society and the workplace, as well as their own cultural values (Evans & Larrabee, 2002). Such awareness will help to prevent career counselors from inadvertently placing their own values on Latina clients (Evans & Larrabee), and thus inappropriately classifying Latina clients as "overly dependent," "enmeshed," and "submissive" based on the involvement of significant others in the decision-making process (Fouad, 1994; Zea et al., 1997). In addition, due to the number of Latinas from lower class backgrounds or currently living in poverty, it is important that career counselors assess their attitudes and biases related to social class (Heppner & O'Brien, chap. 3, this volume).

There are several resources that career counselors could consult to further their knowledge about Latinas or to provide their Latina clients with information. These include popular magazines such as *Latina* (http://www.latinastyle.com), *Catalina* (http://www.catalinamagazine.com), and *Hispanic* (http://www.hispaniconline.com), which often include articles pertaining to careers, education, Latina/o organizations, and best companies for Latina/os. A web site for young Latinas, *¡Soy Unica! ¡Soy Latina!* (http://www.soyunica.gov), has a section on future goals, choices, and decision making. In addition, the following organizations have web sites that provide information and resources for Latinas seeking career guidance: Hispanic Women's Corporation (http://www.hispanicwomen.org),

MANA: A National Latina Organization (http://www.hermana.org), and National Hispana Leadership Institute (http://www.nhli.org). Finally, several career fields have organizations that were specifically developed for their Latino/a members, such as psychology (National Latino Psychological Association, http://w3.arizona.edu/~nlpa), business (National Hispanic Business Association, http://www.nhba.org), and journalism (National Association of Hispanic Journalists, http://www.nahj.org). Career counselors can encourage their Latina clients to seek out such organizations in their respective careers.

Career counselors should have accurate knowledge in a vast domain of vocational-related information, including but not limited to the Latino culture and how cultural values may influence the career development of their clients, the career barriers and supports experienced by Latinas, the treatment and experiences of Latina women across different professional fields and in the labor force, and vocational research on Latinas' career development. Career counselors must be aware of the cultural factors that play a role in Latinas' career development, and implement a tactful counseling method that facilitates the counseling process while maintaining sensitivity to their clients' cultural values. Finally, culturally sensitive career counselors will have the skills to develop a strong alliance with their Latina clients and will have a variety of tools to help their clients build effective coping strategies and decision-making skills for dealing with the challenges they may encounter in the pursuit of their career goals.

Career-counseling practice with Latinas will share common elements of traditional career-counseling approaches and at the same time will include culture-specific factors relevant to the experiences of Latinas. As with most approaches to career counseling, general factors of the process include developing a strong working alliance with the client, and assessment of personal characteristics, interests, skills, work-related values, resources, and decision-making skills. Culture-specific factors that career counselors working with Latina clients should assess include cultural values, gender-role socialization, social support and family's role in career decision making, ethnic-racial and gender identity, discrimination experiences (racism and sexism), perceptions of the college or university cultural environment (Gloria & Rodriguez, 2000), barriers or stressors, generational status, acculturation, and multiple-role management. These issues may be especially important to assess for Latina students at predominantly White college campuses (Gloria & Rodriguez) or working in predominantly White employment settings.

Finally, career counselors should provide a range of career interventions to promote the career development of Latinas. Traditional methods of career counseling (i.e., individual counseling) might include supplemental activities for Latinas, such as connecting them with mentors who will also provide assistance in their career decision making and involving family members in the sessions. Career-counseling groups for Latinas in high school, college, and the workforce can provide an environment for Latinas to learn strategies from other women in their culture for achieving their educational and career aspirations. Psycho-educational workshops and presentations on career planning, especially applying for colleges or graduate school, and interviewing for jobs could be useful. Finally, panel presentations conducted by Latinas who share both the successes and difficulties encountered in their career development as well as the tools and resources needed to manage this process are recommended.

IMPLICATIONS FOR CAREER-COUNSELING TRAINING

Over approximately the last 40 years, counseling psychology has gradually moved away from its roots in career counseling to an emphasis on more clinical-based services (Anderson, 1998; Heppner, O'Brien, Hinkelman, & Flores, 1996). This de-emphasis of career counseling may result in limited training opportunities for vocational counselors and counseling psychologists for working with culturally diverse clients. This shift may negatively affect the quality and effectiveness of career-counseling processes for Latina clients who are in great need of guidance given their long history of educational and occupational underachievement and oppression. Improvements in the career-counseling process for Latinas can come with increased focus on career-counseling and multicultural issues within graduate and predoctoral internship training programs and continuing education activities.

Improving career-counseling training for Latinas' career development involves the simultaneous teaching of career and multicultural counseling competencies to graduate students in counseling and applied psychology programs (Evans & Larrabee, 2002; Flores & Heppner, 2002). Specifically, multicultural career-counseling competencies should be included in didactic courses on general career development and women's career development. These courses should include direct instruction on issues relevant to Latinas' career development and culturally appropriate and sensitive ways of intervening to aid in their career development. Predoctoral psychology internship programs also can offer seminar courses that focus on these issues with the specific Latina populations they serve (e.g., Latina elementary and secondary students, college students, community clients, or veterans). This multicultural career-counseling training should highlight the unique lived experiences of Latinas and the impact of these experiences on their educational and career development.

Experiential training in multicultural counseling also is essential. Within graduate training programs, career-counseling practicum courses can be developed that provide direct training with Latinas. For example, K–12 school-based practica can include workshops and groups that target Latinas who are struggling academically or who are potentially first-generation college students. University-based practica and internship programs can include outreach programs for Latinas adjusting to the university environment and develop liaison relationships with Latina sororities and student organizations. In addition, career-counseling groups specifically for Latinas can be developed and offered. Finally, advanced practica and internship programs can focus on providing services via community agencies that work directly with Latinas, such as women's shelters, community mental health centers, women's leadership programs, and Latino community centers. The goal of such practice-based training is the development of competencies in providing multicultural career counseling to Latinas.

Along with didactic and practical training, graduate training programs should encourage their students to contribute to career development research with Latinas and other culturally diverse people. Again, given their history of educational and occupational underachievement, increased focus on Latinas' career development is warranted. The importance of such research should be reflected in research method and design courses, advanced research seminars, and informal research teams via the emphasis on the investigation of sociocultural and sociopolitical factors that impede or facilitate the career development of Latinas. Finally, career-counseling process and outcome research can be emphasized as an essential aspect of all practice-based training to determine the best career-counseling practices with Latinas through systematic program evaluation.

The development of multicultural career-counseling competencies does not cease when counselors are awarded a graduate degree. In fact, continued training on issues faced by Latinas in education and work settings is necessary. Flores and Heppner (2002) detailed several ways that professionals can continue their development in this area. For example, they can attend conferences that focus on cultural issues. In addition, the professional national conventions include specific presentations and workshops on cultural issues relevant to the career development of Latinas. Along with attendance at professional conferences, Flores and Heppner urged professionals to attend continuing educational workshops that focus on some aspect of cross-cultural competencies (e.g., assessment, counseling specific culturally diverse groups). Another strategy for continued growth as a multiculturally competent career counselor is to read current research on Latinas' career development and to incorporate such research into practice. Finally, greater understanding of the unique lived experiences of Latinas can be produced by reading both nonfiction and fiction literature specifically written by Latinas (Flores & Heppner). Such literature will highlight the diversity of influences on Latinas' lives and ultimately aid professionals in their understanding of Latina career clients.

REFERENCES

Albert, R. D. (1996). A framework and model for understanding Latin American and Latino/Hispanic cultural patterns. In D. Landis & R. S. Bhagat (Eds.), *Handbook of intercultural training* (2nd ed., pp. 327–348). Thousand Oaks, CA: Sage.

Altarriba, J., & Bauer, L. M. (1998). Counseling the Hispanic client: Cuban Americans, Mexican Americans, and Puerto Ricans. *Journal of Counseling and Development, 76,* 389–396.

Alva, S. A. (1991). Academic invulnerability among Mexican-American students: The importance of protective resources and appraisals. *Hispanic Journal of Behavioral Sciences, 13,* 18–34.

Anderson, D. C. (1998). A focus on career: Graduate training in counseling psychology. *Journal of Career Development, 25,* 101–110.

Arbona, C. (1995). Theory and research on racial and ethnic minorities: Hispanic Americans. In F. T. L. Leong (Ed.), *Career development and vocational behavior of racial ethnic minorities* (pp. 37–66). Hillsdale, NJ: Lawrence Erlbaum Associates.

Arbona, C., & Novy, D. M. (1991). Hispanic college students: Are there within-group differences? *Journal of College Student Development, 32,* 335–341.

Arellano, A. R., & Padilla, A. M. (1996). Academic invulnerability among a select group of Latino university students. *Hispanic Journal of Behavioral Sciences, 18,* 485–507.

Arredondo, P. (1996). MCT theory and Latina(o)-American populations. In D. W. Sue, A. E. Ivey, & P. B. Pedersen (Eds.), *A theory of multicultural counseling and therapy* (pp. 217–235). Pacific Grove, CA: Brooks/Cole.

Bandura, A. (1977). Self-efficacy: Toward a unifying theory of behavioral change. *Psychological Review, 84,* 191–215.

Bandura, A. (1977). *Social learning theory.* Englewood Cliffs, NJ: Prentice Hall.

Barajas, H. L., & Pierce, J. L. (2001). The significance of race and gender in school success among Latinas and Latinos in college. *Gender and Society, 15,* 859–878.

Berry, J. W., Trimble, J. E., & Olmedo, E. L. (1986). Assessment of acculturation. In W. J. Lonner & J. W. Berry (Eds.), *Field methods in cross-cultural research* (pp. 291–345). Beverly Hills, CA: Sage.

Betz, N. E., Borgen, F. H., & Harmon, L. W. (1996). *Skills Confidence Inventory: Applications and technical guide.* Palo Alto, CA: Consulting Psychologists Press.

Bingham, R. P., & Ward, C. M. (1994). Career counseling with ethnic minority women. In W. B. Walsh & S. Osipow (Eds.), *Career counseling with women* (pp. 165–195). Hillsdale, NJ: Lawrence Erlbaum Associates.

Bingham, R. P., & Ward, C. M. (1997). Theory into assessment: A model for women of color. *Journal of Career Assessment, 4,* 403–418.

Bobo, M., Hildreth, B. L., & Durodoye, B. (1998). Changing patterns in career choices among African American, Hispanic, and Anglo children. *Professional School Counseling, 1,* 37–42.

Bullington, R. L., & Arbona, C. (2001). Career development tasks of Mexican-American adolescents: An exploratory study. *Journal of Career Development, 28,* 139–153.

Caldera, Y. M., Robitschek, C., Frame, M., & Pannell, M. (2003). Intrapersonal, familial, and cultural factors in the commitment to a career choice of Mexican American and non-Hispanic White college women. *Journal of Counseling Psychology, 50,* 309–323.

Capello, D. C. (1994). Beyond financial aid: Counseling Latina students. *Journal of Multicultural Counseling and Development, 22,* 28–36.

Cardoza, D. (1991). College attendance and persistence among Hispanic women: An examination of some contributing factors. *Sex Roles, 24,* 133–147.

Carrubba, M. D. (2003). *Test of reliability and validity of the Feminist Identity Development Scale, the Attitudes toward Feminism and the Women's Movement Scale, and the Career Aspiration Scale with Mexican-American female adolescents.* Unpublished doctoral dissertation, University of Missouri, Columbia.

Chin, D., & Kameoka, V. A. (2002). Psychosocial and contextual predictors of educational and occupational self-efficacy among Hispanic inner-city adolescents. *Hispanic Journal of Behavioral Sciences, 24,* 448–464.

Church, A. T., Teresa, J. S., Rosebrook, R., & Szendre, D. (1992). Self-efficacy for careers and occupational consideration in minority high school equivalency students. *Journal of Counseling Psychology, 39,* 498–508.

Comas-Diaz, L. (1997). Mental health needs of Latinos with professional status. In J. G. Garcia & M. C. Zea (Eds.), *Psychological interventions and research with Latino populations* (pp. 142–165). Boston: Allyn & Bacon.

Davison Aviles, R. M. D., & Spokane, A. R. (1999). The vocational interests of African American, Asian, Hispanic, and White middle school students. *Measurement and Evaluation in Counseling and Development, 32,* 138–148.

Day, J. D., Borkowski, J. G., Punzo, D., & Howsepian, B. (1994). Enhancing possible selves in Mexican American students. *Motivation and Emotion, 18,* 79–103.

Day, S. X., & Rounds, J. (1998). Universality of vocational interest structure among racial and ethnic minorities. *American Psychologist, 53,* 728–736.

Day, S. X., Rounds, J., & Swaney, K. (1998). The structure of vocational interests for diverse racial/ethnic groups. *Psychological Science, 9,* 40–44.

Delgado-Gaitan, C. (1992). School matters in the Mexican-American home: Socializing children to education. *American Educational Research, 29,* 495–513.

Evans, K. M., & Larrabee, M. J. (2002). Teaching the multicultural counseling competencies and revised career counseling competencies simultaneously. *Journal of Multicultural Counseling and Development, 20,* 21–39.

Falicov, C. J. (1998). *Latino families in therapy: A guide to multicultural practice.* New York: Guilford Press.

Federal Register. (1978, May 4). Washington, DC: U.S. Government Printing Office.

Flores, L. Y., & Dewitz, S. J. (2001, August). *Using social cognitive career theory to predict Mexican American adolescents' postsecondary plans.* Paper presented at the annual meeting of the American Psychological Association, San Francisco, CA.

Flores, L. Y., & Heppner, M. J. (2002). Multicultural career counseling: Ten essentials for training. *Journal of Career Development, 28,* 181–202.

Flores, L. Y., & O'Brien, K. M. (2002). The career development of Mexican American adolescent women: A test of social cognitive career theory. *Journal of Counseling Psychology, 49,* 14–27.

Flores, L. Y., Spanierman, L. B., Armstrong, P. I., & Velez, A. D. (in press). Validity of the Strong Interest Inventory and Skills Confidence Inventory with Mexican American high school students. *Journal of Career Assessment.*

Fouad, N. A. (1993). Cross-cultural vocational assessment. *Career Development Quarterly, 42,* 4–13.

Fouad, N. A. (1994). Career assessment with Latinos/Hispanics. *Journal of Career Assessment, 2,* 226–239.

Fouad, N. A. (1995). Career behavior of Hispanics: Assessment and career intervention. In F. T. L. Leong (Ed.), *Career development and vocational behavior of racial and ethnic minorities* (pp. 165–191). Mahwah, NJ: Lawrence Erlbaum Associates.

Fouad, N. A., & Bingham, R. P. (1995). Career counseling with racial and ethnic minorities. In W. B. Walsh & S. H. Osipow (Eds.), *Handbook of vocational psychology: Theory, research, and practice* (2nd ed., pp. 331–365). Mahwah, NJ: Lawrence Erlbaum Associates.

Fouad, N. A., Harmon, L. W., & Borgen, F. H. (1997). Structure of interests in employed male and female members of U.S. racial-ethnic minority and nonminority groups. *Journal of Counseling Psychology, 44,* 339–345.

Fouad, N. A., & Smith, P. L. (1996). A test of a social cognitive model for middle school students: Math and science. *Journal of Counseling Psychology, 43,* 338–346.

Garza, L. (1998). The influence of pre-college factors on the university experiences of Mexican American women. *Aztlán, 23,* 119–135.

Giachello, A. L. (1996). Latino women. In M. Bayne-Smith (Ed.), *Race, gender, and health* (pp. 121–171). Thousand Oaks, CA: Sage.

Gloria, A. M. (1997). Chicana academic persistence. *Education and Urban Society, 30,* 107–122.

Gloria, A. M. (2001). The cultural construction of Latinas: Practice implications of multiple realities and identities. In D. B. Pope-Davis & H. L. K. Coleman (Eds.), *The intersection of race, class, and gender in multicultural counseling* (pp. 3–24). Thousand Oaks, CA: Sage.

Gloria, A. M., & Robinson Kurpius, S. E. (1996). The validation of the Cultural Congruity Scale and the University Environment Scale with Chicano/a students. *Hispanic Journal of Behavioral Science, 18,* 533–549.

Gloria, A. M., & Rodriguez, E. R. (2000). Counseling Latino university students: Psychosociocultural issues for consideration. *Journal of Counseling and Development, 78,* 145–154.

Gomez, M. J., & Fassinger, R. E. (1994). An initial model of Latina achievement: Acculturation, biculturalism, and achieving styles. *Journal of Counseling Psychology, 41,* 205–215.

Gomez, M. J., Fassinger, R. E., Prosser, J., Cooke, K., Mejia, B., & Luna, J. (2001). Voces abriendo caminos (Voices forging paths): A qualitative study of the career development of notable Latinas. *Journal of Counseling Psychology, 48,* 286–300.

Gonzalez, R., & Padilla, A. M. (1997). The academic resilience of Mexican American high school students. *Hispanic Journal of Behavioral Sciences, 19,* 301–317.

Gowan, M., & Trevino, M. (1998). An examination of gender differences in Mexican-American attitudes toward family and career roles. *Sex Roles, 38,* 1079–1093.

Gysbers, N. C., Heppner, M. J., & Johnston, J. A. (2003). *Career counseling: Process, issues, and techniques* (2nd ed.). Boston: Allyn & Bacon.

Hackett, G., & Betz, N. E. (1981). A self-efficacy approach to the career development of women. *Journal of Vocational Behavior, 18,* 326–339.

Hackett, G., Betz, N. E., Casas, J. M., & Rocha-Singh, I. A. (1992). Gender, ethnicity, and social cognitive factors predicting the academic achievement of students in engineering. *Journal of Counseling Psychology, 39,* 527–538.

Hansen, J. C., Sarma, Z. M., & Collins, R. C. (1999). An evaluation of Holland's model of vocational interests for Chicano/a and Latino/a college students. *Measurement and Evaluation in Counseling and Development, 32,* 2–13.

Harmon, L. W., Hansen, J. C., Borgen, F. H., & Hammer, A. C. (Eds.). (1994). *Strong interest inventory applications and technical guide.* Palo Alto, CA: Consulting Psychologists Press.

Helms, J. E. (1993). *Black and white racial identity.* Westport, CT: Praeger.

Heppner, M. J., O'Brien, K. M., Hinkelman, J. M., & Flores, L. Y. (1996). Training counseling psychologists in career development: Are we our own worst enemies? *The Counseling Psychologist, 24,* 105–125.

Hernandez, A. E. (1995). Do role models influence self efficacy and aspirations in Mexican American at-risk females? *Hispanic Journal of Behavioral Sciences, 17,* 256–263.

Hernandez, A. E., Vargas-Lew, L., & Martinez, C. L. (1994). Intergenerational academic aspirations of Mexican-American females: An examination of mother, daughter, and grandmother triads. *Hispanic Journal of Behavioral Sciences, 16*, 195–204.

Hernandez, J. C. (2000). Understanding the retention of Latino college students. *Journal of College Student Development, 41*, 575–588.

Hernandez, T. J., & Morales, N. E. (1999). Career, culture, and compromise: Career development experiences of Latinas working in higher education. *Career Development Quarterly, 48*, 45–58.

Hess, R. S., & D'Amato, R. C. (1996). High school completion among Mexican American children: Individual and family background variables. *School Psychology Quarterly, 11*, 353–368.

Holland, J. L. (1985). *Making vocational choices: A theory of personalities and work environments.* Odessa, FL: Psychological Assessment Resources.

Holland, J. L., Daiger, D. C., & Power, P. G. (1980). *My vocational situation.* Palo Alto, CA: Consulting Psychologists Press.

Hurtado, A. (1995). Variations, combinations, and evolutions: Latino families in the United States. In R. E. Zambrana (Ed.), *Understanding Latino families: Scholarship, policy, and practice. Understanding families, Vol. 2* (pp. 40–61). Thousand Oaks, CA: Sage.

Hurtado, M. T., & Gauvin, M. (1997). Acculturation and planning for college among youth of Mexican descent. *Hispanic Journal of Behavioral Sciences, 19*, 506–516.

Jackson, G. C., & Healy, C. (1996). Career development profiles and interventions for underrepresented college students. *Career Development Quarterly, 44*, 258–269.

Lango, D. R. (1995). Mexican American female enrollment in graduate programs: A study of characteristics that may predict success. *Hispanic Journal of Behavioral Sciences, 17*, 33–48.

Latinos in education: Early childhood, elementary, secondary, undergraduate, graduate (ED No. 440 817). (1999). Washington, DC: White House Initiative on Educational Excellence for Hispanic Americans.

Lauver, P. J., & Jones, R. M. (1991). Factors associated with perceived career options in American Indian, White, and Hispanic rural high school students. *Journal of Counseling Psychology, 28*, 159–166.

Lent, R. W., Brown, S. D., & Hackett, G. (1994). Toward a unifying social cognitive theory of career and academic interest, choice, and performance. *Journal of Vocational Behavior, 45*, 79–122.

Leong, F. T. L., & Brown, M. T. (1995). Theoretical issues in cross-cultural career development: Cultural validity and cultural specificity. In W. B. Walsh & S. H. Osipow (Eds.), *Handbook of vocational psychology: Theory, research, and practice* (pp. 143–180). Hillsdale, NJ: Lawrence Erlbaum Associates.

Leong, F. T. L., & Hartung, P. (1997). Career assessment with culturally different clients: Proposing an integrative-sequential conceptual framework for cross-cultural career counseling research and practice. *Journal of Career Assessment, 5*, 183–202.

Leong, F. T. L., & Hartung, P. J. (1997). Cross-cultural career assessment: Review and prospects for the new millennium. *Journal of Career Assessment, 8*, 391–401.

Lundberg, D. J., Osborne, W. L., & Miner, C. U. (1997). Career maturity and personality preferences of Mexican American and Anglo American adolescents. *Journal of Career Development, 23*, 203–213.

Marin, G., & Marin, B. V. (1991). *Research with Hispanic populations.* Newbury Park, CA: Sage.

Markus, H., & Nurius, P. (1986). Possible selves. *American Psychologist, 41*, 954–969.

Marsella, A. J., & Leong, F. T. L. (1995). Cross-cultural issues in personality and career assessment. *Journal of Career Assessment, 3*, 202–218.

McNeill, B. W., Prieto, L. R., Niemann, Y. F., Pizarro, M., Vera, E. M., & Gómez, S. P. (2001). Current directions in Chicana/o psychology. *The Counseling Psychologist, 29*, 5–17.

McWhirter, E. H. (1997). Perceived barriers to education and career: Ethnic and gender differences. *Journal of Vocational Behavior, 50*, 124–140.

McWhirter, E. H., Hackett, G., & Bandalos, D. L. (1998). A causal model of the educational plans and career expectations of Mexican American high school girls. *Journal of Counseling Psychology, 45,* 166–181.

Morales, P. C. (1996, August). *Acculturation and vocational identity: The influence of Hispanic familialism.* Paper presented at the annual meeting of the American Psychological Association, Toronto, Canada.

Nevill, D. D., & Super, D. E. (1986). *The Salience Inventory: Theory, application, and research manual.* Palo Alto, CA: Consulting Psychologist Press.

Niemann, Y. F. (2001). Stereotypes about Chicanas and Chicanos: Implications for counseling. *The Counseling Psychologist, 29,* 55–90.

O'Brien, K. M. (1996). *Career Aspiration Scale.* Unpublished manuscript.

O'Brien, V., Kopala, M., & Martinez-Pons, M. (1999). Mathematics self-efficacy, ethnic identity, gender, and career interests related to mathematics and science. *Journal of Educational Research, 92,* 231–235.

Ortiz, V. (1994). Women of color: A demographic overview. In M. B. Zinn & B. T. Dill (Eds.), *Women of color in U.S. society* (pp. 13–40). Philadelphia: Temple University Press.

Perrone, K. M., Sedlacek, W. E., & Alexander, C. M. (2001). Gender and ethnic differences in career goal attainment. *Career Development Quarterly, 50,* 168–178.

Pesquera, B. M. (1991). "Work gave me a lot of confianza": Chicanas' work commitment and work identity. *Aztlán, 20,* 97–118.

Phinney, J. (1989). Stages of ethnic identity development in minority group adolescents. *Journal of Early Adolescence, 9,* 34–49.

Quinoñes, M. (2000). Beyond stereotypes: Exploring the complexities of Latino identity. *Family Therapy Networker, 24,* 63–66.

Ramos, L., & Sanchez, A. R. (1995). Mexican-American high school students: Educational aspirations. *Journal of Multicultural Counseling and Development, 23,* 212–221.

Reyes, O., Kobus, K., & Gillock, K. (1999). Career aspirations of urban, Mexican American adolescent females. *Hispanic Journal of Behavioral Sciences, 21,* 366–382.

Rivera, A. A., Anderson, S. K., & Middleton, V. A. (1999). A career development model for Mexican American women. *Journal of Career Development, 26,* 91–106.

Rivera, L. M., & Chen, E. C. (2001, August). *A test of social cognitive career theory with Hispanic women.* Paper presented at the annual meeting of the American Psychological Association, San Francisco, CA.

Rodriguez, N. (1996). Predicting the academic success of Mexican American and White college students. *Hispanic Journal of Behavioral Sciences, 18,* 329–342.

Rogler, L. H. (1994). International migrations. *American Psychologist, 49,* 701–708.

Rounds, J., & Tracey, T. J. (1996). Cross-cultural structural equivalence of RIASEC models and measures. *Journal of Counseling Psychology, 43,* 310–329.

Santiago-Rivera, A. L., Arredondo, P., & Gallardo-Cooper, M. (2002). *Counseling Latinos and la familia: A practical guide.* Thousand Oaks, CA: Sage.

Schnorr, D., & Ware, H. W. (2001). Moving beyond a deficit model to describe and promote the career development of at-risk youth. *Journal of Career Development, 27,* 247–263.

Segura, D. A. (1991). Ambivalence or continuity? Motherhood and employment among Chicanas and Mexican immigrant women workers. *Aztlán, 20,* 119–150.

Solberg, V. S., O'Brien, K. O., Villarreal, P., Kennel, R., & Davis, B. (1993). Self-efficacy and Hispanic college students: Validation of the College Self-Efficacy Instrument. *Hispanic Journal of Behavioral Sciences, 15,* 80–95.

Solberg, V. S., Valdez, J., & Villarreal, P. (1994). Social support, stress, and Hispanic college adjustment: Test of a diathesis-stress model. *Hispanic Journal of Behavioral Sciences, 16,* 230–239.

Solberg, V. S., & Villarreal, P. (1997). Examination of self-efficacy, social support, and stress as predictors of psychological and physical distress among Hispanic college students. *Hispanic Journal of Behavioral Sciences, 19,* 182–201.

Solorzano, D. G. (1995). The baccalaureate origins of Chicana and Chicano doctorates in the social sciences. *Hispanic Journal of Behavioral Sciences, 17,* 3–32.

Subich, L. M. (1996). Addressing diversity in the process of career assessment. In M. L. Savickas & W. B. Walsh (Eds.), *Handbook of career counseling theory and practice* (pp. 277–289). Palo Alto, CA: Davies-Black.

Sue, D. W., Ivey, A. E., & Pedersen, P. B. (Eds.). (1996). *A theory of multicultural counseling and therapy.* Pacific Grove, CA: Brooks/Cole.

Sue, D. W., & Sue, D. (2003). *Counseling the culturally different: Theory and practice* (4th ed.). New York: Wiley.

Super, D. E. (1984). Career and life development. In D. Brown & L. Brooks (Eds.), *Career choice and development* (pp. 192–234). San Francisco: Jossey-Bass.

Super, D. E., Thompson, A. S., Lindeman, R. H., Jordaan, J. P., & Myers, R. A. (1981). *The Career Development Inventory.* Palo Alto, CA: Consulting Psychologists Press.

Torres, J. B., & Solberg, V. S. (2001). Role of self-efficacy, stress, social integration, and family support in Latino college student persistence and health. *Journal of Vocational Behavior, 59,* 53–63.

U.S. Bureau of the Census. (2000). *Statistical abstract of the United States: 2000* (120th ed.). Washington, DC: U.S. Government Printing Office.

U.S. Bureau of the Census. (2002a). *The Hispanic population in the United States: 2002. Detailed Tables (PPL-165).* Retrieved November 7, 2003, from http://www.census.gov/population/www/socdemo/hispanic/ppl-165.html

U.S. Bureau of the Census. (2002b). *Population projections of the United States by age, sex, and Hispanic origin: 1999 to 2100.* Retrieved November 7, 2003, from http://www.census.gov/population/www/projections/natdet-D1A.html

U.S. Bureau of the Census. (2002c). *Race and Hispanic origin of people by median income and sex: 1947 to 2001.* Retrieved November 7, 2003, from http://www.census.gov/hhes/income/histinc/p02.html

U.S. Bureau of the Census. (2002d). *Statistical abstract of the United States: 2002* (122nd ed.). Washington, DC: U.S. Government Printing Office.

Valencia, A. A. (1994). The attributes of academically successful Mexican-American university male and female students. *Journal of Multicultural Counseling and Development, 22,* 227–238.

Valenzuela, A. (1993). Liberal gender role attitudes and academic achievement among Mexican-origin adolescents in two Houston inner-city Catholic schools. *Hispanic Journal of Behavioral Sciences, 15,* 310–323.

Ward, C. M., & Bingham, R. P. (1993). Career assessment of ethnic minority women. *Journal of Career Assessment, 1,* 246–257.

Waxman, H. C., Huang, S. L., & Padron, Y. N. (1997). Motivation and learning environment differences between resilient and nonresilient Latino middle school students. *Hispanic Journal of Behavioral Sciences, 19,* 137–155.

Weiler, J. (1997). Career development for African American and Latina females. *ERIC/CUE Digest, 125.* (ERIC Document Reproduction Service No. ED410369)

Wyche, K. F., & Graves, S. B. (1992). Minority women in academia: Access and barriers to professional participation. *Psychology of Women Quarterly, 16,* 429–437.

Wycoff, S. E. (1996). Academic performance of Mexican American women: Sources of support that serve as motivating variables. *Journal of Multicultural Counseling and Development, 24,* 146–155.

Young, G. (1992). Chicana college students on the Texas-Mexico border: Tradition and transformation. *Hispanic Journal of Behavioral Sciences, 14,* 341–352.

Zea, M. C., Garcia, J. G., Belgrave, F. Z., & Quezada, T. (1997). Socioeconomic and cultural factors in rehabilitation of Latinos with disabilities. In J. G. Garcia & M. C. Zea (Eds.), *Psychological interventions and research with Latino populations* (pp. 235–254). Boston: Allyn & Bacon.

Chapter 10

A Culturally Oriented Approach for Career Counseling With Native American Women

Charlotte McCloskey
Laurie Mintz
University of Missouri-Columbia

> *When questioned by an anthropologist on what the Indians called America before the White Man came, an Indian said simply, Ours.*
> —Vine Deloria (1996, p. 346)

When discussing multicultural counseling in general, or the career development of racial or ethnic minorities in particular, most often the focus is on African American, Asian American, and Latino individuals. Indeed, it is common to find that multicultural research and writings on career development and counseling address these three groups extensively, yet provide minimal focus on Native American individuals (e.g., Brown, 2003; Peterson & Gonzalez, 2000). In short, Native American people seem to be the forgotten or neglected minority in psychology in general and in the career development literature in particular.

Career issues among Native Americans are severely understudied (Koegel, Donin, Ponterotto, & Spitz, 1995; Turner & Lapan, 2003), and thus there are few resources to assist psychologists in working with Native American career clients (Byers & McCubbin, 2001).[1] A thorough literature search revealed

---

[1]Some information on vocational rehabilitation with Native Americans can be found, but is outside of the scope of this chapter. We refer the reader to Marshall, Sanders, and Hill (2001). Similarly, we located two articles (McCormick & Amundson, 1997; Neumann, McCormick, Amundson, & McLean, 2000) on career counseling with First Nation members (Native people in Canada), but excluded them from our discussion, as they were mainly redundant with the information and suggestions we located on Native Americans.

only two book chapters on the career development of Native American people (Johnson, Swartz, & Martin, 1995; Martin, 1995). Likewise, fewer than 50 published articles present information related to career development and counseling among Native American individuals, and indeed, in the vast majority of these studies, the information is not on Native Americans specifically, but instead includes Native Americans within the category of racial-ethnic minority participants (e.g., Daniels, D'Andrea, & Gaughen, 1998; Leung, 1995; Luzzo, McWhirter, & Hutcheson, 1997; Trusty, 2002; Ward & Bingham, 1993). We could locate only about 13 published articles focused exclusively on career issues among Native Americans (Canabal, 1995; Epperson & Hammond, 1981; Gade, Fuqua, & Hurlburt, 1984; Hansen, Scullard, & Haviland, 2000; Haviland & Hansen, 1988; Herring, 1990, 1992; Juntunen et al., 2001; Krebs, Hurlburt, & Schwartz, 1988; Martin, 1991; Martin & Farris, 1994; Napier, 1996; Turner & Lapan). We also located two studies on Native Americans that, though not focusing solely on career issues or counseling, provided some relevant findings, such as career-counseling help-seeking behaviors and counselor preferences (Bee-Gates, Howard-Pitney, LaFromboise, & Rowe, 1996; Bichsel & Mallinckrodt, 2001). Of these 15 studies, only two (Bichsel & Mallinckrodt; Napier) focused exclusively on the career development of Native American women. In summary, very little information is available regarding career development or career counseling with Native Americans, and almost nothing is known about career development and counseling among Native American women.

The general aim of this chapter is to serve as a catalyst for increased knowledge of America's first peoples, and the specific aim is to stimulate psychologists to provide effective career services for Native women. However, because ours is only the third published chapter on career counseling with Native people, and the first on Native women, much of the information that must be conveyed pertains to Native people in general and not just to Native women. In other words, because basic knowledge about Native people is needed in order to provide effective services to Native women, much of our chapter covers such general knowledge. Of course, when available, we focus on information specific to Native women.

This chapter first places career counseling with Native American women in both historical and current cultural contexts. Specific biases within the field of psychology are then detailed. Subsequently, we present a variety of suggestions and techniques guided by the literature and our own professional experience for effective career counseling with Native American women.

Prior to providing context and suggestions, it is critical for the reader to understand that there is no one "Native" way of existing. According to the U.S. Bureau of the Census (n.d.), there are approximately 4 million Native American people in the United States, encompassing over 500 different federally recognized tribes or nations, such as Cherokee, Kiowa, Lakota, Navajo, and Winnebago, to name just a few. Although there are commonalities across tribes, particularly those that have arisen from a shared history of oppression, each has its own customs, family structures, worldviews, and languages. Similarly, just as we cannot assume that all Native Americans are alike due to tribal differences, practitioners must also refrain from assuming that all members of a particular tribe share the same issues and values. Each individual member of a tribe demonstrates differences in personality, lifestyle, and location. Clearly, practitioners must strive to educate themselves about the specific customs of each particular client.

HISTORICAL AND CURRENT ISSUES FACED BY NATIVE AMERICANS

Before presenting suggestions and techniques for effective career interventions with Native American women, we believe it is important to understand both the historical and current issues that Native American women face. Knowledge of contemporary issues may help to place an individual woman's problems within a cultural context. Likewise, historical issues of oppression continue to impact Native Americans, and thus knowledge of these issues is also important in placing clients' problems into a broader framework. In other words, in accordance with the feminist therapy view, we believe that the "personal is political" (Brown, 1994, p. 50), meaning that an individual client's issues are also a reflection of the broader sociopolitical context and thus an understanding of this context is critical for effective counseling. Supporting this view, Herring (1992) contended that the more aware a counselor is about Native American issues, including history, the more likely the Native American client is to feel supported by the counseling relationship.

Historically, as well as currently, the Native people of this continent faced severe hardships that are often ignored or undocumented by mainstream White culture. This history of oppression, often the result of being cast as "aliens in their own land" (LaFromboise, 1998, p. 138), is documented here with two caveats. First, due to space limitations, we could not provide an exhaustive review and thus some critical issues are covered only superficially and several other issues (e.g., Indian Wars, all aspects of American Indian law, legal definitions of Native American) are not dealt with at all. Practitioners who encounter such issues in their work with clients are encouraged to seek additional information; much pertinent and accurate information can be found on the Internet, as well as through Native American culture centers or Native American studies departments, most often located in large urban areas or on large university campuses. Additionally, there are publications (such as *American Indian Law Review* and *American Indian Quarterly*) and books (such as Nabokov's *Native American Testimony: A Chronicle of Indian-White Relations from Prophecy to the Present* [2003]) that provide information on the topics just listed. Second, although we attempt to present issues in a roughly chronological order, as the reader will see, for the vast majority of issues, history and present-day status collide and thus must be chronicled together. Indeed, historical oppression has a direct link to current living situations and issues.

An Overview of Colonization

In 1492, the colonists from Europe arrived in a land inhabited by people with their own structure, culture, and religious beliefs or, in other words, people native to this land (hence, the terms that we recommend using: Native Americans or Native people or peoples[2]). The arrival of the colonists set into motion unthinkable oppression of Native people. Native people were bombarded with and often forced to adopt religious, moral, and ethical beliefs that were incongruent for them. Native people were faced with war, disease, rape, and forced removal from their homelands. When resources were found on Native lands that the colonists wanted, battles and war arose between the immigrants and the Native peoples (Beauvais & LaBoueff, 1985). Some estimates report that over 90% of Native people of this land were massacred, diseased, or starved by the colonists in the first 200 years (Stannard, 1992). Although Native people in general were oppressed, the violation of Native women was especially horrific. Indeed, it was quite common for Native women and children to be raped and brutalized by colonist men and soldiers from different European nations (Mihesuah, 2003).

Broken Promises and Economically Motivated Oppression

The arrival of the colonists set into motion a series of broken promises and economically motivated oppression of Native people. Indeed, as we document historical and current events in this section, we believe that the reader

---

[2]Other terms found in the literature and used by both Native Americans and others include *Indian, American Indian,* and *Indigenous* people. In addition, tribal affiliation (e.g., Lakota, Cherokee) is used. Also, the terms *tribe(s)* or *nation(s)* are used to refer to one or more specific affiliation groups, whereas *Tribes* or *Nations* can be used to refer to the Native American population as a whole. One interesting though uncommon term is "Red Americans" (Weisbord, 1975). We use the term *Native American* or *Native people(s)* to refer to this diverse and multidimensional race of people. We purposefully choose not to use the terms *American Indians* or *Indians* due to their origin, that, on his first trip to what would become the Americas, Columbus believed he was in India and referred to the people as "Indians."

will often see two clear themes permeating: failed guarantees and financially rooted malice.

Smallpox.   With colonization, Native Americans were exposed to infectious diseases to which they had no immunity, including both measles and smallpox. Indeed, some scholars suggest that Native Americans were the victims of one of the earliest episodes of biological warfare (Patterson & Runge, 2002). O'Connell (1989) stated, "Colonists during the French and Indian Wars resorted to trading smallpox-contaminated blankets to local tribes with immediate and devastating results" (p. 171). Daley and Daley (2003) noted that most Native people believe that blankets handed out by the federal government were responsible for the spread of this deadly epidemic, which killed or severely diminished whole populations of tribes (Daley & Daley).

Most Native people assert that the early U.S. government was initially responsible for introducing smallpox, and there is also evidence that later U.S. governments did little to stop the epidemic. For example, although in 1832 Congress appropriated $12,000 to aid Native people, in this same year, vaccination expenditures for smallpox amounted to only $1,786. The next year, expenditures for the prevention of smallpox were down to $721. The remainder of the funds were spent on non-heath-related expenses, such as missionary work and the "civilization" of the Native people (Unrau, 1990).

Treaties.   According to Canby (1998), "When Europeans . . . established colonies . . . they had little choice but to deal with the Indian tribes as the independent nations that they were. Terms of peace and exchanges of land were . . . accomplished by treaty between the . . . government and the tribes" (p. 96). Beginning with the first treaty in 1787 until the last in 1871, hundreds of treaties were signed between Native people and the U.S. government. Provisions of treaties varied widely, but they commonly included a guarantee of peace, a delineation of land boundaries (with, most often, Native lands going to the government), a provision for Native hunting and fishing rights (often on the ceded land), and regulation of trade and travel. Importantly, as it relates to current relations between the U.S. government and Native people, most treaties also contained a statement that Native tribes recognized the authority of the U.S. government, or placed themselves under its protection (Canby).

In the early years when treaties were negotiated, tribes were often in a position of strength (due, for example, to the government being exhausted by the Revolutionary War and wanting to avoid additional wars). However, as the years went by, the bargaining positions changed significantly and by the end of the treaty period, the government was dictating most of the terms of treaties and some of them even dictated the unthinkable for most Native people: federal authority over tribal affairs (Canby, 1998). In addition, the treaty-making process itself put Native people at a disadvantage, in that treaties were written in English and some of the basic concepts of treaties, such as land ownership, were foreign to the tribal cultures. All of these factors, and others, contributed to an overextension of federal authority into tribal business. Nevertheless, important rights were also guaranteed by the treaties, "and many of these rights continue to be enforceable . . . include[ing] . . . ownership of . . . lands, hunting and fishing rights, and entitlement to certain federal services such as education or health care" (Canby, p. 98). Nevertheless, Congress can unilaterally repeal treaties and can pass laws inconsistent with treaties. Fortunately, for the most part, Congress has been careful to not infringe on rights promised under treaties. One notable exception that will be discussed subsequently is the Termination Era (Canby).

Expansion, Forced Removal, and Indian Territories.   Beginning in the 1800s, the U.S. government began to expand into lands possessed and occupied by Native people, and to forcibly move them onto areas designated as "Indian Territory." In other words, the government took Native homelands, forced Native people to often faraway new lands, and then "gave" these new lands to the Natives, with treaties governing such land possession and rights.

It is critical to note that this forced expansion and removal had the weight of U.S. presidents behind it. In 1807, when addressing his Secretary of War regarding any Native people who resisted expansion into their lands, President Thomas Jefferson stated, "If ever we are constrained to lift the hatchet against any tribe we will never lay it down till that tribe is exterminated. . . . They will kill some of us; we shall destroy all of them" (Stannard, 1992, p. 120). Such tyrannical attitudes and behaviors toward Native Americans spanned into subsequent presidential terms. Indeed, four presidential terms later, Andrew Jackson referred to Native people as "savage dogs" and stated "the whole Cherokee Nation should be scourged" (Stannard, p. 121). Indeed, it was under President Jackson that one of the most well-known forced removals, The Trail of Tears, occurred. The Cherokee Nation, whose ancestral homelands were in the Southeast, was forcibly moved by a proclamation by President Jackson. Thousands of Cherokees died on this winter 1838 march to an Indian territory in what is now Oklahoma.

Whereas the forced travel was often deadly, once in Indian territories, extreme difficulties continued. Native people were not allowed to practice their historical way of life (hunting, harvesting), and were penalized for non-Christian religious or spiritual beliefs. (Strikingly, it was only in 1978 that these penalties were officially removed, with the American Indian Religious Freedom Act.) There was little food, shelter, medical attention, or education available on the Indian territories.

In 1824, the Bureau of Indian Affairs (BIA) was established, with the purpose of overseeing the Indian territories. This same bureau remains in existence today, and among its many other duties, it continues to administer the Indian reservations that eventually sprang from the Indian territories. More detailed information will be presented in a subsequent section on government and tribal relations and the BIA. In addition, because of its import in Native history and current issues, the role of the BIA will also be noted in subsequent sections, such as the one that follows on boarding schools and current educational issues.

Past Boarding Schools and Current Educational Issues. In about 1879, following the relocation to Indian territories, boarding schools were established to force Western ideology on "uncivilized" Native American children. The first of many such schools was Carlisle, a multitribal, coeducational school that isolated students from their tribal cultures in an attempt to assimilate them into dominant culture.

Carlisle, located in military barracks in Carlisle, Pennsylvania, indoctrinated its students with a curriculum based on European ideology, the English language, and the importance of hard manual labor. To further reinforce the value of the work ethic, the school adopted the "outing system," in which student labor was contracted out to local farmers and other businesses. Native languages and customs were banned and Christianity was strongly encouraged, with severe punishment for those who broke these totalitarian rules.

Government officials who sought assimilation rallied to the support of the educational policies employed at the new school. In 1887, the General Allotment Act (commonly referred to as the Dawes Act) was passed, making Carlisle the model for Indian education and giving the BIA authority to use boarding schools to achieve cultural assimilation (Canby, 1998).

Unfortunately and sadly, these schools achieved compulsory assimilation. Native children stayed at these schools for years or even decades, and by the time they returned home, they had been robbed of their ethnic identity. Children returned as outsiders to their families.

Perhaps surprisingly to those new to Native American history, the practice of sending Native children to boarding schools was not exclusive to the early years of American history but continued up until the mid-1970s. Today, the BIA continues to have among its most substantial responsibilities "the provision of education" and has in recent years "phased out its boarding schools in favor of day schools located in reservation communities. The Bureau has also entered contracts permitting local tribal or community control of some of the schools and this trend is likely to continue" (Canby, 1998, p. 47).

To summarize, the education of Native American children was originally an instrument of assimilation and hence has been the focus of much resentment and controversy over the years. Although much improved today (Canby, 1998), strife and distrust regarding education still abound. Indeed, a recent study (Wood & Clay, 1996) found that structural barriers are mainly responsible for Native American high school students currently having significantly lower performance than their White counterparts. Clearly, counselors working with Native high school youth need to be aware of such barriers and thus refrain from making assumptions about an absolute relationship between the potential and the achievement of Native students.

Reservations. As noted in an earlier section, most reservations sprang from the Indian territories to which Native people were forcibly moved. Over the years, Congressional acts and executive orders changed Indian territories into reservations. Today, reservations are lands in which Native people have their own government, judicial system, and education and social services, although they still fall under the umbrella administration of the BIA. Currently, there are approximately 275 lands administered as reservations, varying widely in size. The smallest is less than 100 acres, and the largest (the Navajo reservation) encompasses 16 million acres of land in three states (Arizona, New Mexico, and Utah). The local governing authority on reservations is the tribal government.

Although differences in both size and governance exist across reservations, one important commonality is that most reservations are impoverished and unemployment rates are staggering (Turner & Lapan, 2003). Contributing to the poverty and unemployment is the fact that business development is lacking and thus "money that flows into the reservation, regardless of its source (i.e. government, mining activities, welfare, etc.), finds its way to off reservation pockets such as banks, or grocery, clothing, or liquor stores" (Johnson et al., 1995, p. 106). The unemployment rate on reservations is 45%, 37% higher than the average unemployment rate in the United States (Johnson et al.). Among the approximately 50% of employed Native people on reservations, strikingly, 30% earn wages below the poverty level (Juntunen et al., 2001). In addition, drug and alcohol abuse are common. Indeed, among American Indian women, death rates associated with alcoholism are much higher than among women of all other races. For example, during the period from 1990 to 1992, mortality due to alcoholism among 25- to 34-year-old American Indian and Alaska Native women was nearly 21 in 100,000, in contrast to the rate of 2 in 100,000 for women of other races. Similarly, American Indian and Alaska Native women ages 35 to 44 had a mortality rate due to alcoholism of 47 in 100,000 from 1990 to

1992, which was nearly 10 times the rate of U.S. women of other races (Indian Health Service, 1996; National Women's Health Information Center, n.d.). The current combination of unemployment, poverty, and substance abuse makes reservations among the most disadvantaged areas in the United States.

Despite the difficulties of life on reservations today, they also often are places of great commonality and support for Native American people. On reservations, cultural traditions, language, and spirituality are practiced. In addition, because reservations have their own court and social service systems, they essentially exist as a separate self-governing nation, affording Native peoples a sense of control over their culture and destinies.

In conclusion, although most reservations sprang up initially from forced relocation, today they can be a place of both safety (i.e., commonality) and danger (i.e., poverty) for Native women. Practitioners working with Native women, whether from reservations or not, would be wise to know about the historical roots and current status of reservations.

Government-Tribal Relations and the Bureau of Indian Affairs. Throughout the previous sections, the BIA has been discussed (e.g., in regard to administering reservations and boarding schools). It is important to have an understanding of this rather complex bureau and its current, as well as historical, place in the lives of Native people. To understand the BIA, however, it is first necessary to understand "the special relationship between the federal government and the tribes" (Canby, 1998, p. 33).

At its broadest, the relationship between the government and Native American people includes a mixture of legal duties, moral obligations, and expectations that have arisen from the entire course of dealing between the federal government and the tribes. In its narrowest and most concrete sense, the relationship approximates that of trustee and beneficiary (Canby, 1998, p. 33). Much of this trustee-beneficiary relationship stems from several Supreme Court decisions describing Native tribes as wards of the state, and as dependent on the United States—in other words, these court decisions uphold the notion that the relationship of tribes to the U.S. government "resembles that of a ward to his guardian" (Canby, p. 33). Stated quite simply, the U.S. government holds tribes' resources in its control (i.e., it is the legal titleholder of all Native American land and resources), and is thus morally obliged to deal with these resources fairly and in the best interest of the tribes. Nevertheless, numerous court cases have revolved around disputes in this relationship (Canby) and many Native American people remain understandably resentful of being considered beneficiaries (wards) of the government with respect to their own lands and resources.

Importantly, the primary instrument for carrying out the beneficiary relationship has been the BIA, now located in the Department of the Interior.

At one time, as can be gleaned from previous sections, the BIA's goal was as-similation and the discouragement of tribal self-government. Today, the BIA mainly focuses on administering the beneficiary-trustee relationship, such as through the allotment of funds for education and the management of land and other resources, "although its overall influence on tribal affairs remains great" (Canby, 1998, p. 47).

Over the years, the BIA has been the focus of sharp criticism on a num-ber of counts. For example, it has been asserted that its complex adminis-trative structure eats up too many of the funds that should be spent for the benefit of Native Americans and that "it has 'lost' large portions of those ap-propriations" (Canby, 1998, p. 48). In addition, the BIA has been accused of being more sensitive to non-Native than to Native interests, and of mak-ing political compromises, to the detriment of Native people, with other agencies within the Department of the Interior, such as the National Park Service and the Bureau of Land Management.

Perhaps the most important criticism, from a psychological level that may affect clients, is that although no longer an instrument of assimilation, the BIA remains overly paternalistic and influential within tribal affairs. Part of this undue influence is habitual, and part is that the trustee-beneficiary relationship is "opposed in principle and to some degree in practice to that of tribal independence" (Canby, 1998, p. 55).

An obvious conclusion might be to abolish the BIA. However, this deci-sion is not one unanimously supported by Native peoples. First, more and more Native people are gaining a voice in the BIA, leading it to be fairer and less paternalistic. Second, the BIA is seen as an embodiment of the ben-eficiary-trustee relationship and therefore to end the BIA could mean end-ing this relationship, and "the experience of tribes whose relationship with the Federal Government was terminated in the 1950's was sufficiently dis-mal that any hint of this" draws opposition (Canby, 1998, p. 55). This dis-mal part of Native history is documented in the next section.

The Termination Era. In 1953, the United States government voted to sever its trustee-beneficiary relationships with the Indian tribes (Daley & Daley, 2003). During the termination period, 100 tribes were terminated, 12,000 individuals lost tribal affiliation, and 2.5 million acres of Indian land were lost (Utter, 1993): "While the intentions of many of the supporters of termination had once again been benevolent (one purpose had been to 'free' the Indians from domination by the BIA), the results were generally tragic" (Canby, 1998, p. 26). Specifically, Native lands were sold and pro-ceeds dissipated, thus plunging severed tribes into even more serious eco-nomic difficulties. Subsequently, some of the severed tribes secured legisla-tion to restore their special relationship with the federal government.

Relocation. Around the time that Congress was stressing termination, the BIA was attempting to encourage Native people to leave reservations under its relocation program. Specifically, in response to high unemployment rates on reservations, the BIA offered grants to Native people who left reservations to seek work in various urban centers (Canby, 1998); the BIA also provided one-way transportation to urban centers (Campbell, 1989; Kramer, 1992; Rousseau, 1995). Over 65,000 Native people participated in relocation to urban areas (DuBray, 1992), but many Native people could not obtain the urban housing and employment needed to survive that had been promised to them (Daley & Daley, 2003), and "all too often . . . the effect of the program was to create in the target cities a population of unemployed Indians who suffered all the usual problems of the urban poor along with the added trauma of dislocation" (Canby, p. 27).

Perhaps due to the relocation program, currently, nearly three fifths (59%) of Native Americans live in urban areas (DuBray, 1992). For Native people living in urban areas today, homelessness, violence, poverty, and unemployment remain great problems (Fixico, 2000). Indeed, transportation, housing, and a lack of outreach and advocacy from service agencies can be problematic for Native people in urban areas who are seeking employment (Marshall, Johnson, Martin, Saravanabhavan, & Bradford, 1992).

Indian Health Service. Based on over 300 treaties signed in the 1700s and late 1800s, members of federally recognized tribes are guaranteed health care. The Indian Health Service (IHS) was originally part of the BIA, but in 1955 transferred to the Department of Health and Human Services. The IHS provides health services to approximately 1.5 million American Indians and Alaska Natives (IHS, n.d.). IHS programs are staffed and managed within Native communities, due to the 1975 Indian Self-Determination and Education Assurance Act.

Prior to this, rather than providing quality medical care, the IHS was responsible for many needless sterilizations being performed on Native women. Specifically, between 25% to 50% of Native women between the ages of 15 and 44 may have been sterilized in the 1970s (Mihesuah, 2003). At the IHS hospital in Claremore, Oklahoma, 194 sterilizations were performed in 1 year, which equates to one out of every four women admitted that year. Perhaps even more tragically, 4 of these 194 women were under the age of 20 (Robinson, 1977; Shapiro, 1985). In a report issued by the U.S. General Accounting Office, it was stated that in the 4-year period from 1973 to 1976, the IHS sterilized 3,406 Native women using consent forms that were not in compliance with regulations (Hartmann, 1987; Shapiro). Although this report did not admit blatant coercion, it did imply that Native women might have perceived they had to agree to the procedure

(Shapiro). It is our speculation that these mass sterilizations had, at least in part, an underlying economic motive in that the fewer Native people in existence, the fewer financial and land trusts would need to be honored.

Oppressive History and Mistrust

The previous section briefly documented a long history of oppression faced by Native women. Indeed, Native women have been taken advantage of and blatantly mistreated by a variety of governmental agencies, including those concerned with education and health services (i.e., boarding schools and forced sterilization, respectively). Thus, there often exists an underlying current of mistrust between Native women and mainstream education and health providers and this may be particularly true of health providers working in governmental agencies or health centers. Indeed, Native women's wariness of trusting health providers (including psychologists) outside of their communities is, in our view, a natural consequence of the historical events just outlined. Thus, to work with Native women, it is critical to accurately understand Native American history, as well as the current cultural biases that continue to affect Native women and their trust of mainstream psychologists.

Current Cultural Biases

Native women today continue to face cultural biases that seem to have a financial purpose and that also affect them psychologically. Two such biases are the commodification of Native heritage and peoples, and mass media representations.

The Commodification of Native Women. One very powerful cultural bias faced by Native American women is commodification, which is the use of Native people and symbols as products. Today, Native people are depicted as sports team names and mascots (e.g., Washington Redskins, Cleveland Indians), automobiles (e.g., Jeep Grand Cherokee, Dodge Dakota, Winnebago motor homes), school materials (e.g., Big Chief writing tablets and Warrior pencils), packaged foods (e.g., Land O Lakes butter, Crazy Horse malt liquor), and several clothing lines (e.g., Cherokee brand carried by Target stores, Crazy Horse division of Liz Claiborne).

One striking example of commodification exists in the town in which the authors of this chapter live. There is a local coffee shop whose name is that of a Native American nation (Lakota). This particular nation holds in its history the slaughter of several hundred unarmed men, women, and children by U.S. cavalry in 1890, known now as the Massacre at Wounded Knee. This coffee shop has shamefully used Wounded Knee as a name of one of its coffee blends. In other words, the coffee shop's name is that of a group of people, and the coffee blend is the name of a place where countless numbers of these people were massacred, including elderly men, women, and children. In our opinion, a comparison of this would be to have a coffee shop named "Jews" selling an "Auschwitz" blend of coffee, or a "Cambodians" coffee shop with a "Killing Fields" blend of the day. Such commodification of other groups is thankfully unthinkable but, in the United States today, commodification of Native Americans abounds.

We believe that it is this commodification that sets the stage for the devaluation of Native people (Steele, 1996), as well as the belief that Native people are historical figures and not current individuals. In other words, the common belief of mainstream society is that Native people do not exist anymore and this idea is created and bolstered by their commodification. Likewise, when Native people are presented as objects or things, they cannot be thought of as living, breathing people. The end to such commodification is thus a critical step in validating the experience of Native individuals, and of creating a more supportive environment to work with Native women and Native peoples. Psychologists working with Native individuals must carefully check their offices for any products or art that commodify Native people or that present them as historical figures. Such products and art abound and, unless specific education is provided to psychologists and other service providers, they may not even be aware of such offensive items in their offices.

Mass Media Representations. Another related, current problem is stereotyped and negative media images. In general, Native women are depicted as either maidens or crones (Barbie, 2001; Welch, 1988). (The commonplace term *squaw* will not be used, due to the root origin of the word being a woman's vagina.) The Native crone is often depicted as mindless, savage, and servile. In many media depictions, the Native crone and her male counterpart, the savage, are portrayed as needing to be eradicated in order to allow a safe place for colonists and settlers.

Whereas media images often condemn the crone, the maiden is frequently elevated to "princess" status. In addition, in many stories and media depictions, the Native American princess is portrayed in relation to European American men, often giving up her people and befriending and aiding the enemy (Rountree, 2001). Indeed, it is this image that has helped foster the myths of Pocahontas and Sacagawea.

The story of Pocahontas illustrates just how misleading media images can be. In 1995, Disney released an animated movie about a Powhatan woman known as Pocahontas. According to the web site of the Powhatan

Renape Nation, located at the Rankokus Indian reservation in New Jersey, the Powhatan Nation complained to Disney, noting that the movie distorted "history beyond recognition." Disney's retort was that the film was historically accurate. In response, the Powhatan Nation offered to assist Disney with cultural and historical accuracy. Disney rejected this offer (Crazy Horse, n.d.).

Although the Disney movie presents Pocahontas as a sweet love story in which Pocahontas saves John Smith from being clubbed to death by her father, Chief Powhatan, closer examination reveals that at the time that Pocahontas and John Smith would have known each other, she would have been 10 or 11 years old, and John Smith would have been 30 (Kilpatrick, 1999). Furthermore, many historians have speculated that the interactions between Smith and Pocahontas (whose real name was Matoaka, with Pocahontas actually being a nickname meaning "spoiled child") were contrived and that they hardly knew each other at all (Rountree, 2001). Indeed, according to the Powhatan Nation web site, 17 years after his winter stay with Powhatan's people, John Smith falsified the Pocahontas rescue story. In written accounts Smith made directly after his stay, he never mentioned such an incident and instead reported that he had been treated as an honored guest of Powhatan. (For more information on the true story of Matoaka, please see: http://www.powhatan.org/pocc.html.) In short, the now-famous story of Pocahontas was distorted and falsified.

Similarly fallacious media representations portray Native women wearing buckskins, living in teepees, and riding horses. Such an image was inaccurate 200 years ago, and is certainly wholly distorted today. Such images support outdated and incorrect stereotypes and misconceptions. Psychologists and other service providers must be educated about today's Native women and their experience, as well as about the negative effects of such stereotyped and inaccurate images on Native women, such as internalized racism, feelings of invisibility, and justified, but nevertheless often uncomfortable, feelings of anger, to name just a few. Additional information on such effects are detailed in our final section, when discussing cultural identity development and its potential impact on the career-counseling relationship. Prior to this, however, we detail biases toward Native people that exist within the field of psychology.

BIASES WITHIN THE FIELD OF PSYCHOLOGY

Given that the field of psychology exists within a broader cultural framework, it is not surprising that there exist biases within the field in terms of knowledge of Native American individuals. Three of these biases that are briefly overviewed are ignorance, pathologizing views of Native Americans, and bias in assessment.

Ignorance

As noted at the start of this chapter, the field of psychology has often ignored the experiences of Native American people in general and Native American women in particular. Most of the research and writing in the area of racial-ethnic heritage commonly leaves out the experiences of Native Americans. Although this is not always the fault of the researcher in that it is often difficult (or even impossible) to secure a sufficient Native American sample, this nevertheless leaves psychologists at a distinct disadvantage when working with Native American women, in that much clinical work must be conducted in the absence of research. We hope that this chapter will serve to spur interest in researching and writing about Native people, their concerns, and effective counseling strategies.

Pathologizing View of Native Americans

Until quite recently, most information available about Native American people focused on pathology. For example, many research studies can be found that focus on alcohol and drug abuse and suicide among Native Americans (e.g., Beauvais, Chaves, Oetting, Deffenbacher, & Cornell, 1996; Echohawk, 1997; Middlebrook, Lemaster, Beals, Novins, & Manson, 2001; Taylor, 2000). It is only recently that information presenting a more holistic view of issues and counseling with Native Americans can be found (Duran & Duran, 1995; Garrett & Wilbur, 1999; Herring, 1992; Johnson et al., 1995; LaFromboise, Trimble, & Mohatt, 1990; Martin, 1995; Mihesuah, 2003).

Bias in Assessment

Bias in assessment has been identified as a serious concern when working with Native clients (Duran & Duran, 1995). Specifically, most available psychological tests and measures, including career assessment measures, have not been validated on a Native American sample (Fouad, 1993; Juntunen et al., 2001). Furthermore, many instruments that have been studied reveal differing norms for Native Americans (Juntunen et al.). Indeed, experiences that constitute normal behavior within a Native person's life can be deemed pathological by test instruments like the Minnesota Multiphasic Personality Inventory (MMPI; Duran & Duran). Thus, until inventories are appropriately normed on Native populations, psychologists must either refrain from using them or use them with very great caution (Johnson et al., 1995). Specific issues and suggestions regarding career-counseling assessment are detailed in the following section.

A CULTURALLY ORIENTED APPROACH FOR CAREER
COUNSELING WITH NATIVE AMERICAN WOMEN

This section presents a culturally derived approach for effective career counseling with Native American women. The basis of the model is the work of the scholars whose approach to working with Native peoples has been holistic and respectful (Duran & Duran, 1995; Garrett & Wilbur, 1999; Herring, 1992; Johnson et al., 1995; LaFromboise et al., 1990; Martin, 1995; Mihesuah, 2003). In addition, due to the lack of research and information on Native American career development, this approach is also based on models developed for other ethnic minority women, such as Bingham and Ward's (1994) multilayered approach to career counseling with racial-ethnic minority women.

More specifically, in developing our approach, we attended to the five areas that Bingham and Ward (1994) indicated as having an effect on the career development of racial-ethnic minority women: (a) vocational information, (b) family participation and support, (c) community, role models, and language, (d) socialization, and (e) sexism and racism. In addition, we took into account the seven factors that these scholars note as being facilitative in working with ethnic minority women in career counseling. These seven factors are: (a) establish rapport or culturally appropriate relationship, (b) identify career issues, (c) assess impact of cultural variables, (d) set counseling goals, (e) make culturally appropriate counseling interventions, (f) make decisions, and (g) implementation and follow-up. As the reader will see, however, we do not simply adapt Bingham and Ward's lists for Native American women. Instead, themes are weaved throughout our approach.

The approach that we suggest for effective career counseling with Native American women includes several components, all of which are detailed later. The first component that we discuss is counselor awareness, education, and attitudes regarding Native American issues. The second is an understanding of Native ethnic identity and acculturation and their potential impact on career counseling. Third is the facilitation of a working alliance through culturally appropriate alliance-building behaviors. The fourth, fifth, and sixth components are assessment and intervention regarding accurate career knowledge, barriers to career development, and family and community support. Our seventh component pertains to culturally appropriate strategies to help clients clarify values, interests, and goals. Our eighth component focuses on the appropriateness of traditional quantitative assessments with Native women career clients. Finally, we conclude with some additional ways in which to avoid attrition, and a summary.

Counselor Education, Awareness, and Attitudes

For effective counseling with Native American women, counselors must first be educated concerning Native American history and issues, and also must confront their own biases toward Native people. The first portion of this chapter focused exclusively on historical and current issues faced by Native Americans, and thus the reader has already begun this educative step. As previously noted, we place significant emphasis on education concerning Native American issues because such knowledge has been noted to positively effect counseling (Herring, 1992). Similarly, we believe that having a counselor who is already knowledgeable about Native American issues can, at some level, provide a corrective emotional experience for the client, in that the vast majority of non-Native Americans know little about Native issues, history, and customs, often leaving Native people feeling invisible and ignored by majority culture. Having a counselor who is already knowledgeable can help to provide a unique, and better, experience for the client than they often receive in the outside world and can also have a positive impact on the development of the working alliance.

In addition to reading about Native American history and issues, there are other sources of knowledge and familiarity. For example, many urban areas and reservations have Native American cultural centers. Most large universities have Native American student groups that host cultural events throughout the year, and some universities have Native American studies departments that typically house a host of resources and information. In addition, there are several books that may assist practitioners in developing greater understanding and insight into Native culture. Along with several excellent political and academic writings (e.g., Cook-Lynn, 2001; Deloria & Wildcat, 2001; Huhndorf, 2001; Mihesuah, 2003), two books that practitioners would enjoy are one by Pierre and Long Soldier (1995) on medicine women, and LaDuke's (1999) biographical account of her life as a Native woman. Likewise, novels such as Silko's (1988) *Ceremony* and Momaday's (1999) *House Made of Dawn*, and Alexies's (1994) collection of short stories in *The Lone Ranger and Tonto Fistfight in Heaven* provide helpful illustrations of historical and contemporary Native American life. Finally, movies like *Smoke Signals* (Estes, Rosenfeldt, & Eyre, 1998), *Skins* (Kilik, Pomier, & Eyre, 2002) and *Lakota Woman: Siege at Wounded Knee* (Berner & Pierson, 1994) also provide insight into Native peoples and their lives. Regardless of specific sources used, the key issue is that the counselor must make an effort to gain knowledge of Native history, culture, and current issues. We particularly recommend experiential learning, such as attending a Native American cultural event such as a powwow. Although attending an event as an outsider can be uncomfortable, such attendance provides an important glimpse into culture. For the majority counselor, it also provides the empathy-building experience of being an outsider, something racial-ethnic minority clients often have to cope with on a daily basis.

In addition to gaining concrete knowledge and experiences, counselors must also examine their biases toward Native people. Though perhaps an obvious point, it must be stated that therapists who have a dislike for or lack of respect for certain groups should not work with them (Pinderhughes, 1989). It is also important that non-Native counselors seeking to work with Native American clients examine their underlying motivation. Specifically, Pinderhughes suggested that when counselors work with people of racial-ethnic status or lower socioeconomic status it may be to elevate their feelings of self-worth and importance. This is, of course, potentially harmful: Therapists cannot enter the therapeutic relationship on an ethnocentric or paternalistic mission. A nonpaternalistic stance is particularly critical for Native American clients given the paternalistic (i.e., wards of the state) relationship Native peoples have with the U.S. government. To be effective, therapists cannot approach therapy with the idea that the values of their culture are the best and the only way to do things. Instead, therapists need to believe that they have as much to learn from their clients as their clients have to learn from them. Therapists working with ethnic minority clients must also be able and willing to help such clients appreciate their own cultures and not buy into or support negative cultural images (McNicol & Baker, 1998).

In order to be able to take such a stance with Native American (and other ethnic minority) clients, there are several necessary counselor behaviors and attitudes. First, therapists should be willing to make themselves vulnerable, whether that means letting the client know that they do not know everything or being less directive (Pinderhughes, 1989). Second, and quite importantly, therapists need to be willing and able to examine their own ethnic and cultural identities. Specifically, therapists need to carefully examine the many dimensions of who they are in terms of race, ethnicity, culture, gender, socioeconomic level, access to education, and so on. For most people, power is not uniform: They can be powerful in one area of their lives and powerless in others (Pinderhughes). Indeed, as stated by LaFromboise, Berman, and Sohi (1994):

> A therapist effective with Native Americans must be aware of the attitudes and customs particular to her (or his) own ethnic and cultural heritage and be knowledgeable about alternatives in a client's background, both self-disclosed and those from sources other than the client. In this regard, the therapist's goal is to uncover, respect, and learn to understand the differences in culture, community, and past and present experience. (p. 51)

In summary, for effective counseling with Native American clients, all counselors must be knowledgeable and open to continued learning about

Native history and issues; nonpaternalistic and nonethnocentric; and willing and able to examine their own ethnic identity, bases of power and powerlessness, and motivations for counseling.

Ethnic Identity and Acculturation

As noted previously, for effective work with Native clients, counselors must examine their own ethnic identity. Equally as critical is knowledge of ethnic identity literature both in general and as it pertains to Native Americans specifically. The writings on ethnic identity and its impact on counseling is a rich body of literature, and we encourage the reader to seek deeper knowledge than we can provide in this chapter (e.g., Constantine, 2002; Gloria & Rodriguez, 2000; Helms, 1994; Ponterotto, Fuertes, & Chen, 2000; Trusty, 2002). Indeed, when working with clients of minority racial-ethnic backgrounds, it is important to be aware of the influence of oppression on that person's life, and how it has affected their ethnic identity and acculturation (Garrett & Pinchette, 2000).

There is a dearth of literature on Native American women's racial and ethnic identity development (Fisher & Moradi, 2001; Mihesuah, 2003). Nevertheless, there does exist a recently developed model that specifically focuses on Native American women. Specifically, Mihesuah presented a modern American Indigenous Female Identity model based on Cross (1991) and Parham (1989), both of whom focused on African American identity development. Mihesuah stated that Native Americans live in a society that is dominated by White Americans and therefore must deal with everyday stressors like racism, stereotypes, and oppression. Additionally, she recognized the complex nature of being biracial or multiracial, and specifically noted that a Native woman can be affected not only by White society but by tribal societies as well. We would add that a Native woman might also be affected by sexism, in both mainstream and tribal cultures.

As with her predecessors, Mihesuah (2003) outlined four states that a Native woman follows as she develops her racial-ethnic identity: pre-encounter, encounter, immersion-emersion, and internalization. The first, pre-encounter, is when a Native woman identifies with White culture or focuses little attention on her Native identity. In this stage, a Native woman might see herself as Native, but feel inferior to Whites and responsible for her economic, social, and political status. In the second stage, encounter, a Native woman strives to learn more about her culture and tribal history. This search for knowledge is usually due to a mitigating event, which can be either positive or negative. Regardless, this event leads to a journey in which the Native woman seeks the "truth" of her people and her heritage. The third stage, immersion-emersion, can be volatile and filled with anxiety, confusion, depression, and frustration as the woman tries to define what it means to be Native. At this stage, a Native woman often increases her participation in religious and cultural events and becomes more politically active. This stage is also often marked by a lack of acknowledgement of the non-Native cultural, racial and ethnic parts of herself, and hostility toward Whites or non-Natives. Also in this stage, the Native woman may become judgmental of other persons claiming Native ethnic status and question whether those individuals are indeed Native in the "right ways" or are "Native enough." The fourth and final stage, internalization, is when the Native woman is secure in her identity. In this stage, she is able to discuss racial identity with others in a balanced manner.

Related to stages of ethnic identity formation is the concept of acculturation. Simply defined, acculturation is the psychosocial development of gaining knowledge of cultural values and customs of a new culture while maintaining some measure of affiliation to one's traditional culture (Casas & Pytluk, 1995). LaFromboise et al. (1990) listed five levels of acculturation among Native Americans. The first level is traditional: These individuals generally speak and think in their native language and know little English. They follow old-style religious and cultural rituals. The second level, transitional, includes individuals who often speak both English and their native language in the home. These individuals question traditional religious and cultural rituals, but cannot fully accept dominant culture and values. Those in the third, marginal, level are people who are unable to either comfortably live the cultural heritage of their group or to identify with the dominant society. The fourth level, assimilated, are the group of people who, for the most part, have been accepted by the dominant society, and generally embrace dominant culture and values. Finally, there is the bicultural level: Within this group are those who are for the most part accepted by the dominant society, but who also know and accept their tribal traditions and culture. "They can thus move in either direction, from traditional society to dominant society, with ease" (Martin, 1995, p. 234).

As may be obvious from a reading of the previous descriptions, an individuals level of acculturation may help explain critical aspects of their vocational behavior and attitudes (Gysbers, Heppner, & Johnston, 1998). For example, varying levels of acculturation will impact how similarly to the American mainstream a Native American woman will view the role of occupation in her life (Martin, 1995). Even more specifically, for example, Morgan, Guy, Lee, and Cellini (1986) suggested that Native Americans who follow traditional ways may view employment as much more than an individual pursuit. Supporting this view, in a qualitative study on Native Americans' career perspectives, Juntunen et al. (2001) found a clear tendency among respondents to view career as a direct pathway through which to promote tradition, and for success to be defined in collective terms, such as one's ability to contribute to the well-being of others and to benefit one's home community. Especially pertinent to an understanding of Native women, Juntunen et al. also found that "beyond meeting the needs of the broad . . . [Native American] community, [female] participants indicated that success could be measured by . . . family and the impact one had on children" (p. 279). Clearly, a Native woman's identity development and acculturation stage is critical to understanding the meaning of career in her life.

A Native American woman's stage of identity development and acculturation will also influence the career-counseling process, "from differences in initial help-seeking behavior to racial or ethnic preference for a counselor" (Gysbers et al., 1998, p. 43). In other words, a Native woman's level of acculturation and identity development may impact whether she seeks career services in the first place, although one interesting study (Bee-Gates, Howard-Pitney, LaFromboise, & Rowe, 1996) reported that Native American adolescents were more likely to seek help from a friend, parent, or relative for personal problems and to seek professional guidance for academic and career problems. Nevertheless, acculturation and identity development remain paramount in terms of the degree to which a Native client is able to trust a non-Native (particularly a Caucasian) counselor initially (Ho, 1987). The practitioner must be aware of this and not note it as resistance. Though ideally, in certain stages of identity development (i.e., immersion-emersion), a client would be referred to a Native counselor, this is not always possible (i.e., there is a great shortage of Native counselors). Thus, non-Native counselors who wish to work effectively with Native clients must have awareness and sensitivity to Native issues (LaFromboise et al., 1990).

Indeed, one interesting study with Native American women (Bichsel & Mallinckrodt, 2001) shed light on the impact of identity and traditional Native values on counselor preferences. Specifically, Bichsel and Mallinckrodt found that Native women living on a reservation in Oregon generally preferred a counselor who was female, ethnically similar, and culturally sensitive. As one would predict, "these preferences were stronger for women with high commitment to Native American culture" (Bichsel & Mallinckrodt, p. 858). Also of interest, however, was the finding that a culturally sensitive White counselor was preferred over a culturally insensitive Native counselor, pointing to the hypothesis that cultural knowledge and sensitivity may be even more important than ethnic similarity for traditional Native American female clients.

Along with having an impact on seeking counseling and trusting the counselor, identity development and acculturation influence the appropriateness of specific interventions and stances to career counseling. Some authors have noted that Native Americans' present-time orientation may make career counseling, with its future orientation, difficult (Gysbers et al., 1998). However, more recent work contradicts this notion, finding that career is generally considered a "long-term activity with a strong link to one's contribution to the world" (Juntunen et al., 2001, p. 283). Nevertheless, the practitioner must still keep in mind that "more traditional career interventions would be most appropriate for clients who are highly acculturated, whereas rooting career interventions in a cultural context would be essential for clients who more closely adhere to the practices of their culture" (Gysbers et al., p. 43). As one example, if a Native American woman client reflects a very traditional belief system, it may be helpful to suggest that significant persons such as a medicine man or medicine woman get involved in the counseling process (Garrett & Wilbur, 1999). Nevertheless, counselors need to use great caution when discussing traditional healing and medicine practices with traditional Native American clients. We advise not to explore the topic in the initial interview, but instead establish rapport and wait until the client initiates the conversation. In summary, assessment of acculturation and identity development is paramount to making culturally appropriate interventions in career counseling with Native women.

Though it is clear that knowledge of identity and acculturation are critical for effective counseling, the question remains regarding how to assess such constructs. Although a few scattered instruments exist (e.g., Lysne & Levy, 1997; Bates, Beauvais, & Trimble, 1997; Kim & Abreu, 2001), we believe that such measures are best reserved for research purposes. In counseling, such assessment of identity and acculturation can best be accomplished by an inquiry about language, values, geographic origin or residence, and tribal affiliation (Garrett & Herring, 2001; Garrett & Wilbur, 1999). According to Martin (1995), in assessing how acculturation and identity may be affecting career decision making, the counselor should inquire about several factors, including the client's own perceptions of the acculturative process, and short- and long-term goals related to living on the reservation, if pertinent. More information on such assessment is included later, in sections on both career knowledge and the role of the family and community.

Working Alliance

Brief Definition of Working Alliance and Its Importance.   As in any counseling, the working alliance is of critical importance. Briefly, to review what we assume most readers are already familiar with, the working alliance is a relationship that is formed between a counselor and client who engage in a therapeutic setting. Bordin (1979) outlined three major facets of the working alliance, with the first and second being agreements between the counselor and client on what the goals and tasks are, respectively. The third facet outlined by Bordin is the bond formed by the client and counselor, which makes the tasks and goals important. Several scholars in the field have discussed the working alliance extensively (e.g., Gelso & Fritz, 2001; Gysbers et al., 1998), and we refer the reader to these sources for specific information on general principles for establishing and maintaining a therapeutic alliance, such as active listening, empathy, compassion, and a demonstrated willingness to persist in the work, as well as the early setting of goals that are then checked and rechecked as the relationship forms and develops.

It is imperative to develop a positive working alliance with the client for the multiple general reasons outlined in the working alliance literature, as well as for more Native American client-specific reasons. Specifically, like other racial-ethnic minority clients, Native Americans have high attrition from counseling (Sue & Sue, 1990). This is why in every setting, no matter the type or duration of counseling, the establishment of a good alliance is critical. Indeed, we believe that it is this alliance that can help counselors to prevent the premature termination of Native American clients. In other words, a solid therapeutic alliance is the first step to preventing attrition of Native clients.

Culture-Specific Alliance-Building Behaviors and Suggestions. Along with the general alliance-building behaviors described earlier, there are some specific behaviors that can facilitate alliance building with Native clients. These suggested behaviors may be more or less appropriate depending on a Native woman's identity development and acculturation level, as described earlier. However, some of these alliance-building behaviors will need to be implemented prior to assessing the client's identity and acculturation (i.e., greetings). Thus, at least initially, we suggest erring in the direction of using these specific suggestions and behaviors.

Garrett and Wilbur (1999) suggested seven practical ways of building a working alliance with Native clients, although we see these suggestions as important for both building and maintaining the alliance. First, Garrett and Wilbur warned that, contrary to what is expected in mainstream society, a firm handshake is considered an insult in some traditional Native cultures. Clearly, counselors should refrain from using handshakes at all initially, or should use only a very gentle handshake. Garrett and Wilbur also noted that for some Native people, it is customary to allow some silence after the greeting, as a sign of respect and understanding. Thus, when first meeting a Native client, counselors may include a moment of silence following the greeting. Third, Garrett and Wilbur noted that generosity is an important aspect of Native traditions. Therefore, when working with Native woman clients, it is helpful to initially offer a beverage or food. Fourth, in terms of initial seating, do not sit too close or directly across from the client. Instead, it is more appropriate and more congruent with traditional practices to sit at an angle side by side. Fifth, Garrett and Wilbur advised that traditional Native clients may avert their eyes as a sign of respect; counselors should subtly match this level of eye contact as a sign of both awareness and respect for the client's beliefs. Garrett and Wilbur also mentioned that due to a history of deception and oppression, Native clients will closely read nonverbal and verbal cues, and it is thus imperative that the counselor's nonverbal behaviors reflect assistance and not a desire to control or influence. Related and finally, Garrett and Wilbur noted that traditional Native clients will be seeking alternatives and ideas from the counselor and it is important to give such opinions and choices, but not to exert too much pressure on the client to change.

Along with these seven concrete alliance-building and maintaining behaviors, another set of suggestions that we offer pertains to language. First, a "determination of the clients' level of English proficiency may be necessary. Word recognition, word meanings, spelling, comprehension, narrative analysis, oral language skills, and receptive language skills . . . that will be important in the work setting need to be considered" (Martin, 1995, p. 233). If English skills are lacking, the counselor may need to suggest that clients take a class in English to improve oral and writing skills, and to thus improve their chances of obtaining a good job (Martin).

Along with assessment and intervention around English proficiency, it is also critical to understand the Native oral tradition and linguistic style. Historically and currently, Native people utilize the oral tradition as a way of passing stories from one generation to the next. Oral stories are used to explain history and convey social structures, morals, information, and tribal archives. Indeed, we believe that this oral tradition actually makes the use of talk therapy especially helpful for Native American clients. We also suggest that it is important to not misread long pauses in speech as uncertainty or to interrupt a Native woman client. In some traditional Native communities, there is often a protracted silence time between one person finishing a sentence and another person beginning to speak (Tafoya, 1989). In addition, "Native peoples often use rhetorical embellishment to emphasize a point and are accustomed to talking without interruption until they have stated what they feel needs to be said" (LaFromboise et al., 1994, p. 32). Indeed, many Native Americans who come from traditional communities consider speaking quickly or loudly, or interrupting the speaker as signs of disrespect (Daley & Daley, 2003), and it is thus imperative that counselors refrain from such linguistic behaviors. In addition, sarcasm, used frequently in American society, is not seen as humorous (Daley & Daley) and should not be used.

One final linguistic issue that counselors need to be aware of is gesturing. Specifically, gesturing is a common characteristic of Native people's speech patterns; often, Native people use hand movements, facial expressions, and body movements to communicate a state of mind or intention. Thus, it is imperative that counselors not pathologize such gesturing. Instead, it will behoove the counselor to gain knowledge about the linguistic style of their client's particular tribal culture to keep from insulting or losing trust with the client.

Assessment and Intervention Regarding Barriers to Career Development

Along with taking into account acculturation and identity and utilizing culturally appropriate alliance-building behaviors, counselors must be aware of the very real barriers that Native American women often face. Juntunen et al. (2001) identified such barriers as lack of support from significant others, single parenting, lack of child-care resources, domestic violence, substance abuse, oppression, discrimination, and alienation. Career counselors should be sensitive to these very real barriers and help clients to cope with them, while acknowledging that some are out of the clients' control to overcome.

Assessment and Intervention Regarding Accurate Career Knowledge

As one early step in career counseling with Native women, the counselor must ascertain the client's level of knowledge regarding careers. This suggestion is made because scholars have noted that Native American clients may have inadequate knowledge about vocations (Martin, 1995), and be particularly vulnerable to myths (i.e., inaccurate beliefs) about careers (Herring, 1990). Such limited knowledge and myths may arise or be perpetuated by uninformed career counselors (Herring), families, (Martin, 1991), and continued commodification, stereotyping, and media images of Native women (Herring, 1990; Johnson et al., 1995), as well as by a lack of available career role models for Native Americans.

Role models for Native American women may be particularly lacking. For example, Native Americans are more likely to be enrolled in 2-year rather than 4-year institutions (National Center for Education Statistics, 1999), yet Flowers (2003) reported that only 1% of instructional faculty and staff across all American 2-year colleges were Native American women. Further addressing the importance of role models, particularly in higher education and professional careers, Johnson et al. (1995) stated:

> Social learning theory provides a template upon which some career outcomes can be described. For example, a Native American may experience and observe the limited frequency in which Indian people make career decisions in the technical or scientific fields (i.e. medicine, biomedical engineering, psychologist). Instead, one sees Native Americans as teachers, teacher aides, janitors, bus drivers and so forth; therefore these are career options available or accessible to Native Americans. The notion of being a physician may seem an

inaccessible career option if one has not seen Native Americans in such career roles. (p. 128)

It is imperative that initial attention in career counseling with Native
women be on assessing knowledge and role models and then, if needed, on
providing experiences that increase both. For example, it would behoove
the counselor to gather information on family members' and friends' occupational history, as well as exposure to any other career role models. Then,
useful knowledge enhancing interventions could include "tryout experiences, career exploration seminars, career information interviews, exposure to career information (e.g. occupational informational publications
and computerized career guidance systems) and job shadowing" (Johnson
et al., 1995, p. 126).

One specific technique that we recommend that can help expand the
Native woman client's knowledge about vocational jobs and careers, while
simultaneously helping to clarify interests, values, and skills, is the Missouri
Occupational Card Sort (MOCS; Hansen & Johnston, 1989). This intervention consists of a set of cards, with each card listing an occupational title, associated job tasks, educational level needed for the job, and other information such as the Dictionary of Occupational Title (DOT) code. To use this
card sort, clients are first given a stack of cards and told to make three piles:
occupations they would like, occupations they would not like, and occupations about which they are unsure. After clients have sorted the cards into
three piles, they are to sort the "like" pile according to the different reasons
for their appeal or similarities between them. Subsequently, the "dislike"
pile is sorted according to the different reasons for their lack of appeal or
similarities between them. Clients are also asked to go back through the "in-
different" pile and see if any new ideas emerge from looking over the cards
for a second time. As noted earlier, we recommend the MOCS because it
can help to ascertain what occupations are well suited for the client's attitudes and values, while also giving the career counselor a view of how much
the Native woman knows about careers. In addition, we believe that the
MOCS is particularly well suited for Native American woman clients in that
the process itself is in line with oral tradition and storytelling. In addition, it
gives the counselor an avenue with which to initially assess the role of community and family in career decisions, a critical element of career counseling that is detailed next.

Assessment and Intervention Regarding Family
and Community Support

In listing reasons for likes and dislike of career options during the MOCS,
we predict that the mention of family and community will be made, and this
will give the counselor an initial method with which to begin to explore this

critically important topic. Indeed, there is a growing body of literature that suggests that the family and community are of great importance in career counseling with ethnic minorities in general (Bingham & Ward, 1994; Evansoki & Wu Tse, 1989) and with Native Americans in particular (Garrett & Wilbur, 1999; Johnson et al., 1995; Juntunen et al., 2001; Martin, 1995; Martin & Farris, 1994).

Although family and community are generally important for Native women, the extent of involvement in nuclear and extended families varies by individual. Thus, the counselor needs to fully assess values pertinent to family, homeland, tribal traditions, and community in order to gain a comprehensive understanding of the consequences that career decision making may have for a particular client. Factors to consider include how decisions are made within the family system, client's family roles and responsibilities (including financial responsibilities), family's expectations for the client's career pursuits, and family's willingness to support the client in her pursuits (Martin, 1995).

As noted in the earlier section on acculturation and ethnic identity, for many Native people, career and success are viewed as ways to give back to the community, rather than as an individualistic endeavor (Juntunen et al., 2001). In addition, such a traditional, extended family orientation may mean that individual decision making is subordinated to group decision making. In this vein, establishing a relationship with family members who have a strong influence on the client's decisions and including them in the career-counseling process will be vitally important. However, it is also important to keep in mind that, along with being supportive of and important to career decisions, family and community members can also serve in an unsupportive role, with for example, some respondents in Juntunen et al.'s survey reporting a lack of support from family and community.

Similarly, some respondents in Juntunen et al.'s (2001) survey who had left reservations to pursue career training and then returned reported a sense of alienation. This finding, among others, points to the importance of helping the client examine the impact of living on a reservation or an urban area. Specifically, although high unemployment in reservation communities can make relocating to urban areas a practical option, this choice must also be weighed against the cultural and familial support provided on the reservation. Indeed, for many, maintaining a community connection is an important factor in career decision making (Juntunen et al.). For some clients, the support system found on their reservation may motivate them to live there but to work in urban areas, thus commuting 60 or 70 miles a day (Martin, 1995). When working with clients who make this choice, counselors must help them to anticipate and make plans to cope with difficulties that may come from "living in two worlds" (Juntunen et al., p. 281), while taking into account that the level of difficulty in spanning two worlds will vary according to the client's acculturation level. Similarly, counselors must be aware, when working with clients who gain career training outside the reservation (such as at a university) and then return home to the reservation (often due to a desire to help their own community), that this returning home may be difficult and alienating (Juntunen et al.). Finally, when working with clients who decide to both live and work on a reservation that has limited job opportunities, "then creative job development and traditional work become salient activities for career placement [and] the counselor must be knowledgeable of the reservation labor market" (Martin, p. 238).

In short, when working with Native American clients in career decision making, counselors must remain cognizant of the fact that "the exploration of individual interests, skills, and goals may be less important . . . than is the exploration of the client's role as a member of [a family and] of the community, and the expression of that role through career choice" (Juntunen et al., 2001, p. 283). Thus, "the counselor must help the client make the best life choice, not just the best job choice" (Martin, 1995, p. 238).

Additional Strategies to Clarify Values, Interests, and Goals

Along with the acknowledgement of barriers, the provision of knowledge, and the incorporation of family and community into decision making, there are a few other specific techniques that we suggest as being potentially useful with Native women career clients.

Visualization. LaFromboise et al. (1994) suggested that guided imagery exercises can be effectively used with Native American clients. Juntunen et al. (2001) further noted that "dreaming is also very important . . . [and] dreaming about careers and planning ahead to fulfill those dreams may be a value consistent with traditional values" (p. 283). Thus, we strongly suggest that the reader secure a copy of Morgan and Skovholt's (1978) article on the use of fantasy and daydreams in career counseling. This article includes suggestions regarding the use of both spontaneous and guided fantasy and daydreams in career counseling. In addition, this article includes an actual script for a guided fantasy, as well as suggested methods of processing the fantasy experience. We believe this fantasy script, as well as the suggestions around the use of daydreams in career counseling, would be especially culturally appropriate for use with Native American women.

We further suggest that a guided fantasy approach could be used to confront career myths and stereotypes discussed earlier. Specifically, the client may be asked to visualize a maid, a nurse, or a scientist, with a discussion following of the gender and race of what they imagined the person to be. This exercise can help the client confront myths and also to explore her feelings about the world of work and how it pertains to her as a woman and as a woman of color.

Journaling.   Many practitioners use journaling as a homework assignment to enhance the counseling process (Stone, 1998; Youga, 1995). Such journaling may be especially useful for Native American woman career clients. For example, both unguided (i.e., free flowing) and guided (i.e., specific writing topics) journals could be utilized. In terms of the latter, the career counselor could suggest several different writing exercises that would reflect a more Native American worldview, such as a letter about the client's career journey addressed to the next generations of her family or community. She might also address and honor her ancestors, giving thanks to them for their influence on her career path and learning.

Traditional Quantitative Assessments With Native Women Career Clients

As noted in our first section, bias in assessment is a serious issue when working with Native clients, with many career assessment instruments not normed for use with Native Americans, or, if normed, found inappropriate (Juntunen et al., 2001). Specifically, Native Americans have been found to differ from the norms on the Self-Directed Search (Gade et al., 1984; Krebs et al., 1988). On the other hand, there is evidence that Holland's hexagonal vocational interest structure is an appropriate model for Native Americans, particularly Native American college students (Day & Rounds, 2000; Day, Rounds, & Swaney, 1998; Hansen et al., 2000) and Native American adolescents (Turner & Lapan, 2003). Additionally, the Strong Interest Inventory exhibits validity with Native Americans (Haviland & Hansen, 1988; Lattimore & Borgen, 1999), with one caution: Likely because of oppression and cultural values, the enterprising theme may be minimized when working with Native Americans (Lattimore & Borgen). Our recommendation, then, is that at least with a college population of Native Americans, the Strong Interest Inventory is appropriate.

Nevertheless, for Native clients with limited English skills, such instruments would be wholly inappropriate. Likewise, for the many Native clients who lack occupational knowledge or experience, results on Holland-code-based instruments can be skewed (Johnson et al., 1995). Hence, great caution must be exercised in using such assessments, with both English language proficiency and career knowledge being prerequisites to their use.

Prevention of Attrition and Overall Summary

We believe our culturally guided suggestions will assist counselors in providing effective career services to Native American woman clients, and will also assist in preventing the premature termination that is so common among ethnic and racial minority clients (Sue & Sue, 1990). Two other concepts that we want to emphasize, or reemphasize, are the activity level of the client and the concept of choice. First, "the concept of choice is central to the Native American way of life" (Garrett & Myers, 1996, p. 101) and hence all career interventions must be aimed at providing and encouraging client choice, rather than counselor directedness. Second, as Garrett and Herring (2001) suggested, if the Native client is active in her career counseling she is much more likely to learn from the sessions and return.

In summary, as stated by Gysbers et al. (1998), "It is our position that in order to provide ethical career counseling that truly has the welfare of the client as a paramount goal, counselors must become proficient at providing services within cultural contexts" (p. 39). We hope that this chapter will serve as a foundation for counselors in providing culturally appropriate career counseling to Native American women.

REFERENCES

Alexie, S. (1994). *The Lone Ranger and Tonto fistfight in heaven.* New York: Perennial Press.

American Indian Religious Freedom Act of 1978, Pub. L. No. 95-341, 92 Stat. 469 (1978).

An Act to Provide for the Allotment of Lands in Severalty to Indians on the Various Reservations (General Allotment Act or Dawes Act), 24 Stat. 388-91 (1887).

Barbie, D. (2001). Sacagawea: The making of a myth. In T. Purdue (Ed.), *Sifters: Native American women's lives* (pp. 60–76). New York: Oxford University Press.

Bates, S. C., Beauvais, F., & Trimble, J. E. (1997). American Indian adolescent alcohol involvement and ethnic identification. *Substance Abuse and Misuse, 32,* 2013–2031.

Beauvais, F., Chaves, E. L., Oetting, E. R., Deffenbacher, J. L., & Cornell, G. R. (1996). Drug use, violence, and victimization among White American, Mexican American and American Indian dropouts, students with academic problems, and students in good standing. *Journal of Counseling Psychology, 43,* 292–299.

Beauvais, F., & LaBoueff, S. (1985). Drug and alcohol abuse prevention in American Indian communities. *International Journal of the Addictions, 20,* 139–171.

Bee-Gates, D., Howard-Pitney, B., LaFromboise, T., & Rowe, W. (1996). Help seeking behavior of Native American Indian high school students. *Professional Psychology: Research and Practice, 27,* 495–499.

Berner, F. (Producer), & Pierson, F. (Director). (1994). *Lakota woman* [Film]. Los Angeles, Inter Video.

Bichsel, R. J., & Mallinckrodt, B. (2001). Cultural commitment and the counseling preferences and counselor perceptions of Native American women. *The Counseling Psychologist, 29,* 858–881.

Bingham, R. P., & Ward, C. M. (1994). Career counseling with ethnic minority women. In W. B. Walsh & S. H. Osipow (Eds.), *Career counseling for women* (pp. 165–186). Hillsdale, NJ: Lawrence Erlbaum Associates.

Bordin, E. S. (1979). The generalizability of the working alliance. *Psychotherapy: Theory, Research, and Practice, 16,* 252–260.

Brown, D. (Ed.). (2003). *Career information, career counseling, and career development* (8th ed.). Boston: Allyn & Bacon.

Brown, L. S. (1994). *Subversive dialogs: Theory in feminist therapy.* New York: HarperCollins.

Byers, A. M., & McCubbin, L. D. (2001). Trends in career development research with racial/ethnic minorities: Prospects and challenges. In J. G. Ponterotto, J. M. Casas, L. A. Suzuki, & C. M. Alexander (Eds.), *Handbook of multicultural counseling* (2nd ed., pp. 425–456). Thousand Oaks, CA: Sage.

Campbell, G. R. (1989). The changing dimension of Native American health: A critical understanding of contemporary Native American health issues. *American Indian Culture and Research Journal, 13*, 1–20.

Canabal, M. E. (1995). Native Americans in higher education. *College Student Journal, 29*, 455–457.

Canby, W. C., Jr. (1998). *American Indian law: In a nutshell.* St. Paul, MN: West Group.

Casas, J. M., & Pytluk, S. D. (1995). Hispanic identity development: Implications for research and practice. In J. G. Ponterotto, J. M. Casas, L. A. Suzuki, & C. M. Alexander (Eds.), *Handbook of multicultural counseling* (2nd ed., pp. 155–180). Thousand Oaks, CA: Sage.

Constantine, M. (2002). The intersection of race, ethnicity, gender, and social class in counseling: Examining selves in cultural contexts. *Journal of Multicultural Counseling and Development, 30*, 210–215.

Cook-Lynn, E. (2001). *Anti-Indianism in modern America: A voice from Tatekeya's earth.* Champaign: University of Illinois Press.

Crazy Horse, R. (n.d.). *Pocahontas myth.* Retrieved October 21, 2003, from http://www.powhatan.org/pocc.html

Cross, W. E., Jr. (1991). *Shades of Black: Diversity in African American identity.* Philadelphia: Temple University Press.

Daley, C., & Daley, S. (2003). Care of American Indians and Alaska Natives. In J. Bigby (Ed.), *Cross cultural medicine* (pp. 95–128). Philadelphia: American College of Physicians.

Daniels, J., D'Andrea, M., & Gaughen, K. J. S. (1998). Testing the validity and reliability of the Perceived Employability Scale (PES) among a culturally diverse population. *Journal of Employment Counseling, 35*, 114–123.

Day, S. X., & Rounds, J. (2000). Universality of vocational interest structure among racial and ethnic minorities. *American Psychologist, 53*, 728–736.

Day, S. X., Rounds, J., & Swaney, K. (1998). The structure of vocational interests for diverse racial-ethnic groups. *Psychological Science, 9*, 40–44.

Deloria, V. (1996). Indian humor. In M. Andersen & P. H. Collins (Eds.), *Race, class, and gender: An anthology* (pp. 341–346). Belmont, CA: Wadsworth.

Deloria, V., Jr., & Wildcat, D. R. (2001). *Power and place: Indian education in America.* Golden, CO: Fulcrum.

DuBray, W. (1992). *Human services and American Indians.* St. Paul, MN: West.

Duran, E., & Duran, B. (1995). *Native American postcolonial psychology.* Albany: State University of New York Press.

Echohawk, M. (1997). Suicide: The scourge of Native American people. *Suicide and Life-Threatening Behavior, 27*, 60–67.

Epperson, D. L., & Hammond, D. (1981). Use of interest inventories with Native Americans: A case for local norms. *Journal of Counseling Psychology, 28*, 213–220.

Estes, L., Rosenfeldt, L. (Producers), & Eyre, C. (Director). (1998). *Smoke signals* [Film]. Seattle: ShadowCatcher Entertainment.

Evansoki, P. D., & Wu Tse, F. (1989). Career awareness program for Chinese and Korean American parents. *Journal of Counseling and Development, 67*, 472–474.

Fisher, A. R., & Moradi, B. (2001). Racial and ethnic identity: Recent developments and needed directions. In J. G. Ponterotto, J. M. Casas, L. A. Suzuki, & C. M. Alexander (Eds.), *Handbook of multicultural counseling* (2nd ed., pp. 341–370). Thousand Oaks, CA: Sage.

Fixico, D. L. (2000). *Urban Indian experience in America.* Albuquerque: University of New Mexico Press.

Flowers, L. A. (2003). *Racial and gender faculty diversity among America's two-year college faculty* (Institute of Higher Education Brief No. 1). Gainesville: University of Florida, Institute of Higher Education.

Fouad, N. A. (1993). Cross-cultural vocational assessment. *Career Development Quarterly, 42,* 4–13.

Gade, E. M., Fuqua, D. R., & Hurlburt, G. (1984). Use of the Self-Directed Search with Native American high school students. *Journal of Counseling Psychology, 31,* 584–587.

Garrett, M. T., & Herring, R. D. (2001). Honoring the power of relation: Counseling Native adults. *Journal for Humanistic Counseling, Education, and Development, 40,* 139–161.

Garrett, M. T., & Myers, J. E. (1996). The rule of opposites: A paradigm for counseling Native Americans. *Journal of Multicultural Counseling and Development, 24,* 89–104.

Garrett, M. T., & Pinchette, E. F. (2000). Red as an apple: Native American acculturation and counseling with or without reservation. *Journal of Counseling and Development, 78,* 193–206.

Garrett, M. T., & Wilbur, M. P. (1999). Does the worm live in the ground? Reflections on Native American spirituality. *Journal of Multicultural Counseling and Development, 27,* 193–206.

Gelso, C., & Fritz, B. (2001). *Counseling psychology* (2nd ed.). Fort Worth, TX: Harcourt.

Gloria, A. M., & Rodriguez, E. R. (2000). Counseling Latino university students: Psychosociocultural issues for consideration. *Journal of Counseling and Development, 78,* 145–154.

Gysbers, N. C., Heppner, M. J., & Johnston, J. A. (1998). *Career counseling: Process, issues and techniques.* Needham Heights, MA: Allyn & Bacon.

Hansen, J. C., Scullard, M. G., & Haviland, M. G. (2000). The interest structure of Native American college students. *Journal of Career Assessment, 8,* 159–165.

Hansen, R. N., & Johnston, J. A. (1989). *Missouri Occupational Card Sort* (College Form, 2nd ed.). Columbia: University of Missouri-Columbia, Career Planning and Placement Center.

Hartmann, B. (1987). *Reproductive rights and wrongs.* New York: Harper & Row.

Haviland, M. G., & Hansen, J. C. (1988). Criterion validity of the Strong-Campbell Interest Inventory for American Indian college students. *Measurement and Evaluation in Counseling and Development, 19,* 196–201.

Helms, J. E. (1994). Racial identity and career assessment. *Journal of Career Assessment, 2,* 199–209.

Herring, R. D. (1990). Attacking career myths among Native Americans: Implications for counseling. *The School Counselor, 38,* 13–18.

Herring, R. D. (1992). Seeing a new paradigm: Counseling Native Americans. *Journal of Multicultural Counseling and Development, 20,* 35–43.

Ho, M. K. (1987). *Family therapy with ethnic minorities.* Newbury Park, CA: Sage.

Huhndorf, S. M. (2001). *Going Native: Indians in the American cultural imagination.* Ithaca, NY: Cornell University Press.

Indian Health Service. (1996). *Indian health focus: Women.* Rockville, MD: U.S. Public Health Service.

Indian Health Service. (n.d.). *Indian Health Service Introduction.* Retrieved October 21, 2003, from http://www.ihs.gov/PublicInfo/PublicAffairs/Welcome_Info/IHSintro.asp

Indian Self-Determination and Education Assistance Act of 1975, Pub. L. No. 93-638 (1975).

Johnson, M. J., Swartz, J. L., & Martin, W. E., Jr. (1995). Applications of psychological theories for career development with Native Americans. In F. T. L. Leong (Ed.), *Career development and vocational behavior of racial and ethnic minorities* (pp. 103–133). Hillsdale, NJ: Lawrence Erlbaum Associates.

Juntunen, C. L., Barraclough, D. J., Broneck, C. L., Seibel, G. A., Winrow, S. A., & Morin, P. M. (2001). American Indian perspectives on the career journey. *Journal of Counseling Psychology, 48,* 272–285.

Kilik, J., & Pomier, J. (Producers), & Eyre, C. (Director). (2002). *Skins* [Film]. Los Angeles: First Look Media.

Kilpatrick, J. (1999). *Celluloid Indians: Native Americans and film.* Lincoln: University of Nebraska Press.

Kim, B. S., & Abreu, J. M. (2001). Acculturation measurement: Theory, current instruments, and future directions. In J. G. Ponterotto, J. M. Casas, L. A. Suzuki, & C. M. Alexander (Eds.), *Handbook of multicultural counseling* (2nd ed., pp. 394–424). Thousand Oaks, CA: Sage.

Koegel, H. M., Donin, I., Ponterotto, J. G., & Spitz, S. (1995). Multicultural career development: A methodological critique of 8 years of research in three leading career journals. *Journal of Employment Counseling, 32,* 50–63.

Kramer, B. J. (1992). Health and aging of urban American Indians. *Western Journal of Medicine, 157,* 281–285.

Krebs, E., Hurlburt, G., & Schwartz, C. (1988). Vocational self-estimates and perceived competencies of Native high school students: Implications for vocational guidance counselling. *Canadian Journal of Counselling, 22,* 212–225.

LaDuke, W. (1999). *Last standing woman.* Stillwater, MN: Voyageur Press.

LaFromboise, T. (1998). American Indian mental health policy. In D. R. Atkinson, G. Morten, & D. W. Sue (Eds.), *Counseling American minorities* (pp. 137–158). Boston: McGraw-Hill.

LaFromboise, T. D., Berman, J. S., & Sohi, B. K. (1994). American Indian women. In L. Comas-Díaz & B. Greene (Eds.), *Women of color: Integrating ethnic and gender identities in psychotherapy* (pp. 30–71). New York: Guilford Press.

LaFromboise, T. D., Trimble, J. E., & Mohatt, G. V. (1990). Counseling intervention and American Indian tradition: An integrative approach. *The Counseling Psychologist, 18,* 628–654.

Lattimore, R. R., & Borgen, F. H. (1999). Validity of the 1994 Strong Interest Inventory with racial and ethnic groups in the United States. *Journal of Counseling Psychology, 46,* 185–195.

Leung, S. A. (1995). Career development and counseling: A multicultural perspective. In J. G. Ponterotto, J. M. Casas, L. A. Suzuki, & C. M. Alexander (Eds.), *Handbook of multicultural counseling* (pp. 549–566). Thousand Oaks, CA: Sage.

Luzzo, D. A., McWhirter, E. H., & Hutcheson, K. G. (1997). Evaluating career decision-making factors associated with employment among first-year college students. *Journal of College Student Development, 38,* 166–172.

Lysne, M., & Levy, G. D. (1997). Differences in ethnic identity in Native American adolescents as a function of school context. *Journal of Adolescent Research, 12,* 372–388.

Marshall, C. A., Johnson, M. J., Martin, W. E., Jr., Saravanabhavan, R. C., & Bradford, B. (1992). The rehabilitation needs of American Indians with disabilities in an urban setting. *Journal of Rehabilitation, 58,* 13–21.

Marshall, C. A., Sanders, J. E., & Hill, C. R. (2001). Family voices in rehabilitation research. In C. A. Marshall (Ed.), *Rehabilitation and American Indians with disabilities: A handbook for administrators, practitioners, and researchers* (pp. 165–175). Athens, GA: Elliot & Fitzpatrick.

Martin, W. E., Jr. (1991). Career development and American Indians living on reservations: Cross-cultural factors to consider. *Career Development Quarterly, 39,* 273–283.

Martin, W. E., Jr. (1995). Career development assessment and interventions strategies with American Indians. In F. T. L. Leong (Ed.), *Career development and vocational behavior of racial and ethnic minorities* (pp. 227–248). Hillsdale, NJ: Lawrence Erlbaum Associates.

Martin, W. E., Jr., & Farris, K. K. (1994). A cultural and contextual decision path approach to career assessment with Native Americans: A psychological perspective. *Journal of Career Assessment, 2,* 258–275.

McCormick, R. M., & Amundson, N. E. (1997). A career-life planning model for First Nations people. *Journal of Employment Counseling, 34,* 171–179.

McNicol, S. G., & Baker, J. B. (1998). *Cross cultural practice: Assessment, treatment and training.* New York: Wiley.

Middlebrook, D. L., Lemaster, P. L., Beals, J., Novins, D. K., & Manson, S. M. (2001). Suicide prevention in American Indian and Alaska Native communities: A critical review of programs. *Suicide and Life-Threatening Behavior, 31*, 132–149.

Mihesuah, D. A. (2003). *Indigenous American women: Decolonization, empowerment, activism.* Lincoln: University of Nebraska Press.

Momaday, N. S. (1999). *House made of dawn.* New York: Perennial Press.

Morgan, C. O., Guy, E., Lee, B., & Cellini, H. R. (1986). Rehabilitation services for American Indians: The Navajo experience. *Journal of Rehabilitation, 52*, 25–31.

Morgan, J. I., & Skovholt, T. M. (1978). Using inner experience: Fantasy and daydreams in career counseling. *Journal of Counseling Psychology, 24*, 391–397.

Nabokov, P. (2003). Native American testimony: A chronicle of Indian-White relations from prophecy to the present, 1492–2000. New York: Penguin Books.

Napier, L. A. (1996). Nine Native women: Pursuing the doctorate and aspiring to positions of leadership. In K. D. Arnold, K. D. Noble, & R. F. Subotnik (Eds.), *Remarkable women: Perspectives on female talent development. Perspectives on creativity* (pp. 133–148). Cresskill, NJ: Hampton Press.

National Center for Education Statistics. (1999). *Digest of education statistics.* Washington, DC: Author.

National Women's Health Information Center. (n.d.). *Women of color health data book.* Retrieved January 29, 2003, from http://www.4women.gov/owh/pub/woc/native.htm

Neumann, H., McCormick, R. M., Amundson, N. E., & McLean, H. B. (2000). Career counseling for First Nations youth: Applying the First Nations career-life planning model. *Canadian Journal of Counselling, 34*, 172–185.

O'Connell, R. L. (1989). *Of arms and men: A history of war, weapons, and aggression.* Oxford, UK: Oxford University Press.

Parham, T. A. (1989). Cycles of psychological nigrecence. *The Counseling Psychologist, 17*, 187–226.

Patterson K. B., & Runge, T. (2002). Smallpox and the Native American. *American Journal of Medical Science, 323*, 216–222.

Peterson, N., & Gonzalez, R. C. (2000). *The role of work in people's lives: Applied career counseling and vocational psychology.* Belmont, CA: Wadsworth.

Pierre, M. S., & Long Soldier, T. (1995). *Walking in the sacred manner: Healers, dreamers, and pipe carriers. Medicine women of the plains.* New York: Touchstone.

Pinderhughes, E. (1989). *Understanding race, ethnicity and power: The key to efficacy in clinical practice.* New York: Free Press.

Ponterotto, J. G., Fuertes, J. N., & Chen, E. C. (2000). Models of multicultural counseling. In S. D. Brown & R. W. Lent (Eds.), *Handbook of counseling psychology* (3rd ed., pp. 639–669). New York: Wiley.

Robison, J. (1977, May 22). "U.S. Sterilizes 25 Percent of Indian Women: Study." *Chicago Tribune,* sec. 1, p. 36.

Rountree, H. (2001). Pocahontas: The hostage who became famous. In T. Perdue (Ed.), *Sifters: Native American women's lives* (pp. 14–28). New York: Oxford University Press.

Rousseau, P. (1995). Native-American elders: Health care status. *Clinical Geriatric Medicine, 11*, 83–95.

Shapiro, T. (1985). *Population control politics.* Philadelphia: Temple University Press.

Silko, L. M. (1988). *Ceremony.* New York: Penguin Books.

Stannard, D. (1992). *American holocaust: The conquest of the new world.* New York: Oxford University Press.

Steele, J. (1996). Reduced to images: American Indians in nineteenth century advertising. In S. E. Bird (Ed.), *Dressing in feathers: The construction of the Indian in American popular culture* (pp. 45–64). Boulder, CO: Westview Press.

Stone, M. (1998). Journaling with clients. *Journal of Individual Psychology, 54*, 535–545.

Sue, D. W., & Sue, D. (1990). *Counseling the culturally different: Theory and practice.* New York: Wiley.

Tafoya, T. (1989). Circles and cedar: Native Americans and family therapy. *Journal of Psychotherapy and the Family, 6,* 71–98.

Taylor, M. (2000). The influence of self-efficacy on alcohol use among American Indians. *Cultural Diversity and Ethnic Minority Psychology, 6,* 152–167.

Trusty, J. (2002). Counseling for career development with persons of color. In S. G. Niles (Ed.), *Adult career development: Concepts, issues and practices* (3rd ed., pp. 190–213). Columbus, OH: National Career Development Association.

Turner, S. L., & Lapan, R. T. (2003). Native American adolescent career development. *Journal of Career Development, 30,* 159–172.

U.S. Bureau of the Census. (n.d). *American Indian and Alaska Native populations 2000: Census 2000 brief.* Retrieved December 15, 2003, from http://www.census.gov/prod/2002pubs/c2kbr01-15.pdf

Unrau, W. (1990). The depopulation of the Kansa Indians. In P. K. Stuewe (Ed.), *Kansas revisited: Historical images and perspectives* (pp. 64–75). Lawrence: University of Kansas, Division of Continuing Education.

Utter, J. (1993). *American Indians: Answers to today's questions.* Lake Ann, MI: National Woodlands.

Ward, C. M., & Bingham, R. P. (1993). Career assessment of ethnic minority women. *Journal of Career Assessment, 1,* 246–257.

Weisbord, R. (1975). *Genocide? Birth control and the Black American.* Westport, CT: Greenwood Press.

Welch, D. (1988). American Indian women: Reaching beyond the myth. In C. Calloway (Ed.), *New directions in American Indian history* (pp. 31–48). Norman: University of Oklahoma Press.

Wood, P. B., & Clay, W. C. (1996). Perceived structural barriers and academic performance among American Indian high school students. *Youth and Society, 28,* 40–61.

Youga, J. (1995). Journal writing. In M. Ballou (Ed.), *Psychological interventions: A guide to strategies* (pp. 137–151). Westport, CT: Praeger.

Chapter 11

Career Counseling With Lesbian Clients

Kathleen J. Bieschke
Elizabeth Toepfer-Hendey
Pennsylvania State University

Current career-counseling models were not specifically designed to meet the needs of lesbian career clients. Cook, Heppner, and O'Brien (2002a) proposed an ecological career-counseling perspective for women that seems to be particularly well suited to the needs of lesbian career clients as well. Such a perspective acknowledges the dynamic interplay between the person and the environment as well as the importance of understanding a person in context. At a minimum, lesbian career clients face unique career concerns due to their sexual orientation as well as their gender. Furthermore, like other career clients, lesbians must contend with other aspects of their identity that may be marginalized and unacknowledged in current career-counseling models (e.g., race-ethnicity, socioeconomic status [SES], disability). An ecological model encourages the counselor to carefully consider interventions focused on changing person-environment interactions.

In this chapter, we apply the ecological model (Bronfenbrenner, 1977) to career interventions with lesbian women. First, we articulate the assumptions that we believe underlie this chapter. Next, we describe in depth the ecological model proposed by Bronfenbrenner and its applicability to providing a contextual understanding of the career behavior of lesbian women. We then describe the many factors influencing the contexts in which lesbians live that must be understood in order to get a full picture of their career development. We discuss three areas relevant to the career concerns of lesbian women from an ecological perspective, including vocational choice, role management, and identity management issues. We end the chapter by discussing the application of the ecological model to career counseling with lesbian women.

ASSUMPTIONS

Prior to discussing the ecological model and issues of particular relevance for lesbian career clients, we believe it is important to explicate the assumptions underlying this chapter. Although we elaborate on some of these assumptions in subsequent sections, in general the following beliefs are infused throughout the chapter and serve to inform our beliefs about career counseling with lesbian clients. Knowledge of these assumptions will provide a context for understanding our approach to career counseling with this population:

- Lesbian women and bisexual women present with similar but not identical career-counseling issues. Given that the majority of the writing in this area is focused on lesbian women, our chapter also focuses primarily on this group.
- Lesbian women must attend to issues regarding sexual orientation within a gendered context.
- We agree that "lesbian identity and career development processes are interactive and mutually reciprocal" (Driscoll, Kelley, & Fassinger, 1996, p. 229).
- Similar to McCarn and Fassinger's (1996) theory of identity development specific to lesbian women, we do not believe that being out is necessarily an indication of advanced development.
- Lesbian and bisexual individuals may experience increased stress in comparison to heterosexual individuals but the etiology for this stress stems not from sexual orientation per se but rather from a social context that pathologizes homosexuality (Waldo, 1999).
- For career counseling to be effective for lesbian women, it must take place within a context of affirmation of the client's sexual identity.
- When working with lesbians, career counselors must also be sensitive to multiple diversities, such as SES, race-ethnicity, disability, religion, and culture.
- Career counselors can advocate for the utilization of strengths and normalize experiences related to sexual identity development.
- All counselors and career-counseling work environments are heterosexist to varying degrees.
- Lesbian clients may or may not reveal their sexual orientation to the counselor; it is important to be affirmative of sexual orientation with all clients, not just women who are openly lesbian or bisexual.

ECOLOGICAL PERSPECTIVE

Cook et al. (2002a) advocated for the incorporation of an ecological perspective in career counseling, particularly when working with women. Lesbian women represent at least two marginalized groups in American society (i.e., sexual orientation and gender). Diversity in race as well as SES and educational status can add to the complexity of women's perspectives and life experiences. As developing individuals within environments that are always changing, a lesbian woman's career development is influenced by both internal and external factors. Applying an ecological perspective to career-counseling work with lesbian women allows for the consideration of, and interventions informed by, the dynamic interplay between the individual and the environment. This section provides a brief summary of the importance of considering contextual factors when attempting to understand the career development of lesbians. We then describe the application of Bronfenbrenner's (1977, 1979) theoretical model of human development to career counseling with this population.

The general practice of career counseling includes primary consideration of individual traits with some recognition of contextual factors. The process of career counseling continues to be practiced in a structured manner reminiscent of traditional models of career development (Gysbers, Heppner, & Johnston, 2003). Research and theories addressing women's career development have rapidly expanded over the last 30 years and have incorporated the influence of social and political trends on the individual (Betz & Fitzgerald, 1987; Hackett & Betz, 1981). The social issue of oppression due to gender, race, and other forms of discrimination, however, remains much the same (Fitzgerald, Fassinger, & Betz, 1995).

A variety of theories have evolved that include the consideration of contextual factors in the career development of the individual (Hackett & Betz, 1981; Lent, Brown, & Hackett, 1994; Super, 1990, 1994). Cook et al. (2002a) proposed the application of an ecological counseling perspective when working with women:

> The ecological perspective generally states that human behavior results from the ongoing, dynamic interaction between the person and the environment. Behavior is the result of a multiplicity of factors at the individual, interpersonal, and broader sociocultural levels . . . a person's behavior is . . . a representation of the complex interaction among the myriad factors that constitute her or his life, referred to as the *ecosystem.* (p. 296)

Women's experiences are shaped not only by their own actions and beliefs, but also by societal and group expectations and assumptions.

The ecological counseling perspective is based on the work of Bronfenbrenner (1977, 1979), who proposed a theoretical model of human development that accounts for the developing person in the context of the environment. This theory stresses the interaction between the person and the environment. The individual is conceived of as a developing human being with individual traits and qualities. However, Bronfenbrenner's (1979) model describes an ecological environment in which the individual's development is influenced by the:

> progressive accommodation, throughout the life span, between the growing human organism and the changing environments in which it actually lives and grows. The latter includes not only the immediate setting containing the developing person but also the larger social contexts, both formal and informal, in which these settings are embedded. The changing relation between person and environment is conceived in systems terms. (Bronfenbrenner, 1977, p. 513)

Envisioned as a nested set of structures, Bronfenbrenner (1977) identified four major subsystems that influence human behaviors: the microsystem, mesosystem, exosystem, and macrosystem. An individual's development is influenced by the interaction of these multiple systems. It is important to note that Bronfenbrenner (1979) envisioned developing persons not only as influenced by the environment, but also as dynamic entities that can restructure the microsystems within which they reside. The individual attributes of a person therefore interact with the environment. Understanding key elements of these systems allows for the application of the ecological model to career-counseling interventions for lesbian women. Individual and contextual variables can be actively considered in this model. In an effort to explicate the applicability of Bronfenbrenner's (1977, 1979) model to career counseling with lesbian women, we describe each of the systems in turn and provide examples of how they may be operational in the lives of lesbian women.

The microsystem "is a pattern of activities, roles, and interpersonal relations experienced by the developing person in a given setting with particular physical and material characteristics" (Bronfenbrenner, 1979, p. 22). Interpersonal relations occur within these settings and additional factors of these settings include time, participants, and physical features. People have varying roles in their microsystems and behaviors vary accordingly. For an adult lesbian woman, these settings might include her work, home, and community. She may participate as an employee, partner, parent, advocate, church member, or peer. Relationships in these settings may include supervisor-employee, partner-partner, parent-child, parent-teacher, and volunteer-client. Her expectations and behaviors, depending on her role, may vary in each microsystem.

The mesosystem "comprises the interrelations among two or more settings in which the developing person actively participates (such as, for a child, the relations among home, school, and neighborhood peer group; for an adult, among family, work, and social life)" (Bronfenbrenner, 1979, p. 25). The mesosystem is an interaction of microsystems that contain the developing person at a certain point in time. Individuals experience shifts in roles and expectations across microsystems, and the events in one system can influence individuals' behavior and development in another. In addition, the nature of these interconnections can have a positive or negative influence on the development of individuals. Mesosystem variables can include relations between work and home, and home and peer groups. For a lesbian woman of color, attitudes and behaviors toward lesbian women within her own cultural context may influence her behaviors in other settings. The mesosystem of home and work may also cause conflict. For example, if a lesbian woman has chosen not to divulge her sexual orientation at work and lives with a partner, limiting the interaction between these two systems may create career difficulties and personal strain.

The exosystem is an extension of the mesosystem and the external context in which the prior two systems are embedded. It "refers to one or more settings that do not involve the developing person as an active participant, but in which events occur that affect, or are affected by, what happens in the setting containing the developing person" (Bronfenbrenner, 1979, p. 25). This system includes formal and informal social structures such as the world of work, characteristics of a neighborhood, mass media, social networks, and other influences on an individual. Individuals can be influenced by situations that occur in settings in which they are not present or events that influence a person that they relate to on a regular basis. For example, the partner of a lesbian women who has experienced harassment at work due to sexual orientation (or other marginalized identities) may become fearful of a similar event occurring in her own life.

The fourth and final system Bronfenbrenner proposed is the macrosystem. The macrosystem differs from the preceding systems. It "refers to the overarching institutional patterns of the culture or subculture, such as the economic, social, educational, legal, and political systems, of which micro-, meso-, and exosystems are their concrete manifestations" (Bronfenbrenner, 1977, p. 515). Macrosystems are informal general prototypes that are carriers of information and ideology. They provide overarching institutional patterns of cultures and subcultures (Bronfenbrenner). They contain cultural values, norms, beliefs, and societal ideologies. At a macrosystem level, lesbian women may be influenced by gender stereotyping regarding careers that are deemed appropriate for women. Furthermore, expectations that a heterosexual lifestyle is the norm are also an important part of the macrosystem for lesbian women.

The ecological model of career development as developed by Cook, Heppner, and O'Brien (2002b) recognizes that individual and ecosystem variables are not distinct. Career behaviors evolve from an ongoing interaction between the person and his or her environment. Meaning making is also an important construct in this theory. As defined by Sexton and Griffin (1997), Herr (1999), and others, meaning making is an interpretive process that involves an individual trying to make sense of life events. It is the cognitive process within an individual that can account for variations in career development and behaviors.

Cook et al.'s (2002b) ecological model of career development provides us with core principles to consider as we explore key aspects of lesbian women's experiences. These principles include consideration of individuals' interplay with their ecosystem in understanding career behavior, the dynamic relationships between ecosystem levels, the uniqueness of individuals' experiences and subsystems, and the dynamics of ecosystems on individuals' inter- and intrapersonal experiences. It is also understood that individuals have an influence on their ecosystem in multiple ways. The ecological model of career development is discussed in more detail later in this chapter; this model, however, can provide a framework to consider lesbians' career development as we discuss the contextual issues lesbians face.

THE CONTEXT OF LESBIAN WOMEN

We believe it is important to provide as much context as possible for understanding lesbian career clients (Fitzgerald & Betz, 1994). We begin by discussing from a macrosystem perspective the complexities lesbian women face due to their gender and sexual orientation and, potentially, other marginalized identities. We then go on to describe in detail three issues of particular importance to lesbian women (i.e., vocational choice, role management, and identity management), incorporating an ecological perspective where appropriate. We believe career-counseling interventions are most effective when understanding lesbian women within their own context. Only once we have addressed in detail these contextual issues do we turn to describing career-counseling interventions that can be used with this population.

The Influence of Marginalized Identities

The ecological model of career development (Cook et al., 2002b) contends that individuals live interactionally within ecosystems. Fassinger (1996) noted that "lesbians, because they experience a double or, for women of color, triple minority status in the work world, are subject to even greater discrimination based on the intersection of gender, sexual orientation, and race" (p. 166). Lesbian women can belong to a number of groups of people marginalized in American society due to their race, SES, religious affiliation, or disability status. As members of these groups, they will likely experience discrimination, unequal treatment, and oppression. Gender and racial identity development, and experiences of stigmatization related to other marginalized status, all contribute to a lesbian woman's career development and experience. Understanding of the complexities of women's lives can facilitate counselors' ability to help their clients to integrate aspects of themselves into their career planning. The ecological model allows for the consideration of these multiple environmental influences on the individual and is particularly relevant for informing career interventions due to consideration of individual, microsystem, exosystem, and macrosystem issues.

Sexual Orientation. As is likely obvious, it is important to recognize that sexual orientation has a minority status and that lesbians experience oppression and its effects. An effective career counselor must first approach work with lesbian clients with the understanding that their clients experience oppression, most likely on multiple levels. Waldo (1999) found that gay, lesbian, and bisexual individuals have unique stressful experiences related to their minority status. Stress can result when working in a male-dominated and heterosexist environment. In addition, an effect of this minority status may be that individuals may or may not have had preparation in dealing with oppression, depending on where clients are in their lesbian identity development. The ability to cope with oppression may be mediated by race or other attributes that may also result in oppression. Finally, models of sexual orientation discuss the issue of the decision to be out. Yet cultural, religious, and other contextual factors may have an influence on the decision to be out at work, home, or the community. As mentioned previously, later in this chapter we discuss in detail issues of particular concern to lesbian women, including vocational interests and choice, multiple roles, and identity management in the workplace; here we merely acknowledge the ever-present existence and possible manifestations of societal views based on sexual orientation.

Gender. The impact of gender on lesbian women's career experiences has been the most extensively studied of the issues relevant to diversity, perhaps due to the increase of work completed on gender and women's career behavior in general. Extensive reviews of the vocational development and career counseling of women have been completed over the last three decades (Betz, 1994; Fitzgerald et al., 1995; Gysbers et al., 2003). Although reviewing the breadth of this work is outside the scope of this chapter, key issues relevant to work with lesbian clients in career counseling are presented.

Cook (1993) argued that gender-based differences continue in society and manifest themselves in sex segregation in the labor market. A higher number of women continue in lower paying occupations, make less than their male peers, and underutilize their skills. Gender-role and occupational stereotyping occurs regularly in home, educational, and work settings (Badgett, 1996; Matlin, 1996). Lack of role models and the null environments in these settings continue to act to discourage women from pursuing their career aspirations. Finally, gender-biased career counselors assisting women continue to propagate these beliefs (see Betz, 1994; Cook et al., 2002; Gysbers et al., 2003, for extensive reviews).

The career development of lesbian women has been influenced by this gendered experience. Hetherington and Orzek (1989) and Hetherington (1991) contended that in explaining differences in career development, gender may be more significant than sexual orientation. Lesbians do not escape the gender socialization process. Yet, given that their sexual orientation is gender inappropriate, lesbians may be forced to consider other aspects of gender socialization as well. Furthermore, lesbian women may be affected differently by gender-dominated messages due to experiences and differing needs. For example, there is some evidence to suggest that lesbians as a group value gender-nonconforming behaviors (Morgan & Brown, 1991). Self-concept may be influenced in part by the socialization that occurs and opportunities perceived.

Race. Fukuyama and Ferguson (2000) contended that lesbian, gay, and bisexual (LGB) people of color are confronted with the need to manage multiple oppressions such as racism, sexism, and heterosexism. The authors assume that all phenomena have a cultural context, and that the social structure of the United States is based on a dominant paradigm that marginalizes people who are different and favors heterosexual, White, male, Eurocentric, and Christian values. The values of this paradigm are reflected in psychology, where developmental models have stressed the importance of the individualization of self. However, the development of the individual self is influenced by group memberships. For many people of color, cultural norms have valued the development of collective identities. The notion that identity itself is formed by ecosystem influences is vital to consider when understanding lesbian women's experiences. Many authors have commented on the dearth of research pertaining to lesbian women of color (Alquijay, 1997; Croteau & Bieschke, 1996; Soto, 1997).

The identity of lesbian women of color can be conceptualized through multiple identity models, such as their gender, race, and sexual identity development. Concurrent identity development becomes relevant in terms of issues and barriers with which an individual is confronted. It is thus important to consider key issues relevant to racial, gender, and sexual identity development to understand the whole person.

First, prior to focusing specifically on lesbian women of color, it is important to understand what has been studied regarding career development issues of minority group members (see Leong, 1995; Walsh, Bingham, Brown, & Ward, 2001, for excellent reviews). Gysbers et al. (2003) argued that the Western European worldview has been the basis of career development practice. They outlined tenets to consider when working with lesbian clients of color, including individualism and autonomy, affluence, structure of opportunity open to all who strive, centrality of work in people's lives, and the linearity of career development. These tenets provide a framework to understand how race may influence lesbian women from minority cultures. Identifying culture-specific differences is important, as is attending to clients' within-group variability in gender, social class, and education level. Understanding a lesbian client's worldview, acculturation level, and racial identity development is necessary to provide culturally appropriate career interventions (Gysbers et al.).

Issues that LGB people of color cope with can be applicable to lesbian women of color. Lesbian women may be coping with choosing to be visible and out in their microsystem settings, for example, within the White culture, their ethnic communities, the lesbian community, their work life, or their church community. Davidson and Huenefeld (2002) discussed the case of a Chinese American lesbian woman, Eileen, seeking counseling for career decision making who discussed this dynamic in her life. Eileen's multiple identities, as a woman, a lesbian, and a Chinese American, have an impact on her vision of a career as well as how a career counselor can work to assist her. As the authors suggested, working with Eileen begins with exploring her sense of self as a woman, a lesbian, and a Chinese American. The interplay of Eileen's self-concept and her exosystem are important to consider when assisting with her career development.

This example highlights the differences across ethnic groups that can influence women in their career implementation. In addition, individuals' experience of and ability to manage discrimination due to racism, sexism, and homophobia can have a direct impact on their self-concept, abilities, and desire to succeed. Career counselors must be vigilant in their consideration of gender and race issues when working with lesbian women, however, they must also take into consideration differences related to SES, disability status, and religious affiliation.

SES, Disability, and Religion. Socioeconomic backgrounds vary tremendously. Recent data on the household population of the United States (U.S. Bureau of the Census, 2002) indicated that 26% of people 25 years and over have a bachelor's degree or higher, 12% of people live in poverty, and 28% of families with a female head of household and no husband present have incomes below poverty level. Variability in SES can have a tremendous impact on a lesbian woman's self-concept and exosystem experience. Access to role models, opportunities, and resources can be greatly influenced by family-of-origin SES. If welfare has been part of a family of origin's support network, for example, impressions of societal and government attitudes toward work may influence a woman's expectations and self-concept. In contrast, if part of an upper-class family, perceptions of opportunities and resources will differ. This component of a lesbian's life must be fully assessed in order to understand the individual and exosystem influences.

Disability status can also have an impact on lesbian women's experience. People with physical, learning, and psychological disabilities have a broad range of issues, strengths, and challenges that contribute to their development. In addition, although there is macrosystem recognition of the need for assistance and accommodation through federal laws, there is also stigma and stereotyping in the environment that can have an impact on self-concept and self-efficacy. A career counselor working with a lesbian woman needs to fully assess disability status to understand that woman's perspective, identity development, and outcome expectations. Being familiar with the literature on career development and interventions relevant to the needs of persons with disabilities is vital for the career counselor.

Spirituality and religion have also recently been discussed as contextual factors that contribute to an individual's career development (e.g., Bloch & Richmond, 1997; Colozzi & Colozzi, 2000; Hansen, 1997; Lent et al., 1994) and these issues may be particularly salient for lesbians. The discovery of work that fulfills a quest for meaning, the desire to follow a "calling" related to a personal spiritual need, and the honoring of a client's values specific to spiritual experience are some of the issues discussed. Spirituality is often not addressed in career counseling, yet religion is a social structure that influences the macrosystem messages that clients receive. What is surmised is that many conservative religions judge homosexuality to be against religious doctrine, and lesbian women's experiences and decisions regarding in what settings to be out will be affected by this (see Davidson, 2000, for a fuller discussion of these issues). The stigma related to sexual orientation has influenced opportunities in organized religious settings and may also influence lesbian women's perception of possibilities in the work world.

Summary.   The preceding discussion highlighted why attending to lesbian's multiple identities is important when attempting to understand the career development of lesbian career clients. Although every lesbian career client must attend to the complexities of being both female and lesbian, clearly, other marginalized identities can further complicate the presenting career concerns. Though the preceding discussion was not exhaustive, our hope is that it will prompt career counselors to seek out information about these as well as other identities.

Vocational Choice Issues

In order to fully understand the context of lesbian women, career counselors need to understand the vocational choice issues these clients face. Certainly, our previous discussion of marginalized identities underlies the present one. Furthermore, career counseling with lesbian clients around vocational choice issues must take these identities into account when considering career interventions. Much has been written about vocational choice and implementation issues for lesbian women (e.g., Degges-White & Shoffner, 2002; Hetherington & Orzek, 1989; Morgan & Brown, 1991). In particular, Fassinger (1995, 1996) thoroughly described the existing literature and integrated it with the extensive literature focused on women's career development. But although a wealth of scholarly thought and anecdotal information is available, little of it is based on empirical data (Croteau, Anderson, Distefano, & Kampa-Kokesch, 2000). We now summarize the scholarly and empirical literature relative to three areas that influence vocational choice: identity development, vocational interests, and opportunity structures. Where appropriate, we discuss how this information can be incorporated into an ecological model of career counseling for lesbian women.

Identity Development. Fassinger (1995) asserted that vocational identity is interwoven with other aspects of identity, including gender, race, and sexual orientation. The development and influence of a lesbian identity is seen as unique and distinct from that of a gay male identity. Fassinger discussed in detail how gender-role socialization (which emphasizes one's relationships with others) combined with a repression of sexual desire adds a level of complexity to the process not experienced by gay men. Such factors may result in an extended period of questioning and exploration, which may explain why women tend to come out later in life than men do (Garnets & Kimmel, 1991).

Such a delay has long been posited to have a deleterious effect on lesbian's vocational development (e.g., Fassinger, 1995; Morgan & Brown, 1991; Morrow, 1997). Morgan and Brown stated that women who come out at an earlier age might be better able make an informed career decision, one that takes into account their identity as lesbians. Fassinger discussed four reasons why lesbians' career development might particularly suffer if the exploration of lesbian identity occurs during late adolescence and early adulthood, often when their heterosexual counterparts are thought to be in the throes of career decision making. First, lesbians intensely involved in the coming-out process are often renegotiating their relationships with their family and social networks, exploring their sexuality, and establishing intimate relationships. Little energy may be left to devote to career concerns. Second, coming to terms with one's sexual orientation may result in the elimination of some appealing careers (e.g., teaching), further lengthening the career decision-making process. Third, some lesbians may be faced with the loss of support from their families as well as other important members of their social support system, further complicating career development. For example, Herring (1998) discussed his perception that school counselors may be reluctant or resistant to discussing the influence of sexual orientation on career planning. Finally, Fassinger discussed how coming to terms with one's lesbian identity might result in a temporary loss of self-esteem as well as the alteration of one's self-concept that may further complicate the career-planning process.

Preliminary empirical evidence is supportive of some of these assertions. Results of a qualitative study by Boatwright, Gilbert, Forrest, and Ketzenberger (1996) suggest that lesbian women experience a "second adolescence" in the process of coming out. Furthermore, their results suggest that establishing one's lesbian identity does "delay, disrupt, and in some cases seriously derail the career development process" (p. 210). Their interview data suggest that earlier career decisions are often reexamined and that only after one's personal identity is established can well-considered decisions be made about one's career. Some of the women in their study described feeling "behind" their age-appropriate heterosexual counterparts. Nauta, Saucier, and Woodard (2001) found that lesbian (and gay) college students reported less support for career decision making than heterosexual college students.

Furthermore, given the preceding findings, career counselors may assume that one way they can be of assistance to lesbian career clients is to hasten the identity development process. Clearly, lesbian career clients can struggle with vocational issues at any phase of identity development (Croteau et al., 2000). Yet, career counselors must also understand that contextual factors influence lesbian identity development, particularly in regard to decisions about coming out. Previous identity models seemed to associate advanced development with the decision to widely disclose one's sexual orientation (e.g., Cass, 1984). McCarn and Fassinger (1996) proposed a theory of lesbian identity development that takes into account an individual's unique characteristics (e.g., age, race and ethnicity, class, religion) relative to the identity development process and to decisions about disclosure. In their model, two parallel, reciprocal processes were proposed. Individual sexual identity refers to the person's recognition and acceptance of same-sex attraction. Group membership identity refers to the acceptance of one's membership in an oppressed group. Within each of these processes, an individual may experience the following phases: awareness, exploration, deepening and commitment, and internalization and synthesis. McCarn and Fassinger stressed the importance of not focusing on disclosure as the end goal. Rather, they focused on the process of resolving decisions about disclosure or the manner in which these decisions are resolved as reflective of one's maturity. Furthermore, this model is consistent with a mesosystem perspective as it clearly incorporates the integration of two or more microsystems and does not arbitrarily predetermine one particular outcome.

Career Interests. Given the complexities associated with identity development for lesbians, one might reasonably assume that the formation of career interests is complicated as well. Croteau et al. (2000), in their review of the vocational psychology literature for LGB individuals, concluded that the research in this area has centered around the hypothesis that gender-role socialization influences the development of career interests differently for lesbian and gay individuals and heterosexual individuals. In particular, LGB individuals are assumed to be more gender nontraditional than heterosexual individuals. Croteau et al. reported that some authors (e.g., Fassinger, 1995, 1996; Morgan & Brown, 1991) have commented that this may be perceived as an advantage for lesbian women as they are more likely to resist pressure to pursue gender-traditional interests and occupations that are often associated with lower status and salaries.

Hetherington and Orzek (1989), among others (e.g., Fassinger, 1996), posited that lesbian women may need to be more aware of their earning power than heterosexual women, given that they are unlikely to partner with a male wage earner. Morgan and Brown (1991) broadened this assertion, stating that lesbians often do not assume financial dependency between partners. Furthermore, Morgan and Brown stated that given the lack of legal status afforded lesbian partnerships, work-related benefits one might receive via a partner's employment cannot be assumed. Badgett (2002, p. 8725) also noted the potential economic consequences of "being cut off from family support, being denied housing or access to important public resources, and facing discrimination in employment." Multiple scholars concluded that opting for nontraditional occupations may be one way for lesbians to narrow the wage gap between the sexes and provide themselves the best possible support (Chung, 1995; Fassinger, 1995, 1996; Morgan & Brown). In fact, lesbian women earn significantly more (20%–35%) than other equally skilled women and have higher educational levels than other men and women (Black, Gates, Sanders, & Taylor, 2000).

Opportunity Structure. As discussed earlier, many studies document that sex stereotyping of occupations begins at an early age (e.g., Matlin, 1996). There are no empirical studies that examine how sex stereotyping influences occupational structure for lesbian women specifically. Relative to heterosexual women, however, lesbians tend to hold more nontraditional gender roles (see Morgan & Brown, 1991, for review) and there has been considerable speculation (Fassinger, 1995, 1996; Hetherington & Orzek, 1989; Morgan & Brown) that these liberal gender roles enable women to make vocational choices that are less dependent on sex stereotypes and thus more nontraditional. In addition, as just discussed, lesbian women are less likely to depend on a partner for financial support and this may also influence their consideration of nontraditional occupations, as these occupations often offer higher compensation (Morgan & Brown).

Furthermore, based on the existing literature, Croteau et al. (2000) discussed how scholars have hypothesized that LGB individuals internalize societal vocational stereotypes about lesbian and gay individuals that then influence their perceptions of which occupations are accessible to them (Fassinger, 1995, 1996; Morrow, Gore, & Campbell, 1996). Fassinger (1995) noted that occupational stereotyping is a considerable barrier to lesbian women, and one that is difficult to overcome given that many lesbians choose to remain closeted in the workplace. Thus, lesbian girls and women may have few role models to help guide their decision making about career decisions. Not surprisingly, lesbian (and gay or bisexual) college students expressed more of a preference for role models with the same sexual orientation and gender than did heterosexual college students (Nauta et al., 2001). Although there are no empirical studies that explicitly address whether there are particular professions that are perceived as inappropriate for lesbians, there is some support that careers involving work with children are not seen as appropriate for LGB individuals (Griffin, 1992; Woods & Harbeck, 1992). There is also evidence that the military is not a welcoming work environment for lesbian women (Fassinger, 1995).

Summary. In this section on vocational issues we discussed identity development issues, career interests, and opportunity structure. Lesbian identity development may have the effect of delaying career decision making. Yet, given that lesbians tend to express more nontraditional career interests, they are perceived as having more earning power than their heterosexual counterparts. Lesbian career clients often have fewer role models and thus may find it difficult to make career decisions, particularly relative to occupations that are seen as inappropriate for lesbians.

Role Management Issues

Lesbian women, like their heterosexual counterparts, face numerous issues related to role management. According to Badgett (2002), "Lesbians in families raise children, divvy up housework, take jobs to support their families and care for the family's adult members" (p. 8727). In fact, most lesbians are in long-term relationships at some point in their lives (Black et al., 2000; Peplau, Cochran, & Mays, 1997). Furthermore, given that many lesbians are employed, lesbians must often contend with dual-career relationship issues. In addition, between 22% and 28% of lesbians have children living in the home with them and the majority of these children are under 18 (Black et al.). And like all women, they must negotiate not only their relationships with members of their own household, but also relationships with families of origin and members of their social support network. As stated previously in our description of the macrosystem, lesbians typically contend with role management and role conflict issues in the midst of a societal climate that is heterosexist at its best and homophobic at its worst.

Clearly, one of the primary microsystems for lesbian clients is their partnership status. Lesbian relationships have been shown to be high in dyadic cohesion (Jordan & Deluty, 2000), consistent with theory suggesting that women are relational (e.g., Gilligan, 1982). Lesbian couples often lack both social support from significant others for their relationships and public recognition for their commitment to one another (Jordan & Deluty). Though lesbians are increasingly creating their own traditions (e.g., commitment ceremonies), they must still contend with lack of support from central figures in their lives. For example, lesbians may not be able to visit family on holidays or, if allowed to visit, may not be able to sleep with their partner. Furthermore, lesbians may have to hide relationships from extended or nuclear family members and choose an appropriate sexual identity management strategy at work.

Interestingly, from a mesosystem perspective, disclosure status appears to influence both relationship satisfaction and behavior in the workplace. Jordan and Deluty (2000), based on the results of their empirical study, contended that the meaning of disclosure must be negotiated within the relationship. They theorized that nondisclosure might appear to one's partner as lack of commitment to the relationship, whereas disclosure may signal commitment. In couples with low discrepancy scores (meaning that they agreed on disclosure status) higher relationship satisfaction resulted. Furthermore, when discrepancy was low and disclosure was high, greater relationship satisfaction resulted.

It seems then that lesbian women may be making inferences about an individual's commitment to the relationship based on disclosure status without considering systemic issues. Results from a study conducted by Rostosky and Riggle (2002) illustrated how the exosystem (e.g., workplace policies of the employer of both the individual and her partner), in addition to the individual variable of internalized homophobia, influences disclosure of sexual orientation on the job. Lesbians are not completely unaware of this interaction between partnership status and workplace issues. When asked directly, lesbian workers are able to identify the conflict between one's role as a partner and one's employment status. Peters and Cantrell (1993) found that significantly more lesbians reported conflict between the roles of intimate partner and career or job. The source of that conflict was perceived to be coworker disapproval (either of sexual orientation or intimate partner, or inability to communicate with coworkers or employers about their intimate relationship).

Eldridge and Gilbert (1990) studied a sample of lesbian dual-career couples and found that differences in the career commitment between partners was significantly and negatively related to the relationship satisfaction of both partners. It seems logical that career commitment might be a source of conflict within lesbian relationships given that "lesbians cannot marry their same sex-partners. . . . Lesbians are excluded from the kind of legal framework and public resources that support other families. Lesbian couples lack legal ties to each other that assign inheritance rights, allocate property after a breakup, provide access to income security programs, and make couples eligible for spousal employment benefits" (Badgett, 2002, p. 8728). Moreover, lesbians' inability to marry their partners often eliminates their eligibility for spousal benefits, resulting in a reduction in lesbians' total compensation. A growing number of employers are recognizing domestic partners for the purpose of benefits, in part because of the belief that doing so is right, but also in order to make themselves more attractive to talented lesbian (and gay) workers (Spielman & Winfeld, 1996). Despite such progress, lesbian workers, particularly those who are not professionals, are unlikely to receive domestic partnership benefits.

Lesbian women must also manage relationships with others who may feel they have a claim on their time and energy. Peters and Cantrell (1993) found that lesbians reported interrole conflict between the roles of daughter and intimate partner, the source of which tended to be perceived to be parental disapproval (of intimate partner, sexual orientation, or inability to communicate with parents about intimate relationship). Furthermore, and often more profoundly, lesbian women face threats to their rights as mothers. Badgett (2002) reported that lesbians might face losing custody of their children to a heterosexual father. In addition, in many states lesbian mothers cannot become a legal parent of a child born to or adopted by her lesbian partner and may not have legal rights to visitation or custody of the child if the couple separates. Clearly, these legal disadvantages illustrate that lesbian women face challenges similar to those faced by heterosexual women. Yet, they face these challenges without any legal or economic support. On the other hand, there is some evidence to suggest that lesbian households can be more full than heterosexual households, and often include an identifiable community of family and friends with whom to share the good and bad times (Oerton, 1997). Badgett also reported that "lesbians form relationships with other adults that would typically be recognized as kinship relationships" (p. 8727).

There is also evidence to suggest that lesbians share household tasks more equitably. Kurdek (1998) reported that in a sample of couples without children, compared to both married and gay couples, lesbian couples tended to share more tasks. Compared to married couples, lesbian couples were more likely to split tasks equally. Furthermore, lesbian partners who did household labor were less likely to report symptoms of depression or general distress. Kurdek noted that it seemed lesbian partners performed household tasks because they chose to do so. Badgett (2002) also reported that lesbian couples appear to equally distribute housework more than heterosexuals. She also noted that their negotiations seem to be less influenced by the income of each person than they are in heterosexual or gay male couples. She theorized that this might be due to more egalitarian norms related to contributions of partners and the economic role of women. Relatedly, Peplau et al. (1997) found that for African American lesbian women, unlike their heterosexual counterparts, decisions about partners seemed to be less related to instrumental resources. These authors, similar to Badgett, speculated that given the likelihood of a dual-career relationship as well as financial independence, lesbian women might have the luxury of not worrying about financial equality. Finally, Peters and Cantrell (1993) found that lesbian women spend less time than their heterosexual counterparts fulfilling the roles of homemaker and mother, though both groups reported struggling to juggle their roles at least some of the time.

Summary. Like their heterosexual counterparts, lesbians must contend with role management issues. Lesbians are more likely than heterosexual women to be in partnerships where the division of labor is equitable. Yet, they must contend with heterosexist and homophobic views regarding their roles as mothers, family members, and employees. Lesbians' relationships with their partners are often complicated by negotiations around sexual identity management in many aspects of their lives, including work environments.

Work Environments and Identity Management

Lesbian workers face an omnipresent tension between feeling the need to be out at work and the need to remain closeted. Further complicating this issue, as we discussed previously, is the lack of visible role models (e.g., supervisors, mentors, colleagues) in the workplace, sexual identity development, other salient identities (e.g., racial, religious), partner status, and career field. Many lesbians are uncertain of how to integrate their career with their personal life.

Lesbian workers have adopted a variety of identity management strategies at work. Griffin (1992) proposed a continuum for sexual identity management strategies for LGB individuals. At one end of the continuum is passing. When using this strategy, the lesbian's goal is to be perceived as heterosexual. Thus, personal information is often modified or fabricated to be consistent with a heterosexual lifestyle. Although this strategy is often perceived to offer the most protection from discrimination, it also involves the greatest sacrifice of a sense of self-integrity. Covering is the next identity management strategy on the continuum. Covering involves omitting information that might lead to the perception that a woman identifies as a lesbian. Similar to passing, this strategy is also intended to protect women from workplace hostility. The cost to self-integrity is somewhat less with covering than with passing because the lesbian worker is not providing false information but rather omitting information that might lead to perceptions that she is lesbian. The third strategy on the continuum is implicitly out. With this strategy, the lesbian worker is honest about personal information but does not explicitly label herself as lesbian. The strategy supplies some measure of safety as sexual orientation is not explicit and the option for adopting one of the more protective strategies still exists. The woman's sense of integrity may remain intact, as she is not engaged in actively denying her sexual orientation. The fourth strategy, explicitly out, entails the woman being honest about personal information and explicitly labeling herself as lesbian. Although this strategy affords her a full sense of integrity, it also offers the least protection from discrimination. Workers may adopt multiple identity management strategies, but typically will cluster around one particular point on the continuum. Croteau et al. (2000) stated that the existing empirical research seemed to be supportive of such a continuum. Anderson, Croteau, Chung, and DiStefano (2001) reported promising preliminary psychometric data for a measure designed to assess sexual identity management strategies for gay men and lesbians.

One might assume that being more out at work results in more job satisfaction. Empirical studies to date have yielded mixed findings. Results from some studies (e.g., Day & Schoenrade, 1997; Driscoll et al., 1996; Griffith & Hebl, 2002) indicated that disclosure of identity status might mediate work satisfaction. Croteau et al. (2000), however, concluded that high disclosure at work was associated with greater frequency of discrimination (Croteau & Lark, 1995; Croteau & von Destinon, 1994; Levine & Leonard, 1984) and that disclosure was found to have a positive or no relationship to job satisfaction (Croteau & Lark; Croteau & von Destinon). Waldo (1999) reported that increased outness was related to fewer experiences of indirect heterosexism but was positively related to experiences of direct heterosexism. Furthermore, his results indicated that a higher proportion of men in the organization was related to experiences of direct heterosexism.

An exosystem issue lesbians face is the expectation of being discriminated against in the workplace. Croteau et al. (2000) stated in an exhaustive review of the literature that workplace discrimination was one of the most frequently studied variables subjected to empirical research and lesbians the most studied subpopulation. They concluded that discrimination against LGB workers is insidious. Croteau (1996) reported that 25% to 66% of those sampled reported experiencing discrimination. Furthermore, he stated that LGB respondents in qualitative studies often reported experiencing discrimination or feeling fearful about the potential for discrimination (e.g., Boatwright et al., 1996; Woods & Harbeck, 1992). Other recent studies also suggest that discrimination is commonly encountered in the workplace (House, 2004; Ragins & Cornwell, 2001; Waldo, 1999). Chung (2001) proposed conceptual models for LGB clients that may be helpful to refer to when discussing how to help clients cope with work discrimination and work adjustment.

Another exosystem issue that influences lesbians' decisions about identity management strategies is that many companies do not have domestic partnership benefits. In addition, many workplaces do not have nondiscrimination statements that include sexual orientation as a protected category. Obviously, decisions about identity management must be made within the context of the exosystem. Moreover, examining the relevant microsystems for each client will also guide discussions about identity management issues in the workplace.

One microsystem issue is the specific workplace in which the client works. Quite simply, some workplaces are more affirmative than others and the risk of discrimination varies accordingly (e.g., Day & Schoenrade, 2000). Waldo (1999) conducted a study with 287 participants indicating that LGB individuals who perceived their organizations as intolerant of homosexuality were likely to experience more heterosexism. Increased outness is related to fewer experiences of indirect heterosexism and increased experiences of direct heterosexism. A higher proportion of men in the workplace also predicts experiences of direct heterosexism. Experiences of heterosexism were related to higher levels of psychological distress and health-related problems as well as decreased job satisfaction that then led to stronger intentions to quit and lower satisfaction with health. Lower health satisfaction led to higher levels of absenteeism. Finally, direct heterosexism is more related to negative health outcomes than indirect heterosexism. Button (2001) found that individuals in workplaces with policies intended to recognize and affirm sexual orientation are less likely to experience discrimination. Furthermore, more equitable treatment was related to higher levels of satisfaction and commitment between lesbian and gay employees.

Similarly, career field is another microsystem consideration when making decisions about identity management relative to sexual orientation. Woods and Harbeck (1992) conducted a qualitative study with lesbian physical educators and found that because of the heterosexism prevalent in school systems and because physical educators are negatively stereotyped as being lesbian, teachers often engaged in identity management strategies, similar to those proposed by Griffin (1992).

Examining the interaction between two microsystems is also important. Take, for example, the interaction between a lesbian individual's workplace and her partner status. Rostosky and Riggle (2002) used an ecological perspective "to test the utility of intrapersonal, interpersonal, and work environment factors in explaining the disclosure status of gay male and lesbian individuals in the workplace" (p. 411). Their results indicated that the decision to be out at work was influenced by both assessments of work environment safety and level of internalized homophobia. Having a workplace nondiscrimination policy, being in a relationship with a partner whose workplace has a nondiscrimination policy, and lower levels of internalized homophobia in both partners are associated with being out at work.

Counselors must also attend to the unique issues clients bring to decisions about how to manage their sexual identity in the workplace. For example, some authors have posited that individuals will vary in their need to be out at work (e.g., Driscoll et al., 1996; Griffin, 1992). Moreover, greater levels of internalized homophobia are negatively related to the likelihood of being open about sexual identity in the workplace (Rostosky & Riggle, 2002). Button (2001) found that gay and lesbian identity attitudes were related to both identity management strategies chosen and work attitudes and behaviors.

Summary. Decisions about identity management are ongoing. Lesbians use a variety of identity management strategies in the workplace, ranging from passing to explicitly out. There is equivocal evidence relative to whether being out in the workplace contributes to an increase in job satisfaction. There is considerable evidence that being out relates to increased workplace discrimination. Certainly, decisions about identity management are influenced by workplace characteristics, including the presence of domestic partnership benefits and nondiscrimination policies. Further complicating identity management decisions are the occupational stereotypes associated with a particular career field as well as issues related to partner decisions about disclosure status.

The chapter to this point has outlined issues relevant to consider in providing career counseling to lesbian clients with an ecological perspective. The importance of considering contextual, vocational choice, role management, work environment, and identity management issues has been explored. We now turn to the implications for career interventions.

CAREER INTERVENTIONS

Cook et al. (2002b) stressed the interaction of the individual, microsystem, and macrosystem in explaining career behavior in their approach to career counseling with an ecological perspective. A counselor with an ecological perspective can target individuals' interpretation of life events, how these beliefs mediate their behaviors, as well as their interaction with the environment. Interventions are also planned to create change in the environment. In striving to integrate the ecological model of career counseling into their work, career counselors must first evaluate how their current theoretical perspective addresses sexual identity issues.

Theory as Foundation of Counseling Work

Many career counselors cite the theories of Donald Super, John Holland, and others as informing their career-counseling work. A variety of authors have examined how existing theories of career development can be applied to work with LGB clients. For example, Super's (1990) life-span approach proposed that communities, the economy, societal values, and social groups interact to influence the progression of career stages and the development of a self-concept. Dunkle (1996) contended that gay men and lesbian women progress through the life stages and integrate their sexual orientation into their self-concept. House (2004) contended that Super's approach could inform the understanding of barriers to Caucasian lesbians' career development. John Holland's theory has been extensively utilized in theory and practice, and career counselors should consider the application of this model for their lesbian clients. Mobley and Slaney (1996) examined the relevance of Holland's theory for working with gay and lesbian individuals. They suggested that Holland's (1992) congruence model and Cass' (1979) interpersonal congruency theory need to be considered in assisting gay and lesbian clients. Incongruent choices may be made due to ecological issues such as homophobia in society and in the workplace. Other career theories have also been explored in their applicability to work with LGB clients. Chojnacki and Gelberg (1994) discussed the person-environment approach and stressed the need to understand how lesbian and gay workers are influenced by the environment in order to plan effective interventions. Morrow et al. (1996) applied social-cognitive career theory (Lent et al., 1994) to the career development of lesbian women and gay men. Societal factors influence academic and career development and result in effects on vocational interests, vocational choice, self-efficacy beliefs, and outcome expectations.

Specific to lesbian women, Morgan and Brown (1991) suggested that the theories of Farmer (1985), Astin (1985), and Gottfredson (1981) provide a theoretical understanding of the influence of personal, environmental, and developmental variables on career development. Internal and external factors provide socialization that influences an individual's internal view of the world. Degges-White and Shoffner (2002) applied the theory of work adjustment (Dawis & Lofquist, 1984) when assisting lesbian women with obstacles in the workplace. Discrimination and the decision to disclose sexual orientation can influence career satisfaction, fulfillment of psychological needs, and the use of abilities in the workplace. Responsible career counselors will actively consider how their current theoretical model informs their work with lesbian clients. Similarly, they will also thoughtfully consider whether their work with lesbian clients is ethical.

Ethical Career Counseling With Lesbian Clients

Career counselors must be vigilant in attending to ethical issues in their work with all clients, but there are special considerations when working with lesbian women. Career counselors abide by ethics articulated by professional associations of the counseling profession, including the American Counseling Association (ACA; http://www.counseling.org), the American Psychological Association (APA; http://www.apa.org), and the National Career Development Association (http://www.ncda.org). The codes of ethics of these associations all include guidelines requiring counselors to respect difference and to not engage in any form of discrimination, including those based on sexual orientation. In addition, counselors are required to monitor their boundaries of professional competencies. The APA code of ethics specifically refers to knowledge of sexual orientation issues. ACA also includes knowledge of career development issues in relation to diversity issues as important.

In light of the ethical obligation to achieve competency in working with individuals of diverse sexual orientations, counselors are recommended to learn about best practices and competencies specific to working with the lesbian woman. The Association for Gay, Lesbian, and Bisexual Issues in Counseling (AGLBIC; http://www.aglbic.org/) and the Society for the Psychological Study of Lesbian, Gay, and Bisexual Issues (http://www.apa.org/divisions/div44/) are two professional associations that provide excellent resources to guide competent counseling practice with lesbian women. For example, AGLBIC competencies include not only guidelines for knowledge in human growth and development, social and cultural knowledge, and career development, but also clearly articulated competencies in helping. Helping competencies include the acknowledgement of prejudice as well as the importance of self-awareness and the danger of attempts to change sexual orientation. A close look at the ethical guidelines as well as the competency requirements of these organizations are required activities of any counselor working with lesbian clients. Knowing the applicability of their theoretical orientation to working with lesbian clients and familiarity with the relevant ethical codes and guidelines specific to this population are essential first steps counselors are advised to take prior to seeing lesbian career clients. Applying the ecological model to the career counseling of lesbians also includes understanding the process of career counseling, being aware of their own attitudes toward this population, and being knowledgeable of career-counseling tools and interventions with this population. The remainder of the chapter focuses on these issues in turn and explicitly addresses the importance of maintaining an ecological perspective.

The Process of Career Counseling

Although there is an increased recognition that context can influence career development, individual traits continue to be the primary focus in the practice of many career counselors. Considering the interplay of individual experience and environmental influences is vital in order to truly assist lesbian women. Applying the ecological model to the process of career counseling can expand a counselor's repertoire of strategies to assist clients.

Gysbers et al. (2003) envisioned the process of career counseling to include phases of work. Generally, the process begins with developing a working relationship, exploring areas of concern to enhance self-awareness, and setting goals. Activities include gathering client information on individual attributes and contextual influences as well as generating hypotheses about client behavior. The next phase is problem resolution, which includes developing plans of action and evaluating results. Insight about the self is combined with exploration of the world of work through written and experiential learning, and developing an action plan to find opportunities in the work world. Information gathering about the client, use of assessments, and encouraging experiential activities are all strategies in this model of career counseling. Career counseling can assist with negotiating a career direction, adjusting to work environments and stress, and career success strategies. A counselor can integrate an ecological perspective into any stage of career counseling.

Establishing a working alliance is a core component of career-counseling work. Within the ecological model of career counseling, it is especially important to recognize that the counseling relationship becomes a component of the client's microsystem. The counseling relationship becomes another variable in the client's world and the attitude of the counselor is an important factor in creating change. It is thus very important that counselors be particularly aware of their personal stance toward sexual orientation.

Counselor Self-Awareness and Attitudes

Counselors must be aware of their own biases toward lesbians as well as microsystem and macrosystem influences. On an individual level, they can take an active role in examining their own LGB-affirmative career-counseling stance and analyzing their own sexual and racial identity to facilitate a positive working relationship with a lesbian client. Effectively assisting the client with internalized homophobia, sexism, or racism requires that counselors be aware of their own development, biases, and issues. Morgan and Brown (1991) pointed out the need to "recognize and work to change your own homophobic and heterosexist biases, do not assume that your client is heterosexual . . . [and] avoid perceiving career choices for lesbians as limited by stereotypical vocational roles" (p. 287).

Career counselors must actively examine their own level of internalized homophobia to effectively work with lesbian clients. As individuals within their own ecosystems, counselors must examine messages they have internalized regarding sexual orientation. There are several steps that can be taken to increase self-awareness and expand affirmative attitudes. First, counselors can actively ask themselves questions as they work with (or consider working with) a lesbian client. Questions might include:

• What assumptions am I making about this client due to her sexual orientation?
• How are my own values and beliefs about sexual orientation influencing how I feel about working with this client?
• How am I treating this client differently because of her sexual orientation?

The responses to these questions will guide counselors' efforts to increase self-awareness and expand skills to affirmatively work with lesbian clients. Steps to be taken can include continuing to examine and challenge personal attitudes, becoming familiar with professional literature about lesbian identity and experiences, and involving themselves in activities that expand understanding and experiences with lesbian women. These activities can include reading popular press publications or Internet sites specific to the lesbian community, attending programs and community events within the lesbian community, and actively seeking to engage in activities with individuals from a diverse range of sexual orientations in personal and work settings. Whether residing in urban, suburban, or rural settings, the opportunity to expand awareness exists for counselors seeking out the opportunity. To be ethical, however, it is the counselors' responsibility to be honest about their ability to be bias-free in their work with clients. We believe that all individuals are to varying degrees heterosexist given the privileges associated with a heterosexual orientation in this society (Bieschke, Croteau, Lark, & Vandiver, 2004), and the ethically responsible counselor will seek supervision and consultation when appropriate. If a counselor recognizes and is unable to ameliorate significant feelings of internalized homophobia, referral of the client may be warranted if it is ultimately in the client's best interest.

An effective ecological career counselor values diversity. Because lesbian clients are often in a "hidden" group due to concerns regarding discrimination, there is a need to be sensitive and affirmative to all clients (Bieschke & Matthews, 1996). Fassinger (1991) stated that it is important that counselors "deliberately create a gay affirmative approach that validates a gay sexual orientation, recognizes the oppression faced by gay people, and actively helps them overcome its external and internal effects" (p. 170). Furthermore, there is the need for affirming counselor behaviors, not merely the absence of destructive and homophobic reactions (Atkinson & Hackett, 1988; Betz, 1991; Brown, 1992). Affirming counselor behaviors derive from knowledge of sexual and racial identity development and career issues specific to lesbians. Croteau and Thiel (1993) suggested ways that counselors can attend to the needs of their clients' sexual orientation. Signaling lesbian and gay affirmation through language and actions, enhancing the development of a positive gay or lesbian identity in the context of career development work, and integrating the reality of antigay stigma into discussions can all address issues that impact career development.

Just as it is important to be aware their own biases, counselors need to be aware of biases and homophobia within the counseling agencies in which they work. The interactive nature of the ecosystem with the counseling process requires this. How they are perceived as a member of the organization in which they work will have an influence on the experience of their client. Bieschke and Mathews (1996) surveyed career counselors to learn about factors predictive of higher levels of affirmative behavior with LGB career clients. The most predictive factors were a nonheterosexist organizational climate and the counselor's sexual orientation. Whereas a significant predictor of culturally affirmative behaviors was the extent to which counselors defined a broad diversity of populations as cultural minorities, the organizational climate in the counseling agency created the context for LGB-affirmative career-counseling work. On a microsystem level, counselors can be advocates in analyzing and acting against oppression in their own work settings. To create change it is first important to assess the extent to which their agencies affirm lesbian women's experiences. To enhance the organizational climate, counselors can organize professional training for staff, promote outreach to lesbian groups and individuals, or monitor documents and programs for heterosexist language. On a macrosystem level counselors can advocate for change in community norms and legal rights through advocacy work in their professional organizations and other communities (Gelberg & Chojnacki, 1995). In addition, embracing the role of advocate can enhance the ongoing development of a lesbian-affirming counseling stance. This stance will assist in the additional steps in the process of career counseling, including career interventions and career choice implementation.

Career Counseling Interventions

Gathering information about the client occurs at every stage of career-counseling work. Prince (1997b) defined assessment as methods used to evaluate career concerns such as interviewing and informal and formal assessments. Assessment can include verbal exploration of known interests, values, abilities, self-efficacy status, and decision-making style. An ecological counselor will facilitate exploration of ecological issues that contribute to the client's self-concept. Assessing macrosystem issues for lesbian clients that influence internalization of homophobia, racism, or stereotyping is essential. Exploring and validating societal influences will not only increase counselors' understanding of support systems, but also expand the understanding of client dilemmas. Discussing barriers such as discrimination in the workplace can help normalize experience and help the client to develop coping strategies. Identifying exosystem patterns will enable the client and counselor to plan for targeted interventions. Exploration of the impact of multiple identities, dual relationships, and family issues can also assist in the planning of interventions.

Informal and standardized assessments also assist in the process of information gathering. Informal assessments, such as family-career genograms, card sorts, career fantasy exercises, storytelling, and reflective writing on accomplishments, allow for further assessment of individual and contextual issues. Creatively utilizing these strategies can assist with further exploration of ecosystem issues. For example, expanding a family-career genogram to include social support networks that have influenced career dreams or stereotypes may be helpful. This can also lead to targeting microsystem support systems or areas for advocacy for the client or counselor.

Formal interest assessments are often used in career counseling because of their benefits: "Interest inventories can reveal conflicts between expressed choices and underlying psychological structures. Such inventories may reflect gender role conflicts, and may be indicators of general psychological adjustment and self-esteem" (Spokane, 1994, p. 286). Standardized assessments with lesbian clients should be used with caution. A variety of authors have cautioned about the reliability and validity of formal career assessments with lesbians and gay men (Fassinger, 1995; Hartung et al., 1998; Prince, 1997a, 1997b). Chung (2003) detailed concerns particularly relevant for LGB clients such as reliability and validity and the difficulty in finding reliable measures that assess the constructs of identity development, discrimination coping strategies, and a client's degree of outness. There has been limited research investigating the use of career assessments with lesbians, but findings indicate that counselors should be cautious regarding interpretation with this population (Pope, 1995). Scores on self-report measures may be distorted depending on individuals' comfort with their sexual identity status (Pope & Jelly, 1991). For example, a lesbian woman hesitant about outing herself to her counselor may not answer honestly on an interest inventory that could reveal nonstereotypical gender responses.

Diversity competencies are required in the use of all standardized assessments and counselors must be aware of biases that may influence interpretation. Prince (1997b) cautioned that to fairly test lesbians and gay men, the administrator must consider the possibility of bias in the instrument, as well as within the assessor and the interpretation process itself. Although several measures have been developed for career assessment with LGB persons (e.g., Anderson et al., 2001; Waldo, 1999), their utility for career-counseling work may be limited. Thus, a career counselor must often rely on commonly used assessments, such as the Strong Interest Inventory (SII), Self-Directed Search (SDS), and career maturity measures, if they wish to formally assess their lesbian clients. Because normed groups used to develop inventories such as the Strong Interest Inventory (Harmon, Hansen, Borgen, & Hammer, 1994) are predominately White, well educated, and of unknown sexual orientation status, counselors can use several strategies. Prince suggested that counselors can integrate into the counseling process activities that foster a more equitable use of assessments. Expanding demographic information, history taking, conducting assessment interviews with questions about sexual orientation and community connections, and encouraging individuals through homework assignments that link career assessment results with their sexual orientation may be helpful.

In addition, Mobley and Slaney (1996) pointed to the need to be cautious in interpreting assessments that include Holland's theory. The results of the SDS (Holland, 1994), the SII (Harmon et al., 1994), and the Vocational Preference Inventory (Holland, 1985) may vary depending on individuals' stage of sexual orientation identity status, age, and stage level of outness. As previously discussed, stages of sexual identity status drive not only awareness of self, but comfort in revealing aspects of self to another person. A lesbian woman may feel that the Holland code of realistic is a better fit for her interests, but be reluctant to reveal these interests because of fear of stereotyping or internalized homophobia. The counselor not only needs to be aware of sexual identity status achieved to understand assessment results (Pope, 1995), but also needs to continually understand that individuals may be hesitant to be out to the counselor in the career-counseling process. Different stages of sexual orientation and racial identity status may influence individuals' self-concept, knowledge of interests, and identity status. For lesbian women, gender-role socialization may also influence traditional career interests (such as social activities of helping and nurturing) while discouraging nontraditional interests (realistic activities of working with hands or outdoor activities).

Career counseling includes integration of knowledge of self to create plans for the implementation of career decision making. Manageable goals for implementation can target change in the individual as well as the ecosystem. It is important to encourage clients to consider aspects of themselves for development (e.g., becoming involved in activities to develop work-related skills), as well as creating ecosystem changes (e.g., advocating for changed attitudes at a workplace or for legal changes). An ecological counselor is willing to be more active and include alternative approaches in this stage of work. For example, Cook et al. (2002b) suggested that career counselors include family and peers in the career-counseling process to assist with emotional support. This type of intervention can influence the individual and microsystem.

Gathering Information and Implementing Career Choice

An important part of career counseling is gathering information about the world of work. A lesbian client should be encouraged to explore standard, written career information as well as materials designed specifically for LGB individuals (Green, 1994). Counselors can assist clients in assessing their microsystems to seek out role models and to utilize local and national resources. Lesbian clients can be encouraged to identify lesbian or affirmative heterosexual individuals to contact when conducting informational interviews. Assistance in identifying specific questions pertinent to their concerns and level of outness is important. For example, they may target an individual in their church to discuss a specific field of interest, without discussing their concern about being out in that field. On the other hand, they may next conduct another informational interview with someone in their lesbian community group to discuss further questions. Strategically planning this information gathering will help clients to consider the interplay between their vocational and sexual identity development.

Lesbian women need support and encouragement from important others in their lives (Fassinger, 1996). Nauta et al. (2001) reported also that LGB students had more career role models than heterosexual students. LGB students perceived less support and guidance from others and were more likely to endorse the importance of a career role model's sexual orientation. As counselors, the fact that LGB clients value LGB role models and those who are supportive of LGB clients should lead to help in finding these individuals. For lesbian clients with other minority status, identification of role models with like attributes should also be considered. Counselors not only need to take an active role in finding access to role models for their clients, but can serve as advocates and encourage LGB professionals to serve as role models.

Exploration of the work world also includes internships, job shadowing, and other in-the-career experiences. It is important for counselors to encourage clients to seek out valuable learning opportunities (Etringer, Hillerbrand, & Hetherington, 1990). Lesbian women can seek out internships or externships in businesses owned by LGB community members to connect with role models. Clients can be encouraged to assess career tasks and activities during these experiences as well as workplace climate issues such as heterosexism, gender and racial stereotyping, and other career barriers. Effective consideration of individual and ecosystem issues in career exploration can assist lesbian clients in implementing their job search and in transitioning to, and adjusting to, the world of work.

When assisting lesbian women with job-search strategies, it is essential that counselors acknowledge macrosystem issues. Discrimination toward lesbian women will occur during and after the job search. Gelberg and Chojnacki (1995), Croteau and von Destinon (1994), and others made extensive suggestions regarding issues to be aware of as lesbian clients seek employment. First, an individual woman's issues must be assessed and processed, such as self-efficacy beliefs, individual coping strategies to deal with options compromised by stereotyping, and self-management skills in general. Assessment of microsystem supports and awareness of macrosystem issues are important in this phase. Core issues that clients must consider include issues of self-disclosure in a job search and on the job, dual-career issues, identification of heterosexist workplace environments, and the use of family and community connections. Negotiating job offers and transitioning to a new work environment are also issues to discuss. Choices about work settings and decisions about how to self-disclose on the job search are related to identity development, assessment of the work environment, and other complex issues. It is critical that career counselors assess and plan interventions with their career clients by taking the micro- and macro-system issues into consideration.

As previously discussed, Chung (2001) outlined coping strategies that can be utilized in decisions regarding vocational choice, identity management, and discrimination management. Once on the job, decisions about self-disclosing in the workplace and managing discrimination are core areas for lesbian women. Access to advancement may be limited by discrimination and lack of role models and counselors can be active in encouraging women to seek out resources in their ecosystem. In addition, to mediate these issues, counselors can serve as advocates in the workplace by consulting with employers and proactively identifying role models, as well as serving as mentors and role models themselves.

CONCLUSION

We believe that an ecological approach to career counseling will serve lesbian career clients best given the many contextual issues that influence the career development of these clients. Moreover, an ecological approach acknowledges the dynamic, developmental interplay between the individual and her environment that can serve as the focus of counselors' interventions. Interventions need not be limited to or focused on the client; rather, the counselor should consider interventions that reach beyond the individual, including the counselor's as well as the client's environment. By conceptualizing the client's issues using a contextual framework, a counselor's influence can extend beyond one client to effect change systemically as well.

REFERENCES

Alquijay, M. A. (1997). The relationships among self-esteem, acculturation, and lesbian identity formation in Latina lesbians. In B. Green (Ed.), *Ethnic and cultural diversity among lesbians and gay men: Psychological perspectives on lesbian and gay issues* (Vol. 3, pp. 249–265). Newbury Park, CA: Sage.

Anderson, M. Z., Croteau, J. M., Chung, Y. B., & DiStefano, T. M. (2001). Developing an assessment of sexual identity management for lesbian and gay workers. *Journal of Career Assessment, 9,* 243–260.

Astin, H. S. (1985). The meaning of work in women's lives: A sociopsychological model of career choice and work behavior. *The Counseling Psychologist, 12,* 117–128.

Atkinson, D. R., & Hackett, G. (Eds.). (1988). *Counseling non-ethnic American minorities.* Springfield, IL: Thomas.

Badgett, M. V. L. (1996). Employment and sexual orientation: Disclosure and discrimination in the workplace. *Journal of Gay and Lesbian Social Services, 4,* 29–52.

Badgett, M. V. L. (2002). Lesbians: Social and economic situation. In *International encyclopedia of the social and behavioral sciences* (pp. 8725–8728). Amsterdam: Elsevier.

Betz, N. E. (1991). Implications for counseling psychology training programs: Reactions to the special issue. *The Counseling Psychologist, 19,* 248–252.

Betz, N. E. (1994). Basic issues and concepts in career counseling for women. In W. B. Walsh & S. H. Osipow (Eds.), *Career counseling for women* (pp. 1–41). Hillsdale, NJ: Lawrence Erlbaum Associates.

Betz, N. E., & Fitzgerald, L. F. (1987). *The career psychology of women.* New York: Academic Press.

Bieschke, K. J., Croteau, J. M., Lark, J. S., & Vandiver, B. J. (2004). Toward a discourse of sexual orientation equity in the counseling professions. In J. M. Croteau, J. S. Lark, M. Lidderdale, & Y. B. Chung (Eds.), *Deconstructing heterosexism in the counseling professions: Multicultural narrative voices* (pp. 189–210). Thousand Oaks, CA: Sage.

Bieschke, K. J., & Matthews, C. (1996). Career counselor attitudes and behaviors toward gay, lesbian, and bisexual clients. *Journal of Vocational Behavior, 48,* 243–255.

Black, D., Gates, G., Sanders, S., & Taylor, L. (2000). Demographics of the gay and lesbian population in the United States: Evidence from available systematic data sources. *Demography, 37,* 139–154.

Bloch, D. P., & Richmond, L. J. (Eds.). (1997). *Connections between spirit and work in career development.* Palo Alto, CA: Davies-Black.

Boatwright, K. J., Gilbert, M. S., Forrest, L., & Ketzenberger, K. (1996). Impact of identity development upon career trajectory: Listening to the voices of lesbian women. *Journal of Vocational Behavior, 48,* 210–228.

Bronfenbrenner, U. (1977). Toward an experimental ecology of human development. *American Psychologist, 32,* 513–531.

Bronfenbrenner, U. (1979). *The ecology of human development: Experiments by nature and design.* Cambridge, MA: Harvard University Press.

Brown, L. S. (1992). While waiting for the revolution: The case for a lesbian feminist psychotherapy. *Feminism and Psychology, 2,* 239–253.

Button, S. B. (2001). Organizational efforts to affirm sexual diversity: A cross-level examination. *Journal of Applied Psychology, 86,* 17–28.

Cass, V. C. (1979). Homosexual identity formation: A theoretical model. *Journal of Homosexuality, 4,* 219–235.

Cass, V. C. (1984). Homosexual identity formation: Testing a theoretical model. *Journal of Sex Research, 20,* 143–167.

Chojnacki, J. G., & Gelberg, S. (1994). Toward a conceptualization of career counseling with gay/lesbian/bisexual persons. *Journal of Career Development, 21,* 3–10.

Chung, Y. B. (1995). Career decision making of lesbian, gay, and bisexual individuals. *Career Development Quarterly, 44,* 178–190.

Chung, Y. B. (2001). Work discrimination and coping strategies: Conceptual frameworks for counseling lesbian, gay, and bisexual clients. *Career Development Quarterly, 50,* 33–44.

Chung, Y. B. (2003). Ethical and professional issues in career assessment with lesbian, gay, and bisexual persons. *Journal of Career Assessment, 11,* 96–112.

Colozzi, E. A., & Colozzi, L. C. (2000). College students' callings and careers: An integrated values-oriented perspective. In D. A. Luzzo (Ed.), *Career counseling of college students: An empirical guide to strategies that work* (pp. 63–91). Washington, DC: American Psychological Association.

Cook, E. P. (1993). The gendered context of life: Implications for women's and men's career-life plans. *Career Development Quarterly, 41,* 227–237.

Cook, E. P., Heppner, M. J., & O'Brien, K. M. (2002a). Career development of women of color and white women: Assumptions, conceptualization, and interventions from an ecological perspective. *Career Development Quarterly, 50,* 291–305.

Cook, E. P., Heppner, M. J., & O'Brien, K. M. (2002b). Feminism and women's career development: An ecological perspective. In S. G. Niles (Ed.), *Adult career development: Concepts, issues, and practices* (pp. 168–189). Columbus, OH: National Career Development Association.

Croteau, J. M. (1996). Research on the work experiences of lesbian, gay, and bisexual people: An integrative review of methodology and findings. *Journal of Vocational Behavior, 48,* 195–209.

Croteau, J. M., Anderson, M. Z., Distefano, T. M., & Kampa-Kokesch, S. (2000). Lesbian, gay, and bisexual vocational psychology: Reviewing foundations and planning construction. In R. Perez, K. DeBord, & K. J. Bieschke (Eds.), *Handbook of counseling and psychotherapy with gay, lesbian, and bisexual clients* (pp. 383–408). Washington, DC: American Psychological Association.

Croteau, J. M., & Bieschke, K. J. (1996). Beyond pioneering: An introduction to the special issue on the vocational issues of lesbian women and gay men. *Journal of Vocational Behavior, 48,* 119–124.

Croteau, J. M., & Lark, J. S. (1995). On being lesbian, gay, or bisexual in student affairs: A national survey of experiences on the job. *NASPA Journal, 32,* 189–197.

Croteau, J. M., & Thiel, M. J. (1993). Integrating sexual orientation in career counseling: Acting to end a form of the personal-career dichotomy. *Career Development Quarterly, 42,* 175–179.

Croteau, J. M., & von Destinon, M. (1994). A national survey of job search experiences of lesbian, gay, and bisexual student affairs professionals. *Journal of College Student Development, 35,* 40–45.

Davidson, M. G. (2000). Religion and spirituality. In R. Perez, K. DeBord, & K. J. Bieschke (Eds.), *Handbook of counseling and psychotherapy with gay, lesbian, and bisexual clients* (pp. 409–434). Washington, DC: American Psychological Association.

Davidson, M. M., & Huenefeld, N. (2002). Struggling with two identities: The case of Eileen. *Career Development Quarterly, 50,* 306–310.

Dawis, R. V., & Lofquist, L. V. (1984). *A psychological theory of work adjustment.* Minneapolis: University of Minnesota Press.

Day, N. E., & Schoenrade, P. (1997). Staying in the closet versus coming out: Relationships between communication about sexual orientation and work attitudes. *Personnel Psychology, 50,* 147–163.

Day, N. E., & Schoenrade, P. (2000). The relationship among reported disclosure of sexual orientation, anti-discrimination policies, top management support and work attitudes of gay and lesbian employees. *Personnel Review, 29,* 346–363.

Degges-White, S., & Shoffner, M. F. (2002). Career counseling with lesbian clients: Using the Theory of Work Adjustment as a framework. *Career Development Quarterly, 51,* 87–96.

Driscoll, J. M., Kelley, F. A., & Fassinger, R. E. (1996). Lesbian identity and disclosure in the workplace: Relation to occupational stress and satisfaction. *Journal of Vocational Behavior, 48,* 229–242.

Dunkle, J. H. (1996). Toward an integration of gay and lesbian identity development and Super's life-span approach. *Journal of Vocational Behavior, 48,* 149–159.

Eldridge, N. S., & Gilbert, L. A. (1990). Correlates of relationship satisfaction in lesbian couples. *Psychology of Women Quarterly, 14,* 43–62.

Etringer, B. D., Hillerbrand, E., & Hetherington, C. (1990). The influence of sexual orientation on career decision-making: A research note. *Journal of Homosexuality, 19,* 103–111.

Farmer, H. S. (1985). Model of career and achievement and motivation for women and men. *Journal of Counseling Psychology, 32,* 363–390.

Fassinger, R. E. (1991). The hidden minority: Issues and challenges in working with lesbian women and gay men. *The Counseling Psychologist, 19,* 157–176.

Fassinger, R. E. (1995). From invisibility to integration: Lesbian identity in the workplace. *Career Development Quarterly, 44,* 148–167.

Fassinger, R. E. (1996). Notes from the margins: Integrating lesbian experience into the vocational psychology of women. *Journal of Vocational Behavior, 48,* 160–175.

Fitzgerald, L. F., & Betz, N. E. (1994). Career development in cultural context: The role of gender, race, class, and sexual orientation. In M. Savickas & R. Lent (Eds.), *Convergence in career development theories* (pp. 103–117). Palo Alto, CA: Consulting Psychologists Press.

Fitzgerald, L. F., Fassinger, R. E., & Betz, N. E. (1995). Theoretical advances in the study of women's career development. In W. B. Walsh & S. H. Osipow (Eds.), *Handbook of vocational psychology: Theory, research, and practice* (2nd ed., pp. 67–109). Hillsdale, NJ: Lawrence Erlbaum Associates.

Fukuyama, M. A., & Ferguson, A. D. (2000). Lesbian, gay, and bisexual people of color: Understanding cultural complexity and managing multiple oppressions. In R. Perez, K. DeBord, & K. J. Bieschke (Eds.), *Handbook of counseling and psychotherapy with lesbian, gay, and bisexual clients* (pp. 81–106). Washington, DC: American Psychological Association.

Garnets, L., & Kimmel, D. (1991). Lesbian and gay male dimensions in the psychological study of human diversity. In J. Goodchilds (Ed.), *Psychological perspectives on human diversity in America: The master lectures* (pp. 143–189). Washington, DC: American Psychological Association.

Gelberg, S., & Chojnacki, J. T. (1995). Developmental transitions of gay/lesbian/bisexual-affirmative, heterosexual career counselors. *Career Development Quarterly, 43,* 267–273.

Gottfredson, L. S. (1981). Circumscription and compromise: A developmental theory of occupational aspirations. *Journal of Counseling Psychology, 28,* 545–579.

Green, F. (1994). *Gay yellow pages.* New York: Renaissance House.

Griffin, P. (1992). From hiding out to coming out: Empowering lesbian and gay educators. In K. M. Harbeck (Ed.), *Coming out of the classroom closet* (pp. 167–196). Binghamton, NY: Harrington Park Press.

Griffith, K. H., & Hebl, M. R. (2002). The disclosure dilemma for gay men and lesbians: "Coming out" at work. *Journal of Applied Psychology, 87,* 1191–1199.

Gysbers, N. C., Heppner, M. J., & Johnston, J. A. (2003). *Career counseling: Process, issues, and techniques.* Boston: Allyn & Bacon.

Hackett, G., & Betz, N. E. (1981). A self-efficacy approach to the career development of women. *Journal of Vocational Behavior, 18,* 326–339.

Hansen, L. S. (1997). *Integrative life planning: Critical tasks for career development and changing life patterns.* San Francisco: Jossey-Bass.

Harmon, L. W., Hansen, J. C., Borgen, F. H., & Hammer, A. L. (1994). *Strong Interest Inventory: Applications and technical guide.* Palo Alto, CA: Consulting Psychologists Press.

Hartung, P. J., Vandiver, B. J., Leong, F. T. L., Pope, M., Niles, S. G., & Farrow, B. (1998). Appraising cultural identity in career-development assessment and counseling. *Career Development Quarterly, 46,* 276–293.

Herr, E. L. (1999). Theoretical perspectives on the school-to-work transition: Reactions and recommendations. *Career Development Quarterly, 47,* 359–364.

Herring, R. D. (1998). *Career counseling in schools: Multicultural and developments perspectives.* Alexandria, VA: American Counseling Association.

Hetherington, C. (1991). Life planning and career counseling with gay and lesbian students. In N. J. Evans & V. A. Wall (Eds.), *Beyond tolerance: Gays, lesbians, and bisexuals on-campus* (pp. 131–145). Alexandria, VA: American College Personnel Association Media.

Hetherington, C., & Orzek, A. (1989). Career counseling and life planning with lesbian women. *Journal of Counseling and Development, 68,* 52–57.

Holland, J. L. (1985). *Vocational Preference Inventory.* Odessa, FL: Psychological Assessment Resources.

Holland, J. L. (1992). *Making vocational choices: A theory of vocational personalities and work environments.* Odessa, FL: Psychological Assessment Resources.

Holland, J. L. (1994). *The Self-Directed Search: Professional manual.* Odessa, FL: Psychological Assessment Resources.

House, C. J. C. (2004). Integrating barriers to Caucasian lesbians' career development and Super's life-span, life-space approach. *Career Development Quarterly, 52,* 246–255.

Jordan, K. M., & Deluty, R. H. (2000). Social support, coming out, and relationship satisfaction in lesbian couples. *Journal of Lesbian Studies, 4,* 145–164.

Kurdek, L. A. (1998). The allocation of household labor in gay, lesbian, and heterosexual married couples. In D. L. Anselmi & A. L. Law (Eds.), *Questions of gender: Perspectives and paradox* (pp. 582–591). Boston: McGraw-Hill.

Lent, R. W., Brown, S. D., & Hackett, G. (1994). Toward a unifying social cognitive theory of career and academic interest, choice, and performance. *Journal of Vocational Behavior, 45,* 79–122.

Leong, F. T. (Ed.). (1995). *Career development and vocational behavior of racial and ethnic minorities.* Hillsdale, NJ: Lawrence Erlbaum Associates.

Levine, M. P., & Leonard, R. (1984). Discrimination against lesbians in the work force. *Signs, 9,* 700–710.

Matlin, M. (1996). *The psychology of women.* New York: Holt, Rinehart, and Winston.

McCarn, S. R., & Fassinger, R. E. (1996). Revisioning sexual minority identity formation: A new model of lesbian identity and its implications for counseling and research. *The Counseling Psychologist, 24,* 508–534.

Mobley, M. M., & Slaney, R. B. (1996). Holland's theory: Its relevance for lesbian women and gay men. *Journal of Vocational Behavior, 48,* 125–135.

Morgan, K. S., & Brown, L. S. (1991). Lesbian career development, work behavior, and vocational counseling. *The Counseling Psychologist, 19,* 273–291.

Morrow, S. L. (1997). Career development of lesbian and gay youth: Effects of sexual orientation, coming out, and homophobia. In M. B. Harris (Ed.), *School experiences of gay and lesbian youth: The invisible minority* (pp. 1–15). New York: Haworth Press.

Morrow, S. L., Gore, P. S., & Campbell, B. W. (1996). The application of a sociocognitive framework to the career development of lesbian women and gay men. *Journal of Vocational Behavior, 48,* 136–148.

Nauta, M. M., Saucier, A. M., & Woodard, L. E. (2001). Interpersonal influences on students' academic and career decisions: The impact of sexual orientation. *Career Development Quarterly, 49,* 352–362.

Oerton, S. (1997). "Queer housewives?" Some problems in theorizing the division of domestic labour in lesbian and gay households. *Women's Studies International Forum, 20,* 421–430.

Peplau, L. A., Cochran, S., & Mays, V. (1997). A national survey of the intimate relationships of African-American lesbians and gay men: A look at commitment, satisfaction, sexual behavior, and HIV disease. In B. Greene (Ed.), *Ethnic and cultural diversity among gay men and lesbians* (pp. 11–38). Thousand Oaks, CA: Sage.

Peters, D. K., & Cantrell, P. J. (1993). Gender roles and role conflict in feminist lesbian and heterosexual women. *Sex Roles, 28,* 379–392.

Pope, M. (1995). Career interventions for gay and lesbian clients: A synopsis of practice knowledge and research needs. *Career Development Quarterly, 44,* 191–203.

Pope, M., & Jelly, J. (1991). MBTI, sexual orientation, and career development: Summary. *Proceedings of the 9th International Biennial Conference of the Association for Psychological Type, 9,* 231–238.

Prince, J. P. (1997a). Assessment bias affecting lesbian, gay male and bisexual individuals. *Measurement and Evaluation in Counseling and Development, 30,* 82–87.

Prince, J. P. (1997b). Career assessment with lesbian, gay, and bisexual individuals. *Journal of Career Assessment, 5,* 225–238.

Ragins, B. R., & Cornwell, J. M. (2001). Pink triangles: Antecedents and consequences of perceived workplace discrimination against gay and lesbian employees. *Journal of Applied Psychology, 86,* 1244–1261.

Rostosky, S. S., & Riggle, E. D. B. (2002). "Out" at work: The relation of actor and partner workplace policy and internalized homophobia to disclosure status. *Journal of Counseling Psychology, 49,* 411–419.

Sexton, T. L., & Griffin, B. L. (Eds.). (1997). *Constructivist thinking in counseling practice, research and training.* New York: Teachers College Press.

Society for the Psychological Study of Lesbian, Gay, and Bisexual Issues. Retrieved April 5, 2004, from http://www.apa.org/divisions/div44/

Soto, T. A. (1997). Ethnic minority gay, lesbian, and bisexual publications: A 10-year review. *Division 44 Newsletter, 13,* 13–14.

Spielman, S., & Winfeld, L. (1996). Domestic partner benefits: A bottom line discussion. In A. L. Ellis & E. D. B. Riggle (Eds.), *Sexual identity on the job: Issues and services* (pp. 53–78). Binghamton, NY: Harrington Park Press.

Spokane, A. R. (1994). The resolution of incongruence and the dynamics of person-environment fit. In M. L. Savikas & R. W. Lent (Eds.), *Convergence in career development theories: Implications for science and practice* (pp. 119–137). Palo Alto, CA: Consulting Psychologists Press.

Super, D. (1990). A life-span, life-space approach to career development. In D. Brown & L. Brooks (Eds.), *Career choice and development: Applying contemporary theories to practice* (2nd ed., pp. 197–261). San Francisco: Jossey-Bass.

Super, D. E. (1994). A life span, life space perspective on convergence. In M. L. Savikas & R. W. Lent (Eds.), *Convergence in career development theories: Implications for science and practice* (pp. 63–74). Palo Alto, CA: Consulting Psychologists Press.

U.S. Bureau of the Census. (2002). *American community survey.* Retrieved March 1, 2004, from http://www.census.gov/acs/www/Products/Single/2002/ACS/index.htm

Waldo, C. R. (1999). Working in a majority context: A structural model of heterosexism as minority stress in the workplace. *Journal of Counseling Psychology, 46,* 1–15.

Walsh, W. B., Bingham, R. P., Brown, M. T., & Ward, C. M. (Eds.). (2001). *Career counseling for African Americans.* Mahwah, NJ: Lawrence Erlbaum Associates.

Woods, S. E., & Harbeck, K. M. (1992). Living in two worlds: The identity management strategies used by lesbian physical educators. In K. M. Harbeck (Eds.), *Coming out of the classroom closet* (pp. 141–166). Binghamton, NY: Harrington Park Press.

Chapter **12**

Career Concerns of Immigrant Women: Issues and Implications for Career Counseling

Oksana Yakushko
University of Nebraska–Lincoln

"You should be a teacher," was the well-meaning advice I received concerning the major I should pursue during my studies as an immigrant student in the United States. "Teaching is the best job for women," an American gentleman said, "you can take as much time off as you'd like to be with your children and your schedule also coincides with theirs when they go to school. It will be good for your children and good for you as a mother. Many women here in America find careers that are best for their families and their children." I remember thinking, "But I don't want to be a teacher." Growing up in Soviet Ukraine, in a family of women who were mainly involved in sciences and engineering and who did not arrange their careers around their children, this advice was very puzzling to me. As a child, I wanted to be a cosmonaut like Valentina Tereshkova, the first woman in space, a philosopher, or a biologist—not a teacher. Although I thought I would have children, I never considered shaping my career and work life around being a parent. After all, child-care facilities where I grew up were abundant, accessible, and excellent. The American woman's world of work was vastly different from the one I knew growing up in a foreign country and my immigration to the United States initially resulted in confusion and stagnation in my career development.

The U.S. Bureau of the Census reported that 10.4% or approximately 28 million U.S. citizens and legal residents are immigrants (Schmidley, 2001). Almost half of this group (43.6%) reported on the most recent census that they moved to the U.S. after 1990. Despite this influx, immigrant visibility in

YAKUSHKO

psychological literature is slight (Hovey, 2000; Pernice, 1994; Yoshihama & Horrocks, 2002).

Even less information exists on the psychological impact of immigration on women because research has focused primarily on men (Hondagneu-Sotelo, 1999). The most recent census estimates reveal that approximately 15% more women than men legally immigrated to the United States between 1990 and 2000 (Perry, Vandervate, Auman, & Morris, 2001). Globalization is an economic force that is thrusting many women toward migration to other countries in search of work and is believed will lead to an explosion of women's immigration in the near future (Marsella & Ring, 2003; Seager, 2003). In addition, U.S. immigration law favors admission of spouses and children as well as skilled workers in female-dominated fields such as nursing (Simon, 2001).

Gender and migration have gained attention in such fields as demography, sociology, anthropology, geography, and increasingly in psychology (Hondagneu-Sotelo, 1999). Studies have examined psychological distress (Rodriguez & DeWolfe, 1990), posttraumatic stress symptoms and victimization (Yoshihama & Horrocks, 2002), adaptation strategies (McIntyre & Augusto, 1999), and identity changes (Weeks, 2000) in the lives of immigrant women. In 1992, *Women and Therapy* published a collection of articles on the mental health issues of refugee women (Cole, Rothblum, & Espín).

The majority of immigrant women seek employment after their relocation to the United States (Schmidley, 2001). Information about the career development and career-transition issues of immigrant women remains limited, yet career counseling with immigrant women can be one of the most significant contributors to their positive transition into a new culture. In 1991, the United National Resolution on Women Refugees called on all nations that have ratified refugee agreements to focus on providing women with specific educational opportunities about employment after relocation (Office of the United Nations High Commissioner for Refugees).

This chapter focuses exclusively on the population of immigrant and refugee women in the United States who have migrated within the last 10 years or less and who may be struggling with career-transition and adjustment issues due to relocation. International women students and those who remain in the United States for limited periods of time are not considered. The unique needs of these women are increasingly receiving attention in the career literature (e.g., Yang, Wong, Hwang, & Heppner, 2002).

In this chapter I review existing literature about immigrant women in the United States and develop a framework for understanding and working with their career concerns. I briefly describe the circumstances of relocation and the demographic characteristics of immigrant women in the United States and highlight the theoretical and research scholarship relevant to understanding the career development issues of these women. In particular, I consider social-cognitive learning theory, theories of career transition, ecological theory, and feminist theory. I also present an overview of key influences that shape the career experiences of immigrant women. Finally, I describe specific principles and strategies for career counseling with immigrant women.

DEMOGRAPHIC CHARACTERISTICS OF IMMIGRANT WOMEN

Circumstances of Relocation

Women relocate to the United States in many different ways, under a wide array of relocation circumstances. These circumstances bear significant repercussions for individuals who enter the United States and for their experiences while in this country. In particular, immigrants' work status and work experiences can be directly related to the circumstances of their relocation to the United States. The three primary relocation circumstances are highlighted in this section: legal immigration, refugee relocation, and undocumented or illegal immigration.

Legal Immigration

Legal immigration refers to noncitizens who are granted legal permanent residence (i.e., not citizenship, which provides a right to vote) in the United States by the federal government, or who reside in the United States and will ultimately be granted this status. Legal permanent residence includes the right to remain in the country indefinitely, to be gainfully employed, and to seek the benefits of U.S. citizenship through naturalization (Mulder et al., 2001). A distinction is made between legal immigrants who are new arrivees; *adjustees*, whose status was adjusted after they came to the United States; and *asylees*, who claimed that it was impossible for them to return to their native countries because of war or political persecution (Perry et al., 2001).

The majority of immigrant women are likely to enter the United States on family-sponsored immigrant visas (Malone, Baluja, Costanzo, & Davis, 2003). These visas are granted to individuals who seek to become U.S. citizens or residents (i.e., green card holders) through family connections to citizens or legal residents. One category of such immigrants are mail-order brides. Simons (1999) argued that American males have a higher propensity to marry foreign women and that international marriage brokerage is currently a booming cross-national business.

Women also can gain immigrant visas through a practice that has been termed *brain drain* (Simon, 2001). This brain drain is achieved through immigration policies that allow for legal immigrant status to be granted to those who are deemed to be "persons of extraordinary ability" or to have advanced training or skills in occupations that are important for the U.S. labor market (e.g., nurses). Companies or agencies can sponsor such individuals in gaining legal immigrant status (Malone et al., 2003).

One of the more recent developments in U.S. immigration policy is focused on creating more equal opportunities for individuals of various countries. Each year, the Diversity Lottery Program makes 55,000 immigrant visas available through a lottery to people who come from countries with low rates of immigration to the United States, such as African, Eastern European, and Latin American countries (U.S. Citizenship & Immigration Services, 2005). This program provides opportunities for women to come by themselves or with their families by obtaining legal immigrant status to reside and work in the United States.

Refugees

Another type of immigration status is granted to individuals who are considered refugees. Refugees are defined as those people outside their country of nationality who are unable or unwilling to return to that country because of persecution or a well-founded fear of persecution, which coincides with the definition determined by the 1967 United Nations Protocol on Refugees (Mulder et al., 2001). The U.S. Refugee Act of 1980 (U.S. Department of Health & Human Services, 2005) stated that under circumstances outlined by the United Nations Protocol, the United States will allow a number of individuals from any country to enter the country (Malone et al., 2003). This number is determined by the U.S. President and Congress and has a ceiling, which in the last years has been severely restricted because of U.S. war involvement and fears of foreign terrorism (Sengupta, 2002).

Women are particularly vulnerable as refugees. Although refugees of both genders undergo tremendously difficult experiences as a result of war or persecution, a woman's position as a refugee has been recognized to carry especially horrific repercussions. The Office of the United Nations High Commissioner for Refugees (1991) set forth guidelines for the protection of refugee women worldwide. This document stated that women refugees are at a greater risk of experiencing physical, sexual, economic, and emotional violence and must be protected either through relocation or by local agency services.

Illegal or Undocumented Immigration

The last category of immigrants to the United States consists of those migrating in search of employment and better living conditions. Often referred to pejoratively as illegal aliens or undocumented, the unauthorized migrant population consists primarily of two groups: those entering the United States primarily across land borders without inspection and those entering with legal temporary visas who violate the terms or stay beyond the specified time allotment (Mulder et al., 2001). The U.S. Bureau of the Census estimated that in recent years approximately 5 million individuals remained in the United States without legal documents (Malone et al., 2003).

Ninety-five percent of undocumented immigrants detained in the United States are Mexicans (Portes & Rumbaut, 1996), and their experiences of crossing the borders are often life threatening (Guarnaccia, 1997). In the past, male family members accompanied most Mexican immigrant women, whereas more recently an increasing number of Mexican women have immigrated to the United States alone (Salgado de Snyder, 1994).

Undocumented immigrant women remain in the United States because of economic benefits for their families and themselves and because of hopes of gaining legal resident status. The Immigration Reform and Control Act, which was signed by President Reagan in 1986 (U.S. Department of Homeland Security, 2005), stated that if an individual who has resided in the United States without legal documents can prove to the U.S. government that she has been living there for 10 years or more, she could qualify for legal immigrant status (Rodriguez & DeWolfe, 1990).

The recent terrorist attacks have spurred a new call for reforms of the immigration laws and immigration agencies (Dillon, 2001; Ofari Hutchinson, 2001; Toy, 2002). These reforms are likely to be implemented in the near future and will signify changes for many women immigrants, such as increased government control creating greater fears of imprisonment, deportation, and denial of status. In addition, the current anti-immigrant atmosphere in the United States may create additional difficulties for undocumented immigrants who are now residing here (Garcia, 2002).

THEORIES OF CAREER DEVELOPMENT
AND IMMIGRANT WOMEN

Career-counseling and vocational theories have emerged in the United States in response to pressing social concerns of the times, and large-scale immigration was one of the conditions that fueled the evolution of many of the early career theories (Swanson & Gore, 2002). Recently, many of the theories have been examined for their applicability to diverse U.S. populations. Although none of the theories has been directly tested with immigrant populations, these theories may serve as bases for understanding the career experiences of immigrant women and for theorizing about successful career services for this group of women.

Social-Cognitive Career Theory

Social-cognitive career theory (SCCT) provides a model for career interest, choice, and performance based on career-related experiences, which are shaped by environmental and personal factors (Lent, Brown, & Hackett, 1994). Career-related experiences are expected to lead to the development of self-efficacy that in turn allows individuals to develop positive beliefs about the outcomes of their work. Environmental factors can serve either as barriers or facilitors of career development processes, based on individuals' exposure to experiences and their cognitive appraisals of personal abilities and interests.

Although empirical support for SCCT is "strong and growing" (Swanson & Gore, 2002, p. 247), studies that tested the model with minority populations within the United States show only partial support (e.g., Flores & O'Brien, 2002). Nevertheless, SCCT can serve as a framework for understanding the career development of immigrant women because it takes into account their career experiences prior to relocation, their current self-efficacy in regard to career and work, as well as past and present environmental barriers and facilitators to career development. In my own career development as an immigrant woman, my career self-efficacy was strong because of growing up in Soviet Ukraine but was challenged by experiences of relocating to a society that is more gender segregated in the area of work. Subsequent portions of this chapter focus in greater detail on some of the potential influences on immigrant women's career experiences while in the United States and include SCCT as a theoretical framework for understanding their career development processes.

Theory of Career Transition

The theory of career transition (TCT) was proposed by Abrego and Brammer (1992) and is based on a number of developmental and career-specific theories that relate to midlife career change. This theory has utility for understanding the career development of immigrant women because, for the majority of women who recently migrated to the United States, relocation signifies a shift in their relationship to the world of work. Abrego and Brammer suggested that all work transitions lead to an experience of reorganization of self and the development of new assumptions about oneself and the world. The motivation for change, the magnitude of the transition, the availability of support, the perception of control over one's choices and environment, and one's personal ability to manage anxiety serve as markers for how positive or negative the career shift can be. According to Abrego and Brammer, transition to a new career can involve several phases: immobilization or shock, minimization of change, self-doubt, letting go of negative appraisals, testing new options, search for meaning, and integration or renewal. Many immigrant women, including myself, experience career-related transitions in a new culture as some of the most difficult spaces to negotiate. Although the TCT was developed to address the needs of individuals from majority backgrounds who live in Western or American contexts, the theory can serve as a general guide for conceptualizing the difficulties of immigrant women's transition into a foreign world of work.

Ecological Theory

The ecological model was proposed by Bronfenbrenner (1979), an immigrant from the Soviet Union, and was recently extended to career development and counseling by Cook, Heppner, and O'Brien (2002). Bronfenbrenner suggested that an individual behavior is influenced by four major subsystems: the microsystem (interpersonal interactions in an individual's life such as school or family), the mesosystem (interaction between two or more microsystems), the exosystem (subsystems that influence the individual such as neighborhood or the media), and the macrosystem (societal ideology). Cook et al. proposed that this ecological model can help career counselors to conceptualize the "dynamic interaction between the individual and the environment" in a way that recognizes the complexity of multiple identities and multiple sociocultural influences on individuals (p. 291).

Multiple systems come into play when an immigrant woman seeks to find employment and to develop her career in the United States. For instance, shortly after my relocation to the United States there were times when securing a job was essential not only for personal reasons of meaning and financial stability, but also in order to provide for my family back in the Ukraine. The ecological theory is helpful in conceptualizing the types of issues that may have an impact on the career development and career transitions of immigrant women and can provide an excellent framework for working with the realities immigrant women face in the United States. The

microsystemic, mesosystemic, exosystemic, and macrosystemic levels all
have a significant bearing on the career success of an immigrant woman.

Feminist Theory

Feminist principles have guided scholarship on the career development of
women in what has been described as "the most active and vibrant area of
research in all vocational development" (Fitzgerald, Fassinger, & Betz,
1995, p. 167). Meara (1997) highlighted how gender permeates all aspects
of career development and is the key factor in understanding and formulating all career development theories. Feminist theory has profoundly
shaped how vocational scholars conceptualize career development (e.g.,
Chronister, McWhirter, & Forrest, chap. 5, this volume). Feminist career
scholars have focused on external barriers, such as gender discrimination,
gender bias, differential treatment, and sexual harassment, as well as internal barriers to women's work, such as women's multiple-role conflicts.

Immigrant women experience the gendered worlds of both their own
culture and the host culture. For many immigrant women, gender oppression may take vastly different forms in the public and private spheres. The
Ukraine and Eastern Europe provide good examples of such differences,
where women could often develop in their careers in relatively equal ways
to men but were relegated to lower status in the private sphere of their
homes (e.g., working the double shift). Thus, both the home and host gender cultures shape how immigrant women approach work and their career
development. Immigrant women also face external and internal barriers to
career development that are common to native-born American women.
Feminist theory is essential to any examination of the career development
of immigrant women and to developing career services for this population.

PERSONAL FACTORS INFLUENCING THE CAREER
DEVELOPMENT OF IMMIGRANT WOMEN

Issues that influence the career experiences and development of immigrant women in the United States are numerous and reflect their unique
personal characteristics and the many circumstances of their relocation
and adjustment to a host culture. The working roles of immigrant women
are likely to shift on their relocation and these changes are often based on
the economic survival needs of women and their families (Hogan, 1996;
Menjivar, 1999; Simon, 2001). In order to understand the unique pathways
of immigrant women's career development, it is important to consider the
key influences on women's working lives, especially after they relocate to
the United States.

Diversity of Immigrant Women

Immigration has made the United States one of the most racially and ethnically diverse nations in the world (Marsella & Ring, 2003). Immigrant women who relocate to the United States will not only be representing widely diverse cultural and ethnic groups but also the complexity of human behavior influenced by vast differences in economic status, religious practice, age, educational level, physical ability, sexual orientation, and kinship system (see Table 12.1 for summary).

Cultural and Racial Diversity. The growing racial diversity of the United States is strongly related to the pattern of immigration from countries that have populations of non-White European descent. For example, more than one fourth of foreign-born individuals who reside in the United States come from Mexico (Marsella & Ring, 2003). Among other countries with high numbers of recent immigrants to the United States are the Philippines, China or Hong Kong, Cuba, Vietnam, India, the Dominican Republic, El Salvador, and Korea (Reimers, 1992). Immigrant women who enter the career-counseling process are likely to belong to visible racial minority groups.

Place of Origin. Immigrant women come from a markedly different racial and ethnic context when they arrive here from their country of origin. Onetime director of the Department of Mental Health's Multicultural Services Division, Dr. Giorgis, an Ethiopian immigrant, remarked that in Ethiopia people are not classified by color but by ethnicity and that for many immigrant Ethiopians the "concept of color really doesn't sink in until you have lived in this culture for a long period" (Smith, 2002, p. 87). Gabaccia (1994), a historian, argued that women immigrants to the United States may perceive more similarities (i.e., being a foreigner) than differences across their racial and ethnic backgrounds than U.S.-born minority women. In addition to the unique racial and ethnic composition of women's country of origin, it is important to consider whether they relocated from and to an urban or rural environment. Political climate as well as the economic status of their country of origin will also be significant for understanding the psychosocial factors that influence their career trajectories. Finally, because of the frequent military and political conflicts around the world, counselors must bear in mind the socioeconomic and political relations between the immigrant woman's home country and the United States.

Socioeconomic Status. Attention to socioeconomic status (SES) and its relation to mental health as well as career counseling is increasing (e.g., Heppner & O'Brien, chap. 3, this volume; Lott, 2002). An immigrant

TABLE 12.1
Psychosocial Factors That Can Influence Mental Health
and Career Functioning of Immigrant Women

Factors	Specific Considerations
Place of origin	Racial and ethnic composition of the country of origin
	Urban or rural home and host environments
	Political climate of the country or origin
	Developed, third world, or economy-in-transition economic status of the country
	Home country's relations with the host country
Conditions of migration	Economic
	Political
	Familial
	Educational
	Vocational
Socioeconomic status	Educational level
	Social class status in the home culture
	Financial resources available for migration
	Socioeconomic status of the home country
Demographic factors	Age
	Gender
	Ability level
	Religious practices
	Relationship status and size of the kinship unit
Social support	Proximity of similar ethnic community
	Proximity of other immigrant groups
	Proximity of family and friends
	Proximity of social services for immigrants
Personality factors	Personality traits (e.g., optimism)
	Coping styles
	Worldview
	Achievement motivation
	Resilience
	Rigidity or flexibility
	Cognitive styles
Language proficiency	Knowledge of spoken English
	Knowledge of written English
	Literacy in home language
	Availability of interpreters
Legal status	Legal immigrant (i.e., naturalized citizen, green card holder or permanent alien resident, asylum seeker)
	Refugee
	Undocumented immigrant
	Availability of legal and social services resources
Length since migration	Length of time in the host culture

Note. List of factors and considerations is not comprehensive.

woman's SES will determine her standing in the host environment (Marsella & Ring, 2003) and may be one of the most influential factors in her career development prior and subsequent to her relocation. A woman's SES is likely to be determined by her social status in her home country and the financial resources available to her for migration. The overall SES of her home country can also play a role in the ease of her adjustment to the economically "developed" United States. Finally, a woman's educational level before relocation can contribute to her ability to negotiate the career transition to a new country.

Demographic Factors. Immigrant women represent the full range of human diversity. Immigrant women differ in their age, sexual orientation, ability level, religious practices, and relationship status. For example, lesbian women, similar to heterosexual women, seek to migrate to the United States for personal, economic, and political reasons. Foner (1986) described Jamaican migrant workers in the United States who reported sending financial support to their "girlfriends" back in Jamaica. Espín (1999) wrote about those previously invisible in research: immigrant women for whom migration provided "space and permission to cross boundaries and transform their sexuality and sex roles" (p. 5). Using qualitative methodology, Espín elucidated the experiences of immigrant women for whom migration signified an opportunity to acknowledge and embrace their lesbian sexual identity.

Other demographic factors may be less discernible to an American career counselor because of the uniqueness of immigrant populations. Women's legal status is particularly important to their work opportunities and experiences. Immigrant women who enter and remain in the United States without legal immigration documents are restricted in their choices to domestic and menial labor. Some groups of women who relocate to the United States, often referred to as mail-order brides, are not free to follow their career choices because their immigrant status depends on their marriage to a partner who may be choosing for them because of their legal and psychological dependence. Women refugees can also experience restriction of their career choices because of their unstable status in the host country. In addition, English fluency, which can be essential to immigrant women's adjustments to a new country, may depend on characteristics such as age and cognitive ability.

Career-counseling literature in general, and this volume in particular, highlight the significance of demographic diversity, such as age and sexual orientation (e.g., Bieschke & Toepfer-Hendey, chap. 11, this volume). Immigrant women's career development reflects their complex multiple identities. For instance, a study by Loewy, Clark, and Yakushko (2003) described difficult career transitions faced by Bosnian women refugees who were attempting to reconcile various aspects of their lives, such as their religion, age, and relationship status, as they sought employment in the United States.

Personality Factors. Personality factors play an important role in the adjustment of immigrant women to a new culture and their experiences concerning their careers. Personality traits such as optimism, positive coping styles, achievement motivation, ability to be cognitively flexible rather than rigid, and self-efficacy help determine a woman's ability to make a career transition and begin a new pathway of career development in a host culture. Immigrant women who seek career counseling present the full range of personality factors that will influence their career lives.

Social Support and Relationship Factors

Family and ethnic community have been viewed as the primary environmental resources for immigrant and refugee women (Ben-Sira, 1997). Family can include not only individuals of blood relation, connections with whom may be severed by the relocation, but also persons with whom immigrant women have had prolonged contact during or following their relocation (Gold, 1989). Furthermore, the realities of ethnic enclaves in U.S. metropolitan communities, such as Chinatown, point to the importance many immigrants can attach to their ethnic communities while in a foreign land (Palinkas, 1982). These communities are often sources of social support as well as social networking for women immigrants and these community connections are likely to have enormous impact on employment-seeking strategies (Ben-Sira).

Immigrant women's relationship status and their familial experiences can be some of the most significant contributors to their career development. Women may feel a new sense of freedom in moving away from sharing a household with in-laws and developing their own relational space, which can include entrance into the workforce (Kosmarskaya, 1999). For example, Ybarra (1988) discussed the realities of Mexican women whose relocation to the United States signified for them greater economic power and interpersonal freedom.

Women immigrants may, however, encounter a number of difficulties in their nuclear and extended family due to their relocation, especially if they are in heterosexual married relationships. Viewed in traditional patriarchal societies as the keepers and transmitters of cultural values, women can experience an increased pressure to focus on their families after relocation (Espín, 1999; Narayan, 1997; Simons, 1999; Toren, 2001). Itzhaky and Ribner (1999) found that in a sample of 200 female and male Jewish refugees, women had a much higher sense of responsibility for all aspects of the family than did men. At the same time, women may not have the resources of extended families and the knowledge of local community resources to be able to care for their families to the same degree they were able to in their home culture (Zlotnik, 2000). Weeks (2000) found that women whose male partners gained entrance to the United States for employment purposes experienced the U.S. culture as pressuring them toward even greater gender-role traditionality than their home culture. For example, Weeks described women in her study discussing meeting with Americans who insisted it was greatly important for these women to stay at home in order to care for their husbands.

Immigration has been seen as a source of relational stress for many women. Domestic violence against immigrant women by their partners has been judged to be a grave and all too frequent situation. The National Council for Research on Women (1995) reported that, in a survey of immigrant women in the San Francisco Bay Area, 34% of Latina, 30% of Chinese, and 20% of Filipina women reported experiencing domestic violence since their relocation to the United States. Forty-eight percent of the Latinas in this sample reported that the intensity and frequency of the abuse had increased since their move to the United States. This report also cited a study of Chicana women in the District of Columbia indicating that 77% of immigrant women who were married to U.S. citizens or legal residents are battered. Yoshihama and Horrocks (2002), who studied Japanese American and Japanese immigrant women in the United States, found that the proportion of women in their sample who experienced physical, sexual, and emotional violence in their partnerships was higher than that of the general U.S. population. Russian women refugees in Kosmarskaya's (1999) sample attributed the serious worsening of their marital relationships to the overall instability of the individuals in the immigrant household and specifically to the male partners who were "drinking and unemployed" (p. 192).

A woman whose immigrant status depends on marriage to a U.S. citizen or legal resident may be at even higher risk of domestic violence. Narayan (1995) wrote about mail-order brides and cited that women who enter the United States through this arrangement are more economically, psychologically, and linguistically dependent on their partners than other women, may be rejected by their ethnic communities within the United States, and can be completely unfamiliar with any legal or social resources available to them, leaving them additionally vulnerable to their partners.

Women's access to adequate social support and the atmosphere in their intimate partnerships have significant consequences for their career development in the United States. Ethnic communities, families, friends, and partners can be an asset or a barrier to women's experience of work. The conflict of multiple roles in women's lives can place severe limitations on immigrant women's successful career development (Fitzgerald & Weitzman, 1992). Immigrant women may be required to hold primary responsibility as household managers and parents whereas their resources for help with these responsibilities (e.g., grandparents) may be severely limited. McWhirter, Torres, and Rasheed (1998) also suggested that multiple-role stress can serve as a barrier to a woman's career adjustment process. Betz (chap. 2, this volume) discusses a number of barriers, such as family and career conflicts, that can have a negative impact on women's career development.

Women's Gender Roles

Immigration has been seen both as providing women with an impetus for challenging the gender traditionality of their cultures and families, and as pressuring women toward more traditional gender roles. Various studies have shown that immigrant women reported improvement of their gender-role status as the result of migration because of their perception of increased control over decision making in the household, greater personal autonomy, and the opportunity to challenge their culture's gender stereotypes (Foner, 1986, 2001; Hondagneu-Sotelo, 1994; Pedraza, 1991; Simon, 1992).

Nontraditional gender-role orientation can serve as a facilitator of immigrant women's career transition or adjustment (Betz, chap. 2, this volume). Career counseling with immigrant women can be influenced by gendered beliefs that are either self-facilitating or self-limiting. Immigrant women's experiences within their intimate relationships and within their communities profoundly influence their career expectations, self-efficacy, and choices.

Immigration as a Stressful Event

The process of immigration is almost always a highly stressful life experience. Rumbaut (1991) stated that "migration can produce profound psychological distress even among the most motivated and well-prepared individuals, and even in the most receptive circumstances" (p. 56). The stress experienced by immigrant women can result from a number of factors related to their relocation and adjustment to a new culture. Espín (1999) suggested that among the difficult experiences for immigrant women can be posttraumatic stress, mourning and grieving of multiple losses as the result of moving, and acculturative stress. Transition to a new culture can result in loneliness, loss of self-confidence, strain and fatigue from cognitive overload, a sense of uprootedness, and a perception that they are unable to function competently in the new culture (Espín, 1997; Garza-Guerrero, 1974).

Rodriguez and DeWolfe (1990) documented that in a sample of 90 legal and undocumented immigrants from Mexico, the majority experienced high psychological distress. In a sample of Portuguese-speaking immigrant women, McIntyre and Augusto (1999) documented that women with a prior history of abuse seem to undergo a "supercoping" phase prior to immigration and "collapse" upon their arrival to the United States (p. 387). Weeks (2000) conducted a qualitative study of women whose husbands were relocated to the United States for employment purposes and found that these women similarly described a sense of losing their self-esteem and identity and experienced an intense isolation. Hovey (2000) documented that adult Mexican immigrants can be at risk of experiencing critical levels of depression and suicidal ideation after their relocation.

Refugee women can experience tremendous psychological distress that results from their traumatization history prior to relocation. Refugee women may undergo intense reactions of stress due to forced relocation (Saldana, 1992) and conflicts around having to flee their homes (Roe, 1992). Posttraumatic stress reactions that refugee women experience can be related to their experience of rape and sexual violence (Friedman, 1992), torture (Chester, 1992; Herbst, 1992), or the experiences of war trauma (Bowen, Carscadden, Beighle, & Fleming, 1992; Shepherd, 1992). In addition to depression, anxiety, and posttraumatic stress disorder symptoms, refugee women can respond to their difficulties with culturally unique psychological reactions such as psychosomatic blindness (Van Boemel & Rozee, 1992).

The career development process of immigrant women will be significantly influenced by immigrant women's experiences of stress due to their relocation and its circumstances. Women who seek help with their career development or career transition, especially soon after their relocation, are often functioning under duress and are likely to feel overwhelmed. This stress is mediated by their internal and external resources, including access to career counseling and job training.

Resilience and Resourcefulness of Immigrant Women

For the majority of immigrants, moving to a new culture is viewed as a difficult but hopeful move toward their goals of safety, prosperity, and well-being for themselves and their children (Zajacova, 2002). Voluntary immigration, positive expectations, language skills, and support are associated with more positive mental health outcomes for immigrants (Escobar, Nervi, & Gara, 2000; Hondagneu-Sotelo, 1994; Salgado de Snyder, 1994). Immigrant women can have strong internal resources and may see work involvement as a chance to improve their self-esteem through providing a service to their families and community (Yee, 1992). Immigrant women can also become involved in political activism, which may help buffer them from the disempowering and stressful events of their relocation (Light, 1992).

Women's career development trajectories are influenced by their positive expectations, resilience, and the internal and external resources they can access. Immigrant women can be especially eager to find a suitable career after their relocation because their work will be not only a source of financial security but also a source of self-esteem. The Office of the United Nations High Commission for Refugees (1991) encouraged the nations that host refugee women to focus on aiding women in finding suitable employment as part of their integration into a new community and their healing from the trauma of war or persecution.

Acculturation

Acculturation, or the process of adapting to the values and behaviors (e.g., gender roles) of a new culture, is the most common factor used in discussion of immigrants' mental health needs (Flannery, Reise, & Yu, 2001; Ortega, Rosenheck, Alegria, & Desai, 2000; Salgado de Snyder, 1994). There are, however, inconsistent findings concerning immigrants' acculturation experiences and resulting mental health outcomes: Researchers have puzzled about what acculturation levels, for what immigrant groups, and in what countries can lead to positive mental health outcomes. For example, in a review of five major large-scale studies examining the prevalence of mental disorders among Mexican-born and U.S.-born Mexican Americans living in the United States, data show that Mexican-born immigrants have better mental health profiles than U.S.-born Mexican Americans (Escobar et al., 2000). Mexican-born immigrant women, in particular, had a lower prevalence of serious mental disorders and substance abuse, which may be increased in the U.S.-born Mexican American women because of their experiences of racism. These data indicate that greater acculturation to U.S. culture was directly related to more negative mental health outcomes for Mexican Americans. The authors challenged the notion that Mexican immigrants are helpless and mentally ill and that adapting to U.S. culture necessarily leads to positive mental health outcomes.

On the other hand, acculturation as part of immigrants' response to a new culture has been considered a significant factor in overall functioning. Leong (2001) examined various patterns of acculturation in Asian immigrants to the United States and found that acculturation plays an important role in the career development processes of this group. Berry (1980) described the acculturation process as dependent on individuals' choices about integrating into American society. Berry highlighted the complexity of the acculturation process that must be attended to in addressing the career development of immigrant women. For example, the assumption that increased time since relocation inevitably results in immigrant women's positive adjustment can be inaccurate. The barriers to positive adjustment and acculturative stress can be related less to women's choices regarding the host culture than to the societal atmosphere. The U.S. host culture, with its general anti-immigrant sentiment as well as the cultural realities of racism and sexism, is likely to have a significant effect on immigrant women's career development.

SOCIOCULTURAL FACTORS INFLUENCING IMMIGRANT WOMEN'S CAREER DEVELOPMENT

Immigrant women in the United States can experience a number of difficulties because of multiple oppressive forces that are sociocultural in their nature. These forces are likely to include xenophobia, racism, sexism, poverty, and employment discrimination, as well as other systemic issues.

Xenophobia

The Desk dictionary definition of xenophobia is the "fear and hatred of strangers or foreigners or of anything that is strange or foreign" (1995, p. 642). Xenophobia has been linked to jingoism, which refers to extreme chauvinism or nationalism marked especially by a belligerent foreign policy and ethnocentrism, which is characterized by or based on the attitude that one's own group or culture are superior. Xenophobia has also been identified with an attitudinal orientation of hostility against nonnatives in a given population and viewed as a form of racism that does not use the concept of race as a defining element (Boehnke, Hagan, & Hefler, 1998). Marsella (1997) stated that xenophobia is typically characterized by the rising fear of immigrants and noted that the growing uncertainty in the world can be related to the host culture's rejection of culturally different others. Fear and dislike of immigrants is most likely when the immigrants represent "aliens" who possess different historical, cultural, reproductive, economic, and racial characteristics from the majority individuals within the host culture (Marsella).

The United States has had a long history of mistreatment of immigrants in general and women immigrants in particular (Foner, 2001). Public opinion polls continue to indicate that the majority of Americans would like to either severely restrict or put a moratorium on immigration (DeLaet, 2000). Groups such as the Federation for American Immigration Reform, a national educational and lobbying network, are vocal in expressing their concern about "the adverse effects of out-of-control immigration" (National Council for Research on Women, 1995, p. 3). Another group, Sachem Quality of Life Organization, whose goal is to have the government deport illegal immigrants, condemns illegal immigrants as invaders and criminals who destroy suburban neighborhoods (Sachs & Baker, 2001). The 1986 Reagan-era Immigration Reform and Control Act (U.S. Department of Homeland Security, 2005) sought to set limits on immigration with the rhetoric that immigration fuels U.S. unemployment, depresses wages, and costs jobs for native workers. Proposition 187 (1994) in California (California Department of Education, 2003) revealed a widespread attitude that the provision of social services, education, and nonemergency medical care to undocumented immigrants was burdensome (DeLaet; National Council for Research on Women). Both U.S. and Canadian social agencies that serve immigrant populations have been reporting severe budget cuts or enforced closures of services (Doors Closed to Immigrant Women, 2000).

Blatant discrimination against immigrants has been rationalized on the basis of economic issues, concerns about population growth, and other arguments (Marsella & Ring, 2003). The history of minority populations' treatment within the United States reveals a rhetoric regarding economics, religion, and safety similar to that used to rationalize discriminatory practices against racial minorities, women, and gay and lesbian individuals (Sue & Sue, 1999). Recent economic and crime rate statistics highlight the fallacy of claims that immigration puts economic and social strains on U.S. society (Lee, Martinez, & Rosenfeld, 2001; National Research Council, 1997). As a labor force, immigrants produce nearly $10 billion in profits for the United States. The country's economy is highly dependent on immigrants who are willing to work in low-level, low-paying jobs (National Research Council).

Recent international and national events have brought public and political outcries against immigration to new highs. The American media have highlighted fears and concerns regarding immigrants. U.S. policy sanctions tougher restrictions on immigration and roundups of undocumented immigrants, and may encourage lashing out at those who appear to be foreign (Dillon, 2001; Ofari Hutchinson, 2001; Toy, 2002). The White House administration has severely restricted entrance of refugees to the United States, which carries enormous repercussions for persons awaiting help in relocation camps around the world (Sengupta, 2002).

Xenophobia toward immigrants goes further than punitive policies and unfavorable public debate. Prejudices about immigrants skills and abilities based on their linguistic mastery of English or on the way they choose to dress or behave may also be considered xenophobic. Women immigrants suffer negative consequences brought on by xenophobic attitudes and policies and their career development can be strongly influenced by these attitudes and policies. Women immigrants may perceive the labor market as closed to them because of the general attitude that immigrants are here to get the jobs of native-born Americans. They may also be denied jobs or placed in low-wage, unskilled jobs because of the perception that they lack intelligence due to their lack of English skills or a nonnative accent (Melville, 1988). If women choose to follow their home culture's practices regarding dress, holidays, or social interactions, employers may perceive their behavior as unacceptable. These reactions can further decrease women's career confidence and self-efficacy and carry a negative stimulus value in women's career choices (Betz, chap. 2, this volume).

Racism

For immigrants of color, racism presents a new and painful reality. Although xenophobia and racism may be closely interrelated, considering that the majority of the immigrants to the United States are also non-White, it is useful to distinguish these two oppressions. Lind (1998), in his review of attitudes toward immigrants, highlighted that individuals who are racial minorities and are legal citizens of the United States display a level of intolerance toward immigrants similar to that of White native-born Americans. Lind further asserted that anti-immigration sentiments have been found among Latino and African American leaders because the immigrant workers, who often are willing to take low-wage, nonunionized jobs, have been seen as likely to undermine the efforts of minority labor unions.

Racism has been a tremendous force that affects the realities of immigrant women in the United States. Incredibly, U.S. immigration policies have been shaped by policies that have sought to "control the contamination by the inferior races" (Sinke & Gross, 1992, p. 68). Unquestionably, non-White immigrants to the United States and their subsequent generations have suffered immense abuses and restrictions because of racist attitudes and policies (Comas-Díaz & Greene, 1994; Sue, Ivey, & Pedersen, 1996; Sue & Sue, 1999).

Immigrant women's career development, similar to that of U.S.-born women of color, is likely to be negatively influenced by racism and racist stereotypes. Carter and Cook (1992) provided an excellent outline of a culturally relevant perspective for understanding the career development of visible racial-ethnic minority individuals. They emphasized that, in addition to paying attention to career development theories, career-counseling scholars and practitioners must attend to the historical-cultural perspective of work, the cultural and family system characteristics unique for racial minorities, and the significance of acculturation and racial identity development. McWhirter et al. (1998) stressed that racism is one of the most significant environmental barriers that women of color face in their career adjustment. Bingham, Ward, and Butler (chap. 7, this volume) provide an excellent overview of career-counseling issues with ethnic minority women and other chapters provide information about specific groups of ethnic minority women in the United States.

Gender Discrimination

Gender discrimination and sexism are forces of oppression that affect women globally (Smith, 2000). Patriarchy has power over women in all parts of the world and the process of immigration and its consequences for women are also shaped by societal sexism. Because women are often seen as the carriers and preservers of cultural norms through their primary participation in childbearing and child raising, the pressure on women to assume traditional gender roles in the new culture can be even greater than in their home environment (Espín, 1999; Narayan, 1997; Simons, 1999; Toren, 2001). The mere existence of mail-order brides, often coming from Asia and Eastern Europe, who are likely to be chosen for their submissive, traditionally feminine behaviors, points to the intensity of patriarchal oppression. The prevalence of domestic violence against these brides emphasizes the mind-set that seems to sanction such patriarchy (Simons; Sinke & Gross, 1992).

The dominant society's gender stereotypes of immigrant women can exacerbate the impact of sexism. Yeoh and Huang (2000) found that immigrant women who serve as domestic servants are often portrayed by the host culture as sexually predatory and promiscuous. Weeks (2000), who examined the identity renegotiations of women whose male partners came to the United States to complete their academic work, reported that these immigrant women perceived a much greater pressure for them to assume traditionally feminine roles as wives and mothers than in their home cultures.

Women may view immigration as an opportunity to redefine their gender roles (Espín, 1999; Prieto, 1992). A new location can be used as a space to renegotiate gendered relations, which can provide immigrant women a chance to escape the patriarchal constraints of their own cultures (Willis & Yeoh, 2000). The necessity of and opportunity for employment outside the home often serves as one such escape for immigrant women (Simon, 2001; Willis & Yeoh). Pessar (1987) interviewed women who immigrated from the Dominican Republic and cited the following statement from one of the participants: "If both the husband and wife are earning salaries then they should equally rule the household. In the Dominican Republic it is always the husband who gives the orders to the household. But here, when the two are working, the woman feels herself the equal of the man in ruling the home" (p. 121). In her later work, Pessar (1995) observed that women's opportunities to earn wages often give them the rights to greater autonomy and authority within the household, although the dynamics of how women assert these rights and what these rights mean within different cultures can vary.

In the last three decades, career-counseling literature about the impact of gender stereotyping and sexism on women's career development has experienced tremendous growth. The current volume provides an excellent overview of current theories and empirical findings on diverse women and their career development. This extensive attention to the career development of U.S.-born women, especially women of color, can serve as a guide for those career counselors who work with immigrant women.

Economic Discrimination and Poverty

Economic discrimination, poverty, and employment discrimination are among the most profound influences on immigrant women's career experiences in the United States. The majority of immigrant women must work in order to survive economically (Hogan, 1996; Menjivar, 1999; Simon, 2001). Ben-Sira (1997) suggested that "economic problems and problems of employment are among the most salient instrumental problems of immigrants" (p. 75). Immigrant women are continually overrepresented in the lowest socioeconomic levels of U.S. society and are likely to experience their work as oppressive.

The 2000 population census provided important information about the employment status of foreign-born individuals in the United States (Schmidley, 2001). This report suggested that the unemployment rates are higher for foreign-born populations in the United States than for native-born individuals. Immigrant women who are either noncitizens or have been in the United States for less than 10 years tend to have the lowest reported labor participation, although they may not be reporting their for-cash domestic labor work. In comparison with native-born individuals, foreign-born workers are less likely to occupy managerial or professional specialty occupations (jobs of the middle and higher social classes) and are more likely to work in skilled labor and service-oriented jobs. Immigrant women earn 59 cents for every dollar earned by U.S.-born males in similar occupations and 83 cents for every dollar earned in a similar occupation by an average U.S.-born female. The poverty rate of foreign-born individuals is 16.8% versus 11.2% for native-born persons (Schmidley).

The census data also revealed further differences between immigrant individuals by their country of origin and their gender (Schmidley, 2001). U.S. immigration policy requires different educational levels for individuals from various countries, which reveal both national-origin restrictions and strategies for assuring an influx of menial laborers. The highest percentage of high school completion is required for immigrants from Africa (94.9%), whereas it is 79.6% for immigrants from Central and South America and 33.8% for Mexican immigrants. Poverty rate is the highest for Latin American immigrants: 21.9% versus the national rate of 11.2%. Individuals who migrated from Western Europe and Australia as well as from the "developed" Asian countries often have employment and educational levels closer to that of native-born U.S. individuals. Immigrant women of all nationalities, however, appear to fare worse than men (Schmidley).

Historically, immigrant women have been employed in the United States as domestic workers (Chang, 2001; Messias, 2001). This trend toward hiring immigrant women for jobs such as domestic cleaning, laundry, child care, and elder care may have been spurred by the growing entrance of mostly White U.S.-born women into the workforce (Hondagneu-Sotelo, 1994). Domestic service menial jobs may be the only possibilities open to immigrant women because of their lack of English or lack of legal papers, but also because of general cultural attitudes toward immigrants (Messias). For a great number of immigrant women, regardless of their country of origin, such work signifies a downward shift to a low-wage and low-status dead-end job (Foner, 2001; Hogan, 1996). Hogan stated that "throughout American history, immigrant women often worked at unrewarding and difficult jobs, facing constant hazards, discrimination, exploitation, and even death" (p. 44). Immigrant women's qualifications based on their previous educational and work experience may be unrecognized because of their language problems or difficulties with prerequisite educational and licensing exams (Foner).

The existence of sweatshops in the United States serves as the most vivid illustration of the types of employment discrimination and abuse immigrant women experience. An exhibit in 2002 entitled *Between the Rock and a Hard Place: A History of American Sweatshops From 1920 to the Present* (2002), showed that sweatshops, often connected to the U.S. apparel industry, continue to operate. The web site of this exhibit provides a statement by the U.S. Secretary of Labor Alexis Herman in the wake of publicity about sweatshop abuses in California (Between a Rock and a Hard Place, n.d.). He is quoted as saying:

> In this era of concern for civility, decency, and family values, sweatshops are repugnant to our moral core. It is wrong to value fashion when we do not value the people who make fashion real. . . . Sweatshops reflect too vividly how we as a nation feel about the weakest among us. And it is such an "underground" problem that there is no definitive source on how many sweatshops operate in this country. But we know this: One is one too many.

U.S. sweatshops typically operate by forcing immigrant children and women to work in unsanitary conditions, conditions that have been described as slavery (Branigin, 1995). Pessar (2000) indicated that immigrant women may be willing to work in sweatshop conditions because of their desperate need for money, lack of legal status, and the fact that the sweatshop provides for nontraditional work hours, such as night work.

On the other side of the social class ladder in the United States, immigrant women who have had distinguished academic careers in their homelands often are able to receive special immigration privileges from the U.S. government. The National Science Foundation (2004) estimated that in a single year approximately 18,000 men and 4,500 women with advanced degrees in sciences and engineering immigrate to the United States. These women, however, also experience a downward shift in their status as well as discrimination. Manrique and Manrique (1999) studied women scholars from developing countries in American academia and found that women professors reported that they frequently were harassed by other faculty and students because of their accent and way of dressing. For example, a woman faculty member reported that "during one of her first job interviews, the male professor interviewing her derided her for wearing pants and proceeded to tell her that if this was a common practice in her country of origin, she would be expected to wear something else if she were teaching in his institution" (Manrique & Manrique, p. 112). Manrique and Manrique further highlighted that immigrant women faculty, more than immigrant men, were questioned about their right to teach about American subjects. Women who participated in the study described how their standard of living, social status, and the perceived support for their research were lower than in their country of origin. Thus, even relatively privileged immigrant women experience downward social and status mobility as well as discrimination in their U.S. employment.

Immigrant women's career development in the United States may often begin with low-skill, low-level jobs that offer them no opportunity for professional or personal growth (Espiritu, 1999; Hondagneu-Sotelo, 1999; Menjivar, 1999; Pessar, 1999). Poverty or financial difficulties along with employment discrimination are likely to reflect the working realities of many immigrant women. Social class and its influence on mental health and well-being are receiving greater attention in the psychological literature (e.g., Lott, 2002). Heppner and O'Brien (chap. 3, this volume) provides an excellent source on how to conceptualize and work with social class issues in the career development process.

Oppression Based on Women's Multiple Identities

Xenophobia, racism, sexism, and poverty do not operate independently of each other. Women's multiple identities and their intersectionality mean that women will often experience oppression and discrimination based on numerous sources of prejudice. Although this chapter does not discuss oppression based on immigrant women's religious affiliation, lesbian identity, age, physical ability, or appearance, each of these forces does have an impact on women's career development and adjustment.

CAREER COUNSELING WITH IMMIGRANT WOMEN

The career development path of immigrant women is shaped by both their career experience in their home countries and their relocation to the United States. This fact, although obvious, is important to highlight because immigrant women's career development is not affected by the same factors as U.S.-born women. Immigrant women's circumstances from their childhood to the time of relocation, in their families, immediate communities, schools (if they were allowed to receive an education), and their countries, reflect a unique combination of factors that are likely to be different from those of U.S.-born women. At the same time, after their relocation to the United States, immigrant women can share experiences common to native-born women based on entrance into the Western-American gender, race, and class systems that shape the world of work in the United States.

The following principles can serve as guidelines for career-counseling work with immigrant women. Many of the principles share commonalities with standards that direct the career-counseling process with U.S.-born majority and minority women. These principles, however, continually highlight the distinctive needs of immigrant women in career counseling.

Challenging Assumptions

Ethnocentric and xenophobic attitudes are not foreign to career-counseling practitioners and scholars. A general cultural belief that the United States is the greatest nation in the world permeates nearly all aspects of American society and is reflected in the nearly complete absence of international career-counseling information in U.S. career-counseling training programs. In my experience as an immigrant from the Ukraine, I have been surprised and even offended by the prevalent assumptions of U.S. citizens about gender relations and the world of work for women in my home country. Numerous women from other foreign countries have shared with me similar reactions to gender and cultural stereotypes they have experienced in the United States. It is paramount that career counselors working with immigrant women enter their work with a healthy skepticism regarding traditional cross-cultural assumptions and ready to realize that their knowledge of immigrant women's experiences may be inaccurate.

Immigrant women's career development in their home cultures often does not follow the stereotypes set forth by the American media's representation of women in other countries. Kagitcibasi and Berry (1989), who wrote about women's employment in Pakistan and Turkey, suggested that in many gender-segregated societies women report experiencing more occupational and professional freedom than in gender-integrated societies such as Western Europe or the United States. Women's judgment of their career experiences in both their home and host cultures is shaped by many unique cultural and personal factors, many of which may indeed be alien to an American career counselor.

Immigrant women who are relocating from socialist or postsocialist countries arrive from societies where the majority of women were able to have their own careers. Describing the dual-earner families in Hungary, Clason (1992) stated, "In communist Hungary, full-time employment was both a right and an obligation for every adult" (p. 99). Many socialist and Soviet-block countries (e.g., the former Soviet Union, Eastern European countries, the Republic of China, Cuba) are committed to gender equality and opportunities for women to choose from a wide range of careers. One of the proudest boasts of the Soviet socialist system was that nearly 95% of women were in paid employment and that 30% of the seats in the Supreme Soviet—the Soviet equivalent of the U.S. legislature—were reserved for women (Rule & Noonan, 1996). Clason stated that during the socialist era, "the role of the male as main breadwinner became virtually extinct and household work and childcare at home were considerably reduced" (p. 99).

Career counselors who work with women from former Soviet-block countries or countries with communist governments such as the Republic of China and Cuba should be aware of these social differences in gender equality at work that resulted from communist reformulations of the division of labor. Women from these countries may not have experienced Western job segregation by gender or occupational gender stereotyping and thus may have had opportunities to develop self-concepts, interests, experiences, and self-efficacy in a much wider range of occupations. Subsequently, the transition to an occupationally gender-segregated country such as the United States can have difficult career consequences for these women. These immigrant women can be especially disappointed with occupational limitations set on them by xenophobic restrictions such as the availability of only domestic services or dead-end jobs, by lack of structural support for women's full participation in the workforce such as inadequate child care, and by job-related sexist experiences. An American career counselor who unquestioningly accepts ethnocentric notions that women in other countries have it worse than women in the United States may provide damaging and unethical services to immigrant women clients.

Yet, the world of immigrant women is as diverse as the world. Whereas some immigrant women come to the United States and face gender discrimination in a new way, others migrate from countries where they may not have had any chances previously to develop a career. Colonial history left many women working menial jobs that supported the global capitalist economy (Fall, 2001; Sircar & Kelly, 2001). Furthermore, many countries restrict women's occupational participation because of gender-restrictive religious and political atmospheres (Soni-Sinha, 2001). The experiences of Afghani women under Taliban rule attest to how limited women's access to work and career can be. American career counselors must carefully examine cultural experiences and expectations of a woman's career in order to adapt counseling interventions to diverse women's needs.

Stereotypes, ethnocentric attitudes, and reliance on one's own cultural understanding are difficult to change because they provide a structure for the expectations of how others in foreign countries act and behave. Approaching a session with a beginner's mind can communicate to an immigrant woman that her career counselor is open to learning about and respecting both her culture and her unique position within that culture as well as facilitating the establishment of an alliance (Heppner & Heppner, 2003).

Balancing Openness to Learn With Offering Expertise

Career-counseling scholarship and practice in the United States have had extensive academic and political support and gathered a wealth of knowledge to offer those who seek career-counseling services in this country (Swanson & Gore, 2002). Career counseling has been enriched by growing attention to the diverse career experiences of marginalized populations in the United States. American career counselors can provide women with a number of excellent resources for obtaining a job and establishing a career in their new host country. These resources can include information about job-search skills, access to occupational information, the variety of alternative work environments, and federal, state, and local laws, rules, and regulations.

Using Culturally Valid Career Assessment

Assessment strategies in working with immigrant women can follow principles of career development for American-born women in general and women of color in particular. Lonborg and Hackett (chap. 4, this volume) discuss the purposes and the strategies for career assessment of women. Assessments in career counseling gather information in order to decide on specific counseling strategies to address clients' needs. The gathered information must be meaningful and focus on the client and her environment (Hackett & Lonborg). Career assessment can also be utilized to provide feedback to the client, to share new perspectives, to highlight new ideas, or to stimulate discussions (Hackett & Lonborg). Hackett and Lonborg emphasize that gender must be a central part of the career-assessment process, both by directly assessing how women's gendered experiences have influenced their career development and by using assessment measures with an awareness of gender bias.

Bingham and Ward (1994) highlighted that in the process of career counseling with ethnic minority women, "the counselor must keep in mind that factors such as the counselor's culture, race, ethnicity, or gender can hinder or encourage the disclosure of information" (p. 179). Similarly, immigrant women may not disclose information relevant to their career development needs because of fears of being judged or misunderstood by an American counselor.

The values of a particular culture can have a unique impact on the career development of immigrant women. For example, career choice can be defined markedly differently in countries where factors other than individual volition and interest have an effect on individual career decisions (Hesketh & Rounds, 1995). An interest in math and science can be common among women from countries such as China and the former Soviet Union, where access to occupations considered traditionally male in U.S. culture have not been restricted. Women can also have a stronger interest in math and science owing to the higher prestige given to these occupations in their home culture (Hesketh & Rounds).

A theoretical foundation should guide the assessment of career experiences and needs of immigrant women. Social-cognitive learning theory emphasizes how women's prerelocation career circumstances may have shaped their interests, choice, and performance as well as their self-efficacy beliefs about work. The theory also recognizes the significance of assessing current facilitators and barriers to women's career development, many of which have been discussed in this chapter. The theory of career transition also provides a useful framework for understanding how immigrant women can approach changes in their career development. Career-counseling practitioners may seek to assess women's motivation for change, the magnitude of their career transition, the availability of support, the perception of control over choices and environment, and the personal ability to manage anxiety. Furthermore, various factors in immigrant women's experience related to their career development can be assessed by utilizing the ecological model: Counselors can keep in mind the microsystemic (personal), mesosystemic (family), exosystemic (community), and macrosystemic (societal) factors that influence women's career development. Finally, feminist theory can aid career practitioners in the assessment of women's gender identity development and its influence on their career choices.

If using an existing assessment measure with immigrant women, career counselors must become aware of the limitations of these instruments with diverse women and with racial and ethnic minorities in the United States (see Lonborg & Hackett, chap. 4, this volume; Fouad, 2002, for discussion of the Strong Interest Inventory). Career counselors must also attain knowledge and skills in assessing acculturation and its impact on immigrant women (Leong & Brown, 1995). Additionally, career counselors must be able to use assessment instruments to help immigrant women identify their options, while at the same time keeping in mind that foreign-born women can be unaware of career choices that would seem obvious to native-born women.

Career counselors who work with immigrant women may also seek to assess women's immigration status, time since relocation to the United States, and interaction with governmental agencies around their residence and employment status. Women's language proficiency in both spoken and written English may also be included in the career assessment. In addition, the counselor can inquire about women's levels of literacy in their home language. These factors can play a crucial role in immigrant women's career development processes.

Finally, it is essential that career counselors be aware that career assessment instruments were developed, normed, and researched based on American and Western cultural standards. In conducting assessments with immigrant women, career counselors must inform women that their inferences and recommendations are tentative and that, although tests can provide clients with new and valuable information, results become conclusive only when test results make meaningful sense to individuals being assessed. At the same time, counselors can actively seek to explore cultural validity and applicability of the measures they use.

Using Interpreters or Working With Linguistic Limitations

One of the unique aspects of working with immigrant women is the potential use of interpreters. Establishing rapport with the client when another person is present in the counseling room is likely to be complex. Complications arise when the immigrant woman has concerns about the anonymity of the counseling process based on fears that an interpreter is likely to interact with the woman's ongoing ethnic community (Pernice, 1994).

Immigrant women may be unfamiliar with the U.S. concept of confidentiality with psychological professionals, or may mistrust the concept even when it is understood. Ishisaka, Nguyen, and Okimoto (1985) found that some of their Indochinese clients had to be taught about confidentiality and its use in health settings. Immigrant women who have left politically repressive home environments can understandably be suspicious about the limits of confidentiality and this suspicion will often be heightened by the presence of an interpreter.

Another complication in using an interpreter or conducting a counseling session in a foreign language are differences in language systems. For example, my native language has two levels of how a person can be addressed: "you" can be either an informal *ty* or formal *Vy* and the use of either carries significant ramifications. Using *Vy* denotes respect, often for the person's age and position, but also communicates a more distant, formal relationship (i.e., not a trusting alliance). Using *ty* may seem to convey a lack of respect; it is commonly reserved for people who have established a close rapport with each other. Similarly, in the Indochinese languages, personal pronouns and classifiers are used to reflect important social hierarchies (Pernice, 1994). Therefore, if working with an interpreter or using a foreign language, the counselor must inquire about the linguistic customs of the language of the woman client and keep in mind the potential pitfalls of not communicating in the same language.

Career Interventions With Immigrant Women

One of the first tasks in delivering career interventions to immigrant women is the establishment of rapport. Many immigrant women are likely to be altogether unfamiliar with the processes and goals of counseling and a sufficient level of trust must be established for an immigrant woman to utilize career-counseling interventions. If rapport is not established, an immigrant woman may not return to counseling and may avoid subsequent opportunities to seek professional help. The psychotherapy process literature indicates that one of the key predictors of a client returning for a second session is whether they have formed a strong working alliance in the first session (Tryon & Kane, 1993). Heppner and Heppner (2003) suggested that what affects the beginning of a strong working alliance can be culturally determined.

A career counselor who is mindful of the immigrant woman's needs to learn and trust the process of career counseling can focus on creating a positive safe environment. One of the strategies that can help create such an atmosphere is asking a woman to teach the counselor a few words in her language, such as those for "hello," "thank you," "yes," "no," and "goodbye." Those who frequently work with immigrant women can choose to keep an atlas or a globe in their office and ask women to describe where they came from or tell their story of migration. Following the immigrant woman's lead in the etiquette of communication can be another way to show concern and respect. For example, giving the woman a choice of how and where to sit in the office or accepting gifts for the counselor's time and assistance can communicate respect for cultural norms. Finally, acknowledging to immigrant women that the counselor wants to have a better understanding of them and their culture can help create a culturally and personally affirming therapeutic space.

   Helpful interventions for immigrant women seeking to find jobs and establish careers in a new culture can include a number of components.
These are described in the following subsections.

   Exploring Cultural Norms About Work.   Career counselors can begin the
counseling process by asking women to describe the world of women's work
in their home countries as well as their personal career development jour-
neys prior to relocation. In order to make such conversations more vivid
and meaningful and in light of the fact that it will be difficult for the counselor and the woman to communicate about vastly different cultural experiences, women can be asked to bring objects or pictures that represent their
stories. In presenting information or providing interventions with women,
the counselor can inquire about how certain processes—for example, what
constitutes a normal job search—occur in the women's home countries.

   Job-Search and Interviewing Strategies.   This component can help immigrant women to learn about where to obtain information about available
jobs, how to prepare and deliver a job application, how to interview for positions, and how to follow up their job interviews.

   Self-Assertion Skills.   Self-assertion may be difficult for many women in a
new culture where they are not familiar with the etiquette required for
working within organizations. Women may have come from cultures where
being passive or less communicative, and deferring to an authority are normative for job-search success. Immigrant women, especially from Asian cultures, may be stereotyped by others as being passive and nonassertive and
often can be judged negatively for exhibiting behaviors that would be
deemed as culturally unexpected. Helping women to understand self-
assertion strategies common in the United States and potential stereotypes
about women and ethnically diverse women can be useful. It is also important to help women establish their own self-assertion standards in a new culture that can honor their cultural heritage, their gender identity development, and their interests in particular careers.

   Focus on Organizational Systems, Bureaucracies, and Work Environments.
Women who have recently moved to a foreign culture may not be familiar
with the common structures of the job market in the United States. Inviting
women to watch movies or television programs that can show how organizational systems work within the United States can help them become more
familiar with differences between job environments in their home and host
cultures.

   Working Parent Skills.   Many immigrant women enter the workforce for
the first time in their lives and are making a difficult transition to being
both a family caretaker and a financial provider. Other immigrant women

may have worked full time but are not familiar with the complexities of balancing work and family responsibilities that women in America face. For example, in socialist and postsocialist countries the majority of women are in full-time employment and child care is relatively inexpensive to obtain. For still other women, relocation entails a loss of family and community structures in which children could be cared for by relatives or friends. Career counselors can directly discuss with immigrant women clients how they can adjust to a new gendered system of work as well as how they can deal with changes within their families and communities.

Attending to Facilitators and Barriers of Career Development.   Career interventions with immigrant women can include a direct exploration of the facilitators and barriers to their career development. Highlighting women's strengths and resources as well as brainstorming ideas for dealing with existing difficulties in women's career development processes can provide women with tangible ideas and solutions. For instance, prejudice toward immigrant women's accents may be a barrier to their career opportunities. Counselors may work with women to help them recognize when others are judging them based on their accent and how to address this prejudice in work environments. Career counselors can also help immigrant women reframe having an accent as a positive indication of immigrant women's flexibility, teachability, courage, and innate intelligence. Immigrant women learning a new language late in life are taking on a daunting task and career counselors can help them turn what may be the embarrassment of an accent into a continual reminder of the integrity of their life journey and something of which they can be justly proud. Career counselors can play a role in assisting immigrant women with minimizing the potential negative career implications of speaking and working in a language that is different from that of their home country.

Dealing With Career Transition.   Career-counseling sessions with immigrant women can seek to emphasize the phases of making a career transition, such as immobilization-shock, minimization of change, self-doubt, letting go of negative appraisals, testing new options, search for meaning, and integration-renewal (Abrego & Brammer, 1992). Helping women to establish a plan for dealing with various phases of their transition can facilitate a more positive adjustment to a new world of work.

Creating Workshops and Structured Groups

For the majority of people around the world, individual counseling is truly a foreign worldview concept (Sue & Sue, 1999). Using structured workshops and groups can be more acceptable to immigrant women than attending individual sessions. Structured workshops can be arranged with community organizations that serve immigrants locally. Workshops can focus on issues that broadly influence women's lives: jobs, education, language, relationships, and mental and physical health. For example, Aggarwal (1990) described English as a second language classes, which focused specifically on language skills necessary for employment. Chronister and McWhirter (2005) developed a career intervention program for Mexican immigrant women that was conducted through a domestic violence shelter. In addition to career-related information, workshops and groups can provide immigrant women with needed support from other immigrant women, a space for networking and exchanging of ideas, and helpful advice about how to navigate a new world of work. Career counselors involved in the creation of such workshops can develop professional relationships with organizations and individuals who provide services to immigrant women in their communities. Such collaboration grants access not only to immigrant communities themselves but also to essential information about the context and resources available to immigrant women.

GAINING COMPETENCIES IN WORKING
WITH IMMIGRANT WOMEN

U.S. psychology training in general and career training in particular have historically been undertaken in rather remarkable isolation from the rest of the world. Graduate and professional training programs have given minimal attention to teaching students about international perspectives on mental health or career-counseling processes. This trend appears to be changing based on the increase in articles that focus on cross-cultural applications of career psychology or on describing career-counseling services around the world. International English-language scholarly publications, such as the *International Journal for Educational and Vocational Guidance* and the *International Journal for the Advancement of Counselling*, or career journals published in Australia and Great Britain (e.g., the *British Journal of Guidance and Counselling* and the *Australian Journal of Career Development*) are now available in a number of U.S. libraries. American journals that are focused on career and vocational counseling have also increased the number of articles that include an international focus (see Flores et al., 2003, for a review of international career-counseling literature published in 2002). Although the majority of these international publications focus only on portions of the entire world, such as on the developed countries of Southeast Asia, Australia, and Western Europe, they nevertheless provide a picture of how international career-counseling processes can and do differ from U.S.-based practices.

Counselors' openness to other cultures is stimulated by a general commitment to understanding and challenging ethnocentrism in their own lives and career-counseling work. The *Penguin Atlas of Women in the World*, compiled by Seager (2003), is an excellent statistical and pictorial overview of current issues women face across the globe related to work, literacy, equality, domestic violence, lesbian rights, and motherhood. Watching foreign films, attending international community events, volunteering in local organizations that support immigrants, reading foreign literature, and traveling abroad can all provide career counselors with opportunities to step outside the U.S.-centered worldviews of life and work. The Internet can be an extraordinary resource for helping counselors get specific information about other countries, peoples, and cultures.

CONCLUSION

Based on census estimates, 1 in 10 women in the United States has recently immigrated to this country (Schmidley, 2001). Immigrant women naturally seek to enter the U.S. workforce (National Science Foundation, 1997). For many immigrant women, employment is necessary to survival as well as a necessary component of their dreams for a better life. Globalization, an economic force that is pushing many women to migrate to other countries in search of work, will likely lead to a future explosion of women's immigration (Marsella & Ring, 2003; Seager, 2003). Although immigrant women have been included as part of the racial and ethnic diversity emphasis in career-focused literature, the career-counseling literature has not addressed the realities of immigrant women as a unique group.

The occupational realities of immigrant women and questions of how career services can address their needs is deserving of increased attention. The specificity of how particular assessment and intervention strategies may or may not apply to working with immigrant women can be improved. Issues of xenophobia and ethnocentrism that are pervasive in U.S. culture and bear on career issues for immigrant women should be included in career-counseling training. Training can also introduce a more global perspective on women's worlds of work. By focusing research on immigrant women, counselors can gain greater understanding of how the intersection of multiple identities influences career processes.

Yoshihama and Horrocks (2002) suggested not only that greater understanding of immigrants' psychological issues is necessary for developing policies and services "to respond to this growing population," but that these studies can also provide "valuable cross-cultural information on the etiology and clinical course of mental health problems" (p. 208). Similarly, in their article on the "global vision of counseling psychology," Leong and

Blustein (2000) proposed that the field of counseling psychology must step out from U.S.-focused scholarly isolation and enter into a global dialogue through research and writing. Attending to the issues of immigrant women in the United States is one concrete way that career counseling can increasingly open itself to other cultures and enter the new global era.

REFERENCES

Abrego, P., & Brammer, L. (1992). Counseling adults in midlife career transitions. In H. D. Lea & Z. B. Leibowitz (Eds.), *Adult career development: Concepts, issues, and practices* (2nd ed., pp. 234–254). Alexandria, VA: National Career Development Association.

Aggarwal, P. (1990). English classes for immigrant women: A feminist organizing tool. *Fireweed, 30,* 94–103.

Ben-Sira, Z. (1997). *Immigration, stress, and readjustment.* Westport, CT: Praeger.

Berry, J. W. (1980). Acculturation as varieties of adaptation. In A. M. Padilla (Ed.), *Acculturation: Theory, models, and some new findings* (pp. 9–25). Boulder: CO: Westview Press.

Between a Rock and a Hard Place (n.d.). *A history of American sweatshops from 1820 to present.* Retrieved April 13, 2005, from http://americanhistory.si.edu/sweatshops/index.htm

Bingham, R. P., & Ward, C. M. (1994). Career counseling with ethnic minority women. In W. B. Walsh & S. H. Osipow (Eds.), *Career counseling for women: Contemporary topics in vocational psychology* (pp. 165–195). Hillsdale, NJ: Lawrence Erlbaum Associates.

Boehnke, K., Hagan, J., & Hefler, G. (1998). On the development of xenophobia in Germany: The adolescent years. *Journal of Social Issues, 54,* 585–603.

Bowen, D. J., Carscadden, L., Beighle, K., & Fleming, I. (1992). Post-traumatic stress disorder among Salvadoran women: Empirical evidence and description of treatment. In E. Cole, O. M. Espín, & E. D. Rothblum (Eds.), *Refugee women and their mental health: Shattered societies, shattered lives* (pp. 267–280). New York: Haworth Press.

Branigin, W. (1995, September 10). Sweatshop instead of paradise: Thais lived in fear as slaves at L.A. garment factories. *The Washington Post,* p. A1.

Bronfenbrenner, U. (1979). *The ecology of human development.* Cambridge: Harvard University Press.

California Department of Education. (2003). *Immigration status of students: Fact book 2003.* Retrieved April 12, 2005, from http://www.cde.ca.gov/re/pn/fb/yr03immgstatus

Carter, R. T., & Cook, D. A. (1992). A culturally relevant perspective for understanding the career paths of visible racial/ethnic group people. In H. D. Lea & Z. B. Leibowitz (Eds.), *Adult career development: Concepts, issues, and practices* (2nd ed., pp. 192–217). Alexandria, VA: The National Career Development Association.

Chang, G. (2001). Disposable domestics: Immigrant women workers in the global economy. *Women in Action, 1,* 62–63.

Chester, B. (1992). Women and political torture: Work with refugee survivors in exile. In E. Cole, O. M. Espín, & E. D. Rothblum (Eds.), *Refugee women and their mental health: Shattered societies, shattered lives* (pp. 209–220). New York: Haworth Press.

Chronister, K. M., & McWhirter, E. H. (2005). *An experimental evaluation of two career intervention programs for battered women.* Manuscript submitted for publication.

Clason, C. (1992). Dual-earner families in Hungary: Past, present, and future perspectives. In S. Lewis, D. N. Izraeli, & H. Hootsmans (Eds.), *Dual-earner families: International perspectives* (pp. 99–108). London: Sage.

Cole, E., Espin, O. M., & Rothblum, E. D. (Eds.). (1992). *Refugee women and their mental health: Shared societies, shattered lives.* New York: Haworth Press.

Comas-Díaz, L., & Greene, B. (Eds.). (1994). *Women of color: Integrating ethnic and gender identities in psychotherapy*. New York: Guilford Press.

Cook, E. P., Heppner, M. J., & O'Brien, K. M. (2002). Career development of women of color and White women: Assumptions, conceptualization, and interventions from an ecological perspective. *Career Development Quarterly, 50*, 291–305.

DeLaet, D. L. (2000). *U.S. immigration policy in an age of rights*. Westport, CT: Praeger.

Dillon, S. (2001, October 15). Mexican immigrants face new set of fears. *The New York Times*, p. A14.

Doors Closed to Immigrant Women. (2000, Winter). *Horizons, 13*, 13.

Escobar, J. I., Nervi, C. H., & Gara, M. A. (2000). Immigration and mental health: Mexican Americans in the United States. *Harvard Review of Psychiatry, 8*, 64–72.

Espín, O. M. (1997). *Latina realities: Essays on healing, migration, and sexuality*. Boulder, CO: Westview Press.

Espín, O. M. (1999). *Women crossing boundaries: A psychology of immigration and transformation of sexuality*. New York: Routledge.

Espiritu, E. L. (1999). Gender and labor in Asian immigrant families. *American Behavioral Scientist, 42*, 628–647.

Fall, Y. (2001). Gender and social implications of globalization: An African perspective. In R. M. Kelly, J. H. Bayes, M. Hawkesworth, & B. Young (Eds.), *Gender, globalization, and democratization* (pp. 49–74). Lanham, UK: Rowman & Littlefield.

Fitzgerald, L. F., Fassinger, R. E., & Betz, N. E. (1995). Theoretical advances in the study of women's career development. In W. B. Walsh & S. H. Osipow (Eds.), *Handbook of vocational psychology: Theory, research, and practice* (2nd ed., pp. 67–109). Hillsdale, NJ: Lawrence Erlbaum Associates.

Fitzgerald, L. F., & Weitzman, L. M. (1992). Women's career development: Theory and practice from a feminist perspective. In H. D. Lea & Z. B. Leibowitz (Eds.), *Adult career development: Concepts, issues, and practices* (2nd ed., pp. 124–160). Alexandria, VA: National Career Development Association.

Flannery, W. P., Reise, S. P., & Yu, J. (2001). An empirical comparison of acculturation models. *Personality and Social Psychology Bulletin, 27*, 1035–1045.

Flores, L. Y., & O'Brien, K. M. (2002). The career development of Mexican American adolescent women: A test of social cognitive career theory. *Journal of Counseling Psychology, 49*, 14–27.

Flores, L. Y., Scott, A. B., Wang, Y. W., Yakushko, O., McCloskey, C. M., Spencer, K. G., et al. (2003). Annual review: Practice and research in career counseling and development 2002. *Career Development Quarterly, 52*, 98–131.

Foner, N. (1986). Sex roles and sensibilities: Jamaican women in New York and London. In R. J. Simon & C. J. Brettell (Eds.), *International migration: The female experience* (pp. 185–197). Totowa, NJ: Rowan & Allenheld.

Foner, N. (2001). Benefits and burdens: Immigrant women and work in New York City. In R. J. Simon (Ed.), *Immigrant women* (pp. 1–20). New Brunswick, NJ: Transaction.

Fouad, N. A. (2002). Cross-cultural differences in vocational interests: Between-groups differences on the Strong Interest Inventory. *Journal of Counseling Psychology, 49*, 283–289.

Friedman, A. R. (1992). Rape and domestic violence: The experience of refugee women. In E. Cole, O. M. Espín, & E. D. Rothblum (Eds.), *Refugee women and their mental health: Shattered societies, shattered lives* (pp. 65–78). New York: Haworth Press.

Gabaccia, D. (1994). *From the other side: Women, gender, and immigrant life in the U.S., 1820–1990*. Bloomington: Indiana University Press.

Garcia, A. (2002, Spring). Editorial: No nation of immigrants would treat immigrants this way. *Network news: National Network for Immigrant and Refugee Rights*. Retrieved July 15, 2003, from http://www.nnirr.org/news/news_index.html

Garza-Guerrero, C. (1974). Culture shock: Its mourning and the vicissitudes of identity. *Journal of the American Psychoanalytic Association, 22,* 408–429.

Gold, S. J. (1989). Differential adjustment among new immigrant family members. *Journal of Contemporary Ethnography, 17,* 408–434.

Guarnaccia, P. J. (1997). Social stress and psychological distress among Latinos in the United States. In I. Al-Issa & M. Tousignant (Eds.), *Ethnicity, immigration, and psychopathology* (pp. 71–94). New York: Plenum Press.

Heppner, M. J., & Heppner, P. P. (2003). Identifying process variables in career counseling: A research agenda. *Journal of Vocational Behavior, 62,* 429–452.

Herbst, P. K. R. (1992). From helpless victim to empowered survivor: Oral history as a treatment for survivors of torture. In E. Cole, O. M. Espín, & E. D. Rothblum (Eds.), *Refugee women and their mental health: Shattered societies, shattered lives* (pp. 141–154). New York: Haworth Press.

Hesketh, B., & Rounds, J. (1995). International cross-cultural approaches to career development. In W. B. Walsh & S. H. Osipow (Eds.), *Handbook of vocational psychology: Theory, research, and practice* (2nd ed., pp. 367–390). Hillsdale, NJ: Lawrence Erlbaum Associates.

Hogan, D. G. (1996). Immigrant women in the U.S. and work. In P. J. Dubeck & K. Borman (Eds.), *Women and work: A handbook* (pp. 41–44). New York: Garland.

Hondagneu-Sotelo, P. (1994). *Gendered transitions.* Berkeley: University of California Press.

Hondagneu-Sotelo, P. (1999). Gender and contemporary U.S. immigration. *American Behavioral Scientist, 42,* 565–576.

Hovey, J. D. (2000). Acculturative stress, depression, and suicidal ideation in Mexican immigrants. *Cultural Diversity and Ethnic Minority Psychology, 6,* 134–151.

Ishisaka, H. A., Nguyen, Q. T., & Okimoto, J. T. (1985). The role of culture in the mental health treatment of Indochinese refugees. In T. C. Owan (Ed.), *Southeast Asian mental health: Treatment, prevention, services, training, and research* (DHHS Publication No. AD 85-139). Washington, DC: U.S. Government Printing Office.

Itzhaky, H., & Ribner, D. S. (1999). Gender, values, and the work place: Considerations for immigrant acculturation. *International Social Work, 42,* 127–138.

Kagitcibasi, C., & Berry, J. W. (1989). Cross-cultural psychology: Current research and trends. *Annual Review of Psychology, 40,* 493–531.

Kosmarskaya, N. (1999). Post-Soviet Russian migration from the New Independent States: Experiences of women migrants. In D. Indra (Ed.), *Engendering forced migration: Theory and practice* (pp. 177–199). New York: Berghahn Books.

Lee, M. T., Martinez, R., & Rosenfeld, R. (2001). Does immigration increase homicide? Negative evidence from three border cities. *Sociological Quarterly, 42,* 559–580.

Lent, R. W., Brown, S. D., & Hackett, G. (1994). Toward a unifying social cognitive theory of career and academic interest, choice, and performance. *Journal of Vocational Behavior, 45,* 79–122.

Leong, F. T. L. (2001). The role of acculturation in the career adjustment of Asian American workers: A test of Leong and Chou's (1994) formulations. *Cultural Diversity and Ethnic Minority, 7,* 262–273.

Leong, F. T. L., & Blustein, D. L. (2000). Toward a global vision of counseling psychology. *The Counseling Psychologist, 28,* 5–16.

Leong, F. T. L., & Brown, M. T. (1995). Theoretical issues in cross-cultural career development: Cultural validity and cultural specificity. In W. B. Walsh & S. H. Osipow (Eds.), *Handbook of vocational psychology: Theory, research, and practice* (2nd ed., pp. 143–180). Hillsdale, NJ: Lawrence Erlbaum Associates.

Light, D. (1992). Healing their wounds: Guatemalan refugee women as political activists. In E. Cole, O. M. Espín, & E. D. Rothblum (Eds.), *Refugee women and their mental health: Shattered societies, shattered lives* (pp. 297–308). New York: Haworth Press.

Lind, M. (1998, July/August). Hiring from within. *The Mother Jones.* Retrieved July 15, 2002, from http://www.motherjones.com/mother_jones/JA98

Lott, B. (2002). Cognitive and behavioral distancing from the poor. *American Psychologist, 57,* 100–110.

Loewy, M. I., Clark, H. D., & Yakushko, O. (2003, August). *Adjustment of refugees resettled in the United States: The Kosovar experience.* Paper presented at the meeting of the American Psychological Association, Toronto, Canada.

Malone, N., Baluja, K. F., Costanzo, J. M., & Davis, C. J. (2003, December). *The foreign born population 2000: Census 2000 brief* (Census 2000 Summary File No. C2KBR-34) [Electronic version]. Washington, DC: U.S. Government Printing Office.

Manrique, C. G., & Manrique, G. G. (1999). Third world immigrant women in American higher education. In G. A. Kelson & D. L. DeLaet (Eds.), *Gender and immigration* (pp. 103–126). New York: New York University Press.

Marsella, A. J. (1997). Migration, poverty, and ethnocultural diversity: A global perspective on immigrant and refugee adaptation. *Scandinavian Journal of Work, Health, and Environment, 23,* 28–46.

Marsella, A. J., & Ring, E. (2003). Human migration and immigration: An overview. In L. L. Adler & U. P. Gielen (Eds.), *Migration: Immigration and emigration in international perspective* (pp. 3–22). Westport, CT: Praeger.

McIntyre, T. M., & Augusto, F. (1999). The Martyr Adaptation Syndrome: Psychological sequelae in the adaptation of Portuguese-speaking immigrant women. *Cultural Diversity and Ethnic Minority Psychology, 5,* 387–402.

McWhirter, E. H., Torres, D., & Rasheed, S. (1998). Assessing barriers to women's career adjustment. *Journal of Career Assessment, 6,* 449–479.

Meara, N. M. (1997). Changing the structure of work. *Journal of Career Assessment, 5,* 471–474.

Melville, M. B. (1988). Mexican women in the U.S. wage labor force. In M. B. Melville (Ed.), *Mexicanas at work in the United States* (pp. 1–11). Houston, TX: University of Houston Press.

Menjivar, C. (1999). The intersection of work and gender: Central American immigrant women and employment in California. *American Behavioral Scientist, 42,* 601–627.

Merriam-Webster desk dictionary. (1995). Springfield, MA: Merriam-Webster.

Messias, D. K. H. (2001). Transnational perspectives on women's domestic work: Experiences of Brazilian immigrants in the United States. *Women and Health, 33,* 1–19.

Mulder, T. J., Hollmann, F. W., Lollock, L. R., Cassidy, R. C., Costanzo, J. M., & Baker, J. D. (2001). *U.S. Census Bureau measurement of net international migration to the United States: 1990–2000* [Electronic version]. Washington, DC: U.S. Bureau of the Census, Population Division.

Narayan, U. (1995). "Male-order" brides: Immigrant women, domestic violence and immigration law. *Hypatia, 31,* 104–126.

Narayan, U. (1997). *Dislocating cultures: Identities, traditions, and Third World feminism.* New York: Routledge.

National Council for Research on Women. (1995). Intervening: Immigrant women and domestic violence. *Issues Quarterly, 1,* 12–14.

National Research Council. (1997). *The new Americans: Economic, demographic, and fiscal effects of immigration.* Washington, DC: Author.

National Science Foundation. (2004). Graduate enrollment in science and engineering fields reaches new peak; first-time enrollment of foreign students declines [NSF 04-326]. Retrieved April 14, 2005, from http://www.nsf.gov/sbe/srs/infbrief/nsf04326/start.htm

Ofari Hutchinson, E. (2001, September 14). Beware of backlash: The civil rights of Arab and Muslim Americans may become another casualty of the Sept. 11 terror attacks. *The Mother Jones.* Retrieved July 15, 2002, from http://www.motherjones.com/web_exclusives/commentary/opinion/backlash.html

Office of the United Nations High Commissioner for Refugees. (1991). *Guidelines on the protection of the refugee women.* Geneva: The United Nations. Retrieved July 15, 2002, from http://www.unhcr.ch/cgi-bin/texis/vtx/home

Ortega, A. N., Rosenheck, R., Alegria, M., & Desai, R. A. (2000). Acculturation and the lifetime risk of psychiatric and substance use disorders among Hispanics. *Journal of Nervous and Mental Disease, 188,* 728–735.

Palinkas, L. A. (1982). Ethnicity, identity, and mental health: The use of rhetoric in an immigrant Chinese church. *Journal of Psychoanalytic Anthropology, 5,* 235–258.

Pedraza, S. (1991). Women and migration: The social consequences of gender. *Annual Review of Sociology, 17,* 303–325.

Pernice, R. (1994). Methodological issues in research with refugees and immigrants. *Professional Psychology: Research and Practice, 25,* 207–213.

Perry, M., Vandervate, B., Auman, L., & Morris, K. (2001). Evaluating components of international migration: Legal migrants. *Population Division Working Paper #59.* Washington, DC: U.S. Government. Retrieved July 16, 2002, from http://www.census.gov/population/www/documentation/twps0059.html

Pessar, P. R., & Graham, P. M. (1987). The Dominicans: Women in the household and the garment industry. In N. Foner (Ed.), *New immigrants in New York* (pp. 225–247). New York: Columbia University Press.

Pessar, P. R. (1995). On the homefront and in the workplace: Integrating immigrant women into feminist discourse. *Anthropological Quarterly, 68,* 37–47.

Pessar, P. R. (1999). Engendering migration studies: The case of new immigrants in the United States. *American Behavioral Scientist, 42,* 577–600.

Pessar, P. R. (2000). Sweatshop workers and domestic ideologies: Dominican women in New York apparel industry. In K. Willis & B. Yeoh (Eds.), *Gender and migration* (pp. 193–210). Chetlenham, UK: Elgar Reference Collection.

Portes, A., & Rumbaut, R. G. (1996). *Immigrant America: A portrait.* Berkeley: University of California Press.

Prieto, Y. (1992). Cuban women in New Jersey: Gender relations and change. In D. Gabaccia (Ed.), *Seeking common ground: Multidisciplinary studies of immigrant women in the United States* (pp. 185–202). Westport, CT: Greenwood Press.

Reimers, D. (1992). *Still the golden door: The third world coming to America.* New York: Columbia University Press.

Rodriguez, R., & DeWolfe, A. (1990). Psychological distress among Mexican-American and Mexican women as related to status on the new immigration law. *Journal of Consulting and Clinical Psychology, 58,* 548–553.

Roe, M. D. (1992). Displaced women in setting of continuing armed conflict. In E. Cole, O. M. Espín, & E. D. Rothblum (Eds.), *Refugee women and their mental health: Shattered societies, shattered lives* (pp. 89–104). New York: Haworth Press.

Rule, W., & Noonan, N. C. (1996). *Russian women in politics and society.* Westport, CT: Greenwood Press.

Rumbaut, R. G. (1991). The agony of exile: A study of the migration and adaptation of Indochinese refugee adults and children. In F. L. Ahearn & J. L. Athey (Eds.), *Refugee children: Theory, research, and services* (pp. 53–91). Baltimore: Johns Hopkins University Press.

Sachs, S., & Baker, S. (2001, August 5). Few local issues at anti-immigrant gathering. *The New York Times,* p. A30.

Saldana, D. H. (1992). Coping with stress: A refugee's story. In E. Cole, O. M. Espín, & E. D. Rothblum (Eds.), *Refugee women and their mental health: Shattered societies, shattered lives* (pp. 21–34). New York: Haworth Press.

Salgado de Snyder, V. N. (1994). Mexican women, mental health, and migration: Those who go and those who stay behind. In R. G. Malgady & O. Rodriguez (Eds.), *Theoretical and conceptual issues in Hispanic mental health* (pp. 114–139). Melbourne, FL: Krieger.

Schmidley, A. D. (2001). Profile of the foreign born population in the U.S., 2000. *U.S. Census Bureau Current Population Reports, Series p23-206.* Washington, DC: U.S. Government. Retrieved July 16, 2002, from http://www.census.gov/prod/2002pubs/p23-206.pdf

Seager, J. (2003). *The Penguin atlas of women in the world.* New York: Penguin Books.

Sengupta, S. (2002, June 7). Refugees languishing in camps as the U.S. admits many fewer. *The New York Times,* p. A9.

Shepherd, J. (1992). Post-traumatic stress disorder in Vietnamese women. In E. Cole, O. M. Espín, & E. D. Rothblum (Eds.), *Refugee women and their mental health: Shattered societies, shattered lives* (pp. 281–296). New York: Haworth Press.

Simon, R. J. (1992). Sociology and immigrant women. In D. Gabaccia (Ed.), *Seeking common ground: Multidisciplinary studies of immigrant women in the United States* (pp. 23–40). Westport, CT: Greenwood Press.

Simon, R. J. (Ed.). (2001). *Immigrant women.* New Brunswick, NJ: Transaction.

Simons, L. (1999). Mail order brides: The legal framework and possibilities for change. In G. A. Kelson & D. L. DeLaet (Eds.), *Gender and immigration* (pp. 127–143). New York: New York University Press.

Sinke, S., & Gross, S. (1992). The international marriage market and the sphere of social reproduction: A German case study. In D. Gabaccia (Ed.), *Seeking common ground: Multidisciplinary studies of immigrant women in the United States* (pp. 67–88). Westport, CT: Greenwood Press.

Sircar, A., & Kelly, R. M. (2001). Globalization and Asian Indian immigrant women in the United States. In R. M. Kelly, J. H. Bayes, M. Hawkesworth, & B. Young (Eds.), *Gender, globalization, and democratization* (pp. 95–120). Lanham, UK: Rowman & Littlefield.

Smith, B. G. (Ed.). (2000). *Global feminism since 1945.* London: Routledge.

Smith, D. (2002). Adjusting to America. *Monitor on Psychology, 33,* 86–87.

Soni-Sinha, U. (2001). Income control and household work-sharing. In R. M. Kelly, J. H. Bayes, M. Hawkesworth, & B. Young (Eds.), *Gender, globalization, and democratization* (pp. 121–136). Lanham, UK: Rowman & Littlefield.

Sue, D. W., Ivey, A. E., & Pedersen, P. B. (1996). *A theory of multicultural counseling and therapy.* Pacific Grove, CA: Brooks/Cole.

Sue, D. W., & Sue, D. (1999). *Counseling the culturally different: Theory and practice.* New York: Wiley.

Swanson, J. L., & Gore, P. A. (2002). Advances in vocational psychology: Theory and research. In S. D. Brown & R. W. Lent (Eds.), *Handbook of counseling psychology* (2nd ed., pp. 233–269). New York: Wiley.

Toren, N. (2001). Women and immigrants: Strangers in a strange land. In R. J. Simon (Ed.), *Immigrant women* (pp. 175–196). New Brunswick, NJ: Transaction.

Toy, V. S. (2002, April 28). Immigrant issues sprout like the daisies. *The New York Times,* p. 14LI1.

Tryon, G. S., & Kane, A. S. (1993). Relationship of working alliance to mutual and unilateral termination. *Journal of Counseling Psychology, 40,* 33–36.

U.S. Citizenship and Immigration Services. (2005). *Immigration and through Diversity Lottery.* Retrieved April 14, 2005, from http://uscis.gov/graphics/services/residency/divvisa.htm

U.S. Department of Health and Human Services. (2005). *U.S. Refugee Act of 1980* (INA: Act 411—Office of Refugee Resettlement. Sec. 411 [8 U.S.C. 1521]). Retrieved April 12, 2005, from http://www.acf.hhs.gov/programs/orr/policy/refact1.htm

U.S. Department of Homeland Security. (2005). *Immigration Reform and Control Act of November 6, 1986 (IRCA)* (100 Statutes-at-Large 3359). Retrieved April 12, 2005, from http://uscis.gov/graphics/shared/aboutus/statistics/LegisHist/561.htm

Van Boemel, G. B., & Rozee, P. D. (1992). Treatment for psychosomatic blindness among Cambodian refugee women. In E. Cole, O. M. Espín, & E. D. Rothblum (Eds.), *Refugee women and their mental health: Shattered societies, shattered lives* (pp. 239–266). New York: Haworth Press.

Weeks, K. A. (2000). The Berkeley wives: Identity revision and development among young temporary immigrant women. *Asian Journal of Women's Studies, 2*, 78–89.

Willis, K., & Yeoh, B. (Eds.). (2000). *Gender and migration.* Chetlenham, UK: Elgar Reference Collection.

Yang, E., Wong, S. C., Hwang, M., & Heppner, M. J. (2002). Widening our global view: The development of career counseling services for international students. *Journal of Career Development, 28*, 203–213.

Ybarra, L. (1988). Separating myth from reality: Socio-economic and cultural influences on Chicanas and the world of work. In M. B. Melville (Ed.), *Mexicanas at work in the United States* (pp. 12–23). Houston, TX: University of Houston Press.

Yee, B. W. K. (1992). Markers of successful aging among Vietnamese refugee women. In E. Cole, O. M. Espín, & E. D. Rothblum (Eds.), *Refugee women and their mental health: Shattered societies, shattered lives* (pp. 221–238). New York: Haworth Press.

Yeoh, B. S. A., & Huang, S. (2000). Negotiating public space: Strategies and styles of migrant domestic workers in Singapore. In K. Willis & B. Yeoh (Eds.), *Gender and migration* (pp. 251–272). Chetlenham, UK: Elgar Reference Collection.

Yoshihama, M., & Horrocks, J. (2002). Posttraumatic stress symptoms and victimization among Japanese American women. *Journal of Consulting and Clinical Psychology, 70*, 205–215.

Zajacova, A. (2002). Constructing the reality of the immigrant life. *Journal of Social Distress and the Homeless, 11*, 69–79.

Zlotnik, H. (2000). Migration and the family: The female perspective. In K. Willis & B. Yeoh (Eds.), *Gender and migration* (pp. 27–45). Cheltenham, UK: Elgar Reference Collection.

Chapter 13

Career Counseling for Women in Science, Technology, Engineering, and Mathematics (STEM) Fields

Ruth E. Fassinger
Penelope A. Asay
University of Maryland

Tammy is a 26-year-old White graduate student in biology at a large research university in an urban environment. Already anxious and ambivalent about graduate school, Tammy is stymied by her master's thesis in biology. She feels she does not have the writing skills she needs, but her advisor ignores her fears and keeps pushing her simply to get it done by the impending deadline. As a self-described introvert, she feels isolated from her peers in the program, and she does not know how to find help. Tammy's undergraduate advisor encouraged her to continue with him in graduate school. She found, however, that once she started graduate school, he was not as available and supportive as she had hoped he would be. In fact, she has found that he does not mentor her as much as he did when she was an undergraduate, and he seems to be expressing constant disapproval with her inability to make progress toward her degree.

Tammy is the first member of her family to attend college, and she feels her family does not understand why she is still in school and why it is important to her. Tammy has difficulty explaining the importance of her work to her family, and she feels guilty about spending so much time away from them because of school. She recently became engaged and bought a house with her fiancé. Her fiancé, who is Peruvian, has encouraged her to leave school and find something less stressful. She is now considering leaving school altogether and becoming a gardener, which would enable her to spend more time with her family and not miss out on what she calls "the important things in life." Her fiancé (and her future in-laws) hope that he and

Tammy will start a family soon after they are married. Tammy is unsure how she feels about this.

Tammy reports suffering from a depressive episode several months ago. She concealed her depression from her fiancé, as she did not want to upset him because he was having difficulties at work at the time. Even though her depression is now somewhat abated (she obtained medication from her physician), she occasionally resents having to carry such a burden without the support of her fiancé and family. Tammy speaks passionately about 6 months she spent doing research in the rain forests of South America, and part of her would love to return and continue the work. Another part of her, however, feels she should be concentrating on spending time with her family and creating a home with her future husband, an alternative that seems comforting and safe. She cannot help feeling like a failure, however, and she wonders how she could deteriorate from being such an enthusiastic and promising undergraduate to such a disappointing graduate student.

Beverly is a 30-year-old African American new assistant professor in computer science at a research university in a small Midwestern city. Beverly feels that she is being pulled in all directions in her position. As the only African American in the department, Beverly finds herself overwhelmed with advising and mentoring requests from African American and women students. A group of students have even asked her to help them develop a tutoring program. Beverly knows she does not have the time, but she also knows that no one else will help them. Although she has been in her position for only 6 months, she has been asked by the faculty to chair a committee aimed at recruiting more African American and Latino students into the department. This committee and the mentoring requests are opportunities she would like to consider, but they interfere with her research time. Beverly has a solid research and publication record from her graduate and postdoctorate years, but she knows she has to publish considerably more work to remain a viable candidate for tenure and promotion to associate professor. Unfortunately, Beverly has been given only one graduate assistant for 2 years (most new faculty get two), and she is expected to obtain external funding to continue to fund this assistant and any others she wants. Beverly does not have any experience in grant writing, however, and she wonders what she will do if she does not obtain at least one successful grant to continue funding her only student. No one in her department is responsive when she requests advice regarding external funding.

Despite the cordial attitude of her new colleagues, Beverly notices that she is frequently interrupted in faculty meetings and that her suggestions and comments are largely ignored. She says she feels like a child who is allowed to sit at the grown-up table but expected to keep her mouth shut. She also has heard blatant sexist comments from several of her male colleagues (particularly two from non-Western countries) and she has seen comic strips demeaning women posted on office doors for public viewing. There is only one other woman in the department, a White woman who is being considered for tenure this year. In the few times they have been able to talk about Beverly's experiences in the department, her colleague has advised her to ignore all the "crap" that goes on around her and just concentrate on her work. Beverly is seriously questioning whether she can do that. She knows that, as an African American, she is at risk for a number of stress-related health problems, and she feels that her current stress levels, if maintained, will compromise her health.

Jean is a 36-year-old second-generation Taiwanese American woman working as a scientist in a large chemical company. She was trained as a physical chemist in a Research I university, and is married to a man (also Taiwanese) who is a computer scientist. She has one school-age son and a mother-in-law who also lives with the family. Jean was referred to the company EAP coordinator by her immediate supervisor, who observed that recently she seemed to be getting overly anxious during team meetings (particularly those in which she was presenting to others), and he suggested that she address this before it became a problem and compromised her yearly evaluation. Jean herself reports general feelings of nervousness about her job and near panic when she has to present publicly. These feelings are new to her, and she does not know when or why they began.

On questioning, she reveals that she is feeling pressured to move up in the company, and she has grave doubts about her ability to do so. She has topped out in the promotional tracks as a scientist in her company, and her supervisor is suggesting that she consider moving into a managerial role, offering to send her to training in order to build her skills in this arena. Jean believes that she does not possess the ability to be in leadership roles, and she also is not interested in such roles—she enjoys "doing science," and does not want to change her career direction.

Another reason for her reluctance about taking on management responsibilities lies in Jean's current family situation. Her mother-in-law, recently diagnosed with cancer and undergoing treatment, is quite ill from chemotherapy and requires much care from Jean. Jean's spouse is in favor of her possible promotion into management roles, but he also expresses worry about how they will handle the responsibility of his sick mother and their young child if Jean's work becomes more demanding of her time and energy. Thus, Jean is feeling that his support is ambivalent at best, and she fears bringing on marital difficulties if she pursues this professional path.

Questioning regarding Jean's supervisor's support reveals that he often praises her in a way that highlights her female status, for example, opining that most women could not have completed her projects as successfully as she. Jean does not see this as inappropriate—there are few women in her company, after all, and it is conceivable that there are few qualified women to assume such responsibilities. Jean also observes that she was one of only a few women in her graduate program and the only female postdoctoral student at that same institution. All of this reinforces Jean's belief that women in general and she in particular should not attempt leadership roles.

Tammy, Beverly, and Jean all share the position of being a woman in a science, technology, engineering, or mathematics (STEM) occupational field. An extensive literature suggests that they will experience predictable vocational problems as a result of this position. In addition, these women experience unique difficulties stemming from other aspects of their demographic locations (e.g., race/ethnicity, age, social class, family status) that interact with the realities of their occupational locations. Effective counseling and intervention with these women and others like them requires an understanding of the position of women in STEM fields and the unique issues that they face, as well as knowledge of particular resources that may assist them in their careers.

In this chapter, we first present a review of the general issues facing women who enter STEM fields. Next, we examine each of the three previous cases in the context of the challenges that women encounter in these fields, and outline possible interventions. Finally, we conclude with brief recommendations for changes needed to create healthier STEM workplaces for women.

WOMEN IN SCIENCE, TECHNOLOGY, ENGINEERING, AND MATHEMATICS FIELDS

STEM fields are considered to be crucial to U.S. economic growth and are expanding rapidly. They are expected to increase at three times the overall occupational rate from 2000 to 2010 (National Science Foundation [NSF], 2002). Indeed, the National Science Board (2000) identified addressing the adequacy of the supply of scientists, engineers, and science teachers as one of the top 10 priorities of the early 21st century. As demographic trends indicate, women and minorities represent the greatest increases in workforce participation; thus, it is reasonable to expect that many future STEM workers will be women, including women of color. This is crucial because the numbers of White males, who traditionally have constituted most of the STEM workforce, are decreasing due to high retirement rates and decreased rates of entering STEM fields; for example, the percentage of White male new hires in academic STEM positions decreased from 80% in 1973 to 40% in 1999 (NSF). The resultant employment gaps could be filled by women and racial-ethnic minorities (Bienenstock, 2000). However, despite dramatic increases in the number of doctorates in STEM fields awarded to women (over fivefold during the past 25 years), the continued underrepresentation of women, including women of color, in STEM fields is well documented. In 1999, for example, women made up almost half (47%) of the U.S. college-degreed labor force but represented less than one fourth (24%) of the STEM workforce, with women of color constituting less than one fifth of the total number of women in the STEM workforce and only 4% of the overall STEM workforce (NSF).

Much of the attention to women's relative absence from STEM fields has focused on educational issues and academic women, a reasonable strategy given that the educational system is responsible for producing degree recipients and potential workers. Moreover, tracking and measuring the success of academic women may be easier than following women in nonacademic settings due to proscribed advances through a predictable career trajectory (Sonnert & Holton, 1996b). However, this focus on academe has resulted in a paucity of information about STEM-trained women in nonacademic settings in which they directly or indirectly utilize their formal scientific training (Committee on Women in Science and Engineering, National Research Council, 2001; Davis, 2000). Industry, for example, is the largest employer of science and engineering workers, particularly at the bachelor's (73% in 1997) and master's degree (60% in 1997) levels (National Science Board, 2000). However, women in STEM fields are less likely than men to be employed in the industrial sector: 51% in 1999 versus 68% of men (NSF, 2002). Moreover, women STEM professionals in the industrial sector are far less likely than men to hold management, senior management, or corporate officer roles (Catalyst, 1999; NSF).

In order to understand the career experiences of individual woman scientists and engineers in the workforce, it is first necessary to examine the context of their vocational participation. It is well documented, for example, that patterns of women's participation in the STEM workforce consistently exhibit underrepresentation, underemployment, depressed salaries, field segregation, and absence at the highest levels of achievement (Fassinger, 2002). In the case of underemployment, for example, male scientists and engineers are more likely to be employed full time in their field of highest degree, whereas women are more likely to be unemployed, employed part time, and in fields outside their degree (NSF, 2002). Men are more likely to be employed in business and industry (as noted earlier) and women are more likely to be employed in educational institutions (27% vs. 14% of men; NSF), especially elementary or secondary schools (11% women vs. 4% men) and 2-year colleges (12% women vs. 9% men; National Science Board, 2000).

Field segregation—the clustering of women in biological and social sciences and their relative absence from physical sciences and engineering—is also well documented, and probably is related to the lower numbers of women in business and industry (NSF, 2002). There have been dramatic increases in participation in the social and life sciences by women, but a persistent lack of progress into other STEM fields. NSF figures indicate that, of the 43% of STEM doctorates earned by women overall in 1999, 42% were in social and behavioral sciences and 41% in biological sciences, but only 23% in the physical sciences, and 15% and 18% in engineering and computer science, respectively. Occupational segregation exists within STEM subfields as well: Within engineering, for example, women constituted 15% of chemical and industrial engineers in 1999, but only 6% of mechanical, electrical, and aerospace engineers (NSF). Field segregation also characterizes the experiences of racial/ethnic minority STEM-degreed workers. In 1999, for example, Asians constituted 11% of the STEM workforce, clustered primarily in engineering and computer science, with only 4% in the social sciences. By contrast, African Americans, Hispanics, and Native Americans collectively constituted 7% of the STEM workforce, but were disproportionately likely to earn social science degrees and work in social service occupations (NSF).

Field segregation is strongly related to oft-cited salary discrepancies between men and women. Despite evidence for more equitable salaries in STEM fields relative to the overall workforce, differential rates of compensation persist, particularly with increasing years of experience (NSF, 2002). Moreover, documented compensation patterns remain even when factors such as education, age, and performance are controlled (Phillips & Imhoff, 1997). In 1999, for example, the median annual salary for women scientists and engineers ($50,000) was about 22% less than the median salary for men ($64,000); for those holding their degrees less than 5 years, women's salaries were 83% of men's (NSF). Salary patterns for women of color in STEM fields are similar to those of White women, except for Asian women, who fare slightly better due to their larger percentages in computer science and engineering (where women's salaries are 12% less than men's) versus the social and life sciences (where women's salaries are 23% less than men's; NSF).

Finally, patterns in women's advancement in the STEM workforce indicate persistent difficulties in achieving the same levels of support and recognition for their work as men. For example, in terms of grant support (critical for success in academic science), data indicate that the overall percentage of National Institutes of Health grants received by women is far less than the percentage obtained by men, and increased only slightly over a 9-year period from 1988 (18.3%) to 1997 (22.3%; see Fassinger, 2001). At the highest levels of achievement, it is notable that fewer than 200 women are included in the membership of almost 2,400 in the National Academy of Sciences, most of them concentrated in biologically related sciences and very few in chemistry, physics, or engineering. In terms of leadership roles, women are far less likely than men to be found at the highest levels of management within the STEM-intensive industrial sector, a gap that widens at higher levels and with increased age (NSF, 2002). Within industrial chemistry, for example, only 4% of the upper management of the top U.S. chemical companies in 1997 were women; similarly, a recent study of Fortune 500 companies found that less than 4% of the chairperson, CEO, and VP titles were held by women, that only 11% of women were corporate officers, and that very slow growth rates were projected (to 17% female corporate officers by 2005; Davis, 2000). Moreover, women in management roles tend to have fewer direct and indirect subordinates than men, a gap that also widens with age (NSF, 2000). The lack of women's presence and influence in top levels of management in the STEM industrial sector is a critically important problem because women's consumer preferences shape products in every area, from textiles to cosmetics to health care, and yet their expertise in the management hierarchy remains largely untapped (Widnall, 2000).

Thus, gender-related patterns of participation and achievement in the STEM workforce indicate that women are disadvantaged relative to men. A useful concept for exploring gender-related disadvantage is that of *micro-inequities*, small inequities (e.g., less lab space, slightly lower salaries than men) that do not appear to be important in isolation, but that add up over time to produce cumulative disadvantage for women (Sonnert & Holton, 1996a, 1996b, 1996c; Valian, 1998). For example, one computer simulation study of promotions in a hypothetical company demonstrated that small-scale gender bias—accounting for only 1% of the variability in promotion—resulted in 65% males at the top of an eight-level hierarchy after several promotions (Martell, Lane, & Emrich, 1996). Understanding and addressing micro-inequities and the cumulative disadvantage they cause for women in the workplace is critical to the development and implementation of interventions aimed at the recruitment, retention, and advancement of women workers. A half century of literature on women's career development has produced ample evidence of these pervasive impediments to women's occupation-related choices and behaviors, and has documented a wide range of discriminatory practices in educational and occupational preparation, entry, retention, and advancement (e.g., see Betz, 1994, chap. 2, this volume; Fassinger, 2001, 2002; Fitzgerald & Betz, 1994; Fitzgerald, Fassinger, & Betz, 1995; Phillips & Imhoff, 1997).

In the realm of educational preparation, for example, pervasive bias against females is well documented, and includes such practices as: classroom interaction, language, and communication patterns that exclude or marginalize female students (e.g., use of examples familiar mainly to males, sexist jokes); faculty behavior that ignores or belittles females (e.g., low expectations for female performance, attention focused on males); faculty and peer harassment of female students (e.g., sexual harassment); curriculum content and practices that alienate female students (e.g., use of textbooks that stereotype or marginalize women, lack of interpersonal contact with faculty or peers, more opportunity for males to use equipment and technology, excessive focus on rote learning); extracurricular activities that exclude female students (e.g., women excluded from field experiences and opportunities considered too rough); and the absence in educational institutions of women in positions of power who can serve as mentors, role models, and advocates for female students (see American Association of University Women, 1992; Betz & Fitzgerald, 1987; Fassinger, 2001, 2002; Sadker & Sadker, 1994). Research on the retention of women in STEM college majors indicates that women are more likely than men to expect interactions with faculty, and are more affected by faculty feedback (e.g., criticism) than are men, suggesting the critical importance of overt faculty support for women in STEM fields (Seymour & Hewitt, 1997). Unfortunately, faculty may not perceive the importance of their support; in one study of faculty and female graduate students, students believed that faculty did not care about them, whereas faculty believed that students should be able to determine independently whether they belonged in graduate school (NSF, 2003). For women of color, lesbian women, and women with disabilities, some of these problematic educational practices may be exacerbated by individual and institutionalized bias based on racism, heterosexism, and antidisability prejudice in addition to gender-related bias (see Fassinger, 2002; Pearson & Bechtel, 1989).

    In terms of impediments to advancement, research on the vocational psychology of women indicates that women are consistently disadvantaged despite qualifications, education, experience, and occupational attitudes comparable to those of men (Phillips & Imhoff, 1997). Factors associated with differential advancement opportunities for men and women have been documented consistently in the literature and are both structural and attitudinal, including: the tendency of men to support and promote other men; the relationship between gendered schemas or attitudinal sets that result in lower expectations and poorer evaluations of women relative to men; the prevalence of sexual harassment; tracking of women into a narrow range of positions and tasks; excessive surveillance of women's work; women's exclusion from information-rich "old boy" networks; attitudinal factors in both women and men (e.g., stereotypes of women's abilities and appropriate roles for women); family responsibilities borne mostly by women; negative workplace climate; lack of experiences and resources for advancement (e.g., mentors, organizational support such as adequate lab space and assistants, opportunities to manage others); excessive responsibility for interpersonal relationships and other "shadow jobs" in the workplace; gender socialization patterns that compromise women's confidence and risk-taking ability; and, for women with other marginalized status (e.g., race/ethnicity, sexual orientation, disability), exacerbation of these factors due to additional sources of potential bias (for detailed discussion, see Betz, 1994, chap. 2, this volume; Betz & Fitzgerald, 1987, 1993; Fassinger, 2002; Pearson & Fechter, 1994; Phillips & Imhoff; Valian, 1998).

For example, one study of nine Fortune 500 companies found that barriers to women's advancement into upper management included: recruitment policies that depend on word-of-mouth networking and referrals; lack of opportunity to build and enhance credentials by assignment to corporate committees, task forces, and special projects; and insufficient monitoring of evaluation and compensation systems to make sure women and minorities are being treated fairly (Martin, 1991). A study of medical school faculty in 24 U.S. schools found that women were less satisfied and less productive than their male counterparts, with lack of institutional support (e.g., grants, clerical help) and greater child-care responsibilities implicated in this particular gender gap (Carr et al., 1998). A recent study of eminent female scientists (Wasserman, 2000) identified barriers to advancement such as the unfair or inaccurate assessment of women by men, lack of institutional financial support during the critical early years of their careers, exclusion from old boy networks, lack of mentors, and persistent negative societal attitudes. Studies of women scientists and engineers in the industrial sector indicate that women perceive male managers as "protecting" them from positions seen as "dirty or rough," thus unintentionally excluding them from career assignments in manufacturing or field sites that are critical for promotion (Catalyst, 1992, 1999). Finally, preliminary results from an ongoing study of women academic chemists suggest concurrence with many of these issues, citing isolation, difficulty in establishing visibility, exclusion from informal networking, excessive service and teaching demands, early support replaced by backlash regarding career advancement, and lack of mentoring as the most salient difficulties they faced (Scantlebury, Fassinger, & Richmond, 2003, 2004).

Many of the difficulties women experience in their advancement trajectories both stem from and result in negative or "chilly" organizational climates (Hall & Sandler, 1984). Studies have documented perceptions of the work environment as hostile to women on several dimensions, including sexist attitudes and comments, dual standards and opportunities, informal socializing, remediation policies and practices, and balancing work and personal obligations (e.g., Stokes, Riger, & Sullivan, 1995; see Betz, 1994, and chap. 2, this volume; Betz & Fitzgerald, 1987, for more detailed discussion). In STEM fields, in particular, there is growing recognition that the masculinized climate of science is an additional force that discourages women from pursuing and remaining in scientific fields (Fassinger, 2001). Implicated in an inhospitable climate are: a male model of career success in science that emphasizes competitiveness, combativeness, self-promotion, and aggression; alienating linguistic patterns (e.g., use of masculine images, dirty jokes) that permeate laboratories; narrow views of scientific investigation that emphasize quantity more than quality; the exclusion of females from formal and informal informational and social networks; and resource allocation that favors men and often excludes or disadvantages women. In addition, there is some evidence that women may do science differently from men, concentrating on developing their expertise in a unique niche, rather than competing with other researchers in broader, more mainstream areas. Moreover, women tend to demonstrate lower publication rates than men, although there is evidence that their work is cited more than men's; scholars in this arena suggest that women may focus more on quality than quantity in their work and may take longer on projects by being careful and perfectionistic in their approach, engaging in broader, more comprehensive projects, and placing greater emphasis on mentoring and involving others in their work (Fassinger).

Moreover, organizational policies and practices may unintentionally disadvantage women (Fassinger, 2002; Hewlett, 2002). Academic settings are characterized by rigid promotion and tenure timelines and industrial settings may involve career advancement requirements such as extensive travel and time spent with customers, both of which tend to coincide with women's childbearing years, forcing many women to choose between career and family because they perceive it to be too difficult to manage both roles. Perceptions of a negative workplace climate have critical implications for job satisfaction and turnover; for both women and men, the friendlier they perceive a work environment to be, the longer they plan to stay in the organization (Stokes et al., 1995). In fact, extensive research on job satisfaction has demonstrated strong links to family variables and role conflict, mentoring, social support, income, and occupational rank and type, all areas in which women typically are disadvantaged relative to men (Phillips & Imhoff, 1997). Occupational dissatisfaction also may be linked to a recent finding that regret of field choice among scientists is highest for those in physics and chemistry, areas represented strongly in business and industry (NSF, 2000).

Although many of the problems for women in negotiating male-dominated work environments are rooted in lack of support on the part of men, the absence of other women who might serve as role models and mentors also constitutes a major barrier to achievement (see Betz & Fitzgerald, 1987; Fassinger, 2002). Professional isolation virtually ensures that women will not obtain knowledge that is critical to success. Research, in fact, indicates that women more than men tend to lack information about what is required for career advancement; as they often are excluded from informal networks, they also receive little performance feedback and therefore are less able than men to take corrective action or position themselves for more desirable outcomes (Betz, 1994; Betz & Fitzgerald; Fassinger, 2002). The presence of women in positions of power and influence in organizations and institutions helps to legitimize women and provides models of status attainment with which women can identify, particularly in regard to managing the home-work interface (Fassinger, 2001). However, although research indicates that having mentors has positive effects on women's career advancement, it must be noted that it is exceedingly difficult to obtain mentors due to the lack of women (particularly women characterized by other minority statuses) in the upper ranks of most workplaces, especially those in STEM fields (Fassinger, 2002; Phillips & Imhoff, 1997; Wasserman, 2000). Studies indicate that, in general, individuals tend to receive more support for advancement from same-sex workers, and also that men tend to support other men, whereas women support both women and men (Phillips & Imhoff); taken together, these results suggest that men are far more likely than women to be in relationships in which they are being mentored.

A final well-documented area of challenge in the vocational psychology of women is the home-work interface and, more specifically, the fact that multiple-role responsibilities are borne mostly by women. Research indicates consistently that many women exhibit strong commitment to both work and family roles (Barnett & Hyde, 2001), which often include caring for extended family members (e.g., aging parents) or close friends and community members; thus, multiple-role issues are salient for most women, whether or not they have children of their own (Fassinger, 2001). Although ample evidence points to the beneficial aspects of multiple roles (especially work roles) for women (Barnett & Hyde; Crosby, 1991), the presence of (heterosexual) marriage and children consistently overdetermines women's vocational participation and success, and the impact of parenting roles on one's career trajectory continues to be experienced far more dramatically by women than men (Fitzgerald et al., 1995; Phillips & Imhoff, 1997). For example, for those who received doctorates in sciences and engineering for the period from 1973 to 1995, marriage and family were the most important factors differentiating workforce participation of men and women, associated with increased rates of full-time employment for men, but decreased rates for women (Committee on Women in Science and Engineering, National Research Council, 2001); moreover, the presence of children exhibits a positive association with salary for men, but a negative association with salary for women (NSF, 2002).

Research indicates that, although women's contemporary employment patterns reflect higher levels of employment and smaller families started later in life, their level of responsibility for housework and child care has not changed substantially relative to that of men, and they continue to bear most of the burden of home and family, even in dual-career couples (Fitzgerald et al., 1995; Phillips & Imhoff, 1997). Research indicates that expectations of women and men regarding care of home and children continue to exhibit wide discrepancies, and that men's actual performance of household and child-care tasks is far lower than women's even in relationships perceived to be egalitarian (see Gilbert, 1992). Indeed, in Wasserman's (2000) sample of eminent female scientists, the women with children generally reported that they assumed most of the responsibility for home and children, even though many of them were married to scientists, who presumably understood the rigors of scientific careers. Unfortunately, research suggests that women may feel more comfortable and confident about managing multiple roles if they are pursuing careers in fields traditional for women (Phillips & Imhoff), suggesting that women's plans to combine work and family may contribute to the paucity of women in STEM fields, especially at higher levels of achievement.

Many of the problems that women experience in managing multiple roles can be blamed on structural barriers in the workplace that make role integration difficult. By and large, workplaces have not provided affordable and accessible child care, flexible working arrangements such as job sharing and flextime, liberal parental leave policies, and viable alternative paths to success such as longer tenure timelines (Catalyst, 1996, 2000; Fassinger, 2001, 2002). One recent study of more than 1,000 employers indicated that that only 9% offered on-site child care, 5% assisted workers in paying for child care, and 36% offered information on finding child care (Bond, Galinsky, & Swanberg, 1998). Interestingly, however, data suggest that offering such services actually is fiscally sound; one study of a large banking firm demonstrated savings of $825,000 in absenteeism over 1 year due to a policy of limited emergency child care (Bond et al.). It also is worth noting that research has found that companies with women in top positions were six times more likely to provide child care than companies in which men predominated (Bond et al.), again highlighting the importance of women gaining access to the highest ranks of organizational hierarchies.

Ultimately, the goal of understanding barriers to women's STEM workforce participation is to use this knowledge to guide the design of interventions that organizations can implement in the recruitment, retention, and advancement of women, and that mental health professionals can use to help individual women survive in a context of systemic discrimination and lack of support. Many scholars argue that until a "critical mass" (15%–38%) of women in an organization or field is reached, no real changes will occur in the way that occupation is conceived and practiced (e.g., Wasserman, 2000); research supports this notion in the finding that women's performance is judged more positively when their presence in an organization reaches about one third (Fassinger, 2001). Indeed, results of the Project Access study suggest that only when percentages of men and women approach equality do barriers to women in those environments really begin to dissipate (Sonnert & Holton, 1996b, 1996c). However, increasing occupational specialization and persistent isolation suggest that even when small numbers of women are present, opportunities for interaction and mutual support may be infrequent, and some research suggests that as numbers of women approach 15% of an organization, they are even more isolated by the majority because of their threat to those in power (Wharton & Baron, 1987). Moreover, women who have achieved seniority in the current STEM workforce likely occupy those positions in part because they have been successful at adapting to the masculinized norms of the scientific workplace. They may have little investment in changing the workplace culture, rendering necessary the influx of women over several professional generations before the workplace culture can be transformed. The implication is that difficulties faced by women in the STEM workforce are not problems that can be resolved quickly or easily, and the development of effective interventions—by both organizations and mental health professionals—requires long-term commitment.

The vocational psychology literature, focused as it is on counseling and psychoeducational activities aimed at enhancing vocationally relevant attitudes and behaviors (e.g., occupational choices, decision-making skills, task self-efficacy, attitudinal barriers), and on interventions delivered to individuals and small groups, offers a wealth of information on which to draw in conceptualizing interventions to help women in STEM fields. It also suggests a direction for broader, systemic changes needed to make workplaces more viable for women. We draw from this literature in the following analyses of the three cases presented at the beginning of this chapter.

CASE ANALYSES AND INTERVENTIONS

Counseling Tammy: What Are the Issues?

Tammy is struggling with a number of issues that are contributing to her disappointing and unproductive graduate school experience. Tammy, a bright student as an undergraduate, seems to be a disappointment now that she is a graduate student. Her advisor had high expectations of her, but now that she is struggling, he does not offer the support or guidance she needs. Despite Tammy's expression of concern about her ability to write a thesis, her advisor is not helping her with the writing process or product. Rather, Tammy is left to figure out the thesis-writing process by herself. The fact that her advisor had more time for her when she was a promising and eager undergraduate rather than a struggling, disheartened graduate student suggests that he is either unaware of the help she needs or unable (or unwilling) to provide it. Such lack of mentorship and guidance is a pervasive problem for women in STEM fields. Tammy finds herself suddenly struggling with failure and support withdrawn, an experience common for women in STEM fields, and illustrative of the oft-cited "pipeline" problem in the sciences: the higher the movement up the hierarchy, the greater the likelihood that women will have been lost. Women who excel are expected to continue to do so, and any faltering may be viewed as confirmation of women's inability to excel in the sciences. Compounded by gender socialization that teaches women to downplay their achievements and doubt their abilities, it is perhaps unsurprising that Tammy would experience her current difficulties as disappointment, discouragement, and self-doubt.

Social support networks are especially important to women in the sciences, and Tammy has a number of roadblocks in her path. As a first-generation college student, Tammy has had to struggle with an experience and institution unknown to her parents, and she has been unable to seek their informed counsel in negotiating the academic environment. This experience can be isolating and confusing, as students often struggle with issues (e.g., intellectual demands) that their peers seem to handle more easily and their families do not understand. Given her family's difficulty with the fact that she is still in school, they probably expected Tammy to complete her degree and move into the world that is familiar to them, the work world. The added pressure of trying to communicate the importance of her intellectual growth to them is difficult for Tammy, as it emphasizes an uncomfortable rift between the opportunities and experience she has and the more limited worldview of her family. This disparity may be contributing to Tammy's feelings of guilt for selfishly spending time on an endeavor that is so incomprehensible to the people she loves.

Tammy also does not seem to be getting the support she needs from her fiancé, someone from whom she felt she needed to hide her depression. It is possible that, coming from another culture, his expectations about his future wife's education and career may reflect fairly traditional beliefs about marriage and motherhood. These expectations may be blatantly or subtly pressed on Tammy, as she already is manifesting the strain by considering the comfortable and safe (and more gender-stereotypic) alternative of staying at home and gardening. In addition to lack of support from her advisor, family, and fiancé, Tammy also does not feel connected with other students in her program, leaving her with virtually no one to help her through her current difficulties and decisions.

As the literature in women's mental health suggests, Tammy's depression probably is the result of internalizing her graduate school difficulties as feelings of personal failure and frustration. Concealing her despair from those to whom she was closest illustrates the desperate lack of connectedness she is experiencing. She did not want to bother her fiancé, who was dealing with his own difficulties, and she believed she had to deal with the depression in a way that did not disrupt her close relationships. She may have even feared that sharing her struggle with her family would lead to increased questioning about her continuing with graduate school, making her feel even less affirmed and more pressured to justify her decision (e.g., "Why stay if you're so miserable?" or, even worse, "Why did you choose to do this in the first place?"). Faced with the prospect of having to justify herself to her family and burden her fiancé, Tammy chose to suffer in silence.

What Are Possible Interventions for Tammy?

Tammy's lack of instinctual knowledge about how to write a thesis has caused her to question not the system of which she is a part, but rather herself. She sees the problem as a shortcoming on her part, although it is clear that at least some of the blame rests on a program (or advisor) that does not provide adequate support, guidance, and mentoring of students. To have received enthusiastic encouragement previously and now have it withdrawn as she encounters a difficult and ambiguous task probably confirms Tammy's worst fears about herself, leading her to believe she is not fit for the field she has chosen (something she has very likely heard before). Productive therapeutic work with Tammy will necessitate an analysis of the gendered structure of her graduate program and very basic consciousness raising about the common problems encountered by women in STEM fields. This will help Tammy recognize that her problems are not rooted in personal failings, and may lift some of the depression she is experiencing.

It is important to help Tammy establish the academic and interpersonal supports she is lacking. A first priority would be to acknowledge the looming deadline for her thesis and talk with Tammy about options for completion (e.g., an extension, a paring down or refocusing of the experiment she is doing). Tammy also might seek assistance in the form of a writing tutor and support group of some kind. A writing tutor will give her the guidance and structure she needs to help her with the actual writing of the thesis, and a support group will help her to avoid discouragement and self-doubt. There may be a program for women in the sciences at her institution, and it is likely that support groups for graduate students (particularly thesis or dissertation support groups) also may exist. As Tammy feels isolated from others in her program, it would be beneficial for her to connect with students (especially women) who may be experiencing similar difficulties. Tammy also may turn to online resources, such as MentorNet, an online mentoring network for women in STEM fields (MentorNet, 2004). MentorNet pairs undergraduate, graduate, and postdoctoral students with mentors in academia and industry. It also provides an electronic forum for discussions about graduate school, work-life balance, and career planning.

A significant focus of counseling with Tammy will need to address her career self-efficacy. Given the likelihood that gender socialization has taught her to doubt her abilities as a woman in the sciences and experience guilt when pursuing her own goals, it is entirely possible that Tammy does not feel capable of making a decision about her future that involves anything other than safe, comforting possibilities (i.e., gardening). In addition to challenging the assumption that a career in gardening is safe (in fact, anything other than amateur work will necessitate schooling in landscape architecture or a similar field, and most assuredly will move her, once again, into a male-dominated arena), interventions designed at giving Tammy a chance to recognize and internalize some of her successes may strengthen her enough to begin to think beyond safety and comfort. For example, Tammy may be encouraged to construct a lifeline of milestones and accomplishments in her academic life, and this visual representation of the path she has traveled may help her to appreciate the challenges she has already overcome. Another technique may be to introduce bibliotherapy, having Tammy read about women scientists in order to contextualize her struggles in light of the lives of those who have gone before. As a budding scientist herself, Tammy will likely enjoy and absorb any information she is given about women in STEM fields. Tammy also may benefit from exploration of her early experiences in the sciences, particularly the ways in which family, teacher, peer, and self expectations may have shaped the current conflicts (both internal and external) she now is facing. All of these strategies may help to rebuild Tammy's enthusiasm and confidence so that she can reconsider more readily her previously chosen career path, and can decide whether she wishes to pursue it from a position of strength rather than retreat.

Another important aspect of work with Tammy will be to help her clarify her values. With the pull to be a wife and mother coming from her fiancé and his family and the pull to spend more time with her own family, Tammy may find herself yielding to external pressures rather than making a conscious decision about what she wants for herself. She once had considerable passion about working in rain forests, a rather adventurous aspiration given her current anxieties and gravitation toward the comfort of home life. What happened to this career aspiration, and how much of that passion does she retain? How does her current thesis project connect (or not) with that aspiration? Even if she no longer seriously considers a career working in rain forests, what aspects of that dream does she value strongly enough to actualize, realistically, in her current career plan? Clarifying Tammy's values may involve a variety of techniques, including values card sorts, guided imagery (e.g., an imaginary day in the future), or formal career testing (including computer-guided assessment). Focusing Tammy on articulating more clearly the aspects of her future possibilities that are most appealing to her may help her to bridge what now seem like two very dichotomous and disparate worlds—her academic life and her personal life—and ultimately may lead her to more integrated life choices.

Counseling Beverly: What Are the Issues?

Beverly's situation is common among women of color in STEM fields. As the first African American in the department, Beverly is facing the pressure of African American and female students interested in her as an advisor and mentor. Students seeking out role models and mentors are inclined to find faculty with whom they identify, often those of the same race/ethnicity and gender, if such faculty exist. Beverly also may be the first or one of the few African Americans or women they have seen in their field, and this recognition that someone like them can do computer science is a powerful motivator for students. Beverly, who almost certainly has gone through her undergraduate and graduate careers without having the kind of African American female role model she can be to these students, naturally feels pulled to help them. Unfortunately, the need is so great that she cannot possibly work with all the students who seek her out. Moreover, the department's efforts to recruit more underrepresented students will likely increase the need for her advising and mentoring in the future, a prospect that is undoubtedly quite daunting. Even if she does not formally mentor most of the students who seek her out, she may find that she is called on frequently as an informal resource. With such demands on her time from needy students, Beverly is put in a no-win position: If she gives herself over to mentoring activities and other shadow jobs, she will almost surely not get enough research done to merit eventual tenure, but if she focuses on research and minimizes attention to students, she will feel that she is failing at one of her core responsibilities and pleasures as a faculty member.

Beverly also likely feels that every move she makes in her department is being scrutinized. The pressure on the first female African American faculty member to be perfect is considerable, because her success (or failure) will very likely influence her department in future hiring decisions and thus affect the professional lives of others like her who will follow. The burdens of tokenism—feeling that she is representing her race and gender, and also being treated by others as if she does—add to the pressure of an already stressful job. Beverly again faces a double bind, in that there are negative consequences whether she accepts or refuses the various professional responsibilities she is being asked to assume, and the disappointment of some people that she is bound to cause will be noticed and remembered.

There also is indication in this case that Beverly is being challenged by the chilly climate of science in her department. Her only female colleague, apparently familiar with the sexist attitudes of some of the faculty, offers no guidance or support. Women in STEM fields often face subtle and blatant sexism, which may be most obvious in male colleagues who come from cultures in which sexism is deeply embedded. The climate in Beverly's department is characterized by egregious manifestations of sexism, and it appears that her department chair either is oblivious to it or even may collude in it, given that the other female in the department apparently has given up and decided to tolerate it. Although Beverly's publication record is good at present, the sexist (and probably racist) beliefs of her colleagues put her in a position of having to be twice as accomplished as her White male counterparts to be considered half as good. Moreover, if she was hired in any kind of a special attempt to bring in female or minority faculty members, her colleagues (even those who voted in her favor) probably harbor the assumption that she was hired because of her race and gender, not her talents. Most women in STEM fields (probably including Beverly) have encountered teachers, professors, and colleagues who assert directly or indirectly that women do not belong in the sciences. Experiencing such blatant sexism at her new job may not be entirely surprising to Beverly, but it most certainly is discouraging and frightening, as these are the people who will be making decisions about her professional performance and prospects for a very long time.

Beverly also faces limitations in resource allocation common to women who work in STEM fields, because she is competing with men (who are likely more aggressive and competitive in obtaining what they want) for lab space, funding, graduate assistants, desirable teaching assignments, and other tangible benefits. Having only one research assistant puts Beverly at a considerable disadvantage because it seriously affects her ability to establish her research program. With limited research assistance, it is virtually impossible for Beverly to write grant proposals and conduct research simultaneously. In addition, Beverly may do science differently from her male colleagues, putting her energy into broad, complex, interdisciplinary projects that take a lot of time and require a great deal of collaboration. If this is the case, Beverly almost certainly will be punished in the tenure process as she will likely produce fewer publications than are expected. Finally, the inability or reluctance of Beverly's colleagues to help her with her resource-related problems, though typical for women in STEM fields, also highlights the isolation she faces in her work on a daily basis.

What Are Possible Interventions for Beverly?

Effective therapeutic work with Beverly needs to focus first on helping her to locate sources of support, for both her job-related tasks and her emotional reactions to her position. A first step would be to ready her to approach her department chair and discuss expectations and work-load issues. It will be important for the chair to articulate clearly to Beverly exactly what will be considered in the tenure process, what is important for the establishment of her career, and what she may reasonably refuse without negative consequences. Beverly's sharing of the fact that she has female and African American students clamoring for help also may enlighten the chair regarding her pressures as the first African American female faculty member, and also can help him to justify the need for more female faculty and faculty of color. Even if hiring additional faculty is not feasible at present, the department could be encouraged to invite more women and people of color as colloquium speakers, thus enhancing the networking opportunities for students without putting additional demands on Beverly's time. Establishing a relationship with her chair also may provide Beverly with useful guidance and an ally (or, at least, a somewhat sympathetic ear).

Beverly's institution may have a Black faculty and staff association (or similar organization) that would help her to establish a network of colleagues who have negotiated the same difficulties she faces. Particularly useful would be other African American women (preferably in the sciences if they exist), and a senior female faculty member might offer a great deal of wisdom not only about how to handle oneself personally, but also about the politics and unwritten normative practices of the institution. Depending on the size and composition of the institution, connecting with other women may necessitate establishing a network of professionals at nearby institutions or even nationally; if this is done with women in STEM fields, it may lead additionally to fruitful grant collaborations for Beverly. The campus equity office also would serve as a valuable resource in helping Beverly address the sexism she is encountering from her colleagues, and would aid her in assessing any personal action she might take.

Beverly also may be interested in networking and professional opportunities at the national level. A number of national STEM organizations concerned with the problems of women and minorities in their fields have implemented various kinds of initiatives aimed at providing support, networking, mentoring, and enhancement of professional skills. The American Chemical Society, for example, has a Women Chemists Committee, which offers a wide range of resources for its members, and similar structures exist in physics, computer science, and engineering professional organizations (a new publication from the NSF [NSF, 2003] outlines virtually every existing NSF-funded program designed to aid women and girls in STEM fields). Networking and skills training may help Beverly to learn strategies for contributing in faculty meetings despite the unwelcome climate. Learning to address the dismissive attitudes of her colleagues in an effective way also may help Beverly to feel and establish overtly her legitimacy and worth.

Yet another source of support for Beverly is the grants office at her institution, as well as program officers at funding organizations such as the NSF and the National Institutes of Health. Personnel in such positions are an excellent source of information about what sources of external funding are available, and also can help her to shape her work in order to obtain particular kinds of funding. Moreover, many funding agencies offer grants to young or new investigators, to women and minorities, and specifically for training and mentoring, all of which may benefit Beverly. Although Beverly's colleagues do not appear to be particularly helpful to her in this area, good program officers at organizations such as the NSF will spend time discussing preliminary ideas and proposals with applicants in order to ensure that their proposals meet program requirements and obtain a fair review.

Additional therapeutic work with Beverly might focus on helping her to reframe the conflicts she is experiencing and prioritize appropriately. Beverly, like most women, probably has been socialized to put others before herself. Thus, it might help her to consider that time and effort expended on establishing herself firmly in her career (i.e., prioritizing research) actually will be of benefit to students in the long run. Essentially, the way that Beverly will be able to help students most effectively is to progress in her position, secure tenure, and become a permanent fixture in the institution. In this reframing, taking care of herself by publishing (which she may regard as selfish and uncaring) can be viewed as maximizing her potential to take care of and be there for others, because she is protecting herself in order to protect them. This reframing also may serve to broaden Beverly's conception of the kind of help she needs to give to students, and may encourage her toward more indirect forms of support—helping students to establish their own networks and external contacts (including electronic resources, such as MentorNet, with which her students are likely to be especially comfortable). Beverly also should establish a connection at the college counseling center so that she may refer students struggling with academic and personal issues. In this way, she would not be ignoring the pleas of students seeking help, nor would she be taking on the commitment to work with them directly.

Finally, although it may be disheartening for Beverly to consider the possibility of negative future events, it is crucial that she keep thorough documentation of her professional life. She must follow up and document promises, decisions, and requests in writing, she must save electronic communications, and she should document the time she spends in advising, mentoring, service, and shadow jobs. Such documentation will provide evidence of both the formal and informal responsibilities in which Beverly is engaged, and she can use this information to demonstrate to her chair and to the departmental promotion and tenure committee how she is spending her time. This may allow her to renegotiate assignments in an ongoing way, and also will prepare her to address debates that might arise over her eventual tenure and promotion. Finally, therapeutic work with Beverly should help to focus her on lifestyle habits that will ensure her continued health. Encouraging her to pursue activities such as exercising, socializing, and nurturing hobbies outside of academe may help Beverly to stay energized, focused, and calm in her very stressful position.

Counseling Jean: What Are the Issues?

Jean is struggling with substantial multiple-role conflicts that are quite characteristic of working women (particularly those in STEM fields), and are probably exacerbated by her stage of life (young mother) and her cultural background. Although Jean is married, the primary responsibility for child care clearly rests on her shoulders. Added to this responsibility is Jean's duty to her ailing mother-in-law, a common occurrence in a generation of contemporary women caring not only for their children, but also for elderly parents. In addition, although both members of the couple work, there is evidence in this case that Jean's career pursuits may be viewed as secondary to her husband's, who may be considered the primary breadwinner by everyone in the family. Spousal help with child care and elder care is not known, but clearly Jean feels that her career decisions are contingent on fulfilling her family duties, whereas her husband's are not. In fact, her husband has expressed concern about Jean's career advancement affecting their lives, but he does not appear to have considered any adjustment in his career situation to accommodate Jean's advancement. As a Taiwanese American man, he may have fairly traditional expectations about her duty to his mother and their child, particularly because the child is male. Her mother-in-law also may hold such notions, and Jean may receive considerable chastisement if she is not perceived to be devoting adequate attention to her home and family members. Jean's son even may have been enlisted by his father or grandmother to discourage Jean from spending time away from the family. The fact that Jean is worried about causing a marital rift by pursuing a managerial path suggests that her career advancement may be viewed as a threat to all or most members of the family. Unfortunately, Jean is unlikely to find direct assistance from her company, as the structure of most workplaces does not accommodate the personal and home-related needs of working women, particularly in the context of being considered for managerial roles.

Jean's other major obstacle concerns her lack of leadership self-efficacy and her development of persistent anxiety in recent team meetings. As the onset of Jean's anxiety coincides with the suggestion that she pursue a new career path, it is reasonable to conceptualize these two issues as linked. Many women formally trained in STEM fields experience individuals, institutions, and systems that question their ability to perform in the sciences. Such external challenges also trigger internal questioning and a sense of insecurity in one's own abilities, knowledge, and skills. The resultant self-doubt can manifest itself even in the wake of apparent external support. Jean is being encouraged (although she views it as being pressured) to stretch herself and join the managerial ranks, but she is uncomfortable with the idea of leaving her area of expertise. Despite the offer of additional training in the skills she would need to succeed, and the support of her supervisor (who presumably has an accurate assessment of her potential in management), Jean's self-concept does not allow her to consider such a role, and her Taiwanese cultural background also likely contributes to her reluctance to enact behaviors seen as aggressive and inappropriate for her gender. Jean is wedged into a niche in her field that she has been able to carve out for herself, and leaving this niche may render her vulnerable to public criticism and failure in a way that she is not prepared to handle. The anxiety she is experiencing in team meetings may be reflective of her discomfort in being singled out, a feeling not uncommon to women in STEM fields, for whom attracting notice in a male-dominated environment can lead to detrimental consequences, even in a seemingly positive arena such as career advancement.

Jean also seems to have internalized the sexist climate in STEM fields, evidenced by her self-professed doubting of women's abilities to achieve in the scientific workplace. The pervasive isolation surrounding the work lives of women in STEM occupations and the profound lack of women mentors, role models, or even colleagues can cause even the most determined women to question the right of women to occupy STEM positions. They are likely to have experienced considerable difficulty combating the stereotypes encountered in school and in their professional lives, and as they near the tops of their fields (where the pipeline problem virtually ensures a paucity of women), their stereotypes may simply be confirmed by the lack of female colleagues. Jean may feel that she is one of the lucky ones to have advanced as far as she has, and that she should not press her luck by venturing into a new arena in which she seems almost certain to fail.

What Are Possible Interventions for Jean?

One of the most crucial and immediate interventions needed with Jean is to help her to connect with women in similar circumstances. In many ways, it was inevitable that Jean reach this crossroads in her personal and career lives. Having apparently internalized the societal stereotype that limits the career paths and possibilities for women in STEM fields, Jean is unprepared to consider a path beyond her current position. Because one of Jean's obstacles is a limited vision of what women in science might do, her thinking may be expanded by exposure to other STEM women in a diversity of jobs. In addition to the organizational and technological resources noted previously, another online resource to consider is WomenTechWorld.org, an online component of the WomenTech Project run by the Institute for Women in Trades, Technology, and Science. WomenTechWorld.org provides an opportunity for women in technology and science fields to connect with other women in a variety of ways, from posting on message boards, to reading "Her Stories" about women in a variety of science and technology jobs, to utilizing career and mentoring information provided online. Jean may benefit from reading the stories and electronically chatting with women who are in STEM fields. She also may find advice, guidance, and inspiration from women (particularly women of her own cultural background) who are managing professional positions and maintaining a family life.

In conjunction with helping Jean to develop external support networks, therapeutic work also must focus on her internal struggles. As with many anxiety-related problems, simple insight regarding the causes of her recent difficulties with public speaking is unlikely to result in immediate relief for Jean, which might be addressed most effectively with a variety of relaxation and visualization techniques. For example, Jean may be asked to imagine the circumstances in which she is feeling anxious, and these experiences can be analyzed sequentially to ascertain the severity of anxiety at each step and identify both the cause and the accompanying thought patterns that may be exacerbating her anxiety. Jean can be taught ways to manage and combat her anxiety both in anticipation of and during the anxiety-producing circumstances. Seeing her own ability to manage her anxiety and overcome a difficult challenge, Jean may build some of the self-efficacy she is lacking.

As Jean's views of her possibilities as a woman expand and as she observes her own ability to handle her anxiety growing stronger, she might explore her reluctance to pursue the leadership role being offered to her. Exploring the gendered messages she has received both implicitly and explicitly (including her supervisor's comments), and placing those messages in her cultural context as a Taiwanese American woman and her work context as a woman in a scientific field will be important in helping Jean to sort out the effects of these messages and perhaps rethink them. This work also might include readying Jean for additional information gathering and discussion with her supervisor. For example, Jean might be encouraged to sample some of the leadership training sessions on a trial basis, or she might make contact (and perhaps spend a day) with women in similar positions in her own or other companies to clarify in her mind exactly what her managerial duties might entail. Additionally, discussions between Jean and her supervisor might focus on the specifics of managing her family roles in addition to her leadership roles in the company, with arrangements perhaps made to accommodate Jean's needs.

A final therapeutic goal for Jean is to address some of her difficulties at home, particularly regarding her obvious caretaking overload and her fear of her husband's anger or disapproval. Couples counseling might prove quite beneficial for Jean and her spouse, especially in terms of opening a dialogue between them that Jean might be too frightened to initiate or maintain. Counseling can provide a safe space for both partners to articulate their fears and work out compromises that are optimal for both of them, personally and professionally. For example, they might decide together to hire a nursing assistant to care for Jean's mother-in-law, or they might decide that Jean's husband will shave several hours a week off his job in order to spend more time at home. Given the inevitable stresses of raising a child and caring for a mother-in-law, couples counseling also might provide a time and place for Jean and her husband to reconnect with one another. At the very least, knowing where she stands with her spouse vis-à-vis her career opportunities will provide Jean with more solid information on which to base her decisions. Getting Jean's spouse into counseling may be difficult, however, given that he is both male and from a background that does not encourage speaking with mental health professionals, factors that may predispose him to be reluctant about seeking help. If true, then Jean will need strategies for engaging her spouse in a dialogue outside of counseling. Regardless of the venue, it is critically important to help Jean claim the opportunity to consider her array of choices as real choices, and not default decisions resulting from her own or her family's unexamined expectations.

CONCLUSION

Our focus in this chapter was on providing information for the development of interventions aimed at helping women like Tammy, Beverly, and Jean to resolve their personal struggles. However, we also note that none of these women faced additional barriers related to sexual orientation or disability, and their socioeconomic status background is unknown, so it is not clear to what extent social class also affects their unique circumstances. It also should be abundantly clear that individual solutions are wholly inadequate for addressing the structural barriers that render educational and work environments so difficult for women in STEM fields. Sweeping changes are needed (see Fassinger, 2002, for detailed discussion). Such changes should include: developing educational and workplace policies that affirm and support all workers (e.g., equitably distributed benefits, antidiscrimination statements); instituting educational and workplace practices that help to counter discriminatory attitudes (e.g., training in diversity, transparent performance review and reward systems); implementing social policies and laws that support families in all of their diverse forms (e.g., accessible child care, medical and legal benefits that are available to all families); and, finally, transforming gender-socialization practices so that all individuals have the freedom and support to actualize into their best selves.

REFERENCES

American Association of University Women. (1992). *How schools shortchange girls: The AAUW report*. New York: Marlowe.

Barnett, R. C., & Hyde, J. S. (2001). Women, men, work, and family: An expansionist perspective. *American Psychologist, 56,* 781–796.

Betz, N. E. (1994). Basic issues and concepts in career counseling for women. In W. B. Walsh & S. H. Osipow (Eds.), *Career counseling for women* (pp. 1–42). Hillsdale, NJ: Lawrence Erlbaum Associates.

Betz, N. E., & Fitzgerald, L. F. (1987). *The career psychology of women.* New York: Academic Press.

Betz, N. E., & Fitzgerald, L. F. (1993). Individuality and diversity: Theory and research in counseling psychology. *Annual Review of Psychology, 44,* 343–381.

Bienenstock, A. (2000, May). *The scientific, technical, and engineering workforce for the 21st century: The federal perspective.* Paper presented at the Chemical Sciences Roundtable, National Research Council, Washington, DC.

Bond, J. T., Galinsky, E., & Swanberg, J. (1998). *The 1997 study of the changing workforce.* New York: Families and Work Institute.

Carr, P. L., Ash, A. S., Friedman, R. H., Scaramuccii, A., Barnett, R. C., Szalacha, L., et al. (1998). Relation of family responsibilities and gender to the productivity and career satisfaction of medical faculty. *Annals of Internal Medicine, 129,* 532–538.

Catalyst. (1992). *Women in engineering: An untapped resource.* www.catalystwomen.org

Catalyst. (1996). *Making work flexible: Policy to practice.* www.catlystwomen.org

Catalyst. (1999). *Women scientists in industry: Making it in both management and technical roles.* www.catalystwomen.org

Catalyst. (2000). *Flexible work arrangements III: A ten-year retrospective of part-time arrangements.* www.catalystwomen.org

Committee on Women in Science and Engineering, National Research Council. (2001). *From scarcity to visibility: Gender differences in the careers of doctoral scientists and engineers.* Washington, DC: National Academy Press.

Crosby, F. J. (1991). *Juggling.* New York: Free Press.

Davis, S. (2000, May). *An oddity no longer: Women scientists in the chemical industry.* Paper presented at the Chemical Sciences Roundtable, National Research Council, Washington, DC.

Fassinger, R. E. (2001). Women in nontraditional work fields. In J. Worrell (Ed.), *Encyclopedia of women and gender* (Vol. 2, pp. 1169–1180). San Diego, CA: Academic Press.

Fassinger, R. E. (2002). Hitting the ceiling: Gendered barriers to occupational entry, advancement, and achievement. In L. Diamant & J. Lee (Eds.), *The psychology of sex, gender, and jobs: Issues and solutions* (pp. 21–46). Westport, CT: Greenwood Press.

Fitzgerald, L. F., & Betz, N. E. (1994). Career development in cultural context: The role of gender, race, class, and sexual orientation. In M. L. Savickas & R. W. Lent (Eds.), *Convergence in theories of career choice and development* (pp. 103–118). Palo Alto, CA: Consulting Psychologists Press.

Fitzgerald, L. F., Fassinger, R. E., & Betz, N. E. (1995). Theoretical advances in the study of women's career development. In W. B. Walsh & S. H. Osipow (Eds.), *Handbook of vocational psychology* (2nd ed., pp. 67–109). Hillsdale, NJ: Lawrence Erlbaum Associates.

Gilbert, L. A. (1992). Gender and counseling psychology: Current knowledge and directions for research and social action. In S. D. Brown & R. W. Lent (Eds.), *Handbook of counseling psychology* (2nd ed., pp. 383–418). New York: Wiley.

Hall, R., & Sandler, B. (1984). *The classroom climate: A chilly one for women?* Washington, DC: Association of American Colleges and Universities, Program on the Status and Education of Women.

Hewlett, S. A. (2002). Executive women and the myth of having it all. *Harvard Business Review, 80*(4), 66–73.

Martell, R. F., Lane, D. M., & Emrich, C. (1996). Male-female differences: A computer simulation. *American Psychologist, 51,* 157–158.

Martin, L. (1991). *A report on the glass ceiling initiative.* Washington, DC: U.S. Department of Labor.

http://www.mentornet.net

National Science Board. (2000). *Science and engineering indicators: 2000.* Arlington, VA: Author.

National Science Foundation. (2000). *Women, minorities, and persons with disabilities in science and engineering: 2000.* Arlington, VA: Author.

National Science Foundation. (2002). *Science and engineering indicators: 2002.* Washington, DC: Author.

National Science Foundation. (2003). *New formulas for America's workforce: Girls in science and engineering.* Washington, DC: Author.

Pearson, W., Jr., & Bechtel, H. K. (1989). *Blacks, science, and American education.* New Brunswick, NJ: Rutgers University Press.

Pearson, W., Jr., & Fechter, A. (Eds.). (1994). *Who will do science? Educating the next generation.* Baltimore, MD: Johns Hopkins University Press.

Phillips, S. D., & Imhoff, A. R. (1997). Women and career development: A decade of research. *Annual Review of Psychology, 48,* 31–59.

Sadker, M., & Sadker, D. (1994). *Failing at fairness: How our schools cheat girls.* New York: Simon & Schuster.

Scantlebury, K., Fassinger, R. E., & Richmond, G. (2003, September). *Grace under fire: Women chemists' perseverance in and dedication to chemistry.* Paper presented at the 226th American Chemical Society meeting, New York.

Scantlebury, K., Fassinger, R. E., & Richmond, G. (2004, April). *There is no crying in chemistry: The lives of female academic chemists.* Paper presented at the National Association of Research in Science Teaching, Vancouver, Canada.

Seymour, E., & Hewitt, N. M. (1997). *Talking about leaving: Why undergraduates leave the sciences.* Boulder, CO: Westview Press.

Sonnert, G., & Holton, R. (1996a). Career patterns of women and men in the sciences. *American Scientist, 84,* 63–71.

Sonnert, G., & Holton, G. (1996b). *Gender differences in science careers: The Project Access study.* New Brunswick, NJ: Rutgers University Press.

Sonnert, G., & Holton, G. (1996c). *Who succeeds in science? The gender dimension.* New Brunswick, NJ: Rutgers University Press.

Stokes, J., Riger, S., & Sullivan, M. (1995). Measuring perceptions of the working environment for women in corporate settings. *Psychology of Women Quarterly, 19,* 533–549.

Valian, V. (1998). *Why so slow? The advancement of women.* Cambridge, MA: MIT Press.

Wasserman, E. R. (2000). *The door in the dream: Conversations with eminent women in science.* Washington, DC: Joseph Henry Press.

Wharton, A. S., & Baron, J. N. (1987). So happy together? The impact of gender segregation on men at work. *American Sociological Review, 52,* 574–587.

Widnall, S. (2000, April). *Digits of Pi: Barriers and enablers for women in engineering.* Paper presented at the southeast regional meeting of the National Academy of Engineering, Georgia Tech University, Atlanta.

http://www.womentechworld.org

Chapter 14

Career Counseling for Women in Management

Joyce E. A. Russell
The University of Maryland

Over the past 50 years, the influx of women into the workforce and their growing interest in managerial careers has been one of the major developments in American society (Bowen & Hisrich, 1986). In fact, in the United States, the proportion of women managers more than doubled between 1970 and 1987, increasing from 16% to 38%, and rose to 45% in 2002 (Powell, 1988; Powell & Graves, 2003). In fact, management was traditionally considered a male occupation in the United States, yet today is seen as sex neutral. Around the world, women have also made gains in management representation, although not to the same degree as in the United States. For example, from 1980 to 2000, the number of women managers increased from 14% to 26% in Australia, 25% to 35% in Canada, and 16% to 29% in Sweden (Powell & Graves). Despite the gains women have made entering managerial positions, there still remains a large gap between the proportion of women in management overall and the proportion of women in top management positions. In all countries, the proportion of women decreases at progressively higher levels in the managerial ranks (Powell & Graves).

Because of the increasing numbers of women entering managerial positions, researchers and practitioners have examined some of the career-related issues facing women as they move into this occupation. Although male and female managers share some similar experiences in career development, they also encounter some unique issues resulting in different career tactics, plans, and career progression. In the present chapter I review the major issues confronting women in management and discuss strategies and counseling techniques that may provide assistance to women managers, emphasizing the issues facing women who currently are managers. It is assumed that the career issues facing men and women in management differ to some degree, and that the concerns confronting women themselves vary as well because women managers are considered to be a heterogeneous group with respect to their career plans and progress.

In this chapter, I integrate literature from a variety of disciplines, including vocational behavior, counseling psychology, industrial and organizational psychology, and organizational behavior. To date, very few attempts have been made to combine the research from these distinct fields in order to describe career counseling for women in management. For example, researchers in the areas of vocational behavior and counseling psychology have examined career-counseling issues and strategies for employed women in general, identifying relevant theories, barriers, and work-family issues facing women, pertinent counseling strategies, and counselor biases in treating women. At the same time, researchers in the areas of industrial and organizational psychology and organizational behavior have documented obstacles confronting women managers and assistance strategies, yet with little emphasis on career-counseling concerns. In this chapter I attempt to merge this diverse literature in order to discuss career-counseling issues for women in management.

CAREER DEVELOPMENT FOR WOMEN VERSUS MEN MANAGERS

In general, most of the research on career development has focused on the issues facing men, assuming that similar issues also confront women (Betz & Fitzgerald, 1987). Almost two decades ago, however, researchers suggested that the career development of women may be different from that of men due to differences in attitudes, role expectations, behaviors, and sanctions arising from the socialization process (Borman & Guido-DiBrito, 1986). Gutek and Larwood (1987) argued that a theory for women's career development must be separate from a theory of men's career development because women face unique opportunities and problems. Women and men have different expectations regarding the perceived appropriateness of jobs for them, women face more constraints in the workplace (e.g., gender stereotypes and biases in hiring and promotion decisions), and marital and parental roles have a differential impact on the career progress of women versus men. Relative to men, women have divergent career perspectives, choices, priorities, and patterns that need to be understood.

Having a separate theory for women's career development does not, however, mean that women's career achievements are any less important than those of men or that some women do not fit the male model of work and careers. The premise behind a separate theory is that women on the whole face a set of opportunities and problems distinct from those of most men (Morrison, White, Van Velsor, & the Center for Creative Leadership, 1987) and that career theories for men do not fit many women's lives and development. A separate theory of women's career development should address career preparation, societal opportunities and constraints, and the influence of marriage, pregnancy, and children on career choices (Gutek & Larwood, 1987). More so than men, women often focus their life on work-related and non-work-related factors (e.g., their relationships and their families) and are interested in finding a balance between those worlds (Smith, 2000).

In management positions in particular, Powell (1988) noted that the career development process is unique for men and women managers, although this is diminishing to some degree. Men and women managers face similar management functions and goals, yet the process of reaching those goals differs (Carr-Ruffino, 1993). They may share similar levels of work motivation, yet they make different career choices due to their socialization experiences and the opportunities available to them (Astin, 1984). The career patterns for male and female managers differ whether in the United States or other countries (Brown & Ridge, 2002). Women managers often do not advance as far in the organizational hierarchy as their male counterparts. Male managers often have more mentors, are more likely to be in line positions, have greater professional status, and occupy higher positions than women managers. Moreover, men and women managers have different career tactics and plans. Men are more likely than women to assume personal control for their own careers by developing long-range career plans, whereas women often believe that their superiors will look out for their career progress and opportunities.

Kirchmeyer (1998) examined four possible determinants of managerial career success to see if they impacted men's and women's careers differently: human capital (experience, tenure, career interruptions, professional degree), individual (masculinity, femininity), interpersonal (mentor, superior support, network support), and family (spouse, nonemployed spouse, children). She found that the women managers earned less than the men, but perceived their careers to be equally successful. They also achieved the same hierarchical levels as the men despite their lower incomes.

Marital and parental factors are likely to lead to differences among male and female managers. Women with families experience more difficulties pursuing careers in management than men with families. Furthermore, married male managers are more likely than female managers to have a stay-at-home spouse who takes care of family responsibilities. Because women who are part of a dual-career couple still handle most of the household activities, having a family appears to pose a greater constraint on a woman's career than on a man's. This is particularly true in a time-greedy career such as management.

LABOR TRENDS FOR WOMEN'S PARTICIPATION IN MANAGEMENT

Women Entering Management Positions

Over the past several decades, women have made progress in entering managerial positions. This may be due to changes in cultural norms, federal legislation banning gender discrimination in employment practices, increased opportunities for women to obtain training or advanced education, delays in childbearing, and the women's movement (e.g., consciousness raising; Hammer-Higgins & Atwood, 1989). In 1970, women compromised only 16% of managers, a figure that increased to 26% in 1980, and to 39.3% in 1988 (Powell, 1988; U.S. Bureau of the Census, 1990). By 2002, women made up 46% of the executive, administrative, and managerial positions in the United States (U.S. Department of Labor, Bureau of Labor Statistics, 2003). Even during the sluggish U.S. economy from 2001 to 2003, women were making steady progress moving into management positions (Armour, 2003). The number of women filling lower and mid-level management positions has continually increased. Despite the fact that more women are entering management positions, they are not entering leadership positions in all types of industries. For example, companies in the high-tech industry (e.g., computer hardware and software, telecommunications, Internet services) report lower numbers of women in leadership positions compared to their Fortune 500 counterparts (Catalyst, 2003a).

Women Entering Top Management

Even though women have been entering management positions in record numbers, relatively few women have made it to top management. The greatest number of women managers exists at the lowest levels, followed by the middle levels, thus, the lower managerial ranks have become sex neutral, whereas the top managerial levels remain male intensive (Powell & Graves, 2003). The proportion of women in top management or "clout" positions that wield the most power and influence (e.g., chief executive officer, chairman, vice chairman, president, chief operating officer, senior executive vice president, executive vice president) has remained low and a glass ceiling still exists (Catalyst, 2000b; Powell & Graves). As of 2002, the proportion of women in corporate officer positions in Fortune 500 corporations was only 15.7%, up from 12.5% in 2000 and 8.7% in 1995 (Catalyst, 2003c). As of 2003, there were eight female CEOs in the U.S. Fortune 500 firms and nine more in the Fortune 501-1000 firms. Women of color comprised only 1.6% of corporate officers. Two senior management positions that are still predominately male include CFOs (chief financial officers) and general counsel positions (7.1% and 16.1%, are women, respectively). Despite the fact that CEOs state that women need line experience, only 9.9% of line corporate officer positions are held by women. Women are still predominately in staff positions, whereas men are mostly in line positions.

Several reasons explain why women make up such a small percentage of top management positions. One factor making it difficult for women to reach the senior jobs is that they face greater demands regarding family issues (e.g., housework, child care, marriage), and may experience more career interruptions than male managers (Rothwell, 1986). Another view is that many women managers have not been in organizations long enough to have entered into the senior management ranks. For example, many women have not yet accumulated the 25 years of work experience necessary to move into senior management, or 35 years of experience to sit in the CEO's chair ("For Women," 1992). A survey by Catalyst found that 79% of women and 90% of CEOs said the primary obstacle to women moving into top management is their limited line (general management) experience (Wellington, Kropf, & Gerkovich, 2003). Other reasons offered include the glass ceiling, or sex discrimination in promotion practices, fewer training opportunities to prepare women to advance, and less interest among women for moving into senior management (Powell, 1999). A recent study by Catalyst (2004d), however, indicated that female executives are just as likely as male colleagues to aspire to the CEO job, and this was true even for women with children at home. Catalyst found that women and men Fortune 1000 executives shared equal ambitions and similar strategies for reaching the top jobs, including consistently exceeding performance expectations, successfully managing others, seeking high-visibility assignments, and demonstrating expertise.

Women in Corporate Director Positions

Generally, board of directors positions are reserved for those with significant executive experience. Women generally hold few board seats in the United States and elsewhere despite the fact that having women on boards is economically advantageous to a firm. Statistics for 2003 indicated that women held 13.6% of all board seats in the U.S. Fortune 500 firms, up from 12.4% in 2001 and 9.6% in 1995. Women of color held 3% of board seats, an increase of only .5% from 1999 (Catalyst, 2003c). Women held only 11.2% of board director positions in Canada, and the number of U.S. companies with at least one board seat held by a woman is nearly double that of Canadian companies (e.g., 89.2% of Fortune 500 companies have at least one board seat held by a woman versus 48.6% of Canadian Fortune 500 firms; Catalyst, 2004f). In Europe and Asia, women are far less represented on boards (Gundry, Ben-Yoseph, & Posig, 2002).

Given the lower numbers of women in CEO positions, Hillman, Cannella, and Harris (2002) were curious to know the degree to which women and minorities served on boards and what characteristics they needed to be chosen. By tracking a group of White male and female, and African American male and female board members serving in Fortune 1000 firms, they found that the women and minorities were more likely to come from non-business backgrounds and more likely to hold advanced degrees. Consistent with other research, they felt that women and minorities needed the advanced degrees more than White males in order to be chosen for directorship positions. Similarly, Sheridan (2002) found that women who gained appointments on corporate boards in Australia not only had to be well educated and able to demonstrate a strong track record in their field, but also had to have many valuable business contacts. Maman (2000) found similar results for women accessing board positions in Israel.

Women of Color in Management Positions: Trends

Women of color continue to face a concrete ceiling as they work toward career advancement in business. Giscombe and Mattis (2002) found that 38% of women of color saw no change regarding the opportunities for women in their ethnic group and only 47% thought things had improved. African American women expressed the most negative views (e.g., having to fit into the corporate environment, not having influential mentors, limited networking, lack of company role models, lack of high-visibility assignments).

According to the Equal Employment Opportunity (2001) reports, 85.1% of officials and managers from private employers with 100 or more employees or federal contractors with 50 or more employees are White, which means that only 14.9% of the officials or managers are minorities. This figure is broken down as follows: 6.5% are Black (3.5% male, 3% female), 4.7% are Hispanic (3% male, 1.6% female), 3.4% Asian and Pacific Islander (2.2% male, 1.2% female), and 0.4% are Native American or Native Alaskan (0.2% male, 0.1% female; Occupational Employment, 2001).

It should be noted that women of color remained a relatively small proportion of the workforce from 1990 to 2001, growing from 11% in 1990 to 14.5% in 2001 (a 33% increase in the private sector). African American women represented 7.6% of the workforce in 2001, followed by Hispanic women at 4.7%, Asian women at 2.1%, and Native American women at 0.3%.

Although women of color remain a relatively small percentage of all officials and managers, their increase in the decade between 1990 and 2001 was dramatic, with increases of 75% for African American women, 130% for Hispanic women, 135% for Asian women, and 87% for Native American women. It is still important to note that this is still a small percentage of the total number of managers and officials in the private sector.

Reports from Equal Employment Opportunity statistics indicate that women of color have common experiences in their movement from white collar positions into management (Occupational Employment, 2001). Consistently, legal services, physician offices, and architectural, engineering, and related services are among the industries with the highest odds for minority women moving from white collar jobs into management jobs. As the report reveals, however, this is not necessarily good news because these industries have managers with lower employment status. The industries where women of color consistently seem to confront low probabilities of movement into management are department stores, pharmaceutical and medicine manufacturing, and depository credit intermediation.

Like White women, women of color face hurdles moving into senior management positions. For example, African American women represent an important and growing source of talent, yet they currently represent only 1.1% of corporate officers in Fortune 500 companies (Catalyst, 2004b). Interestingly, 37% of African American women see their opportunities for advancement to senior management positions declining over time, in contrast to Latinas and Asian women, who are more likely to see opportunities slightly increasing (Catalyst).

Women Dropping Out of Management Positions

Women and men managers differ in their propensity to quit their jobs and leave their employers voluntarily. Women managers' decisions to quit or stay are influenced by career-related concerns more so than family-related concerns. Female managers who are frustrated at their lack of career opportunities are more likely to quit their jobs than are frustrated male managers. Interestingly, women managers who receive a promotion are less likely to quit their jobs than are male managers who receive a promotion. As Stroh, Brett, and Reilly (1996) pointed out, women managers seem to have a lower tolerance for denied career opportunities and a greater appreciation for granted career opportunities than male managers.

Women who leave their current managerial jobs often due so in order to change employers, start their own business, work part time, work out of their homes, job share, or stay at home to be full-time homemakers (Lipovenko, 1987; Marjamaa & Hoffman, 2002; Maynard, 1988; Schwartz, 1989; Taylor, 1986; Williams, 1988). Some women have changed employers in order to work for a more compatible firm (Nicholson & West, 1988). Few women have actually left corporations solely for family reasons, although when these reasons were cited, they were viewed as temporary. In fact, Rosin and Korabik (1990) noted that women who reported being likely to leave organizations felt this way due to office politics and limited opportunities to progress, rather than marital or family factors. One report found that 73% of the women managers who quit large companies moved to another company, whereas only 7% left to become full-time homemakers (Garland, 1991).

Women Entrepreneurs

As noted, some women managers have dropped out of management in order to start their own firms. Women-owned business firms represent the fastest growth segment of privately held business firms. In 2002, nearly one half (46%) of all privately held businesses in the United States were either 50% owned or majority owned by women, employing 18.1 million people and generating $2.3 trillion in sales (Catalyst, 2003b). In fact, women are starting businesses at a faster rate than their male counterparts and the majority of these (59%) are sole proprietorships (relative to 38% of businesses owned by men; National Foundation for Women Business Owners, 1999). In some areas of the United Kingdom, 67% of all new businesses are being started by women (Simms, 2003). Interestingly, businesses owned by women of color are growing twice as fast as all women-owned firms and more than four times faster than the national average ("Number of Minority," 2002). Despite the increase in women entrepreneurs, women still face barriers with getting money from banks and venture capital firms (Wasserman, 2002).

Men and women often become entrepreneurs for the same reasons: to be their own boss, have greater independence, and control their own destiny (Prince, 2002). There are, however, reasons unique to women's decision to become entrepreneurs. Many women managers became entrepreneurs because they desired autonomy and felt stifled by the rigidity of organizations and homogeneity of the management ranks (e.g., primarily all White males). Others wanted to have more control over their lives or have a more comfortable balance between work and family responsibilities (Prince, 2002; Wasserman, 2002). Still others wanted to escape "hostile" corporate America and the glass ceiling (Daily, Certo, & Dalton, 1999). In fact, 44% of women business owners who left their former positions due to the glass ceiling felt their contributions were not recognized, compared to 17% of men business owners (National Foundation for Women Business

Owners, 1998). It seems that women who start their own businesses are able to better use, satisfy, and maintain high levels of skills than they would if they continued working in many corporations (Alvarez & Meyer, 1998). Women also start their own businesses as a way to change things (by hiring women) and make a difference in their communities. In fact, 92% of women entrepreneurs support charitable and community organizations (National Foundation for Women Business Owners, 2000).

Future Trends for Women's Management Participation

Although women are expected to continue to increase their participation in management, their participation rate may remain below 50%. Powell (1988) offered several reasons for this rate, including enormous family constraints and pressures, limited managerial aspirations of women, minimal organizational support for family issues, and discriminatory hiring practices for management positions. In addition, some firms are reporting difficulties locating women applicants for managerial positions (Merrick, 2002).

It is expected that women will increase their numbers in senior management positions as they move up the ranks, however, there are several reasons why the present imbalance may continue to exist: sex discrimination in hiring for middle and upper management positions, sex discrimination in the development of lower level managers so that they are unprepared to move up, and less interest among women to move up in management careers (Powell, 1988). Sellers (2003) noted in *Fortune's Annual List of the Most Powerful Women* that some women are choosing not to move into high-level jobs. One explanation might be that women perceive a mismatch between themselves and the masculine characteristics required of a senior management job. For example, the intense job demands for high effort, competition, and achievement require an almost total surrender to the job (and greater work-family conflicts), which are viewed as more problematic for women than men (van Vianen & Fischer, 2002).

Women themselves are not optimistic about being completely accepted as executives in corporate America. Researchers have also predicted that no more than a handful of women will reach the senior management level of U.S. Fortune 100 corporations within the next decades due to continuing barriers (Hunsaker & Hunsaker, 1991; Morrison et al., 1987). Others noted that in firms throughout the world, it is unlikely that a critical mass of women in positions of economic power will appear soon. They believe this would require a major restructuring of power in these societies that is not likely to occur in the near future (Adler & Izraeli, 1988). Because the number of "executive, administrative, and managerial workers" is projected to only increase by 16.4% from 1998 to 2008 (a slower growth rate than the 19.8% rate in the previous decade), women's opportunities may be further restricted (Braddock, 1999).

ISSUES AND STRATEGIES FOR COUNSELING
WOMEN IN MANAGEMENT

There are a number of factors that counselors should consider when helping women managers cope with the barriers they experience. First, they should be aware of their role and their own stereotypic biases as counselors. In addition, they should be cognizant of the issues and barriers women managers face. They should tailor their counseling efforts to the career phase the woman manager is in (e.g., early, middle, or late). Furthermore, they should recognize that women managers are a diverse group, and are confronted with unique experiences that require distinct assistance strategies. For example, women managers comprise reentry women, members of dual-career couples, minorities, token women, and women in international assignments, among others.

Counselors should be committed to understanding women in a societal context, and should use intervention models that are appropriate to this context. They must recognize that women's careers can only be understood in relation to the social structure in which they live (Richardson & Johnson, 1984). The primary counseling focus should be on removing barriers or obstacles to career choice or advancement by examining attitudes of significant others, discrimination in the workplace, and other barriers posed by the social, political, and economic systems. Counselors should educate clients about marketplace realities and teach them strategies to overcome or cope with these issues (Brown, Brooks, & Associates, 1990). They should also weigh the benefits and risks associated with providing sex-segregated training. Finally, they should be aware of future changes in managers' jobs and in organizations to know which issues and topics to emphasize (e.g., global issues, teamwork).

Although a number of problems confront women and men managers, some issues are unique or more prevalent to women, and some of the barriers facing women are similar to those they encounter in other nontraditional careers. In most cases, they are better prepared for getting into the job than knowing how to survive in it on a daily basis. As a result, they may become disillusioned and experience lower job satisfaction than expected. Prior to providing assistance, counselors need to identify the source of women managers' concerns and the external and internal barriers they perceive to exist (Brown et al., 1990; Budman, 2002; Fitzgerald & Betz, 1983; Powell, 1988; Rosen, Templeton, & Kichline, 1981; Terborg, 1977).

External Barriers Facing Women Managers and Assistance Strategies

Women managers may encounter a number of external barriers, including discriminatory attitudes and sex-role stereotypes and discriminatory practices in the workplace (e.g., biased treatment, unequal compensation, limited access to training and developmental opportunities, slower advancement and fewer promotion opportunities, backlash, sexual harassment). In addition, women managers may experience social isolation due to tokenism, lack of female role models, and limited access to mentoring relationships and informal networks (Hammer-Higgins & Atwood, 1989; Kanter, 1977a).

Although all women face barriers to the managerial field, women of color often face even more. For example, African American women are confronted with negative, race-based stereotypes, more frequent questioning of their credibility and authority, and a lack of institutional support. They experience a "double outsider" status (being both women and African American) and consequently report exclusion from informal networks (Catalyst, 2004b).

Discriminatory Attitudes and Sex-Role Stereotypes

In a survey, women executives cited male stereotyping and preconceptions as the strongest factor holding them back from advancement. These preconceptions were that women were uncommitted to careers, unwilling to work long hours, not aggressive enough, and unwilling to relocate, and that they had limited skills (Catalyst, 1998). Women across the world report stereotypes and preconceptions (Budman, 2002). Researchers have noted that although today female bosses are more accepted, biases still remain (Armour, 2003). Some women say that they have had customers tell them that they want to talk to a man. According to a Gallup poll, 70% of men are accepting of female bosses compared to 66% of women. In another Gallup survey, they asked people in 22 countries: "If you were taking a new job and had your choice of a boss, would you prefer to work for a man or a woman?" All over the globe, more respondents expressed a preference for a male boss (Simmons, 2001). This preference for a male boss has, however, decreased gradually over time. For example, in 2000, 45% of men and 50% of women preferred a male boss, whereas in 1975 over 60% of men and women preferred male bosses (Simmons). Another study found that supervisors who had a female manager perceived lower job responsibility and were more likely to look for another job than did those with a male manager (Valentine, Godkin, & Turner, 2002). Employers may prefer male bosses because of the perception that the characteristics of effective leaders are more masculine than feminine.

Research conducted in the 1970s and 1980s (Powell & Butterfield, 1979, 1989) found that women and men described a good manager as possessing predominately masculine characteristics (e.g., assertiveness, independence, willingness to take risks). Recently, Powell, Butterfield, and Parent (2002) updated their study to determine whether these findings still applied today. Contrary to expectations, they found that good managers were still perceived as predominately masculine. Even among business students there still exists a gap between views of men and women toward the role of women (Tomkiewicz & Bass, 2003). In addition, in high-tech companies, the corporate culture is seen as exclusionary and does not support women's advancement. This is due to myths about women's talents, ambitions, and commitments, lack of acceptance of women in leadership roles, and lack of a commitment to diversity from senior leaders (Catalyst, 2003a).

In summary, although views have changed somewhat over time, the role of the manager is still seen as more consistent with masculine characteristics (Rutherford, 2001), and this is true in the United States and around the world (Sauers, Kennedy, & O'Sullivan, 2002). This means that women managers are at a disadvantage: If they engage in masculine characteristics, they do not meet the requirements of the female gender role (e.g., niceness and deference to the authority of men), but if they display feminine characteristics, then they do not meet the requirements of the leader stereotype (Powell & Graves, 2003). This is not expected to change anytime soon because the power in organizations is still predominately held by men (i.e., they are in the top management positions). In addition, women aspiring to managerial careers may be disillusioned about what it will take to become an effective manager.

Interestingly, although many of the masculine characteristics are seen as positive, some are increasingly being questioned. As the role of managers has changed over time, some masculine characteristics are posing problems for managers. For example, today managers who are seen as cold and arrogant, less sensitive or caring to their employees, and more likely to bully them are disliked more and are more likely to be fired than in the past (Merrick, 2002).

Overall, male executives believe things have gotten easier for women due to affirmative action, equal employment policies, and less overt discrimination. Women executives, on the other hand, do not appear to be as optimistic, perhaps because they have experienced subtle forms of discrimination. In fact, as of 2004, women executives of Fortune 1000 firms still reported gender-based stereotypes as a barrier to their career advancement not faced by male executives (Catalyst, 2004d).

Accuracy of Sex-Role Stereotypes for Management: Are Men and Women Really Different in Terms of Behaviors as Leaders? There has been mixed evidence over the past three decades as to whether men and women differ as leaders

(Butterfield & Grinnell, 1999), although some have found differences (Bass, Avolio, & Atwater, 1996). Eagly, Karau, and Makhijani (1995) conducted a meta-analysis to look at sex differences in leader effectiveness. They found that overall women and men did not differ in their effectiveness as leaders. Results varied, however, depending on how male intensive the setting was. In military settings (male-intensive settings), men were rated as more effective than women. Women were rated as more effective in less male-intensive settings (e.g., education, government, social service). Neither men nor women were more effective in business settings. In addition, they found that whereas men were more effective in lower level managerial jobs, women were more effective in middle-level management jobs (requiring more interpersonal skills).

In a more recent meta-analytic study, Eagly and Johannesen-Schmidt (2001) found that women managers were more likely to be good leaders than men in equivalent positions. Examining the results of 45 studies on leaders in business, Eagly and Johannesen-Schmidt found that women were more likely to be transformational leaders (e.g., demonstrating charisma, inspiring their workers, developing their skills and creativity, showing individual consideration). This is important because research has indicated that transformational leaders create the most productive and satisfying work environments. Women also rated higher on using contingent rewards with employees. Men, on the other hand, rated higher on using management by exception (corrective action with employees; Eagly, 2002; Eagly & Johannesen-Schmidt, 2001). Valentine and Godkin (2000) also found that individuals who had female managers perceived their jobs to be more relationship oriented than did those with male managers. It seems that women rate higher than men in behaviors that contribute to their effectiveness as leaders and lower than men in behaviors that would detract from their effectiveness (Powell & Graves, 2003).

As Powell and Graves (2003) noted, situational factors influence the effectiveness of men and women as leaders. These factors include the nature of the organizational setting and leader role, the proportions of male leaders and followers, and the managerial level of the position. Thus, some leader roles are more congenial to male leaders, whereas others are more congenial to female leaders. In addition, Powell and Graves indicated that the evidence refutes the stereotypes that men are better leaders and that better leaders are masculine. Today, effective leadership requires a combination of traditionally feminine (e.g., individualized consideration), sex-neutral (e.g., inspirational motivation, charisma), and masculine (e.g., contingent rewards) behaviors (Powell & Graves, p. 151).

Women Managers Are Not Career Committed Due to Family Obligations. Managers are expected to spend a significant amount of time at work. Often, women managers are viewed as being unable or unwilling to commit the necessary time to be effective managers due to their involvement in their families. Gallos (1989) noted that women are seen as failures if they limit their work time to parent their children or if they refuse to be workaholics. If they are unsure about their home demands and relationships, they appear unfocused or look like they do not have the required inner drive. If they do choose to leave the organization to gain more control over their lives, they may be seen as less career committed or motivated.

Although some organizations have started allowing women managers to work part time, most firms are resistant to managers working less than 40 hours a week. In some cases, it is believed that part-timers will not be able to contribute anything useful to the firm. In addition, managers are expected to be employed full time so they can be easily accessible to their subordinates and colleagues. Interestingly, this view ignores the fact that many managers are unavailable anyway due to travel, attendance at meetings, and closed-door policies.

Recently, Catalyst (2003a) reported that one barrier for women leaders in high-tech firms was the conflicting demands of work and career. Women indicated inflexible demands of work schedules and long hours, insufficient support for flexible schedules and sabbaticals, and incompatible career-building and family-building cycles (e.g., taking time off to have children makes it difficult for women to climb back on the career track). This is very similar to the burdens women face in the finance field. Most senior finance jobs have little flexibility regarding hours, travel, and relocation, which makes them problematic for women with families (Hayward, 2002).

Discrimination in the Workplace

Women managers still experience various forms of discrimination in the workplace. These include biased treatment on the job, compensation discrimination, subtle forms of discrimination, public scrutiny, limited access to training and development opportunities, lower advancement and fewer promotion opportunities, discrimination due to backlash, and sexual harassment.

Biased Treatment on the Job. Cox and Harquail (1991) reported bias in the allocation of raises and promotions for a sample of male and female managers. The bias was primarily due to systematic gender-related differences in starting salaries, starting job levels, and company seniority. Korabik and Van Kampen (1995) found that women managers experienced more work stressors than male managers due to prejudiced attitudes by the opposite sex, promotion beneath their competence, and exclusion from informal networks. Eagly (2002) indicated evidence of prejudice and discriminatory treatment of women in terms of obtaining leadership roles and being evaluated as leaders. Similarly, Abelson (2001) documented that two thirds of the more than 400 women from seven financial services firms that were surveyed indicated that they believed they must work harder than men for the same rewards. Rindfleish (2002) found that 37% of senior managerial women working in the private sector in Australia had experienced sex discrimination and 55% of those in the public sector had reported such discrimination (e.g., being excluded from meetings, sexual harassment).

The Equal Employment Opportunity statistics reveal the industries where women have made the most formal charges of discrimination. This is important for illustrating that women experience and report discrimination in a variety of industries in the United States. For all racial-ethnic groups, engineering and management services seem to be the industry with the lowest rate of formal discrimination Equal Employment Opportunity Commission charges. Industries with the highest charges of discrimination brought against them are: agricultural services for White women, automotive dealers and service stations for African American women, special trade contractors for Hispanic women, apparel and other textile products for Asian women, and social services for Native American women. The results also indicate that African American women file charges at a greater rate than other women, followed by Native American women and Hispanic women, White women, and then Asian women.

Compensation Discrimination. Women managers experience a number of psychological and economic barriers that keep them in lower level and dead-end jobs that serve to deflate their self-esteem. They may be discriminated against in the allocation of salaries and in hiring and promotion decisions. For example, only 62% of female executives (relative to 72% of men) believed they were paid fairly compared to others in their department (Bates, 2002). Most experts believe the wage gap between men and women still exists. Part of the problem is that salaries are often set based on previous salary history (which is lower for women) thereby perpetuating the gender pay gap ("Thin on Top!," 2002). As of 1985, women managers earned 64.6% of men's wages and by 2001 it had only gone up to 66.6% (Wasserman, 2002). Median weekly 2001 salaries for U.S. female and male full-time executives and managers were $706 for women compared to $1060 for men (U.S. Department of Labor, Bureau of Labor Statistics, 2002b). The salary gap between male and female managers actually widens as they move up the management hierarchy (Brown, 1988). Interestingly, Lavelle (2001) found a significant difference between the salaries of the highest paid male and female executives. For the 20 highest paid male executives, total compensation averaged $138.5 million, whereas the 20 best-paid females earned about $11.2 million each.

Subtle Forms of Discrimination. Sometimes, rather than overt biases (e.g., inappropriate jokes, hostile confrontations, overt discrimination), women experience subtle, sometimes unspoken, and often unconscious devaluing messages called *micro-inequities*, and these have a powerful impact on interactions (Catalyst, 2004a). Some researchers indicate that the more senior women get, the more subtle the barriers become, and the more profoundly they operate (Lavelle, 2001). Women must be aware of these messages and develop strategies for professionally handling them (rather than getting defensive or emotional). Sometimes women refer to the discrimination they experience as an inhospitable corporate culture (Catalyst, 2004d). For example, one study found that female executives were less satisfied than their male counterparts with their level of involvement and influence in decisions affecting their departments and their companies (Bates, 2002).

Public Scrutiny. Because there are so few women CEOs or senior executives, whatever they do seems to make the press (Tischler, 2004). For example, many new female CEOs have ended up on the cover of *Fortune* magazine or other prominent business magazines or newspapers with articles highlighting the challenges they will face. For example, the cover of the June 9, 2003 issue of *Fortune* had the picture of Sallie Krawcheck, the new chair and CEO of Smith Barney, with the title "Can Sallie save Citi? Is she up to the job?" (Rynecki, 2003). Although some articles like this are written about male CEOs, many of them escape the public scrutiny that a female CEO must endure. For example, Brenda Barnes was considered a real contender for the top job at PepsiCo when CEO Roger Enrico retired. But, at the age of 43 she stepped down because she believed the job toll outstripped the rewards (e.g., getting up very early, working 11–12 hours a day, trying to balance children and family, extensive traveling, numerous job relocations). Interestingly, she believes, despite all of her accomplishments at PepsiCo and in other firms since that time, that she has been forever branded as the woman who walked away. Krefting (2002) examined articles in the U.S. business press on male and female executives and found that prominently featured articles on women executives provided some positive accounts, but many more negative portrayals of women's competence and likeability as executives, whereas similar issues were not raised in the coverage of male executives.

Limited Access to Training and Developmental Opportunities. Women and men managers differ in their access to key developmental experiences during their careers (Powell & Graves, 2003). Men are more likely to be given "stretch" developmental assignments, which enable them to learn to handle a variety of responsibilities in the spotlight and under fire. For example, male managers are often given jobs that require them to handle high stakes (e.g., rigid deadlines, pressure from senior management, high visibility, responsibility for key decisions), manage business diversity (e.g., handle multiple functions, groups, products, customers, markets), and deal with external pressure (e.g., negotiate with unions, cope with serious community problems). In contrast, women managers are placed into jobs that require them to function on their own with little support. They are more likely to be excluded from key networks and receive little encouragement. These differences in jobs are important because the developmental challenges men face in their jobs contribute to their career advancement, and women managers may be less prepared to move up in the organization (Ohlott, Ruderman, & McCauley, 1994).

Catalyst (2003a) reported that women in high-tech firms felt that their companies did not strategically and objectively identify and develop talent. Women were not given access to key experiences or training programs, and were not part of programs to identify and develop talent, and the firms had ineffective hiring practices for attracting and recruiting qualified women. In addition, the metrics used to measure performance and provide feedback were underemphasized and not objective enough.

Men are sent to more formal training programs, industry meetings, professional conferences, and off-site developmental activities and receive greater financial support from their employers for outside educational programs (e.g., part-time MBA degrees). As a result, these activities have a greater influence on male managers' than female managers' objective career success (Tharenou, Latimer, & Conroy, 1994).

Married women are also offered fewer job opportunities requiring relocation than are married men, particularly for relocations involving international assignments. For example, only 13% of U.S. managers sent abroad are women, even though women represent 45% of managers overall (Powell & Graves, 2003). Women may be perceived to be less willing to relocate, even though in reality women do not express less willingness to relocate than men. They may also be seen as less suitable for international assignments despite the fact that most women who work abroad report that being a female has a positive or neutral impact on their effectiveness (Catalyst, 2000b). The consequences of the fewer relocation opportunities for women means that they may be restricted or constrained in their objective career success (Eby, Allen, & Douthitt, 1999).

Biased Performance Evaluations and Slower Advancement (Glass and Concrete Ceiling). Women may suffer in advancing into the managerial ranks, partly due to the way women are evaluated on the job. Specifically, women managers may be subject to greater discrimination in performance evaluations and promotions (Powell & Graves, 2003). If managers make biased performance evaluations, these can have a devastating effect on an employee's career advancement. A meta-analysis of laboratory studies of sex differences in evaluations of leaders found a tendency for female leaders to be evaluated less favorably than male leaders. This was true when the female leaders used a stereotypically masculine leadership style, occupied a traditionally male-intensive leader role, and were evaluated by men (Eagly, Makhijani, & Klonsky, 1992). Another study found that even though male and female cadets did not differ on any objective measures of military performance, male cadets were believed to possess the motivation and leadership qualities necessary for military performance, whereas women were believed to possess more feminine attributes that impaired military performance (Boldry, Wood, & Kashy, 2001). Thus, although men's attitudes have become more favorable over time, they still hold more negative attitudes toward women as leaders than women do (Powell & Graves).

Women managers do not experience the rapid promotions typical of their male counterparts. One reason is that they are initially placed into low-status, low-power staff positions with little opportunity for advancement (Gallos, 1989). Or, if they are in line positions, it is usually in departments that are considered to be dead-end areas (e.g., highly routinized jobs such as clerical or staff). Although they may advance in a staff area or low-status line area, they are not on a career path leading to senior management. To move into senior management, they would need to be in positions that are responsible for profits and losses (e.g., marketing, plant management; Garland, 1991). Male managers, on the other hand, are often placed into upwardly mobile, fast-track, line positions with a more direct route to senior management (Carr-Ruffino, 1993; Hammer-Higgins & Atwood, 1989). Even today, women executives of Fortune 1000 firms indicated that the one barrier prohibiting them from reaching senior management jobs was a lack of general management, operations, or line experience (Catalyst, 2004d; Lavelle, 2001).

Another reason women managers may not advance as quickly as men in organizations is due to discrimination, or the glass ceiling (Glass Ceilings, 2003). The glass ceiling is defined as "a barrier so subtle that it is transparent, yet so strong that it prevents women and minorities from moving up in the management hierarchy" (Morrison & Von Glinow, 1990, p. 200). The glass ceiling is pervasive across countries. In the United Kingdom, for example, 52% of women executives think that the glass ceiling still exists ("Female High Flyers," 2002). For women minorities, it has often been called a "concrete ceiling" because they have even more difficulties moving into higher management ranks (Tomlinson, 2001).

The glass ceiling may exist for several reasons. First, many organizations do not have systematic procedures in place for moving individuals up into the highest management ranks. As a result, decisions are often unstructured and unscrutinized, enabling them to be biased without fear of retribution or accountability (Powell & Butterfield, 1994). In addition, as noted earlier, senior management positions are often see as traditionally masculine; thus decision makers may have masculine stereotypes in mind as they make their selections of top managers. And because most people making the decisions about senior management vacancies are male, they may choose others like themselves (homosocial reproduction; Kanter, 1977b). In addition, women may be less likely to apply for top management positions if they feel disadvantaged, and they may not be as aggressive in fighting for promotions. Recognizing that women historically have been excluded from higher level, nontraditional managerial positions, they may feel that their efforts will be met with resistance (Carr-Ruffino, 1993; Rizzo, Mendez, & Brosnan, 1990).

Discrimination Due to Backlash. Equal employment opportunity guidelines and affirmative action policies have been implemented to resolve some of the discrimination experienced by working women. One consequence of these policies, ironically, has been backlash against women, that is, actions have been taken against women because men believe women have received preferential treatment. In a Catalyst (2003b) study, men and women in their 20s and 30s had different perceptions of diversity-related issues. For example, 62% of men thought that women were paid a comparable salary to men for doing similar work in the organization, whereas only 30% of women agreed with this. In addition, 30% of men thought that a woman would be promoted over a man in their organization, whereas only 10% of women thought this.

The consequences of these attitudes is that men may resent women if they believe women have received special treatment. Although they may hire women as managers, they may offer them lower starting salaries and later try to undermine their effectiveness. Jacobson and Koch (1977) found that women were rated less favorably if they were seen as hired due to affirmative action policies rather than for their meritorious performance. Their performance and accomplishments were undervalued by their colleagues and superiors. In essence, backlash can have serious consequences for the career progress of women.

Sexual Harassment. Over the past decades, sexual harassment has been recognized as one of the most pervasive and serious problems facing workers, particularly women (Fitzgerald & Betz, 1983; Gutek, 1985). Although both sexes may be the targets of sexual harassment, women are more likely to be harassed. In 2001, over 15,000 sexual harassment complaints were filed with the U.S. Equal Employment Opportunity Commission (14% were filed by men). It is a cross-cultural phenomenon occurring in numerous countries (Powell & Graves, 2003).

Women who are managers are not protected from sexual harassment. In cases where peers or superiors resent the presence of female managers, they may engage in harassing behaviors to further isolate women managers or to make them feel uncomfortable enough to leave. Female victims were harassed more by their immediate or higher level supervisors (28%) than by their subordinates (3%), although, generally, coworkers and other employees without supervisor authority over victims are the most common harassers of women and men. The effects of sexual harassment can include loss of productivity, need for medical assistance and emotional counseling, being transferred or quitting work, using sick leave, and using leave without pay. In 1990, 10% of women managers quit their jobs because of sexual harassment (Gutek, Cohen, & Konrad, 1990). Harassment negatively affects physical health (e.g., headaches, sleep disturbance, fatigue), mental health (e.g., loss of self-esteem and self-confidence, anxiety, depression), and general attitudes about work (e.g., lower organizational commitment or job satisfaction; Dansky & Kilpatrick, 1997). Sexual harassment affects not only the victims, but also other employees' views of the work environment (e.g., being seen as hostile). In addition, the costs associated with sexual harassment can be enormous (e.g., the U.S. federal government estimated costs of $327 million over a 2-year period; Powell & Graves, 2003).

Social Isolation

Women managers may experience social isolation in organizations for a number of reasons. If they are one of few women managers in a group, they may be seen as tokens and excluded from informal group activities. In addition, they may have few, if any, female role models to emulate and share experiences with. Also, male managers may experience discomfort working with female colleagues or bosses and may limit their contact with them. Consequently, women managers may have less contact with their peers and subordinates, and less access to informal networks and mentoring relationships.

Tokenism.   Most organizations have few, if any, women managers, and even when an organization has several women managers, they may be located throughout the firm so that there are only one or two in each department. As a result, each woman manager stands out in her group and may have difficulty fitting in with her male colleagues. If the woman manager is also a member of a minority group, she may feel the effects of social isolation to an even greater extent.

Women managers who are members of skewed groups (e.g., 85% males, 15% females) may experience even more stress and gender stereotyping than women managers who are members of more balanced groups (e.g., approximately equal numbers of male and females; Kanter, 1977b). This is because tokens are highly visible to others, and face additional performance pressures (i.e., they may be singled out for being female rather than for being successful; Davidson & Cooper, 1988). Lortie-Lussier and Rinfret (2002) compared the proportions of women managers on attitudes of coworkers and found that when there were 20% women (relative to 9%), men made more positive evaluations of women's participation in the organization and of their status. When there were 45% women managers, the men recognized their managerial talents better. Tharenou (2001) noted that in firms with mostly males in middle and upper management, women had a lower rate of advancement than men.

The differences between tokens and dominants (e.g., White male managers) may become exaggerated by the dominant members in the group, a process called *boundary heightening*. The dominant members (e.g., White males), either consciously or unconsciously, engage in discussions or activities that serve to exclude the token (e.g., woman). For example, they may discuss auto mechanics and playing football in an attempt to let the woman know that she is not one of them. In skewed groups, the dominant members are more likely to stereotype women tokens. Role encapsulation takes place such that the women's characteristics become distorted or misperceived, and they are classified according to their gender even if their personal characteristics are not consistent with the stereotypes. For instance, they may be assigned the role of taking notes in a meeting or getting coffee for male colleagues, or be assigned routine detail tasks (Kanter, 1977b).

Several strategies have been recommended for women to help them cope with their experiences as tokens. First, they need to become indispensable to their groups in some way. For example, they could develop a special area of expertise that is highly valued by the groups. In addition, they need to develop the skills required of successful dominants. These include having a power base, and being perceived as having self-confidence, taking risks, and supporting important group causes (Fairhurst & Snavely, 1983). Counselors should offer token members opportunities to discuss any problems they are experiencing to reduce the amount of social isolation they feel. In addition, they should work with them to develop effective coping strategies.

Few Female Role Models. Women managers have few, if any, women above them in organizations to serve as role models. Without effective role models, women managers may be unsure how to address the unique issues they experience (e.g., tokenism, sexual harassment, work-family conflict, social isolation). Even in cases where higher level women managers are available, they may not be able or willing to serve as role models for women below them. For instance, women at higher levels are faced with their own set of difficulties that require an enormous amount of their time and attention. In addition, because there are few women at higher levels in organization, their behavior is salient to others. Recognizing this, they are often careful about the amount of attention they bestow on their female subordinates relative to their male subordinates, to avoid charges of favoritism.

Women executives reported that the lack of role models was a critical barrier making it difficult to get a CEO job (Catalyst, 2004d). In high-tech firms, this is especially true for women managers, who report feeling isolated due to a lack of senior women role models, a lack of access to networks and relationships, and a lack of mentors (Catalyst, 2003a). In firms that have more women in senior positions who serve as mentors and role models (e.g., Citigroup), lower level women managers feel a stronger sense of support and encouragement (Fagerberg, 2003). Tharenou (2001) noted that women who were in a climate of encouragement were more likely to move into upper management.

Limited Access to Mentoring Relationships. Mentoring is considered to be a critical aspect of the professional development and advancement of men and women in organizations. As one author noted, "For a man, having a mentor is a good idea. For a woman, it's a must" (Sepehri, 2003, p. 57). Mentoring serves two primary functions for protégés. Career development functions include sponsoring employees for promotions, helping them learn the ropes and prepare for advancement, offering challenging assignments to develop them, providing exposure and visibility for protégés, and coaching them. Psychosocial functions include improving protégés' sense of competence and identity, providing them with psychological support, building their confidence, offering acceptance and confirmation, and providing personal counseling (Kram, 1985).

Mentoring relationships have numerous benefits for individuals and organizations. Generally, protégés are better educated, better paid, less mobile, and more job satisfied (Hunt & Michael, 1983). In addition, they earn more money at a younger age, and are more likely to follow a career plan (Borman & Colson, 1984). In fact, some firms consider mentoring to be so beneficial that they have established formal mentoring programs for all employees or for women and minority employees. Thus, mentors significantly contribute to their protégés' objective and subjective career success.

Most women managers believe that mentors are critical for success. Women are more likely than men to cite "help from above" as one of the essential factors they lacked if they do not reach senior managerial positions (Burke, 1992). Women managers may need mentors even more than men because of the discrimination and work-related obstacles they encounter. Mentors could buffer women from overt and covert discrimination and help them to overcome obstacles to attaining top management positions. This is particularly true for women managers of color (Tomlinson, 2001).

For women managers, mentoring is especially needed at two stages of their career development. In the early phase, mentoring teaches women the ropes in the organization and shows them how to build their image and become team players. Mentors are needed to provide encouragement, support, and advice, and to make sure that women receive credit for their work. In later career stages, when women are trying to make it into higher management, mentoring provides them with endorsements to advance and helps them gain the respect of their colleagues and superiors (Westoff, 1986). Mentors also sponsor their protégés to help them move up in the corporation. In both stages, it is important for women to receive professional and emotional support from their mentors in addition to work-related assistance. If women managers experience social isolation from their peers and subordinates, they will need to be able to discuss this with their mentors and learn to cope with it.

Despite the importance of mentoring for women, women are less likely than men to be mentors or protégés. They are less likely to be mentors because there are very few women in higher level positions in organizations. In addition, women face greater barriers to developing informal mentoring relationships than men. Male mentors may be reluctant to select female protégés because of concerns about possible sexual innuendoes or because they want to select other men. Also, women are more hesitant to initiate mentoring relationships with men for fear that these actions might be seen as sexual advances (Ragins, 1999). One difficulty with cross-gender mentoring relationships is that women managers argue that even with supportive male mentors, men can never fully understand or empathize with the constraints facing a woman in a male-dominated environment. Male mentors may have difficulty counseling their female protégés on how to deal with being a token or being isolated from their peers, or giving them guidance on work-family issues and thus may not be able to fulfill female protégés' mentoring needs.

Because women are often excluded from informal organizational networks and often occupy a token status, they are less likely to be chosen as protégés. They have less access to mentors and more difficulty finding a mentor (Fox & Schuhmann, 2001; Hunsaker & Hunsaker, 1991). Williams (1988) reported that most successful men have had at least one sponsor who suggested them for a promotion, but male mentors have been less likely to take on women. When men have chosen protégés, they have often done so not to help "promote the protégés' dream" but to show the organization's commitment to promoting women or to develop talent (Fitt & Newton, 1981; Kanter, 1977a).

Women managers should be encouraged to find informal mentors and to also develop several less intense relationships (e.g., sponsors, guides, peer pals) to fulfill mentoring functions. Having multiple mentors may avoid the speculation common to cross-gender relationships, as well as provide women managers with several sources of support (Gersick & Kram, 2002; Kram, 1983). It is important, however, for women to have male mentors in addition to female mentors because men may provide more career outcomes given their greater power in organizations (Ragins & Cotton, 1999). Another strategy is for organizations to establish formal mentoring relationships (along with supporting informal mentoring) to be sure that each individual is given access to a mentor. Mentors should be encouraged to provide stretch (challenging) assignments to help develop their protégés. Booz Allen Hamilton and Goldman Sachs are two firms that have established formal mentoring programs where women are assigned mentors early in their careers (Fagerberg, 2003).

Limited Access to Informal Networks and Communication Channels. Networking involves linkages and communication between people at vertical and lateral levels. It takes place through grapevines, conferences, workshops, phone calls, parties, and mutual friends, and by sharing books, newsletters, and articles (Rizzo et al., 1990). The value of networking is that it provides individuals with moral support or political backing, inside information, and access to those who make decisions related to advancement. Most successful managers use networks so they can trade information, technical expertise, and advice, as well as garner support.

For years, women have expressed their frustration at being excluded from the informal networks in organizations (Catalyst, 1998, 2004d). The "old boy's network" has consisted primarily of White male managers who effectively serve to control the power and resources of the organization. Women managers have traditionally been denied access to the important informal networks and interactions in organizations. Experts agree that being excluded from male-dominated social networks is one of the greatest barriers to women moving up the management ranks (Lavelle, 2001).

Exclusion of women managers from informal networks may exist for a number of reasons. Women may have been boycotted because they were not considered viable candidates for promotions and equal status in the organization. They may also have been excluded because men were uncomfortable communicating with women or wanted to maintain their dominance over women (Kanter, 1977b). In addition, the token status of many women managers has served to exclude them from important informal networks (Terborg, 1977). Although White males may be assumed to have the requisite characteristics to be part of the managerial circle, women and minorities may not be considered acceptable (i.e., the "cloning affect"). Women may have to pass certain tests concerning behavior, attitudes, and values before they can be considered acceptable to the group (Rizzo & Mendez, 1991).

The danger of excluding women from important informal networks is that their career progress may be hindered as they attempt to move up the corporate ladder. This can be further exacerbated by any childrearing responsibilities or restrictions on job mobility (e.g., spouse's job offers). In addition, for the organization's welfare, the omission of women from important networks affects the quality of resources available in those groups (Campbell, 1988).

Another outcome of excluding women from old boy's networks has been the formation by many women of their own networks. "New girl's networks" have been created in occupational groups, organizational groups, and regional circles (Catalyst, 1999). For example, a number of networking groups currently exist for managerial and professional women, including the National Association for Female Executives, Catalyst, the American Society of Professional and Executive Women, and the American Business Women's Association. In addition to general women in management networks, there are also many networks established to help women of color. Women's networks are formally organized to help women learn the importance of building contacts and to develop their networking skills. They also focus on career advancement strategies and creating a better workplace for women. By 1999, 33% of Fortune 100 companies had women's networks, including Kimberly-Clark, McGraw-Hill, 3M, Ford, IBM, Hewlett-Packard, Procter & Gamble, Motorola, Merck, Dow Chemical, Xerox, McDonald's, and Texas Instruments (Catalyst).

General Electric (GE) has been a pioneer in developing talent. Their women's network is an integral part of their employee development. Today, the General Electric Women's Network is active in 118 hubs in 60 countries. Most importantly, the CEO regularly visits geographic business unit leaders and network leaders to review business strategy and discuss talent needs. Network activities give his senior executive management team the opportunity to meet with the high-potential female talent pool. GE was recently honored by Catalyst for their initiative, Developing Women Leaders: Synergistic Forces Driving Change, which aligns the company's performance management and succession planning system with those of their women's network to provide women with the information, tools, and experiences to become leaders. Based on GE's initiatives, representation of women corporate officers increased from 5% to 13% between 1998 and 2002, representation of women senior executives increased from 9% to 14%, and women at the executive board level increased from 18% to 21% (Catalyst, 2004c).

Goldman Sachs also has many women's networks. One called New Mother's Network and Mother Mentoring is designed to connect new mothers so they can get advice on dealing with the stresses of maternity leave and coming back to work. Given the increase in women returning to

Goldman after maternity leave, they feel the program has been successful (Fagerberg, 2003).

Although networking with other women is an effective strategy to assist executive women, women managers will still need to establish informal networks with male managers if they are to have access to important organizational information and advancement strategies. They also need to make sure they develop contacts with individuals in positions of authority who have information and high status (usually males). Interestingly, when women have had the opportunity to become integrated into the workplace, they have been perceived as being more central to interactions and more successful at building informal networks than men.

Internal Barriers Facing Women Managers and Assistance Strategies

Women managers may have difficulties advancing in management due to some internal barriers they perceive. They may believe they lack the necessary skills to be successful in management, that they will not be suited to the work, or that they will be intimidated by men and that they will have to be too competitive or will have to outperform men. The barriers that women perceive may be reinforced by their families, communities, and society, and these barriers may bar women from maintaining a career in management or advancing into higher management.

Perceptions Regarding Skills

Skills or perceptions that women need to improve to be even more effective as managers include gaining a greater awareness of politics and the use of power and influence, assertiveness and communication skills, networking skills, negotiating skills, self-confidence, and career management.

Awareness of Politics and Use of Power and Influence. Some estimate that 75% of managers who are forced out of their jobs fail because of organizational politics (Carr-Ruffino, 1993). Women are often more vulnerable to political games and subject to more disempowering messages (e.g., subtle exclusion, stealing ideas and credit; Smith, 2000). Women managers often avoid office politics and power and seem to be less interested in the inner workings of organizations, the authority hierarchy and chain of command, and power sources, perhaps because they have traditionally been excluded from the informal power networks. Recently, women executives indicated that one of the barriers keeping them from becoming CEOs was a lack of awareness of organizational politics (Catalyst, 2004d). Carr-Ruffino provided valuable strategies for handling political games.

Assertiveness and Communication Skills.   Women managers need to be encouraged to be more confident and assertive about stating their own needs and refusing to back down even if the immediate response is not receptive. In addition, when the situation calls for a direct approach, women leaders need to be able to take quick action that may not call for a participative style (i.e., solicit and build on employees' views). Furthermore, counselors can encourage women to stop others from engaging in demeaning behaviors toward them (e.g., interrupting them when they talk, excluding them from decision making). In addition, counselors can help women managers develop stronger support systems and networks and share their expertise with other women.

Networking.   Women managers often concentrate almost exclusively on their own job performance, rather than trying to build alliances and garner power for themselves. As one woman leader pointed out, "Many women take the tack that if they do their job, keep their nose down, and work very hard, they will be recognized. They don't understand that they have to reach out and tell people how they are doing. They have to market themselves" (Wasserman, 2002, p. 40). In addition, once women leaders are appointed to managerial positions, they need to take advantage of their "status as symbols of change" (Adler, 1999). They have an opportunity to influence others and create change and should be ready to do this. Singh, Kumra, and Vinnicombe (2002) found that men were more likely to use networking, ingratiation, and self-promotion strategies than women.

Negotiating.   As noted earlier, there are salary differences between women and men managers, and one reason for this difference is the degree to which women negotiate. Research indicates that women do not negotiate as often or as "hard" as men and they are less likely to negotiate for themselves (Babcock & Laschever, 2003; Wasserman, 2002). In addition, women's expectations for salaries and compensation are often lower than men's. As of 2003, women MBAs anticipated an average starting salary of $78,700, whereas male MBAs expected to earn an average of $84,100. Women should be encouraged to take negotiations courses to enhance their skills in this area.

Confidence in Skills.   Women managers may lack confidence in their abilities to handle financial matters, projects requiring math or technical skills, or situations requiring problem-solving and decision-making skills. Relative to men, women managers may experience greater fear of failure, lower self-esteem, and more sex-role conflict (Borman & Guido-DiBrito, 1986). Women are more likely than men to doubt their abilities, which can further undermine their performance. For example, Sellers (2003) pointed out that many women are reluctant to point out their accomplishments. Relative to men, they have the tendency to overdo professional modesty by stating that they are not ready for stretch assignments. They may also subscribe to the think manager, think male mode, which further limits their confidence to put themselves forward for promotion (Vinnicombe & Singh, 2002). One female manager quoted Eleanor Roosevelt, who said, "No one can make you inferior without your consent" (Wasserman, 2002, p. 41).

Career Management. Women managers often do not actively manage their career goals to the extent that their male colleagues do. Rosen et al. (1981) found that women managers reported that they had fuzzy career goals. They had a tendency to suppress their ambitions and goals, while expecting their superiors to acknowledge their achievements and direct their career progress. Often, women are more reticent to talk about their abilities and achievements with the people who should be kept informed (e.g., superiors). Male managers, on the other hand, are usually more proactive in planning their own career progress and letting others know of their accomplishments (Carr-Ruffino, 1993). Callanan and Greenhaus (1990) found that women managers and professionals reported being more undecided about their long-term goals than their male counterparts. They speculated that women may anticipate extensive work-family conflict, which makes it difficult for them to plan their career goals and aspirations.

Women managers need to develop clearer career goals and objectives and construct action plans to implement their goals. When preparing career goals and plans, they need to take into consideration other important life goals (e.g., family, personal) so that they can balance these roles and resolve any role conflicts. When deciding on a firm, they should carefully look at the culture and values of each potential employer and the firm's demonstrated commitment to women's advancement (e.g., representation of women in corporate office positions). Furthermore, they should talk to people who work there to better understand the organization's reputation for working with women.

To assist women, counselors need to help them to understand their attitudes toward career planning and help them establish goals, set priorities, and develop action plans. In addition, they can help them to enhance their financial, political, and technical skills and build their self-esteem so that they are more comfortable using these skills. If the women managers are averse to taking risks, counselors must provide them with support and encourage them to get additional assistance (e.g., role models, mentors, support groups). Moreover, counselors should advise women to obtain career-related information, performance feedback, and challenging job assignments from their superiors. As Callanan and Greenhaus (1990) noted, career management assistance is crucial for reducing fears and anxieties and improving self-confidence among managers and professionals.

Work-Family Issues

Women managers may encounter a number of work-family issues and conflicts. As Catalyst (1996) noted, 72% of female vice presidents and top leaders in Fortune 1000 firms are married and 64% have children. Women may have concerns over child-care issues, experience role conflict and overload, and feel that they have to sacrifice their careers for their marital and parental responsibilities. Many women managers who combine a demanding career and a family encounter a variety of problems and conflicts. They may be faced with practical problems or career restrictions resulting from excessive work commitments (e.g., limited time) and the primacy of their husbands' careers. They may also experience psychological problems such as limited support from others, concerns over home and child care, psychological burnout, and role conflicts (Burke & McKeen, 1992; Loerch, Russell, & Rush, 1989). The concerns over achieving a balance between work and life management still exist today (Hammonds, 2004). As of 2004, 51% of women executives of Fortune 1000 firms reported difficulty in achieving a balance in their lives (Catalyst, 2004d).

In the financial services industry, the norms for working long hours are strong. Thus, many women do not have children and wonder how they would be able to manage multiple roles if they did (Abelson, 2001). Interestingly, in a study examining managers who overwork (i.e., working 61 hours or more per week), Brett and Stroh (2003) found that 99% of the men who overworked had wives who were not employed and children living at home, whereas the majority (89%) of the women who overworked had husbands who worked full time. Whereas fewer women than men had children, those with children had husbands who helped more with child care as well as additional child-care assistance. Interestingly, they also found that women managers who worked longer hours were significantly more satisfied with their family lives than those who worked shorter hours, although they felt more alienated from their families.

Kirchmeyer (1998) found that women managers reported more career interruptions than male managers due to family demands that worked against their career success (e.g., lower income). As a result of these interruptions, women's subsequent advancement and earnings may be likely to suffer and they may achieve lower long-term objective career success (Judiesch & Lyness, 1999; Schneer & Reitman, 1997).

Excessive Work Commitments and Limited Time. Due to the large time commitment involved in a managerial career, many women managers feel unable to devote much time to their personal lives. One survey reported that in 1986, 75% of all male managers were married, whereas only 58% of female managers were married (Powell, 1988). Schwartz (1989) reported that 90% of executive men have children by age 40, whereas only 35% of executive women do. Interestingly, in 2002, more than one third of the women in the Fortune 50 Most Powerful Women list had stay-at-home husbands (Sellers, 2003). These women would not have been able to take on a demanding senior management job without a stay-at-home spouse.

Organizations often demand that managers work long hours, travel extensively, and relocate frequently (especially in high-tech or finance fields). They assume that managers are solely dedicated to their careers and do not have other major life demands (e.g., home and child care), a perception that is truer for male than for female managers. Men at the executive levels of corporations often have wives who are traditional homemakers and who provide a support system at home. Women at the same level may be unmarried or have working spouses. For these women, a full-time caretaker of the home or children typically does not exist. Thus, for women managers, the rigorous demands of a managerial career may pose undue hardships on them because they bear the primary responsibilities for child and home care (Ogintz, 1983). Women managers may have difficulties competing with male peers who have fewer family and housekeeping burdens. Women may put in fewer hours at work due to family commitments, resulting in less visibility, and consequently they may be less likely to be included in formal and informal networks. They may choose different managerial positions from their male peers in order to provide time for home maintenance. Unfortunately, these career choices may be out of the mainstream for fast-track career promotions.

Recently, Tischler (2004) suggested that one reason women may be underrepresented in the corner office (i.e., CEO) is that although they may work as hard as men, they may not compete as hard as men. In other words, men put in more hours, are more willing to relocate, and are more comfortable putting their work ahead of their personal commitments. Being a CEO is a global, 24-hour-a-day job that a person has to give his or her life to. Statistics reveal that male managers work more hours per week (46.1) than their female counterparts (40.4; U.S. Department of Labor, Bureau of Labor Statistics, 2002a). Some women may not be interested in doing this because they also want to spend time in their other life roles.

The Primacy of the Husband's Career.   In many dual-career couples, the husband's career is considered to be the most important one when decisions are made regarding opportunities for advancement. In 2003, 60% of men stated that their careers were primary relative to the careers of their spouses, but only 31% of women stated this (Catalyst, 2003b). One of the consequences of these views is that some women managers may have to turn down promotion opportunities or geographic moves if their husband's career will not benefit. In fact, one earlier study noted that 79% of women had moved at least once for their husbands' careers, whereas only 2% reported that their husbands had moved primarily for the benefit of the wives' careers (Deitch & Sanderson, 1987). This poses particular difficulties for women managers as they try to advance in the management hierarchy. Another problem is that organizations may show more concern for their male managers' careers if they believe them to be more important. If they expect women managers to make career sacrifices for the sake of their families, they may perceive them to be less committed to the organization, and therefore may make fewer efforts to retain or advance them in the organization.

Limited Support by Others.   Women managers often express concern that they have limited support for a nontraditional career from their significant others, in addition to husband's colleagues, in-laws, parents, friends, and married professionals. They perceive that others disapprove of the time they spend away from their home and child-care responsibilities, and expend considerable energy worrying about others' attitudes. These fears may be legitimate given that, Etzion (1987) noted, women managers who experienced success and self-fulfillment on the job were also more likely to experience failure and dissatisfaction in their personal lives.

Concerns Over Home and Child Care.   Despite the increasing amount of home and child-care assistance provided by husbands, women still assume the primary responsibilities for these areas. One study found that working mothers spend about 80 hours on work, child care, and household chores, whereas working fathers average about 50 hours per week (Barnett & Rivers, 1992). Many individuals believe that employed women work the equivalent of two jobs (Betz & Fitzgerald, 1987). In management positions, there is a sex difference in family structure. As women move up into higher managerial levels, they are less likely to be married or to have children than men with similar responsibilities. In general, the more successful the man is in objective terms, the more likely he is to have a spouse and children, whereas the opposite is true for women (Catalyst, 1996; Hewlett, 2002).

Because women have the primary responsibility for home and child care, they experience a number of concerns. Often, they report difficulties finding time for household tasks and locating high-quality, affordable child care. They experience guilt over leaving their children for their careers, and they have trouble taking time off work to care for sick children. Women managers in particular experience difficulties due to the heavy demands of their jobs. Given the extensive time commitments and pressures, women managers must be able to work in a relatively uninterrupted fashion if they are to advance, which means it is imperative that reliable child-care assistance be available. Few organizations have embraced the idea of providing child-care assistance and many are resistant to allowing managers to work part time to accommodate their personal lives.

Helping Women Managers to Deal With Work-Family Issues.   Counselors can provide assistance to help women managers cope with work-family issues and conflict. Most interventions focus on helping women managers achieve a balance in their lives. They may be taught how to negotiate with others at home or at work regarding hours, projects, benefits, and obligations (Gallos, 1989). Family and marital counseling may be useful to clarify expectations that women and their significant others have regarding their roles and responsibilities. In addition, women managers who are single mothers may find counseling beneficial for addressing unique issues they face, such as financial stress, loneliness, single parenting, developing new relationships, autonomy, and legal issues.

Counselors need to provide women managers with strategies for coping with role conflict, including: eliminating unsupportive relationships, limiting obligations taken on, redefining involvements, manipulating schedules to accommodate demands, delegating tasks and roles, and seeking support and assistance from others. Hall (1972) suggested three coping strategies for use: Type I structural role redefinition (i.e., changing the expectations of others to reduce the number of obligations), Type II personal role redefinition (i.e., changing one's own perceptions of one's role demands), and Type III reactive role behavior (i.e., attempting to meet all role demands and please everyone). Hall reported a positive relationship between using Type I and II coping strategies and satisfaction, and a negative relationship between using the Type III coping strategy and satisfaction. Recent research suggests that women managers' multiple roles result in benefits in terms of their life satisfaction, self-esteem, and self-acceptance (Ruderman, Ohlott, Panzer, & King, 2002). Counselors need to examine this research in order to better assist women executives.

BARRIERS AND STRATEGIES FOR WOMEN AT VARYING CAREER STAGES AND MANAGEMENT LEVELS

Women managers may experience unique barriers as a function of their level of managerial rank. These are described in the sections that follow.

Women During Early Career

Barriers

Business schools are increasingly struggling to attract women applicants. For example, women make up 36% of MBA students, 47% of medical students, and 49% of law school students (Sellers, 2003). In a 2003 survey of what MBA women really want in their careers, the highest priority was flexibility in the workplace. Even during the first 3 years after graduation, women's top priorities were balancing personal life and career, working with increasingly challenging tasks, and reaching a managerial level.

Women who do enter managerial positions have been advised to think about a career in management as if they are taking on a foreign assignment (Hennig & Jardim, 1977). As an example, Ivarsson and Ekehammar (2001) found that those women who moved into management positions (relative to those who had the same aspirations but did not get into management) had a more instrumental personality profile (e.g., high masculinity, high achievement, and power motivation), supporting the notion that women have to be more like men to get into management. Women managers face some unique hurdles. Some of these include:

1. Being assigned jobs that are not initially challenging.
2. Being rewarded for conforming to standards rather than being creative, leading to feelings of frustration and discontent.
3. Receiving few formal performance appraisals or poorly conducted appraisals, making them confused about the required performance standards and how they can improve.
4. Holding unrealistically high expectations about the degree to which they will be able to apply their new skills in the real world.
5. Being placed in low-visibility or safe positions (e.g., personnel, public relations) with few opportunities to make decisions relating to corporate policy or affecting the bottom line.
6. Being excluded from informal networks, leading to feelings of isolation and limited control; being bypassed for promotions to more influential positions.
7. Being seen as a threat to higher level superiors who may have less education.

Strategies

Counselors can work with women who are aspiring to a managerial career to determine their career maturity levels, vocational preferences, attitudes about family-work conflict, and sex-role self-concepts. A variety of interventions can be used, including structured exercises for career and life planning, group counseling, career homework assignments, and one-on-one counseling to explore educational and vocational options (Kimbrough, 1981). Workshops may be useful to help women determine a lifeline, clarify roles, assess vocational interests, and express their feelings regarding working in a managerial career.

Counselors can use similar interventions with women who are trying to enter into management. They can encourage them to participate in career-planning workshops and self-assessments in order to identify their career interests and abilities and desires for career growth. They can also assist them in formulating their short- and long-term career plans and developing specific action plans with goals and timetables (Hunsaker & Hunsaker, 1991). Other programs that may be particularly beneficial for these women include more flexible academic programs (e.g., work-study programs, part-time and evening professional programs) and counseling for career development and placement.

During the early career period, some women experience a considerable amount of stress due to family and career issues and conflicts (Gallos, 1989). They may be seeking to find the proper balance between their various roles while receiving pressures from work or family for greater involvement. Counselors can provide special advising to address work-family questions and conflicts. In addition, they can prepare women for anticipating the difficulties they may experience in a male-dominated field. For example, Milwid (1983) noted that few professional women had given much thought to the dynamics of working with men. Few expected any difficulties, yet most experienced psychological stress during the first 2 years. She recommended that counselors offer a variety of support to young professional women in male-dominated fields. Also, counselors could help women managers develop interpersonal power, handle office politics, prevent and deal with sexual harassment, avoid being stereotyped, work with others, becoming visible to top management, reduce stress, be assertive, and take risks (Hammer-Higgins & Atwood, 1989; Milwid).

To enhance their careers, there are a number of things that women themselves can do. Most importantly, they should focus on demonstrating competence and building credibility during their early career period. They should accept difficult and highly visible stretch assignments and job transfers to domestic or international locations. Furthermore, they should set goals, establish mentoring relationships, and network with others. In addition, they should take advantage of opportunities to further their education (e.g., part-time MBA programs) in order to develop their skills and knowledge. They might also want to develop coping strategies for dealing with stress from the demands of their work and family roles (Carr-Ruffino, 1993; Catalyst, 2000d; Powell & Graves, 2003).

Women During Mid-Career or Middle-Level Management

Barriers

Morrison et al. (1987) noted that women may be seduced into thinking they have made it in the business world because they experience fewer difficulties in getting into management today than they have in years past.

These same women, however, often become disillusioned when they confront barriers as they try to move up into management. Researchers have found that women are more satisfied earlier in their careers than at the midpoint because the work environment becomes less supportive (Reitman & Schneer, 1997). Some of the barriers women face as they move up into higher management include the following:

1. Limited access to important opportunities (e.g., overseas assignments, mainstream jobs).
2. Limited support among male colleagues and higher level executives.
3. Difficulties balancing work and family lives due to the excessive time commitments required of higher level managerial positions.
4. Hostility from younger men who resent women for creating stress for them (e.g., making men take on more home and child care).
5. Few female role models.
6. Less support from higher level women than expected because these women are fearful of appearing biased.
7. Denial by some women that problems exist.
8. Having little room to make mistakes due to their salient status as tokens.
9. Discrimination.
10. Having to prove themselves to their male peers.
11. The glass ceiling.

Strategies

As some women move into middle-management positions, they often reassess their lives in terms of their work, family, and personal roles (Gordon, Beatty, & Whelan-Berry, 2002). As Gersick and Kram (2002) noted, women managers at midlife have several developmental issues to address, such as finding a role in life, making career-family trade-offs, and coming into their own. Although these tasks are also important for men, they are more complicated for women due to strong norms about gender and careers.

Women in middle management comprise a diverse group. Some women may have made personal sacrifices (e.g., not getting married or having children) in order to move into management. These women may question whether it was worth it. Other women may have grown children by this time and have more independence in their lives (Gallos, 1989). Older women whose husbands have retired may have more time to devote to their careers because they no longer have to provide support for their husbands' careers.

Counselors serve an important role in assisting women in middle management to understand their life roles and involvements, and in making effective career changes when necessary. Life-span developmental counseling is necessary to help women manage their multiple roles. Counselors must encourage their clients to spend some time thinking about their roles and potential role strains, and make them aware that a constant reassessment of changing needs may be necessary. At a minimum, they should help them develop skills in setting realistic goals and clarifying values, managing time effectively, being assertive, and negotiating with others. Furthermore, they should help women evaluate their options and develop effective coping strategies. Middle management is a critical developmental period for women because they can experience many rich work challenges. In fact, Kirchmeyer (2002) found that over time women middle managers changed their gender self-perceptions (i.e., increased masculinity) as a function of their increased income and promotions.

Interestingly, there is more advice and assistance available to help women enter management than to help them survive once on board. Counselors need to offer support to women, particularly during the mid-career period. One of the reasons why counseling is so critical during this period is that some women report lower job satisfaction, often because of ineffective working relationships they have with male peers, superiors, and subordinates. They may experience sexual harassment, lack of cooperation from other workers, isolation, and limited faith in their abilities (Haring-Hidore & Beyard-Tyler, 1984).

Personal counseling is needed to assist women managers in coping with dissatisfaction, depression, anxiety, poor self-esteem or confidence, and career-related issues. Career counselors can prepare women for understanding these issues and learning how to cope with them. They can use cognitive restructuring techniques to enable women to develop new ways of viewing themselves and other women (Kahn, 1988). Cognitive career counseling might be beneficial for enabling them to eliminate roadblocks they have to reaching their career goals (e.g., having unrealistic expectations, experiencing burnout). Additionally, counselors can focus on consciousness raising, building a support system, and providing role models. During this period, women managers may need to be empowered so that they have feelings of control and self-efficacy, and can think independently and resist organizational pressures to conform (Rizzo & Mendez, 1991).

Counselors can work with women to help them take proactive career actions such as career planning, setting goals, seeking mentors and membership in informal networks, obtaining career-related information, and developing needed skills and education (Hunsaker & Hunsaker, 1991; Powell, 1988). They can employ behavioral and psychological skills training to address women managers' deficits in stress and time management, and enhance their skills in assertiveness, communication, and negotiations. If the women managers decide to leave their career field, counselors can provide grief counseling to help them discuss their loss (e.g., opportunities, dreams, relationships). If they decide to continue in their current job, counselors can help them develop negotiation skills to use with their employers to try to make their current job or work relationships more satisfying.

Women Advancing Into Top Management

Barriers

As noted earlier, one reason why corporate America is seen as hostile to women managers is the glass ceiling. Another reason women have difficulties moving up into top management is because of others' perceptions of their ability. Although they may have the necessary education and skills to move up, women are not often perceived to have the political savvy required of senior managers. In many cases, women do not have the power they need because they lack political clout and powerful mentors or sponsors. Top executives may be fearful of giving women too much power because women are seen as different and less predictable (Blum & Smith, 1988). Often, women use different types of power from men. For example, women may try to show their power by being nurturing and supportive. Their male colleagues, however, may not view this as being powerful. Often women are placed in jobs that further aggravate the situation. For example, they may be denied access to challenging assignments or put in situations where they are neither expected nor encouraged to take risks or where their authority or positional power is undermined by their superiors (Burke & McKeen, 1992). If the women themselves feel insecure about their authority and communicate this insecurity to their subordinates, their subordinates may in turn resist their authority, perpetuating a self-sustaining cycle that discounts women managers' abilities (Carr-Ruffino, 1993; Wiley, 1987).

Women perceive a number of barriers in top management positions that may explain their disenchantment and increasing dropout rates. Women believe that it is harder for women than men to advance. They observe that men hold the most important jobs, and that it is unlikely that they will be able to move beyond the level of vice president. They feel stuck in less challenging jobs (e.g., purchasing, public relations, personnel; Hunsaker & Hunsaker, 1991). Because they see few women being promoted for their efforts, the costs are perceived as being too great and the rewards too few (Hammer-Higgins & Atwood, 1989). Women are aware of the fact that they are not paid as well as their male counterparts. In fact, some women experience salary discrimination because they "have a husband who works" (Williams, 1988, p. 134). Many successful women managers have reported encountering biases in their careers. They become frustrated when their expectations are not realized. In addition, they face considerable work-family demands if they are married or have children.

Strategies

Counselors must recognize that the organizational climate in top management is not the same for men and women managers. Counselors need to help women managers develop the skills needed to break the glass ceiling (e.g., political savvy). For example, women managers generally have to earn their power, whereas male managers are initially ascribed more power due to their gender (Stechert, 1986). Women must therefore demonstrate to superiors that they are involved in important decisions and are proficient at office politics (e.g., gaining support, developing a power base).

Some strategies that women managers can be taught for increasing power include being proactive in career planning, being exceptionally competent, acquiring needed resources and information, developing credibility among peers, developing connections with people who have power, taking risks, and being able to take criticism and implement suggestions (Carr-Ruffino, 1993; Haskell, 1985). In addition, women managers need to be taught how to use several different influence strategies, including reason, friendliness, bargaining, assertiveness, coalition building, appeals to higher authorities, and sanctions (Kipnis & Schmidt, 1982). Generally, women managers moving up into middle and upper level management have primarily used institutional sanctions for influencing others rather than persuasive strategies, yet persuasive strategies may be more effective (Kipnis & Cosentino, 1969). It may be that women need to build up their confidence in using a variety of influence strategies before they can be expected to do so with any frequency.

To obtain positions on corporate boards, a variety of strategies have been suggested for women, including: creating a public image and high profile, taking a proactive approach (e.g., self-promote and document achievements), using the media for self-promotion, establishing strong networks (especially with CEOs and other board members), and acquiring upper management line experience (Burgess & Tharenou, 2002).

GLOBAL ISSUES FOR WOMEN MANAGERS

Women comprise over 50% of the world's population, yet in no country do they constitute close to half of the corporate managers. Although the number of women managers has increased over the last decades, their numbers are substantially below those for men. In addition, the higher the rank within the organization, the fewer the women that will be found there. This

pattern of unequal representation of women prevails in countries throughout the world, although there are differences in women's prospects for entry and promotion in management positions (Adler & Izraeli, 1988). According to a survey of 420 firms in nine Western European countries
(Belgium, France, Germany, Italy, Netherlands, Portugal, Spain, Switzer-
land, United Kingdom), only 49% of the firms had ever employed a woman
manager. Of the remaining 51%, 15% stated they would never consider
promoting a woman into management. The firms with the most women
managers included the United Kingdom (83% of the firms), France (74%),
and Portugal (67%). These figures may be misleading, however, because in
each of the countries only a small fraction of the total number of managers
is women (8%, 9%, 13% respectively). Italy reported the fewest number of
companies (12%) having women managers, and firms in Germany, Italy,
and the Netherlands reported no women in top management. In addition,
most firms surveyed did not have any programs implemented to increase
women's participation rates into management positions (Management
Centre Europe, 1982).

In Asian countries in particular, it is difficult for women to advance into
management positions. Women in China, Vietnam, Korea, Japan, Hong
Kong, and other Asian countries may face stronger barriers to advancement
than their American counterparts. For example, in Japan, women are expected to marry young and devote themselves to child rearing. It is difficult
for them to keep full-time positions once they have children because there
is little company support and Japanese management is male dominated
(Yamaguchi, 1999). Even Hong Kong, which is considered one of the more
progressive Asian countries in terms of workplace practices, has few women
managers. By 1999, only 22% of all managers were women, up from 16% in
1993. Interestingly, Asian women may seemingly condone some of the barriers they experience by believing that men are more qualified (Marshall,
1999). Of course, many Asian women have decided to attend business
schools in the United States and their applications to MBA programs have
increased, hoping to shatter the glass ceiling when they return home or stay
in the United States to work as managers (Schellhardt, 1999).

Similarities

Despite the differences among countries in culture, level of technological
and economic development, and availability of resources (e.g., human, material), similar factors affect women's participation rates in management
and their career patterns. Women managers worldwide share a number of
barriers, including structural (e.g., legal restrictions, cultural sanctions, social norms, stereotypes, discrimination, historical policies, corporate obstacles, educational barriers) and psychological (e.g., difficulties coping with

role expectations and conflict, lack of political skills, disinterest in pursuing management careers; Adler & Izraeli, 1988; Chan, 1988). In most countries, if not all, management is considered to be a masculine career field and is heavily dominated by men, especially at the senior levels (Bu & McKeen, 2002; Harris, 2002). Even in countries (e.g., Indonesia) where women are more highly educated than men, women are underrepresented in management positions (Crockett, 1988). Women managers are typically located in less powerful, lower paid, and lower status positions than their male counterparts (Chan; Hearn & Parkin, 1988).

Across countries, women managers experience credibility problems, blocked mobility, discrimination, and stereotypes. These stereotypes were found to be pervasive across most countries (e.g., France, Canada, Japan, Singapore, Indonesia, United States). They include the beliefs that successful managers have masculine attributes (Crockett, 1988), that women do not have the commitment and involvement required of careers in managements, that women value their family lives more than their careers (Antal & Krebsbach-Gnath, 1988; Crockett; Symons, 1988), that married women or mothers are unsuitable for jobs requiring frequent travel or long hours, that men are emotionally more stable than women and are intellectually superior (Crockett), and that others will not want to work for women managers (Chan, 1988). Women managers in various countries also experience similar isolation and loneliness in management positions, especially at higher levels. They share similar feelings of having limited authority and poor career prospects (Chan). In fact, given the time-intensive nature of managerial positions, in most countries where women are managers, they are less likely than men to be married or parents. Women expatriates also see their international assignments as a less useful career moves than men, and are subject to more problems in their host locations (Selmer & Leung, 2002).

Differences

Across countries there are differences in the proportion of women in management and their prospects for entry and promotion into management. These variations may be due to differences in fundamental assumptions about women's role in management. In some countries (e.g., the United States), women managers are expected to assimilate into the corporate culture, and effectiveness is measured against male norms. Essentially, there is one best way to manage. In other countries (e.g., France, Sweden), the underlying assumption is that there are multiple effective ways to manage. Women managers are expected to be different from male managers, and organizations attempt to set up conditions that enable women and men to make unique, equally important contributions (Adler & Izraeli, 1988). Interestingly, powerful international women (e.g., on the Fortune Top 50 list) are more likely to have had family connections than powerful U.S. women (Sellers, 2003). Although it is more likely that sons are given a family business, if a daughter can show she can run the business, she may be given the reins.

Differences among women managers worldwide exist due to varying cultural traditions and social norms, level and form of economic development, social policies, access to education, and organizational processes (Adler & Izraeli, 1988). Cultural traditions and social norms may dictate women's participation rates in management. For example, the social norm in Japan due to the paternalistic system indicates that for women to achieve senior management positions, they must be the appropriate age and unmarried (Steinhoff & Tanaka, 1988). In other countries (e.g., Fiji, Indonesia), women born into elite classes are ascribed leadership positions (Crockett, 1988; Renshaw, 1988). In countries where the roles of women as wife and mother are central (e.g., Israel), women are discouraged from becoming managers (Izraeli, 1988). Economic developments also affect women's access and opportunities in management positions. For example, Singapore's rapid economic growth in the 1980s led to an increase in women's participation rates in management. However, women were still concentrated in traditional functions (e.g., personnel, administrative services, public relations, consumer affairs) and in lower and middle management positions (Chan, 1988). Social policies (e.g., legislation, allocation of resources) that differ across countries have also impacted women's participation in management. Some countries such as the United States have policies (e.g., affirmative action) that actively promote women's participation in management (Brown, 1988). Others (e.g., Singapore, South Africa) have governmental policies that discourage women's labor force participation (Chan; Erwee, 1988). Women's access to education also differs across countries, affecting their subsequent selection and advancement in management positions. For example, in the United States, Canada, and Israel, women are often recruited directly from universities for management positions, whereas in the United Kingdom, a university degree is less important. Organizational processes differ for women in various countries. For example, in some countries (e.g., Japan), women are excluded from geographic transfers, which are critical to advancement into senior-level management positions (Steinhoff & Tanaka).

Assistance Strategies

Various strategies have been utilized to assist women managers from different cultures. Mentoring and sponsorship have been considered critical for women managers, although the degree to which women managers enjoy these activities has varied. For example, women managers in the United

States and Canada receive more sponsorship than in France (Symons, 1988). Similar social policies across countries serve to encourage or discourage women's participation and survival in management careers, including the availability of child care, parental leave, and flexible working arrangements. For example, in Germany, child care is government subsidized, although in most German schools children have half-day schedules, making it difficult for women mangers to combine their parental and work roles (Antal & Krebsbach-Gnath, 1988). Across countries, formal education is considered to be an important criterion for women's participation and advancement in management. In addition, in most countries women managers in the public sector fare better than they do in the private sector, perhaps due to specified criteria and public control (Adler & Izraeli, 1988).

Career counselors need to recognize the similarities and differences among women managers of various cultures if they are to provide relevant assistance. In most cases, women will need to receive education and training to build their self-confidence and develop their political and networking skills. Across countries, women managers have reported a need for support from counselors, practitioners, family members, peers, superiors, and subordinates (Renshaw, 1988).

Research is also needed to examine issues facing repatriates. Some work done in this area has noted that female repatriated managers reported that the reentry phase is haphazard and ill planned. Women repatriates express concerns over how an international assignment affects their career progress, and some indicated that on their return they were placed into jobs that did not utilize their skills and experiences (Linehan & Scullion, 2002). Mentoring and networking would be valuable to assist them with their career growth. Clearly, more research is needed in this area and organizations should become more involved in establishing programs to assist women expatriates and repatriates (Bu & McKeen, 2002).

ORGANIZATIONAL EFFORTS TO ASSIST WOMEN MANAGERS

This chapter has described strategies counselors can use to help women adjust or fit into existing organizational cultures. Increasingly more firms have become woman friendly by implementing programs to assist women managers. These organizations have provided special training for women managers addressing intrapersonal, interpersonal, and technical areas. Often the focus is on improving communication and assertiveness skills, enhancing goal setting, building confidence, and developing greater expertise in substantive topics (e.g., finances, problem analysis, planning and decision making, leadership, team dynamics).

Other strategies that organizations have used to assist women managers have included offering career-planning services (e.g., personal counseling, workshops, managerial coaching, job postings) and developmental programs (e.g., assessment centers, job rotation, additional training opportunities, formal mentoring programs). Work-family issues have also been addressed through workshops that focus on work-family conflicts, and through offering leave for child care, flexible work arrangements, relaxed organizational policies on travel and transfers, child-care support, and child-care referral systems.

Career-Planning Assistance

Women managers could greatly benefit from career assistance. Younger women could be counseled on the range of options possible for themselves, and senior women could be coached to consider their long-term aspirations and seek out strategic developmental experiences (Gersick & Kram, 2002). Career development programs that include succession planning, high-potential identification, mentoring, network groups, and individual development planning or career pathing would be very beneficial for grooming women into higher levels of management (Giscombe & Mattis, 2002; Marjamaa & Hoffman, 2002). Some organizations have provided career-planning programs to assist women managers (Russell, 1991). For example, Gulf Oil initiated a program that included assessment, individual advising, and a career-planning workshop. The issues for the workshop discussion consisted of career versus family-life issues, strategies for making and implementing educational and career plans, goal setting, decision making, identification of organizational career resources and opportunities, communication skills, and relevant academic programs at nearby schools. In the high-tech field, women should be given career assistance to plan out the types of job experiences they will need to move up in leadership. Counselors could encourage them to gain a broad base of professional experience, take on critical company assignments, and develop track records (Catalyst, 2003a).

Training, Development, and Networking Opportunities

For women to advance into managerial positions, particularly top management, they need to be given challenging job assignments and developmental opportunities. They should have access to stretch assignments and training and development activities such as executive MBAs or executive leadership workshops.

Some firms (e.g., Capital Cities, ABC) have found that their women managers are predominately liberal arts graduates who need additional financial and management training. As a result, they have enrolled them in management development programs (e.g., Smith Management program at Smith College). Other firms (e.g., Merck, Corning, Gannett) have provided training courses for women managers to make them better equipped, more confident, and more competitive for higher level managerial positions (Williams, 1988).

One of the most important ways to develop women is to provide them with good performance feedback and to place them in succession planning programs. Harley-Davidson brings together all senior leaders within each functional area to discuss employee performance, bench strength, and potential to make sure that all managers see employees' talents. As a result, they have seen growth in the representation of women in their senior ranks from 5% of vice presidents in 1995 to 17% in 2003. In addition, 29% of their corporate officers are women (Catalyst, 2004c). In the high-tech field, it is especially important for women leaders to expand their social networks by keeping in touch with past and present employers and colleagues (Catalyst, 2003a).

Separate Training for Women in Business

Today, there are still a number of organizations (e.g., Catalyst) and conferences set up specifically for women (e.g., the Women's Leadership Conference sponsored by the Conference Board; Women in Leadership Summit sponsored by Linkage, Inc.). Topics addressed in women's leadership conferences generally include: building organizational allies and networking, women in technology fields, mentoring programs, membership on boards, self-promotion for career and financial advancement, effective negotiation techniques, managing work and family, attracting women to male-dominated fields, and strategies for retaining senior women. In addition, assertiveness training courses for women in business are still being offered (e.g., American Management Association). Some of the purported benefits include: helping women deal with conflicts confronting women in business, overcoming obstacles to assertiveness, building and projecting a positive image, managing stress, and using assertive communication techniques. The idea behind separate training programs for women managers is that they can share their concerns with other women executives in a comfortable, supportive, informal learning environment. The Women's Leadership Program offered by the Center for Creative Leadership is geared for women in middle- and senior-level management. Staffed only by women, it is designed to provide female managers with a safe setting to discuss women's leadership and work experiences.

Women may gain some benefits from participating in sex-segregated classes. They may be able to establish a network of female peers by sharing their experiences with other competent women. They are also given the opportunity to observe effective female role models, and can participate in stereotype-free career planning (Powell & Graves, 2003). They may have opportunities to discuss some of the unique issues they experience in management (e.g., discrimination, harassment, tokenism, social isolation, stereotyping). Classes may be needed for women to gain additional skills in areas they are less exposed to, including building self-esteem, learning new behaviors for managing interpersonal conflict, developing leadership and team-building skills, and enhancing political skills and influence strategies. Other women may need coaching in being less dominating and aggressive so that they can do a better job of collaborating with colleagues, subordinates, and senior managers (Strout, 2001).

In some organizations (e.g., Capital Cities, ABC) women have been sent to additional financial and management training to build their self-confidence and the confidence of their male peers toward them (Williams, 1988). In addition, women can receive help with career planning, and learn the perceptions, strategies, and behavioral skills needed to fit into the corporate arena. Whereas all of these skills may be needed for some male managers, they are considered critical for women managers.

Work-Family Assistance

There are numerous things that organizations can do to alleviate work-family pressures on women managers. These can include child-care and elder-care programs, financial assistance toward the cost of child care, on-site or near-site child-care centers that provide all-day and after-school care, and flexible work arrangements. Merck and Deloitte & Touche LLP were both very successful in designing flexible work arrangements that would appeal to their employees (Catalyst, 2003a).

Organizations also need to make sure that the corporate culture supports women managers when they participate in these programs. For example, if none of the senior women have taken part in these programs (e.g., job sharing, part-time work, flexible hours) then most women managers will be reluctant to take advantage of the programs. If this is the case, they may feel they have to choose between having a family and a career as a woman executive. Burke (2002) found that managerial women reporting organizational values more supportive of work and personal-life balance also reported greater job and career satisfaction, less work stress, less intention to quit, greater family satisfaction, fewer psychosomatic symptoms, and more positive emotional well-being.

At Citigroup, women managers have reported that the environment is a friendly place for women with children given the flexible work arrangements that people feel comfortable using. Similarly, at Booz Allen Hamilton, there are "internal opportunities" or part-time work schedules to enable women managers and consultants to continue to work at the firm after having children (Fagerberg, 2003). These examples are not the norm, however. Today in the United States the average hours worked weekly by employed women has increased. Employees are also spending more unpaid hours using the Internet to work at home without cutting back on hours at the work site. These trends have resulted in a time crunch for many workers. Thus, organizations are increasingly pressuring employees to work long hours wherever they are and whether they want to or not (U.S. Department of Labor, Bureau of Labor Statistics, 1999). Managers in particular face pressure by senior executives who work long hours to mimic their behavior; otherwise they may be committing career suicide (Hewlett, 2002).

As Hall (1989) mentioned over a decade ago, senior executives need to reexamine their assumptions about what constitutes a "good" executive, a "good" career, and a "good" parent in today's times. He also stated that firms should examine the effectiveness of their executive succession systems for advancing women into higher management. Finally, he recommended that top managers establish a task force to examine work-family issues throughout the organization. The task force should be charged with developing recommendations that top managers can implement. Gersick and Kram (2002) also suggested that employers reconsider their assumptions about what successful careers look like. For example, men have often followed a linear career path to climb the corporate ladder and this model has been viewed as the successful career model. Unfortunately, women's careers often do not follow this direct path due to work-family issues and trade-offs.

Addressing Discrimination and Advancing Women

Counselors need to be able to understand the types of discrimination women managers experience to assist them in one-on-one interventions or in workshops. The barriers that women managers are confronted with are important for counselors to be aware of so they can provide sex discrimination counseling to women (i.e., provide women involved in legal suits with information, support, and direction).

Powell and Graves (2003) suggested three types of actions that organizations can take to address discrimination issues facing women: promote non-discrimination in the treatment of people and decisions about people (i.e., adherence to equal employment opportunity laws); promote diversity among employees in all jobs and at all levels (i.e., greater numbers of diverse employees at different organizational levels); and promote inclusion of employees from all groups in the organizational culture (i.e., engage in practices to help all employees feel valued and comfortable in the workplace).

It is critical for organizations to assist women in their moves into higher managerial positions. A recent study by Catalyst (2004e) revealed that companies with a higher representation of women in senior management positions financially outperformed companies with few women at the top. Thus, firms that recruit, retain, and advance women seem to have a competitive advantage in the global marketplace. To create lasting change and move women, especially women of color, into management positions, Catalyst (2004e) recommended the following:

- Benchmark (via salary, function, and time in job grade) the firm's progress of women in management with that of men.
- Integrate diversity goals with the firm's strategic goals.
- Ensure commitment of senior management to change (keep the CEO involved and committed).
- Actively involve women, particularly women of color, in the firm's performance development programs (e.g., provide opportunities for line and general management assignments and other high-visibility assignments).
- Support the formation and maintenance of networks and mentoring opportunities that support women, especially women of color.
- Review work-life policies and practices to ensure that they allow flexibility and address the needs of those with extended or nontraditional families.
- Hold managers accountable for diversity practices (e.g., review managers' performance evaluations by gender and race to uncover any systematic biases, create and enforce financial incentives for progress on diversity goals).

To address sexual harassment issues, organizations must create cultures that reject sexual harassment. They should have strong written policies against it, educate employees about what it involves, and establish formal grievance procedures to deal with allegations of harassment. New employees should receive information about sexual harassment policies in their orientation, and managers should be trained regarding the policies, the forms of sexual harassment, and the proper responses to allegations of harassment (Powell & Graves, 2003).

As noted earlier, individuals still describe leaders in stereotypical terms that favor males over females. They express personal preferences for male over female leaders, and they hold attitudes that make it more difficult for female leaders to be effective in their roles (Powell & Graves, 2003). In order to create a working environment in which both men and women have an equal chance to be effective as leaders, stereotypes and prejudices against women leaders must be confronted. To specifically deal with sex-role stereotypes, Rizzo and Mendez (1991) offered some suggestions for organizations that are still valuable today. These include:

- Illustrate that there are examples of successful managers who are women. Announce the appointment of individuals to leadership roles and point out their special skills, expertise, and accomplishments.
- Support women entering management to enable them to remain in management.
- Provide women managers with challenging situations so that they can demonstrate their ability to succeed and their male colleagues can observe them as effective.
- Promote women managers out of lower level positions. Make sure the performance measurement and reward system motivates managers to refrain from sex discrimination in decisions.
- Sponsor organizational workshops to focus on the prevalence and dangers of stereotypes.
- Move women managers into male-dominated positions in organizations (e.g., line positions). Monitor for gossip about the reasons for leader appointments and try to quell untrue rumors (Falkenberg, 1990).
- Build women's self-confidence by giving them feedback, allowing them to take risks, and offering rewards.

Some firms have implemented some of these strategies or diversity awareness programs for addressing sex-role stereotypes. Despite the fact that 75% of Fortune 500 firms have formally stated diversity programs, only 33% of African American women felt that these programs effectively created supportive environments (Catalyst, 2004b). As Giscombe and Mattis (2002) found, there was a split between the diversity ideals espoused by the senior leadership and the perception of women of color regarding the effectiveness of the diversity initiatives.

Brooks, Fenwick, and Walker (2003) found that despite increased support for Equal Employment Opportunity initiatives in a firm over a 5-year period, there was no accompanying significant change in the proportion of women in management positions. Thus, it is important to examine these programs to make sure they are effectively meeting the needs of all women. Some firms that have done an outstanding job of creating programs to better manage diversity were recently honored by Catalyst (Catalyst, 2004c). For example, Shell was honored for their initiative, Valuing and Leveraging Diversity, because their program focuses on developing and advancing women and people of color. Shell's efforts have met with tremendous success, given that currently women comprise 57% of its corporate officers. Between 1997 and 2003, women's representation at the senior executive level increased from 8% to 32%, at the senior management level from 7% to 14%, and at the middle management level from 9% to 22%. Likewise, Harley-Davidson's Optimizing Talent: A Culture of Empowerment is a program that encourages the development and promotion of diverse talent through intensive employee development and empowerment.

DIRECTIONS FOR FUTURE RESEARCH

Today, some subscribe to the belief that less research on women managers is needed because most of the problems they face have been solved. Others contend that research is needed more today than ever before because discrimination and barriers still exist for women, although they are much more subtle and difficult to detect. More innovative research methodologies may be necessary to tease out the difficulties and dilemmas confronting women managers.

Although a considerable amount of research has been conducted on issues, barriers, and concerns facing women in management, very little research has specifically focused on career-counseling strategies that may prove useful to this population. In fact, research on women in management and on career counseling has not overlapped to any great extent. This is unfortunate because research is clearly needed to identify the types of counseling that can assist women managers.

Researchers need to identify why some women may not be entering MBA programs or management careers, and why others are dropping out. Exit interviews with women leaving management positions may prove useful in identifying barriers and strategies needed to maintain a managerial career. With their findings, counselors may be better able to assist women in entering or surviving in careers in management. For example, some types of coping strategies or counseling techniques may prove useful as women enter management careers. Other strategies may be more beneficial to help women managers survive once they are in a management career. Longitudinal research is needed to uncover the differences in the issues confronting women as they move through their careers. In addition, it would be valuable to follow those women who drop out of corporations and start their own firms to see what types of assistance would be most beneficial for them.

Research that examines the types of barriers that exist for women at varying levels of management or at varying stages in their careers is needed. Up to now, much of the research has assumed that women managers are a homogenous group, sharing similar problems. Researchers need to identify the unique issues that may be applicable to various managerial women in order to recommend effective counseling for each subgroup (Russell & Rush, 1987). For example, women in higher level management positions may face different pressures from male peers than women who are in lower level management. In addition, researchers should examine issues and strategies unique to women managers from different industries (e.g., high tech, finance, entertainment, retail) as well as the private and public sector, as different fields may pose varying challenges for women (Rindfleish, 2002). Issues unique to women of color should also be documented because these women face double marginalization in the corporate world (Giscombe & Mattis, 2002).

It is also important to investigate the issues confronting women managers who exhibit different career patterns. Any number of classification systems could be used, including Super's (1957) system, which identifies women according to the centrality of their workforce participation and homemaking, or Zytowski's (1969) career patterns for women, which classify women by the time of their career entry (early, late) and participation (low, high). It would be interesting to see the issues and barriers facing women in management who vary with respect to their participation (pattern) in their career and home lives. We might expect women who enter management careers after raising their children to experience different concerns from women entering management as singles or new wives or mothers.

It would be meaningful to see the similarities and differences in the feelings experienced by men and women managers in various career stages (e.g., maintenance). For example, during middle career, if both male and female managers experience low self-esteem, is it for the same reasons? Her feelings may be due to sex-role issues and discrimination whereas his may be due to career plateauing. Clearly, the underlying rationale for their concerns and perceptions must be identified before appropriate counseling can be provided.

Research is needed that identifies the unique issues facing different subgroups of women managers, such as minorities, reentry women, and dual-career couples. For some of these women (e.g., African Americans), it seems important to examine how the double effects of tokenism may serve to isolate them and what counseling they may need. Also, issues and assistance may differ for women managers who work in varying sizes and types of organizations (e.g., manufacturing vs. services, private vs. public sector, profit vs. nonprofit). In addition, research with women managers of a broader, more global nature is needed, including issues confronting women managers of various cultures and countries. The book edited by Adler and Izraeli (1988) is an important step in this direction. Global research should also examine the attitudes of men and women in different countries toward women managers. For example, Cordano, Owen, Scherer, and Munoz (2002) translated the Women as Managers Scale into Spanish and surveyed views of individuals in the United States and Chile. More research of this nature is needed.

Although women managers should be the target population for much of the research called for, the attitudes and behaviors of men should also be investigated. This includes men in their work and home roles (e.g., spouses, fathers, peers, superiors, subordinates). It is important to further understand men's perceptions of women managers and to determine the amount and type of support they provide to women managers. Researchers should try to discern to what degree men are aware of the barriers facing women, and what their role is in contributing to or minimizing some of the problems.

Research is needed that examines the relative effectiveness of women managers and the nature of the contributions they make to organizations (Adler & Izraeli, 1988). In addition, very little research has evaluated the relative effectiveness of interventions used to assist women managers, despite the fact that this research is critical. Research is needed that examines the relative importance of various assistance strategies (e.g., mentoring, coping strategies, individual counseling) and to determine when each strategy is most effective. It is important to see how these strategies address problems of low job satisfaction, low self-esteem, feelings of powerlessness in dealing with inequities, and organizational commitment. Researchers should examine the financial and psychological costs associated with various programs, the necessary refinements to maximize benefits and reduce negative features, and any unintentional negative consequences such programs may have on managers. Finally, research is needed to determine the effectiveness of both individual strategies employed by women managers and organizational strategies adopted by firms for dealing with the issues and concerns facing women managers.

CONCLUSION

Women managers continue to experience a number of external and internal barriers that hinder their effectiveness in organizations. Although some progress has been made in remediating these difficulties, in some cases the problems have simply become more subtle and difficult to detect. Given the coming U.S. labor shortage predicted to hit by 2010, it will be critical for U.S. firms to redesign their jobs to hold onto their talented women managers (Tischler, 2004).

Career counselors must recognize that women managers comprise a diverse group; across management levels and career phases, they report unique concerns and require different types of assistance. Even within levels and phases, they may confront varying barriers due to their marital and parental status as well as their age, race, and personality characteristics. In addition, as Portello and Long (2001) noted, workplace stress management interventions aimed at female managers should facilitate an exploration of the significance of the stressor in order to determine ways of coping and reducing stress.

Counselors need to recognize that organizations are not static, so that the skills women managers need are constantly changing. Today, organizations are much more competitive and operate in a global, changing environment. Successful managers, regardless of gender, need to develop skills to demonstrate the contribution they can make to the organization as a whole. This means they need to be more innovative and proactive about change. Some of the personal skills required include taking a broader perspective, being more creative, advocating a vision for the firm, and being persistent about ideas. Some of the interpersonal skills required include using teams and participative management and empowering peers and subordinates. Many researchers believe that women already possess the characteristics needed for future organizations. For example, many women have the interpersonal and transformational leadership skills considered critical in the increasingly service-driven marketplace (Aburdene & Naisbitt, 1992; Catalyst, 1987; Rizzo & Mendez, 1991). Counselors and practitioners need to encourage women to use these skills and at the same time urge organizations to more fully appreciate the unique contributions women managers can make. Women managers should also be encouraged to receive executive coaching, one-on-one coaching in which an individual receives personalized assistance based on her unique strengths and areas for development.

A variety of career-counseling efforts are needed to assist women managers in dealing with the issues they face in organizations. Some of these include career-planning workshops and self-assessments, cognitive career counseling, and individual and group counseling. At the same time, organizations must adopt more innovative techniques and interventions to alter their structure to meet the needs of women managers. The future will continue to require change at both the individual and organizational levels to address the issues confronting women managers. Women managers will probably have to continue to learn how to fit into the male managerial model. Likewise, organizations will need to continue to offer them assistance (e.g., counseling) to help them assimilate into the corporate culture. However, organizations will also need to make greater strides in altering their organizational structures (e.g., offering flexible work arrangements, child care) to enable women managers to provide the unique contributions they are capable of making. Future research will be needed to determine the relative effectiveness of these approaches for assisting women as they enter, survive, and advance in management careers in the decades ahead.

REFERENCES

Abelson, R. (2001, July 26). A survey of Wall Street finds women disheartened. *The New York Times*, p. C1.

Aburdene, P., & Naisbitt, J. (1992). *Megatrends for women.* New York: Villard Books.

Adler, N. J. (1999). Global leaders: Women of influence. In G. N. Powell (Ed.), *Handbook of gender and work* (pp. 239–261). Thousand Oaks, CA: Sage.

Adler, N. J., & Izraeli, D. N. (Eds.). (1988). *Women in management worldwide.* Armonk, NY: Sharpe.

Alvarez, S. A., & Meyer, G. D. (1998). *Why do women become entrepreneurs? Frontiers of entrepreneurship research.* Wellesley, MA: Babson College.

Antal, A. B., & Krebsbach-Gnath, C. (1988). Women in management: Unused resources in the Federal Republic of Germany. In N. J. Adler & D. N. Izraeli (Eds.), *Women in management worldwide* (pp. 141–156). Armonk, NY: Sharpe.

Armour, S. (2003, June 25). More women cruise to the top. *USA Today*, p. 3B.

Astin, H. S. (1984). The meaning of work in women's lives: A sociopsychological model of career choice and work behavior. *The Counseling Psychologist, 12,* 117–126.

Babcock, L., & Laschever, S. (2003). *Women don't ask: Negotiation and the gender divide.* Princeton, NJ: Princeton University Press.

Barnett, R. C., & Rivers, C. (1992, February). The myth of the miserable working woman. *Working Woman,* pp. 62–65, 83, 88.

Bass, B. M., Avolio, B. J., & Atwater, L. (1996). The transformational and transactional leadership of men and women. *Applied Psychology, 45,* 5–34.

Bates, S. (2002, April). Top female managers see gender gap in salaries. *HR Magazine, 47,* 12.

Betz, N. E., & Fitzgerald, L. F. (1987). *The career psychology of women.* Orlando, FL: Academic Press.

Blum, L., & Smith, V. (1988). Women's mobility in the corporation: A critique of the politics of optimism. *Journal of Women in Culture and Society, 13,* 528–545.

Boldry, J., Wood, W., & Kashy, C. A. (2001). Gender stereotypes and the evaluation of men and women in military training. *Journal of Social Issues, 57,* 689–705.

Borman, C. A., & Colson, S. (1984). Mentoring: An effective career guidance technique. *Vocational Guidance Journal, 3,* 192–197.

Borman, C. A., & Guido-DiBrito, F. (1986). The career development of women: Helping Cinderella lose her complex. *Journal of Career Development, 12,* 250–261.

Bowen, D. D., & Hisrich, R. D. (1986). The female entrepreneur: A career development perspective. *Academy of Management Review, 11,* 393–407.

Braddock, D. (1999). Occupational employment projections to 2008. *Monthly Labor Review, 11,* 61–72.

Brett, J. M., & Stroh, L. K. (2003). Working 61 plus hours a week: Why do managers do it? *Journal of Applied Psychology, 88,* 67–78.

Brooks, I., Fenwick, G., & Walker, B. (2003). The effect of changing perceptions of EEO on the appointment of women to management and supervisory positions in a public sector organization. *New Zealand Journal of Industrial Relations, 28,* 23–43.

Brown, D., Brooks, L., & Associates. (Eds.). (1990). *Career choice and development: Applying contemporary theories to practice* (2nd ed.). San Francisco: Jossey-Bass.

Brown, L. K. (1988). Female managers in the United States and in Europe: Corporate boards, M.B.A. credentials, and the image-illusion of progress. In N. J. Adler & D. N. Izraeli (Eds.), *Women in management worldwide* (pp. 265–275). Armonk, NY: Sharpe.

Brown, L. K., & Ridge, S. (2002). Moving into management: Gender segregation and its effect on managerial attainment. *Women in Management Review, 17,* 318–327.

Bu, N., & McKeen, C. A. (2002). Introduction: Enhancing women's international mobility and career success. *Women in Management Review, 17,* 48–50.

Budman, M. (2002). What's holding back European women? *Across the Board, 39,* 71–72.

Burgess, Z., & Tharenou, P. (2002). Women board directors: Characteristics of the few. *Journal of Business Ethics, 37,* 39–49.

Burke, R. J. (2002). Organizational values, job experiences and satisfactions among managerial and professional women and men: Advantage men? *Women in Management Review, 17,* 228–242.

Burke, R. J., & McKeen, C. A. (1992). Women in management. In C. L. Cooper & I. T. Robertson (Eds.), *International review of industrial and organizational psychology* (pp. 245–283). New York: Wiley.

Butterfield, D. A., & Grinnell, J. P. (1999). "Re-viewing" gender, leadership, and managerial behavior: Do three decades of research tell us anything? In G. N. Powell (Ed.), *Handbook of gender and work* (pp. 223–238). Thousand Oaks, CA: Sage.

Callanan, G. A., & Greenhaus, J. H. (1990). The career indecision of managers and professionals: Development of a scale and test of a model. *Journal of Vocational Behavior, 37,* 79–103.

Campbell, K. E. (1988). Gender differences in job-related networks. *Work and Occupations, 15,* 179–200.

Carr-Ruffino, N. (1993). *The promotable woman: Advancing through leadership skills* (2nd ed.). Belmont, CA: Wadsworth.

Catalyst. (1987). A matter of personal ability, not gender. *Management Solutions, 32*(11), 38–45.

Catalyst. (1996). *Women in corporate leadership: Progress and prospects.* New York: Author.

Catalyst. (1998). *Advancing women in business: The Catalyst guide.* San Francisco: Jossey-Bass.

Catalyst. (1999). *Creating women's networks: A how-to guide for women and companies.* San Francisco: Jossey-Bass.

Catalyst. (2000a). *Cracking the glass ceiling: Catalyst's research on women in corporate management 1995–2000.* New York: Author.

Catalyst. (2000b). *Passport to opportunity: U.S. women in global business.* New York: Author.

Catalyst. (2000c). *Women and the MBA: Gateway to opportunity.* New York: Author.

Catalyst. (2003a). *Bit by bit: Catalyst's guide to advancing women in high tech.* Retrieved August 11, 2004, from http://www.catalystwomen.org

Catalyst. (2003b). *U.S. demographic fact sheet: Study findings and background statistics for the next generation of leaders.* Retrieved August 11, 2004, from http://www.catalystwomen.org/press room/factsheets/images/factsu8.jpg

Catalyst. (2003c). *2003 Catalyst census of women board directors.* Retrieved August 11, 2004, from http://www.catalystwomen.org

Catalyst. (2004a). *Action steps for human resource executives.* Retrieved August 11, 2004, from http://www.catalystwomen.org

Catalyst. (2004b, February 18). *Catalyst report outlines unique challenges faced by African-American women in business.* Retrieved August 11, 2004, from http://www.catalystwomen.org/press_ room/releases.htm

Catalyst. (2004c, January 15). *General Electric, Harley-Davidson, and Shell Oil Company earn prestigious Catalyst Award for efforts to advance women employees.* Retrieved August 11, 2004, from http://www.catalystwomen.org/press_room/releases.htm

Catalyst. (2004d, June 24). *New Catalyst study finds female executives are just as likely as male colleagues to aspire to CEO job.* Retrieved August 11, 2004, from http://www.catalystwomen.org/ press_room/releases.htm

Catalyst. (2004e, January 24). *New Catalyst study reveals financial performance is higher for companies with more women at the top.* Retrieved August 11, 2004, from http://www.catalystwomen.org/ press_room/releases.htm

Catalyst. (2004f, February 19). *1 in 9 corporate directors of FP500 are women in latest count.* Retrieved August 11, 2004, from http://www.catalystwomen.org/press_room/releases.htm

Chan, A. (1988). Women managers in Singapore: Citizens for tomorrow's economy. In N. J. Adler & D. N. Izraeli (Eds.), *Women in management worldwide* (pp. 54–73). Armonk, NY: Sharpe.

Cordano, M., Owen, C. L., Scherer, R. F., & Munoz, C. G. (2002). Expanding opportunities for cross-cultural research: The development of a Spanish women as managers scale. *International Journal of Management, 19,* 290–299.

Cox, T. H., & Harquail, C. V. (1991). Career paths and career success in the early career stages of male and female MBAs. *Journal of Vocational Behavior, 39,* 54–75.

Crockett, V. R. (1988). Women in management in Indonesia. In N. J. Adler & D. N. Izraeli (Eds.), *Women in management worldwide* (pp. 74–102). Armonk, NY: Sharpe.

Daily, C., Certo, S., & Dalton, D. (1999). Entrepreneurial ventures as an avenue to the top? Assessing the advancement of female CEOs and directors in the Inc. 100. *Journal of Developmental Entrepreneurship, 4,* 19–34.

Dansky, B. S., & Kilpatrick, D. G. (1997). Effects of sexual harassment. In W. O'Donohue (Ed.), *Sexual harassment: Theory, research, and treatment* (pp. 152–174). Boston: Allyn & Bacon.

Davidson, M. J., & Cooper, C. L. (1988). The pressures on women managers. *Management Decision, 25,* 57–63.

Deitch, C. H., & Sanderson, S. W. (1987). Geographic constraints on married women's careers. *Work and Occupations, 14,* 616–634.

Eagly, A. H. (2002, August). *Leadership styles of women and men.* Paper presented at the meeting of the Academy of Management, Denver, CO.

Eagly, A. H., & Johannesen-Schmidt, M. C. (2001). The leadership styles of women and men. *Journal of Social Issues, 57,* 781–797.

Eagly, A. H., Karau, S. J., & Makhijani, M. G. (1995). Gender and the effectiveness of leaders: A meta-analysis. *Psychological Bulletin, 117,* 125–145.

Eagly, A. H., Makhijani, M. G., & Klonsky, B. G. (1992). Gender and the evaluation of leaders: A meta-analysis. *Psychological Bulletin, 111,* 3–22.

Eby, L. T., Allen, T. D., & Douthitt, S. S. (1999). The role of nonperformance factors on job-related relocations opportunities: A field study and laboratory experiment. *Organizational Behavior and Human Decision Processes, 79,* 29–55.

Erwee, R. (1988). South African women: Changing career patterns. In N. J. Adler & D. N. Izraeli (Eds.), *Women in management worldwide* (pp. 213–225). Armonk, NY: Sharpe.

Etzion, D. (1987). Burning out in management: A comparison of women and men in match organizational positions. *Israel Social Science Research, 5,* 147–163.

Fagerberg, P. (2003, December). The top women employers 2003. *MBA Jungle,* U1–U14.

Fairhurst, G. T., & Snavely, B. K. (1983). Majority and token minority group relationships: Power acquisition and communication. *Academy of Management Review, 8,* 292–300.

Falkenberg, L. (1990). Improving the accuracy of stereotypes within the workplace. *Journal of Management, 16,* 107–118.

Female high flyers still "banging heads" against the glass ceiling. (2002). *Women in Management Review, 17,* 95–96.

Fitt, L., & Newton, D. (1981). When the mentor is a man and the protégé is a woman. *Harvard Business Review, 59,* 56–60.

Fitzgerald, L. F., & Betz, N. E. (1983). Issues in the vocational psychology of women. In W. B. Walsh & S. H. Osipow (Eds.), *Handbook of vocational psychology* (Vol. 1, pp. 83–159). Hillsdale, NJ: Lawrence Erlbaum Associates.

For women, senior management jobs are in sight. (1992). *Women in Management, 2*(3), 2.

Fox, R. L., & Schuhmann, R. A. (2001). Mentoring experiences of women city managers: Are women disadvantaged? *American Review of Public Administration, 31,* 381–392.

Gallos, J. V. (1989). Exploring women's development: Implications for career theory, practice, and research. In M. B. Arthur, D. T. Hall, & B. S. Lawrence (Eds.), *Handbook of career theory* (pp. 110–132). New York: Cambridge University Press.

Garland, S. B. (1991, September 2). How to keep women managers on the corporate ladder. *Business Week, 9,* 64.

Gersick, C. J. G., & Kram, K. E. (2002). High-achieving women at midlife: An exploratory study. *Journal of Management Inquiry, 11,* 104–127.

Giscombe, K., & Mattis, M. C. (2002). Leveling the playing field for women of color in corporate management: Is the business case enough? *Journal of Business Ethics, 37,* 103–112.

(2003). *Glass ceilings: The status of women as managers in the private sector.* Retrieved September 25, 2003, from http://www.eeoc.gov/stats/reports/glass.html

Gordon, J. R., Beatty, J. E., & Whelan-Berry, K. S. (2002). The midlife transition of professional women with children. *Women in Management Review, 17,* 328–341.

Gundry, L. K., Ben-Yoseph, M., & Posig, M. (2002). The status of women's entrepreneurship: Pathways to future entrepreneurship development and education. *New England Journal of Entrepreneurship, 5,* 39–50.

Gutek, B. A. (1985). *Sex and the workplace.* San Francisco: Jossey-Bass.

Gutek, B. A., Cohen, A. G., & Konrad, A. M. (1990). Predicting social-sexual behavior at work: A contact hypothesis. *Academy of Management Journal, 33,* 560–577.

Gutek, B. A., & Larwood, L. (Eds.). (1987). *Women's career development.* Newbury Park, CA: Sage.

Hall, D. T. (1972). A model of coping with role conflict: The role behavior of college educated women. *Administrative Science Quarterly, 17,* 471–486.

Hall, D. T. (1989). Moving beyond the "Mommy track": An organization change approach. *Personnel, 66*(12), 23–29.

Hammer-Higgins, P., & Atwood, V. A. (1989). The Management Game: An educational intervention for counseling women with nontraditional career goals. *Career Development Quarterly, 38,* 6–23.

Hammonds, K. H. (2004, October). Balance is bunk! *Fast Company, 87,* 68–76.

Haring-Hidore, M., & Beyard-Tyler, K. (1984). Counseling and research on nontraditional careers: A caveat. *Vocational Guidance Quarterly, 33,* 113–119.

Harris, H. (2002). Think international manager, think male: Why are women not selected for international management assignments? *Thunderbird International Business Review, 44,* 175–203.

Haskell, J. R. (1985). Women blocked by corporate politics. *Management World, 14*(9), 12–15.

Hayward, C. (2002, March). The ascent of women. *Financial Management,* 18–21.

Hearn, J., & Parkin, P. W. (1988). Women, men, and leadership: A critical review of assumptions, practices, and change in industrialized nations. In N. J. Adler & D. N. Izraeli (Eds.), *Women in management worldwide* (pp. 17–40). Armonk, NY: Sharpe.

Hennig, M., & Jardim, A. (1977). *The managerial women.* Garden City, NY: Anchor Press/ Doubleday.

Hewlett, S. A. (2002). Executive women and the myth of having it all. *Harvard Business Review, 80*(4), 66–73.

Hillman, A. J., Cannella, A. A., & Harris, I. C. (2002). Women and minorities in the boardroom: How do directors differ? *Journal of Management, 28,* 747–763.

Hunsaker, J. S., & Hunsaker, P. (1991). *Strategies and skills for managerial women.* Cincinnati, OH: South-Western.

Hunt, D., & Michael, C. (1983). Mentorship: A career training and developmental tool. *Academy of Management Review, 8,* 474–485.

Ivarsson, S. M., & Ekehammar, B. (2001). Women's entry into management: Comparing women managers and nonmanagers. *Journal of Managerial Psychology, 16,* 301–314.

Izraeli, D. N. (1988). Women's movement into management in Israel. In N. J. Adler & D. N. Izraeli (Eds.), *Women in management worldwide* (pp. 186–212). Armonk, NY: Sharpe.

Jacobson, M. B., & Koch, W. (1977). Women as leaders: Performance evaluations as a function of method of leader selection. *Organization Behavior and Human Performance, 20,* 149–157.

Judiesch, M. K., & Lyness, K. S. (1999). Left behind? The impact of leaves of absence on managers' career success. *Academy of Management Journal, 42,* 641–651.

Kahn, S. E. (1988). Feminism and career counseling with women. *Journal of Career Development, 14,* 242–248.

Kanter, R. M. (1977a). *Men and women of the corporation.* New York: Basic Books.

Kanter, R. M. (1977b). Some effects or proportions on group life: Skewed sex rations and responses to token women. *American Journal of Sociology, 82,* 965–990.

Kimbrough, F. H. (1981). Effects of a group career/life planning counseling model on the sex role and career self-concept of female undergraduates. *Dissertation Abstracts International, 42*(3), 291-A. (UMI No. 8118274)

Kipnis, D., & Cosentino, J. (1969). Use of leadership powers in industry. *Journal of Applied Research, 53,* 460–466.

Kipnis, D., & Schmidt, S. (1982). *Respondent's guide to the profiles of organizational influence strategies.* San Diego, CA: University Associates.

Kirchmeyer, C. (1998). Determinants of managerial career success: Evidence and explanation of male/female differences. *Journal of Management, 24,* 673–692.

Kirchmeyer, C. (2002). Change and stability in managers' gender roles. *Journal of Applied Psychology, 87,* 929–939.

Korabik, K., & Van Kampen, J. (1995). Gender, social support and coping with work stressors among managers. *Journal of Social Behavior and Personality, 10,* 135–148.

Kram, K. (1983). Phases of the mentor relationship. *Academy of Management Journal, 26,* 608–625.

Kram, K. E. (1985). *Mentoring at work: Developmental relationships in organizational life.* Glenview, IL: Scott, Foresman.

Krefting, L. A. (2002). Re-presenting women executives: Valorization and devalorization in US business press. *Women in Management Review, 17,* 104–119.

Lavelle, L. (2001, April 23). *For female CEOs, it's stingy at the top.* Retrieved November 24, 2003, from http://www.businessweek.com/magazine/content/01_17/b3729116.htm

Linehan, M., & Scullion, H. (2002). Repatriation of female executives: Empirical evidence from Europe. *Women in Management Review, 17,* 80–88.

Lipovenko, D. (1987, February 26). Mom's choosing nursery over career. *Globe and Mail Report on Business Magazine,* B1–B2.

Loerch, K. J., Russell, J. E. A., & Rush, M. C. (1989). The relationship among family domain variables and work-family conflict for men and women. *Journal of Vocational Behavior, 35,* 288–308.

Lortie-Lussier, M., & Rinfret, N. (2002). The proportion of women managers: Where is the critical mass? *Journal of Applied Social Psychology, 32,* 1974–1991.

Maman, D. (2000). Who accumulates directorships of big business firms in Israel? Organization structure, social capital and human capital. *Human Relations, 53,* 603–630.

Management Centre Europe. (1982). An upward climb for women in Europe (Executive report). *Management Review, 71*(9), 56–57.

Marjamaa, L., & Hoffman, K. E. (2002). Follow the leaders: How to keep high-performing women at your bank. *Community Banker, 11*(4), 16–22.

Marshall, S. (1999, May 21). Executive action: Women stereotyping women. *Asian Wall Street Journal,* p. 3.

Maynard, R. (1988, January 15). Thanks, but no thanks. *Globe and Mail Report on Business Magazine,* 26–34.

Merrick, B. G. (2002). The ethics of hiring in the new workplace: Men and women managers face changing stereotypes discover correlative patterns for success. *Competitiveness Review, 12,* 94–114.

Milwid, B. (1983). Breaking in: Experiences in male-dominated professions. *Women and Therapy, 2*, 67–69.

Morrison, A. M., & Von Glinow, M. A. (1990). Women and minorities in management. *American Psychologist, 45*, 200–208.

Morrison, A. M., White, R. P., Van Velsor, E., & the Center for Creative Leadership. (1987). *Breaking the glass ceiling: Can women reach the top of America's largest corporations?* Reading, MA: Addison-Wesley.

National Foundation for Women Business Owners. (1998). *Women business owners of color: Challenges and accomplishments.* Washington, DC: Author.

National Foundation for Women Business Owners. (1999). *Characteristics of women entrepreneurs worldwide are revealed.* Washington, DC: Author.

National Foundation for Women Business Owners. (2000). *Survey finds business owners are philanthropic leaders.* Washington, DC: Author.

Nicholson, N., & West, M. (1988). *Managerial job change: Men and women in transition.* New York: Cambridge University Press.

Number of minority women-owned businesses expected to reach 1.2 million in 2002. (2002). *Women in Management Review, 17*, 93–94.

Occupational employment in private industry by race/ethnic group/sex, and by industry, United States, 2001. Retrieved September 25, 2003, from http://www.eeoc.gov/stats/jobpat/2001/national.html

Ogintz, E. (1983, December 18). Career mothers outnumber housewives. *Bryan-College Station Eagle*, pp. 1A, 12A.

Ohlott, P. J., Ruderman, M. N., & McCauley, C. D. (1994). Gender differences in managers' developmental experiences. *Academy of Management Journal, 37*, 46–67.

Portello, J. Y., & Long, B. C. (2001). Appraisals and coping with workplace interpersonal stress: A model for women managers. *Journal of Counseling Psychology, 48*, 144–156.

Powell, G. N. (1988). *Women and men in management.* Newbury Park, CA: Sage.

Powell, G. N. (1999). Reflections on the glass ceiling: Recent trends and future prospects. In G. N. Powell (Ed.), *Handbook of gender and work* (pp. 325–345). Thousand Oaks, CA: Sage.

Powell, G. N., & Butterfield, D. A. (1979). The "good manager": Masculine or androgynous? *Academy of Management Journal, 22*, 395–403.

Powell, G. N., & Butterfield, D. A. (1989). The "good manager": Did androgyny fare better in the 1980s? *Group and Organization Studies, 14*, 216–233.

Powell, G. N., & Butterfield, D. A. (1994). Investigating the "glass ceiling" phenomenon: An empirical study of actual promotions to top management. *Academy of Management Journal, 37*, 68–86.

Powell, G. N., Butterfield, D. A., & Parent, J. D. (2002). Gender and managerial stereotypes: Have the times changed? *Journal of Management, 28*, 177–193.

Powell, G. N., & Graves, L. M. (2003). *Women and men in management* (3rd ed.). Thousand Oaks, CA: Sage.

Prince, D. (2002). Leaving corporate life for a saucy start-up. *Management Today*, 66–68.

Ragins, B. R. (1999). Gender and mentoring relationships: A review and research agenda for the next decade. In G. N. Powell (Ed.), *Handbook of gender and work* (pp. 347–370). Thousand Oaks, CA: Sage.

Ragins, B. R., & Cotton, J. L. (1999). Mentor functions and outcomes: A comparison of men and women in formal and informal mentoring relationships. *Journal of Applied Psychology, 84*, 529–550.

Reitman, F., & Schneer, J. A. (1997, August). *Snapshots of early managerial careers of men and women post- and preorganizational restructuring.* Paper presented at the annual meeting of the Academy of Management, Cincinnati, OH.

Renshaw, J. R. (1988). Women in management in the Pacific Islands: Exploring Pacific stereotypes. In N. J. Adler & D. N. Izraeli (Eds.), *Women in management worldwide* (pp. 122–140). Armonk, NY: Sharpe.

Richardson, M. S., & Johnson, M. (1984). Counseling women. In S. D. Brown & R. W. Lent (Eds.), *Handbook of counseling psychology* (pp. 832–877). New York: Wiley.

Rindfleish, J. (2002). Senior management women and gender equity: A comparison of public and private sector women in Australia. *Equal Opportunities International, 21*(7), 37–39.

Rizzo, A. M., & Mendez, C. (1991). *The integration of women in management: A guide for human resources and management development specialists.* New York: Quorum Books.

Rosen, B., Templeton, M. E., & Kichline, K. (1981). Early career experiences of women in management. *Business Horizons, 24,* 26–29.

Rosin, H. M., & Korabik, K. (1990). Marital and family correlates of women managers' attrition from organizations. *Journal of Vocational Behavior, 37,* 104–120.

Rothwell, S. (1986). Manpower matters: Women's career developments. *Journal of General Management, 11,* 88–93.

Ruderman, M. N., Ohlott, P. J., Panzer, K., & King, S. N. (2002). Benefits of multiple roles for managerial women. *Academy of Management Journal, 45,* 369–386.

Russell, J. E. A. (1991). Career development interventions in organizations. *Journal of Vocational Behavior, 38,* 237–287.

Russell, J. E. A., & Rush, M. (1987). A comparative study of age-related variation in women's views of a career in management. *Journal of Vocational Behavior, 30,* 280–294.

Rutherford, S. (2001). Any difference? An analysis of gender and divisional management styles in a large airline. *Gender, Work and Organization, 8,* 326–345.

Rynecki, D. (2003, June 9). Ca Sallie save citi, restore Sandy's reputation, and earn her $30 million paycheck? *Fortune, 147*(11), 68–78.

Sauers, D. A., Kennedy, J. C., & O'Sullivan, D. (2002). Managerial sex role stereotyping: A New Zealand perspective. *Women in Management Review, 17,* 342–347.

Schellhardt, T. D. (1999, June 1). Managers and managing: Asian women seeking MBAs in U.S. schools. *The Wall Street Journal,* p. 4.

Schneer, J. A., & Reitman, F. (1997). The interrupted managerial career path: A longitudinal study of MBAs. *Journal of Vocational Behavior, 51,* 411–434.

Schwartz, F. N. (1989). Management women and the new facts of life. *Harvard Business Review, 67*(1), 65–76.

Sellers, P. (2003, October 13). Power: Do women really want it? *Fortune, 148,* 80–118.

Selmer, J., & Leung, A. S. M. (2002). Career management issues of female business expatriates. *Career Development International, 7,* 348–358.

Sepehri, P. (2003, December). How to pick the right mentor. *MBA Jungle,* 57.

Sheridan, A. (2002). What you know and who you know: Successful women's experiences of accessing board positions. *Career Development International, 7,* 203–210.

Simmons, W. W. (2001, January 11). When it comes to choosing a boss, Americans will prefer men. *Gallup News Service.* Retrieved September 10, 2001, from http://www.gallup.com

Simms, J. (2003, January 1). Business: Women at the top—You've got male. *Accountancy,* p. 1.

Singh, V., Kumra, S., & Vinnicombe, S. (2002). Gender and impression management: Playing the promotion game. *Journal of Business Ethics, 37,* 77–84.

Smith, D. M. (2000). *Women at work: Leadership for the next century.* Upper Saddle River, NJ: Prentice Hall.

Stechert, K. B. (1986). *Sweet success: How to understand the men in your business life and win with your own rules.* New York: Macmillan.

Steinhoff, P. G., & Tanaka, K. (1988). Women managers in Japan. In N. J. Adler & D. N. Izraeli (Eds.), *Women in management worldwide* (pp. 103–121). Armonk, NY: Sharpe.

Stroh, L. K., Brett, J. M., & Reilly, A. H. (1996). Family structure, glass ceiling, and traditional explanations for the differential rate of turnover of female and male managers. *Journal of Vocational Behavior, 49,* 99–118.

Strout, E. (2001). New rules for female executives: Helpful or harmful? *Sales and Marketing Management, 153*(11), 12–15.

Super, D. E. (1957). *The psychology of careers.* New York: Harper & Row.

Symons, G. L. (1988). Women's occupational careers in business: Managers and entrepreneurs in France and in Canada. In N. J. Adler & D. N. Izraeli (Eds.), *Women in management worldwide* (pp. 41–53). Armonk, NY: Sharpe.

Taylor, A., III. (1986, August 18). Why women managers are bailing out. *Fortune,* 16–23.

Terborg, J. R. (1977). Women in management: A research review. *Journal of Applied Psychology, 62,* 647–664.

Tharenou, P. (2001). Going up? Do traits and informal social processes predict advancing in management? *Academy of Management Journal, 44,* 1005–1017.

Tharenou, P., Latimer, S., & Conroy, D. (1994). How do you make it to the top? An examination of influences on women's and men's managerial advancement. *Academy of Management Journal, 37,* 899–931.

Thin on top! Why men earn more and get promoted faster. (2002). *Women in Management Review, 17,* 92–93.

Tischler, L. (2004, February). Where are the women? *Fast Company,* 52–60.

Tomkiewicz, J., & Bass, K. (2003). Attitudes toward women and management attributes: An update. *International Journal of Management, 20,* 62–68.

Tomlinson, A. (2001). Concrete ceiling harder to break than glass for women of color. *Canadian HR Reporter, 14*(22), 7, 13.

Trost, C. (1989, November 22). New approach forced by shifts in population. *The Wall Street Journal,* pp. B1, B4.

U.S. Bureau of the Census. (1990). *Statistical abstracts of the United States, 1990.* Washington, DC: U.S. Department of Commerce.

U.S. Department of Labor, Bureau of Labor Statistics. (1999). Hours of work. In *Report on the American workforce 1999* (pp. 80–109). Washington, DC: Author.

U.S. Department of Labor, Bureau of Labor Statistics. (2002a). *Current population survey, business.* Author.

U.S. Department of Labor, Bureau of Labor Statistics. (2002b). *Highlights of women's earnings.* Author.

U.S. Department of Labor, Bureau of Labor Statistics. (2003). *Employed persons by occupations, sex, and age.* Retrieved September 25, 2003, from ftp://ftp.bls.gov/pub/special.reequests/lf/aat9.txt

Valentine, S., & Godkin, L. (2000). Supervisor gender, leadership style, and perceived job design. *Women in Management Review, 15,* 117–126.

Valentine, S., Godkin, L., & Turner, J. H. (2002). Women's management, perceived job responsibility, and job search intention. *Women in Management Review, 17,* 29–38.

van Vianen, A. E. M., & Fischer, A. H. (2002). Illuminating the glass ceiling: The role of organizational culture preferences. *Journal of Occupational and Organizational Psychology,* 315–323.

Vinnicombe, S., & Singh, V. (2002). Sex role stereotyping and requisites of successful top managers. *Women in Management Review, 17,* 120–130.

Wasserman, E. (2002, December/January). Breakthrough: Women in business. *MBA Jungle,* 39–46.

Wellington, S., Kropf, M. B., & Gerkovich, P. R. (2003). What's holding women back? *Harvard Business Review, 81*(6), 18–29.

Westoff, L. A. (1986, October). Mentor or lover. *Working Woman,* 116–119.

Wiley, K. W. (1987, June). Up against the ceiling. *Savvy,* 51–52, 71.

Williams, M. J. (1988, September 12). Women beat the corporate game. *Fortune,* 128–138.

Yamaguchi, M. (1999, February 9). Japan shuns career women. *The Arizona Republic,* p. E10.

Zytowski, D. G. (1969). Toward a theory of career development for women. *Personnel and Guidance Journal, 47,* 660–664.

Author Index

513

H

Subject Index

Role overload, 109, 110
Role Salience Inventory (RSI), 29
Role-sharing, 197
RSI, *see* Role Salience Inventory
Russian women refugees, 399

S

Sachem Quality of Life Organization, 403
Salary gap, *see* Income gap
Salience Inventory (SI), 138, 151, 302
Same-sex families/partnerships
    beneficial effects of multiple roles, 49–50
    dual-earners, 197
Sanger, Margaret, 3
Satisficing, 108
SAW, *see* Section for the Advancement of
        Women
SCCT, *see* Social-cognitive career theory
Scholastic achievement tests, 136
Schools, *see* Elementary schools; High
        schools
SCI, *see* Skills Confidence Inventory
Science, Technology, Engineering, and
        Mathematics (STEM) fields
    bias in educational preparation, 433–434
    case analyses and interventions, 439–450
    changes needed in, 450–451
    common experiences of women in,
        427–430
    critical mass of women in, 438–439
    demographic trends, 430–431, 432, 433
    differential advancement opportunities
        in, 434–436
    field segregation in, 431–432
    microinequities concept of gender bias
        and, 433
    multiple-role issues for women and,
        437–438
    organizational climate and, 435–436
    patterns of women's advancement,
        432–433
    professional isolation of women, 436–437
    salary gap, 432
    structural barriers facing women, 438
    underemployment of women in, 431
Sciences, women's participation in, 6, 50
SCT, *see* Social-cognitive theory
SDS, *see* Self-Directed Search
Second Sex, The, 4

Secondary schools, career education and,
        30–32
Section for the Advancement of Women
        (SAW), 5
Selection bias, 122, 123
Self-assertion skills, 416
Self-care, 209
Self-concept, assessing, 28
Self-Directed Search (SDS), 28, 56, 130,
        132–133, 260, 300, 343, 377
Self-effacement, 253–254
Self-efficacy, 22–23
    assessing, 137, 146–148, 301–302
    Latinas and, 287–289, 290, 293
    low outcome expectations and, 52–54
    in social-cognitive theory, 249
Self-efficacy expectations, 112–113
Self-esteem, 57
Self-reports
    behavioral, 125
    lesbian clients and, 376–377
Self-talk, 113
Sensitivity, 61
Sex, conceptual meaning, 198
Sex bias
    concerns about in tests and inventories,
        121–125
    interest measures and, 26–27
Sex discrimination
    immigrant women and, 406–407
    "subtle," 149–150
    women managers and, 461
Sex equity, labor market and, 6–7
Sex restrictiveness, in interest inventories,
        123–124
Sex-role stereotyping, *see* Gender-role ster-
        eotyping
Sex segregation
    lesbians and, 357–358
    occupational, 204–205
Sexual harassment
    as barrier to workplace equity, 64–65
    career-counseling assessments and, 30
    categories of, 64
    women managers and, 471–472, 499
    in the workplace, 8–9, 206
Sexual identity development, 15
Sexual identity management, 32
Sexual orientation
    Asian women and, 255
    lesbians and, 357
Shell, 500–501